Upper Peninsula
of Michigan

Lake
Michigan

Lake
Huron

Traverse City

N
W E
S

Michigan

Bay City

Alma
Saginaw

Muskegon

Flint

Grand Rapids

Lansing

Pontiac

Lake
St. Clair

Kalamazoo Battle Creek

Jackson

Canada

Lake Erie

Indiana

Ohio

Consumers Power Company
Electric Service Area

Area Served by Consumers Power
● Division Headquarters Cities

FUTURE
BUILDERS

FUTURE BUILDERS

The Story of Michigan's Consumers Power Company

GEORGE BUSH

New York
St. Louis
San Francisco
Düsseldorf
Johannesburg
Kuala Lumpur
London
Mexico
Montreal
New Delhi

McGRAW-HILL BOOK COMPANY

Panama
Rio de Janeiro
Singapore
Sydney
Toronto

Library of Congress Cataloging in Publication Data

Bush, George, date
  Future builders.

  Includes bibliographical references.
  1. Consumers Power Company.   I. Title.
  HD9688.U54C63   338.7'61'3636209774   72-4428
  LSBN 0-07-009298-2

HQ
9688
.U54
C63

1234567890 HDMM 76543

Cop. 2

The editors for this book were W. Hodson Mogan and Lydia Maiorca,
the designer was Naomi Auerbach, and its production was supervised
by Teresa F. Leaden. It was set in Alphatype Caledo by University Graphics, Inc.

It was printed by Halliday Lithograph Corporation and bound by The Maple
Press Company.

For Susanna and Richard, Who Are the Future

Contents

Preface

M ost business histories are hard to read. That's because they are crammed with detail of no interest even to the fact-hungry audience of nonfiction. Yet the underlying stories are often fascinating—if you can just find them.

I tried to structure this history of Consumers Power Company of Michigan, one of our country's leading energy utilities, in a way that the book might fill the needs of the specialist, without slowing down the narrative for the general reader.

In the main text, the story of Consumers Power is told as the adventure in future building that it is. Exposition has been held to a minimum: I included what interested me and left out everything else.

The other section of the book, Notes and Comments, is an expansion of the footnote device. Here, by means of numbered references that appear in the main text, industrial historians and students of public utilities can delve more deeply into their special interests.

One problem has been that history doesn't stop. Consumers Power is very much alive, and every day important events occur that influence its course. I have tried to keep up with these events until the very last possible moment before press time, but it's almost certain that some of the most recent reportage will be outdated by the time you read this book. This is particularly true of Consumers' financial situation and future planning; such matters always are in a state of flux.

I would have been unable to complete this work in less than the two years dictated by practical considerations were it not for the fact that most of the historical research had already been compiled by E. Hardy Luther, who retired in 1963 as general personnel development supervisor of Consumers Power after forty-two years with the company and associated businesses. Some of the Notes and Comments, especially in the early-history chapters, are quoted almost verbatim from Luther's "Song of Service," an unpublished manuscript he prepared over the period of a decade as the official historian of Consumers Power and its predecessor companies.

Nor could I have written *Future Builders* without the unstinting support of Romney Wheeler, Consumers Power vice-president of public relations, and the help of Ty Cross, one of my Detroit newspaper colleagues in the late 1940s and now director of public information for the company.

My thanks also go out to many other Consumers Power people, past and present, who gave generously of their time and experience in long interview sessions, most prominently among them A. H. Aymond, the company's chairman of the board, president, and chief executive officer, whose ever-open door and completely candid approach to my task set the example for everyone in his organization. All records were placed at my disposal. No question I asked remained unanswered, and the answers were never evasive. Nor did Aymond or any of his executives ever try to influence my conclusions on the various controversial matters that inevitably are part of any company's affairs.

Al Aymond's interest in the project was shared by James H. Campbell, president and chief operating officer until his death in January 1972, and I am deeply indebted to him and his memory for his elucidations, incisive comments, and good company.

Others at Consumers Power who helped whenever I called on them included Harry R. Wall, vice-chairman of the board of directors and former senior vice-president in charge of electric operations; John B. Simpson, senior vice-president in charge of gas operations; Russell C. Youngdahl, senior vice-president in charge of electric construction and operations; Walter Boris, financial vice-president; Harold P. Graves, vice-president and general counsel; John W. Kluberg, vice-president and controller; Birum G. Campbell, Jr., vice-president of personnel (formerly in charge of marketing); Frank Brewer, manager of the company's Jackson division; Louis D. McDowell, executive assistant for division managers; Robert L. Haueter, electric production superintendent (nuclear); E. H. Kaiser, director of power resources and system planning; Richard C. Hyatt, Jackson division line supervisor; and Doris Carr, file supervisor, recently retired.

Robert B. Atwater, Consumers' executive director of fuel supply, reviewed the manuscript and corrected technical errors. Mrs. Marian DeNato of Consumers Power was at my disposal for secretarial assistance whenever I visited or telephoned the company. Donald Stoutt, supervisor of editorial production in the Consumers Power public relations department, generously and most competently handled the vilest job of all: he read the whole script word for word at least twice, in galley and page proofs, to catch typos and assorted inconsistencies.

Among former Consumers Power people who helped fill me in on the company's past were Robert D. Allen, until 1970 the company's senior vice-president in charge of electric and general engineering (now a vice-president of the Bechtel Corp., San Francisco); as well as a host of fine men on the retired list: Delbert Ford, Rolla G. England, LeRoy L. Benedict, George

Clark, Grover Hemstreet, Don McGowan, Herman L. Fruech-tenicht, Claude A. Mulligan, Lyman Robinson, E. V. Sayles, Raymond K. Smith, Horace Brewer, and James H. Foote, former chief engineer of Consumers Power and son of the company's founding engineer, J. B. Foote.

I also wish to express my appreciation to the members of the Panhandle-Trunkline system and its subsidiaries who introduced me to the excitement of natural gas pipeline operations and offshore gas exploration: King Sanders, chairman of the board of Panhandle Eastern Pipe Line Company; Stanford Wallace, another former Detroit newsman and now Panhandle's director of public relations; Mack Price, the company's manager of public relations; Raymond E. Fairchild, Gulf Coast exploration manager of Panhandle's Anadarko Production Co.; and Virgil Kincheloe, J. B. Sellers, and Thomas McPherson, of Trunkline Gas Company.

Others who provided material for this manuscript include Herbert Spendlove, editor of the *Jackson Citizen Patriot,* and Clare Sergeant, librarian of the city of Jackson.

My thanks also go to Rudy Plaisance, of Golden Meadows, Louisiana, captain of the huge offshore platform *Ocean Driller* for being such a pleasant host aboard his wondrous contraption; to Herb Latch, the helicopter pilot who deposited me gently on *Ocean Driller;* and to the two ladies—if they will forgive this outmoded compliment—who wore down their pretty finger-nails on typewriter keys, Mrs. Avis Powell, of Doylestown, Pennsylvania, and Mrs. Ruth Houston, of Jackson, Michigan.

Last, but certainly not least, I am indebted to my two good friends and long-time associates, Jim Riggs and Jim Autry of *Better Homes and Gardens,* without whose indulgence I probably would have been unable to take on this assignment; two yet older friends and mentors, Laurence J. Henderson, night city editor of the *Detroit News,* since retired, who first showed me the lovely land of Michigan's Lower Peninsula, and Charles T. Haun, the venerable (but sentimental-tough as ever) words-

and-pictures sage of the Detroit Free Press, who advised me many years ago that a long book wasn't so hard to write if you wrote it one chapter at a time; and finally Jack Hess, another friend and a former fellow magazine editor who, as the then editor of corporate histories at McGraw-Hill, launched me on this project.

George Bush

FUTURE
BUILDERS

Today

Ask almost anyone in Michigan which of all industries he considers most essential, and his answer will be the automobile industry. In Los Angeles, until recently at least, the reply would be aerospace. In Gary, Indiana, the respondent still says steel. All these answers are wrong.

In an industrial society, the most essential industry is energy. Without it, everything stops. When energy utilities are not allowed to grow, nothing else can grow. It's like flipping off the future switch.

On the lush lands of southern Michigan, late spring lies like a heavy blanket on a fevered man. Moisture steams from fields and scattered forests. Highways shimmer in a glaring haze. Shade gets ever scarcer even on the home-proud residential streets whose old elms are dying. There is something almost symbolic about the demise of these tall trees. The America of the porch swing, of the green wonder of safe and tranquil afternoons, is all but gone.

On Wednesday, June 16, 1971, tree surgeons performed their power-tooled autopsies on two disease-riddled elms that had roofed a stately lawn on Jackson's Fourth Street, and then they trucked away the corpses. It was not the happiest of homecomings that evening for fifty-six-year-old A. H. Aymond, chairman of the board and chief executive of Consumers Power Company.[1] An attorney by profession and a public utilities man by choice and fortune, Aymond had spent long hours at the office and pulled into his driveway barely in time to be blinded by the last red rays of the now almost unobstructed setting sun. But the elms, much as he had loved them, were the least of Al Aymond's problems. He had other, far more pressing—and depressing—matters on his mind.

Still, he was the exemplary, jovial host as he took me up the steps to his screened porch and on into the kitchen. His wife Betty, a trim, vivacious, dark-haired woman, was awaiting us, with almonds and Greek olives ready on a tray. Al Aymond's smooth, deceptively young face showed strain as he mixed drinks, munched nervously on appetizers, and made light of a tough day with small talk. Betty shot him apprehensive glances. Even I, who hardly knew him, could tell that he held in his temper, just as he disciplined his blond hair to adhesive perfection and bossed the sharp creases on his trousers, the shirt cuffs that wouldn't dare smudge, and the conservative tie that never strayed from dead center.

But the explosion was bound to come, and it did after we had finished dinner, as the festive candles on the table flickered before a coming wind. I think we had been talking about

3

Villa d'Este, a great resort hotel on Lake Como where the Aymonds had spent a few days the previous autumn and which I had visited in the course of researching a magazine piece. Suddenly Aymond switched subjects, unable to contain himself any longer. The vision of Italian lakes evaporated. Mirage gave way to reality. "You know what the Public Service Commission told us today?" he burst out. He was still smiling, but his smile was now a tight and bitter parody, the smile of a man who would like to take all blows with good grace, but can't. "The commission turned down our rate increase. They told us, 'We know you're bleeding, but you're not dead yet, so you don't need a blood transfusion.' Can't they see what's happening?"

And then it all spilled out: the gnawing frustration of a man trying to do his job in a country at odds with itself; the help-lessness of a life-tempered idealist who, like any youngster, would prefer a life of easy plentitude and perfect justice, of air as pure and water as sparkling as they had been in the days of the wide-open spaces, but who had learned that the less a society is willing to face facts, the more elusive the ideal becomes.

The facts were that a nation cannot consume more than it produces; that it cannot spend more money than it makes; that America, with more than 203 million bellies to feed, could not return to cottage industry even if it wanted to; that unemployment and hunger are the worst pollutants of all. Disenchanted with a glut of goodies that bring no real happiness, sickened by glib answers that gloss over all real problems, Americans could well demand a better future. The politicians, no less glibly than before, could promise it to them, but if there was to be a viable future at all, it would be up to men like Aymond. A. H. Aymond's Consumers Power Company somehow must provide the power, light, and heat without which much of Michigan and its nearly nine million people cannot exist.

On that sweltering June day of 1971, this task seemed close

A. H. AYMOND

The chairman of the board of Consumers Power Company at his Jackson home. He doesn't get a chance to relax on his back porch very often.
(Consumers Power photo by Rus Arnold)

to impossible. The Michigan Public Service Commission's refusal to allow the rate increase that Consumers Power Company needed desperately to keep its services abreast of the state's demands threatened to be the proverbial straw that breaks the camel's back.

That June 16 was the thirty-sixth day of a strike by 5,400 of Consumers Power's 11,900 employees, a strike that was to last 112 days, the longest in the company's history. Supervisory and other nonunion personnel kept the customers supplied with electricity and gas, risking and sometimes suffering physical assault, but they were unable to keep up with vital maintenance, and major equipment failures were an ever-present peril.[2]

It was the 296th day on which a $120 million nuclear plant, whose construction had been approved by the Atomic Energy Commission, stood idle at Palisades, near South Haven on Lake Michigan, while hearings continued on whether the plant should be allowed to operate. Each idle month added $1 million to the cost of the project: interest payments on the investment had to be made whether the plant operated or not. This waste, together with the only slightly less staggering expense of buying power from other utilities to fill the gap, ultimately would be reflected in the bills paid by the company's customers. In order to put a stop to this drain, Consumers had given in to the demands of an environmentalist group to build thermal-pollution safeguards considered by many impartial scientific experts to be unnecessary. Even so, the issue was still in doubt.

It was the 183rd day of delay, resulting from the petition of another environmentalist interveners' group, concerning authorization to build yet another nuclear plant, at Midland. Originally, this plant's completion had been planned for February 1975. By now, however, it was apparent that the hearings would drag on for many more months. For this and other reasons—among them AEC staff delays in processing the application, and a reduction of workweek hours by the primary contractor—Midland could not possibly go into operation before May 1977, and then not at 100 percent capacity. Not before May 1978, at best, could it be expected to run full tilt—a delay of approximately forty months. The fact that the plant's output would be sorely needed to power the Michigan economy long before then, and that its clean nuclear system would do away with nearly two dozen smokestacks now fouling the air over Midland, seemed to bother no one—no one, that is, except the people of Midland, who were tired of the stinking smoke, and of course Consumers Power and The Dow Chemical Company, which planned to purchase most of its steam for chemical processing from the Midland nuclear plant.

And now, to top it off, the Michigan Public Service Commission had issued a preliminary decision rejecting an application by Consumers Power Company for an interim electric rate increase of $7 million for the year, an amount that actually had been recommended by the commission's professional staff.[3] Even if the increase had been granted, it would not have covered the company's burgeoning costs. Fuel prices had gone up 41 percent over the past two years. As a result, the company's earnings on common stock had decreased to $2.81 from $3.16 the previous June and now stood nearly 25 percent below the fair return required on a public utility's investment.[4] The stock was down to $30 from a high of $54 — sad enough for the pension funds, mutual funds, and individuals that already held the shares, but worse yet for the future of the company and Michigan's general economy. With declining earnings and depressed share prices, Consumers Power would find it increasingly difficult to compete for the investment dollars it desperately needed to finance its expansion program. At conservative estimates, the demands on the company's system would increase 50 percent by 1976, requiring $1.4 billion in additional capital, raised largely through sales of bonds and common and preferred stocks. On June 16, 1971, Aymond could not visualize how this might be accomplished in the light of steadily eroding earnings.

In a free economy, investment flows naturally to where it may expect the most return. This is as it should be. Growth potential is thus encouraged, and weakness is usually nipped before too much damage is done. But in that same free economy, public utilities—their profits being controlled by state regulation—can find themselves in a precarious situation. When a state's utilities commission is insensitive to the demands of the marketplace and sets a company's rates too low, it's like sending your horse into the Preakness with its legs hobbled. The poor beast might just as well stay out of the race.

If this simile strikes the reader as too ripe, it's only because I have not yet succeeded in making clear the symbiotic interdependence between energy utilities and the society they serve. Consumers Power Company is one of the nation's ten largest investor-owned operating utilities, and it's the third largest that sells both electricity and gas. In 1971, the company supplied some 20 billion kilowatthours to its nearly 1,113,000 electric customers and 334 billion cubic feet of natural gas to its 880,000 gas customers. Over 60 percent of all the people in Michigan—some 1,543,000 breadwinners and their families—depend for their livelihoods on industries and businesses that could not function without the energy supplied to them by Consumers Power. Among the company's energy-dependent customers are several major General Motors and Ford plants, key installations of U.S. Steel and Dow Chemical, many manufacturers of vital automobile parts, and dozens of others, including food processors, like the Kellogg Company, and pharmaceutical companies, like Upjohn.

Consumers Power's gas and electric territories, which sometimes but not always overlap, cover most of Michigan's Lower Peninsula, from the Straits of Mackinac south to the Ohio and Indiana borders; from Lakes Huron, St. Clair, and Erie west to Lake Michigan. The only major population center in the state which Consumers Power does not serve is the city of Detroit, but even here the company's existence is essential to uninterrupted electric operation. Since 1962, Consumers

Power and The Detroit Edison Company have joined in the Michigan Power Pool, an arrangement whereby the two companies are linked with 138,000- and 345,000-volt ties and share each other's generating capacities, comprising a total of 10,000 megawatts. Each company engages in mutually planned and agreed-upon expansion programs, thereby achieving important economies, and each buys power from the other as need dictates.[5] Beyond that, since 1969, Consumers Power, together with Detroit Edison, has been a member of MIIO, the Michigan-Indiana-Illinois-Ohio group, whose participants are interconnected with extra-high voltage lines and back one another up in emergencies—forestalling such blackouts as the one that hit the East coast in 1965.[6] The Canadian province of Ontario is also tied to Consumers Power and Detroit Edison through yet another, similar arrangement.[7] Thus not only the company's own customers but also some 1,500,000 in the Detroit Edison territory and almost six million others across immediate state lines depend, to a not inconsiderable degree, on the ability of Consumers Power to generate enough electricity to meet the demands made on its system. Moreover, Consumers Power belongs to the ECAR group of twenty-six utilities in eight East Central states—some of them as distant as Pennsylvania, Maryland, and Virginia—and must stand ready at all times to back up power deficiencies in these far-flung areas.[8]

Michigan's population grows at a rate of 1.27 percent a year. Its industrial output rises at an annual rate of 2.96 percent. This productivity increase is far from enough. Along with our country's other industrial states, Michigan's per-man-hour output must rise drastically if the United States is to remain competitive in the world's markets. American wages are higher than those anywhere else, and it's obvious that the more a worker is paid, the more he must produce to earn his keep: international economics are not based on charity. Now, even if the old Puritan work ethic still ruled our attitudes—even if we had not become a leisure-oriented society—there is a limit to the best worker's strength as a creature of muscle and bone. The extra strength required for increased production must come from manufactured energy. Thus, energy output is the basis (and a measure) of a nation's standard of living, not because of gadgets like electric toothbrushes and can openers, but because of the productivity it generates. Already many of our country's products, including automobiles, are being undersold by foreign imports made by cheaper labor. We are changing from a producer nation into a consumer nation. This is untenable in the long run. No country can afford to spend more money than it takes in. Quality of workmanship aside, our only hope lies in the intelligent application of manufactured energy.

Consumers Power's capitalization in June 1971 stood at $1.7 billion. To keep up with anticipated energy demands, this capitalization would have to nearly double in five years.[9] That's what A. H. Aymond was so upset about that hot June evening: Michigan's future—as indeed the country's future—depends on the precarious future of its energy utilities.[10]

Trouble always comes in bunches. That's no accident: the affairs of man are intertwined. Bad breeds bad as good breeds good, and no one knows the turning point until it has been passed. Consumers Power had been on top of the world in the early sixties. Good had bred good to the point where, in several succeeding years, the company could raise the pay of its employees, increase the dividends it paid its stockholders, reduce—voluntarily—the rates charged its customers, and still could keep building for the future. Then, almost imperceptibly at first, came Vietnam. And bad begat bad.

The nation, for the first time in its history, faced struggle without understanding its purpose, fought a war without real expectation of victory, experienced prosperity without enjoying it. Guns and butter don't mix—even when guns fire on the installment plan. A flippant Confucius might have concluded that he who sits on a fence gets goosed; worse yet, our country found itself nearly disemboweled. Resources went to waste. Inflation ran rampant. Don't-give-a-damnism flourished. The dollar gap widened. Promises, easily given, were just as easily betrayed. Society lost its continuity, as youth, understandably alienated by the pointlessness of it all, ceased trying to succeed its elders and instead decided to dump them. The issue became Utopia versus the Establishment.

The alter ego of Establishment is big industry—capitalist industry. Public utilities, since they affect everyone, are among the most visible of industries. Populist politicians are not unaware of that fact. Thus, once again, the utilities became prime targets in a period of social upheaval, and Consumers Power was no exception. But this time the point of attack was not profiteering, as it had been in the trust-busting days of the New Deal 1930s. By 1970, everyone interested in such matters knew that profits of utilities are limited by public regulation; utility issues are not ordinarily found in glamour-stock portfolios. Instead, the leverage now was ecology, that esoteric dictionary word which had almost overnight become a slogan: the new science in which everyone could qualify as an expert provided he was emotional enough—the respectable marijuana of the masses in a frustrated, drug-happy, scapegoat-happy time. Most of its addicts couldn't tell the difference between a British thermal unit, a milliroentgen, and a megawatt, but they knew, with the absolute conviction granted only to the half-informed, that all power pollutes.

True, there was plenty to be concerned about. The nation had indeed abused its environment shamefully over the years, though probably as much out of ignorance and apathy as out of greed. And when it came to power generation, there could be no doubt that there's no smoke without fire, and no soot and sulfur without smoke. The more responsible of the utilities had been aware of this long before the public was, but their drive for cleaner, more expensive fuels than high-sulfur coal—so far as they were available—had often been frustrated by the pressure of state utility commissions (!) which objected to such improvements as devices to raise rates. Municipally owned power plants, politically the most responsive to demands for the lowest possible rates, were and still are among the dirtiest. Consumers Power, however, had been one of the first utilities which back in the early 1950s had already begun to install expensive ($400,000 to $700,000) electrostatic precipitators in its chimneys to reduce the fly ashes of smoke, years before the public had begun to associate soot with anything but paychecks. More than that, beginning in 1924, the company had started on a vast reforestation program of its lands along Michigan's rivers, planting more than twenty-two million trees over the years and turning thousands of acres of its properties over to state and local governments as recreation areas.[11] But now, in the 1970s, the company suddenly found itself accused of being a spoiler of the environment.

Ironically, the target was nuclear energy, the cleanest and potentially the most economical way to generate the huge electric requirements of the future. Only two other generating techniques have conceivably less effect on the environment. One is hydroelectric generation, which turns the force of falling water into electric energy; the other is steam turbines fired by natural gas. Neither is practical today. In the relatively flat country of Michigan, where streams have so little drop that electric pioneers had to clock corks bobbing downstream to spot stretches where the flow was strongest, the few dams that still remain in operation supply less than 3 percent of the Consumers Power system's needs. Even in the mountainous West, dams are not nearly as important in the power picture as they once were. And as for natural gas as a power-plant fuel, there is hardly enough to go around these days for heating; available reserves are short of meeting demands, particularly industrial demands.

Consumers Power, as we shall see, had been among the first companies to set its sights on nuclear energy. It was thus also one of the first to suffer the slings and arrows of outraged Unconsciousness I. Not that many people worried about the possibility of a nuclear accident. Even the most uninformed had finally come to realize that plants are not bombs. No angina pectoris case has ever blown himself up with a nitroglycerin pill. Nor was there widespread concern about radiation emanating from reactor plants. Atomic Energy Commission safety standards provide for an allowable maximum that is less than 1/1,000 of average natural background radiation. If you stood next to a nuclear plant all day, you would be exposed to less radiation than would enter your system if you drank a can of tomato juice. Instead, environmentalists zeroed in on the vague threat of "thermal pollution," one which could be neither proved nor disproved and which therefore made for a publicizable debate: the possible effect on aquatic fauna and flora of the warm water discharged by nuclear plants.

All steam generating plants produce waste heat. All return cooling water to its source at a higher temperature than they originally get it. In nuclear plants none of the steam heat is dissipated up the chimney, so the discharged water is somewhat hotter, and there is admittedly a lot of it, but it still runs out at less than body temperature.

For Consumers Power, the test case was its Palisades plant, which was completed in 1970 and whose 800,000-kilowatt generating unit, the largest ever installed in Michigan, could light all the streets, homes, and offices of a city of 1 million people. When it came time to put in the less than 100 tons of nuclear fuel that could do the job of 6.7 million tons of dirty coal, a hastily activated group of environmentalists, which called itself the Michigan Steelhead and Salmon Fishermen's Association but which was led and financed by Chicago interests, intervened at the AEC hearings on granting the plant an operating license. As we already know, and shall learn about in more detail later, Consumers Power eventually yielded to the group's demands. The company agreed to install cooling towers and other additional safeguards that will cost $29 million to build, add about $5 million a year in extra overhead costs, and use up about 10 percent of the plant's power output. Future decisions of the AEC might make the cooling towers unnecessary, but for the moment this compromise was all the company had to go on.

In any case, by June 16, 1971, the operating license had not been granted. Palisades did not go into even partial operation until 1972 — at least two years behind schedule. Worst of all, however, the Palisades case set a precedent, as was its apparent purpose in the first place. It resulted, in turn, in delaying the construction of the company's next nuclear project, a $500-million plant at Midland, which would not only generate 1.3 million kilowatts (500,000 more than the Palisades plant) but also supply The Dow Chemical Company with vast quantities of steam for use in its processes. Dow Chemical now gets this steam by burning coal—hardly an enlightened environmentalist's choice of fuel. Moreover, there is no doubt that the success of the Palisades intervention will also rub off on the expansion plans of other utility companies, and this in the face of the most critical energy shortage ever faced by the nation. As one of the leading interveners admitted candidly to a Consumers Power executive in private conversation, "I know you are a fine company. Everybody knows it. That's the point. If we can stop you, we can stop anybody."

Being singled out for compliments while getting kicked in the teeth was not a new experience for Consumers Power. Once before, in the country's convulsion of the 1930s, it had been among the prime targets in Franklin Delano Roosevelt's war on investor-owned utilities. At that time, too, many of the company's antagonists had agreed that Consumers was a good outfit; they told Wendell Wilkie, who was then Consumers' boss, that if only all the other utilities were run like his, he wouldn't have so many problems.

Consumers Power, then the largest and most important operating unit of Commonwealth & Southern Corporation, one of the utility giants of the holding-company era, survived the 1930s battle between government and private power interests. Ending up as an independent company, Consumers Power probably even benefited from the reorganization that the New

Deal forced on the utilities industry. Perhaps, Consumers Power eventually may benefit also from the current onslaught. Sooner or later, it would seem, even the dimmest, most politically motivated mind will come to recognize that energy utilities must not be bled but nurtured, and even the most hysterical environmentalist will come to realize that a proper balance must be struck between protection and productivity if our nation is to have a future. If nothing else, the negative effects of today's anti-utility actions should serve to define more clearly the parameters of constructive utility controls.

Consumers Power had its origins on the Michigan frontier. It grew with Michigan, and Michigan grew with it. To feel our way into the future, we must know the present; to understand the present, we must know the past. History is all of one piece. Let's have a look.

Yesterday

1

Michigan Fever

*Come all you Yankee farmers who'd like to
change your lot,
Who've spunk enough to travel beyond your
native spot,
And leave the village where Ma and Pa do stay,
Come, follow me and settle in Michi-gan-i-a.*[1]

They called it the Territorial Road, this being its official
name, and sometimes the St. Joseph Road, since the old
French fort at St. Joseph on the western shore of Michigan was
its destination. In either case, the term "road" was something
of an exaggeration. But then those spunky Yankees who headed
out into the promised land were not averse to applying a little
positive thinking. Their "road" was but an old Indian trail
with clumps of underbrush to snag a walker's tired feet and
tree stumps cut so high they often caught on wagon axles. It
was deeply rutted from the wheels that had churned through
mud left by drenching spring rains and summer showers, and
there were other places where the trail passed through swamps
that were deep mud the year around. It was a narrow trail,
walled in by forests so dense they scarcely admitted any
light, and there were long stretches where the trail was barely
wide enough for wagons.

The year was 1829. The month was July. Michigan was not

yet a state; another eight years were to pass before its admission to the Union on January 26, 1837. The trail, following the route of today's Interstate 94, cut through a wilderness that was still Indian country, although no war whoops had been heard here now for years, not since Governor Lewis Cass of the Michigan Territory had purchased the lands south of the Grand River at a treaty powwow in Chicago in 1821. It was a rich land of many varied soils, a gently rolling countryside sculpted by the glaciers of four ice ages. These glaciers, alternately pushing down from the Arctic and receding over the period of a million years, had wiped out vast tropical forests washed by warm, life-bearing seas. The glaciers excavated the Great Lakes, and they pitted the land between these huge lakes with countless smaller lakes and built the paths of many rivers. As the ice cap retreated, it left a legacy of many different kinds of earth and rock superimposed on the limestone formed from the ancient sea's crustacean shells and corals. If there ever was a rich earth, this was it; and with its great diversity of soils you couldn't have found better land for growing all manner of crops.

But on this third day of July 1829, those rich crops were still a Yankee dream. Horace Blackman was one of the Yankees. He also had the dream of Michigan, a dream persuasive enough to make him leave behind the schoolteacher bride he had just married in Worcester, Massachusetts. With little more than $300 in his pocket, he had set out for the new territory the month before. Now he and his two companions were on their second day out of Ann Arbor, already a prospering frontier community with some two hundred inhabitants, a frame church, and a log jail. The church steeple had been the three men's last landmark of civilization. Since then they had seen little else but swamp and forest.

Blackman, as swarthy as his name implied, was in his late twenties then, and most of his face was covered by a straggly beard. He was a hard man, sinewy and well-muscled, as one had to be to brave the wilderness. Even more rugged was his equally tall companion, Alex Laverty, an experienced pioneer who had made it once from Detroit, then seat of the territorial government, all the way up to Fort Mackinac, which was as far as you could go without mounting an elaborate expedition.

Laverty was something of a mystery. He had fought in the War of 1812, this much was sure; there were rumors that he had been a captain in the New York Militia, that his real name was Lafferty, and that there must have been a good reason for him to drop his title and change his name. The third man was even bigger than either Blackman or Laverty. He was Pe-Wy-Tum, a huge Potawatomi Indian guide with a shuffling, flat-footed, surefooted walk so fast that he seemed to glide. This forest was his old stamping ground; the Potawatomis, one of the Algonquin tribes, occupied most of Michigan's southern tier.

It had been a long day. The sun, only two hours short of setting, shot its blinding light straight down the trail, blazing through chinks in the canopy formed by the hardwoods' inter-lacing branches. Blackman squinted and cussed. His face was covered with mosquito welts; his body drenched in sweat. Often in the course of this day and other days before it on his foot-weary way from Detroit to Ann Arbor and beyond, he had been tempted to take off his long-sleeved flannel shirt. But Blackman wasn't the foolhardy type. He had heard somewhere that good rough flannel, worn next to the skin during the day, kept a man healthy, especially when he was perspiring, by protecting him against chills and infection.[2] In any case, the mosquitoes would have eaten him alive. Blackman had no fear of wolves, of which there were plenty around at campfire time, but whenever he heard the buzz of a mosquito near his head, he was tempted to run, and he might have indeed if he hadn't been so tired.

"He says we'll be there soon," Laverty said, referring to Pe-Wy-Tum, who had scouted ahead. "He says the village is just on the other side of the river up ahead."

Blackman grunted his doubts, but sure enough, the almost

solid forest of maple and oak, elm and ash ended abruptly a short distance ahead. Through the last trees he could see a cool and sparkling stream, and on the other side of the stream there stretched a field of Indian corn. Toward the horizon, shimmering in the haze of late afternoon, several low, dome-shaped Potawatomi wigwams huddled against a grove of oaks. The wigwams were built of bent saplings, in the manner of Algonquin Indians, and were covered with reed mats and stripped bark.[3] Blackman didn't worry about the Indians. There was no danger here. By now they were used to sharing their land with the white man. What interested Blackman most for the moment was the stream, which the Indians called the Washtenong-sepe and which now is called the Grand River. Blackman let out a yell of joy, tossed his rifle on the level bank, and threw himself headlong into the shallow water where the trail crossed the stream. It crossed here because this was the only safe ford for miles in either direction. On the other side, the trail split, one branch shooting out southward toward Indiana and thence to Chicago, and the other heading due west to St. Joseph.

By the time the sun had set, the three men had forded the Grand River, and in the summer dusk they made their camp in a burr oak opening on the river's western bank. The Indians paid no attention to them, not this evening, or through the black night, alive with animal sounds and rustlings. But at sunrise the next morning, Blackman and Laverty staged an impromptu July Fourth celebration on this fifty-third anniversary of American independence, firing their rifles in salute and squandering the ammunition they had carried in their packs. The Indians, hearing the shots, came over to the white men's camp, first hesitantly, one by one, and then in droves when they saw there was no danger. Laverty orated in English and in imitation Potawatomi dialect. The crack of Pe-Wy-Tum's rifle sounded applause, and the whole commotion amused the Indians greatly. They brought corn and potatoes and fish and game for a banquet on the prairie ground, and everybody drank ceremonial toasts of the river water. (When Laverty's wife—she was either his second or his third— later heard about this, she wrote to a friend, "Can you imagine Alex drinking a toast in water?")

It wasn't until the next day that the men began to explore the land. They scouted upstream and downstream for a few miles, and eventually Blackman found a spot to his liking, a flat place where the grass grew 4 feet high, bordered by a forest of oak which wasn't too dense to cope with. The old trees stood fairly far apart here, and there was not too much undergrowth between them. The land wouldn't be easy to clear, but it wouldn't be as hard as some, and between the strong trees of this oak opening and the tall grass of the clearings there was great promise of fertility. Nearby ripples in the stream indicated good waterpower at hand to turn mill wheels.

Town location required a careful survey, a study of the lay of the land and its approaches from all directions. Blackman decided that the southeast quarter of Section 34, T2 R1W furnished the best opportunity for platting. He struck his claim stake, and then it was time for more "sepe" water toasts. The Indian trail passed directly through Blackman's land; the river's bank was of hard soil and quite level, and yet it was high enough for good drainage. A creek ran through the northerly part of the section. To the southwest there was a swamp along the river, but it was far enough away not to be objectionable.

After staking out on this location, Blackman returned to Ann Arbor, where he bade farewell to his two companions. He then traveled by foot to Monroe to the land office to pay his $2 per acre for his 160-acre claim, and he wrote to his brother Russell in Berkshire, New York, to join him in Ann Arbor and bring $320 so that they could locate another 160 acres on the east side of the river.

While waiting for his brother, Horace hired out to chop wood and clear land near Ann Arbor. When Russell finally showed up late in August, he had only a couple of hundred dollars, not enough to buy the land on the east bank. Nevertheless, Horace purchased a pair of oxen and a wagon, and the two Blackman brothers, together with three hired men, set off again along the Indian trail to Horace's claim. They felled timber, cleared the land, and built a log house. They planned a village, whose main street was to pass their house. As yet, this village had no name. It wasn't until the next year that a group of volunteers, blazing and grading the trail into a "road" as far as Blackman's location, decided to call it Jacksonburgh in honor of Andrew Jackson, the hero of New Orleans and then the seventh President of the United States. The name of the settlement was later changed to Jackson for short, and Blackman's first house of logs stood where Trail Street now crosses the Grand River. Oddly enough, this is practically the present site of the Consumers Power Company Trail Street building.

Meanwhile, of course, other settlers had come, and also land speculators and squatters. Some speculators from Ann Arbor were the first to arrive. Having heard of Blackman's claim, they bought three quarter sections of land directly south of, and diagonally upstream from, the Blackman purchase in order to obtain control of the river waterpower. Then came the squatters. On January 1, 1830, Congress had reduced the price of land to $1.25 per acre and passed the "squatter act," under which settlers could preempt 80 acres for $100 or twice 80 acres for $200 and pay for their claims over two years' time. But this was not so easy as it seemed. Under the Land Act of 1820, the government auctioned off the quarter sections, and those men with the most cash in their pockets got most of the land. So the squatters had to be on guard against land speculators and against the possibility that wealthy farmers would bid up the price. These speculators and farmers, most of whom were from the East, had sharp-eyed scouts roaming all over the territory, and naturally they were always on the lookout for quarter sections that had already been improved. The only practical thing for the squatters to do was to show up at the land auction armed to the teeth and wearing a no-nonsense look on their rough, work-worn faces. They toted rifles and carried hanging ropes to scare off the speculators, and sometimes the speculators chickened out and the squatters could keep their land.

For Blackman and the other settlers, it was still fairly easy pickings to obtain the kind of ground they wanted. Michigan's total population in 1830 was only about 31,000, and that included everybody who stuck around long enough to be counted. That's not very many people for so large an area. The reason for the lack of population was that although no major battles had ever been fought right here, Michigan's exploration and subsequent settlement had been delayed by almost continuous hostilities ever since Cadillac founded Detroit in 1701. First the British fought the French in a series of wars that lasted until 1760. Then the American Revolutionaries fought the British, and eventually there came the War of 1812, which actually lasted almost until New Year's Day of 1815. In the meantime there was the ever-present threat of Indians, who sometimes went on the warpath on their own, but who were more often egged on and armed by the various colonial adversaries. Treaties with the Indians were slow to be made, and without such treaties settlers could not get clear title to their land.

What's more, a report in 1815 by the Surveyor General of the United States, Edward Tiffin, had served to give Michigan a bad name. Tiffin's men, dispatched to survey 2 million acres in southeastern Michigan for settlement, had found so many lakes and swamps and so much poor land in this particular region that they concluded, "Not more than one acre in one hundred . . . would . . . admit of cultivation." As a result, the veterans of 1812 were rewarded for their services with land in Missouri and Illinois instead of Michigan. Not until Henry R. Schoolcraft, serving as geologist on Cass's 1820 expedition into the wilds beyond Lake Superior and Lake Michigan, discovered a huge nugget of pure copper at the mouth of the Ontonagon River in the Upper Peninsula did public attention focus favorably on the Michigan Territory. Cass hadn't lost a single man on his 4,200-mile trek, which was rather promising in itself. And then, no one anywhere had ever seen a rich chunk of copper like Schoolcraft's, almost 4 feet square and 18 inches thick.

Even so, settlers were slow to come. In 1825, with the warlike Chippewa still threatening the Saginaw Valley, only 92,332 acres of Michigan land were auctioned off in Detroit. This meant that there were at most 1,154 new families that year, and actually probably fewer than that since some of them no doubt bought more than 80 acres. In the second half of the 1820s land sales dropped even below that figure, and it wasn't until 1831, when 217,943 acres were sold, that "Michigan fever," as it was called, really started burning hot. In 1833, the land sales went to 447,780 acres, and by 1836 they topped 4 million, more than were sold in any other state or territory. [4]

Only the Saginaw Valley had lagged behind in development and was still hardly settled—an island of wilderness in the midst of a land that was being rapidly tamed. That was because the Chippewas regarded it as holy territory and kept all white men and even halfbreeds out. Under the Cass Treaty of 1819 these warlike Indians insisted on perpetual hunting and fishing rights for the entire Saginaw Valley area, and in addition they received 50,000 of its most beautiful acres as their reservation. Settlers were afraid of them and clung to communities along the trail that ran from Detroit to Saginaw, and it wasn't until 1834—barely before Michigan's statehood—that they dared to explore the Chippewa hunting preserve west of the Saginaw Trail. [5]

Nothing, however, deterred the pioneers from expanding their settlements in western Michigan. One town after another sprang up along the Territorial Road (not to be confused with today's highway called Territorial Road north of Jackson). Settlers purchased land at the forks of the Kalamazoo River in 1831; this became the site of Albion. Battle Creek, also on the Territorial Road to St. Joseph, got its start the same year. By that time, the old trail was at last in the process of really becoming a road. Remaining tree stumps were chopped as close to the ground as possible, and what was left of underbrush was rooted out. In some particularly swampy areas, logs were placed side by side to form what was called a "corduroy." It was a bumpy, bone-shaking way to travel, but at least you didn't get stuck quite so often.

That same year, too, a settler by the name of Titus Bronson founded Kalamazoo. He chose a beautiful site in a burr oak opening on the Kalamazoo River and platted a town which he named Bronson, after himself. When, four years later, some other residents who disliked him changed the settlement's name to Kalamazoo, adopting the Indian name of the river, Bronson picked up and moved farther west to Illinois. No one quite knows where.

Kalamazoo was ideally situated. Not only was it on the Territorial Road, which eventually went all the way to St. Joseph on Lake Michigan, but it was also blessed with water-power and river transportation. When the water ran high enough, ships laden with merchandise came up the Kalamazoo River from the lake and, in turn, carried away produce from the farms in the Kalamazoo area. By 1856, wealthy Kalamazoo had 16,000 inhabitants; its own newspaper, the *Kalamazoo Gazette;*[6] and its seat of higher learning, Kalamazoo College. The Grand Rapids and Indiana Railroad was in the process of being built through town, and the community was important enough so that in August of that year, Abraham Lincoln spoke at a local political rally. Blackman's Jacksonburgh, by then called Jackson, had also fared well. It now counted about five thousand population, and it had an even greater claim to political fame: Under its stately oaks a meeting had been held in 1854 that led to the creation of the Republican party.

But Kalamazoo was the key city in western Michigan as far as the early history of what we now call the utilities industry is concerned. And 1856 was the key year. For on May 8 of that year twenty individuals and Kalamazoo business firms subscribed $27,000 of a proposed $30,000 capital issue for a firm to be known as the Kalamazoo Gas Light Company.[7] Articles of association were filed on December 8, and four days later the *Gazette* reported that "The gas used by this company is made from resin with Aubin's Patent Generator. It is said that gas from resin will yield twice as much light as the same quantity of gas made from coal. The work of laying pipes is to be commenced immediately, and will be completed by August 1, 1857."[8]

For once—and it probably wasn't so rare then as it is now—the work progressed faster than plans called for. On July 3, nearly one whole month ahead of schedule, the *Gazette* announced jubilantly, if not altogether grammatically, "We are now a gas lighted city. Except here and there a slight difficulty, incident to getting started, which will soon be remedied, the success of our enterprise is complete. Our business houses are most beautifully and brilliantly illuminated every evening, and the effect, especially on the main street, is gorgeous and almost enchanting."

Meanwhile, the village council of Jackson, sometime in 1856, had granted to one Edward Coen "the right and privilege to erect and maintain a gas works and conduits for public distribution." There was, however, a provision inherent in the permit that the plant had to go into operation within a stated number of months. Apparently Coen missed his deadline, for the following year—when Kalamazoo already had its gas—Coen and his associates had to apply all over again, this time to the city of Jackson, which had just been incorporated. Coen then built his coal-gas plant on the west side of Mechanic Street between Luther Street (now Pearl Street) and the Grand River.[9]

Such were the humble beginnings of the two earliest predecessors of Consumers Power Company. With their advent, the state of Michigan, barely born and but one short generation

BY 1856, JACKSON WAS MORE THAN A ONE-HORSE TOWN

That was the year brothers J. Z. and J. D. Ballard established their livery stable on Columbus Street near Pearl to serve as a depot for stagecoaches traveling from Jackson to Adrian and Jonesville. Jackson's first artesian well was discovered on the site of their barn. (Ambrotype by N. E. Allen, courtesy of Eunice Ballard, granddaughter of J. D. Ballard)

removed from the frontier, entered the magic gaslight era. Gone were the primitive cabins such as Blackman and Laverty had built, cabins that had no glass in the windows and where oiled paper or scraped buckskin served to keep out the weather. In the towns and villages, neat little clapboard houses were going up, and soon these houses would wink cozily in the evening hours, windows aglimmer with the gaslights of neighborly warmth and hospitality.

2

The Early Light

Basic to all civilization is the use of tools. Some tools—such as ax and hammer—serve only the man who handles them (although, of course, the products he makes with them may serve his fellowmen as well). Other tools are collective. Fire was the first of these. It warmed not only the savage who lit it, but also other members of his tribe. With the advance of civilization, collective tools became increasingly common and served ever larger publics. The wagon supplemented the horse. The steam train superseded the stagecoach. The flivver grew into the bus. Central sources of power, eventually shared by millions of people, supplanted candle and lantern, wood stove and fireplace.

In the mid-nineteenth century, the land had been conquered and settled. America stood at the threshold of the great era of the collective tool, and manufactured gas was among the first implements of this industrial revolution.

Jean Baptiste van Helmont, a Belgian, had discovered way

back in 1609 that fuels in the process of combustion "belched
forth a wild spirit." Later, a British clergyman from Yorkshire,
John Clayton, heated some coal in a closed vessel and observed
that "The Spirit which issued out caught Fire at the Flame of
a Candle." Clayton filled animal bladders with his "Spirit,"
and he seemed to have had a lot of fun with his new toy: "When
I had a mind to divert Strangers or Friends," he wrote, "I
have frequently taken one of these Bladders, and pricking a
Hole therein with a Pin, and compressing gently the Bladder
near the Flame of a Candle till it once took Fire, it would
then continue flaming till all the Spirit was compressed out of
the Bladder, which was the more surprising, because no one
could discern any Difference in the Appearance between these
Bladders and those which were filled with Common Air."[1]

It was another century before William Murdock, a Scotsman
residing in Cornwall, put gas to practical use. Murdock discovered in 1792 that gas obtained by distillation from coal,
wood, and other flammable substances burns with great
brilliance when lit. He did his distilling in an iron retort and
conducted the resultant gas a distance of 70 feet through tin,
iron, and copper tubes to a room in his house. Then he cut
openings of various shapes and sizes in the tube to determine
which would give the best light.

As it happened, Murdock worked at that time for James
Watt, developer of the steam engine, whose name was later
appropriated to identify a common measurement of electricity.
But in this instance Watt was involved with gas, and he applied
his employee's discovery to the lighting of his factory in
Birmingham, England. That's as far as Watt went with it,
thereby missing a good bet. The first English patent for the
making of coal gas instead accrued in 1804 to one Frederick
Albert Winsor, a flashy promoter of uncertain nationality[2] who
went all out with advertising, exhibitions, and demonstrations
to sell the process he had somehow gotten hold of.

Winsor ran into bitter opposition. Commenting on the new
invention, Sir Walter Scott wrote to a friend, "There is a mad-

man proposing to light London with—what do you think? Why, with smoke!" Eventually, however, Winsor had his way, leaden pipes were laid in London's Pall Mall, and a part of that famous street was lighted with gas. This paved the way for the world's first gas company, the London and Westminster Gas Light and Coke Company, which was incorporated in 1810 and got its royal charter two years later. Even Sir Walter came around after a bit. Not only did he illuminate his own home with gas, but later, being apparently at least as good a business-man as he was a poet, he actually became chairman of the board of the Edinburgh Oil Gas Company.

In the United States, gas was first used for public lighting in Baltimore, and thereby hangs an interesting little tale. At the turn of the eighteenth century there lived in Philadelphia a most remarkable man, Charles Willson Peale, whose many varied talents rivaled those of his friend and correspondent, Thomas Jefferson. Peale was not only one of the most out-standing portrait painters of his day, but in addition he was a naturalist, a dentist, a farmer, a showman, and the owner of a museum which, not surprisingly, specialized in Peale paintings. Along with all these activities, Peale somehow found the time to sire and raise seven equally talented and artistic sons. One of these was Rembrandt Peale, who, true to his given name and his paternal inheritance, became a painter like his father. Also like his father, Rembrandt was a dilettante and a showman as well. Since the elder Peale had already cornered the museum market in Philadelphia, Rembrandt built a showplace of his own in Baltimore. There he exhibited not only his paintings, but also various collections of stuffed birds, Indian relics, and such curiosities as the skeleton of a mastodon. However, Rembrandt's restless mind was forever searching for additional attractions, and in 1816 he hit on the idea of using illuminating gas made from pine tar, which had just been patented by one of his father's friends, Dr. Benjamin Kugler.[3] Peale's advertisement in the *Baltimore Gazette* of June 13, 1816, proclaimed:

GAS LIGHTS

WITHOUT OIL, TALLOW, WICKS OR SMOKE

It is not necessary to invite attention to the gas lights by which my salon of paintings is illuminated; those who have seen the ring beset with gems of light are sufficiently disposed to spread their reputation; the purpose of this notice is merely to say that the Museum will be illuminated every evening until the public curiosity shall be gratified—Rembrandt Peale.

Indeed, the exhibition made such a hit that within two weeks, the city council passed an ordinance authorizing the Gas Light Company of Baltimore to go into business. In retrospect, this quick decision by the city fathers of Baltimore is more than a little surprising, and not only because governmental bodies were no more given to fast action in those days than they are today. What made the acceptance so amazing is that the public had great reservations about this new, spectacular development. Many respectable citizens argued that artificial illumination interfered with the divine plan that the world should be dark at night. There were even those who claimed that illuminating the streets would induce people to stay out-of-doors, thus causing them to catch colds in the night

REMBRANDT PEALE

As his self-portrait indicates, Peale was a reasonably talented painter. More important, he was an extremely apt showman. To publicize his museum in Baltimore, he staged the first public demonstration of illuminating gas in the United States (right). The date was June 13, 1816. (Consolidated of Baltimore)

air, and that the unwanted light would frighten horses, encourage thieves, and increase drunkenness and depravity.[4] Thus, after 'the establishment of the New World's first gas company in Maryland's largest city, the new invention was very slow to spread, and as late as 1850 only thirty American communities had gas plants.[5]

Many of these early plants started right off making gas from coal. This generally was the cheapest method, and it had the advantage of yielding certain by-products—such as coke, tar, and ammonia—which also could be sold. However, in Kalamazoo the original source was pine resin, which was bought from a nearby lumber mill and which, because of this convenience, seemed like a good idea at the time. But real trouble lay just ahead.

The first Kalamazoo plant, which is believed to have been located on Harrison Street near the present site of the Riverside Foundry, consisted of a retort house where the resin was distilled, an office shack, and several resin storage sheds. The main building was 30 feet high. It contained a gas holder with a capacity of 12,250 cubic feet. About 2½ miles of pipe had been laid in the street. When the operation started, the

company had eighty customers using about five hundred burners. It was a deceptively auspicious beginning.

One day early in September 1857, barely two months after the jubilant inauguration of the service, half a dozen of the company's major stockholders met at the plant office, whose most imposing item of furniture was an immense rolltop desk. All the faces were glum.

"At this rate," said Jeremiah Woodbury, the company's president, his knobby index finger traveling down the scrawled entries in a ledger, "we'll go broke in another six months."

Stephen S. Cobb, one of the stockholders, held up a copy of the *Gazette*. "Our good friend, the editor, isn't helping us any," he said bitterly. "The honeymoon is over. You've all seen the paper. It says right here that only the wealthiest families can afford us."[6]

"Well," said Woodbury, "it's the truth. We've got to charge

KALAMAZOO IN 1856

That's what Main Street (now Michigan Avenue) looked like when the first predecessor company of Consumers was founded by Jeremiah Wood-bury. If you look carefully, you will discover some streetlights, then still fueled with kerosene. (Kalamazoo Public Museum)

$7 for 1,000 cubic feet of our resin gas. If we charged less, we'd go broke even faster. When they first started in New York, they charged $10."

"What's the rate there now?" asked Cobb.

"Six dollars, last I heard. But their costs are lower. They're now using coal." Woodbury pulled some dog-eared notes out of his jacket pocket. "We can estimate that 1 ton of coal will make 8,000 cubic feet of gas," he said. "Assuming we switched to coal, each ton would leave us 45 bushels of coke, for which we can get 30 cents a bushel. Altogether, by selling the coke and the tar, we'd defray the wages of the two men in the works. This leaves us with just the cost of the coal, and that won't amount to much more than the resin, even if prices go up."[7]

There was a long silence, broken at last by James A. Walker, who acted as treasurer of the little company. "Seems to me that there is only one thing to do," he said. "We've got to

. . . AND TWENTY YEARS LATER

Now Kalamazoo was no longer a frontier town. Impressive new buildings had gone up, older ones had been refurbished, and the city was illuminated by gas. Both photographs were taken almost from the same spot, looking west from Portage Street. (Kalamazoo Public Museum)

switch from resin to coal. We've got $3,000 in the kitty. That's not enough. But I'll tell you something, gentlemen. We can still let out another $3,000 worth of stock. We might be able to go on that. The big question is, should we solicit new shareholders, or do we want to add to our own subscriptions?"

Woodbury looked around the little room. "It may be throwing good money after bad," he said, "but I've got faith in our project, and I am willing to risk it."

"I'll go along with you," said Cobb, "and I guess the other fellows here will too."

They did, and so the company was saved. Three months later, with additional investment and some borrowed funds, a new coal plant had been erected, and the equipment had been changed. The price of gas went down. But the editor of the *Gazette* still wasn't totally satisfied. On January 22, 1858, he reported: "The Gas Company of Kalamazoo uses Jackson coal which produces a very good light but fills the atmosphere with a sulphurous vapor." This item may well have been the first ecology editorial printed in the state of Michigan—even then there were people who wanted to benefit from technological progress without submitting to the laws of chemistry and physics.

Not so, however, in Pontiac, which was still a village of fewer than 5,000 inhabitants. Here, the *Weekly Gazette* of August 24, 1860, announced: "It gives us sincere pleasure to say that we are soon to have gas in Pontiac. Four able and capable businessmen . . . have taken the matter in hand, formed themselves into a stock company, have purchased the right to use Mr. A. K. Tupper's Improved Gas Generator, and have employed Mr. Tupper to superintend the operations of erecting gas works of sufficient capacity to supply the whole city."[8] When the work dragged on and on and Tupper still hadn't got his job done by November, the *Weekly Gazette*, which apparently was a Republican paper, complained, "The question is, shall we have gaslight to read the news of Lincoln's election by next Tuesday night?"

The first gas was finally sold in Pontiac in January of the following year. It was made from resin—the men in Pontiac evidently hadn't heard about the near-disaster in Kalamazoo. So Pontiac went through the same experience, only worse. Soon after the Civil War broke out in April 1861, the price of resin rose so high that the plant had to be shut down completely. When operations resumed at last, Pontiac was also using coal, and the rate was pegged at $4.80 per 1,000 cubic feet in the fall of 1864. Other Michigan communities soon had their gas companies too. By 1870, the remaining four of the seven predecessor gas companies of Consumers Power had been founded, and all were in the black: the East Saginaw Gas Light Co. (1863), Saginaw Gas Light Co. (1868), and those in Bay City and Flint.[9]

Let's have a quick look at what the manufacture of coal gas involved. The coal was not burned—it was "cooked"; that is, it was heated in airless retorts to a temperature somewhere between 1000 and 1200° C. The resultant gas was driven off, collected, and purified. The retorts in which this distillation took place were long and narrow and usually made of clay. In cross section, they resembled the letter "D" laid on its back, and for this reason they were often called "D-type" retorts. They usually were stacked on top of one another in a series of banks. Stoking them by hand was quite an art, since the face of a retort—the opening through which it had to be fed—was only about 18 by 28 inches, but the body of the chamber was some 9 feet long. The efficiency of the whole operation—how much gas was produced per pound of coal—depended entirely on the skill of the stoker.

Then, in 1873, a new type of gas plant was built in Phoenixville, Pennsylvania. It used a more sophisticated process that had been patented by Professor T. S. C. Lowe the year before. The gas obtained by Lowe's method is commonly called "water

EARLY GAS RETORTS

At the beginning, manufactured gas was made mostly in hand-operated clay retorts, commonly called "D retorts" because of their shape in cross section. This picture shows several banks of them at the Owosso Gas Light Company, where they were still used in the 1920s. (Consumers Power Company)

gas," but this is a somewhat misleading term since water, as such, does not enter it. What happens is that steam is passed through incandescent coke or anthracite in the retort, resulting in a chemical breakdown and realignment of hydrocarbons. To further enrich or "carburate" the resultant water gas, oil then is usually sprayed over checker bricks heated by the coal or coke used in the process. This, in turn, gasifies the oil, and the oil gas mixes with the water gas to produce a much richer gas with a considerably higher heat value. In later years, when heating rather than lighting became the purpose of the gas utility, carburated water gas came into general use.

But the original gas business was primarily a lighting business, based on the illumination achieved as the carbon particles in the gas burned. The more such particles were in the gas, the brighter the light. Candlepower, a unit of light intensity, became the quality measure of gas, and every plant had a photometer that regularly checked the output.

The development of early gas fixtures consisted mainly of enlarging the area over which the gas was spread for incineration of its carbon particles. All factors being equal, it stood to reason that the larger the light source, the more illumination it would yield. There were generally two types of tips through which the gas jets came. One type had a rounded top with a slit in it. The other type had two openings that were angled toward each other at 45 degrees from the perpendicular; it produced a spread-out but relatively thin flame pattern. The light from either source was called "fishtail" or "batwing," depending on how a person viewed the pattern.

In 1850, Robert Wilhelm von Bunsen invented the blue-flame gas burner named after him. By introducing a jet of air along with the gas, he was able to produce an intensely hot

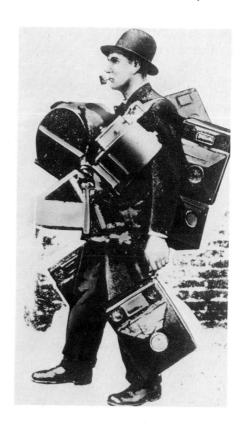

OFF TO WORK

The men who installed early gas meters had to make their rounds on foot, carrying their tools and materials.
(Consolidated of Baltimore)

flame which was economical and smokeless. The bunsen principle paved the way for heat application, but this was still some time off. In the meanwhile, the so-called Welsbach fixtures and mantles were developed, which employed the bunsen-type flame to heat certain metals to incandescence. In their manufacture, the woven material of the mantle was dipped into a metallic solution. Then, after installation in the lamp, the mantle was burned. This destroyed the woven material but left the metallic meshwork intact as a concentrated light source, much as in today's camping lanterns that are fed by gasoline and bottled gas and in outdoor lights that burn natural gas. Of course, people had to be extremely careful with these fixtures. The metal meshwork was extremely fragile, and when it was touched it crumbled, necessitating purchase of a new one.

The Welsbach lights were soft and pleasing and were generally considered to be of better quality than the early electric light. But the system had two major faults. One was heat. The other was that any gas lighting—especially on a large scale—was cumbersome, at best, to operate. Another big problem was cost. In the late 1860s, for instance, the price of gas in New York City went down as low as $3.50 per 1,000 cubic feet,[10] but this was still thought to be quite expensive by the standards of those days, and when the much cheaper kerosene lamp came on the market at about that time, it proved a powerful competitor. Gas as an illuminant was finally dealt the death blow by the advent of Thomas Edison's electric incandescent lamp. Only the increasing development of the heating potential of gas saved the early companies, including the predecessors of Consumers Power Company, from demise.

But the inherent elegance of gas fixtures and their romantic glow has not been forgotten to this day. Even now, gas lamps and electric outdoor lights resembling the old gas fixtures are big sellers, for they suggest the wonderfully secure mood of the gaslight era, a mood that has not been recaptured since.

Within a few decades of its frontier days, Michigan had become a cozy, even gracious place to live. Lighted streets were safe streets, lighted homes invited evening company, and lighted halls allowed for theater and other evening entertainments. There is little doubt that without gaslight to bridge the years between the candle and the electric bulb, it would have taken America far longer to achieve cultural maturity.

3

Powers' Towers

One afternoon in May 1880, Fred Powers, age thirteen, tiptoed across the living room of his parents' home in Grand Rapids. He poked his head into its cozy kitchen, saw that the coast was clear, and quickly stuffed his pockets with oatmeal cookies from a jar. Still on tiptoe, he opened the back door as silently as he could, but as he was about to close it behind him, the knob slipped from his hand and the door banged shut.

"Freddy," he heard his mother's voice from an upstairs window, "where are you going?"

"To Grandpa's," the boy yelled back, and by that time he was running. The important thing was to get out of earshot fast, so that he couldn't be called back to do his chores. Any stolen hour spent with his grandfather was well worth getting scolded for later. Old William T. Powers ruled a fascinating world of machines and gadgets where something interesting happened every minute. Young Fred loved all the smells and noises at the Powers factory—the heady aroma of freshly cut timber, the pungent odors of varnish and machine oil, the ear-piercing screech of circular gang saws as they bit into wood and slit thick planks into siding and flooring. He loved to watch as skillful workmen rubbed furniture to a fine finish, and he liked the way all the men at the mill treated him with affection and his grandfather with respect. But best of all were those precious hours in his grandfather's private workshop behind the mill, where the elder Powers experimented with just about every new scientific and mechanical invention of the day. Sometimes the old man even allowed the boy to "help."

Of course, William Powers was an old man only in his grandson's eyes. Born in 1820, Powers was just turning sixty then, and he was a man of robust health and energy, but the muttonchops that were in fashion then tended to make men look older than their years and lent them that air of patriarchal authority not easily achieved by the clean-shaven.

Powers, a native of Bristol, New Hampshire, had come to Grand Rapids in 1847 with his family, hoping like so many other young pioneers to make his fortune on Michigan's forest frontier. A cabinetmaker by trade, he couldn't have chosen a more favorable spot. Grand Rapids lay on the "Grand River Road," another important avenue of settlements like the Territorial Road of Jackson and Kalamazoo. Villages like Farmington, Brighton, Howell, Grand Rapids, and Grand Haven grew up along this immigrant trail in the 1830s, foreshadowing the day when it would become Interstate 96. Lansing, now the state capital, didn't get its start until the very year Powers came to Michigan, but Grand Rapids was already sixteen years old by then, having been founded by fur trader Louis Campau in 1831.[1] Even prior to that time, in 1823, a Baptist mission for the Indians had been established there. The town grew up at the rapids of the Grand River, from which it derived its name. Thanks to the fall of the river at this point, there was abundant waterpower to be harnessed, and the location of the settlement was made all the more fortuitous by the fact that small steamships had no difficulty coming up from Lake Michigan as far as the rapids. The town's first industry had been stucco and plaster, obtained from nearby gypsum pits. Soon there followed a woolens factory, a wagon works, and a pottery. Still, it was a sleepy little frontier town when Powers first arrived, and he rented a room in a small shop at the corner of Franklin and Ionia Streets where he made furniture by hand.

Powers grew and prospered along with Grand Rapids. He was in partnership for a while with Ebenezer M. Ball; then he dissolved the partnership and established his own lumber and furniture business in 1855. He installed the first circular saw in Grand Rapids and later built a machine with a "gang" of circular saws—again a first for that town. Right after the Civil War he bought frontage on the Grand River and constructed the West Side Power Canal, whose flow turned the wheels that made his saws work. All in all, Powers built more than thirty houses, mills, stores, factories, and other structures, including a grand opera auditorium which he proudly called the Powers Opera House and which later became a movie theater. The building through which one gained access to this auditorium still stands today; it is known as the Powers Building, and for some years it housed the local Consumers Power Company offices.[2]

By the time Bill Powers' grandson Fred was thirteen, Grand Rapids had grown into a bustling city of some thirty-two thousand people and was the second largest in the state. By the end of the Civil War, a rapid industrialization had come to Michigan. Detroit was building locomotives, steam engines, and stoves. Kalamazoo produced carriages, mill equipment, pharmaceuticals, and even pianos and melodions. Saginaw and Bay City had sawmills. Flint became known as the center for the manufacture of wagons and carriages. Grand Rapids turned out freight cars, elevators, pumps, paints, varnish, tools, and surgical instruments, and it was well on the way to becoming world famous for its furniture. A real urban life was developing everywhere. Wealthy residents built magnificent homes. Floors were luxuriously carpeted. Fine furnishings took the place of rough, homemade tables and stools. There were waterworks and fire companies. More and more streets were being paved. And more and more streets shone with gaslights at night.

On this afternoon of 1880, it was precisely the subject of lighting that occupied Powers' mind, as it had for several years. When young Fred arrived breathlessly at the workshop, Powers was poring over a report on a newfangled electrical device designed by one Charles F. Brush of Cleveland. Brush had been working on arc lamps and dynamos for a long time and had finally designed a dynamo that produced a nearly constant current of sufficiently high voltage to light up to sixteen arc lamps on one circuit.[3] The first such light, resulting from the flow of electricity between two carbon poles, had been demonstrated in 1808 by Sir Humphrey Davy in England. In this experiment, current was supplied from a battery of 2,000 cells, and pieces of charcoal were used as carbons. Davy touched these pieces of charcoal together and then drew them apart, forming an arc that gave off an intense light. Another Englishman, Michael Faraday, discovered in 1831 that current is generated in an electrical conductor when it is moved between poles of a magnet. Faraday's original dynamo had been a great technical achievement, but he made no attempt to turn it to practical use. Now, at last, Brush had come up with an arc-lighting mechanism that promised to work under practical conditions outside the laboratory.

"See this thing here, Freddy," said Powers, reaching for one of the lamps Brush had sent to him from his shop in Cleveland. "It doesn't look like much, but before long lights like this will make the nights as bright as day, brighter than gaslights. We'll put these lamps on tall towers, much higher than houses, and every street will have its own moon regardless of the weather."

"You're going to do that right here in Grand Rapids?" asked Fred.

"That's right," Powers said. This was nothing really new to Fred. The boy had merely feigned surprise in an effort to stall for time, trying to figure out what to say. What could a boy say to a grandfather he worshiped when that man was about to commit the biggest error of his life? All Fred knew was that he somehow had to dissuade his grandfather from making a fool of himself. By now the whole town was talking about Powers' plan to light up the city with this latest brainstorm, and many people were happily betting that it wouldn't work. More than once during the past weeks Fred had been forced to defend his family's honor with his fists when classmates kidded him about his grandfather's man-made moons. The trouble was that even when Fred won these fights, as he usually did, this did not remedy the situation; deep down he knew that the old man would fail, and he had good reasons for his doubts.

Two years earlier, in the biggest adventure of Fred's young life, Grandfather Powers had borrowed him from his parents and taken him all the way to New York by train. There, in that big, overwhelming city, the older man and the excited boy had taken a carriage to a glassblower's shop on Mott Street where a crate filled with balloon-shaped glass objects had been waiting for them. Inside each of these glass bulbs was a small brown cardboard strip covered with a fragile glass finish a fraction of an inch in thickness. The cardboard assembly was held in place by two thin wires that came through at the base of the bulb. His grandfather had told Fred that by connecting these wires to metal projections that stuck out of a box which he called a "battery," the glass bulbs would glow brightly, giving off a stronger light than any other man-made lamp. Grandfather Powers had designed the bulbs himself and was convinced that they would work. Fred was equally sure—after all, his grandfather was infallible! But when they finally got back to their hotel, where Powers had such a battery, and he connected his first bulb, it not only glowed so feebly one could hardly see it in the daylight, but the light flickered out almost immediately.

Grandfather Powers had tried one after another of his bulbs, but none of them worked any better. Again accompanied by the boy, he then returned to the glassblowers and ordered some more bulbs made, instructing the craftsmen on the modifications he wanted. But the new batch turned out to be equally disappointing.[4]

Fred remembered all this well, and he was now beset by the terrible fear that his grandfather was just as wrong about the new arc lamps as he had been about his old incandescent bulbs. The first failure had been private, shared only by the boy. But if the old man failed again, the fiasco would be public, and after all his big pronouncements Powers would be the laughing stock of Grand Rapids.

"What if it doesn't work?" Fred stuttered. "Grandpa, you remember. . . ."

"Don't you worry about that for a minute," Powers laughed. "I know it's going to work. I'll tell you what, boy. When we get everything set up, you can throw the switch!" As an afterthought he added, almost as if speaking to himself, "It had better work. I just put a lot of money into it, and so did your father."

Only two months earlier, on March 22, 1880, Powers had organized the Grand Rapids Electric Light and Power Company with a total capitalization of $100,000, spread among eight farsighted investors.[5] The company had immediately purchased its first dynamo, the sixteen-light Brush arc machine, together with the lamps, wire, and other materials. The dynamo was now being installed in the plant, at the corner of Pearl and Front Streets, of the Wolverine Chair Company, of which Powers was an official. A covered bridge led to the plant from the downtown side of the river. Waterpower to propel the dynamo was rented from a nearby lumber mill.

July 24 was the target date. Powers looked forward to it with great hopes; young Fred, with terrible trepidation. The arc lights were set up in The Powers Opera House and in Sweet's Hotel, as well as in several leading stores.[6] Wires were strung up and connected. Finally everything was ready, just in time for the big day.

Already in the morning hours of that sunny summer Saturday of 1880, Grand Rapids folks who had nothing better to do started collecting in little crowds around The Powers Opera House, where two of the sixteen arc lights were strung on wires to illuminate the building's facade. Shoppers on their way to downtown stores stopped to look in wonderment at those strange contraptions, which, inconceivable as it must have seemed at that time, would somehow fashion light out of a nothingness called electricity. Workmen hammered away at a small grandstand that faced the entrance. Here was where the local dignitaries would be enthroned this evening to make speeches and to listen with half an ear to the speeches of others as replete with commonplace public phrases as their own, but mostly to witness the illumination which had been promised once young Fred Powers pulled the wooden handle on a simple switch installed by the door of his grandfather's opera house. All day long the crowds gathered and dissolved, a continuously changing panorama of curious faces, all waiting for the big event. By evening, as the summer's late sunlight faded into dusk, a band had assembled in the street. Their tuning up lent the falling night a festive mood, and more and more people, attracted by the sounds of horns and drums, milled in the street to watch the amazing exhibition.

The night was warm. Buntings, resurrected from Fourth of July celebrations, hung still in the humid air of the hot Michigan summer. Young Fred, dressed in his church suit, was drenched with the perspiration of excitement. He stood next to his tall grandfather in the doorway, reverting in his anxiety to a child's manner of stepping from one foot onto the other, unable to keep still. Fred was worried and elated all at the same time. Never had he felt so strongly the beating of his heart. He barely heard the speeches. He did not even listen as his grandfather finished his brief address: "And now, ladies and gentlemen, my grandson Fred here—most of you fine

POWERS OPERA HOUSE IN 1880

It was on Pearl Street in Grand Rapids that William Powers first demonstrated his arc lights. The arcade in the third building from the left marked the spot where Powers' grandson, Fred, threw the switch. This photograph, taken prior to the event, shows Pearl Street looking east from Campau Square. (Grand Rapids Press photo)

people know him—will turn on the lights. I can think of no one more appropriate for this honorable task than a young man of his generation, for it is his generation that will live with all the wonders that electricity can bring. Fred, go ahead now."

Fred stood there, lost in his own world, not moving, and Grandfather Bill Powers had to give him a gentle nudge, saying again under his breath, "Go ahead, Fred. Go ahead now!" before the boy snapped to. Fred raised his hand and grabbed the handle.

The street was silent. Faces in the crowd shimmered like pale disks in the darkness. Fred pulled the switch. Metal closed on metal—and a gasp went through the crowd. The street was as dark as before. Nothing had happend.

There was a sudden swell of voices—murmurs, snickering,

some laughter. Instinctively the bandmaster launched his musicians into another brassy tune. Fred was close to tears. Biting his lower lip, he looked up at his grandfather. He wanted to yell: "I told you so!"

Powers understood. He put his big cabinetmaker's hand on the boy's shoulder. "Buck up," he said. "We'll get it fixed." Then he moved the switch back up to its off position. "You stay right here, Fred," he said. "I'm going to see what's happened." He left the doorway and pushed his way through the restless crowd.

A local politician, who had greedily assumed the role of master of ceremonies for the occasion, motioned for the band

WHERE THE LIGHT CAME FROM

The hydroelectric power for grandfather Powers' arc lights was provided by the West Side Power Canal, which paralleled the Grand River. The generating equipment was connected to the waterwheels of his Wolverine Chair Company (extreme left), whose intake racks are visible just beyond the structure. The little wheelhouse with the Giant Clothing sign on it, between the canal and the river, belonged to the Grand Rapids Brush Co. and furnished power to their factory located on the west side of Front Street. This photograph was taken in the early 1880s from the old Pearl Street bridge. The Wolverine Chair building stood on the northeast corner of Front and Pearl Streets between Front Street and the canal. (Courtesy of L. L. Benedict)

to stop playing and then intoned his apologia with the bluff humor of a circus barker whose star attraction has failed to present himself on cue. But Fred heard none of this and couldn't have cared less about "unforeseen circumstances." It had happened just as he had expected. No longer would his grandfather be the big man of Grand Rapids; instead, he'd be looked on as a clown. The band blared out again, drowning out most of the talk and chuckles of the spectators. Minutes passed as Fred stood lost in a trance of mortification.

Suddenly grandfather was back again. A smile on his face, he clapped the boy on the back. "Okay, Fred," he said. "Go ahead."

Fred looked at him questioningly. He couldn't face up to a second failure. It would be more than he could bear. "Don't you worry, boy," Powers whispered to him. "It's all fixed. Somebody just forgot to hook up a little wire." With a sudden rush of desperate decision Fred reached up and pulled the switch once more.

In that instant he was blinded by a blast of light. The roar of the crowd swelled around him lifting his spirits to triumphant heights. In the harsh, unaccustomed glare he saw his grandfather smiling and eagerly shaking the hands of the many well-wishers who now pressed forward, and the boy's choked-back tears turned into tears of laughter. Fred felt himself raised on strong shoulders. It was the greatest night of his life.

Grandfather Powers' powerful arc lamps also shone the next night and the next. They kept shining night after night. Fred was happy. Grand Rapids was happy. And the store-keepers of Grand Rapids were especially happy. The Star Clothing Company, one of the establishments where lamps had been set up, advertised in the *Daily Eagle* that the shop would stay open until nine o'clock each evening to give customers a chance to examine the electric lights—and, of course, to do some buying in the bargain. Other businesses, afraid to be left behind in the competition, also clamored for arc lamps. Merchants could rent the lamps for $120 a year apiece, with the electricity thrown in "free" as part of the deal. Within a few weeks the original sixteen-light machine was moved to Powers' sawmill at the lower end of the West Side Canal, and an even larger machine to feed many more lights was installed with it. By the following spring Powers had obtained a contract from the city for streetlighting, and on June 29, 1881, the brilliance of 16,000 candles' worth of electricity blazed from a cluster of eight Brush lanterns of 2,000 candlepower each, mounted on a nearly 200-foot-tall steel tower near the corner of Pearl and Ottawa Streets. Here was indeed the man-made moon Powers had promised the boy — a fantastic concentration of light, high above the street.

Of course this was hardly the most practical method of illumination. Yet it's quite understandable that it must have seemed the most natural way to light up a town in those days. After all, there had been no prior experience with strong lights except those of the sun and moon. Both of these shone from the sky, and it was only reasonable to assume that man's imitation should shine from up there too. As it happened, the city of Grand Rapids got away from the tower concept almost immediately after the inaugural demonstrations and in a burst of good sense asked Bill Powers to install individual arc lamps on 10-foot iron posts at various important corners of Monroe and Canal Streets — a total of twelve light posts that provided illumination where it was needed, instead of way up in the air. This was in August 1881. But some time after that, and nobody knows why, the city changed its mind and returned to a system of tall towers, now built of steel girders with brass couplings, like those in most communities to which early electricity had come.

These immense towers, which were anywhere from about 100 to 200 and more feet tall, gave the streets below an eerie atmosphere of glaring light and deep darkness. You were blinded when you looked up at the lamps, and the roofs of the houses and the tops of trees were well lighted indeed, but down below, under the eaves and the tree branches, everything

POWERS' FIRST TOWER

This wooden tower, erected in 1881, was located on the present site of the Michigan Trust Company building. It was at first thought that the tall beacon, blazing with 16,000 candlepower, would illuminate the entire city. (Courtesy of Mrs. Emery Thomas)

that was not directly exposed was swallowed by shadows. However, Bill Powers' towers and other three-legged giants like them did have their delightful aspects, and for these they were deeply mourned by the younger generation, if not by their elders, when the towers finally passed from the scene, some as late as the 1920s. One of the charms of the towers was that they offered a daredevil challenge to be climbed, a venture which was not without risk because of their dizzying height and also, of course, because there was hot wire on top. Luckily, there were surprisingly few accidents over the years.

The other intriguing aspect of the towers — much safer except for its implicit threat to wallpaper and flat paint — was that arc-light carbons eventually burned out and had to be changed. Kids collected these smudgy black tips and used them as crayons. "Pencil men," as youngsters came to call the men who serviced arc lamps, were always followed on their rounds like Pied Pipers, as all the boys and girls vied for the discarded carbon tips. This remained a favorite pastime for several decades. As one might expect, young Fred Powers in Grand Rapids was one of its earliest enthusiasts.

William T. Powers, already in that first summer of electric streetlights and store lights, purchased additional land for his Grand Rapids Electric Light and Power Company, as well as waterpower consisting of 16 "runs of stone" on the West Side Canal. A run of stone was a miller's measure of power at a power site, based on the locally accepted standard size of a grindstone. A dam of a certain size on a certain stream was figured to have enough power to run a certain number of these stones. Thus run of stone became the measure of a man's share of the available water energy. To utilize his run of stone, Powers installed large waterwheels, erected permanent buildings on the adjoining land he'd bought, and even added a steam plant to provide for constant running in case his waterpower failed as a result of ice, flood, low water, or any other cause.

The electric business in Grand Rapids looked so good that another entrepreneur, H. D. Wallen, Jr., started a second electric plant at the Michigan Iron Works the following year and founded a stock company known as the Michigan Iron Works Electric Light and Power Company. Wallen operated in competition with Powers until 1884, but in the end Powers bought him out, and Wallen's plant was absorbed into the Grand Rapids Electric Light and Power Company.

Powers' central station of 1880 was in all likelihood the world's first commercial hydroelectric installation.[7] It predated by two years the commonly accepted birth date of commercial electricity—1882—the year when a small hydroelectric central station in Appleton, Wisconsin, and Thomas Alva Edison's original central steam station on Pearl Street in New York City began their operations. Both of these supplied energy only for Edison's incandescent lamps, which were then still in an early and quite inefficient stage. The fact that the birth of electric utilities has been pegged somewhat erroneously on these two installations is probably due to Edison's great fame and influence. Actually, the very first central power station of any kind seems to have been a steam plant of the California Electric Light Company in San Francisco, which was already generating electricity for arc lighting in 1879.[8]

In Saginaw, too, an electric company was formed prior to the official 1882 birth date. Here, a gentlemen by the name of Alexander Swift, of Cincinnati, formed the Swift Electric Light Company, which was franchised on July 15, 1881. Swift was also involved with the Saginaw Gas Light Company, one of the seven predecessor gas companies of Consumers Power mentioned in the previous chapter.[9] In addition, he was active in the lumber business in Saginaw. Thus, like Powers, Swift was a man of considerable prestige and influence, and it is not surprising that he too pioneered this new development.

Swift's electric apparatus was the invention of Hiram S. Maxim, who has since become better known for his machine gun.[10] Indeed, Maxim's light didn't seem to cause nearly the same stir in Saginaw that Brush's had occasioned in Grand

Rapids. The *Saginaw Daily Courier*[11] reported the local light demonstrations, but its only coverage other than a plain announcement of the fact was the wry observation that "electric light is playing hob with evening street flirtations." Such a lack of record, however, is not necessarily conclusive. The general format of newspapers in those days was such that local happenings were rarely reported, and when they were, they were usually relegated to the last page. The idea seemed to be that everyone knew what happened in the community anyway.

In the absence of reliable eyewitness accounts, all we know for sure today is that this second electric predecessor company of Consumers Power gave its first exhibitions at the Bancroft House in Saginaw and the Fraser House—later the Hotel Wenona—in Bay City and that apparently the first demonstration had to be postponed for some weeks. To run his generators, Swift made arrangements with a sawmill near the Fraser House at Sixth and Water Streets, ran wires from the mill to the hotel, and installed some incandescent lamps of sixteen candlepower each for the demonstration. His streetlamps, however, were 2,000-candlepower arc lights, which easily outshone all existing gas fixtures.[12] On November 9, 1881, Bay City gave the Swift Company a contract to light the streets, and the first installation called for seventy such powerful arc lamps mounted on 45-foot poles, as well as a steel tower at the corner of Center and Jefferson Streets which blazed out 36,000 candlepower from its lofty 220-foot summit. The tall tower's light could be seen in Saginaw Bay for a distance of twelve miles, but as may be expected, its local illumination was not particularly effective despite the great intensity, since most of the illumination was obscured by shade trees and houses below the lights. After the authorities of Bay City had had a taste of the tower, they wished it were down. One stormy afternoon in 1885 their wish was granted; the tower was blown loose and tumbled down in a heap. Fortunately no one was hurt and no great damage was done.

Meanwhile, electric pioneers were also hard at work in other

Michigan communities. Early in 1882, J. L. Willett organized the Peoples Electric Light Company in the then small town of Flint with initial capital of $75,000,[13] and in 1884 a group of Jackson businessmen, banding together as the Mitchell-Reid Company, purchased a small dynamo and set it up in a mill driven by power from the Grand River at Holton Dam. A small Edison incandescent light plant for store illumination was started the same year in Jackson, and it operated in a plant on Otsego Avenue, just east of Francis Street, under the name of Jackson Electric Light and Power Company, later called Edison Electric Light Company.[14] On October 30, 1885, the Kalamazoo Electric Company was organized,[15] and in later years there followed the Battle Creek Electric Light and Power Company (1887) and the Edison Electric Light & Motor Company in Pontiac (1888).

These, then, were the electric predecessors of Consumers Power, and like its gas predecessors they were seven in number. Their successes with store-light demonstrations and streetlamps did not guarantee survival, however. All these little companies struggled along in a most venturesome business that was based on a futuristic vision and married to all the risks that such vision entails. It was a highly competitive business — indeed, a free-for-all.

Often, competing companies were organized to render the same service to the same territory. By 1900, for example, Grand Rapids had four competitive utility operations.[16] This competition, coupled with constant technological change, made the period one of great financial danger linked at best to a pitifully small reward. Many of the companies never paid a dividend and were often forced to go out of business, selling their plants at much less than the original investment. Among the companies which suffered this fate were also some of Consumers Power's predecessor companies, including those in Jackson, Pontiac, and Flint. Even the powerful Swift Company in Saginaw eventually had to sell out at a loss of half its $200,-000 cash investment.[17]

Among the reasons for the precarious financial situation of

the early companies were undoubtedly those dangers incident to the establishment of any new line of business for which the public has not yet developed a true want. What's more, the utilization of machinery and equipment had not yet reached a stable level of technical perfection. Particularly in the electric business, with its various methods of generation, distribution, and utilization, nothing was certain except rapid and violent change.[18] Names like Brush, Thomson-Houston, Maxim, and Edison suggest only a few of the many electrical systems introduced in this "competitive epoch of America's utilities."[19]

In those early days, too, there was no regulation of utilities as we now know it. The common-law concept of England, that this business is clothed with a public interest and therefore subject to regulation, had not yet been applied. But the industry did have one important distinction even then from other competitive types of enterprises. Since public streets and highways had to be used for the laying of gas mains and the running of electric distribution lines, it was necessary to obtain franchises from the local municipal authorities. There was a precedent for this requirement. Franchises for laying water mains had been required for many years, and street railways were subject to franchising long before their electrification, when horses still pulled the cars. Sometimes these early franchises, in addition to granting permission for the use of streets, actually incorporated some elements of rudimentary regulation. In the case of street railways, there were requirements with respect to the extent to which streets had to be paved and kept clear of snow. Often, and not just in the case of street railways, there were even limitations on how much a company could charge for its service.

But true regulation was still a long time off, although—at least in retrospect—its eventual coming must have seemed inevitable even to the early utility entrepreneurs like Powers, indeed as inevitable as the fact that the industry had to become centralized in order to accomplish its function as a total public service. This period of consolidation, and with it the industry's phenomenal growth, was soon to be at hand.

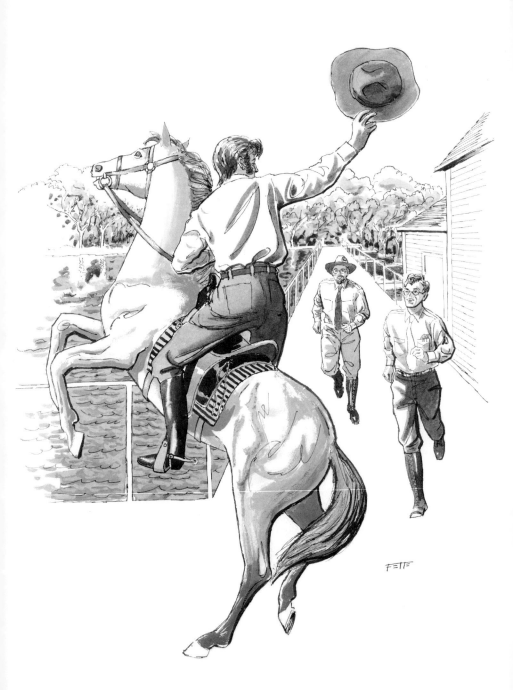

4

Foote Hold

It was only natural that the earliest hydroelectric stations grew up where waterpower was already being put to productive use—in lumber mills and flour mills. Thus the miller's craft, as much as the carpenter's, provided a ready springboard for those who wished to plunge into the electric business, and the fact that the father of the utilities complex we now know as Consumers Power Company was originally a miller by trade is no more surprising than the fact that William Powers, of Grand Rapids, had been a cabinetmaker.

The miller was William Augustine Foote, born on June 9, 1854, in Adrian, Michigan, where his father, Augustus N. Foote, had been brought as a seven-year-old boy from western New York State.[1] W. A. Foote, as he came to be called (the use of initials befitting a man of his eventual station), was educated in the public schools of Adrian and learned the miller's trade in his native city. He was still a very young man when he first manifested his talent for entrepreneurship:

he became so interested in a new roller process of flour grinding that he went to Minneapolis to study this method in the great mills that processed the grain from the Plains states. After working in the Twin Cities area for some time, he returned to Adrian and asked a local man of some means, James Berry, who was an old friend and business associate of Foote's father, to back him in a flour mill of his own. Berry consented. He was intrigued by the young man's staunch and straightforward salesmanship and by the idea that stone rollers would be more efficient than steel rollers. Berry could not possibly have guessed that stone rollers, unlike the old millstones, were not appropriate to the task. The venture, as one may surmise, was hardly a success.

But it so happened that in about 1884, the Thomson-Houston electric people asked Foote for permission to install an arc-light generator in his mill. They were in the process of obtaining a contract for twelve streetlights and needed a power source.[2] Foote agreed readily enough: his business could use any income it could get.

Now, day after day, Foote heard the humming of the Thomson-Houston dynamo. He used to stand there in his mill, watching the new electric machinery working away, dreaming. To be sure, his dreams were modest in terms of today's electric uses. Nobody had yet invented, let alone thought about, most of the machinery and appliances, conveniences, and amusements that now derive from this wondrous power, but Foote did foresee the time when all cities, their streets and homes as well, would be lit by electricity. Perhaps even then he could look far enough into the future to project his two major contributions—the transmission of high voltage from distant power plants to their markets and the linking of many communities and central power plants into one interconnected network. In any case, he decided that henceforth electric service would be his field of endeavor, and just as he had once embarked on setting up his own mill, he now made up his mind to build his own electric plant.

W. A. FOOTE

A formal portrait of the founder of
Consumers Power Company many
years after he had first become
intrigued with the Thomson-Houston
dynamo installed in his flour mill.
(Consumers Power Company
collection)

And so the thirty-year-old miller once again went to the now disenchanted Mr. Berry and asked him for more money. The man listened patiently, but shook his head. "Nothing doing, Will," he said in his pedantic, peculiarly high voice. "We're having enough trouble with your mill as it is. That's what comes from latching on to newfangled ideas that haven't proved out yet. A man ought to stick to what he knows best. I'm sorry, but I'm not interested."

W. A. Foote was a man of few words. "Well," he said in his calm and measured tones, "I suppose I can't really blame you. I trust you'll understand that I'll have to get my financing somewhere else."

Berry was not an unkind person. He still liked Foote, despite the money he had cost him. He looked at the young fellow who sat there in his office, a slight man of medium height with a broad mustache and well-trimmed, light brown Vandyke beard, and blue eyes that missed little. He was neatly but modestly dressed and was full of self-confidence without being obnoxious. "Why don't you go to see John Allen," Berry said, chuckling. "I wouldn't send you to that foxy farmer if he didn't have buckets of money to spare. I guess if he loses some of it he won't hurt any. Go see what you can do."

Foote took this bit of good advice and did manage to get Allen to finance him. He signed his mill over to Berry (who eventually got it to pay off by converting to steel rollers) and built himself an electric plant with a small Thomson-Houston six-light generator. From that moment on, Foote was strictly a utilities man.

One of the first things Foote did was to recruit his seventeen-year-old brother as bookkeeper. This was a stroke of genius, for James Berry Foote—J. B. for short—had all the technical talent which W. A. himself did not possess but which was vital to success in this new field. J. B. was an engineer by instinct. You didn't have to tell him how anything worked. He took a look, thought about what he had seen, and assimilated it instantly. Along with his ledger duties, J. B. soon took over as the engineering head of the company, despite his youth. It was the beginning of a lifelong team effort: W. A. Foote, the shrewd money-raiser and entrepreneur, and J. B. Foote, the practical engineer who provided the technical wherewithal for his brother's ambitions.[3] Henceforth the younger Foote, not unlike his brother in physical stature and looks, and yet with a clean-shaven face revealing an introspective, studious softness not apparent in the other's stern demeanor, was always at W. A.'s beck and call. Indeed, it is doubtful that W. A. could have succeeded without him.

Contrary to the expectations of his erstwhile sponsor in the milling business, W. A. Foote made an instant success of his electric enterprise. But for some reason that no one knows, he was not satisfied with the Adrian venture—perhaps because he didn't have enough waterpower for what he wanted to do, which was to build a high-speed generator. Within a year he sold the little electric plant to a Captain Jerome H. Fee[4] and, taking brother J. B. in tow, went on to Jackson. There, in 1886, he became associated with Samuel Jarvis, foreman of an iron and engine works in Lansing, who felt that he could build the high-speed machine that Foote wanted.

As may be recalled from the previous chapter, Jackson already had some electric service, but it didn't amount to very much. The Jackson Electric Light and Power Company, with its power station on the south side of Otsego Avenue (then known as Mill Street), had been operating an Edison store-lighting system for two years, and the Mitchell-Reid Company ran a tiny portable engine in a riverbank shed behind the city's waterworks pump station, with even more modest results. Both outfits were trying to supply incandescent lighting, and neither was doing very well. Downtown streets were still lit with gas, and on the outskirts naphtha lamps provided the illumination. Foote was not impressed. Powers, he knew, had bedazzled Grand Rapids with his arc lights, and Swift seemed to be getting along well in Bay City, as was Willett in Flint. Why not W. A. Foote in Jackson? Here was his chance.

"Gentlemen," Foote told the members of the Jackson Common Council, "there is no reason why this city should lag behind the other great and growing cities of this state. I ask your permission to erect poles, stretch wires, and place a few electric streetlights on downtown thoroughfares. I am not, at this point, asking for a franchise, only for permission to demonstrate the superiority of my arc lights."

The Common Council consented, and Foote's demonstration turned out to be an epoch-making event in the history of Jackson. If anything, the downtown districts where he dis-

played his "dishpan" lights—carbon points beneath large tin
reflectors—attracted an even greater crowd of jubilant citizens
than had Powers' earlier performance in Grand Rapids.[5] Not
surprisingly, the council gave Foote a franchise almost on the
spot.

Foote and Jarvis maintained the Jackson Electric Light Works
as a partnership for two years; then additional funds became
necessary for expansion, and the company was incorporated in
March 1888 with an original capitalization of $75,000, divided
into 3,000 shares of $25 each. This was shortly raised to
$100,000. Jarvis was president of the corporation, and W. A.
Foote was its general manager. Foote's father, Augustus, was
named secretary and treasurer.[6] Soon J. B. Foote became
manager of the works, freeing W. A. to look at new fields.

In fact, W. A. Foote, the tireless promoter, already was well
on his way. In 1886, shortly after obtaining the Jackson
franchise, he had brought an electric dynamo to Battle Creek,
and the following year, again with Jarvis, had organized the
Battle Creek Electric Light and Power Company.[7] That same
year, he had made the necessary arrangements to light the
streets and carry on a general electric light business in Albion,
and together with Jarvis and Eugene P. Robertson, of the
Albion City Bank, had organized the Albion Electric Light
Company.[8] There was no stopping him now.

Not that the world, in its own cruelly impersonal way, didn't
try often enough. The trouble was simply availability of money.
As Foote's operations expanded, there was a constant need
for new equipment and for workmen to install and repair the
lines and operate the plants. The equipment had to be bought,
and the men had to be paid, and this was not easy since Foote
was saddled even then with the ever-present problem of
utilities: that expansion must be financed and services provided long before there is any return on the capital.

Like all great promoters, W. A. Foote possessed an uncanny
ability to persuade men richer than himself to back him with

their cash. He was equally adept at stalling off his creditors. There was the time, for instance, when he was far in arrears on the fuel for his power plants in Jackson and Albion. He had bought several carloads of coal on credit, which was quite a lot of coal for the size of his operations in those days, and the bill was correspondingly steep in terms of his ability to pay it off. The coal dealer finally lost his patience; he stormed into Foote's threadbare little office threatening to dun him if he wasn't paid right there and then. A few minutes later the coal man was back on the sidewalk, no longer angry but definitely in a daze. "You know," he told a friend who was waiting for him, "I can't believe what I just did. I went in there to get my

FOOTE'S EARLY HEADQUARTERS

In 1888, W. A. Foote incorporated the Jackson Electric Light Works and established himself in this frame building on a setback facing Mechanic Street near the corner of Trail. The photograph probably was made in the 1920s, since the street transmission tower in the background was not developed until about that time. (Consumers Power photo)

money or else, and here this fellow got me to take a six-months note on what he owes me, and before I knew it I promised to send him six more cars of coal on credit besides." Still shaking his head in disbelief, he walked off down the street.[9]

Despite W. A. Foote's expertise in handling creditors, he lived a hand-to-mouth existence for many years, for he wasn't the only man who desperately needed money to help his business keep up with Michigan's phenomenal burgeoning. By 1890, the state's population stood at 2,093,889 — almost double what it had been just twenty years earlier and some sixty times the head count at the time of its admission to the Union.[10] New businesses were springing up everywhere, and every one of them needed money to get started. Existing businesses suffered an equal want of funds. Bay City, Grand Haven, and Detroit required money for their expanding shipyards. Grand Rapids had to finance its growing furniture companies. Flint wanted to build more and more wagons and carriages. And in the seemingly endless forest that then stretched northward toward the Straits, lumbermen were putting up mills and vying with one another for the financing of their machinery. Indeed, wherever Foote went, he had plenty of competition. In Jackson, Nathan S. Potter, of the City Bank, was his biggest backer. In Kalamazoo, Foote got money from a Mr. Ritchey and the firm of Nichols & Shepard. But, as time went on, such local resources were far from enough. W. A. didn't know where to turn.

One of Foote's earliest employees was George Stecker, who lived in Albion not far from a roller-skating rink that Foote turned into a steam power plant. Stecker hadn't yet completed high school when he went to work for Foote in 1889 as a fireman at $25 per month. He worked twelve hours a day, seven days a week, and as little as Foote paid young Stecker, he couldn't always afford it. Stecker and others often went for weeks without pay, and there were many times when W. A. paid Stecker on Friday afternoon and then borrowed the money back from him bright and early on Monday morning to meet

GEORGE STECKER

By the time this photograph was taken at an awards ceremony, the old engineer had long since stopped worrying about having to lend his wages to his boss.
(Consumers Power photo)

some pressing bills. This happened so often that Stecker learned not to spend much on weekends. When Stecker got married, Foote was generous in turn; he lent him the money for the license—but then asked him to come back at seven o'clock that night because he couldn't afford to hire anybody else for the shift. Neighbors, not altogether without cause, used to say in those days that the Footes and their people "got along on tea and potato peelings."[11]

Keeping their belts tight didn't seem to constrain W. A. and J. B. in the slightest, however. Both were men of tremendous faith. They never lacked confidence. J. B.'s son, James Harold Foote, a hale and hearty eighty years old at the time of this writing (1971), still remembers many discussions between his uncle and father during which important decisions were made. It was the brothers' custom always to have a little chat on Sunday. W. A. attended the First Methodist Church in Jackson, and J. B. went to Ida F. Stiles Memorial Methodist Church on Lansing Avenue (now the Calvary Church). James H. Foote recalls that "Uncle Willy usually had Sunday dinner somewhere around two o'clock, and after church it was very common for him to take his family home, and then while they were cooking dinner, he'd come over and he and Father would sit there talking. I was privileged to keep my mouth shut and my ears open while they discussed the plans of the week."

In the decisions arrived at during these informal meetings, neither of the two brothers ever gave in to circumstances, regardless of other people's opinions and what seemed to be the trends of the times. Once the Footes felt that something was the correct thing to do, they went ahead and did it. "This is the right thing," W. A. used to say, "and right will prevail."

Today, such words would sound a little pompous. But they didn't then. The men who built our country had to have a staunch, almost immutable belief in themselves and in what they wanted to do; their simple will to get a job done, no matter what the difficulties, gave us our inheritance. Admittedly, Horatio Alger successes came to pass more readily in that most exciting period of our history when the whole continent was pioneered, civilized, and industrialized, all within the span of just two or three generations. But even so, success was reserved, as it always is, to those rare personalities who, by dint of talent, luck, and vision, succeeded in almost everything that they attempt. People like that always seem to find themselves in the right place at the right time; circumstances have a way of fitting their abilities and ambitions. To some degree, of course, such men create the situations that make them flourish, and it is not unreasonable to suppose that W. A. Foote would have been a success no matter when and where he might have lived or what he might have done.

The decision which, more than any other, gave W. A. Foote the key to the future was on the face of it an obvious one — that the best way to obtain power was to get it where it was amply available.

From his operations in Albion and Battle Creek, W. A. Foote knew the economies of producing power from naturally flowing water rather than by burning coal, which had to be bought and paid for. In both towns sufficient waterpower for their still modest needs was available practically next door. But what about those localities that didn't have water flow that could be dammed effectively or where the electric power which could thus be created was not enough to fill the need?

Just when W. A. Foote conceived his scheme to import electricity from distant hydropower sites is not known. Perhaps he had already dreamed of it way back when he was still watching the Thomson-Houston dynamo in his flour mill. If so, he didn't tell anyone about it. Not even in 1895, when he took over the Ceresco Mill and Hydraulic Company, Ltd., and began accumulating waterpower rights in Calhoun County was there any indication that he did this for the purpose of electric power generation. The company had been set up for the purpose of buying and selling real estate; building and operating flour mills; producing, selling, and using waterpower devices; and buying and selling all kinds of merchandise—and this, and nothing else, is just what the Ceresco Company did.[12]

One day in 1896, while visiting Kalamazoo—where W. A. had firmly decided he would eventually gain control of the Kalamazoo Electric Company[13]—he suggested to J. B. and Stecker, who were accompanying him, that they might take a ride up the Kalamazoo River toward Allegan and look at that interesting country. Allegan lies only some 25 miles northwest of Kalamazoo, but in the old days, with horse and wagon, this involved quite an expedition, and the three men figured that to do it right, they would certainly need a couple of days. They journeyed through that lovely green, rolling land so reminiscent of the English countryside. The road, bumpy and dusty, parelleled the river most of the way, but was rarely in sight of it, and the men had to push through dense forest and underbrush to reach its bank. By Michigan standards, the Kalamazoo is a rapidly moving stream. Between Plainwell and Allegan it drops about 100 feet. At one spot along that stretch, W. A. stood for many minutes, just staring at the water.

"Now, if we put a hydro plant right here, we'd really have something," he said. "How far would you guess we are from Kalamazoo?"

"I'd say about 22 miles," J. B. said. "Not more than 25 anyway."

W. A. nodded and stood in silence for a few more minutes. "Those mill outfits at Plainwell, Otsego, and Allegan are using 30 feet of the drop," he said then. "That leaves 70. You can get a lot of power out of 70 feet, and we could sure use it. Can you build a transmission line 25 miles long and still have power left at the other end?"

"I don't know, Will," said J. B. "It's never been done before, not that I heard. There'd be a lot of problems all right. What do you think, George?"

"It's worth a try, Mr. Foote," Stecker said, "but the devil of it is, we really won't know if it works until we've built it. Twenty-some miles of wire, that's a lot of wire." Stecker was probably thinking about power loss, but W. A. didn't worry himself too much about the technical aspects. He figured that J. B. and Stecker could lick most anything along those lines. What W. A. Foote worried about, as always, was money. "That's not only a lot of wire," he said, "it's a lot of everything else too. We'll have to make surveys and buy riparian rights and build dams. The wire is the least of it." Without cracking a smile, he looked at the two other men and said, "If necessary, we'll use iron wire. That way, if it doesn't work, we can always sell it off for fencing."

W. A. had made his big decision on the spot. Only here and in other similar out-country locations could he get the power he needed at a price that he could afford to ask his backers for. Only from streams like the Kalamazoo could he supply the industrial centers of Michigan the way he wanted to.

With Charles Frisbie, of Jackson, who was one of the directors of the Ceresco Company, as his partner and with William G. Fargo, also of Jackson, as engineer, Foote immediately launched into surveys of the area and purchased real estate and riparian rights along much of the Kalamazoo between Plainwell and Allegan. Four power sites were plotted: one between Plainwell and Otsego, to be known as Plainwell Dam; one, 2 miles downstream from Otsego, just below the Kalamazoo's confluence with Pine Creek, which was to be called the Pine Creek Dam but which was later named Otsego Dam; and a third, 4 miles farther still downstream, to be called Trowbridge Dam, for the township in which it was located. The fourth site, just outside the upstream city limits of Allegan, was not named and was never developed.

Trowbridge Dam was the first to go under construction. Local people called it the "Big Dam." No wonder—such a big earthmoving project had never before been seen in Michigan. William G. Fargo, who with his Fargo Engineering Company of Jackson would now team up with Foote for many years and many ventures, began excavations in the spring of 1898. This was not an easy job. In the East, such dams as were then built could be anchored in the bedrock natural to the area, but in west central Michigan, substantial rock was not indigenous. Fargo's men had to cope with soft soil. After diverting the stream by means of temporary earthworks, they built the dam itself, much as a child would build one in a sandbox, except that they did have horses and some primitive machinery to help them. They hitched up teams of horses to big scoops (called "scrapers") that were dragged along in the dirt. Each scoop had a pair of handles, and a workman walked behind it, holding these handles, and with his weight and the bulging muscles of his arms and back, he pressed the scoop into the ground like a plow. The horses strained and the men sweated and cursed, and when the scoops were full they were brought over to where the dirt was wanted, and it was dumped out.

Scoop after scoop of earth was piled up until the barricade was built up high enough and tamped tight enough to form a dam that could contain a pond of water 22 feet deep. Trowbridge's spillway itself was 80 feet long, and it had three tainter gates[14] of timber, 12½ by 24 feet in dimension. The dam's penstock—its pit for the wheel that drove the dynamo —was 74 by 90 feet, an underwater cave walled in by timber and masonry rubble. This hydraulic unit was designed to yield 2,000 horsepower, driving a 2,500-volt General Electric generator.[15] A wooden powerhouse, set on a suspended foundation of stone and timber, covered the wheel pit. Fargo managed to complete the job in little more than a year, and by September 20, 1899, all the machinery was installed, and the wires strung. Trowbridge was ready for its first big test.

So was the engineering team—J. B. Foote and his right-hand man, George Stecker. Until the moment when water roared through the penstock, ramming the wheel into motion, no one, not even J. B. and George themselves, could be absolutely sure that this very iffy project would work. Electric technology was not yet so far advanced as to be predictable by calculation. The approach was largely empirical: try it and see. If the results were as hoped for, everything was fine. If not, one looked for the bug in the system and often had to start all over again from scratch. But Trowbridge was too complex for this, and it had cost too much. On the bank, next to the dam, a transformer stood ready to step the voltage up to 22,000, an unprecedented pressure. From this transformer, the line led 24 miles into Kalamazoo, an unprecedented distance, and over cheap, low-quality iron wire at that. Would this pioneer effort really work? If it didn't, it could well doom W. A. Foote's dreams, and those of J. B. Foote and George Stecker as well.

Stecker was a simple, unassuming man. It may be recalled that he hadn't even completed high school when he went to work. Already as a boy he'd made up his mind to go into the electric business, and he had been begging the linemen of the Albion Electric Company to let him tend the solder pot for them—without pay. Later, when he'd finally gotten on the payroll, one of his jobs was to unload all the coal for the Albion plant by hand. At the same time, exhausted as he had to be at night from this backbreaking labor, he'd completed his high school studies after hours. Now, ten years older but still a young man in his mid-twenties, he was the project's chief engineer under J. B. Foote. This was the time and place to prove his mettle.

First he designed a regulator that would maintain a steady electric load even as demands on the line changed from minute to minute, for electric railways were just coming into widespread use, and one of Trowbridge's purposes was to supply the trolleys that stopped and started, slowed down and speeded up, all day long and of course without notice.[16] The next problem was that to carry a steady load over a high-voltage line, there had to be some means of switching the electricity from one line to another in case of trouble, like a short circuit, which could happen at any time and often did. Such high-voltage switching had never been done before, and no such switch was on the market. Stecker tackled the challenge and came up with an air-break switch, which became known as the "Stecker switch," but he figured it wasn't quite good enough to handle such a heavy load. At last, after months of work, J. B. and Stecker developed a circuit breaker that blocked the high-voltage flow by means of an oil barrier. It had been built in a machine shop in Jackson, where a German workman dubbed it the "wagon box" because that's what its oil tank reminded him of. A set of three such wagon-box switches were now installed at Trowbridge, and everything was set to go.[17]

When the big moment came, J. B. was waiting at the Kalamazoo end of the line to see whether the lights would go on. W. A. Foote and George Stecker, the latter standing by in case any minor trouble developed, were at the dam for its inauguration. W. A. didn't make a big thing of it. He gave the go-ahead order simply by nodding to the man in charge of the powerhouse. "Okay," was all he said. His matter-of-fact face gave away nothing that went on inside him as the gate was opened.

Water burst through the penstock and gushed down into the stream below the dam, raising a spray of white out of the

WAGON-BOX SWITCHES

These old circuit breakers may not have looked like much, but they were really something. In fact, this set of three remained in service at Trowbridge for more than fifty years after the device, capable of handling high voltages, was invented by J. B. Foote and George Stecker. Eventually, of course, more sophisticated models were developed on the basis of the prototype. (Consumers Power photo)

sudden turbulence. The generator sang, wires crackled, and an incandescent bulb in the powerhouse flared into light. W. A. Foote's expression still did not change. What had happened so far didn't prove anything. Only J. B. in Kalamazoo could tell whether the power from the dam actually had reached all the way into the city, but W. A. at Trowbridge had to sweat it out. There was no immediate way to get word to him; telephones had existed for some time, but long-distance lines were still rare, particularly in the back country.[18] W. A. left the powerhouse. Outside he formally shook Fargo's hand. "Thank you," he said simply. Then he went off by himself and paced back and forth on the dam, dressed in knickers and high-laced boots, his wide-brimmed hat clamped tightly on his head against a gusty wind. Stecker also came out, but remained near the power-house. He was standing by for trouble.

One hour passed. Two hours. Still no message from J. B. at the Kalamazoo end of the line. A low sun glinted yellow through the autumn-dry trees. W. A. Foote was still pacing, inscrutable as he always was in periods of stress. The minutes dragged. Suddenly there was a commotion in the crowd that lined the Kalamazoo's western bank. W. A. turned and quickened his steps. George Stecker came running. A horse galloped up the dam road, raising dust and foaming at the mouth and neighing as its rider reined it to a rearing, sliding halt. The horseman waved his hat and let out a rebel yell. "It's workin'," he shouted. "The lights is workin'!"

Stecker sighed with relief. He was almost dizzy for a moment, and he didn't notice W. A. coming up to him. Foote put his hand on Stecker's shoulder. Stecker looked up. Foote was grinning. "Well, George," he said softly so that no one else could hear him, "I guess after this I won't have to borrow your wages anymore."

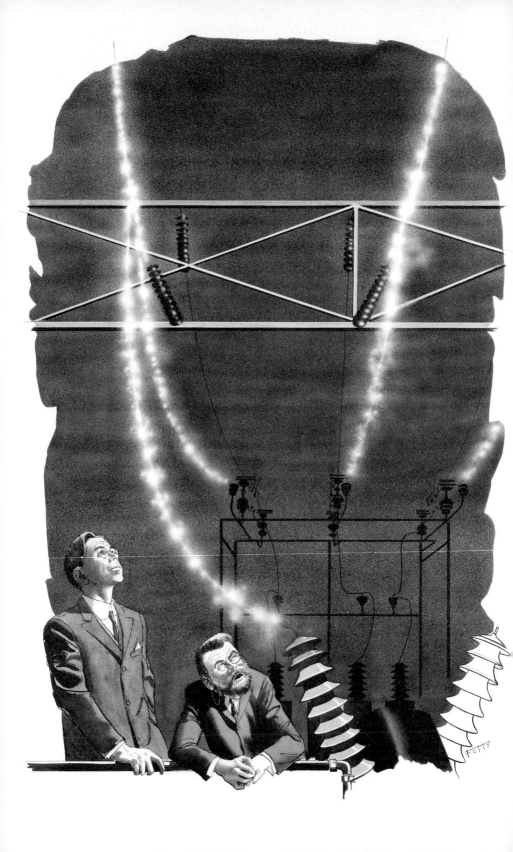

5

High Voltage

Today, Trowbridge and the other dams Foote built along the Kalamazoo — Otsego Dam and Plainwell Number 1 and Number 2 — are no longer active. As the jargon of the electric business has it, they are "down," shut down, that is, but they are still standing. They are being maintained by the Michigan Department of Natural Resources within the river park lands donated by Consumers Power to the state. The old tainter gates, whose timber eventually was replaced with iron, are a little rusty now; the only time they're worked is in the autumn when conservation men fill the dam ponds in order to attract ducks and geese winging their way south for the winter. The flowage lands turn into a jungle of marsh grasses and reeds in spring and summer, lush and green, and the rapid waters below the spillways of the dams are favorites with fishermen, for that's exactly the kind of water that trout like. Trowbridge's original wooden powerhouse was destroyed by fire in 1911 and was replaced with an attractive structure of red brick. You can get quite close to it, walking up the dam from the west bank, the side on which the horseback rider delivered J. B. Foote's message, but on the dam itself a fence bars your way, which is as it should be, for it's quite a drop.

J. B.'s wagon-box switches are not at Trowbridge anymore. They've been taken out and, last anyone knew, were stored in one of the Consumers Power warehouses in Jackson. Not that they are useless museum pieces. If the dam were still active, they'd be right there, clicking along. They looked strangely unsophisticated; yet they were a brilliant mechanism, and they performed their job for about fifty-five years, until well after World War II. As time went on, the wagon boxes handled even higher voltages without any trouble, first 40,000 at Trowbridge in 1903 and later as much as 70,000 here and at other dams.[1]

WHERE J. B. WAITED FOR THE JUICE FROM TROWBRIDGE

The high-voltage line from Trowbridge Dam fed into this switchboard of the original Kalamazoo steam plant at the corner of Water and Edwards Streets. (Consumers Power photo)

MICHIGAN'S FIRST BIG DAM

*Here is Trowbridge in 1899, two years after completion of the project
which proved that electricity could be transmitted over relatively long
distances—in this case, an astounding 24 miles. The wooden powerhouse
was destroyed by fire some years later. The dam still exists, but it is no
longer in operation.* (General Electric Company photo)

Only W. A. Foote's money-saving iron wire gave a little difficulty at first. It contracted in the cold of Michigan's winter, and
as a result it sometimes broke. But this shortcoming was soon
fixed. As the Trowbridge venture proved successful, it became
easier for W. A. to raise money, and the iron lines were replaced
with more expensive aluminum wire. Modern as this sounds,
the early-day transmission lines looked nothing like they do
today. They were strung on wooden poles, not much more than
20 feet tall. Eventually such poles were replaced with slightly
higher "windmill towers" of steel—so called because that's
what they were originally designed for. They were three-legged
structures, coming to a point at the top. You can still see
windmill towers like that on many middle western farms. [2]

With Trowbridge, the future course of Foote's electrical
enterprises became clearly charted. High-voltage power
sources could be utilized to supply distant communities, and
by the same token the electrical services in these communities
could be interconnected, forming a network of usefulness for
the citizens of Michigan.

W. A. Foote had already taken the first step in this direction before Trowbridge was built. To establish a firmer base for the dam's operation, he and his associates had bought the controlling interest in the Kalamazoo Electric Company in 1898, just as excavations began on the dam. The next year he changed the name of the company to Kalamazoo Valley Electric.[3] The pole transmission line from Trowbridge to Kalamazoo fed into the steam plant at the corner of Water and Edwards Streets, which had been acquired with the purchase, and it was here that J. B. had been waiting for the "juice" to start flowing on that first day.[4] Almost immediately work was started on an extension of the Trowbridge line from Kalamazoo to Foote's Battle Creek operation.[5] The new interconnecting line, built mostly along open highway, was if anything even more subject to the usual vicissitudes of pole transmission: lightning, branches broken in windstorms, sleet, and—not the least of the potential hazards—hunters trying to potshot birds off their wire perch. More than ever the success of this extension demonstrated to Foote's faithful backers the validity of his ideas.

It also convinced other people to go into the electric business. One of these was George Erwin, and that decision put him in a real quandary for a long while. Erwin often sat in his flat-bottom rowboat in the middle of the Muskegon River, gently floating along, his fishing line dangling in the blue-green water of that fine stream, which cuts through western Michigan just about halfway up the Lower Peninsula. Erwin had fished the river for many summers, ever since he'd been a boy, and as he grew older his expeditions had carried him farther and farther up the stream, all the way up to the town of Big Rapids, 50 miles northeast of his home. As he looked around him into the pine stands on the Muskegon's banks, the sweet smell of the white pines coming to him in the soft, warm summer air, he knew that for all practical purposes he owned this fine river.

Not that the river was really his, no more than the lands along it were, by either inheritance or purchase, but for four years he had been slowly accumulating, acre by acre, the rights to let the Muskegon flow over its banks and cover the adjoining soil. He hadn't done this just for a hobby. The chubby, kindly faced real estate man from Muskegon, then forty-two years old, knew exactly what he was after. The only trouble was that he didn't know how to go about getting it. He wanted to dam up the Muskegon River and sell electricity.

Erwin didn't understand the first thing about electricity. He was not a J. B. Foote who could pick up this alien art by instinct. But he did know that flowing water somehow manufactures electricity and that the more a river falls, the more electricity can be produced. With the drop of the Muskegon River, which he had experienced often enough in his rowboat, there obviously was a great potential. This thought, and no more than that, had been on his mind when he started buying up the flowage rights he needed for the ponds above his dream dams. He didn't even have a clear idea where he would put the dams, so he simply bought landrights all over the place. These were not very expensive, rarely even as much as $5 an acre, but even so, not being a rich man, he had soon run out of money. Luckily, one day just as Erwin had been about to give up the whole project for lack of funds, another Muskegon businessman, John G. Emery, Jr., had thrown in his lot with him. "I think you're right," Emery had agreed. "Water running downhill will make more money than water that's left idle. I'll take an interest with you in that business."

That solved the problem for awhile, but Emery was no more of an electric man that his friend Erwin. And as still more cash was required, the two men somehow managed to interest yet other businessmen who were equally unqualified for the power business, including Thomas Hume, of the lumber partnership Hackley and Hume. Undaunted, these men formed the Grand Rapids–Muskegon Water Power Electric Company — a grand and impressive name which had nothing behind it but some hopes.

Erwin had battled bravely for his flowage land, for there

were others who wanted those acres too. There had been, for instance, a man by the name of Daniel McCool, boss of a cement company at Newaygo about halfway up the stream, who intended to build a dam himself, though apparently not for electric generation. McCool's men went out telling the farmers, whose land Erwin already had under option, that Erwin was broke and that McCool had bought him out. The landowners, believing the story, had torn up the Erwin options and taken a dollar or two for new options from McCool's people. This was evident fraud, but in those days people weren't as likely to go to court as they are now. Instead, they usually took care of such matters themselves. Not in a Wild West manner though; Michigan was not a shoot-out state. All one night Erwin sat up writing dozens of identical letters to McCool saying, "You having obtained the option from me by misrepresentation, I hereby rescind same and return the consideration paid for it." Then Erwin called on all the land-owners, explained to them that he wasn't bankrupt, gave them the money to refund to McCool, and had them sign the letters. So all the McCool options were returned, and Erwin was in the saddle again. And as Erwin said later, "Well, those cement boys were madder than wet hens, and they said if I ever came to Newaygo again, they would put me in jail."[6]

At last Erwin had all the land he thought he needed, but he didn't know where to turn. He could only see one outside chance. Maybe he could persuade that engineer, J. B. Foote, he'd heard about, to come to work for him, even if only on a consulting basis. Erwin and two of his partners, Emery and Hume, traveled all the way down to Jackson to see if Foote might help them out. They didn't get to see J. B., however. It was W. A. who met them, and they explained to him what they wanted. Emery said apologetically that they could not pay J. B. for the work but that once they got going and started selling their electricity in the cities of Grand Rapids and Muskegon, there would be a royalty arrangement that he hoped would be acceptable to all concerned. Such was their offer.

But they had a big surprise coming. They didn't know any more about W. A. Foote than they knew about electricity.

"No," W. A. said firmly. "My brother works for nobody but me. Anyway, that's not the way to do business. Not anymore. Say Fargo gets your dam built—I know you've been talking to him about it—and we construct the hydro plant for you and put in the transmission lines to Grand Rapids and Muskegon, it won't really mean all that much. You'll be capable of putting out more power than those towns need right now. Where do you go from there? I've got the territory down here, so you can't get that, and I don't think anybody at this point can build a line all the way over to the eastern part of the state. You'd lose too much power over that great a distance."

This was something that Erwin and his friends hadn't really thought about. In fact, it is rather doubtful that they even knew they had to have high-voltage pressure feeding into a long-haul line—that if they didn't, they'd hardly get anything out at the other end. Much as they tried to hide it, the three associates looked somewhat crestfallen.

"How much money have you got tied up in this business now?" Foote asked them.

"About $130,000," Erwin answered.

"All right," Foote said, "I'll buy out half your interest, and we'll build the dam for you."

The Muskegon men were dumbfounded by this proposition. It wasn't at all what they had expected. Yet, considering all the money that they had tied up and the fact that there was hardly any chance in sight of putting their plans into fruition, it was a tempting offer. "Well," Hume said, "it's George Erwin's scheme. If he says to sell you a half interest, that's all right with me."

Erwin was clearly on the spot. His two partners were looking at him expecting an answer. They were in just as deep as he was. He had started it all, and it was up to him to bail them out. But he was a businessman at heart, and he had bargained before. "Never," he said. "That's out of the question. Mr. Foote, you wouldn't be making this proposition to us if you didn't want to get in up there. It is not only that you've got something we want, we've got something you want. Half is too much, but we might consider letting you in for a third as a silent partner."

"Fair enough," Foote said before Erwin had even stopped speaking. "I'll go for that."

And so it happened that Foote extended his interests northward and became a director of the Grand Rapids–Muskegon Water Power Electric Company, later called the Grand Rapids–Muskegon Power Company.[7] At the first meeting of the directors that W. A. Foote attended on November 29, 1904, $5 million worth of twenty-five-year bonds were authorized for issue, with the Michigan Trust Company of Grand Rapids designated as trustee of the mortgage. Half a million was to be certified immediately to finance construction of the dam, to equip the dam with the necessary machinery, and to build a transmission line to Grand Rapids.

Rogers Dam, about 7 miles downstream from Big Rapids, was completed early in 1906, and it turned out to be an even more ambitious project than Trowbridge. Built as an earth embankment over concrete core walls, it had three sections with a total length of 635 feet and held a "head" of water up to 40 feet high—nearly the height of a four-story house.

Still in operation today, the dam impounds the river in a pond covering 608 of the acres George Erwin had so laboriously collected over the years. When it was inaugurated on March 15 of that year, its original power plant consisted of two penstocks 19 by 114 feet in dimension, and turbines that yielded a total of 6,000 horsepower. The generators put out 7,200 volts, stepped up by three transformers to 72,000 volts, the highest voltage in use anywhere in the world at that time.[8]

No less an achievement was the transmission line, which stretched a total of 89.5 miles—16.6 miles from Rogers to Croton, then another 17 to Kent City, and 21.5 more to Grand

Rapids. At Kent City, the line branched to Muskegon, extending 34.4 miles to a brick substation in Muskegon Heights.[9]

Even before the completion of Rogers Dam, work was already under way on a yet larger hydroelectric project at Croton, between 16 and 17 miles below Rogers. With a larger stream flow and a little higher head, it was possible to develop nearly 15,000 horsepower at this point of the Muskegon River. By September 1907, construction on the mammoth project—670 feet long and with a 238-foot spillway—was well under way, and it came time to show it off. On three successive days, a special bunting-decorated Pere Marquette train left from the Grand Rapids Union Depot at ten in the morning, its four coaches jam-packed with everybody who was anybody: manufacturers, city officials, bankers, businessmen, and politicians. W. A. Foote himself was on hand to show his important guests to their seats, as were George Erwin and other high company officials.[10] At Erwin, a small station (so named in George Erwin's honor) just north of Newaygo, the train branched off onto the power company's 5-mile-long private rail line, over which in these past fifteen months of construction more than one thousand cars of material had been brought to the dam site. The mood was that of a celebration, as everyone shared in the immense pride that Michigan was home to this huge enterprise. There was much eating, good fellowship, and singing, including a special song whose lyrics had been written by one H. VanderPloeg, a Dutchman from Holland, Michigan. It was called the "Song of Croton Dam" and was sung to the tune of "Marching through Georgia." According to the September 8 *Grand Rapids Herald,* 200 guests, after being shown the plant, gathered under tent tops at long tables "tastefully arranged and loaded with good things to eat . . . served in a manner that would have been a credit to many first-class hotels. Cigars were passed at the conclusion of the splendid New England dinner and then came the call to the [baseball] grounds."

That same year, too, most of the Croton transmission line was built. It was to carry 110,000 volts, an unprecedented, violent electric pressure that the pin-type insulators used on the 70,000-volt Rogers line could not stand up against—they'd burn out and short the line in no time flat. J. B. Foote had heard that General Electric was developing a new kind of insulator, a series of five porcelain disks (called "bells" in the electrical jargon) which were to be suspended one under another from the tower, to hold up the high-tension line. So J. B. went to Schenectady, New York, to look over these Hewlett-Buck insulators.[11] He liked them. But there was one problem: the bells had to be connected to one another and to the tower and to the heavy line as well. This connecting hardware had to be tensile enough to hold the line and at the same time be very strong—as a result, it cracked the porcelain bells. Nothing . . . worked. "What the heck," J. B. said, "No point in being complicated about it. Why not anneal some of that line wire, thread it through the porcelain bells, and fasten the bells on with Crosby clips? That way you'll put next to no strain on the porcelain, and you'll get the job done." This improvisation may not have been the fanciest way to do it—but it was good enough, and it worked. Once again J. B.'s genius had paved the way for his brother's plans.

When Croton went into operation in July 1908, transmitting 100,000 volts to Grand Rapids, word of its success spread all over the world.[12] Soon distinguished engineers from Russia, France, England, Japan, Italy, and even India came to Jackson and Grand Rapids to learn more about this pacesetting achievement. By today's standards that doesn't sound terribly exciting, but it certainly was then. These visitors often traveled for several weeks by train, ship, and wagon to reach Croton Dam. Although western Michigan was developing rapidly, it was still way off the beaten track. English visitors especially came over in droves. The Empire was rich, and British investors were interested in building up electric power in their islands. Their expectations of western Michigan were often quite differ-

LEARNING TO CONTROL ELECTRIC POWER

All manner of devices, such as these forks, known as "goat horns," were used in early tests of high-potential switches at Trowbridge. This particular experiment involved a charge of 40 amperes at 18,000 volts. The Trowbridge line's operational capacity was 22,000 volts, a first in the industry. (General Electric Company Photo)

ent from what they found. To get to Croton from Grand Rapids once the dam was finished, they had to take a train 40 miles up to White Cloud and then a wagon over from there—this at a period in history when English train service was already excellent. One Englishman, staying at the Morton House in Grand Rapids, was told that he'd have to be ready to catch the Pere Marquette at seven o'clock the next morning. Well before that, George Erwin knocked at his door. The Englishman said that he hadn't had his bath yet. "The train's going to go whether you've had your bath or not," Erwin shouted through the door. "We've got to get going. If we don't catch it, we're out of luck." There was a long silence. "Oh," said the Englishman finally. "I'm so sorry. I thought we might catch the next one." Erwin yelled back, "Well, that'll be the day after tomorrow."

Among Croton's most distinguished visitors—although he hadn't come all the way from Europe, but only from Schenec-

STEINMETZ AT TROWBRIDGE

*In this 1901 photograph, the gentleman reclining under the sun shelter at
left (see arrow) is believed to be Dr. Charles Steinmetz, the wizard
of General Electric.* (Michigan Historical Commission)

tady—was Dr. Charles P. Steinmetz. The celebrated "wizard"
of General Electric was extremely interested in the corona
phenomenon, those jagged little ghosts of dancing fire that
formed on the transmission wire when the electric pressure was
pushed beyond 90,000 volts. The story is told of the great scien-
tist standing behind the Wealthy Street substation in Grand
Rapids one clear, dark night, gazing at the magnificent yellow-
blue spectacle of liberated electricity. He stood there for the
longest time, just watching in awe. Then he turned to his
companions and said, "To think, gentlemen, that this has
never been done before."

W. A. Foote was not awed. He was not the type to be dazzled
by the proclivities of nature. To his practical, utilitarian mind,
God had provided these wonders only to be of use to man. Nor
was W. A. Foote awed by his own accomplishment in amply
arranging such use. Even as Croton made history, he was already thinking of yet longer transmission lines carrying

140,000 volts—all the way from the wilderness rivers of the Manistee and the Au Sable, farther to the north.

The demand for power was becoming ever greater. Within a year of the start of Croton's operation, Foote was already building a new steam station in Grand Rapids, later called the Wealthy Street steam plant, to supply power during those low-water periods when the dams didn't work. The biggest factor in this burgeoning demand was the traction business. Electric railroads suddenly boomed, proliferating even more rapidly than streetlighting and commercial power, and they soon constituted the financial backbone of the electric utilities business.[13]

6

Here She Comes!

The years of the industrial revolution were an exciting time in our land. Technology seemed to come up with a new wonder almost every day—not distant accomplishments like today's moon shots, in which the vast majority of people can participate only secondhand, but down-to-earth, practical developments that affected everyone's everyday life. Gaslight was one of these; electric light was another. So was the railroad, powered by steam locomotives whose clanking wheels, chugging cylinders, and distant hooting conjured up glorious visions of adventure all across our country. Then there was the telephone. And more "simple" devices like the water tap: just think of the thrill it must have been to turn on water for the first time instead of pumping it out of a well by hand. Eventually, of course, the automobile came along, and that turned out to be the biggest thrill of all, for there is nothing as exciting to mankind as power and speed, and when you can be at the controls yourself, that naturally beats everything.

But long before Americans ever dreamed of zooming along an interstate highway at 75 miles per hour, and with plenty of horses to spare at that—even long before braving a dirt road at 20 miles an hour became the American family's big Sunday adventure—long before that, just riding through town in an electric streetcar, its bells clanging and its metal wheels screeching on the rails, was a real escapade.

This new kind of adventure came to Jackson, Michigan, on a hot, sunny Sunday in September 1891. It was, if anything, an even more intoxicating day for the people of this city than that Saturday eleven years earlier had been for the Grand Rapids folk when young Fred Powers turned on his grandfather's arc lights. Again it was electricity that caused all the excitement, but electric technology had come a long way in those years, and the new power stations could produce enough "juice" to send heavy cars loaded with passengers thundering through a city at the unbelievable speed of 10 miles an hour, or even faster where local ordinances and good tracks permitted such ardor.

Horse-drawn streetcars, which announced their coming by the gentle tinkle of a bell on the horse's collar, had been around for a whole decade. A law of 1882—probably the first speed law in the city of Jackson—had solemnly ordained that no streetcar could be operated at more than 6 miles an hour. This ordinance was passed after it had been reported to the City Council that a number of pedestrians had lost their rubbers in the deep mud of Main Street (now Michigan Avenue) because they had to jump out of the way of the streetcar horses. According to the *Jackson Citizen Patriot*, the tracks started at a turntable at Michigan and Dwight, where a huge barn housed thirty horses in assorted colors but all smelling pretty much the same and imparting their distinct odor to the whole neighborhood. As the newspaper's description of the horsecar operation had it:

> A gentlemen in sideburns and derby alighted, followed by a lady in an enormous silk hat and a trailing gown that reached the sidewalk. Yes, she got off the streetcar backwards. The driver, who

also deigned to take the nickel fares through a slit in the door, took a fresh chew of plug tobacco while an extra horse was brought from the stable. The car was turned around on the wooden turntable and began its leisurely trip back "to town" and on out to First Street. At Jackson Street there was an extra horse waiting to help pull the load to the top of the hill with much cracking of whips and occasional profanity that all streetcar drivers thought was necessary before the horse would understand what was wanted. When the traffic was heavy, there was a good deal of scratching before the car reached the brow of the hill.[1]

Jackson apparently had three horsecar lines which later were converted to electricity. Busiest was the line that ran through the city's industrial center on what is now Michigan Avenue. It used to be called the "Old Belt Line." The Fuller Buggy Company, the Jackson Cart Works, the Hutchinson Manufacturing Company, the National Wheel Company, and the Lewis Spring Company all were located along its tracks. Another route went from Michigan Avenue at Mechanic Street to the old state prison, and a third line led up Michigan Avenue to First Street and down on High or Morrell Street.[2] The first horsecars ran on "strap" rails spiked down on heavy timbers. The driver stood on an open platform, one hand always ready to grab the brake in case of a runaway; his other hand held a well-worn whip. When he came to a switch, he stopped and alighted, levering it over with a rod. Inside, passengers sat facing one another, their backs to the windows. When they sat up tightly against one another—provided that no fat persons were aboard—each side could seat ten travelers. In winter, a small hard-coal stove provided a modest measure of warmth.

But in September 1891, the Jackson Street Railway Company was ready at last with its faster and infinitely more luxurious electric vehicles.[3] Company officials and city councilmen and officers, together with representatives of the press, were honored guests on the first trip, which left the former horse barn at East Main and Dwight at exactly 3 P.M. on Saturday, September 19. With N. B. Niles—a representative of the Edison Electric Company of New York, which had manufactured the cars—acting as motorman for this special occasion, the assembled personages "bowled along merrily until the first switch was reached, which being unfortunately a little out-of-place and the paving stone in the same condition, the forward wheels of the car were thrown off the track."[4] No damage was done, however, and within a few minutes, with everyone lending a hand, the wheels had been worked back into their proper places, and the happy inaugural trip continued. Main Street was thronged, and the people were "more than jubilant," the *Jackson Daily Citizen* reported a couple of days later. But they hadn't seen anything yet. The real thrill was reserved for Sunday, when everybody could ride the beautiful new cars. And what a thriller of a day it turned out to be!

Dr. J. H. Innis was standing at his window at the corner of First and Franklin to watch Car No. 3 rumble down his street. It was 12:30 P.M., and the good doctor was looking forward to eating his Sunday dinner just as soon as he had observed this latest spectacle of science. From outside he could hear someone yell, "Here she comes!" and indeed "she" did come, bells clanging. People were cheering and waving, and then suddenly right in front of the doctor's house the car's trolley wheel slipped from the overhead wire. This touched off a fantastic series of unbelievable happenings: the spring-legged trolley wheel pole jumped up and struck a telephone wire hanging nearby. The telephone wire snapped in two, whipped through the air, and fell on the trolley wire. At that very instant a resounding crack right next to where Dr. Innis stood nearly made him jump out of his boots. Instinctively turning toward the sound, he saw his wooden telephone box burst into flames. While the doctor yelled for a pail of water to extinguish the blaze, a man out on the street pushed his way through the crowd and sprinted to the nearest firebox to turn in an alarm. The horse-drawn machines of the fire department reached the scene about five minutes later, and just as the chemical engine crossed the streetcar tracks, a broken end of the now "live" telephone wire struck one of the horses on the leg.

Dying, the electrocuted horse fell against its harness mate, knocking the other horse to the ground and burning its shoulder where the metal on the collar touched its flesh and transmitted the current. John Beacraft, driver of the chemical engine, jumped from his rig and rushed to the front. The telephone wire still lay on the dead horse. Beacraft, like most people of his day, didn't yet understand the nature of electricity. All he knew was that it was the wire which had done all the damage, and he bent down to lift it off the horse.

"Don't!" somebody yelled. "Don't touch it!" and a young man brought Beacraft down with a flying tackle, which no doubt saved his life.

Dr. Innis was not the only resident in the neighborhood who had to fight a fire while all this commotion went on. A number of other telephones in the area were burned out, including that of the fire chief, who, when the alarm sounded, was at his home on Second Street. He immediately ran to his phone to learn the location of the fire, only to find the instrument in flames. He cut the wire with his jackknife, which was taking quite a chance, but then he didn't know any better either. Then he raced out in the direction of the alarm, actually arriving in time to assist.

This first day's debacle could have turned out to be much worse than it did; even so, it was the only bad experience Jackson ever had with its electric cars. Not that anything more serious would have stopped them: people in those days recognized much more readily than we do today that some risk is the inevitable price of progress. In any case, a guard wire above the live trolley wire was soon installed to lessen the chance of a telephone wire striking it, and for many years thereafter electric streetcars served Jackson well and safely, as they did countless other cities throughout the state. It wasn't long before "Here she comes!" changed from a cry of excitement to a sigh of routine as passengers waited at street corners, sometimes freezing in the cold Michigan winter weather, for their streetcar to finally come by.

Traction lines, as the electrics were called, played a vital role in the development of the early electric companies, and W. A. Foote's Jackson Electric Light Co. was no exception. While the early traction lines in the southern part of the state had no actual corporate relationships with Consumers Power or its predecessor companies, they were affiliated organizations and later became part of the same holding company.

Electric companies had been started primarily for street-lighting, but it wasn't very long before one of their most important functions became that of furnishing electricity for the trolleys. Indeed, for a time this was their most stable business, and it was often impossible for them to obtain bond financing unless they could show that they had traction contracts. True, this period was relatively short, but during the forty years or so that it lasted traction was a most exciting business, and one without which our cities would not have developed the way they did. Evidently, individual carriages and hacks could not cope with heavy traffic, nor indeed could horse-drawn trams. Steam locomotives were out of the question because of their smoke. But with electrics offering fast, frequent, and efficient mass transportation, residential and industrial areas could develop in the suburbs, and—no less important—these street-cars gave city dwellers who did not yet have cars the chance to enjoy outings to amusement parks and recreation areas on the outskirts of their towns.[5]

City streetcars were not the only traction lines. Perhaps the most interesting development was the electric "interurban," a term which simply meant a streetcar-like conveyance that ran between different towns. Like city streetcars, the interurbans have long since yielded to the automobile, but in the light of today's traffic congestion it's interesting to speculate on how much more pleasant life might be right now had their rights-of-way somehow been kept intact and their services modernized and expanded to meet modern commuter needs.

For a look at the heyday of interurbans we must jump forward in time to the turn of the century. W. A. Foote first became involved in the electric railway business when the Jackson streetcar line went bankrupt and Foote, as its major creditor, became the receiver for the defunct firm. Then, along about 1900, Foote got interested in building an interurban from Jackson to Ann Arbor. In this venture he was associated with William A. Boland, a native of Jackson who eventually became a New York financier and promoter of electric properties,[6]

NOBODY SAID CHEESE

By 1905, Jackson had known electric streetcars for almost fifteen years, but the passengers on this one looked mighty somber as they posed stiffly for posterity on Francis Street at Sharpe Creek. The problem, of course, was that hand-held photographic shutters were considerably slower than streetcars in those days. The motorman (left) was Alec Simerski; the conductor, Charles Griffing. Passengers included Mrs. Harry Hanaflin (on the running board, dressed in white), who did smile, and Judge Peck's son and daughter-in-law (in the rear of the car), who frowned. (Photo given to Consumers Power by the late Charles Griffing, formerly of Michigan Center)

and with William G. Fargo, of the Fargo Engineering Company of Jackson, the specialist in dam building whose association with W. A. Foote dated back to 1895 and who had built Trowbridge for him.

In recent years it has become a political (and popular) sport to "debunk" the deeds of men like Foote who shaped the future life of our land; the industrial pioneers of our early days have been accused in facile retrospect of raping our resources and pillaging our people. On closer examination, this may hold true for some of them, but certainly not for all our pioneer entrepreneurs. Many, in fact, were highly principled men, and W. A. Foote was one of these—so much so that his standards sometimes got in the way of doing profitable business. That's exactly what happened when Foote got together with Boland to build the interurban, and so here we again meet the father of Consumers Power, but now in a moment of failure rather than success.

The electric interurban business looked like a gold mine in those days. The first line in Michigan, popularly called the "Ypsi-Ann" because it ran between Ypsilanti and Ann Arbor, showed such fabulous earnings despite its modest size that it soon attracted the attention of Detroit capitalists, who acquired it in 1898 and connected it with a line they built from Detroit to Ypsilanti. This became the nucleus of what later developed into the Detroit United System, whose prime movers were two strong-willed gentlemen by the names of J. D. Hawks and S. F. Angus. Among the Hawks-Angus projects was the extension of the line from Ann Arbor to Jackson. It is not surprising that the idea of expansion occurred to Hawks and Angus at precisely the same time that Foote and Boland got ready to build their own interurban starting at the other end, from Jackson to Ann Arbor, and eventually all the way to Detroit. Whenever there is a need that can be met, a supplier comes on the scene sooner or later; when two suppliers show up at the same time, you have the makings of some exciting competition.

And so the stage was set for a unique race: two electric interurbans being built simultaneously from opposite directions, with victory—in the form of paying passengers—going to that competitor who first finished laying his tracks and got his cars moving.[7]

It was late one autumn afternoon in 1901, and Boland and W. A. Foote, together with Fargo, had completed an inspection of their project. Both lines were beyond the midpoint by then; along some stretches they paralleled each other within a stone's throw. But Hawks-Angus had the jump on Boland-Foote. The Detroit outfit was rapidly approaching the outskirts of Jackson, while Foote's line had not yet even reached Dexter and was still some 20 miles short of Ann Arbor.

"We've only got one chance of making it," Boland said. The three men were standing in a construction shack near Michigan Center. Spread out before them, on a rough wooden table, lay a map that showed the day-by-day progress of the competitive line, much as a general's chart reflects the fortunes of his battle. "The only way to beat them," Boland said, his voice gruff and his face red with agitation, "is to get a few more hundred men on the job and just push through. Lay the rails. Don't worry about grading. Don't worry about rights-of-way. That's what Hawks and Angus are doing, and by golly those bastards will get away with it if we don't watch out."

"And what," asked W. A. Foote, who did not approve of cussing even in its mildest forms, "what happens if we don't adopt the means of these whatever-you-call-'em?"

"Then we might as well quit right here," Boland said.

Foote looked questioningly at Fargo, his engineer. "Bill, can we lay the tracks now and then fix 'em up later so that people can ride comfortably?"

"I suppose we could improve it some after it's built," Fargo said, "but I can't see where it would ever be a real good line unless you built it all over again. It's pretty late to start your grading once the tracks are down and the cars are running."

"Well, gentlemen," Foote said in his slow, deliberate voice, cutting the argument short, "in that case it's not worth any further discussion. We'll build it right and take our chances. If Hawks and Angus beat us, so be it."

"But Mr. Foote," said Boland, for few people ever called W. A. by his first name or initials to his face, no matter what their own importance might have been, "if that's really your decision, then I can't see going on with the construction. Why throw good money after bad?"

"Oh, I don't think it's as bad as all that," Foote said. "For one thing, we'll sure get as far as Dexter, and who knows, this may turn out to be a profitable operation by itself someday. Also, the way I see it, we can run a spur down to Wolf Lake from Michigan Center and pick up a lot of Sunday riders. But most important, gentlemen, is that we're learning something about the interurban business. Next time, we'll win."

The outcome of the race was not finally decided until the following year, although it had been a foregone conclusion for many months. Foote and Boland kept building in their slow, careful way, carving out an excellent roadbed on private rights-of-way, and in the end they did make it into Dexter. But the Hawks-Angus people, anxious to beat their competition, con-

PRESSING FORWARD WITH STEAM

This steam locomotive of the Michigan Construction Company was used in building W. A. Foote's Boland line in 1901. The elegant gentleman relaxing in the horse-drawn carriage at the left is Ed Travis, the construction superintendent. (Photo given to Consumers Power Company by Charles Griffing in 1968)

THE RACE FOOTE LOST

*The Boland line (foreground) and the competitive Hawks-Angus line
crossed the Michigan Central Railroad within a couple of hundred feet of
each other at Ballard Road, just east of Michigan Center. Hawks-Angus,
building from Ann Arbor to Jackson, finished their interurban first. W. A.
Foote and his partner, William A. Boland, then stopped building toward
Ann Arbor and terminated their traction operation at Grass Lake.* (Photo
courtesy of the late Edith King)

tinued to lay rails wherever it was most convenient, which was
usually right on the public highway and on the streets of towns,
and they did only a bare minimum of grading—anything to get
the job done fast. Inevitably Hawks and Angus won the race,
but it was nothing to be proud of. Their interurban turned out
to be just about the worst rattletrap railroad anyone had ever
seen. Jackson old-timers who traveled the Hawks-Angus line
to Ann Arbor still remember it for its rough and most uncomfortable ride.

Ultimately the Boland line, as the Foote-Boland operation
was called, salvaged the tracks it had laid into Dexter, giving
up altogether on that run, and merely served Michigan Center,
Grass Lake, and Wolf Lake out of Jackson. Much more important than this little operation, however, was that the whole
experience became a practical lesson in interurban entrepreneurship, just as W. A. Foote had predicted. Sure enough, a

short time later the Foote brothers joined Boland in the construction of another, more successful interurban which ran west from Jackson to Battle Creek and which eventually absorbed a line between Battle Creek and Kalamazoo that had been built by other interests and was powered by electricity from Trowbridge Dam.

Foote's continued involvement in the interurban business had even more far-reaching consequences. Before we go into that, however, let's get a glimpse of what working on the railroad — or, more precisely, the Jackson–Battle Creek interurban — was like. This is important, for it gives us a sense of the spirit of those exciting times, when improvisation was the key.

The storyteller here is Grant Cochran, now dead for some years, who started his lifelong career of employment by Consumers Power predecessors and affiliates at the time the interurbans were built. Cochran, a construction man, had been working for the Austin Western Company of Chicago, which specialized in earth-handling jobs, but as it happened, Cochran's wife had a home in Michigan Center, and he returned there with her when she had to recuperate after a long illness. It was at this point that Foote's engineering consultant, Bill Fargo, met Cochran and asked him to help out with grading on the Boland Line. Eventually Cochran became construction supervisor on the Jackson–Battle Creek project. The fact that Cochran had no prior experience working with rails made no difference — he was summoned in an emergency when a foreman goofed on the job. As Cochran told it, shortly before his death, in a tape-recorded interview with E. Hardy Luther, the official historian of Consumers Power Company:

> I went over there and [they] had thirteen dump cars frozen full of dirt, and we had to pick them all out. I had never laid a foot of steel rail in my life before. We came up in Albion there and had what is known as a switch engine in the yards there. When they came to go around those curves in the town, they were so short that the tender and the engine would come together and would kick part of the wheels off the track every time. As the tender was made all of timber — oak timber — we took a crosscut saw

and sawed the corners right straight down to give us more room to go around the curves. By doing that we were able to go around all curves that happened to be in the town. . . . I laid the track but I didn't know how to bend the rails, didn't know how to shape them according to specifications, degree of curve, and all that. So we said, "We'll do it anyway." We started here and we drove spikes so when we bent the rails we could get the proper degree of curve. We laid the curve out and then we bent those rails by putting down spikes and taking crowbars until they were round. Well, I got the first curve done just below the bridge that went over the river and the railroad track. Charlie Sawyer, who was one of the old engineers, came to me and said, "How did you get this curve in here so good?" I said, "I don't know, it's a mystery to me." He said, "Didn't you know we had a Jim Crow that could bend them and set them at any degree you wanted?" I said, "No, I didn't know that. Nobody told me anything about it." Then he took me into the storeroom and showed me this. It was a long bar probably 14 feet across, and in the middle was this dial and things you clamped onto the rail that you could set any degree you wanted. A couple of men would go around and around, follow the rail right out, and when they got through they had a curve. . . .

The line to Battle Creek was by no means an overnight success. At one point the project was almost forced into bankruptcy by the Railway Company General of Philadelphia, which had done some financing on the venture and saw its initial failure as a chance to take it over. That this did not happen may be largely credited to W. A. Foote's old and faithful backer, Nathan S. Potter, of the Jackson City Bank. Just in the nick of time, when the Philadelphia outfit was about to foreclose, Potter managed to get E. W. Clark & Co., also of Philadelphia, to put up the required funds.[8]

It is here that we encounter the wondrous weave of circumstance, the joining of right place and right time; for when the Clark people came out to Michigan to inspect the interurban, they also became interested in Foote's other ideas.[9] From that moment on, as we shall see, E. W. Clark & Co. played an increasingly vital role in the formation of Consumers Power Company.

7

Of Men and Money

W. A. Foote had been somewhat premature in promising George Stecker at the opening of Trowbridge Dam that he wouldn't have to borrow Stecker's wages anymore. As it turned out, Foote's money problems were far from over. Even as his interests expanded rapidly at the beginning of the century, his was a wealth on paper only. Cash flow remained precarious, to say the least. There were often evenings when Foote waited in his office for the day's receipts of streetcar fares to come in so that he could meet his payroll. Once Stecker went three months without pay altogether. He finally talked to Foote and asked whether he could be advanced $50. Foote couldn't give him even that much, since if he paid Stecker, he would have to pay all the others too. In the end he gave Stecker $3 on account. Of course, that wouldn't go very far now, but in those days it was enough to tide him over; a dozen eggs cost 12 cents, a man's "fancy suit" went for about $9, and coal sold for 85 cents a ton.

Raising capital for new construction presented an even more serious problem. Foote's companies kept on borrowing from one another, trying to stay ahead of the sheriff. About 1904, when the Foote people were consolidating their properties from Jackson west to Kalamazoo into Commonwealth Power Company, the situation started to look a little more promising. W. A. had been able to make contact with the N. W. Harris interests in Chicago, an investment banking firm. According to a retrospective editorial published in the *Jackson Patriot* many years later, Foote at that time walked into the newspaper office and said, "I have an item which may be of interest to Jackson people. N. W. Harris and Company have agreed to underwrite the Commonwealth securities." That didn't appear to be very startling. "What does that mean?" the reporter asked. "It means," replied Foote, very quietly, "that now the Commonwealth Company will have enough money to carry on completion of its waterpower projects."

After this, W. A. was able to relax a little. He did some traveling. He even went abroad. Once he sailed to Europe and caught the next ship back—he found ocean travel so relaxing. But this comfortable period was short-lived. In 1907 a severe depression hit the country, and Foote was no more exempt from its ravages that anyone else. If anything, his problems were greater than most people's. Croton Dam was nearing completion, and he was in dire need of money just at a time when it was hardest to get. By then, at the age of fifty-three, he had gained effective control of the electric business, both commercial and municipal, in five major Michigan cities—Jackson, Albion, Battle Creek, Kalamazoo, and Grand Rapids—as well as a number of smaller communities like Big Rapids, Coopersville, Grandville, and Lowell. In Grand Rapids, he and his associates had managed to eliminate all competition by gaining a dominant influence in the Grand Rapids Light and Power Company, which had been founded by William T. Powers.[1] In Muskegon some competition remained,[2] but Foote's hold in the area was substantial. In addition, he had interests in the

Boland line, the Battle Creek–Jackson interurban, and the Kalamazoo Valley Traction Company, which continued the interurban run from Battle Creek to Kalamazoo. He had Trowbridge, Rogers, and several other dams. But in ever-expanding his operations, he was faced with a never-ending need for funds. Chicago financing, substantial as it was, did not suffice. The big money was in the East—in New York, Philadelphia, and Boston—and Foote had not yet been able to crack this source of capital.

E. W. Clark & Co., of Philadelphia, whose representatives Foote first encountered when they came to inspect the Battle Creek line at the behest of Nathan Potter, was one of the big Eastern money firms. It had been established by Enoch Clark, a young man from New England who, in 1837, had arrived in Philadelphia to do his apprenticeship with some kinsmen by the name of Allen. The Allens were developing a lottery business, which was then regarded as a legitimate means of securing capital for private business undertakings as well as for public concerns; indeed, the promoters of lotteries held a highly respectable place in American business and became forerunners of investment underwriting and stockbrokerage enterprises.[3]

Before long, Enoch Clark established his own firm, and later his two sons, Edward White Clark and Clarence H. Clark, were associated with him. (In the course of time Edward White Clark had five sons, three of whom ultimately became directors of Consumers Power Company.) Another of Enoch's associates was the notorious Jay Cooke, who, after parting company with Clark, was eventually credited with the major financing of the Civil War for the Union government and whose own financial collapse in 1873 with an overcommitment to the Northern Pacific Railroad set off the worst financial panic of the nineteenth century.

Clark soon carried on a nationwide business, as far as our young nation extended at that time. His first really significant undertaking was the sale of Mexican War bonds. One profitable tract acquired by Enoch Clark in settlement of a debt was in the heart of Chicago. Clark Street derives its name from the fact that it ran through that tract.

The panic of 1857 wrecked the original Clark firm, and it went into liquidation. Jay Cooke withdrew, and the Philadelphia firm was reorganized under Clark's two sons, who soon became interested in railroad financing. Later it was a natural step from steam trains to electric railways and electric companies. The Clarks' first Michigan venture came into fruition on April 17, 1900, when the electric Grand Rapids Railway was incorporated as successor to the earlier Consolidated Street Railway Company of that city. This enterprise brought the Clarks together with a thrifty Michigan man of Dutch stock by the name of Anton G. Hodenpyl, who was forty-eight years old and cut of the same cloth as W. A. Foote. But where Foote concerned himself with the consolidation of electric properties, Hodenpyl's interest lay in the consolidation of financing, for he could sense even then that concentrated and interlocking capital was essential to build up utilities to the point where American industry could really get moving. His genius foreshadowed the holding-company period of our utilities, a highly controversial time that eventually had to go. Yet this period was essential to the spectacular growth of the American economy.

Here lies one of the paradoxes that affect history time and again. Every society in the process of industrialization has to amass capital. To accomplish this, labor has to produce more than it consumes. As a result, the workingman earns less than he contributes; he pays with his sweat for the machinery that later makes the lives of his descendants, and perhaps even his own life, easier and more luxurious. In short, the initial capital-building period of our industrial revolution employed a sort of collective savings system. The still-developing socialist countries are not exempt from this tight-belt regimen; instead of running capitalistic sweatshops, they rationalize legalistics to create political prisoners, who then work in slave-labor camps, such as those in Siberia, or they establish "voluntary" communes to produce the capital the country needs: dams, power plants, factories, and machinery. In a capitalist society, the paradox sets in when the required wealth has been created; the working people are no longer peasants then, but are increasingly participating citizens with rising expectations, and in their new position they find the power to condemn—and often scuttle—the system which got them where they are. It's all part of the natural flow of a society's development. There is no villainy, as such, on either side—neither on capital's nor on labor's.

Hodenpyl, to be sure, was a capitalist, and he was certainly no villain. One of Hodenpyl's great interests was nature. He loved trees and wild flowers; in fact, according to a onetime neighbor, "He loved trees so well that he knew the name of every one of them and he patted them as though they were his pets."⁴ Grand Rapids still has its 40-acre Hodenpyl Woods, which he donated to his native city in 1912. Moreover, Hodenpyl was a genial man, possessing a human sympathy that appealed to everyone. Once Burton R. Laraway, who was a humble clerk in Hodenpyl's organization before he went to work for Consumers Power, informed Hodenpyl that he was about to get married. Hodenpyl gave him a piece of highly unusual advice, considering that it came from a businessman of his time. Hodenpyl told Laraway to think the marriage over carefully. "Once you're married," he said, "always remember that your family must come first, ahead of business and all else."

Above all, Hodenpyl was conscientious and totally dependable. When he was still a very young man and working in the lumber business, his boss, Robert B. Woodcock, happened to return to the office late one night, and there was Hodenpyl bent over the account books. "What's the trouble?" Woodcock asked him. "The balance is off," young Hodenpyl said. Woodcock frowned. "That's not good," he said. "How much are we off?" and he looked over the boy's shoulder. "Right here," Hodenpyl said, pointing at a figure, "That should be 1 cent more." Woodcock started laughing. "Don't waste your time on that," he said. "Simply charge it off." Hodenpyl looked at him very seriously and answered, "No, Mr. Woodcock. If I did that, I'd be letting dollars go by."[5] Now, this might have been a very smart trick had Hodenpyl known that Woodcock was returning to the office that night, but such wasn't the case, and thus this little incident sheds considerable light on what Hodenpyl was all about—and part of this was being a natural-born banker.

Anton G. Hodenpyl was born on November 7, 1852, just a few years before Consumers Power's earliest predecessor companies were started in Kalamazoo and Jackson. He was the son of Peter J. G. Hodenpyl, and from his father he must have inherited his important trait of easily venturing into the new; the elder Hodenpyl was among the first spunky merchants in Grand Rapids who had their names arranged in small gas jets across their storefronts in 1857.[6]

Young Hodenpyl was only about thirty years old when the idea of founding a trust company first occurred to him. Today the thought of a trust company—a bank organized to hold funds in trust and to use these funds with vigilance and ability—hardly seems remarkable, but in 1880 it was a rather original idea. There were no trust companies in Michigan then, not even laws to provide for them. It took Hodenpyl nine years to get the necessary bill introduced and passed, but finally on July 15, 1889, the Michigan Trust Company, the first in the state, was organized in Grand Rapids with $200,000 capital.[7] Among the business leaders Hodenpyl attracted as stockholders in his venture were many prominent western Michigan lumbermen and bankers.[8] Hodenpyl was a "perfect steam engine for business,"[9] and with the backing of his influential stockholders, he made Michigan Trust prosper. Soon Hodenpyl thought it should have an office building of its own. In his customary venturesome way, he proposed a ten-story building. Again, in the light of today, there would be nothing unusual about such a proposal; in fact, it might be considered modest for such an important enterprise. But in 1891 buildings of such height were rare even in New York, which was then still a sprawling expanse of one- to six-story buildings, and only Chicago had several structures taller than ten stories. In Michigan, Hodenpyl's edifice, completed in 1892, was a real first.

This, then, was the kind of man whose fate eventually became inextricably interwoven with W. A. Foote's. When Hodenpyl first moved into his new Michigan Trust Building, their association still lay some years in the future, but already their paths were destined to cross.

As we examine history's complex tapestry, we must now select another thread and follow it back to February 24, 1856, the same year that the first gas predecessor company was founded in Kalamazoo. On this date, Henry D. Walbridge was born in that selfsame city, nephew of a pioneer real estate developer. Young Henry—whom everybody called Harry— didn't have much schooling. He had attended only the "open grades." Alert, handsome, and redheaded, he was, unflattering as this may sound, a "floater"—a fellow who didn't seem to care much about anything at that time and who relied on his good looks to win the hand of the daughter of an important man in Wabash, Indiana.[10] The marriage, however, gave Walbridge much more than a well-situated wife. Her father was connected with the gas company in Wabash, and it was through him that Harry learned to keep books and became acquainted with the gas business. Even more important, he now became ambitious.

Meanwhile, in Grand Rapids, there were two brothers, Francis B. and Thomas D. Gilbert, the latter one of the original stockholders of the Michigan Trust Company. In 1856, these two men launched the Grand Rapids Gas Light Company.[11] In 1882, having heard somehow of Henry Walbridge, they prevailed upon him to come join the outfit. During the thirteen years that followed, Walbridge worked his way up to general manager, but he didn't hold the post for long. He went to

MICHIGAN'S FIRST
"SKYSCRAPER"

*Anton G. Hodenpyl, financial
father of Consumers Power,
demonstrated his venture-
someness from the very start
of his career. He organized
the Michigan Trust Company,
first in the state, in 1889,
and before long he built this
ten-story office building in
Grand Rapids as the bank's
headquarters. The "sky-
scraper," of a height rare in
those days, was completed in
1892. It stood on Pearl Street,
just one block from the
Powers Opera House.* (Photo
courtesy of Grand Rapids
Public Library)

Detroit in 1898 to become president of the Backus Heating Company, and almost immediately thereafter he joined the Detroit City Gas Company as general manager. That company was owned by an early gas utilities man by the name of Emerson McMillin, and when McMillin managed also to gain control of the Grand Rapids Gas Light Company in 1901, Walbridge returned to his erstwhile organization and became its president.[12]

Now an important encounter takes place; two threads weave and form a strand. Walbridge, having rapidly moved up in the world, meets Hodenpyl, and they become close friends. "Harry and Tony formed an intellectual team," says the same cousin[13] who once called Walbridge a "floater." "Harry's and Tony's friends were among the elite of Grand Rapids. They both did their part socially. Harry and Tony were one, intellectually, socially, and in business."

Walbridge was in the gas business, and Hodenpyl was in the money business. "All these little companies," Walbridge told Hodenpyl, "they all have their problems. Anybody with enough backing could buy into them strong, one after another, and with

THE MONEYMEN
*Hodenpyl (left) and Henry D.
Walbridge (above), shown here in
their later years, formed a partnership that eventually grew into one
of the nation's most important
utility holding companies.* (Consumers Power Company collection)

some more money, he could really build them up." Whether
this was offered as a suggestion is doubtful, but Hodenpyl
thought long and hard about it. He had already taken part in
the organization of several utilities, including the gas companies
in Grand Rapids, Kalamazoo, and Jackson,[14] and as a financier
he was attracted to this young industry with its high capital
requirements. One day in 1903 he said to Walbridge, "Let's
go!"

The two men joined forces to form Hodenpyl-Walbridge &
Company and established their headquarters *not* in Grand
Rapids but at the font of capital—on Wall Street in New York
City.[15] Their move to this financial and business center of the
East was wholly logical, and with the same logic, as the years

went on, the fulcrum of Michigan's utilities was shifted to New York and remained there until the end of the holding-company period. The Hodenpyl-Walbridge move to the East presaged the important time when Consumers Power would no longer be a local business but the principal operation of a utilities complex that covered many parts of the nation.

One of Hodenpyl-Walbridge's first moves was the organization of the Saginaw City Gas Company in 1901, which they achieved by gaining control of, and merging with, the East Saginaw Gas Light Company and the Saginaw Gas Light Company, two of the original seven predecessor gas companies. In 1902, they organized the Pontiac Light Company in a masterful business coup. At the time of its organization, this company had no assets other than cash, and with this cash they offered to buy out, for $175,000, the Pontiac Gas and Electric Company, formed earlier by a merger of the Pontiac Gas Light Company with the Medbury Electric Light Company.[16] Convincing the stockholders was no problem—it turned out that the company's major owner, with 1,996 of its 2,000 shares, was none other than Henry Walbridge, who had been accumulating them for some time.[17] In 1903, too, there was a consolidation of the public utility companies in Springfield, Illinois, into the Springfield Railway & Light Company. Hodenpyl-Walbridge and the E. W. Clark people of Philadelphia teamed up for this venture, as Hodenpyl and Clark already had for the earlier-mentioned Grand Rapids Railway, of which Hodenpyl was president and C. M. Clark was vice-president. They cooperated again later in the same year to form the Saginaw–Bay City Railway & Light Company, a consolidation of all the utilities and traction lines then operating in Saginaw and Bay City.

Hodenpyl-Walbridge and the Clark people didn't restrict their activities to the Middle West. In 1904 they merged several gas, electric, and traction utilities in Rochester, New York, and it was, in fact, this undertaking which put Hodenpyl-Walbridge really on the map. One day in 1906, Walbridge, who happened to be in Pontiac at the time, received a telegram from his partner: "Your presence in New York urgently required for meeting with Vanderbilt Monday." Since it was already Saturday, Walbridge didn't have much time to prepare for the trip, but he did make it to New York in time and was welcomed at Grand Central Station with all the turn-of-the-century pomp and circumstance that befitted a gentleman who had dealings with the baron of the New York Central Railroad. A hansom cab whisked him immediately to the Wall Street offices, where several high-powered negotiators for the Vanderbilt interests, as well as Anton Hodenpyl, were already waiting. On the way down from the station, George Hardy, Hodenpyl's right-hand man and eventually his partner, briefed Walbridge on the situation. New York Central was interested in buying the Rochester properties and was willing to pay an exorbitant price. "Since when is Cornelius Vanderbilt interested in gas and electricity?" Walbridge asked Hardy.

"Oh, that isn't it at all," Hardy laughed. "What Vanderbilt really wants is our traction lines. He wants to make them part of the New York Central. Mr. Hodenpyl asked me to tell you that he feels we ought to sell, but he'd appreciate it if you'd be tough about it so they'll raise the ante."

Walbridge played his part well, resisting up to the last minute Hodenpyl's blandishments to go for the initial New York Central offer. By the afternoon of the next day, their strategy bore fruit. Vanderbilt's people came back with a bid so high that the sale netted Hodenpyl and Walbridge more than $1 million. They signed, and from that moment on their firm had a truly secure foundation.

Other Eastern properties developed by Hodenpyl-Walbridge in the early days were located in Fulton, New York, and in Williamsport and Johnstown, Pennsylvania. In addition, they consolidated a number of properties in Illinois and Indiana — among them the Peoria Light Company and the Evansville Light Company, both embracing the gas and electric businesses in their respective communities. Two years later, in 1908, they organized the Union Railway Gas and Electric Company, which in turn merged the Springfield, Peoria, and Evansville properties as well as the Rockford & Interurban Railway Company.

But all this was only the beginning. The geographic spread of the Hodenpyl-Walbridge interests foreshadowed the ultimate mutation of their firm into The Commonwealth & Southern Corporation, one of America's utility giants in the coming holding-company days.

In Michigan, too, this consolidation was starting to take form. Here, Hodenpyl and Walbridge were concentrating on the lower Grand Valley and the communities along the Saginaw Road, from the outskirts of Detroit north to Bay City. The

JACKSON IN 1905

It was a bustling, growing city in those days, with electric streetcars and wide, busy sidewalks. Streets were illuminated by W. A. Foote with General Electric magnetite arc lamps (see arrow), then generally known as "luminous arc lights." It was the first commercial installation of this type of lamp. Shown here is Main Street, now Michigan Avenue, looking east from Jackson Street. (Photo courtesy of George Korten)

two men were, at the start, interested mostly in gas companies, but their properties included some electric and traction companies, too, and in effect they soon controlled most of eastern Michigan's power outside of Detroit. At the same time, W. A. Foote's own utilities empire was taking shape in western Michigan, not yet nearly so rich in cash and business influence, but in its own way no less impressive. The 1904 merger of his properties into the Commonwealth Power Company, headquartered in Jackson, was his first step in the direction of big business.[18] Not that the resources at his disposal there were so huge as to warrant that term. At the start, the Commonwealth Power Company supplied only 2,472 electric and gas customers, spread over all the communities that it supplied, but the handwriting was on the wall. While small-town utilities were not yet big business, there was no doubt even then that such eventually would be the case. The growth potential was inherent not only in the increased demand for power by residents and businesses but also in the increasing number of potential customers as Michigan's towns developed and grew. By the same token, it was inevitable that the Foote interests eventually would come face-to-face with those of Hodenpyl and Walbridge. There were only two possibilities then—to clash or to combine their forces.

8

A Matter of Chance

If Michigan's lumbermen had been conservation-minded, it is quite possible that The Commonwealth & Southern Corporation never would have been founded and that Consumers Power never would have been born—at least not in the form that we know it today. But the lumbermen were ravagers, and they changed the face of Michigan. Their cry was "cut and get out," a slogan that would make any self-respecting environmentalist rush to the barricades. But there were no environmentalists in those days and no ecological barricades. Everybody just laughed all the way to the bank.

Michigan was a magnificent forest wilderness when the white man first came. About one-third of the way up its Lower Peninsula, the oak stands gave way to vast forests of virgin pine. The land looked much the way northern Ontario and Quebec still do today. What's more, Michigan's white pine was the best lumber in the world. Who could resist making a killing? And the killing was made easy, for the timber was

TRAIN ON THE LOGGING FRONTIER

Soon you couldn't see the forest for the trees that had been carried off.
(Michigan State Archives)

largely accessible to streams on which the logs could be floated
to sawmills and the market. At that time, towns were springing
up all over the treeless plains of the Middle West, and timber
was needed for building. Chicago, the most important distributing center, was readily reached by cheap water transportation
from Michigan, and so down the river and across the lake went
the trees.

Michigan's lumber operations reached their peak in 1888.
In that year alone more than 4 billion board feet were sawed.[1]
In addition, the state's lumber mills manufactured millions of
shingles, staves, pickets, railroad ties, and square timbers.
Nobody really knows just how much wood was cut. And even
though after 1888 Michigan's timber business declined, it was
still ahead of that of every other state in 1900.

Those were great days for the lumbermen. Their life was
rugged, full of hard work and fun. Logging was carried on
mostly during the winter so that the logs could be hauled on
sleds to the riverbanks. In autumn, the lumberjacks (or shanty
boys, as they were called at first) came to Michigan by ship,
train, or wagon. At the last stop they shouldered their "tur-
keys"—denim bags that contained their clothes and other
possessions—and set out on foot for their camps deep in the

forests near rivers and tributary streams. These camps usually consisted of at least one bunkhouse where the lumberjacks lived, a mess hall where they ate, an office shack, and stables. Life started before daybreak. The great pines were felled, branches were trimmed off, and the huge trunks were sawed into lengths that could be handled. At dusk, the men returned to camp for a hot supper and an hour or so of horseplay before their weariness won out. If there was a fiddler in the camp, it was all to the good, but a jew's harp was enough, and anybody could play that. The men danced jigs and "buck and wing," and when they got too tired to dance they sat around the stove in the bunkhouse and told stories. Unbelievable exploits of mythical characters developed: of Paul Bunyan and Babe, his big blue ox; of Joe Kadunk, the famous second cook of lumberjack lore who had supposedly invented blueberry pie.

With spring came thaws and rains. Streams swelled. The logs that had been piled along the banks during the winter were rolled into the water. They sped lakeward, bobbing, spinning, plunging, and crashing together. Daredevil log handlers called "river hogs" followed along on the banks. They set adrift any logs that floated to shore, and they broke up jams at curves and shallow spots until the floating timber reached the mills that were to saw them. Here, at the mouths of all large rivers, the logs were captured by booms formed of logs chained together and were sorted out by their hammered "log marks" that served as their owner's identification. No sooner had the logs arrived in a mill town than the lumberjacks followed them, pockets bulging with pay saved over the long winter. Saloons, gambling dens, and whorehouses flourished; drunken fights were the order of night and day.

For many years it seemed that Michigan's forests were inexhaustible. But nothing is. The ruthless cutting left Michigan in desolation. Its land was bare, littered with the slashings from the great trees and the smashed corpses of trees too small to cut. The dried litter became prime fuel for forest fires, which sometimes wiped out whole communities. Today, with new stands of timber at last covering those wastes, it is hard to visualize this wretched scene. What's amazing is that the lumbermen did not see it either, until it was too late. Most of them never thought about tomorrow.

Edward F. Loud and his three brothers, owners of the H. M. Loud Sons' Company,[2] were exceptions. As their saws bit deeper and deeper into the pine stands along the Au Sable River, they could visualize the growing gloom when "the whistle that called the crews to labor no longer sounded, when the last board was cut and the wheels had ceased to turn, and the curtain would be rung down and our towns be but a memory of their former greatness."[3]

The towns Loud was thinking about specifically were those of Oscoda and Au Sable, but of course the same was true of other Michigan river cities that depended on lumber for their livelihood. One must remember that in those days, not even the wildest dreamer envisioned the time when tourists, campers, hunters, and fishermen would come by the thousands, bringing with them an entirely new industry. They would have liked it even better then, especially the Au Sable, which the French had called the "Sandy River," for that was the time when silver-scaled grayling lay in the stream "like cordwood" and were so trustful that they could be taken with fly, worm, or grass-hopper. The "sports" of those bygone days used to pursue the fabulous fighter with casts of four dropper flies and a stretcher, and they never even reeled in the line until five fish were hooked all at once. Daily catches were astronomical. Grayling were taken by the hundreds and thrown on the banks to die. No wonder that this game fish soon shared the same fate as virgin pine—none was left. But unlike timber, there could be no second growth of grayling. In their place there came trout—brook, rainbow, and brown, in that order, and it's trout that bring fishermen to the Au Sable today.[4]

Of course, neither Edward Loud nor his brothers—Henry, William, and George—were concerned with such esoteric, futuristic considerations, especially as pertaining to fish. It is even doubtful that they thought much about the long-run economic picture of the state. What they were mostly worried about, and with good reason, was that their firm would collapse when the lumber was depleted.

One day in 1905, the telephone shrilled in the Loud Company offices. Ed Loud, a short, heavy-set man then in his fifties, pulled himself from his chair, unhooked the receiver, and leaned toward the mouthpiece of the wall apparatus. A man was calling from Bay City. The connection was poor, and Loud did not catch his name. "I'd like to know," the caller said, "if you folks own land up there on the Au Sable where water can be dammed up."

"Sure we do," Loud replied.

There was a pause. "We might be able to do some business," the man said. "I'll come up and see you."[5]

Loud settled back down at his desk. "What did this man want?" he asked himself. The caller evidently couldn't be thinking about a new lumber-milling operation; there was no point in making any further investments in this dying business. Electric power? Loud had heard something about that. Maybe that was it.

"Say, Jack, come over here for a minute," he called to John McKenna, his surveyor and timber estimator. "You got anything special to do the next couple of weeks?"

McKenna shook his head. "I'll tell you what I'd like you to do," Loud said. "I want you to make up a map of the whole river, all the way from its source to Oscoda. Show all the lands that we own, and try to get the names and addresses of the owners of all the other river lands."

Loud had underestimated the job. It took McKenna not just a couple weeks, but a couple years to map the Au Sable. It was a good thing that the Bay City man never showed up, for it's pretty difficult to do business with a man when you don't really know what you've got to sell him. The reason the survey took so long was that no real map of the area existed. The government map showed points where streams crossed section lines, but where the waters meandered within the sections was largely a matter of conjecture. Nor was there any way to ascertain the exact sites of possible flowage lands unless all the banks in the likely locations were measured for their height—a laborious, time-consuming job.

Month after month the survey continued. McKenna and Ed Loud eventually acquired a "wanigan," a primitive, flat-bottom type of houseboat made of sections of planking that could be easily disassembled and carried by wagon to some point upstream, where it was then reassembled and floated or poled downstream with the current. The boat had a simple bunk room for a cabin, topped by a flat roof where extra men could sleep under a tent when the cabin got filled up to the point of suffocation. There was a small, flat deck forward of the cabin as well as astern, from which it was easy to jump ashore when the wanigan was beached. On trip after wanigan trip, Loud and McKenna measured the stream and its flow, and between trips they negotiated for flowage lands, for by now Loud had sold himself on going into the power-dam business, whether or not the Bay City man ever called back.

Luckily, land could be obtained cheaply. Loud's treasury was rather low, but the property he was after had little value. It was purely speculative, and Loud moved slowly and with caution in acquiring it. Eventually his company owned both banks of the Au Sable practically all the way from Oscoda to Mio, a distance of more than 40 miles even as the crow flies, and their property included almost all those flowage lands that would be needed if dams were built. There were, however, a number of sections belonging to the state which, up to that time, had been withheld from public sale. When these were offered at last, Loud and McKenna went to Lansing, expecting to pay no more than $1.50 an acre at the auction.

"One dollar!" Loud called after the auctioneer had read out the first description and asked for a bid. A slight, gray-haired man, standing nearby, spoke up even before the auctioneer could raise his gavel. "One dollar and a half," the little man said. Loud raised his bid to $2. The other bidder glanced curiously at Loud, and countered with "Two and a half." The auctioneer grinned with glee, and he got happier and happier as the two competitive bidders ran the price up to $10 an acre. Loud was the winner in the end. He got the 160-acre parcel for $1,600, but there were still nearly 2,000 acres to go!

"Do you know that man?" Loud whispered to McKenna.

"Never saw him," McKenna whispered back.

"Well, " Loud said, shaking his touseled gray hair, "we can't quit now. We've just got to keep going."

The auctioneer started on his next description. The small hall was getting hot and stuffy. Loud drew his fingers under his collar, wiped the sweat from his big mustache, and rejoined with "Five dollars" when the other bidder opened with four. This time, much to the delight of state officials present, the price ran to $15 an acre before the unknown bidder gave up. By noon, Loud had acquired nearly 1,000 acres and had committed himself to payments of more than $12,000, a figure he would be hard put to meet. And yet there was still more land to be purchased. He returned to the hotel for lunch. His adversary was standing in the lobby. The man looked up and smiled when he saw Loud enter and walked up to him. "Mr. Loud," he said, "my name is Arthur Watkins. No hard feelings, I hope. Won't you join me in my room for a drink?" Loud consented pleasantly enough. Business was business, and he could see no reason for not taking a drink together, although he had to admit to himself that he'd never before taken a drink which, in effect, had already cost him a small fortune and might cost him even more that afternoon.

When Watkins opened the door of his room, a lanky man rose from a chair. Shaking Loud's hand, this other visitor introduced himself as W. A. Foote. "You really want those properties, don't you?" Foote said.

"That's right," Loud answered, "and I aim to get them."

Foote nodded. "I can see you do," he said. "Well, I'm going to call off Mr. Watkins here. No point in breaking you," he smiled.

Watkins poured some bourbon for Loud, and the men settled down to talk. Foote and Loud explained to each other what they were after, and in the end they agreed that they had better get together, for neither was in a position to finance the dams they had in mind. What's more, the two men took an instant liking to each other.

A few weeks later Loud took Foote and Fargo down the river on his wanigan. Also along on the trip was Andrew Cooke, vice-president of the Harris Trust and Savings Bank of Chicago, who had looked after the financing of some of Foote's other developments. Cooke seemed to be impressed with the Au Sable's potential and indicated that his bank would not be adverse to backing the project. But then the general economic situation intervened, as it so often does. Foote eventually had to inform Loud that prospects of getting the necessary funds were nearly hopeless, and told him that he was free to negotiate with other parties. All Foote asked was that Loud let him know before such negotiations took place. This Loud promised to do.

Months passed. It was now the summer of 1908. Loud had long given up his dreams of building dams on the Au Sable. He had resigned himself to having thrown away money on the flowage lands and was casting about for some new enterprise that would rescue the family company. One day he traveled down to Detroit to look into some business prospects and put up at the Cadillac Hotel. This old hotel, at the corner of Washington and Michigan Boulevards, was an imposing edifice, six stories high, with turretlike towers at its four corners, and decked out with an elaborate gay-nineties elegance. There were electric streetcar tracks on Michigan Avenue, but this was the only sign of modernity around this imitation castle. Horse-drawn carriages and wagons filled the air with summer dust, and Ed Loud had to brush off his jacket when he entered the ornate lobby.

The Cadillac Hotel had been built by Daniel Scotten, who had made his fortune in tobacco in 1880. Scotten considered it a monument to himself, and it was indeed the showplace of Michigan. The hotel had been named for Antoine de la Mothe Cadillac, the founder of Detroit, and it was the first such tribute—there was no Cadillac Square in those days, no Cadillac Avenue, no Cadillac automobile. The hotel catered to presidents, to actors and actresses, and to visiting baseball teams of the American League, all except Connie Mack's Athletics, for Connie was a frugal man and used to put his boys up at less expensive hostelries.[6] It was a luxurious establishment indeed and just the right kind of place to make important business connections. The dining room served fresh strawberries all the year round and had floors and wainscoting of the finest imported marble. The bar—and this was where Loud's dusty boots first took him after the long trip to Detroit— was the finest and most luxurious wet spot west of New York. Its ceiling was inlaid with gold. Heavy rugs covered the floor. The Cadillac crests in the rugs had been woven in Austria. All in all, this plush emporium presented quite a contrast to the sandy and now almost treeless wilderness of the Au Sable country, from which Loud had just come and from which he had to draw his living—and then some, if he intended to continue frequenting the expensive Cadillac Hotel.

"Hi there," a deep bubbling voice called to him from the gleaming oak bar. "It's Loud, isn't it? Looks like you've come a far piece." The voice belonged to a man of imposing stature, well over 6 feet tall, wide and barrel-chested as a wrestler, with a smile-crinkled, monumental face framed by a heavy gray pompadour. Loud hardly knew the man, despite his unforgettable appearance; he had met him perhaps once or twice, and for the moment he couldn't remember the name. But then remembering names wasn't exactly in Loud's line of work, while it was certainly a basic stock-in-trade for the massive gentleman who leaned on the bar as if he were trying to crush it.

DANIEL SCOTTEN'S CADILLAC HOTEL

Detroit's most opulent hotel exemplified the height of gay nineties elegance and was no doubt the scene of many fateful encounters, among them the 1908 chance meeting that led to the birth of Consumers Power. (Burton Historical Collection, Detroit Public Library)

"I'm John Weadock, one of those damn Bay City Weadocks," the big man chuckled, quickly filling in the evident memory gap of the dusty, tired-looking arrival from the lumber country. "How's things up on the old Au Sable?"

Loud wasn't the type of man to take refuge in equivocations. "Could be a whole lot better," he said. He remembered Weadock now: one of those big-time lawyers who had their fingers in every pie.

Indeed, though barely forty-eight years old, John C. Weadock was among New York's most influential attorneys. A farm boy of Irish parentage, he had been born, the youngest of seven sons, to Louis and Mary Weadock near St. Marys, Ohio, on February 18, 1860. After the death of his parents, young Weadock had joined his eldest brother, Thomas, in Bay City, Michigan, and attended high school there. Eventually he taught school himself, in Hampton Township and the village of Freeland, and evenings he read law in his brother's office. But teaching, even if only for a meal ticket, wasn't Weadock's métier. With his big, burly figure he soon latched on to a purser's job on the *L. G. Mason*, a small river steamer that carried passengers and light freight between Saginaw and Bay City. The passengers were mostly lumber boys out for brawls and bawdy houses, and it was Weadock's job to keep the ship reasonably clean, toss off the drunks, and knock sense into the fighters. That was his income and his job. In between he kept on reading law books, and suddenly he was an attorney. He was lovable of manner when he wasn't bouncing sots, keen of mind as a fox, and homegrown as a turnip, and before he even knew it himself he was a big success, making up for the fun time he'd spent on the river. By 1903, he was one of the organizers and a large shareholder of the Traction and Power Company in Bay City. Later he served as the company's

THE MEETING PLACE

Here is one end of the bar where Loud and Weadock met. In this particular case, the stiff posing so typical of old photographs seems entirely appropriate. (Michigan State Archives)

president, and in 1907 he moved his law practice to New York as requested by "Father Anton" Hodenpyl, who wanted this astute attorney close by. Within a few years Weadock would be the behind-the-scenes kingmaker of Hodenpyl's utilities empire, right up to the point of crowning the last of its caesars, Wendell Willkie, in the *Götterdammerung* of Roosevelt's New Deal, but for the moment utilities as big business hadn't even been conceived. Weadock was about to act the marriage broker and then become the midwife.

"Listen, Ed," Weadock said to Loud after the two men had visited for some time over their glasses. "Do you people own lands on the Au Sable that might be suitable for power development?"

This question, as Loud later recalled, fairly took his breath away. He had no idea of Weadock's association with Hodenpyl-Walbridge, and even if he had known about it, there would have been no reason for him to be aware of the fact that these men were interested in the power business. As it was, the question came to him straight out of the blue, months after he had forced himself to forget about all those wasted years of surveying the river and the money spent in buying up its barren banks. "I should say we do," he answered, and he promptly told Weadock about the river's marvelous possibilities. "Is it under option or tied up in any way?" Weadock asked him. Loud answered that it wasn't.

"Now, that's mighty interesting," the lawyer said. There was always laughter in Weadock's voice, no matter what he said. "Why don't you come to New York and see the people I work with. Tell them what you have and let's talk it over. They are nice people and they won't hurt you."

"All right," Loud agreed. "I'll go. Just tell me when."

Weadock must have telephoned or telegraphed to New York, for that very evening, as Loud was eating in the hotel's gilded dining room, Weadock joined him at his table and suggested a date. "How about next Friday," he said, "would that suit you?"

THE LION FROM BAY CITY

No other man exerted more influence in the history of Consumers Power than John C. Weadock, the self-taught Bay City lawyer who became one of Wall Street's most influential attorneys. Of course, this photograph was made many years after his chance meeting with Ed Loud. No portrait of young Weadock seems to have survived. (Consumers Power photo)

It suited Loud just fine, but he remembered that there was one thing he had to do before he could start negotiations with a clear conscience. He called up W. A. Foote and told him of his intention of presenting the Au Sable River project to a New York combine.

"Who are you going to see there?" Foote asked.

"Hodenpyl-Walbridge & Company," Loud answered.

This must have given Foote quite a jolt. If he had any potential competitors, these were the men. They were selling gas in Jackson and Kalamazoo while he was selling electricity, and gas was the big money-maker. "Don't do it," Foote told Loud. "They're gas people and not power people. They'll tie you up in such a way that nothing can be done with the project."

Loud answered that he had already agreed to go and was going. "Well, I'm very sorry to hear that," Foote said. "I think you're making a great mistake." Foote paused. For several long moments, Loud heard nothing but the crackling of the phone wires. Then Foote asked a surprising question: "Have you any objection to my going with you?" he said.

"None whatever," Loud replied, and it was arranged that Foote would join him on the train for New York.[7]

When the two went to the office of Hodenpyl-Walbridge & Company that Friday morning of their arrival, Loud was surprised to find that Cooke, of the Harris Bank, had joined the party—the same Cooke whose bank had eventually turned down the original request for financing. But Cooke soon explained that his organization still had no interest in the project, that he had come at the request of W. A. Foote to tell the Hodenpyl-Walbridge people, among them a gentleman by the name of William M. Eaton, of his trip down the Au Sable and how much he had been impressed with the river's possibilities. Indeed, Cooke had no sooner done so and explained the financial pressures that had made it impossible for Harris to finance the Au Sable development than he excused himself and left the room.

Loud then tried to present his proposition. "The way I see it, gentlemen," he said, "we could handle this in one of two ways. . . ." But Foote put a hand on his arm and simply took over. Loud was utterly amazed. After all, Foote had no interest or rights in the Au Sable property, optional or otherwise. Foote was polite enough about the interruption. "I hope you don't mind," he said, "but it might be better if I explained the proposition." It wasn't very long before Foote's purpose became apparent to Loud: he had known that Foote controlled other power developments, but had no idea of how really important they were; nor had he suspected how Foote's developments could conceivably be dovetailed with the holdings of the New York group. Within minutes, Loud realized that without Foote he was a mere landowner in a buyer's market. With Foote in on the deal, however, Loud had leverage. The real issue was not how much Loud could sell for, or how much financing he could get, but on what basis the Foote and Hodenpyl-Walbridge interests could be amalgamated through the Au Sable River proposition. In that very instant, without any papers needing to be signed, Foote became Loud's spokesman.

It would be nice to be able to report that the marriage was consummated right on the spot. But it wasn't. Joining big enterprises and buying up a river isn't something that gets done in five minutes. At the moment Loud couldn't even put a money value on his firm's holdings. The negotiations turned out to be a lengthy affair—and the actual joining did not take place until 1909—but the talks concerned detail rather than principle. The overall outcome was a foregone conclusion all along, as indeed it had been ever since the fortuitous chance meeting of Loud and Weadock in Detroit: the formation of one of America's most important utility complexes.[8]

9

The Spirit of 1910

Consumers Power was born into an exciting time—that glorious teen age before World War I catapulted our country into adulthood. Like all youngsters, the United States then was totally preoccupied with itself, feeling no longer bound to its Old World parents, struggling to find its own identity. Still awkward in its grown-up dress, it was not yet accustomed to strong muscles and long limbs. Its voice, trying so hard to be heard, was harsh and strident, not well modulated as it had been in its infancy, when it still looked to Europe's capitals for a measure of guidance, nor yet so firmly self-assured as it was to become in later years. Indeed, our young country suffered all the contradictions and convulsions so typical of youth. Caution never subdued its exuberance. It ravenously pursued success. It suffered deep guilt when it had fun. And like all teen-agers, it loved its first adult-size toy—the horseless carriage.

HE PRESSED THE STARTER ON GENERAL MOTORS

William Crapo Durant, shown here with the Durant car he built, also was in the utilities business: he owned a sizable chunk of Flint Light and Power. Durant later gained control of Buick and founded General Motors. (The Bettmann Archive, Inc.)

For Michigan, this obstreperous piece of machinery was a true godsend. With the lumber industry dying, the state's economic future looked anything but bright. But then came the automobile, and by astounding coincidence a number of natural-born mechanics who were intrigued by its endless tinkering possibilities lived and worked at that time in various Michigan cities. On the outskirts of Detroit, about 1891, Henry Ford had begun toying with the idea of adapting an internal-combustion engine to the horseless carriage. He talked over the idea with his wife Clara, and on the spur of the moment—at least that's how the story goes—he asked her to get a piece of paper so that he could sketch out his thoughts. Clara found a sheet of music on their organ. On the blank back of this sheet, Ford proceeded to outline his proposed machine for the first time, explaining it to his wife as he sketched. He realized, however, that he must learn more about electricity, and forthwith he made appropriate inquiries at the Edison Illuminating Company in Detroit. They asked him whether he wanted a job. He thought he might, and for a short time he worked for the company as an engineer. As we shall see, Ford's connection with the electric utilities industry was far from unique among the pioneer auto builders —a circumstance that was to influence the growth of Consumers Power Company.

Also in the 1890s, Ransom E. Olds took his savings and bought his father's interest in a business in Lansing that handled marine and stationary gasoline engines. After five years of experimenting, he completed the first Oldsmobile in 1897. In Flint, David D. Buick was building cars too, and here another interesting connection with the utilities industry cropped up. One of the prime movers in early Flint had been Henry H. Crapo, who had brought with him to Michigan a part of the capital amassed by his family in New Bedford, Massachusetts, where the French-descended Crapos were mariners and shipbuilders. In Flint, echoing with buzz saws and rich with timber money, Crapo augmented his fortune in the lumber business; reclaimed 1,100 acres of swamp, where he then raised topgrade cattle; and ran for governor and made it. As early as 1879, his daughter, Rebecca C. Durant, had been a stockholder of the City of Flint Gas Light Company, and in 1903, her son, William Crapo Durant, became one of the owners of the electric utility later known as the Flint Light and Power Company. This was the same Durant who later gained control of the Buick Motor Company,[1] transferred it temporarily to Jackson and then back to Flint, and in 1908 founded the General Motors Company with Buick as its basis.[2] Durant soon acquired the Olds Motor Works and even tried to buy out the Ford Motor Company.[3]

Durant's temporary move to Jackson was highly significant in the automobile–utility industries relationship. It was in Jackson, where the Buick assembly operations were installed in the plant of the Imperial Wheel Company, owned by the Durant-Dort family, that Durant met William M. Eaton, manager of the Jackson Gas Company—the same Eaton who in 1907 was to join the Hodenpyl-Walbridge team, and who eventually was involved in the aforementioned negotiations with Foote and Loud on behalf of the Hodenpyl interests. Eaton later served for two years as president of General Motors Company as a favor to Durant, who preferred to stay in the background.[4]

The relationship between Consumers Power and General Motors might have been closer still had Hodenpyl and his associates been as visionary when it came to automobiles as they were about the future of utilities. At one point Hodenpyl was invited to participate in the financing of GM and turned it down. He shared the deep-seated feeling of most business-men of his day that the automobile had come about as far as it could and that there was little future in it. In fact, there was the time in 1911 when General Motors stock was offered to several of the company's own officers and found no takers.[5] If hindsight were the only qualification, we'd all be millionaires.

Certainly the early car business did not look exactly prom-ising of huge rewards. Just like the utilities business, it was highly fractionated. In 1910, when Henry Ford's Model T sold for $950 and he had just moved into his new Highland Park plant, where he was soon to establish assembly-line mass production, considerably fewer than 500,000 cars and trucks were bumping along America's dirt roads.[6] These vehicles represented at least forty makes, of which only Buick, Cadillac, Oldsmobile, and Ford are still around today.[7]

But in both the automobile and the utilities industries, as in most technological fields, the thrust for consolidation already was apparent. The period of ruthless competition between small businesses was beginning to give way to the domination by large concerns and associations. Railroads had been the first to form pools. To counter their cooperative practices, the

Sherman Antitrust Act became law in 1890, but this legislation had little immediate effect, and the movement toward concentrated business went right along, aided to a large degree by New Jersey's General Corporations Act of 1899, which permitted the organization of holding companies without specific legislative action.

The unchecked growth of big business, inevitable and essential as it was during this explosive period of early industrialization, quite understandably brought with it widespread public resentment and concern. Political leaders such as William Jennings Bryan, Robert M. LaFollette, Theodore Roosevelt, and William H. Taft pushed for reforms in both government and business. Laws for the regulation of railroads, banks, and industries came into being.[8] The country did not seem to know which way to go, what business philosophy to follow. On the one hand, Americans believed fervently in money and success. On the other, they were afraid of bigness. Yet this was the time when money was desired largely for the pleasure of its making and as a measure of accomplishment. Money for the sake of the indolence and gadgets it could buy did not become a public idol until much later. Everybody wanted to make his fortune; in fact, everyone rather expected to. But of course those who didn't make their fortunes resented those who did, and in their workaday lives they felt increasingly at the mercy of the big corporations.

At the same time, American business lived in a schizoid dream. Men were in business for profit, naturally. But unlike the "realistic" businessmen of Europe, Americans were imbued with a sense of mission. They knew they were accomplishing an overall good. In their quest to reduce costs, they were not only interested in greater profits but wanted to make their products and services more available. They were shocked to find themselves pictured as monsters in the populist press, the dollar sign the symbol of their evil. For even the biggest among them only *used* dollars but *believed* in men. J. P. Morgan amazed the Money Trust Investigation Committee of the House of Representatives when he testified that "a man I do not trust could not get money from me on all the bonds in Christendom."[9] Lest we dismiss this as fatuity, we must remember that in those days there was rarely time and opportunity for the complex legalities now taken for granted in business life. By the traditions of a frontier society, a man's word had to be his bond; without trust in individual integrity, America's economic development would have been aborted at an early stage.

Such was the cross-purpose spirit of 1910, when the Foote, Hodenpyl, and Clark interests set out together to conquer the utilities business. The collapse of the country's old laissez faire approach was particularly apparent in their fields. Utilities, at their beginnings, had functioned pretty much like any other kind of business, although gas and electric companies as well as traction lines were of course dependent on public rights-of-way and always had to obtain franchises to function. The idea, however, that a business serving the public as a whole is inherently different from other businesses was based on much more than the mere use of streets. The public service concept had its roots back in the Middle Ages under English common law. The concept also found expression toward the end of the seventeenth century, when Sir Mathew Hale, Lord Chief Justice of the King's Bench, ruled that if there was a wharf where all persons in the port must load and unload their goods, then this wharf and all its adjuncts "are affected with a publick interest and they cease to be *juris privati* only."[10]

Why only a wharf, say, or a railroad or a power utility should fall under that definition is open to question; common sense suggests that the same principle could be applied equally to a small town's only general store. But be that as it may, the American spirit of 1910, although it certainly no longer held that government best which governed least, did not yet clamor for controlling even a small part of the business affairs now under bureaucratic regulation. In the United States, the public service principle was applied at first only to railroads and then targeted on the gas and electric utilities.

The movement to regulate railroads and their rates had swept through the country, especially the states of the Middle West, in about 1870 largely as a result of the Granger movement, whose principal force was the National Grange of the Patrons of Husbandry, a powerful farmers' organization. Railroad commissions were established in several states, including Michigan. In 1909 the bipartisan three-man Michigan Railroad Commission was given jurisdiction over electric rates and utility securities.[11]

Thus, in the early 1900s, Michigan's utility men faced an ever-increasing two-pronged pressure—the populist campaign against trusts and the push for public service regulation—and all this precisely at a time when they were deeply immersed in the problems of raising money and constructing new facilities, indeed struggling to exist. What's more, two forces pulled within their industry, one toward a simplification of corporate structure and the other against it. Both of these forces had good reasons behind them. Simplification obviously meant savings, resulting in lower rates for consumers and greater profits for owners. This consideration had led to the organization in 1904 of Commonwealth Power Company, by which W. A. Foote brought together the electric operations in Jackson, Albion, Battle Creek, and Kalamazoo to form an interconnected system. The Hodenpyl-Walbridge group similarly pursued consolidation, and for that purpose, also in 1904, had organized The Michigan Light Company, a holding company under the 1899 New Jersey law, to bring together their holdings in various gas properties.

But there were equally good reasons for complicating the corporate structures of utilities, and these reasons had to do with the problems of raising money. Once a company had floated a bond issue backed by a general mortgage, any new expansion had to be tied into this old mortgage, and as a consequence the company faced severe growth limitations. To bypass this hurdle, different operations of the same basic company were often set up under separate corporations so that they could be financed more easily. In fact, it was not at all uncommon in the electric business to organize a separate corporation for each dam that was to be built.

The result, when Foote, Hodenpyl, and Clark finally got together, was a jumble of individual companies—albeit under one umbrella—whose structure could hold fascination only for a footnote-happy student of corporate legalistics in search of an esoteric Ph.D. Suffice it to say here that the consolidation was achieved in 1910 by organizing the Consumers Power Company of Maine as a holding company for all the electric properties in Michigan. Then, as a final step in strengthening the merger, the Commonwealth Power Railway and Light Company was established, bringing together representations of the common stock of Consumers Power Company and The Michigan Light Company of New Jersey as well as a number of electric railways in Michigan and other utilities in Illinois, Indiana, and Ohio controlled by the Hodenpyl-Walbridge and Clark interests. In short, Commonwealth Power Railway and Light became the big daddy of all joint enterprises.[12]

Not surprisingly, the newspapers of the day made much of the fact that Consumers Power was being incorporated under the laws of the state of Maine. It certainly looked like somebody was pulling a fast one. Not so. What happened was simply this: the original plan had been to pour all the Hodenpyl-Walbridge and Clark electric properties in Michigan into Foote's Commonwealth Power Company. At the same time, its name was to be changed to Consumers Power. With all its new assets, this revamped company was to expand its capitalization to $20 million and float a $35-million bond issue. Consumers Power was intended to be an operating company, running all the Michigan properties as one—and that's where the whole scheme ran afoul of the Michigan Railroad Commission, which had just gained jurisdiction over the financing of operating utilities.

For one thing, the commission admittedly wasn't quite sure how it was to exercise its authority: a case like that hadn't come up before. For another, Foote and Hodenpyl were equally inexperienced in dealing with regulatory agencies; it was the first time for them too. And so they made a couple of big mistakes. Thinking of security issues purely as representing a capitalization of earnings, they were wholly unprepared to present evidence on the value of the properties involved. It would seem that they brushed off the whole commission matter as a formality. The stockholder meeting authorizing the reorganization was held on March 8, 1910, only twenty-three days before the April 1 deadline on certain options essential to the merger; there was indeed a charming innocence about expecting a governmental body to deliberate on so complex a proposition in barely three weeks. Yet the deadline had to be met, or the whole deal was off.

The commission, despite its uncertainties, bravely arranged for Professor Mortimer E. Cooley, of the University of Michigan, to make an appraisal of the properties, but this was obviously a lost cause. Cooley would have had to start from scratch.

Ten days before the deadline, Foote and Hodenpyl held a hurried meeting in Weadock's oak-paneled law offices in New York. For once in his life, Foote seemed disheartened. He sat on the edge of a deep easy chair, supporting his forehead on the heels of his hands. He wouldn't look up as he spoke of his great disappointment that now everything seemed to have been for naught. He didn't even raise his head at first when Weadock suggested that there might be a way out of the dilemma. "Anton," Weadock said to Hodenpyl, who was pacing up and down in the office, "you've organized companies in Maine before, and there was never any problem, right?"

Hodenpyl nodded, somewhat impatiently. "But that doesn't

help us in Michigan," he said. "A holding company is one thing. An operating company is something else again. You'd still have to get approvals from the Railroad Commission on all the financing."

"My friend," Weadock said, chuckling and rising from behind his desk, "we've just solved the problem. We'll set up Consumers as a holding company for Mr. Foote's Commonwealth and the other Michigan properties. That way we'll simply have two holding companies, one over another. No difficulty there. Let's go up to Augusta."

And so it happened that Consumers Power started its existence as a holding company under the laws of Maine. The April 1 deadline was met, and the consolidation took place as planned. Nor was the Michigan Railroad Commission circumvented in any way. The only difference was that the capitalization required for expansion was now sought by the individual underlying companies. On this simplified basis, all the bond issues were authorized by the commission in due time and without any special difficulties. Meanwhile, Consumers Power as a holding company provided no less efficiency than it would have as an operating company: it achieved unified control over its operating units by centralizing the various management functions. And that was, of course, the idea in the first place.

Consumers Power remained a Maine corporation until 1968. It is now a Michigan corporation. The changeover could have been made sooner but wasn't, simply for the reason that the cost of the reorganization would have been greater than any possible gain to be derived from such a move, and there was no point in spending the money. There was no other cause for delaying the transfer—the state of Michigan had long before then realized the importance of utility expansion to the growth of its economy, and all the limitations on financing that had prompted the move to Maine were no longer on the books. In any case, Consumers Power was launched on its extraterritorial

career, and nobody ever had any reason to regret this arrangement, neither the men in the company nor the rapidly growing
number of customers in Consumers Power territory to whose
very existence, as citizens of an industrial state, electric power
became increasingly essential.

10

The Au Sable Days

Istory weaves its tapestry in wondrous complexities and
with threads of many hues and textures. That's what
makes it so fascinating: how all the loose ends are knotted
unexpectedly into a meaningful composition—unexpectedly
at the time, that is, for no man really directs his fate, no
matter how Machiavellian he may be. But looking back, the
design makes perfect logic. Just take all the threads of this
story: the tenacious fiber that took Hodenpyl from Michigan
to New York and back again; the tough wire of Foote's career,
hard and gleaming, thrusting out from western Michigan; the
silken strands of lawyer Weadock's web; the Harris lifeline
from Chicago, knotted here and there, seeking no further
hold but ready to be used; and finally the blue-satin swatch
of the Au Sable, almost a forgotten possession, carried to
Detroit by Loud as excess baggage. Then there was the knot
that tied all the threads together at the old Cadillac Hotel. Of
these threads, the Au Sable's was perhaps the most important.

This river was not only crucial to the formation of Consumers Power Company but also vital to its existence for many years afterward.

The river's reaches had embraced a lovely land before the lumbering began, when the French voyageurs and fur traders traveling the west shore of Lake Huron had sought it out for shelter, and later when fishermen had built little villages at the stream's mouth. Actually, the Au Sable is a skein of many rivers—its north branch, middle branch, south branch, and lots of other little tributaries—rushing east from the Grayling area of Michigan's hilly spine, across a slanting, sandy tableland to the waters of Lake Huron. It is a fast stream with much power, favored today by canoeists and inner-tube enthusiasts.

ED LOUD AND FRIENDS

Lumberman Loud is second from the left in the front row. Kneeling to his right in this 1912 picture is W. M. Eaton. The man in the front row center is unidentified. Jacob Hekma lounges to the far right. The men in the back row are (left to right) George Johnston, H. H. Crowell, George Luther, C. W. Tippy, Frank Howe, R. E. Richardson, and an unidentified gentleman, probably one of the investors. (Consumers Power Company collection)

PIONEERS OF AU SABLE POWER

In this rare photograph, taken on the Au Sable River, you will find (left to right) C. M. Clark, Bill Fargo, Anton Hodenpyl, George Hardy, C. E. Sawyer, W. A. Foote, and E. W. Clark. (Michigan Historical Commission)

Almost all of it flows through what are now the Au Sable State and Huron National Forests. State Highway 72, between Grayling and Harrisville, pursues the river's course through the pine barrens, flanked by white pine, red pine, jack pine, and spruce grown tall again over the past sixty years. State Highway 76/55, from Grayling to Tawas City, roughly parallels the stream beds some miles to the south. U.S. 23, along lower Michigan's eastern shore, crosses the river's mouth at Oscoda. From these major highways, narrow sand roads lead into a wilderness. Here the Au Sable is still healing the wounds left by lumbermen whose saws and fires deprived the river of its trees, whose logs buffeted and tore its banks, and who indeed cheated it of much of its water, for with the forest gone, the climate changed and less rain fell.

After construction of the Au Sable dams, the lands owned by Consumers Power on the lower half of the river were guarded as a wilderness area. Only a few cabins were permitted, and a vast reforestation program was launched.[1] The six hydropower dams on the Au Sable River built with Hoden-pyl-Walbridge and Clark money are still operative. Of course they supply only a small portion of today's power needs—Consumers Power's river hydro constitutes only 3 percent of its total output—but in the early days hydro was the biggest source of power, and the Au Sable dams were the company's most spectacular producers.

Of course all those millions of dollars it took to build the Au Sable dams didn't come personally from Hodenpyl or even the Clarks. These men were essentially financial managers and stock promoters, though this is not meant in any negative, derogatory sense. Their strength lay in their ability to obtain capital by placing bond issues with financial institutions in search of secure, worthwhile investments that could weather the test of time. Luckily there are always people to be found who would employ their money profitably, and where big money is involved these people are no fools—especially when, as with bankers, it isn't their own money but funds left in their trust. They must know all about an enterprise before they write their checks. Investigating potential investments is a laborious process, a poring over books and complex cash-flow projections, but occasionally some of it is fun, and that's exactly what it was on the Au Sable, where a constant procession of bankers from Chicago, New York, and Philadelphia, and even from as far away as England and Scotland, traversed the river's wilderness to inspect the locations of the dams their money was to build.

Ed Loud, the lumberman, had been bought out. He now was comfortably unemployed. He had no function with Consumers Power, but of all the men involved in the Au Sable projects, he knew and loved the river country best.[2] Not surprisingly, he was always happy to show it off to visitors. Instead of a solitary wanigan, Loud now had a fleet of three. In deference to the Au Sable's French heritage, these houseboats bore French names: *Habitant, Voyageur,* and *Dormant,* the last appropriately serving as sleeping quarters for the honored guests. Visiting bankers had the time of their lives aboard the wanigans. They ate well, drank heartily, and sunned themselves, and when they got really ambitious they fished for grayling from the flat tops of the boats' superstructures. W. A. Foote didn't hold with the drinking. He was a severe Methodist and an elder of his church—at one point he even fired some workmen who had been seen smoking on the job—but he slowly got used to the worldly ways of the cosmopolitan financiers and kept up his end by sipping lemonade and calling it the "Foote cocktail." Life aboard the wanigans was far from luxurious, however. The moneymen shared a hand-operated toilet and washed up in a lavatory supplied with river water by means of a small mechanical pump.

These were some expeditions. Up toward the headwaters of the Au Sable, on sandy logging roads, bumped the creaking wagons that carried the bankers, dressed in seedy outdoor costumery for the occasion, and the knocked-down sections of the 40-foot-long wanigans. When finally the desired point upstream was reached, crews of workmen assembled the houseboats, and down the river, with much cheering and horseplay, rode all those distinguished personages for whom this was an entirely new thrill. They slept on one boat and ate their fill on another, which also had a recreation room where they played cards at night. The third craft housed the galley and slept the crew, and the whole convoy—unseaworthy as it was—looked maritime as anything, in its own ramshackle way, since the boats were equipped with portholes instead of windows. The river trips became even more complicated and exciting after some of the dams were built, for then the heavy boats had to be portaged around the earthworks, and they had to be poled in the dam ponds where there was no current. This was a labor in which the bankers liked to take a hand, if only for a little while, until they retired to their lounge chairs on the decks, sweating profusely and in need of drink. They

LIFE ABOARD THE WANIGANS

Potential investors in the Au Sable projects traveled upstream by horse and wagon, along with the knocked-down sections of 40-foot-long "wanigan" houseboats. When the upstream destination was reached, the wanigans were assembled (above), and the bankers were on their merry way, drifting downriver to look over possible damsites. Fishing from the top deck was a favorite sport (below). Note the riverbank beyond, ravaged by lumbering and forest fires.

The bankers welcomed roughing it. In the picture at the right, George Hardy brushes his teeth with Au Sable water, Anton Hodenpyl is buttoning his shirt, and Philadelphia financier E. W. Clark looks as though he just woke up. These photographs were taken about 1912. (Michigan Historical Commission)

didn't always come up with the money—raising capital is never a simple process—but the old Au Sable got talked about far and wide.

Cooke Dam, named in honor of Andrew Cooke, of the Harris Trust Company, was the first to be built.[3] It was in November 1909, several months before the merger was finalized, that Grant Cochran, whom we remember as the construction supervisor on Foote's Jackson–Battle Creek traction project, was called over from Grand Rapids, where the Wealthy Street steam plant was nearing completion, to take charge of the dam. Cochran and his men had to start from scratch. The damsite was 14 miles up the river from Oscoda, and at that time there was only one little house, owned by a man named John Bissonette, between it and the town. November in Michigan is a time of storms. Cold winds start blowing from the Canadian north, and the lakes churn up in whitecaps. Cochran and his men lugged hay and blankets for bedding and a few pots to cook their meals in. They put the hay on the ground and the blankets over the hay, and they camped out in the open until huts were built. The men also constructed a wobbly wooden bridge across the river so they could work on the other side. Cochran could use all the help he could get. Soon after his men had begun to cut timber for the trestle, a boy about eleven years old rode up to him out of the stripped timberlands one morning. The boy, astride a rather ragged pony, identified himself as Charlie Bissonette (he was later known as "Bud" Bissonette at Consumers Power). He said he was the son of the squatter down in the woods, and he asked Cochran for a job. Cochran decided that the boy wasn't yet muscled enough for a hard day's labor but that he could use him anyway. Whenever a special piece of timber was needed, the boy could ride his pony into the barrens where the cutting crews were working and tell them exactly what was wanted. "But listen here," Cochran said in his rough Irish workingman's voice. "We don't want anybody standing around idle. When I've got no messages for you to carry, you get off that little pony of yours, grab a bucket, and carry water to my men. I don't care if they're thirsty or not. You just keep moving."

Cochran himself kept moving too. Cooke Dam was finished in 1911, and long before it was completed, Five Channels Dam had already been started farther up the river. When Cochran was done with a piece of machinery at Cooke, he immediately had it moved up to Five Channels. Meanwhile, Loud Dam was started before Five Channels was finished, and the equipment was transferred there in turn. In this way Cochran actually managed to get three dams built in less than four years—a record achievement. In the end, there were six dams altogether: Foote, Cooke, Five Channels, Loud, Alcona, and Mio, the last farthest up the Au Sable, almost at the junction of its east and west branches, and today right off Highway 72 about 10 miles east of the village of Luzerne.

Cooke Dam, like Croton in western Michigan before it, brought with it a new breakthrough in the electric utility business. The power from the Au Sable River was to be transmitted through Saginaw and Bay City into Flint, Zilwaukee, and Owosso, a greater distance than had ever been attempted before. The wires were to stretch 151 miles. Transmission over a line of this length would suffer even greater power loss than had been true of the Croton–Grand Rapids venture. To overcome this challenge, it was decided to step up the pressure to 140,000 volts. Again, such a high voltage had never before been achieved. New towers were required. So was a new insulator, one yet more resistant than the type J. B. Foote had dreamed up for the Croton line. Even a new conductor wire had to be developed to carry this fantastic voltage and to span a distance of 530 feet between towers, which were placed that far apart for economic reasons, without breaking.

A considerable investment was needed to bring the ambitious Au Sable project to fruition. Indeed, so much money was involved that for a time it looked as though the 140,000-volt line would never be built. Even today, some sixty years later, J. B. Foote's son, Harold, still remembers the day when his father, who was ordinarily not a man to show much emotion, came back jubilantly from a trip to the Hodenpyl offices in New York. "They gave me two and a half million dollars," J. B. kept saying. "Just think, they gave me two and a half million dollars, and we're really going ahead!"

And so, once again, J. B. Foote was on the job. This time, of course, he had a lot of experience with high-tension lines to back him up, and he could draw on the results of the Steinmetz experiments in deciding on wire that would suffer the least power loss over such a great distance. You will recall that Dr. Steinmetz, of the General Electric laboratories, had come to

A NUTSHELL HISTORY OF TRANSMISSION LINES

In this picture, photographed north of Grand Rapids in the early 1920s, you will find the transmission lines of three different periods side by side. The 75,000-volt pole line with its pin insulators (right) is similar to the line that was built from Rogers Dam about 1906. The steel tower (left) approaches modern construction. It was used for 140,000 volts after Tippy Dam on the Manistee River was built at the end of World War I. The pointed windmill steel tower (center background) was the type used for 100,000 volts from Croton in about 1908. (Michigan Historical Commission)

Croton to study the corona phenomenon, those curious luminous crowns of electricity that appear when the atmosphere
surrounding a conductor is ionized, but where the difference
of potential is not so great as to cause sparking. On ship masts
and airplane wings, this effect is called "St. Elmo's fire," and
it's quite meaningless except for its beauty. But on high-tension
lines it means leakage of power—only a little at a time, but
over a great distance enough to make a considerable difference.
J. B. had the Steinmetz conclusions to draw on, and also his
own practical know-how. He came up with a number of
innovations that later became standard for 140,000-volt lines
throughout the country and proved their worth over the years.
Among them were a stiffer tower that tapered up to the bottom
crossarms and from that point upward continued parallel to the
tower's top, the use of cap-and-pin insulators and their specific
arrangement, and the strongest wire yet designed for the
commercial transmission of electricity.[4] The Au Sable line
turned out to be another very real triumph in the electrical
world.[5]

But the completion of the line brought more than fame and
fortune to the Foote family. It fulfilled a vision that the two
brothers had had all along—that of an interconnected system,
operated on a system-wide basis. Up until this time, the power
generated by a facility had been transmitted to its specific
market. There had been neither enough sources of sufficient
power nor enough transmission lines to make such an interconnection possible. Now conditions were ripe for setting
up a dispatching center with overall control of all the plants
and lines.[6]

The new Au Sable line was carried on from Bay City,
Saginaw, and Flint to Owosso, where it connected with the
old transmission system of the Commonwealth Power Company
through a substation that hooked up to a line to Charlotte.
Similarly, the Commonwealth system now was being connected
to that of the Grand Rapids–Muskegon Power Company by
means of a new 140,000-volt line between Kalamazoo and

Grand Rapids.[7] But while building physical facilities requires merely capital, it takes an even scarcer commodity to run them once they're built—qualified men. And that was the major difficulty in getting the new interconnected system going, for there was no one in the Foote organization, not even J. B. Foote, who had any knowledge or experience in the area of coordinating electric services; in fact there were few such men anywhere in the country at that time. After months of talent scouting, the search finally narrowed down to one man, Timothy A. Kenney, who, although he was only thirty years old, had already worked his way up from office clerk to assistant operating manager at New York's Hudson River Power Transmission Company.[8] Hudson River Power operated an interconnected system of sorts, a rather modest affair which was neither as extensive as Michigan's new consolidated network nor equipped for similar high voltages.[9] It is no wonder that Kenney jumped at the chance to go to work as assistant manager of the Au Sable Electric Company under J. B. Foote, its famous chief engineer. Kenney arrived in Jackson and immediately proceeded to build up a dispatching organization at the Trail Street steam plant. His team would be the brain of the whole power network: directing voltage, frequency, and load adjustments; switching communities from one line to another when more power was needed or trouble developed; turning on and shutting down generators as loads required at the moment.

Except for those technical improvements, particularly in the field of automation, which have been introduced in the years since, Kenney's nerve center performed even in those early days the same functions in essentially the same ways that Consumers Power's central dispatching center on Parnall Road, on the northern outskirts of Jackson, handles today.[10] Thus Kenney's headquarters was not just a forerunner but actually the beginning of electric utility distribution as we now know it.[11] The fact that he was able to create such a center, establish its procedures, and recruit and train good men to run it went far to prove his worth.[12] It was thanks largely to this essential contribution, without which Consumers Power could not have functioned as an entity, that Kenney became president of the company twenty years later, an office he held until his death in 1938.

T. A. Kenney was not the only new face of the Au Sable days. With the Foote-Hodenpyl-Clark merger, and the vastly increased scope of the resulting utilities complex, this time of transition brought a host of men to Consumers Power and its allied companies who were destined to help stake out the future of the enterprise and to build it to the point where it was ready to meet the challenges and responsibilities of an entirely new and different era.

Most important among the new men at the executive level were those who came into the organization through the Hodenpyl group. Regardless of their origins—as we shall see, they came largely from backgrounds that were no more "sophisticated" than the Foote family's—they imported a certain Eastern polish and assurance that was quite novel to Michigan's grass-roots utilities. Almost from their earliest beginnings, these new men had been trained to think in terms of country-wide enterprises, of money in the millions, of power that bridged—even transgressed—the visions and ambitions of small-town businessmen; and they were men who had been tutored in the somewhat aristocratic manner then prevalent on Wall Street. Like Hodenpyl and Walbridge, they had become men of the world, and a greater contrast between them and the roughhewn pillars of the Foote edifices, like George Stecker and Grant Cochran, could hardly be imagined. Yet, despite those disparate qualities, or perhaps because of them, their admixture produced a most effective blend. The organization could now function at all levels. From Bissonette's backwoods cabin to FDR's White House, no doors were closed henceforth to Consumers Power men. Almost from one day to the next, the Au Sable era transformed the old predecessor companies into an institution of national importance.

It is difficult to allocate preeminence among men doing their work honestly and well. Who is to say which one is the most important? Hierarchy offers the easy escape from this dilemma. So let us begin with George Hardy, who, in 1911, suddenly became one of the kingpins in Consumers Power's power structure.

George Hardy certainly had the stuff, a quality of matter-of-fact gumption wedded to utter dependability. This was obvious even when he was still a youth. His first job was with Ford and Bender, a company that trained and supplied court stenographers and private secretaries, who in those days were almost exclusively male. When Hardy got the job, he still was in his teens, having left school very early to make a living. He asked Mr. Bender at what time he was to report for work. Bender said, "Oh, you'd better get in early that first morning." Hardy, who had a solid old-fashioned respect for his elders, asked no more questions and showed up at four o'clock in the morning. He sat on the curb until seven, when at last, a janitor showed up and let him in.

Getting up before dawn came naturally to the Hardy family. George Wood Hardy, George Hardy's father, had been one of the sturdy pioneers who matched their muscles against New Hampshire's rocky soil. The elder Hardy had then joined the gold rush and nearly died of fever while crossing the Isthmus of Panama on his way to California. Young George was born in Grand Rapids in 1868, where his father had settled when the West had not proved itself so golden after all. His mother was Harriett Hall, a daughter of the town's first city treasurer. She was a schoolteacher of sorts, and one of her pupils, at that time ten years old, happened to be Anton Hodenpyl. It is doubtful, however, that this formed the connection so important in George Hardy's later life—he hadn't even been born yet. Chances are that Hardy and Hodenpyl

GEORGE HARDY
After Hodenpyl and Walbridge parted company, Hardy became Hodenpyl's partner. In this stuffy boardroom portrait, taken in his later life, it's hard to find the courageous young bank clerk who once coolly stopped a holdup.
(Consumers Power photo)

first met when Hodenpyl wanted a clerk at his Michigan Trust Company and Hardy was sent over by Ford and Bender as an office temporary. After a while Hodenpyl offered Hardy a steady job at $25 a month, exactly what he was making. Upon hearing of the attempted seduction of their employee, Ford and Bender offered Hardy $100 a month to stay. This was a temptation because that sum was the extent of the young man's ambition; but, for one thing, Hardy liked Hodenpyl, and for another, as he said later, he wouldn't really have enjoyed staying with an outfit that was unwilling to pay him what he was worth until the pressure was on.

Soon after Hardy's arrival at Michigan Trust, he became a teller, and here his gumption made itself manifest almost immediately. One day a strange man came in and demanded to see some negotiable notes the bank held for a certain customer. Hardy refused of course; these notes were not a stranger's business. The man leaned against the window and hissed, "Suppose I force you to give them to me?" Hardy looked him coolly in the eye and said, "Why, I'd just turn you over to the fellow behind you." The man whirled around, and there stood the guard. George Hardy, instinctively distrusting this customer, had quietly put his foot on the alarm button during the exchange. The intruder scuffled with the guard and fled. From that moment on, Hodenpyl no doubt thought of Hardy as a young man of considerable promise and involved him increasingly in his affairs.

Year after year in the late 1800s George Hardy's name appeared in the minutes of the predecessor gas companies which Hodenpyl was beginning to control. When Hodenpyl left Michigan Trust to set up his office in New York, Hardy succeeded him as vice-president, and in 1903 he joined Hodenpyl-Walbridge & Company in the East. From then on he was employed full time in the utility business, working out of Wall Street and serving as an officer, in one capacity or another, of the various Hodenpyl companies and, during the consolidation period, of the various subsidiary companies. Here is where he met his test; it must have been a rather strenuous task to take the formerly isolated properties and bring to them financial unity.

Hardy's private life also served to prepare him for the position of great responsibility he was soon to hold. Today, the mere fact that someone lives in the same suburban community as someone else has relatively little effect on his business life, but neither cars nor roads were yet dependable enough in the early 1900s as a means of daily on-time transportation. Commuting by railroad, neighbors were constantly thrown together. Friendships developed, deals were made. When Hodenpyl first went to New York, he established his residence on 57th Street near Fifth Avenue, just around the corner from millionaires row. Later he moved near Locust Valley on Long Island, where his fellow residents included Theodore Roosevelt, of Sagamore Hill, and J. P. Morgan, of U.S. Steel. Hodenpyl's next-door neighbor was Charles Coffin, head of General Electric. Hardy proved himself no less adept in selecting a neighborhood. He made his home in Englewood, New Jersey, then the stamping grounds of many of the younger generation of prominent New York business and financial men, including Thomas Lamont, partner in J. P. Morgan and Company, and industrialist Henry P. Davidson, later head of the American Red Cross during World War I. All in all, George Hardy was rather well prepared for the next big step in his career.

In 1911 Anton Hodenpyl and Henry Walbridge went their separate ways, and George Hardy became Hodenpyl's partner. Nobody knows why the two old associates fell out just after the major accomplishment of their lives. Both men were much too loyal even to tell intimates about it. Henry Walbridge had come a long way from being a "floater." If anything, he had become perhaps too positive a man; he possessed none of Hodenpyl's gentleness and flexibility. Walbridge was often hard to deal with and sometimes totally irascible, always ruled by driving business instincts and an unshakable conviction that he alone was right.[13] No doubt there were personality conflicts — possibly even some financial irregularities. There is some evidence that Walbridge's departure was precipitated by the fact that George Hardy had uncovered some type of dishonesty on Walbridge's part and that Hardy went to Hodenpyl threatening to resign unless Walbridge left. Be that as it may, the particulars must remain hidden from our view. In any case, Walbridge departed; much as in a divorce there was a settlement of assets, and Walbridge took the Pennsylvania properties with him. More important to our story is that Consumers Power was now ruled by Hodenpyl, Hardy & Company. Theirs was the power behind the throne, of course; neither Hodenpyl nor Hardy ever occupied chief operating posts. Rather, they kept their hands on the money tap, and when all is said and done, this is the key position; without money, future builders cannot build.

Another new face was that of Bernard Capen Cobb, the man destined to succeed W. A. Foote as president of Consumers Power Company. As was the case with George Hardy, B. C. Cobb's relatively humble personal beginnings were totally obscured by his eventual development. Not that he withheld them from public scrutiny. As the son of a Boston, Massachusetts, minister who was later called to Grand Rapids, Cobb had grown up in genteel scholarship modesty, first attending Boston Latin School and then graduating from Phillips-Andover Academy with the class of 1891.[14] He started his career as a clerk with the Grand Rapids and Indiana Railroad;[15] indeed, he was working at this job during summers while he still went to school. Later he worked up to cashier at the Grand Rapids Storage and Transfer Company, and in 1896 he joined Grand Rapids Gas Light Company as a clerk.

This impressive man, who looked and acted as if he had been born with a golden spoon in his mouth (the silver-spoon cliché would not do him justice), hadn't even worn a white collar all along. In his early gas company days he drove a coal wagon on occasion. But nothing of the soot-faced teamster remained into his later years. By the time Cobb appeared at Consumers Power, he was the impeccable Beau Brummel of the utilities business who was always dressed as if he were going to an exclusive party. His sartorial trademarks were white piping on his vest and a pearl stickpin in his tie. Cobb's general demeanor dovetailed with his imperious appearance. An injury to his right eye had made the lid droop slightly, endowing him with a haughty, penetrating stare. No Hollywood casting director could have found a better actor to play the role of a Wall Street tycoon. For the time being, however, young Cobb, still eagerly on his way up, progressed from clerk to purchasing agent at Grand Rapids Gas and finally became assistant to the general manager. He met Walbridge and became his protégé.

In 1889, then only twenty-nine years old, Cobb went to Detroit as general superintendent of the Detroit City Gas Company, which, along with Grand Rapids Gas Light, was controlled by the newly organized American Light and Traction Company. Two years later he took the big step into the top-executive suite. When Walbridge left American Light and Traction, he took Cobb with him and made him vice-president and general manager of the Saginaw City Gas Company. From then on Cobb was really in the inner circle. In 1903, when Hodenpyl-Walbridge & Company and E. W. Clark & Co. organized the Saginaw–Bay City Railway & Light Company, B. C. Cobb was placed in charge of the combined operations. His next stop was New York, where undoubtedly he felt in some ways more at home than he had in Michigan. As a native of Boston and descendant on his father's side from people who came to this country on the *Mayflower,* and on his mother's from passengers on the *Mary and John,* the first ship to enter Boston Harbor, Cobb's Wall Street companions were more to his liking than the workaday pragmatists of Grand Rapids and Saginaw. In short, he acted a very convincing snob—but this did not diminish his great qualities as an executive. When Walbridge quit Hodenpyl, he again wanted to take Cobb with him. But this time Cobb declined and instead took a hand in organizing the new Hodenpyl-Hardy Company, of which he now became vice-president as well as chairman of the operating committees of all its electric, gas, and transportation properties, among them, of course, Consumers Power. Thus, almost from the very beginning of the Au Sable days, Cobb began to share the saddle with W. A. Foote.

Then there was Jacob Hekma, later secretary and treasurer of Consumers Power, who represented the new America just as Cobb did the old. Hekma had been brought to this country from the Netherlands as a five-year-old boy. Not only that, he'd had considerable trouble getting here. The steamer *Amsterdam,* on which he, his mother, a brother, and a sister were passengers, struck a sandbar in the ship graveyard of the Grand Banks between Nova Scotia and Newfoundland on July 30, 1884. Luckily, the sea was relatively calm. All the passengers were able to take to boats and reach the desolate coast. For almost a week, they huddled on the beach, awaiting rescue parties. Life was not much easier when Mrs. Hekma and her children at last joined Nickolas Hekma, the father, in Grand Rapids. Nickolas Hekma worked as a laborer and handyman at whatever job he could find. Among others, he worked for Hodenpyl. Jacob completed two years of high school. That was enough. The family needed money, and Jacob had to go to work. "My son is a smart boy," the elder Hekma told Hodenpyl. "Perhaps you can give him a job." Hodenpyl replied, "I've noticed him helping you. Tell him to go into the office and see Mr. Hardy." And so Jacob Hekma started with Michigan Trust as an office boy. In 1904, a few months after George Hardy had joined Hodenpyl in New York, he phoned Hekma and asked him whether he'd be interested in coming to work for him. This was a big decision for the young Dutch bank clerk, who knew what he wanted but was not yet at all sure of himself. He went to see Lewis H. Withey, the Michigan Trust Company's original president, and told him of the offer.

"Mr. Withey," he said, "you know this is a big decision for me. I've been here nine years now, and I don't want to leave if there's a future for me. You know I come from across the railroad tracks. Do you think there is a chance that I'll ever become an executive officer of the trust company?" Withey stared off into space, avoiding Hekma's eyes, and took his time replying.

"Jacob," he finally said, still not looking directly at the young man, "I see no reason why not." That evening Hekma telephoned George Hardy and accepted the job in New York. The banker's pause before he had answered Hekma's question, combined with the hypocritical reply, had made up the young fellow's mind for him. Michigan Trust thus lost a good man, and Hodenpyl—and Consumers Power—gained one. Before long, Hekma became a financial leader in the public utilities field; he was made partner of Hodenpyl-Hardy in 1914, and later a director.

On the operational level there was Charles Worth Tippy, an experienced gas man who had held responsible positions with several of the Hodenpyl properties and was soon to become general manager of Consumers Power Company.[16] Others who also appeared on the scene at about that time included William H. Barthold, who had started with the Grand

Rapids Gas Light Company in 1896 and was to become a Consumers Power vice-president,[17] and Burton R. Laraway, another graduate of the Michigan Trust Company, who was to hold a variety of financial executive positions in the organization.[18] Like Barthold and most of the other new men to become involved with Consumers Power in the Au Sable days, Laraway came in via the Hodenpyl group.[19]

The fact that most of the newcomers were Hodenpyl-Walbridge men did not undermine W. A. Foote's authority. He was the undisputed president of Consumers Power Company. In addition, he and his brother and other stalwarts of his original organization served variously as president, vice-president, or director or on the executive and operating committees of the various underlying operating properties.[20] Nor did the infusion of so many gas men detract from the Foote brothers' importance. A little-known fact is that W. A. Foote was something of a gas man himself, although this had never been his major interest. Certainly as far back as 1897 he had thought in terms of combining electric, gas, and rail operations, and from about 1898 to 1902 he served as vice-president of the Battle Creek Gas Company.[21]

But there is no doubt that after the consolidation, the influence of the Foote brothers did diminish, though for entirely different reasons. The powerful flow of the Au Sable brought a new era to the utilities industry in Michigan, and it also ushered out the past.

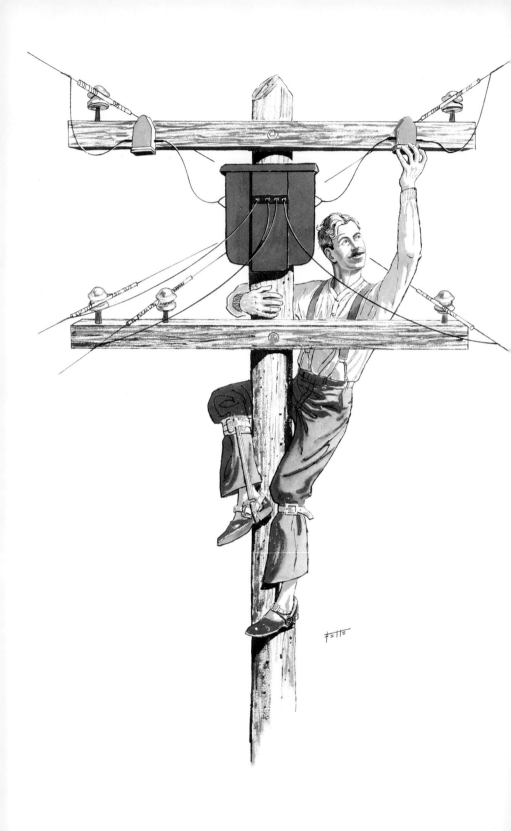

11

The Foote Legacy

One day early in November 1913, Grant Cochran, the indefatigable Au Sable construction supervisor, telephoned J. B. Foote, who was off on one of his periodic visits to the Hodenpyl-Hardy offices in New York City. Cochran had wonderful news for the chief engineer of Consumers Power. Loud Dam wasn't supposed to be finished until New Year's Day, but Cochran's practical system of leapfrogging machinery from one dam to the next had put the project well ahead of schedule. He would be ready, Cochran said, trying to suppress the pride in his voice, to hand over the completed Loud Dam to the company on Thanksgiving Day.

Jubilant as J. B. Foote had been when the financing for his new 140,000-volt Au Sable transmission line came through a couple of years earlier, he had by now returned to his own imperturbable, introverted self. "Now, Mr. Cochran, that's very nice," he said in his dry, rather flat Middle Western voice. "We're all real pleased by the way you've handled this.

J. B. FOOTE

This photograph of the founding engineer of Consumers Power was taken about 1917. The photographer is unknown. (Consumers Power Company collection, courtesy of H. J. Burton)

You go out and buy yourself and everybody else a turkey for Thanksgiving." And without a perceptible pause he added: "And when can you get started on Mio Dam?"

Such was J. B.'s way. He was intent on getting the job done and little else. All the accolades he had received as one of the country's outstanding electrical engineers—albeit without formal engineering training—never had gone to his head.[1] J. B.'s sober attitude didn't bother Cochran a bit. He was rather inclined to be single-minded about work himself. The Mio project, he knew, would be even more difficult than the others. It had been necessary at all the Au Sable hydro sites to bring in every piece of machinery and all the cement and the other supplies by unloading everything from the standard-gauge Detroit and Mackinac Railway at the town of Au Sable and reloading it on the narrow gauge Au Sable and Northwestern, whose lilliputian tracks cut through the river's wilderness. Now, for the Mio job, Cochran would have to transport every single bit of dam-building material and equipment nearly 15 miles by horse-drawn wagons through log-strewn timber country after unloading the railcars at the tiny hamlet of Cummins. Some of the pieces he had to move weighed as much as 30 tons. Cochran did not resent J. B.'s matter-of-factness about this backbreaking assignment. He was used to that with the Foote brothers. In any case, he knew that J. B. never asked anybody to do anything that he wouldn't have been willing to undertake himself.

There was the time, for instance, much talked about by Consumers Power people, when J. B. was on his way to his father-in-law's for a visit. Passing the corner of Edgewood and North Streets in Jackson, he saw a couple of electric linemen staring up a 50-foot pole—a pole so tall that two ordinary poles had been spliced together to achieve the necessary height. This particular pole had an 8-foot sidearm joined to it by means of an angle brace, and way out there, so that it would escape a tangle of tree branches, hung the wire the linemen were expected to work on. Quite naturally they didn't particularly enjoy the prospect of playing acrobats.

"To hell with that," one of these men said, just as Foote went by. "I'm not going to bust my neck. The crazy guy who dreamed this up can darn well try and do it himself." J. B. Foote stopped. He didn't get mad. "Give me your climbers, please," he said to the lineman who had spoken. The man didn't know who Foote was, but apparently he remembered having seen him around the company. He shrugged. "Go ahead," he said. Foote strapped on the climbers and went right up the pole and out on the sidearm, accomplished whatever needed doing, and didn't even bother to make his point by identifying himself to the lineman after he'd come back down.

And there was that early Sunday morning when the lights didn't go on in J. B. Foote's house. Figuring out where the trouble was, Foote hiked up the street in his undershirt and trousers to a transformer at the corner of Ganson Street and Steward Avenue, strapped on a pair of climbers over his bedroom slippers, and proceeded to replace the fuses on a pole transformer. "No point in getting everybody up this early in the morning," he said to his family.

Exploits such as these evoke images of a husky, energetic man, but this in fact was not the case. During most of his adult life, J. B. suffered from a kidney ailment that made it impossible for him to eliminate the poisons from his body naturally, by urination. Precisely during the time of the Au Sable's development, his illness became so critical that specialists in Chicago gave him only a few months to live. The doctors underestimated J. B.'s tenacity, however. One of them had told him that he might be able to prolong his life a little if he moved to a warm climate, like Florida's, where he would perspire more freely. Instead of moving, J. B. imported the subtropics to Michigan in his own inspired way—in the form of Turkish-bath cabinets. He arranged for these steam boxes to be installed in his home and all around the Consumers Power system, and every few hours, no matter where his work took him, he climbed into one of these cabinets to sweat out the toxins. He managed to stay alive for another dozen years that way, but he became increasingly debilitated and less able to keep his hands on the reins. His sight went first.[2] By the time he died on May 3, 1924, at the age of fifty-seven, he was almost blind and had been nearly inactive for several years.[3]

W. A. Foote also withdrew slowly from the business. He was president of Consumers Power, to be sure, and fulfilled all the duties of his office. But he was a builder of the future, rather than an administrator of what had been built in the past. His dream of consolidation had been accomplished. From here on, the company could only grow. It could build more power plants and transmission lines and sell more gas and electricity—none of which really challenged W. A. Foote's imagination. Something else now occupied his mind, something he had long been interested in but had never had much time for: electric railways.

At the turn of the century, as we may recall, the streetcar line in Jackson had gone bankrupt, and W. A. Foote had become its receiver. Shortly afterward he joined up with William A. Boland in the somewhat ill-fated Boland line, which never quite made it from Jackson to Ann Arbor. Still later, he was involved, again with Boland, in the interurban from Jackson to Battle Creek and on to Kalamazoo. But in 1906 Foote had dropped out of the traction business to devote himself full time to his basic electric properties. Now, some five years later, he was convinced that by dropping out he had missed one of the main chances of his life, and he wasn't the kind of man to let it go at that. He felt that at long last his time had come to get into electric traction in a major way. All the generating capacity and transmission lines he needed were now at his disposal, and of course his partners, Hodenpyl and Clark, had been involved in traction from the start; indeed it had been the consolidation of the street railway properties in Grand Rapids that had brought the two financiers together in the first place. Hodenpyl and Clark controlled the Saginaw–Bay City Railway & Light Company, incorporated in 1903, which in turn controlled the stock in various gas, electric, and traction companies in the areas of these two cities.[4] In addition, they had the Grand Rapids Railway Company.[5] As far as W. A. Foote was concerned, this made for a pretty good beginning. Thanks to his connections with Hodenpyl and Clark, he was back on the ground floor of the traction business. To reach the top floor, all he now had to do was scamper up the stairs.

Why did W. A. Foote suddenly decide to take on this new

ELECTRIC TRACTION IN SAGINAW . . .

*Hodenpyl and Clark's Saginaw–Bay City interurban (left), as well as lo-
cal trolleys, still ran in 1925, when this photograph was taken, but motor
vehicles long ago had begun to cut into income.* (Consumers Power
photo)

challenge? Here he was, an honored and successful man in his
late fifties; his hair and goatee were turning white, and his
daughter Edna (Mrs. Luke C. Bootes) had presented him with
two grandsons.[6] He loved family trips in his Franklin Model
H four-cylinder seven-passenger touring car, and now that he
didn't have to face down his creditors anymore, he did a lot
of traveling. He journeyed to the Mediterranean every year,
usually on a cruise, and once he even took his son-in-law,
Bill Tefft, to Egypt. He could have enjoyed more of this easy
living. But that wouldn't have been W. A. Foote.

No doubt a number of factors were involved in his renewed
pursuit of the traction business. His restless pioneer personality was one. Men like W. A. Foote have to build, or they
can't be happy. But even more important, perhaps, since
Foote was a practical man, loomed the pragmatic consideration
that traction was the best business of the bunch. Railways
were by far the biggest money-makers of all the utilities, gas
was in second place, and electricity brought up the rear. Power

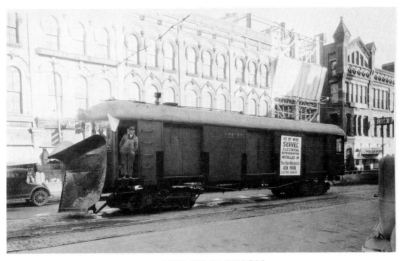

... AND IN JACKSON

*Interurban car with snowplow on the Foote-Boland line from Jackson to
Battle Creek and Kalamazoo. Here, too, electric traction eventually was
forced to yield to private automobiles.* (Photo by R. J. Gusenbar)

companies couldn't even get bankers to take their bonds unless
they had contracts to supply traction companies with energy.

And so in 1911, together with Hodenpyl-Hardy and E. W.
Clark, Foote became involved in two new corporations, a
holding company and an operating company, and through them
regained control of the very railway properties he had sold
a few years earlier. These old Foote properties had been
taken over in 1906 by Myron Mills, of Port Huron, who was
then in the process of building himself a little electric traction
empire in southern Michigan. Mills, through his Michigan United Railways Company, had brought together the interurban
lines from St. Johns through Lansing to Jackson, from Jackson to
Battle Creek and Kalamazoo, and from Lansing to Owosso.
In addition, he controlled the streetcar lines in Battle Creek,
Kalamazoo, Jackson, and Lansing.[7]

How did W. A. Foote get his old interurbans back, plus all
the other Mills properties? Very simply—with Hodenpyl and
Clark financing. Over a period of months they bought heavily

into the stock of Mills's Michigan United. It was a turn-of-the-century equivalent of today's proxy fights. The outcome was a foregone conclusion. Foote-Hodenpyl-Clark ended up with enough shares to make it practical and profitable for the Mills interests to agree to lease the properties of Michigan United Railways for a period of 999 years to the new operating company founded by Foote, Hodenpyl-Hardy, and Clark. This operating company was called Michigan United Traction, and all its shares were owned by the Michigan Railway Company, a new holding company that Foote, Hodenpyl-Hardy, and Clark had set up for this very purpose.[8] Thus, almost overnight, W. A. Foote was once again a railroad man—and he wasted no time getting even deeper into the business.

One day he called up George Erwin, the chubby real estate man from Muskegon who knew nothing about hydroelectric generation but had shown such a fabulous talent for buying up flowage lands along the Muskegon River, and at bargain prices at that. "How would you like to go back to work?" Foote asked him. "We've got something going here that's right in your line."

"And what might that be?" Erwin asked Foote after agreeing that it would be fun to be active again.

"Well," Foote said, "we're starting a new outfit, the Michigan Railway Engineering Company, and I'd very much like you to come down to Kalamazoo and run it."

"But I don't know anything about building railroads," Erwin replied. "I don't even enjoy riding them. Are you sure you want me?"

"Don't worry about that," Foote said. "Bill Fargo will handle the arithmetic, and Grant Cochran is going to boss the job."

"Then why me? And why Kalamazoo?"

"I'd like you to move to Kalamazoo," Foote said, "because it will look a lot better and sit a lot better with the politicians if a local man starts buying up all the land and dickering with city hall than if an outsider comes in from Muskegon."

"Now I get you," Erwin laughed. "You want me to go shopping."

Soon after, Erwin moved to Kalamazoo and quietly began accumulating rights-of-way for a railbed between Kalamazoo and Grand Rapids. This new 45-mile-long interurban line would hook up to the already existing network spanning Kalamazoo, Battle Creek, Albion, Jackson, Lansing, and Owosso. It was W. A. Foote's plan to interconnect the electric railways in the busy center of Michigan, just as he had interconnected the electric companies. No doubt it was also on his mind to eventually extend this interurban system northward to Saginaw and Bay City, linking it to other existing properties.

It was an ambitious project in every respect. The Kalamazoo–Grand Rapids Railway was to be better and faster than any other traction line, even Foote's own. True, when constructing interurbans, Foote had always insisted on well-graded roadbeds—an insistence, as will be recalled, that resulted in his being beaten by Hawks-Angus in the race to complete a line between Jackson and Ann Arbor. Now W. A. Foote set himself yet higher standards. His new electric line would have a roadbed like that of regular steam trains, a base ballasted throughout and with a minimum of grades and curves. There was to be a private right-of-way not only through the countryside but also in Grand Rapids and Kalamazoo, as well as in Battle Creek for a spur to Monteith Junction. Furthermore, the line was to operate at 2,400 volts, four times that of most interurbans.[9]

Much to W. A.'s chagrin, construction had to get under way without Grant Cochran's lending his talent to the job. Cochran was busy on the Au Sable dams, and J. B. Foote was reluctant to let him go. W. A. understood. He knew that when his brother said he needed someone, he really needed him. The problem was that men like Cochran, even then, were few and far between, and naturally he was needed everywhere at once. Before long, with the Au Sable dams progressing at about as fast a clip as the infusion of money allowed, J. B. moved him over to Albion to build an important substation.

Meanwhile, the Kalamazoo–Grand Rapids line was lengthening, but not at the speed for which W. A. had hoped. Perhaps he had a premonition that he had to hurry. Anyway, one Saturday his patience ran out, and he telephoned Cochran in Albion. "How soon can you get over to Wayland?" Foote asked without a preamble. Wayland is about one-third of the way down from Grand Rapids toward Kalamazoo.

"I can get over there tonight if it's necessary," Cochran said. He wouldn't have been nearly so cocky if he hadn't had Cartwright Goss by his side. Cart Goss, a longtime Cochran sidekick, was just installing electrical equipment in the nearly completed substation. Cochran had first bumped into Goss while working on Plainwell Dam, between Otsego and Plainwell on the Kalamazoo River. At the time of their meeting Goss had been the operator of a traction engine Cochran had been forced to rent in an emergency. Cochran had been so impressed with Goss that he had hired him on the spot. Now, with Foote's phone call, Cochran was happier than ever that he had done so.

"I can tell Cart Goss what we expect to do," Cochran said, "and he can finish the job."

"Did you say you can come tonight?" W. A. Foote asked.

"That's right, Mr. Foote."

"Well," W. A. said, "Mr. J. B. Foote would be very unhappy if that Albion job isn't done just right. Maybe you'd better stay there and make sure. It will be good enough if you get over here Monday morning."[10]

Considering that it was only Saturday afternoon, with still more than an hour to go until quitting time, and that Wayland was only about 100 miles over dirt roads, Cochran figured that he had plenty of time—by Foote brothers' standards anyway—to get the Albion job under control. As far as Cochran's new assignment to the Kalamazoo–Grand Rapids line was concerned, W. A.'s instructions had been simply to take over. "Tell them you're the boss," W. A. had told him. "They'll believe you."

Good thing that being a boss came naturally to Cochran. There was labor trouble on the line, and more trouble with the Grand Rapids–Holland Railway people where the two lines crossed each other, and yet more trouble because often there wasn't enough equipment around to do the job properly. At one point it even came near to an internal war between two of Foote's most valuable men. Cochran needed a power pump. The crew building a bridge to carry the tracks over Plaster Creek had only a hand pump to use. They'd pump the water down, preparatory to pouring concrete for the span supports, and then it was quitting time, and the men wouldn't work at night. Of course by morning the forms had filled up with water again, and the pumping had to start all over—and so it went, day after day. A gasoline-driven power pump was the only answer, and Cochran knew just where to get it. There was one over at the Wealthy Street plant in Grand Rapids. So Cochran took some tools, tossed them in a small truck, and drove on up with one of his foremen. "Nothing doing," said the man in charge at Wealthy Street. "Mr. Stecker gave us orders not to let anyone have the tools."

It must be understood that the only connection between the railway construction company and Consumers Power was that they were part of the same holding-company family. Stecker worked for Consumers Power. Cochran worked, at this moment, for the railway construction company. Of course Foote ran them both. Cochran was only a working stiff without a fancy education, but he had no pigeonhole mind. He fully understood that this was all one enterprise. "That pump isn't doing the company any good being locked up here," he said, getting hot under his collar by this time. "You still can't have it," Stecker's assistant said.

"That's what you think," Cochran yelled. He turned to one of his helpers, pointed to the truck, and ordered, "Get that ax out of there and knock the lock off the door."

A few days later Cochran was summoned to Jackson. By that time he was rather contrite, having taken the law into his own hands. For all he knew he'd violated some important company rule. Hesitantly he explained to W. A. Foote about breaking into the storeroom of the Wealthy Street plant. "Never mind about that," Foote said impatiently. "Did you get the bridge up?"

"Yes, Mr. Foote," Cochran answered. "We pumped the water out in about five hours and poured concrete all in the same day."

"Good," W. A. nodded. "Any time you need equipment that's lying idle, you just go and get it. We haven't got any time to waste." [11]

But even when nobody wastes time, building a railroad is no overnight job. It had been on November 15, 1912, that the Michigan Railroad Commission approved the proposed route from Kalamazoo's northern boundary to the southern city limits of Grand Rapids. The following year, with the railroad still far from being completed, the company had purchased a section of an existing steam railway between Battle Creek and Allegan from the Detroit, Toledo and Milwaukee Railroad. [12] This Battle Creek–Allegan leg continued to run under steam power for awhile, but was soon converted to electric operation. The line being built between Kalamazoo and Grand Rapids intersected it at Monteith Junction, and their meeting point was to become the center of the entire system.

Another year passed. It was now 1914. In the world's capitals the days chased each other feverishly, as they always do in times of crisis. World War I was about to engulf Europe. But for W. A. Foote, months flowed like cold molasses. His new venture was advancing mile by mile in a laborious, creeping process, exciting only to Cochran on the scene. It was a daily frustration to Foote, who, apart from routine company business, now had little to do. He spent most of his waking hours at his Jackson office, and of course he took periodic inspection trips around the system and paid occasional visits to Hodenpyl-Hardy in New York. He and his wife, Ida, now lived in a sumptuous home on Jackson's Michigan Avenue, a home far different from Foote's earlier abodes. Restless, he used to wander up and down the mansion's grand circular staircase; he felt constricted by the heavy furniture, the Victorian doodads that cluttered every available surface, the Persian rugs that covered the carpeting and often made him stumble. No, this was not his world. He had to get out of this stuffy, ornate prison. He packed up his wife, his brother, and his nephew; had his chauffeur crank up the Franklin; and headed south on rutted roads. The only good stretch of highway was in Wayne County, where for a few miles the Foote family whizzed along on concrete pavement. W. A. stepped on the gas as much as he dared.

"Say, this is just great," he exclaimed, his voice fighting the wind that whipped through the automobile. But it was here that his vision of the future failed him. He could not imagine this concrete road expanding, stretching ever outward and growing branches until it covered the whole country. He knew of Ford's new assembly line in Highland Park, which was beginning to spew out low-cost automobiles by the thousands, but just as he could not see a country of highways, he could not visualize a nation of cars. W. A. had been born into the time of railroads, and he was going to die in that time. His young nephew, Harold, did see, and for the first and only time in his life, he dared openly to disagree with his uncle. They had stopped at a grade crossing and were waiting for a train to pass when W. A. Foote suddenly said, "You know, I think we ought to buy the Pere Marquette." This was a brand-new idea, but it did not take his brother by surprise. J. B. nodded quietly. "We'll electrify it," he said. "That's right," W. A. answered. "Then we'll have all of Michigan right up to Mackinaw."

Harold leaned over from the back seat. "But Uncle Will," he said. "Railroads are finished. The Pere Marquette is bankrupt right now. In another few years everybody will be driving automobiles."

W. A. laughed, "You still have a lot to learn, young fellow," he said. "Automobiles are great for family outings like this, but they're no way to get anyplace fast. And what about freight? Why, I see the day when we'll have not just one line, but two, one for high-speed passenger trains, and the other for cargo. Michigan is growing so fast that we'll have a hard time keeping up."

That was more or less the end of the discussion. Harold was abashed that he had gone even that far. But from that moment on, the project was very much alive. W. A. attacked it with all his pioneering zest. He commissioned Bill Fargo, his old engineer, to inspect the Pere Marquette property, which, as it turned out, could be had for the bargain price of $5 million. One of Fargo's men, a fellow by the name of F. B. Keel, had all the fun. His job was to bicycle hundreds of miles over all the Pere Marquette tracks to get a bird's-eye view of the condition of the line and to see how much it would cost to recondition it. So, W. A. dreamed and Keel biked, and J. B. and George Stecker played cloak and dagger at the Grass Lake substation of the old Boland line, where, in a secret arrangement with the Westinghouse Company, they set up a 5,000-volt rectifier. Night after night, after the last passenger trolley had finished its 11 P.M. run from Page Avenue in Jackson to Michigan Center, and Grass Lake, the 600-volt interurban was thrown over to 5,000 volts, and the little old trolley became an experimental train to see whether the high voltage would work on an interurban—for on the long stretches of the Pere Marquette, low voltage would never do; the many substations required would become too expensive.

While all this hush-hush work was going on, W. A. tried to keep himself amused in other ways. While on a trip to Miami in October of 1914, he had chartered a 45-foot fishing yacht and had fallen in love with the sea. There were only a half dozen houses on Miami Beach at that time—the area was just beginning to be developed—and W. A. bought several lots. He also wanted a boat, and he commissioned his nephew to go to the Matthews Boat Company in Buffalo to arrange for the design of a 66-foot cabin cruiser. By April of 1915, the boat was ready for delivery. Since W. A. was the president of a big corporation, arrangements had been made for the Twentieth Century Limited, the crack train of that day between Chicago and New York, to make a special stop at Port Clinton, where the boatyard was, to let W. A. and Harold off so that they could accept delivery.

Harold's bags were all packed, and he was waiting for his uncle to pick him up when the phone rang, shortly before eight on the morning of April 12. His aunt was on the line. "Harold, come over here," she said, her voice breaking. "Something terrible has happened." Harold rushed over to his uncle's mansion, arriving just in time to hear him pronounced dead of a heart attack. W. A. Foote had collapsed on the driveway just as he was about to get into his car to start the trip.

W. A.'s Pere Marquette dream died with him. At the funeral, there was still talk about it, but eventually the project was abandoned, and the Chesapeake & Ohio bought the Pere Marquette. Since then, of course, many miles of the road have been abandoned, and much of the old main line is now side-track. Harold Foote, as a young man, had seen the future more clearly than his uncle; the railroads were dying even as the older generation of entrepreneurs was still trying to expand them.

Man's vision, even at its best, is limited by his past successes, and its is in this way that history gives newcomers a chance. America's great sailing ships, the "clippers," were the envy of the world, and our country became so engrossed in them that it never realized that the future belonged to steamships. As a result, the British took over our maritime leadership. In turn, the British were so in love with their steamships that they never noticed the airplane roaring overhead, and America became the leader in the aviation industry, which spelled the doom of the British transatlantic liners. A successful past can be a burden indeed, and so it was for W. A. Foote, who thought in terms of railroads when the automobile was already on the

W. A. FOOTE'S LAST TRIUMPH . . .

This photo, taken circa 1913, shows the main right-of-way construction north of Martin for the Grand Rapids–Kalamazoo interurban line, which was inaugurated only a few weeks after W. A. Foote's death in 1915. (Consumers Power collection)

ascent. His death, shortly before his sixty-first birthday, spared him the recognition of his own limitations. But it also deprived him of a new triumph, albeit a deceiving one.

On May 5, 1915, Foote's electric train from Grand Rapids to Kalamazoo made its inaugural run with company officers, civic grandees, and joyous newspapermen aboard, and the journalists had plenty to write about. It was the fastest interurban yet, making the 47-mile run in forty-two minutes at an average speed of 66 miles per hour. Soon speeds up to over 100 miles per hour were achieved. It was without doubt the finest electric railroad in Michigan. Its terminals were in the heart of the business districts, convenient to hotels, theaters, and shops. Schedules provided for eighteen trains each way every day. No place on the line had a grade of over 1 percent, and the sharpest curve was 3 percent. The comfortable cars, which rode as smoothly as pullmans, carried eighty-five passengers and were divided into several sections, including a parlor, which required an additional fare of 25 cents. A washroom divided a general passenger section from a smoker.

The line did a big business from the start, far beyond the expectations of the company, and it was soon announced that the system would be extended south to Elkhart, Indiana, passing through Vicksburg, Centreville, Three Rivers, and White Pigeon. In addition, it was to be extended west to Dowagiac, connecting with a road recently completed to Benton Harbor. An issue of the *Michigan Investor* predicted enthusiastically that Kalamazoo would become the terminal of one of the greatest electric railroad networks in the United States. These grandiose plans never materialized. The age of the automobile was here, its technology given additional impetus by the big war in Europe. Passenger trains were finished, even though they didn't know it yet.

There is no doubt that W. A. Foote was wrong about the Pere Marquette. His railroad ambition was a futile dream which, had it come to fruition, might well have sapped the

... WAS THE FASTEST INTERURBAN OF THEM ALL
Foote's Grand Rapids–Kalamazoo interurban achieved speeds up to 100 miles an hour and was a great success for many years. This photograph was taken at the Kalamazoo station in the 1920s. (Consumers Power photo)

financial strength of the Hodenpyl-Hardy enterprise. Yet his dream brought about one of those magnificent ironies with which history often surprises its participants. Foote's Pere Marquette project, though ill-fated in every other respect, resulted indirectly in the extension of the Consumers Power domain almost all the way up to the Straits of Mackinac.

It will be recalled that when Consumers Power Company was first recognized, its territory ended more or less at the upper reaches of the Muskegon River on the west and of the Au Sable on the east. North of these streams there still lay wilderness; communities were small and scattered, not worth the cost of bringing them into an interconnected electric system. But an electrified Pere Marquette required power right up to Mackinaw City, and this power had to come from somewhere in the area. High-voltage transmission from the existing Consumers Power hydro sites and steam plants farther south would have been too costly. To obtain this power from closer sources, Foote had seen to it that the Michigan Railway Company gained control of the Manistee Power & Light Company and the Manistee County Electric Company. Note that he did not acquire the stock directly for Consumers Power. Apparently he didn't consider this worthwhile, and it wasn't until a few months after his death that the properties became part of Consumers Power. Thus, even in his miscalculation of the future of electric railroads, W. A. Foote rounded out his heritage. For all practical purposes, he bequeathed to Consumers Power a statewide electric system.

Actually, in his own inimitable way. W. A. Foote had been involved in the northern properties for a number of years. He was aware that the Manistee River offered some of the best waterpower sites in Michigan. The only problem was that the area was so far out of the way. In 1907, when Foote became interested in that region, it wasn't yet worth buying. Foote contented himself with taking an option on flowage lands owned by Clyde J. Holmes, a bright, energetic Grand Rapids lawyer in his thirties who had become interested in hydropower exploitation several years earlier. Holmes's original idea was to build a dam with a 103-foot head just above High Bridge, not far from a place where Tippy Dam was later constructed. In fact, Holmes might well have gone through with his dam project and become Foote's competitor had it not been for a disaster that occurred more than 2,000 miles away—the San Francisco earthquake. Holmes's financing was supposed to have come, for the most part, from Rudolph G. Spreckels, the San Francisco sugar tycoon. But Spreckels, rich as he was, now needed the money to rebuild his wrecked California installations and didn't have any left to invest in Michigan.[13] It was at this point that Foote took out his option. In the process of the negotiations he got to like Clyde Holmes so much that he asked the young attorney whether he would care to work for him. "I am a practicing lawyer," said Holmes, "and I would be glad to work for you on a per diem basis as your work requires. That's the only sort of arrangement that I would consider."

"And what would you charge per diem?" inquired Foote. Holmes named his figure, which was in the neighborhood of $20 a day, a not inconsiderable sum in those years. "All right," said W. A. Foote. "You're retained for 365 days a year." For the next six years Holmes was Foote's personal attorney. Much of his work, including land acquisitions, was connected directly with the power business. In 1908, he organized the Manistee County Electric Company and remained its president until it was absorbed by Consumers Power.[14] In later years, he became general counsel for various divisions of the Consumers Power companies and, still later, vice-president and director of the company. In the meantime, however, as president of the Manistee Company he built Stronach Dam on the Pine River, which is sometimes called the south branch of the Manistee.[15] The dam supplied power to Manistee and Cadillac[16] as well as power for the construction of Junction Dam, later renamed Charles W. Tippy Dam. By 1918 Tippy Dam had been linked to Grand Rapids and into the Consumers Power network with a 140,000-volt power line. Except for local additions, the system was complete.

It is difficult, in retrospect, to assess a man like W. A. Foote except in terms of his accomplishments. Flesh and blood return to dust; only the works of man remain. What manner of man is he who would build beyond his own personal needs? What makes a man a future builder? What motivates him? Ambition, drive, fame, a vision beyond himself—all these are necessary ingredients. So are the will to do for others and an unlimited faith in oneself. Such single-mindedness is often confused with ruthlessness by persons of less strength. Like other future builders, W. A. Foote allowed no obstacles to stand in his way. But this did not make him ruthless. For a picture of his essence as a man we must be content with glimpses.

Fifty years later, Clyde Holmes remembered the one instruction W. A. Foote gave him when he hired him as a lawyer in 1907: "Never go back on your word. If you have promised anything, carry through with it, but be careful what you promise." There is another telling incident which happened when one of Foote's agents was trying to buy some land for the right-of-way of an interurban line. The agent told Foote that the price asked for the land was too high. Foote asked him to whom the land belonged. When told that a widow owned it, Foote said, "Go ahead and pay her price."

W. A. died a rich man, not in cash perhaps, but certainly in assets. His widow eventually left the two daughters about $7 million. Several years after W. A.'s death, Justin R. Whiting, then chairman of the board of Consumers Power, asked Harold Foote, J. B.'s son and W. A.'s nephew, into his office one day. "I have a very personal question," Whiting said. "There is something I don't understand. When Mr. W. A. died, why did your father get such a small share of his estate?" The small share Whiting was referring to was on the order of 5 percent, and even this was not part of the estate, but a gift from W. A.'s widow.

"Mr. Whiting," Harold Foote said, "Uncle Will died intestate." Whiting stared unbelievingly at Harold Foote. "No will?" he asked. Harold answered, "No will." Whiting could only shake his head in wonderment.

This is indeed what happened. W. A. did not leave his brother one cent. J. B. had always been on a salary, a generous one to be sure, but hardly in keeping with his great contributions. This would make it seem that W. A. was less than fair to his brother. But there is another explanation. J. B. lived totally in his brother's shadow. W. A. managed all J. B.'s affairs, even to the point of building a big house for him on West Washington Street in Jackson in 1912. W. A. simply treated him as a junior member of his immediate family. Courts don't recognize such feelings unless they are set down in writing. The real explanation is probably that W. A. Foote's untimely death astonished no one more than himself. He just never expected to die and had made no provision for it. Perhaps this is what distinguishes future builders. They expect to live forever — and, in a sense, they do.[17]

12

Labor Pains

Consumers Power's birth as an operating company in both the gas and electric areas was a slow and painful process, made all the more difficult by the fact that it spanned the inflation years of World War I and the depressions that preceded and followed the conflict. This was a period when even experienced and well-connected moneymen like Hodenpyl, Hardy, and Clark found it extremely hard to raise the necessary funds for maintaining services, let alone finance the expansion required to keep up with Michigan's growth.

Michigan was rapidly developing into an urban, industrial state. Its population, which stood at 2.4 million in the year 1900, had climbed to nearly 3.7 million by 1920. The growth was most marked in the automobile cities, and a true population shift was taking place. In 1890, when Michigan had about two million inhabitants, only 35 percent of them lived in towns of 2,500 or more population. By 1920 this situation was practically reversed; now 61 percent—more than 2.2 million people—occupied the state's towns and cities.[1]

During the blustery, cold month of March 1917, German submarines sent five American ships to the bottom of the Atlantic. On April 2, an enraged President Wilson asked Congress for a declaration of war. Congress complied with a joint resolution on April 6. Almost overnight the country plunged into a war economy from which no industry was exempt. Consumers Power's capacities soon became inadequate. Construction's appetite for new capital seemed insatiable. The price of labor, fuel, and material doubled, and in some cases even tripled, without commensurate increases in electric and gas rates. The cost of money whirled right along on the inflationary spiral—a situation uncomfortably familiar to anyone who has lived in the United States during the schizophrenic period of the war in Vietnam, when Washington tried the precarious high-wire act of a guns-and-butter economy. The parallel between these two periods is overwhelming. Their causes were different, but their sad results were the same. During the war in Vietnam, our new consumer society lived in unprecedented affluence, spending more on luxuries than it ever had before, while borrowing from itself to finance a draining, piecemeal war. In World War I, pure ignorance had still been at work: the country had no prior experience with wartime economic pressures in an industrial society. All business—especially that dependent on heavy capital financing—was sorely squeezed. Consumers Power and the Michigan Light Company were no exceptions.

Consumers Power, its president now the suave and impeccable B. C. Cobb, was no longer a holding company.[2] Its long-pursued petition to do business in Michigan finally had been granted by the Michigan Railroad Commission on July 22, 1915, and it was now an operating company—a development W. A. Foote had looked forward to for many years, but had not been privileged to witness.[3] Michigan Light, too, had become an operating company. This new Michigan corporation had taken over the gas properties of the New Jersey holding company, the Michigan Light Company, in

1913, and its charter ran the whole gamut of producing and supplying gas and electricity for lighting, fuel, and other purposes.[4]

While the going was tough at both companies, the situation at the gas affiliate was considerably less serious. Thanks largely to a new technological development, which Michigan Light had spearheaded, this company was able to face the war years of labor scarcity without too much concern. Prior to 1915, gas had been manufactured in the D-type retorts (previously described in Chapter 2), whose units were of relatively small capacity and had to be fired individually by hand.[5] The manufacturing plants also were equipped with water-gas generators, used primarily for peak-hour operations. Water gas has two great advantages over coal gas. At the consumer's end, it yields much more heat; this was an increasingly important factor as heating rather than lighting became the prime purpose of the gas utility. At the manufacturer's end, the advantage of water gas is that the production process requires much less preparation time; it can be started up at any moment as needs increase in periods of heavy use. However, the old water-gas plants were not automatic. All the valves were hand-operated, and an attendant skittered around the iron-plate operating floor from valve to valve, a time-consuming process.[6]

Under James A. Brown, then assistant gas engineer under Barthold and later a director of Consumers Power, both the coal-gas and the water-gas processes were drastically improved, just in the nick of time.[7] In 1917, shortly after America's entry into the war but before its pressures were yet felt, Brown arranged for the construction of a battery of twenty-one new-type ovens that were far superior to the old retorts. These ovens were adaptations of the ordinary by-product coke ovens used in steel plants where the purpose of the units was to manufacture coke, with gas as a by-product. Brown and his men redesigned these more efficient ovens so that they yielded gas as the main product and coke as the by-product. Most of the work that previously had been done by hand was taken care of by machinery with these new units, from the unloading of coal from railroad cars to the removal of the coke from the ovens. Brown's installation of the new units in the Jackson plant in August 1918 was probably the first or second in the United States.[8] Improvements were also made in the water-gas process. Now, instead of having hand-operated valves and controls all over the plant, they were brought to one central point in a console, and here the operation was made quite automatic by the use of cams, levers, and a motor. This improvement did not increase the productivity of the water-gas units, but was important in saving manpower, a vital consideration as the war economy encroached increasingly on civilian enterprises.

The situation at Consumers Power was considerably more critical. As an electric utility, it required much more capital investment than Michigan Light. Consumers Power's income, both gross and net, had increased rapidly between 1910 and 1914, and so had its capitalization: from $12 million to nearly $23 million.[9] In times of growth and prosperity, business management generally tends to see the future in the rosiest terms, and this was a case in point. Ninety-three construction jobs, including several dams, were in progress when the war started. Additions were under way for the steam-generating plants in Grand Rapids, Battle Creek, Jackson, and Flint.[10] Construction had been started on Junction Dam, Foote Dam, and Alcona Dam.[11]

Then the roof caved in. Funds were transferred from one city to another in a never-ending race to meet current expenses. Creditors were stalled. Officials called on suppliers, persuading them to delay demands for payment and to take long-term notes for settlement of accounts. Hodenpyl, who was in semi-retirement by this time, returned to a more active role and managed to obtain loans from the War Finance Corporation.[12] Thanks largely to these loans, most of the projects were carried to completion. The Alcona hydro installation,

JAMES A. BROWN
Brown rose from the post of assistant gas engineer to become a director of the company. No wonder: It was largely his work that paved the way for Consumers' success in the gas business.
(Consumers Power photo)

however, had to be abandoned, and it was not resumed until well after the war. This dam, whose construction had been started in the winter of 1916–1917, ran into quicksand trouble which necessitated major changes in design, and there just wasn't enough money to pay for it. The company's cash squeeze eventually got so serious that employees were issued metal holders for pencil stubs, and nobody got a new pencil until he could show that his old one was so worn down that it could no longer be stuck into a sharpener. This sort of paper-clip-hoarding office management became even more pronounced with the 1921 recession.[13] At the same time, construction money got so tight that overzealous Consumers Power crews sometimes foraged into the dark of night to pilfer poles for their lines from telephone company pole piles.[14]

As if inflation and depression were not enough of a burden on Consumers Power, even nature seemed to conspire against the company. On February 22, 1922, a giant sleet storm blew in across Lake Michigan and threw Consumers Power into the biggest crisis of its history. The sleet froze even as it reached the ground. Within hours, the state was buried under untold megatons of ice. Tree branches snapped under glittering burdens twenty to thirty times their weight. Wires fell and were frozen into the ice that covered the ground. Poles and towers toppled. With the transmission lines down, practically the whole system was immobilized. Hydro plants in the western part of the state were cut off entirely for several days. In the cities, Consumers Power men scrambled to start every old steam

THE 1922 SLEET STORM
*Cadillac was just about at
ground zero, and that's what
the town looked like after the
blow (clockwise from top left)
on Granite Street, Prospect
Street, Haring Street, and
Cass Street.* (Consumers
Power photos)

generating plant they could find, trying desperately to keep local distribution wires loaded until the transmission damage was repaired. But nobody could really assess the extent of the destruction. All communications were out. Travel by road was impossible; the state was one big skating rink covered by a glare 4 inches thick.

Leroy L. Benedict, later vice-president of electric transmission, was division superintendent in Grand Rapids at that time. His steam plant couldn't cope with the demand. The city was more than half dark. Benedict was thirty-five then, still young enough to be adventurous, and during World War I he'd daydreamed about being in the Air Corps. If you couldn't telephone, and if you couldn't drive, then the only way to see what was going on was from the air. Here was his chance. He got out his binoculars, rode to the Grand Rapids airfield (such as it was in those days), and chartered a plane. His idea was to follow the transmission line to Croton Dam and then continue over the Manistee territory and finally land in Cadillac so that the plane could be refueled for the way home. "Hey," he yelled at a lineman he passed on his way to the field. "You, fellah, lend me your bearskin coat!"

He climbed into the open cockpit. The pilot got in behind him. Contact! And the flimsy little biplane roared and shivered down the runway, the pilot pouring on the throttle as hard as he could. Benedict saw the end of the field rushing up at him faster and faster. As if by an unseen hand, the auxiliary joystick in his cockpit was yanked all the way back, and still the machine wouldn't take off. They were almost at the edge of the field—the trees were coming up in an awful hurry, and then suddenly the world turned upside down. A front wheel had broken through the ice. The plane flipped over. Benedict crawled out. So did the pilot. Both men were shaken but unharmed. "You know, you're goddam lucky," someone told Benedict at the airfield shack. "I know," said Benedict. "Oh no, you don't," the man said. "You'd have been a heck of a lot worse off up at Cadillac." Puzzled, Benedict asked him why. "No place to land up there," the man said dryly.[15]

When Consumers Power men finally did get a look at all the damage, they estimated that it would take two months to replace the transmission lines, but they didn't reckon with the fervor of the crews. Unbelievable as it may seem, the linemen closed most of the gaps in just ten days, establishing a new record for overhead emergency construction. They repaired some 215 steel towers, erected countless temporary wood towers, and restrung some 300 miles of wire. Some areas required nearly total reconstruction. Around Cadillac, for instance, three-quarters of the poles and wires were on the ground and frozen fast under several inches of ice. The transmission line from nearly completed Junction Dam (later renamed Tippy Dam) was down for 17 miles out of Cadillac, and the little steam plant in town couldn't carry the load alone. This was probably just as well because there wasn't any load to carry, for all the distribution wires to the houses were down too. In this area, which had been in the center of the storm, it took about a month before service was restored even on a temporary basis, and then crews worked all through the following summer to put the system back in permanent shape.[16]

The loss to Consumers Power ran into the millions—a loss the company could ill afford at that time. Replacing the lines and towers actually constituted only part of the bill.[17] Among the biggest items was the amount of coal burned in the steam plants while the water of the Au Sable, Manistee, and Muskegon Rivers was going to waste. Today one is apt to minimize the importance of hydro plants, at least in the Middle West, but at that time Consumers Power generated at least half its electric power with water.[18] In 1920, the nearest year for which statistics are available, the company derived 101,000 horsepower of its 202,000-horsepower generating capacity from hydro installations,[19] and this was before some of the dams were completed that were in use at the time of the 1922 destruction. The sleet storm was a bitter blow indeed, and it took some time before the company managed to recover financially from this historic disaster.

One of the major problems that came with the war years was that Consumers Power could not earn enough from its electric rates to cope with the inflation and provide an adequate return on the investment at the same time. The company had always kept its rates as low as possible. This was simply good business. Low rates expanded the market. In the early days, a flat rate had been standard practice; customers paid a certain sum, regardless of how much they used. Perhaps the measure of quantity was not then thought essential; more important, no method had yet been developed to obtain it.

Soon, however, some kind of metering became necessary. Flat-rate use, except for restricted services such as street-lighting, tended to get out of hand. Where the flat rate was set to cover the cost of providing service to a large user, the price was too high for the small customer, and it was harder to get him to buy. When, on the other hand, the flat rate was predicated on the small user, the company lost money supplying the big customer. Necessity once again became the mother of invention, and meters were developed. But they were expensive—too expensive to be installed with small customers. Consequently, some other way of measuring had to be found. Different companies used different methods. Detroit Edison, for example, based its rate on the relationship between the number of rooms in a residence and the possible demand of that residence's customer.[20] The measuring standard developed for Consumers Power by Frank Newton, formerly a staff member of the Wisconsin Railroad Commission who had been hired by the company to deal with rate-regulation problems, was based on an actual count of the wattage and horsepower (one horsepower equaling 746 watts) of lights, motors, and other electric devices. There were certain exclusions such as lights in closets and basements, because these were generally little used.[21]

With a complex of hydro and steam generators feeding a single transmission system for distribution in the various localities, costs became statewide rather than local. Consequently, it seemed logical that rates should also be statewide rather than differ from community to community. The Michigan Railroad Commission eventually authorized such statewide rates, and starting in about 1915, Consumers Power charged a monthly rate of 9 cents per kilowatthour for the first 30 kilowatthours and 3 cents per kilowatthour beyond that. Of course this wasn't enough once the inflation really got started, and eventually the base consumption increment changed to 60 kilowatthours from 30 kilowatthours to provide greater income.

Yet even this was far from enough. Consumers Power was caught in the squeeze between costs and insufficient income. This situation was not at all unique. Most other utilities were in the same bind. Way out in Oregon, for instance, the Public Service Commission of that state commented that it was time "to realize that good service can be obtained only by just and equitable treatment. No starved horse ever pulled a heavy load. The utilities have been deprived of the power to make a just profit. They must also be protected."[22]

The utility situation throughout the nation was in fact so serious that it brought forth an exchange of letters between President Wilson and Secretary of the Treasury William G. McAdoo.[23] In his letter to Wilson, McAdoo warned that public utilities must not be permitted to be weakened.

"It may be," he wrote, "that state and local authorities do not always appreciate the close connection between the soundness and efficiency of the local utilities and the national strength and vigor and do not resort with sufficient promptness to the call for remedial measures." Like the great politician he was, McAdoo then expressed confidence that "all such state and local authorities will respond promptly to the national needs when the matter is fairly and properly brought before them." President Wilson, in his reply, echoed McAdoo's pep-talk optimism. But the two gentlemen's confidence was not altogether warranted. The persuasive tones of their official letters budged a few utility commissions, but the Michigan Railroad Commission was not among them. The commission allowed Consumers Power to do little more than increase the number of hours in the higher-rate increments, and when in 1919 the watchdog body's name was changed to Michigan Public Utilities Commission and its jurisdiction extended to fix gas rates, that end of the business fared no better. If anything, the situation in the gas business was even more serious—and the traction business fared worst of all.

We remember that back in 1907 electric railways were in first place in earnings, gas in second place, and electric service in third. Now, fourteen years later, the situation was reversed. Electric was on top, and traction was on the bottom—and a very poor third at that. Operating costs were mounting; yet there was a general feeling on the part of the public that streetcars and electric interurbans should charge no more for tickets than they did before the war. What's more, in some localities so-called jitney buses were beginning to hurt street railway traffic. "Jitney" was the slang term for 5 cents, the price charged in the 1920s by the many private persons who started hauling people in their cars. This term hung on long after the fares went up, and in some cities, such as Miami Beach, jitneys running along certain streets and stopping on demand to board or discharge passengers kept operating into the 1940s. In other communities, however, jitneys were soon replaced by gasoline-powered buses as we now know them. In any case, the handwriting was on the wall, or more specifically on the ledgers of the traction companies. Their day was definitely drawing to a close. This, of course, also had an indirect effect on Consumers Power's earnings, even though the traction lines were not its own properties but those of the parent holding company, Commonwealth Power, Railway & Light.[24] Still, Consumers Power furnished electricity for the operation of 463 miles of interurban railway and 227 miles of street railway, and their lower

C. W. TIPPY
He was a president everyone would have voted for. (Photo by Fernand de Gueldre)

earnings were definitely reflected in the electric company's profit picture.[25]

It was a good thing that during those very difficult days Consumers Power had a peach of an operating boss. When a company is saddled with financial problems, the life of its staff is rarely a bed of roses, quite apart from having to turn in pencil stubs. Keeping up employee morale is more important than ever. Nobody could have been better suited to accomplish this than Charles W. Tippy. One winter day, a new employee couldn't get his car rolling in the alley next to the old Jackson office. The automobile was stuck in the snow, and when he stepped on the gas, the wheels just dug in deeper and deeper. Suddenly a tall, husky man materialized, bent himself to the task, and pushed the car out of the ruts. "Do you know who that was?" the employee was asked later. "That was our general manager."

C. W. Tippy was that kind of a guy. If the stuck employee hadn't been new, he would have recognized his boss and might even have called him by his first name. Tippy knew everybody, and everybody knew him. But he wasn't just "nice." He was smart as anything, understood the business, and had a magnificent, dry sense of humor. The house in Berrien County where he had been born on March 6, 1876, was located in Michigan, but the sawmill operated by his father sat across the boundary in Indiana. As Tippy commented some years later, "Under present rulings, we would probably have been under the jurisdiction of the Interstate Commerce Commission." Evidently he didn't think much of government interference.

The Tippy family moved to New Carlisle, Indiana, a few miles west of South Bend, when he was still a child, and it was there that he spent his boyhood before going off to Purdue to study mechanical engineering with a specialty in chemistry. Even before college, he got "gas tar on his heels" by spending summers in the gasworks at Grand Rapids, where a brother, B. O. Tippy, was superintendent. Young Tippy's first job was turning iron borings mixed with salt to rust them for making iron oxide, which was used as a purifying material. He was a general roustabout for some time, working for just about anybody in the plant — the blacksmith, the engineer, the water-gas maker, and the stoker — and he really learned the business from the tar-covered ground up. After his graduation in 1899, Tippy started as a chemist with Detroit City Gas at a salary of $50 a month, and was later promoted to assistant superintendent. It was here that he first met B. C. Cobb, who at that time was purchasing agent of the McMillin-owned Detroit company. In 1902, Tippy and his wife, the former Margaret Deacon, moved to Fulton, New York, where he took over a natural gas company (probably Noble Moss & Company) just as the natural gas supply had practically run out. He built a manufactured gas plant there, and as he gleefully reported later, "We were in direct competition with the electric company for commercial lighting, and we succeeded in taking about half of their business away from them." Of course, this was more than ten years before he became an electric man himself, ten years he was to spend as a Hodenpyl-Walbridge gas man in New York, Pennsylvania, and Texas. In 1910, Tippy finally returned to Michigan, being assigned to the Detroit office of Hodenpyl-Walbridge as assistant to W. M. Eaton, then director of distribution in Michigan.[26] It may seem a little peculiar that Tippy, a highly experienced gas man, suddenly became general manager of Consumers Power, an electric outfit, when it changed into an operating company in 1915. But Tippy was the kind of man who could learn just about anything in a hurry, and he didn't remain a stranger to the electric business for very long.

One reason why Consumers Power functioned so well under Tippy's management was that he would not tolerate yes-men. He always insisted that everybody express his own judgment at executive meetings. He would listen to all that was said before making his decision, and even then he welcomed criticism. Sometimes he withdrew his decision after listening to comments, and he did this with a smile and some remark like, "I guess I'm outvoted; we'll do it your way." Under such a system, all his men knew they were expected to express their honest convictions; there was no shilly-shallying, and nobody was unduly upset when his own views were not accepted.

Indeed, Tippy was always open to new ways of doing things when they had merit, and he went along enthusiastically when Hodenpyl-Hardy decided in 1920 to take an entirely new approach in obtaining financing for Consumers Power Company's pressing expansion needs.

It is one of the fundamental characteristics of public utilities that the internal generation of capital funds is limited. Public utility regulation requires quite rightly that utility earnings be reasonably remunerative but not excessive. This means that the rates authorized by the state commissions are at best sufficient to pay for operating expenses and taxes, cover depreciation, and provide a fair return on the value of the property. In short, the customer pays the cost of serving him today, but cannot be required to contribute money for improvements and expansions. All this must come from new capital. True, moneys

ALL SPRUCED UP FOR THE PHOTOG
Electric line crew posing with repair truck sometime in the 1920s.
(Consumers Power photo)

held in reserve, such as for depreciation, can be invested in capital improvements, but in a growing company this is far from enough.

For years the financing of large business undertakings—not just utilities—had come from accumulated wealth, with most capital infusions handled by bankers. This investment market was taxed to the utmost by World War I. Big money dried up rapidly under the demands of the armament industry, and it became necessary to raise capital in many little dribbles instead of a few big chunks. The sale of Liberty bonds tapped for the first time the savings of the middle class and opened up a vast new investment market, and it was to this market that industry now turned.[27] The ownership of securities, until then quite limited, became widespread. Of course the utilities industry also bid for this new capital market, and the most logical way to go about it was to sell securities directly to the utility's customers, with the utility's employees acting as the sales force.

The first company to do this, California's Pacific Gas and Electric, had launched its customer-ownership program in 1914, even before the colorful advent of Liberty-bond rallies.[28] At that time, Fred W. Hoover, later a vice-president of Consumers Power, was still working in California. After Hoover had joined Hodenpyl-Hardy, he brought up the Pacific Gas and Electric experience during a New York meeting at which financial problems were the topic of discussion, and B. C. Cobb sent Hoover to California for a briefing on the methods Pacific Gas and Electric had used in its customer-ownership drive.[29] Hoover then went to Jackson to sell Tippy on the plan. Tippy immediately saw the merit of the new idea, and soon everybody at Consumers Power was out selling preferred stock—office workers, meter readers, and linemen. They had an attractive offer to put before their customers: each share cost $95 and paid a dividend of $7, representing a yield of 7.37 percent. The first shares were sold in September 1920, and the campaign quickly gained momentum. The customer-ownership plan offered additional benefits. For one thing, it was good public relations to have the company's customers possess a better understanding of the utility business. For another, it presented a wonderful opportunity to educate employees in the affairs of their company.

But it wasn't all smooth sailing. At that time, Henry Ford, who was even then beginning to enlarge his auto-maker's horizons to encompass his own peculiar visions of social reform, had declared a personal war against Wall Street, and his propaganda organ, the *Dearborn Independent,* vigorously pursued the vendetta. Now it so happened that the dividends on the Consumers Power preferred were mailed from New York in envelopes that carried a Wall Street return address, and this created considerable opposition, threatening Consumers Power Company's plans for customer ownership. But Hodenpyl-Hardy were not to be licked by such sloganeering. Within a week of hearing about this unexpected difficulty, they moved the stock transfer office from unspeakably evil

Wall Street in New York to utterly respectable Jackson, Michigan, and henceforth Consumers Power Company's dividend letters carried comforting Jackson postmarks. It was an altogether appropriate response: when simplistic attempts are made to defeat you, the countermove must be as superficial as the attack—a lesson which far too few businessmen have really learned even to this day.

While the shrewd device of changing the postmark's venue may seem underhanded to those who tend to blame the world's miseries wholly on financial men, Consumers Power Company's customer-ownership program was strictly aboveboard. As the late W. A. Foote would have said, "It was the only right way." For the shares sold were in preferred stock of the operating company, not in common stock of the holding company, and thus the shareholders were close to the actual source of earnings.[30] This clean, unequivocal method was not always followed by some other big utilities, notably Samuel Insull's Chicago-based empire, whose luckless investors, their funds tied up in paper companies, were wiped out in 1932 when Insull's holding pyramid collapsed.[31]

For Consumers Power Company's customers it turned out to be an excellent investment, however, and the way it was handled accrued to the company's everlasting credit. As we shall see later, Hodenpyl-Hardy's decision to sell the preferred stock of Consumers Power and its other operating companies did much to enhance the good reputation of the Commonwealth utilities when Franklin Delano Roosevelt's "brain trusters" set out to smash the public utilities and their holding companies. But those dark clouds were still far below the horizon, and in the meanwhile, Consumers Power Company's customers went enthusiastically for the ownership idea. They could buy the stock on a nine-payment plan, $10 down and $10 per share for seven months, with $15 as the final payment. Employees, in addition to getting commissions on the sales they made, could buy the stock over twenty-four months with payments of $3.50 each.[32]

By the end of 1920, sales totaled 6,378 shares.[33] By the end of 1921, nearly $2 million worth of cumulative preferred stock had been sold, and the share value had gone up $5 to its $100 par. In 1922 it was decided to increase the company's $40-million capitalization by another $10 million in preferred. At the same time, management came up with the splendid idea that dividends under the customer-ownership plan were to be made payable monthly so as to be used by customer owners in payment of their utility bills. This concept was about as close to participatory ownership in a cooperative enterprise as one could get. The customer, in effect, invested in the service he received. By 1923, even though with easier money the dividend on new issues was now reduced to rates varying from 6 to 6.6 percent, nearly $5 million more capital had been raised.[34]

Hoover, being the most knowledgeable Consumers Power man in this area, was in charge of the program. Working closely with him was Dan E. Karn, an Indiana farmer's son destined to become the president of Consumers Power thirty years later.[35] Karn, who had come to the company in 1916 from a Commonwealth affiliate, the Central Illinois Light Company in Peoria, was appointed assistant to general manager Tippy in 1922 after first working in steam heating at Grand Rapids and later in the rate department of Frank Newton in Jackson.

Customer ownership was far from the only innovation that took place under Tippy's stewardship. Appliance sales also started becoming significant at that time, less as a direct profit function than as a means of stimulating additional power consumption. Like all truly successful and lasting ventures, the appliance business was of great benefit to both parties. The housewife had an easier life, and the company could expand its services.

In recent years, utilities have been accused of speeding the world down the path of pollution by stimulating the use of more and more electric conveniences, just as the automobile industry has been indicted as a co-conspirator for selling automobiles. True enough, human contentment cannot be based on the possession of an electric can opener or an automobile that has more power than a sensible man needs. If people find happiness in gadgets, it is neither the gadgets' fault nor the gadget makers', but that of the individual who thinks that such goodies represent nirvana. It's easy to forget that car makers did not force Americans to buy the 100 million automobiles and trucks they drive and that the utility companies did not coerce people to fill their homes with appliances. Both genres of equipment are basically very real conveniences, and to scapegoat industry for the people's choice to avail themselves of these conveniences is a spurious argument that indicts industry less than it insults the public, for it implies that the average person cannot make wise decisions. But in the 1920s, Big Brother had not yet reared his solicitous head, and most people were still ornery and independent enough not to want to be kept by self-appointed guardians. In any case, they enjoyed the usefulness of appliances and bought more and more of them, first small items like toasters and grills, and later ranges, electric refrigerators, and washing machines.[36]

Sometimes, salesmen as well as the customers got carried away by all those wonderful things that were now available. In one of the early appliance campaigns, electric irons were sold door-to-door like Fuller brushes. Among the most zealous salesmen in this drive was a gentleman assigned to the Manistee territory. Soon after he had plunged enthusiastically into the venture, Consumers Power Company's Manistee manager, Charles Kressler, received a desperate call from a local housewife. "Could you please send that nice man back who sold me my iron? He forgot to show me how to use it on the telephone."

Kressler, interrupted in a busy day's work, couldn't figure out for the moment what she was talking about. "What do you mean," he said, "use the iron on the telephone?" It turned out that the lady didn't have electricity in her house—telephones arrived before electric service became common—and she was understandably confused by all this new technology.

All through that time, C. W. Tippy kept his hand in the gas business of course. It will be recalled that at the same time he was associated with Consumers Power, he was also general manager of Michigan Light, the gas company. His dual office foreshadowed the not-too-distant moment when the electric and gas operations would at last be merged to form the across-the-board operating organization of today. In fact this consolidation had been in preparation for about four years before it finally came to fruition on June 24, 1922. On that day, at a special meeting of the stockholders of the Michigan Light Company, all its property was conveyed to Consumers Power, and Michigan Light ceased to exist.[37] It was another step in the simplification of corporate structure.[38] With it, the birth of Consumers Power was complete.

13

Growing Like Topsy

Ohne day, in the early fall of 1911, a horse and buggy rumbled into Reed City in Michigan's Osceola County, about halfway up the Lower Peninsula. Its passengers, two perfectly respectable-looking men of somewhat less than average height, alighted at King's Hotel, near the railroad-track end of Upton Street. The men were dusty and thirsty after their 15-mile ride north from Big Rapids, where they had rented the conveyance. They could just as well have taken the train all the way up to Reed City and then obtained the horse and buggy on the spot, but they figured that this might have caused some comment in that little village of fewer than seventeen hundred souls, and if there was one thing the two travelers wanted to avoid, it was being conspicuous. The less people paid attention to them, the better they liked it.

The two men, one of them slight but wiry, and the other comfortably padded around his middle and sporting a porkpie hat pushed back from his somewhat petulant face, walked into the hotel and up to its desk to register. Their handwriting was not so sure as it might have been, since both of them used false names. The one with the porkpie hat and incipient pot signed in as R. E. Smith. The stringy fellow, applying more cunning, registered as James Jules, which was, however, not nearly so farfetched an alias as one might presume since his given name was Jules anyway, and he had decided to use it so that he could be absolutely sure of paying attention when Smith addressed him by his assumed name in front of strangers.

The two men left their bags in the room they shared, splashed some water on their faces and down their parched throats; and, although it was already rather late in the afternoon, they immediately started to survey the territory—or, as it might have been called in later parlance, to case the joint.

THE SPY WHO WENT OUT IN THE HEAT

Jules Lang, who helped in the undercover canvass of Reed City, as he looked in his later years. This photograph was taken in 1955, long after his retirement. (Consumers Power photo)

"How about lending me your handkerchief, Mr. Jules?" the man in the porkpie said in his lazy Dixie drawl when they had stepped out of the hotel and back into the sun again. "With pleasure," Mr. Jules replied, and handed his partner a shredded rag that might have been white in its youth. Furtively looking up and down the street, Smith checked to see whether anyone was watching. Then he quickly tied the handkerchief to the buggy's nearest front wheel spoke. This dark deed done, the two men climbed aboard the buggy, and after some persuasion their tired horse got under way.

Following a map of the town, which Mr. Jules kept surreptitiously folded on his lap along with a piece of paper and a stubby pencil, they navigated over to Roth Street and on that modest thoroughfare continued north toward the town's mill-pond. Soon the first object of their search came into sight, George Westover's small hydro plant, which straddled a narrow millrace between the pond and the Hersey River. Feigning unconcern, the two men first crossed the Grand Rapids & Indiana railroad tracks and then the bridges over the millrace and the river and traveled about a mile up the road in their buggy before turning around again. This time, on passing the electric plant, Mr. Jules gave it and its pole line a long, hard look and rapidly jotted something down on his piece of paper. Then they followed the pole line back into town, and if anyone had looked closely, he would have noticed that both passengers' lips were moving as if the men were talking to themselves.

In a sense they were doing just that. They were watching the handkerchief and by this means were counting the revolutions of the wheel, whose circumference they had measured before arriving in Reed City. Clearly these two characters were not engaged in some second-rate caper, like a grocery store burglary or even a bank job. Theirs was evidently a much more important mission, something on the order of international espionage. They kept counting under their breath, and Jules kept scribbling and drawing little diagrams, especially when they passed the town's bigger business enterprises, like the Babcock Grain Co., J. T. Barry's Marble and Granite

Works, Theo Schmidt's farm implement establishment, and the Stoddard Bros. hardware store. When night fell, the twosome were at it again after a simple supper, this time paying particular attention and making check marks in the dark every time they passed a building from which lights shone.

There was no doubt about it—the men were spies all right. Their nefarious employer: the Hodenpyl-Foote combine. Their mission: to measure the local electric company's pole line and to count the streetlights and all the other electric lights in the community. The last of these assignments was rather challenging when it came to domestic illumination. Few homes as yet had electricity, and the few electric bulbs in private use tended to be small and dim, their feeble glow easily confused with that of gaslights or kerosene lanterns when they could not be seen directly from outside.

The purpose of this mysterious cloak-and-dagger exercise was to determine the worth of the Reed City electric property; Foote's forerunner of Consumers Power Company was looking forward to going on a shopping spree among the many, mostly run-down little municipal and privately operated plants in western Michigan. Secrecy was indicated so as not to drive up their asking price. A team of four men handled the investigations. These four were uniquely qualified, not because of any prior espionage experience, but because they'd been imported for this purpose from the Kansas City Electric Light Company and thus presumably were unknown in Michigan. The Reed City spy with the porkpie hat was R. E. Richardson, Mr. Jules's real name was Jules H. Lang, and there were two others, B. S. "Hap" Eppes and R. R. Thomson, who were at this point off on a similar job elsewhere in enemy territory.[1]

The quartet's discreet inquiries did not result in many purchases, however, since it turned out that there were more urgent demands on available investment capital at that time. Several years were to pass before Consumers Power had enough money for the acquisitions it desired. In Reed City, for instance, George Westover continued to operate his hydro plant until 1921, and then the property became a municipal plant.[2] Not until April 1, 1926, did Consumers Power's original intention here materialize. On that date, finally, and without any further secret-service work, the Reed City operation was purchased for $100,000, most of it payable on an installment plan.[3]

Reed City was but one of many acquisitions during this period. Where capital had been tight before, it was amply available now. The postwar depression had ended. The boom of the teeming twenties had begun. Stocks were going up, and their rising prices attracted hordes of new investors to corporate securities. Michigan's automobile industry spearheaded the peacetime prosperity, pouring out cars by the tens of thousands. The state's population increased from 3.7 million in 1920 to more than 4.8 million in 1930. Real estate boomed along with production and employment. So did bootlegging. Michigan, because of its convenient location, became a center for rumrunners who smuggled in their wares from Canada by boat. With the rumrunners came gangsters, including Detroit's notorious Purple Gang, but for the average citizen the gangsters were only headline entertainment, almost as exciting and not nearly so tiring as dancing the Charleston. Mr. Michigan was mostly concerned with his new car, which now had a closed body, balloon tires, shatterproof glass, and sometimes four-wheel brakes. His wife, in turn, was in love with her new appliances. The utilities business, along with the flourishing economy, had at last hit on good times. Starting in 1922, Consumers Power's earnings increased every year. The degree of prosperity varied, but the increases were never less than 9 percent, and in 1928 they went up nearly 20 percent. Even 1929, the year of the stock market crash, still produced a rise in revenues. All told, gross earnings grew from $15 million in 1922 to $33.4 million in 1929, and the company's net income rose from $4.2 million to $14.3 million over the same period.[4] Growth was the byword of the decade.

Like Reed City's electric plant, most of the properties

acquired by Consumers Power during the boom of the 1920s were relatively small. It didn't take higher mathematics to measure their pole lines—a handkerchief in wheel orbit could still have done the job: the municipal systems in St. Johns, Climax, Bronson, and Stockbridge, for instance, and privately held properties in Linden, Frankenmuth, Big Rapids, and other quiet, off-the-beaten-track communities.[5] If anything, municipal plants were a drug on the market. Small operations burned up a lot of coal in relation to the electric power they produced, and with the high price of coal their costs had become prohibitive. Some cities that formerly boasted about their municipal plants were suddenly willing to donate their systems, and in some cases even pay a bonus to get good public utility service, with its much more reasonable rates.

But there were also a number of larger, more important acquisitions. In June 1923, at a receiver's sale, Consumers Power purchased the Citizens Electric Company of Battle Creek for $701,000, adding 5,500 customers to its system with the stroke of a pen upon a check, and two years later bought the output of the Wolverine Power Company's plants on the Tittabawassee River, amounting to 10,500 kilowatts, or 32,000 megawatthours per year. Even more significant were the purchases of the Lansing Fuel and Gas Company, the Thornapple Gas and Electric Company, the Southern Michigan Light and Power Company, and the gas properties in Ionia, Charlotte, and Grand Ledge.[6]

Consumers Power's growth did not stop with buying other properties.[7] Already in 1923, foreshadowing future expansion even within its existing territory, the company closed two industrial power contracts totaling 29,000 horsepower—equal to the demands of a city of 100,000 population—and plunged into a huge building program. Construction on the 12,000-horsepower Alcona Dam project on the Au Sable, interrupted in 1917, was resumed.[8] Work also was started on the Grand Rapids steam heating plant, the 60,000-horsepower Saginaw River plant near Zilwaukee, and the neighboring Saginaw

River gas plant to service both Saginaw and Bay City. At the same time, new electric distribution lines and gas mains went in all over the company's burgeoning territory.

Nowadays when we move into a house, it's usually already hooked up to electricity or gas or both; and even if we build a new house, we simply connect it to whatever services are locally available. Such was not the case then. Utilities grew into new areas by putting in distribution systems and soliciting customers at the same time. Often different utility companies tried to expand into the same territory. Such rivalries generally ended up with one company in control and the other giving up when it couldn't sell enough customers to make the effort worthwhile. In the very early days, the competition could be quite rough. In Jackson in the 1880s, for instance, the men of the Jackson Gas Light and Fuel Company, horning in on the Jackson Gas Light Company, yanked the latter's meters right out of the cellars, tossed them out the back doors, and hooked into the service with their own mains.

By the 1920s the utilities business had become more civilized. More often than not, companies competing for new territory worked out an informal gentleman's agreement that carved up the territories between them. This was not entirely legal, of course. America's business philosophy, unlike that of most other capitalist countries, has always favored competition and opposed cartels, sometimes to the great detriment of all parties involved, including the customer. (Today this is especially apparent in the struggle of our airlines for survival; they must, under Civil Aeronautics Board regulations, compete against one another on routes that often don't offer enough passengers to go around.) No wonder, then, that natural monopoly businesses, such as utilities, frequently took matters in their own hands and worked things out pragmatically between them, for it just didn't make sense to have competing electric distribution lines or gas mains running side by side without either company's serving enough customers to make low rates economically viable, or even warrant the investment.

Side-by-side service sometimes happened, of course. In Bay City, for example, Consumers Power and the municipality still compete; in fact the city, as the result of an old agreement, has its wires strung on Consumers Power's poles. It buys the power from Consumers and, being exempt from taxation, is able to sell it to the residents at a lower rate than Consumers Power does. The only reason that Consumers Power can hang on under these circumstances is that its service is so good that many residents opt for it even though they have to pay a little more. Similarly, in the immediate environs of the old city limits of Pontiac, there is still electric competition between Detroit Edison and Consumers Power, which serves the city itself. Situations such as this are not particularly desirable; nobody enjoys them, and it was to forestall that sort of free-for-all in the area between Detroit and Pontiac that Consumers Power made one of the shrewdest moves in all its history.

What happened was that Consumers Power started pushing its gas mains out of Pontiac southeastward through Bloomfield Hills and Birmingham to Royal Oak and Ferndale. At that time Woodward Avenue was still pretty much a rural highway, with small communities strung out along it. Some increase in the population here must have been expected, but in the 1920s no one in his wildest imagination could have envisioned Detroit's phenomenal growth that followed World War II. The wish to preempt this still rather marginal territory probably was inherent in the simple instinct of all business to expand—a motivation that must have been especially strong for the men of the Pontiac division, whose main thrust had to be in gas sales, since, electrically, Detroit Edison completely surrounded the division's territory. The division was then managed by Birum G. Campbell, Sr., father of James H. Campbell, who was to serve as president of Consumers Power from 1960 until his death early in 1972, and of B. G. Campbell, Jr., now the company's personnel vice-president. The elder Campbell was a longtime gas man who had been secretary of the Jackson Gas Company and later assistant manager of the affiliate in Springfield, Illinois, before being assigned to Pontiac. He was an aggressive campaigner and an excellent promoter. He had to be, for one of his big problems was that the potential customers along Woodward Avenue were essentially Detroit-oriented people. They read the *Detroit Free Press* in the mornings and the *Detroit News* and the since defunct *Detroit Times* in the afternoons. They paid little attention to the Royal Oak paper, which was about as far as Campbell's advertising budget could go; financially it just doesn't make sense to advertise in big-circulation papers to reach only a handful of their readers. So it was largely a personal selling job to persuade the people along Woodward Avenue to stop cooking with electricity, or with oil, kerosene, or wood, and to buy the gas service instead. Campbell won them over by supplying them with gas ranges on a trial-rent basis at low cost.[9] But this was far from Campbell's major problem. He was worried about eventual competition from the Detroit Gas Company, which could work its way up Woodward Avenue just as easily as Consumers Power could work its way down. Campbell brought up this matter one day in a discussion with James A. Brown, later a vice-president of the company,[10] who was in charge of all gas operations in Michigan, and Bill Barthold, who supervised the holding company's gas interests out of the New York office. "If we are worried about Detroit Gas, then they must be worried about us too," Brown said. "I think I know how to handle that situation."

So it happened that Brown went down to the Detroit City Gas Company, where he had worked in his youth under B. C. Cobb before the latter took him along when he joined Hodenpyl-Walbridge. With his old friends there, Brown arrived at an informal agreement whereby Consumers Power and Detroit City Gas divided the territory north of Detroit between them, the demarcation line being Eight Mile Road. Apparently, Michigan Federated Utilities was in on the deal too, for the eastern boundary of Consumers Power coincided with the Macomb County line. (In 1934, the territory was extended to Lake

St. Clair.) The compact between Consumers Power and Detroit City Gas was challenged only once. It happened in the late twenties when Consumers Power Company put a gas line straight south from Pontiac to Farmington and its solicitors collided head on with salesmen from Detroit City Gas. Within a few hours after hearing about it, Brown was on his way to the Pittsburgh headquarters of one of Andrew W. Mellon's utility holding companies, which controlled Detroit City Gas.

No sooner had Brown walked into the office of the particular executive whom he had come to see than the man rose and said, "Well, Mr. Brown, I know why you have come," and reached over and unrolled a map that showed the Detroit area shaded in red and labeled "Detroit City Gas"; the area to the west and northwest shaded in green and labeled "Michigan Federated Utilities"; and all Oakland County shaded in blue and labeled "Consumers Power." "Yes, I know," the man said contritely, "I know that this agreement exists. All I can tell you is that we are sorry. You can go back to your people in Michigan and tell them that they'll not be bothered by us anymore."[11]

Indeed, Consumers Power's expansion north of Eight Mile Road continued without further interference. The marvel of it is that today this area is probably the company's single most lucrative territory for residential gas sales. With Detroit's megalopolis having solidly engulfed suburbia and swelling ever northward toward Flint, the revenues from this market constitute more than one-third of the company's gas income. Brown, Barthold, and Campbell, Sr., couldn't possibly have left a richer legacy.

What makes this territory north of Eight Mile Road so profitable for Consumers Power today is that most of the houses are heated with gas. This was, however, not the case when the company began serving the territory. The gas distributed then was manufactured gas, not the natural gas of today, and the cost of manufactured gas priced it out of the space-heating market, where it couldn't compete with coal.

The prime domestic use of gas was for cooking, and this naturally tended to limit the amount of gas that could be sold. Even a family that lived by the cheaper-by-the-dozen principle kept the burners going only a relatively small part of the time. But there was another logical use for gas on which Brown had kept an eager eye over the years—and this was automatic water heating.

Gas water heaters had been around for some time. The earliest models were installed right in the bathrooms and were lit only when a member of the family felt a sudden urge for cleanliness, a desire frequently suppressed until bathing got to be less bothersome. After houses were piped for both hot and cold water, the so-called sidearm or tank heater came into use. You went down to the basement and lit the heater, in which a gas flame flickered around a coil of water taken from an ordinary pressure tank, and after you had enough hot water for your purposes, you turned off the heater—otherwise you'd end up with boiling water all over the basement. Needless to say, once the heater was turned off and all the hot water was used, nothing but cold water came from the hot-water faucets until you got the heater going again.

Next, manufacturers came up with an instantaneous heater that had cold water running in at one end of a gas-heated coil and coming out hot at the other. This contraption's main handicap lay in the fact that the burners had to be very large to heat the flowing water, and fuel bills were impractically high as a result.[12] It was followed by storage-type heaters that had thermostats controlling the heating in insulated tanks. But these, too, were relatively expensive to operate, since the heater was going almost all the time. The reason was that when the thermostat shut off the burner, leaving only the pilot flame on, air circulation quickly cooled off the water despite the insulation of the tank.

For sixteen long years Brown kept watch on all patents and developments in the water-heater field, hoping that eventually something would turn up that showed real promise. Finally he had enough. The way manufacturers were going about the problem would evidently never result in a product of such steady but low gas consumption that it would pay the home-owner to install one and a utility company to fuel it. "If we want a heater that will get us any business," Brown told B. C. Cobb, "we'll have to design it ourselves." Cobb said: "Go to it."

This Brown did. He went to William J. Handley, Sr., who had been with the gas company in Jackson for twenty-four years and, together with Campbell, Sr., had been heavily involved in water-heater testing during much of that time. Brown and Handley put their heads together and came up with such a simple, logical design that it is surprising no one had thought of it before. It was a combination of a tank of excellent insula-tion to retain heat in the stored water, a low-consumption burner, and a pilot light powerful enough so that it could do its share of water heating when the burner was turned off. A long flue resulted in minimum waste of burner heat. This in turn improved venting. The burner could be of such low capacity that it used no more gas than the old-fashioned gas jets that were formerly employed for lighting. Between the improved vent and the heater's U-tube construction, the reverse flow of cool air was kept at a minimum when the burner was turned off—and this alone did away with the key problem of other water heaters.

Brown tried to get one manufacturer after another to pro-duce the U-tube heater, but not a single one was interested. None of them believed that there would be enough of a market. Brown went back to Cobb. "What would you say if we went into the water-heater business ourselves?" he suggested. Again Cobb gave him the go-ahead.

So Brown and Handley first built half a dozen, then a hundred, and then another hundred. In November 1926, the Handley-Brown Heater Company was launched, and Handley resigned from his position as superintendent of gas distribution in the Jackson district to devote full time to managing the new concern.[13] Within the first year of its operation, more water

HOTTEST CAR ON THE ROAD

Here's how R. N. Woodman, star salesman of Consumers Power's Pontiac district, fixed up his buggy in 1927 to promote the new gas water heater developed by Brown and Handley. (Photo by Welch Studio for Consumers Power Company)

heaters were sold than had been marketed by Consumers Power in all the previous years. Not only Consumers Power but also other utility companies soon began ordering the heaters for resale to their customers. Most important, however, was the fact that Consumers Power could now deliver more gas around the clock. Consumers Power's customers were cleaning up, and so, as a result, was the company.

In the first six months of 1927, the Pontiac district alone sold 449 Handley-Brown heaters, nearly 75 percent of its quota for the year.[14] Locally called the "Consumers Special Gas Water Heater," the appliance was advertised on spare-tire covers of employees' personal cars, and the division's star salesman, R. N. Woodman, ballyhooed it by mounting a platform over the rear bumper of his automobile on which the heater was displayed. An electric appliance campaign was also under way. In Kalamazoo, ingenious Harry Bell operated a truck equipped

THESE LADIES SOLD ELECTRIC COOKING

Home service demonstrations like this were sponsored by Consumers Power throughout its electric service territory. (Consumers Power photo)

as a repair shop and traveling store that was stocked with light bulbs,[15] toasters, flatirons, curling irons, and the like.[16]

Merchandising took on a modern look. In Jackson, the sales department had established a "Home Economy Bureau" in 1920, with a pleasant and pretty lady in charge. Maude Mercer's duties consisted of demonstrating appliances and assisting at social events of all kinds. By October 1926, Miss Mercer, now called Jackson's "Girl in White," went on the air over WIBJ, the city's Capital Theater Broadcasting Station, with a daily radio show, "Tonight's Dinner." Radio was still fairly new then, and Consumers Power made the most of its half-hour program by airing homey employee relations along with Miss Mercer's cookery: from time to time the Consumers Power Employee Quartet, the Men's Glee Club, and the Girls' Glee Club were featured on the show.[17] The idea of the home-economics approach to appliance selling soon spread to Grand Rapids. Here, Mrs. Dorothy Swift, a graduate of the Battle Creek College of Home Economics, ran an "ideal electric kitchen," which was advertised as having "all the efficiency of high-power office equipment." *The Au Sable News* reported: "You switch on the heat, switch on the ice machine, and the kitchen cabinet is as thoroughly equipped as the modern office desk."[18] This was probably a slight exaggeration, not at all an unusual device in sales promotion, then or now. The picture, worth at least 1,000 words, which accompanied the item, showed a white sink and drainboard in the open, supported by a single leg; the range, a high-oven affair on tall legs; a huge white refrigerator; and a kitchen table, looking somewhat lost in all this mechanical affluence.

Consumers Power also operated an "inspection of customers' premises" service whose fieldmen visited homes to show people the tricks of technological living and to make repairs and adjustments on their new and often mysterious appliances. Sales promotion went far beyond the housewifely domain, however. Specialists in gas, power, and lighting engineering called on industrial customers to help them utilize Consumers Power's services more efficiently, i.e., reduce their monthly utility bills. This may sound like cutting your own throat, but big bills are just as bad for a company furnishing energy as they are for the customers who have to pay them. Under B. C. Cobb's presidency the sales promotion department's primary task became to promote satisfied customers.[19] Not surprisingly, there were more and more of them each year. In 1921 the company's gas customers had numbered 60,291. By 1929 they totaled 162,590. Over the same years the number of electric customers increased from 130,421 to 296,036.[20]

This near tripling—and more than doubling—of Consumers Power's customers would not have been possible, of course, without concomitant advances in technology. The company's new plants, both electric[21] and gas,[22] incorporated all the latest improvements, while existing installations were brought similarly up to date. Production thus became ever more efficient and economical, enabling the company to supply an ever-larger audience at increasingly reasonable rates.

In the gas plants, for instance, coal gas and water gas were now nearly always made side by side. It will be recalled from an earlier chapter that the process of making water gas could be started up and shut down almost at a moment's notice; however, water gas was more expensive per cubic foot than coal gas. The latter, on the other hand, while cheaper, had to be produced around the clock since once the coal ovens cooled down, it took a long time to start them up again. The side-by-side operation helped solve one of the utility industry's most challenging problems: how to meet constantly fluctuating demands without overproducing at any given time. Enough coal gas was manufactured all day and all night to fill the anticipated average "base-load" requirements, and at those special times of the day when the demand went up, such as when everybody was home cooking supper, water-gas production was cut in to meet the "peak load." Then, when the peak was over, the water gas was shut down again. One reason why coal gas was

THE LATEST (1925) IN GAS PLANTS

Among the technological improvements in gas manufacturing were Koppers oven batteries like this one at the Jackson gas plant. These new ovens did not have to be stoked by hand and incorporated other automatic devices that made operations more efficient. (Consumers Power photo)

cheaper was that its by-products, like tar, ammonia, and especially coke, could be sold. This reduced the overhead.

Sometimes, of course, parts of the coal-gas process had to
be shut down for necessary maintenance. One of the chemicals
that is burned out of coal as it becomes coke is sulfur, and if
too much of the sulfur sneaked into the gas mains, the customers got yellow—or, worse yet, reddish—flames, which
meant that the gas was not heating efficiently. To remove the
sulfur, coal gas was run through wood chips mixed with iron
oxide. The wood shavings acted merely as a cushion, but the
iron oxide grabbed onto the sulfur and retained it. After some
time, the oxide became so sulfur-saturated that it couldn't
hold any more, and then the contents of these filter boxes had
to be changed. They were, of course, full of gas. Men could

NO MORE SKITTERING FROM VALVE TO VALVE

*Men who ran the early water-gas machinery had to rush from valve to
valve all over the skiddy operating floor. New equipment developed in
the late 1920s concentrated controls in consoles (foreground). This picture
shows installation in Royal Oak in 1932. (Consumers Power photo)*

work in them for only short periods of time, and then they had to go out for air. They could have used gas masks, but most everybody figured that this was too clumsy. So the gas men settled for headaches and let it go at that. Their jobs, altogether, were a lot more dirty and hazardous than those of the electric men—provided that the electric men had learned not to be grounded while touching hot wire.

Not that the electric men didn't have their own headaches. But these were not of the toxic kind. Electric headaches came, as they still do today, from power failures which interrupted the supply to substations that distributed the electricity. The major causes of disruptions have been the same throughout the history of this utility: equipment failure, mechanical interference, planned interruptions for construction and maintenance work, accidents (like out-of-control automobiles bowling over poles), and, of course, bad weather—lightning, wind, and sleet. New technology reduced equipment failure considerably. By 1924, Consumers Power's electric service was 99.7 percent reliable; out of every average 100 hours, the juice was off for only 1.8 minutes, or about three hours per year. To cut this down even further, duplicate lines and apparatus were slowly being installed so that maintenance work could be done without killing circuits; it is hardly more pleasant for a customer to have his electricity shut off when he knows about it in advance than when it happens suddenly as the result of a storm. It was, however, in the area of atmospheric disturbances that some of the most important advances took place.

Lightning had been a bugaboo since the very first day of electric transmission. Dr. Steinmetz, the electrical wizard from Schenectady in the Foote days, already had been concerned with this problem. Now another General Electric man was following in Steinmetz's footsteps. His name was K. B. McEachron. In 1928, McEachron had just devised the world's first million-volt artificial lightning generator and was looking for a transmission line to try it out on. At a convention that year he met Grover Hemstreet, of Consumers Power's transmission department, and was in turn introduced to William W. Tefft, W. A. Foote's son-in-law, who had succeeded J. B. Foote as the company's chief engineer on the latter's death in 1924.[23] "I think we've got just what you're looking for," Tefft told him. "What would you say to a 100,000-volt line that's 50 miles long?"

"I'd say great," McEachron replied enthusiastically, but with a certain amount of skepticism. "How can you possibly afford to take a line like that out of service?"

Tefft explained to him that Foote's original high-tension line from Croton to Grand Rapids had been paralleled in the meantime by two other lines and that during the anticipated changeover of the company's western division from 30 to 60 cycles, the old line wouldn't be used very much. Most of the older systems were on 30 cycles because this was closer to the requirements of electric railways; also, there was less voltage loss in transmission over great distances. But at the receiving end, 60 cycles was cheaper for the customer and more efficient —with the old 30, one could actually see a flicker in the shadow of a bulb. The changeover would be costly; among the many problems was that all the customers' motors had to be rewired at the company's expense. This and other considerations had already delayed the inevitable switch for some years. But now the company was ready to have a go at it.[24] "Just bring your lightning generator to Michigan," Tefft said, "and you can have our Croton line." McEachron didn't hesitate for even a second. "It's a deal," he said, and happily shook Bill Tefft's outstretched hand.

A few months later, in the spring of 1929, McEachron's infernal machine, somewhat resembling the military rocket launchers of a later day, arrived at Croton on its truck chassis. McEachron, who in a manner of speaking was after striking results, got them. He fired his million volts at the old transmission line again and again and found that most of the earlier ideas about the behavior of lightning were wrong. True, artificial lightning is more predictable than the natural variety, but the Croton experiments were conclusive enough to lead to a number of effective protection devices that are still in use today. For instance, everybody had believed transmission towers to be grounded just because they had four steel legs sticking into the earth, or maybe a big metal anchor shaped like a basket. Not so: lightning, snubbing these lures, kept right on traveling over the electric line, and when it reached transformers, they blew. McEachron found that it was necessary in some places—especially in the dry, sandy soil of western Michigan—to drive ground rods as much as 100 feet into the earth to reach a moisture level sufficient to act as a ground. Sometimes even that wasn't deep down enough, and a counterpoise wire had to be buried parallel with the line.[25] These improvements and others eventually reduced lightning-caused

McEACHRON'S INFERNAL MACHINE

K. B. McEachron, of General Electric, brought this artificial lightning generator to Croton in 1929. His million-volt experiments contributed greatly to the knowledge of lightning behavior and new grounding methods. The transmission tower is the "windmill" model then in widespread use. (Consumers Power photo)

outages from about thirty per year per 100 miles of line to only about three or four. Consumers Power had taken another important step forward in its drive for more efficient service.

Indeed, in the Twenties, there seemed to be no end to all the good things that the morrow would bring. Few men retain their twenty-twenty vision in such times. Optimism is the ectoplasm of prosperity—its alter ego, its parent and nursemaid, its child and ultimately its executioner. The progression of symptoms is familiar even to Monday-morning quarterbacks. Expansion starts at the conjunction of hope and opportunity. Later, even as opportunity fades, hope hardens into certainty, Phantasmagoria vary with the times: a chicken in every pot, color TV in every home, no work and all play, plants that triple productivity to serve markets as yet unborn—take your pick. No doubt some promising young economist will come along sooner or later and develop a business-cycle chart based on the number of dreams per square head.

One of these dreams, as the fanciful Twenties roared toward the terrible Thirties, was "superpower." Electricity, so the dream went, was to be produced at giant hydroelectric installations or at mine heads right next to the coal to be burned. The generated power then could be transmitted many hundreds of miles, even thousands of miles, to population centers. Basically, it was a grandiose enlargement of Foote's early idea when he started building dams on Michigan's northern rivers. Imaginative writers, and even some utility people who should have known better, went wild about the concept. What these good people forgot completely was that with increasing distances, transmission becomes prohibitively expensive. The dreamers also forgot that steam plants require not only coal but also tremendous quantities of water, for coal only heats the water, and it's water turned to steam that runs the turbines. Even greater quantities of water are then used to cool the condensers that convert the steam back to water for reuse.

Often steam plants need more water than the cities they supply, and there are few mines, if any, with that much water next door. Consumers Power wasted no time on this fantasy. B. C. Cobb, at the helm, was a level-headed man, and he quickly squelched the superpower nonsense. Instead he envisioned another form of cross-country transmission: the tying together of separately owned electric systems so that they could help one another out when emergencies arose. Being a cautious realist rather than a helter-skelter visionary, he foresaw the power grids which now cover the country and without which blackouts and brownouts would be a far greater threat today.

Cobb didn't get very far with his idea, but he made a good start. A 32-mile-long 132,000-volt line was built to link Consumers Power with Detroit Edison between Jackson and Ypsilanti.[26] The switches to snychronize the two independent systems were thrown on February 23, 1928. Some fanfare celebrated the event, but it didn't get nearly as much publicity as many other happenings of considerably less importance.

Cobb was a realist, too, when it came to investor ownership. Already in 1926, he had warned an overenthusiastic assembly of executives and salespeople that while the company's stocks were "sound and well seasoned," they must never be called safe.[27] With uncanny foresight he injected an even stronger note of caution into his 1929 New Year's greeting to the staff: "Let's not make any promises," he said, "for promises are sometimes broken. . . ." If these precise words don't exactly indicate pessimism, the general tone of his message certainly did.[28] Sure enough, nine months later the stock market collapsed.

Yet Cobb was not totally adverse to the trimmings of prosperity. Perhaps our young economist, busy on business-cycle theories, could make a case that depressions are heralded by the construction of imposing office buildings on the part of heretofore conservative firms. Consumers Power, financially glowing, was no exception. On July 13, 1927, under threatening skies, a new eleven-story general office building on Jackson's West Michigan avenue was dedicated amidst a cacophony of firecrackers and "The Star Spangled Banner"—the same building that was renovated almost to the point of reconstruction just before the 1970 recession. However, before the fire-crackers got cracking for the grand opening, the building was kept in darkness and the leaden clouds heightened the gloom. Assembled employees and honored guests stumbled over the furniture and one another. At last the magic moment came. C. W. Tippy, the genial general manager, struck a pre-repeal bottle against the granite arch of the doorway. The pre-repeal champagne bottle, as Tippy carefully explained, contained water from the thirteen Michigan rivers on which Consumers Power operated its generating plants. Then Clark W. Brown, the mayor, pulled one of the switches so amply available in the utility business, and floor by floor the building burst into light, whereupon the dignitaries quit bumping into one another. A thunderstorm broke soon afterward.

The new general office building, blessed with barely two more years of prosperity in that particular cycle, was not a white elephant, however. The blossoming company's headquarters had been housed in a growing group of makeshift buildings where it was often necessary to walk through someone else's private office before reaching one's own. The new building was necessary, all right, not only for efficiency, but also for employee morale. Not that employees had fared poorly during these good years; employees almost everywhere benefited from the prosperity, and those of Consumers Power probably more than most. The company had introduced a pioneer group insurance plan in 1923; it paid reasonable wages; and its personnel and instruction department, under Harry Burton, concerned itself with a gamut of activities that were quite advanced for that time, from accident prevention and health promotion to social and athletic programs. The department even ran a library service and sponsored Boy Scout troops. Consumers Power's two Jackson employee organizations, the men's Good Fellowship Club and the women's Commonwealth Club, built a recreation center on Clark Lake, south of the city, which is still in use today. Lest all this sound too paternal for today's mood, we must consider that until not so long ago most

THE OLD

W. A. Foote's Commonwealth Power headquarters in Jackson, already located at the corner of Hayes and Michigan, as it looked circa 1910. (Consumers Power collection)

AND THE NEW

Speakers-platform guests at the 1927 dedication of the new general office building of Consumers Power Company (right) included, above from left, Mrs. W. A. Foote, C. W. Tippy, William W. Tefft, E. J. Bechtel, Clark W. Brown, Howard Pett, H. G. Beebe, and D. T. McKone. The dedication attracted a big crowd (left) despite the threatening weather. The general office building has since undergone a major face-lifting in modern architectural style. (Photos by R. J. Gusenbar (above and left) and Consumers Power (right))

CONSUMERS POWER CO.

CONSUMERS POWER
COMPANY BUILDING

people who worked for a company really felt they were a part of it. This attitude benefited employers of course, and there is no doubt that some of them took unfair advantage of the loyalty so freely and conscientiously given. But in some measure the employees must have benefited also, for by all accounts they seemed to be generally happier than most wage earners are today. This is no mean consideration, for with so many waking hours spent at work, life can be mighty sad for those whose only purpose is the paycheck.

The bosses were different too. With but a few exceptions they were paternal autocrats, self-styled fathers of their corporate families. A small minority, like Consumers Power's Tippy, were "democratic," or, as the more current saying goes, "real people." Some were more fatherly than autocratic; Hodenpyl— whom everybody referred to as "Father Anton"—belonged to that delightful group. Yet others were just plain mean. And then there were some who were hard to figure out, embodiments (some real, some fanciful) of the cliché of the man of iron with the heart of gold.

B. C. Cobb was one of these. For real? No one can say. Outwardly he was a tyrant. It's not unreasonable to suppose that behind his back he was called an SOB more often than any other man in the company. One of his early inspection trips, his first to Battle Creek, set the standard for the years to follow. His reputation as a stickler for order and cleanliness had preceded him. So had rumors of his peremptory manner. Everybody was sprucing up and shaking in his boots. Only the cleaning woman, busily scrubbing and polishing, kept her perspective. "Who is that Mr. Cobb, anyhow?" she asked of no one in particular. "You'd think it was the second coming of Jesus." But underneath Cobb's hard, glossy, immaculately groomed exterior, there did seem to hide a gentle self. It didn't sneak out very often. Maybe he figured he had no time for that. In fifteen hectic years he had first shored up Consumers Power against the pressures of war and postwar recession and then built the company into one of the nation's leading utilities. More than that, he ran the whole Commonwealth Power holding-company complex, which grew under his leadership until it controlled the utilities in a sizable portion of the Eastern United States—and he did all this without ever soiling his beautifully manicured hands on the sleazy opportunities for manipulation that holding-company management offered.

The record shows that Cobb was slender and of medium height, no more than 5 feet 9 inches. Yet all the men alive who knew him remember him as being tall—tall and impressive. Such was his personality. Good thing it was, too, for the company, for suddenly the Roaring Twenties went out with a bang and a whimper. Well-dressed men tried selling apples at street corners; jobless veterans marched on Washington; Samuel Insull's utility holding empire collapsed out in Chicago, leaving its investors penniless; and Presidential candidate Franklin Delano Roosevelt promised to "get" all the "Insulls." As every schoolboy used to know, FDR assumed office in 1932. As utility men knew even better, it wasn't long after that before the New Deal adopted the Socialist Party stance on utilities and declared war against them.

14

King Cobb

In Birmingham, Alabama, one day in 1928, a public utilities executive by the name of Thomas W. Martin sat in his comfortable office and contemplated a chart mounted on the wall next to his desk. So far it had not been too busy a morning for him, and as he often did in his spare moments, Martin took pleasure in surveying his domain. He was president of Southeastern Power & Light Company, and the chart diagramed his company's network, which covered not only Alabama but also Mississippi, Georgia, and part of Florida. Martin relished the feeling of being chief of such an important organization.

Suddenly the phone rang, rudely interrupting his reveries. With his feet still propped on the desk and leaning back in his swivel chair, Martin picked up the receiver.

"There's a person-to-person call for you from a Mr. Cobb in New York," his secretary said.

Martin had met Cobb, of course, but knew him only slightly, through such contacts as the get-togethers of professional associations offered. Cobb, on the other hand, knew much about Martin; he had, in fact, devoted considerable thought to him over these past few months, and by now he knew just about all there was to know about Martin and his company. Cobb's conclusion was that Martin was a very competent man and that he ran a fine show.

"By all means," Martin told his secretary. "Please put him on." There was a click on the line, and then Cobb's high, nasal voice came over the wire. "Hello," he said. "This is B. C. Cobb," and without any further preliminary conversation Cobb immediately came to the point: "Mr. Martin, I want you in my office Friday morning at eight. I just acquired control of your company."

Martin kept his cool. He quickly reviewed the railroad schedules in his mind. "Let's make it nine-thirty," he suggested. "That's fine," Cobb said. "See you then. Goodbye." And he hung up.[1]

The sudden news of the take-over must have come as a considerable shock to Martin. He didn't have any idea that Cobb had been amassing Southeastern's shares by picking them up in the open market. Southeastern had no stock transfer agent in New York, and word of the transactions had never reached Birmingham. It goes without saying that Cobb did not buy control of Martin's company for himself, or even in his capacity as president of Consumers Power. When Cobb had ordered his agents to raid the Alabama company, he had done so wearing another of his many hats—that of president of The Commonwealth Power Corporation, the parent holding company which controlled Consumers Power.

Since that day in 1910 when Hodenpyl-Walbridge had organized Commonwealth Power Railway & Light, their holding company had burgeoned with the times and become ever more complex. Commonwealth Power Railway & Light originally brought together various gas, electric, and traction properties in Michigan, Indiana, and Illinois. It functioned basically as an investment trust in that it combined the earnings of these properties and thus presented a financial situation attractive to investors. In addition, it acted as a service company, providing engineering and construction assistance to its properties. Meanwhile, Hodenpyl-Walbridge (later Hodenpyl-Hardy) exercised the management functions and, in conjunction with E. W. Clark & Co., the Philadelphia investment house, concerned itself with the raising of capital.[2]

One of Commonwealth's early problems was that the traction business went sour. Jitney competition began cutting into the profits of electric railways, and with the rapid proliferation of automobiles and buses in the early 1920s, the handwriting was on the wall; still, as is the way of business, attempts were made to stave off the inevitable. Following the principle that "if you can't lick 'em, join 'em," Cobb asked John Collins, who was in charge of the traction lines, to try out bus operations. This was a difficult idea to swallow for an old-timer like Collins who had grown up with streetcars and interurbans. Collins resisted as much as anyone could resist Cobb, but in the end he agreed to buy one bus.

When the vehicle, a Reo Speed Wagon, was delivered, everybody stood around and gaped. Not because it was a gasoline-driven autobus—such conveyances were all too familiar to traction people by that time—but because no one had ever seen one like it before: the bus came equipped with a cowcatcher, just as if it had been an electric interurban. That's how Collins had ordered it; evidently the traction mentality could not be reconciled with the bus business.

Cobb, who had been appointed the chief operating officer of Commonwealth Power Railway & Light at the same time that he took on the presidency of Consumers Power, soon decided that it was folly for the holding company to continue to advance funds to its faltering traction properties.[3] A plan to drop the traction lines took shape, and in January 1924 an offer was made to the stockholders of Commonwealth Power Railway & Light to exchange their securities for those of two new companies, the Commonwealth Power Corporation and the Electric Railway Securities Company. As their respective names suggest, Commonwealth Power assumed the utility properties, and Electric Railway Securities took over the transportation companies, the latter for the sole purpose of their liquidation.[4] Thus divested of its increasingly doubtful rail operations, Commonwealth showed mounting profits, further enhancing Cobb's renown as one of the country's most astute utility executives.

Cobb's acquisition of Southeastern, whether Martin enjoyed it or not, was not Commonwealth's first venture south of the Mason-Dixon line. Indeed it had been Cobb's outstanding reputation that had brought into Commonwealth Power its first Southern property several years earlier—a property destined to play a crucial role in the history not only of the holding company and Consumers Power but also of the whole American utilities industry. This Southern company was The Tennessee Electric Power Company, which generated its electricity at Hales Bar Dam on the Tennessee River near Chattanooga. This company owned the distribution systems in Chattanooga and large parts of the state, and in addition, as subsidiaries, it controlled the Nashville Railway & Light Company, the Toccoa Power Company, and the Lookout Inclined Railway and Lookout Mountain Railway Companies on lovely, tourist-famous Lookout Mountain at the corner of the states of Tennessee and Georgia.

It was this Tennessee Electric Power Company which would become the direct target of Roosevelt's attack on privately owned public utilities; it was here, in this company's territory, that the federal government's Tennessee Valley Authority would spell the doom of the utilities complex Hodenpyl and his associates had built. But in 1922, when Tennessee Electric Power began its liaison with Commonwealth, Roosevelt was not yet even a gleam in the eye of the Democratic National Committee; only two years earlier, as running mate on the James M. Cox ticket, the young former assistant secretary of the Navy had incurred a stunning defeat by the Warren Harding–Calvin

Coolidge team and at this moment was recovering at Warm Springs, Georgia, from a poliomyelitis attack he had suffered the previous summer. In the whole country at that time there were perhaps at most a handful of men who understood, beyond the point of parlor speculation, that America's old order would soon yield to a new one, and it is doubtful that among these few even a single one could have put his finger on Tennessee as one of the major battlegrounds in the coming conflict, let alone on FDR as the new order's standard-bearer. In 1922, with the postwar recession fading rapidly, the future held nothing but promise for utilities, as indeed it did for all sound businesses. The men who controlled Hales Bar Dam on the Tennessee River, eager to participate to the fullest in the millennium, approached Hodenpyl-Hardy with an offer to become part of the Commonwealth group—but only on one condition, namely, that B. C. Cobb take over the reins as chief executive in Tennessee, just as he was Consumers Power's indomitable boss in Michigan. An agreement soon was reached. For the first three years of the arrangement, Cobb, assisted by various Hodenpyl-Hardy experts, would operate the Tennessee company as a separate entity; then, in 1925, it would become a full-fledged subsidiary of Commonwealth Power Corporation.[5]

Thus by the late twenties, with Tennessee's voluntary enlistment and Southeastern's forced draft, Cobb's kingdom stretched from the Great Lakes to the Gulf of Mexico. Its properties operated in the states of Michigan, Illinois, Ohio, Indiana, Tennessee, Alabama, Georgia, Mississippi, and Florida.[6] Its services encompassed factories and homes in the industrial North, the farm-center communities of the Ohio Valley, the growing cities of the mountain South, and the awakening cracker country. It was a giant complex—and further complexities were yet to follow.

Bernard Capen Cobb ran the whole show out of his New York headquarters on Wall Street (later moved to Pine Street), and he did so with an iron hand. His was by no means an

THE IMPECCABLE B. C. COBB

At the height of his career as president of Consumers Power and chairman of the board of Commonwealth & Southern Corporation, this irascible but softhearted tyrant had an eagle eye that recorded every detail and overlooked no trespasses. He was respected by all, feared by many, and loved by those who knew him best. (Photo by Blank-Stoller)

absentee rule. He visited all the properties at least once a year, and as president of Consumers Power he came to Michigan more often than that.

One might wonder how a man can run any company, let alone a bunch of big ones, without keeping on top of everything personally, at all times. This is a mistaken notion. The bigger a business, the more power is delegated; only the most impor-

AS IT MUST TO ALL MEN . . .

Still ramrod-straight and elegant as he neared his seventy-ninth birthday, B. C. Cobb attended the 1949 dedication of the big steam plant near Muskegon named in his honor. Standing at his side is W. M. Lewis, who had retired two years earlier as Muskegon division manager. A few minutes later, Cobb burst into tears. (Consumers Power photo)

tant decisions are made at the apex of the pyramid. Obviously no chief executive can be bothered with all the day-to-day details of operations. Cobb couldn't be either, but there was a big difference between him and the average run of corporate boss, for he had the unusual capacity to concern himself with petty details without ever losing sight of the big picture. His memory for the picayune was so phenomenal, in fact, that it

251

caused more than a little apprehension whenever he visited one of the properties.

There was the day, for instance, when on one of his inspection trips to Consumers Power, Cobb spotted a bullet-riddled "Danger—High Voltage—Keep Away" sign on a transmission tower near Grand Rapids. Someone had used the sign for target practice, a not uncommon sport even before the advent of the generation gap.

"Make sure that this sign gets changed," Cobb told Tippy, his Michigan right-hand man. Tippy, his mind on more important matters, promptly forgot about it. One year later, on the next system-wide inspection trip, Cobb made it a special point to return for a look at the violated transmission tower. Sure enough, the sign had not been replaced.

"Still the same five bullet holes," Cobb snarled, his voice more than ever squeezing out of the corner of his mouth. "I told you to change that damn sign." And he proceeded to chew out his general manager in front of everybody. Was Cobb a monstrous despot? Perhaps. But then, perhaps not. When Tippy died in 1933, Cobb bawled like a baby, again in front of everybody.[7]

Cobb was no less detail-minded on his visits to the other properties. At a steam generating plant of The Ohio Edison Company he once stumbled over a warped threshold. The following year, erect and elegant, Cobb promptly strutted right back to the same door to check what had been done about the hurdle. Luckily for Ohio's general manager, the threshold had been replaced.

Cobb's visits were like military inspections. He ran his fingers over windowsills to see whether there was dust—all he lacked was the white glove. He led his inspection parades as a colonel would. The property's general manager marched behind him like a trusted major, and lesser officers trotted behind the general manager. Thus Cobb stormed one day into the office of Howard Pett, then Consumers Power's Jackson district manager. Pett's desk was piled high with papers, scattered every which way. Cobb halted abruptly, turned back to Tippy, and barked: "Charley, who lives here?" Tippy reluctantly told him. Cobb shook his head as if he couldn't believe the mess he saw. "This is a helluva way to keep house," he said, and with that he stepped up to the littered desk and swept everything onto the floor. "Tell that district manager of yours," he instructed Tippy, "that a man can work on only one piece of paper at one time."

The Michigan crew eventually resigned itself to Cobb's passion for neatness, to his eagle eye that spotted eggshells after an incautious lunch. The men even got a kick out of it. One of their favorite jokes was to twist pictures out of position on the walls before Cobb's visits; it was predictable that he would stop whatever he was doing, walk right over, and straighten things up. Naturally there were many apocryphal stories about him; a man like that generates his own legends. One of these tales had Cobb, annoyed because a member of his executive staff was always late for meetings, walk up to the culprit and demand his watch. Cobb then was supposed to have taken the watch and thrown it out the window with the remark, "Better get yourself a new one that keeps proper time." But it's doubtful that this ever happened. Cobb had too much respect for private property.

Some of the shrewder judges of human nature among the Consumers Power employees did not let Cobbism get to them. They were aware that the man's bluster was only skin-deep. Where others quaked, they did not hesitate to speak up, sensing instinctively that Cobb had tremendous respect for anybody who knew his own mind and stood up for it—provided that there was something in that mind.

One night, Frank Gavian, the superintendent at Saginaw, was sitting at his desk making up the payroll. Suddenly Cobb, beetle-browed and frowning, walked in through Gavian's open office door. "Frank," he said, "I don't want you to waste your time on this. Why don't you get some clerk to do it?" Without looking up Gavian replied: "Because you're too goddamn tight." Cobb simply turned around and walked out the door. He knew better than to oppose a good argument.[8] Even secretaries, who were still pretty low on the totem pole in those days, could get away with back talk if they had the guts. Once when Cobb was dictating a letter to his sister, who was about to undergo a thyroid operation, he patronizingly asked a secretary whether she really knew how to spell "thyroid". "If I don't, Mr. Cobb," the lady blazed at him, "that's what I've got my dictionary for." He looked at her as if to say, "Why you little whippersnapper," but then he couldn't help smiling, and he never challenged her spelling again.[9]

A man's character is much like an intricate mosaic: without the seemingly most unimportant pieces, the picture is often so incomplete as to be incomprehensible. For this reason, Cobb's relationship to a young boy, the son of an old friend, is more revealing of the man's depth than any number of his important business decisions. The boy was Claude Mulligan, son of a Canadian physician who had owned some land on Bras Coupe Lake in Quebec, north of Ottawa. Dr. Edward A. Mulligan sold the place to a gentleman by the name of Charles Hazen, who was connected with the magazine *Field and Stream*. Hazen then got together a group of successful men from New York and Philadelphia to form a fishing and hunting club. The nearest train stop was Maniwaki; here the members (having paid $1,000 for the privilege of belonging, a bargain by today's country-club standards) hired horses and rode the last 20 miles into the wilderness. Eventually a road was built that took them almost all the way in by car. As it happened, Bras Coupe—so named after a one-armed French trapper who had once lived at the lake—became a sort of unofficial vacation headquarters of Cobb's companies. Many of the top executives belonged, as did a number of men on their way up. Cobb came for at least two weeks every year, often for four. Dr. Mulligan had kept his own cottage even though he'd sold the property, and whenever Cobb felt like going trolling, he ambled over to the Mulligan cottage and informed the doctor's son that such was his intention. "You're going fishing with me today," he'd tell the boy. Cobb never asked; he always ordered.

The years passed, and the Mulligan lad grew into a young man of considerable self-assurance. A clash was bound to come, and it did. One night at the clubhouse, Cobb, in one of his crustier moods and being a rather chauvinistic Yankee, had some unkind things to say about Canadian sportsmanship as opposed to the United States variety. Eighteen-year-old Mulligan, of course, was a Canadian; he didn't like Cobb's vitriolic comments, and said so. Cobb persisted. Finally Claude Mulligan had enough. He walked out on Cobb, letting the screen door slam shut behind him. They did not go fishing again together that year. The following summer, Cobb and Mulligan bumped into each other at an outfitter's place in Maniwaki. The youngster politely greeted Cobb, as he had been brought up to do, but kept his distance. Cobb, however, came over to the young man and took him by his lapels.

"You know," he said contritely, "The last time we were together we quarreled. I have thought about it and it was my fault, and I apologize to you." And then Cobb added with a shy smile, "When you get through college you're still going to work for me, aren't you?"

No sensitive, generous man could possibly turn his back on such an openhearted attempt to make amends, and Mulligan didn't either. He joined Consumers Power just as Cobb wished him to, worked his way up, and long after Cobb was gone culminated his career as vice-president in charge of divisions and customer service.

Cobb, who liked children but believed firmly in the old-fashioned way of raising them, in later years also took an interest in Claude Mulligan's son, Ted, and devoted much effort to teaching the young chap manners. Conversations usually went like this. Cobb: "Well, Ted, how are you?" Ted: "Very well." Cobb: "Very well, what?" Ted: "Very well, thank you." Cobb: "Very well, thank you, what?" Ted: "Very well, thank you, sir." And Cobb would nod, satisfied for the moment with his accomplishment. At a dinner at Cobb's cottage one night, Cobb asked twelve-year-old Ted whether he liked rice. Ted said: "No." Cobb, as usual, prompted: "No, what?" Ted, finally catching on, said, "No sir, thank you," and Cobb growled, "Well, you're going to eat rice tonight anyway, whether you like it or not.[10]

That's how B. C. Cobb ran his company, too, and it stood him in good stead, for as Commonwealth Power grew, Cobb's authority as a member of the old Hodenpyl team was increasingly challenged. Rivalry and power play within the organization became pronounced with the acquisition of the Southern companies. T. W. Martin, though he had allowed Southeastern to get away from him, was an able, highly independent man. If he hadn't been, Cobb would not have kept him on after gaining control. Martin not only remained Southeastern's chief executive but also became a member of Cobb's board of Commonwealth directors. Still, Martin resented quite naturally that he and his company had been kidnapped rather than invited to Cobb's court, and although he and Cobb worked together, they never became friends. This may be quite understandable, but it created problems within the organization. For some years, indeed until Roosevelt's attack pulled them together against their common enemy, the Northern and Southern companies formed two distinct camps within the Commonwealth framework. It has been said that the two factions would hardly talk to each other unless it was absolutely necessary. Even if that is an exaggeration, a strong partisanship certainly existed, and it was vitally important that final authority rest with a man who could make it stick that one and all had to eat their rice whether they liked it or not.

The second challenge was more subtle, but at the same time

all the more serious, since it was backed by the ultimate artillery of the business world, namely, money. Just exactly how this pressure came about is impossible to reconstruct; the details are buried in the minds of men long dead. But it all seemed to have started in 1925 when Bonbright & Company, the New York investment house, became an underwriter for Consumers Power in connection with the sale of $5 million of preferred stock.[11] Then, three years later, Consumers Power's board of directors agreed to sell to Bonbright a new series of thirty-year bonds in the amount of nearly $11.5 million.[12] Nothing especially startling about this sort of thing, except that Bonbright's attorneys were the law firm of Winthrop, Stimson, Putnam & Roberts.

One of this firm's members was Edward P. Stevens, son of Ray P. Stevens, of Stevens & Wood, an engineering and construction company incorporated in Maryland and working out of offices in Youngstown, Ohio. Nothing particularly exciting about this either, except that Ray Stevens owned a substantial interest in the Penn-Ohio Edison Company, which operated a generating station on the Ohio River and served as a holding company for utility properties in the Newcastle, Pennsylvania, and Youngstown, Ohio, areas. This made Stevens a neighbor, for in nearby Akron, Ohio, there was the Northern Ohio Power & Light Company, one of the Hodenpyl-Hardy-Clark properties.[13] Now, somehow, everybody got together—quite probably because of the Stevens-Bonbright relationship—and the whole picture changed.

On May 5, 1928, Hodenpyl, Hardy & Company joined with Stevens & Wood to organize Allied Power & Light Corporation (Delaware) as a holding company for Commonwealth Power and Penn-Ohio Edison. Less than two weeks later, on May 16, Allied Power & Light (New York) was formed to supervise the operating subsidiaries.[14] Stevens & Wood was absorbed as a general engineering and construction subsidiary. Cobb found himself promoted upstairs to become chairman of the board of

Allied Power, while Ray Stevens got the job of the man on the spot: president. And, most important of all because it evidenced the shift of power, Hodenpyl-Hardy went out of business.

Anton Hodenpyl had long been retired; now it was George E. Hardy's turn. Whether Hardy was forced out or decided that the time had come for him to take it easy is an open question. Circumstantial evidence points to the former: George Hardy's son, Anton G. Hardy, who was also an officer of the company, retired from the scene along with his father. Not that George Hardy necessarily minded his retirement. In the earlier days, when his friends used to tell him that they would not retire but die with their boots on, his reply was apt to be, "I expect to die with my boots on too, but I've reached the stage where I want some say as to what boots I wear." In any case, the only boots George Hardy continued to wear in the utilities kingdom he had helped to shape were those of a member of Consumers Power's board of directors, a post he held until 1949, the year of his death.

Cobb, however, held on to the top position in the new superimposed holding-company structure, and he did have several old Hodenpyl-Hardy teammates to back him up in the second echelon. Jacob Hekma and Tim Kenney held two of the three vice-presidential spots, and Harry G. Kessler, another longtime Consumers Power hand and the company's controller, became Allied Power's controller as well.[15]

Before long, substantial holdings in Commonwealth Power, Penn-Ohio Edison, and other utility companies were shifted to Allied Power & Light (Delaware), which now sat at the apex of the pyramid. But this new company had hardly been organized when plans were afoot for further consolidations. On May 23, 1929, The Commonwealth & Southern Corporation was organized under the laws of the state of Delaware; this corporation in turn acquired sizable interests in Commonwealth Power, Southeastern Power & Light, and Penn-Ohio Edison, and eventually it absorbed all the assets and assumed all the liabilities of Allied Power & Light (Delaware).[16] The

THE BOYS OF COMMONWEALTH & SOUTHERN

Cobb's crew took time out from a meeting in Chattanooga, Tenn., about 1930, to ride to the top of Lookout Mountain aboard the C&S-owned funicular. The men are, left to right (top row), Dan Karn, S. W. Webb, Samuel Ball, Burt Laraway, G. M. Brower, Fred Hansen (a reporter for the New York Financial Chronicle)*, H. H. Koelbel, William Lewis, and F. W. Hoover; (second row) W. G. Cobb (no relation to B. C. Cobb), D. M. Mackie, J. K. Swanson, B. G. Campbell, Sr., and J. A. Cleveland; (third row) W. A. Scott, Eugene Holcomb, Jo Conn Guild, Jr., and Frank Haas (of Southern Indiana Gas & Electric); and finally at the bottom, doing their clowning best to hold up the holding company, F. A. Beard, Howard Pett, B. S. Eppes, Charles Kressler, and C. I. Weaver (of Springfield Light Heat & Power, Springfield, Ohio).* (Consumers Power collection, from F. W. Hoover)

restructuring became complete a year later, on March 29, 1930, when Commonwealth & Southern (Delaware) created Commonwealth & Southern (New York) to take over Allied Power & Light (New York)[17] in a replay of the familiar pincer maneuver of the holding-company game. Commonwealth & Southern (Delaware and New York) now ran the whole show.

What happened to King Cobb in the process? Did he follow George Hardy into honored oblivion? Let us not stretch the suspense any longer. As he would have said, "Heck no!" In the shuffle, the unsinkable B. C. Cobb ended up as chairman of the board *and* president not only of the two Commonwealth & Southern Corporations but also of the subsidiary holding company, Allied Power & Light, and in addition he was president and director of two more companies at the second level, Commonwealth Power and Penn-Ohio Edison, and a director of Martin's Southeastern Power & Light.[18] Needless to say, he also remained president of Consumers Power, the biggest revenue producer among all Commonwealth & Southern's operating companies. In 1932, according to *Poor's Registry of Directors of the United States,* he was a director of seventeen different companies; most of these, to be sure, were part of the Commonwealth & Southern group, but they also included such supergiants as American Superpower Corporation and The United Corporation, which will soon enter this narrative, as well as two grass-roots operations in his home territory of Michigan, the Bank of Saginaw and The Union and Peoples National Bank of Jackson.

It's hardly surprising that Cobb prevailed. He wasn't a man to say die, not as long as there was any breath left in his body. Many years later, when his heart gave out and he lay under an oxygen tent in a New York City hospital, the specialists gave him but a few more hours to live. All visitors except his most immediate family were barred that night; so were all hospital attendants not directly concerned with administering to his needs, and no deliveries, flowers, presents, or even newspapers were permitted.

The room was hushed except for Cobb's feeble, labored breathing. Suddenly, at about seven the next morning, Cobb's pitifully wasted arm shot out from under the oxygen tent; his hand groped on the night stand. His daughter, Alice, rushed to his side, trying to help. She heard him say in a voice so weak that it was barely audible, but gruff and crochety as ever: "Where the heck's my *New York Times?* I'm not dead yet!"[19] In fact, Cobb resisted death for another six months, and read his *New York Times* even on his last morning.

If death had a hard time subduing Cobb, the living evidently had no chance. When the stock market crashed in October 1929, Cobb was up at Bras Coupe on a vacation. He let the market crash and continued hunting.

It was precisely Cobb's relentless drive, combined with his organizing ability and infinite attention to detail, which was needed in the building of Consumers Power and Cobb's other utilities. His two obsessions were to make his companies strong in service to the people and to keep the country strong. He could not tolerate inefficiency in company operations, or in government. He could not tolerate dishonesty. He was an arch foe of socialism and all that it stood for, not because he wished ill for the people, but because he considered it unjust and inefficient. Inspector Walter Henry Thompson, of Scotland Yard, in his book *Assignment: Churchill* said, "When you work for Churchill, nothing is easy and everything is worth what it costs." The same might well have been said of Cobb. Despite his hardness, or perhaps because of it, Consumers Power probably never had a better boss.

But even strong men like Cobb cannot prevail totally on their own. They need support not only from a loyal staff below but also from some force above. Every boss has a boss. Every company has its kingmaker. In the case of Cobb and Commonwealth & Southern, and all the Hodenpyl manipulations and consolidations that led up to it, it is not unreasonable to state that the power behind the throne was old John C. Weadock.

We remember Weadock as the imposing lawyer from Bay

City, who in 1908 had brought Loud, the lumberman of the Au Sable, together with Hodenpyl-Walbridge & Company. It had been Weadock who arranged the marriage and then delivered the baby when Consumers Power was born. As attorney to the Hodenpyl interests he masterminded the growth of the holding-company structure. Now, close to seventy years old, the onetime riverboat purser who had put the bounce on drunken lumberjacks was no less impressive than he had been in his youth. The years had not bent his more than 6-foot stature; his 200-odd pounds still seemed all muscle and not flab, and the white mane crowning his massive face gave him immense dignity. Wall Street lawyer though he was, he would hold court in his office with his big feet up on his desk, coat and vest stripped off, in a dickey and shirt-sleeves, as befitted a country boy from Bay City who had made good in the big time but had never let it swell his head.

Weadock, of course, did not control the capital. He'd made his pile, to be sure, but his wasn't the kind of money it takes to manipulate vast corporations. The only explanation for his power is that he knew everything and everybody, and with this knowledge and by dint of personality he exerted tremendous influence on the affairs of Commonwealth & Southern and its predecessors. It was Weadock, by all accounts, who had picked Cobb to become president of Consumers Power when Foote died. It had been Weadock who had chosen Cobb to run the holding-company operation. It was Weadock who would bring in Wendell Willkie to take over when illness did to Cobb what no man could and subdued him. And it was still Weadock who, years later, brought in Justin R. Whiting to replace Willkie when the latter resigned to run against Roosevelt in the 1940 Presidential election.

It's interesting that the advent of the law office of Winthrop, Stimson, Putnam & Roberts did not diminish Weadock's power as a kingmaker. Starting with the Bonbright deal of 1925, this law firm took over much of the work that had been previously

handled by Weadock. But while Weadock somehow maintained his position as the power behind the throne, he was not
the power above it. The real power hovered, unseen and rarely
felt, way above Cobb and Weadock in the stratosphere of
American capitalism—the super holding companies of the
world's richest investment banking houses. And even these did
not determine the eventual fate of Commonwealth & Southern
and Consumers Power. The ultimate authority, as always, was
the tide of social change.

15

Powers Above the Throne

One of the passengers aboard the *S.S. Exilona* when she sailed into New York Harbor in May 1934, after a twenty-four-day crossing from Smyrna, Turkey, was a bent and sick old man who, despite his frailty, bore the unmistakable aura of a personage of much importance. His elegant topcoat hung loosely on his short, slight frame; a gray homburg covered his sparse white hair; his eyes, behind a pince-nez, peered out from a shrunken face whose only remaining feature of prominence was a big white walrus mustache.

The old man turned to his companion at the railing. With a nod toward the Manhattan skyline emerging from the fog, he delivered himself of one of those incisive comments which become ever more significant the longer you think about them. If two men, he said, had walked down Fifth Avenue a year ago, in May of 1933, one with a bottle of whisky in his pocket and the other jingling gold coins in his, the one with the whisky would have been considered the criminal, and the man with the gold the respectable citizen. Take the same two fellows today, the old man continued, and the man with the gold would be the criminal, and the one with the whisky would be the honest man.[1]

The septuagenarian's comment was no idle observation. He was on his way home, not as a leisured traveler after a vacation but as a prisoner of the United States government extradited from exile to face a variety of complex charges arising out of stock manipulations.

"What I did when I did it was honest," he said to his guard, for such was his companion on this voyage.

"Now, through changed conditions, what I did may or may not be called honest. Politics demand, therefore, that I be brought to trial; but what is really being brought to trial is the system I represented."[2]

The speaker was Samuel Insull, then seventy-four years old, London-born into the lowest margin of the English lower middle class, a descendant of generations of the "respectable poor," who at the pinnacle of his astounding career had been personally worth several hundred million dollars and had controlled many hundreds of millions more. As a brash young man, Insull had elbowed his way into the early electric business as Thomas Edison's indispensable private secretary. By 1889, at the age of thirty, he was one of the original directors of the newly founded Edison General Electric Company (now General Electric). Soon he was boss of Chicago Edison and built the Harrison Street central power station. But this was only the beginning. With his shrewd, self-educated mind and his gambler's lack of caution, he pyramided company upon company until he monopolized the utilities business in some five thousand communities spread over thirty-two states. The aggregate market value of his companies' securities eventually topped the $3-billion mark.

But Insull was an unregenerate individualist, and he refused to knuckle under to the New York investment bankers. Of course they got even with him. His downfall came in 1931,

SAMUEL INSULL
AFTER EXTRADITION
He still looked every inch a millionaire aboard the train that brought him to Chicago to face trial. (The Bettmann Archive, Inc.)

when, optimistic as ever, he raised funds for expansion by borrowing from his own companies, shifting paper fortunes with supreme confidence even as the country slipped into the abyss of depression. When the right moment came, J. P. Morgan's traders on the floor of the New York Stock Exchange drummed down the price of Insull securities. Insull tried to hold up the market, but no man can keep buying his own securities forever. In one week alone, the stocks of Insull's International Utilities Investment Company, his Commonwealth Edison, and his Middle West Utilities dropped by $150 million.[3] Panic selling then wiped out Insull and his stockholders.

Forced out of his collapsing companies, Insull moved to Paris to live in obscurity on a modest pension income. It was then that the politicians finished the job which the House of Morgan had begun. Democrats, from aldermen to Presidential candidate, ran for office on the Insull "scandal." Formal indictments followed, and Insull fled first to Italy and then to Greece.

The story of his extradition deserves a quick review, for it was symptomatic of the government's attitude toward utilities at that time. Not content with having collected political interest (at usurious rates) on the Insull matter, Roosevelt's administration made it a cause célèbre. When, for legal reasons, an embezzlement charge did not produce Insull's extradition from Greece, the government indicted him on charges of using the mails to defraud, and when that didn't work, they charged him with violations of the Bankruptcy Act. This held no water either, and so Washington resorted to extralegal means by putting financial pressure on Greece. Still, the Greeks refused to extradite Insull, but ordered him to leave the country.

Insull decided to charter a small vessel and safeguard his freedom by cruising the high seas. Meanwhile, pressured by the State Department, Congress passed a special bill authorizing Insull's arrest in any country where the United States enjoyed extraterritorial rights. Turkey was such a treaty nation, and when Insull's ship put in at Istanbul to take on fuel and supplies, he was arrested, and after several days' imprisonment he was delivered to the United States Embassy. The big chase was over, and justice had triumphed.

On Insull's return to the United States, he was found innocent of mail fraud. Even a jury composed of "little" people, naturally inclined to suspect security dealings, decided that the government had no case. Next, after a brief trial, Insull was acquitted on the first of several Illinois embezzlement charges, after which the state's attorney general quickly dismissed the others, recognizing that his legal footing here was no sounder than it had been before. Finally, at Insull's trial for alleged bankruptcy violations, the federal judge, after hearing the evidence, instructed the jury to bring in a verdict of not guilty.[4] And that was the end of the Insull scandal. Three years later, a man without a country, Insull fell dead while waiting for a train in the Paris subway. Nobody knows whether his wallet had been stolen, but police found only the equivalent of 8 cents in French currency on his body.

Insull's fascinating tale, from rags to riches and thence to ruin, is not told here, albeit in a sadly telegraphic version, to evoke sympathy for the utility holding-company tycoons of the

1920s. Their practices, whether at Commonwealth Edison or at Commonwealth & Southern, were certainly not always above reproach: the real world does not run on fairy stories, and only children, imbeciles, and frauds profess undying faith in shining-armor knights. It is only reasonable to suppose that Insull, just like any other man, did not always live strictly within the law, or that even if he did, then not necessarily within the yet narrower limits of total ethics. A small man's petty tricks and subterfuges are no more moral than a big man's market manipulations. No doubt Insull committed his quota of mistakes, and since he was a big man they were whoppers.

It will be recalled, for instance, that in the customer-ownership days, Insull sold shares in his holding companies rather than the operating companies; this had the unfortunate effect of separating his shareholders from the actual source of income and involved them in the lofty gambles of holding-company maneuvers. Consumers Power's Cobb did not approve of this dangerous practice and spoke out against it on several occasions, including at meetings of intra-industrial associations such as the National Electric Light Association, predecessor of today's Edison Electric Institute.[5] In fact, Cobb did not approve of Insull any more than he did of his methods, and didn't like him at all as a man. Once Cobb kept Insull cooling his heels in the outer office for more than an hour (and it took a man like Cobb to pull this on a man like Insull, and a man like Cobb to have an Insull wait for him). Insull later admitted to Cobb, when the two men met accidentally in Europe in 1932, that he probably had been wrong in the way he had exposed his shareholders to the risks of paper pyramids.

Nor is the Insull story told here because of any direct relationship to Consumers Power or Commonwealth & Southern. There was none. Insull's utility group was, in fact, one of the only three major operations in the whole country that remained independent of New York's investment banking houses, so there wasn't even any Wall Street link.[6]

Still, the Insull case exerted a tremendous influence on the fate of all utilities. The scandal broke just at a time when the public temper, rubbed raw by crash and depression, blamed capitalism for all its ills. The utilities, because of their quasi-public nature, were prime targets, and no real distinction was made between those which ran a relatively clean ship and those which didn't. As it happened, all the Hodenpyl utilities had a long-standing tradition of high business ethics. There was, for instance, an inside rumor that Walbridge had been removed because he believed that he could buy anyone, provided he paid the right price. It only stands to reason that such a rumor, whether true or false, doesn't get started in an organization where bribery and the like are taken for granted as part of the routine of doing business.

Of the three cardinal sins charged against utility holding companies, Commonwealth & Southern was certainly innocent. One of these abuses, common in the industry, was overcharging operating companies for the functions performed by the service company of the particular group. C&S warded off this evil by distributing the shares in its service company (Commonwealth & Southern of New York) to the operating companies in proportion to their gross earnings. Consumers Power, being the largest revenue producer of the group, held the largest single block, almost 24 percent of the 90,000 outstanding shares. The next largest holding (in 1930) was that of the Georgia Power Company, with slightly more than 16 percent. The result of this equitable arrangement was that if, by any chance, the operating companies of C&S were overcharged, the money eventually came back to them in their proportionate shares of dividends. Of course, in order to have this system operate successfully over a period of years, adjustments in the holdings of the operating companies were made from time to time to keep them in line with their current gross-earnings relationship to the other properties.[7]

Another holding-company sin was to arrange "upstream loans" from the operating companies, so that in effect the underlying properties financed the parent company instead of the other way around, as was supposed to be the basic purpose of the structure. Insull often raised funds in this manner, but C&S never did.

The third device for holding-company enrichment, which C&S also avoided, was the writing up of asset values, commonly called "loading the rate base," which made it possible to charge exaggerated rates to customers.[8] This was automatically against C&S principles, and for a very pragmatic reason: its operating philosophy was to have the lowest possible rates in order to attract the most customers.

But even the purest lily-white record could not have saved Commonwealth & Southern in the long run. Big as it was, with its common stockholdings in five Northern and six Southern operating companies, by 1930 it no longer occupied the apex of the power structure. In the final spasm of the holding-company period, the real power was becoming increasingly concentrated in the stratosphere of American capitalism—the super holding companies of the world's richest investment banking houses.

It had been in the early 1920s that bond houses, one by one, awoke to the fact that they could make tremendous profits out of handling utility securities—far greater profits than could be derived from actually operating them. Operating profits, it will be recalled, were limited then, as they are now, by regulatory agencies to a fair return on the investment, the fair return not being a specific percentage but just high enough so that utilities could compete with other conservative investments in the capital market. The utility bond business, however, was not limited by such considerations: a company's earnings, and therefore the rates it charged its customers, were not involved at all. Bond profits came out of underwriting charges, sales commissions, and trading profits—and here the sky was the limit.

To start with, the country's growing utilities were continually financing new expansions. There was a constant floating of new bond issues, with the national average running about 10 percent of a company's total capitalization per year. Just the initial sales of these bonds earned sizable commissions for the investment houses that handled the underwriting, but this was by far not the whole potential. Most people don't hold bonds until maturity; there is a steady turnover. Once a house was in the business of marketing a particular company's bonds, it retained the function of making a market for these bonds, i.e., maintaining a relatively stable price range by trading them on the open market. It takes a lot of capital to make a market: you've got to be able to take up the slack when securities are offered for sale and there are no buyers around within a reasonable distance of the current price. But the beauty of it is this: over a period of time you can accumulate large holdings bought at or near the bottom of the permissible price range, and at the right moment you can then sell these holdings in an up market and make a big profit. With the numerous fluctuations that take place during the life of a bond, the possibility of such trading profits is evidently enormous.

Moreover, as utilities sought to become more efficient, they were in a constant process of consolidation. Each consolidation yielded double commissions for the bond houses, one for calling in old issues, and the other for floating new ones. Both commissions were on the total capitalization — and with companies whose capitalizations were in the hundreds or even tens of millions, that really mounted up. This is where most people misunderstand business. The real money rarely has been in selling goods and services, but in the handling of money itself. This is why — and for no other reason — first the smaller bond houses and later the big Wall Street powers became interested in utilities.

At the beginning, the smaller houses created holding companies in order to acquire operating utilities. Some of them, like the Hodenpyl and Clark groups, had an advantage in that they already controlled a nucleus of operating companies. But the richest and most intrepid of the investment bankers went one step further. They didn't bother with the operating companies at all. They founded investment trusts, sold the securities of these trusts to the public (which in itself generated commissions), and then used the proceeds to buy into existing holding companies.

The first super holding company involved in the history of Consumers Power was the American Superpower Corporation, which had been organized in Delaware on October 26, 1923, primarily to acquire and hold securities in electric light and power companies.[9] Among American Superpower's early directors were in fact George E. Hardy and B. C. Cobb, but the control was in the hands of Bonbright & Company — the same New York investment firm which suddenly appeared in 1925 as the underwriter in a Consumers Power preferred stock sale and which was later instrumental in the merger with Stevens & Wood to form Allied Power & Light. Fascinating, isn't it, how the strands do form an ever-tighter web! But wait: the story isn't over yet.

By itself, American Superpower never really became more than a medium-sized investment trust. It owned substantial minority interests in a number of large electric power companies, but never achieved sufficient diversification to exert more than a nominal influence in the electric utilities business.[10] Certainly the company must have fallen far short of the expectations of its original incorporators. These men no doubt intended, by means of interlocking directorships, to dominate major segments of the industry. Now don't get the wrong idea: American Superpower was merely stopped a little short of the summit and couldn't make it the rest of the way without roping up with the most powerful pyramid climber of them all, J. P. Morgan. Not the legendary John Pierpont Morgan, of course — he had been dead since 1913 — but the House of Morgan, J. P. Morgan & Co., the investment banking firm now led by the son who bore the old man's name and had inherited his fortune and his talents.

It was in January 1929 that J. P. Morgan & Co. announced the formation of The United Corporation, whose deceptively simple appellation meant exactly what it implied. With a capitalization twenty times as great as that of U.S. Steel, United's purpose was to gain the same place in America's electric and gas utilities that American Telephone and Telegraph held in its own domain (where, incidentally, Morgan already had complete control of the bond business). Morgan didn't go it alone on United. Involved with him in this, the House of Morgan's most audacious concept—literally to unite the whole utilities industry—were Drexel & Co. and of course Bonbright & Company, with its American Superpower Corporation.[11]

If United indeed intended to become the AT&T of the power business, it did not accomplish its objective. FDR saw to that. But in the meanwhile, and with amazing speed, United "became interested," as the saying goes, in a number of major utility companies whose securities in the aggregate were valued at more than $2 billion. Among them were the United Gas Improvement Company, Niagara Hudson Power, Columbia Gas & Electric, Consolidated Gas of New York, Public Service Corp. of New Jersey, and—as you've probably guessed by now—B. C. Cobb's Commonwealth & Southern.

Not that the House of Morgan dominated Commonwealth & Southern in any day-to-day sense. Even less did it influence the routine affairs of Commonwealth's underlying properties, such as Consumers Power. United's holdings in Commonwealth & Southern were actually rather modest, but when added to those of American Superpower, Electric Bond & Share, and United Gas Improvement, they amounted to slightly more than 25 percent. This was a rather substantial chunk, considering that these holding companies really constituted one single interest, tied together by Bonbright's control of Superpower and its relationship to Electric Bond & Share.[12]

It is next to impossible to find one's way through the maze of the holding-company relationships of that wild period. The Federal Trade and Securities Exchange Commissions spent years trying to untangle all the threads, and even then could not come up with any comprehensive picture. Suffice it to say here that the power of The United Corporation extended far beyond the power of those companies with which it had formal affiliations. One by one, all the major utility holding companies that were controlled out of New York fell into United's sphere of influence. Wholesale nepotism at the directors' level had been one of the time-honored Morgan methods by which this was achieved. On almost every board there was somebody's brother or brother-in-law, son or son-in-law, or old friend from college days. Such connections, vague as they may seem, are very real. To anyone with a realistic turn of mind, there can be little doubt that few, if any, major decisions were made by New York-controlled utilities without the tacit agreement of The United Corporation.

This semisubservient relationship to super holding companies caused more than a little trouble within the utilities themselves. Throughout the holding-company period an ever-widening gulf developed between the service-oriented executives of the operating companies and the moneymen of Wall Street. Certainly no love was lost between the Jackson managers of Consumers Power and most of the New Yorkers, who were always peering over their shoulders. Cobb (although he was respected rather than loved) was an exception; but then he had started as an operating man in Michigan and belonged to the old Hodenpyl team. Later, Wendell Willkie, who followed Cobb, was even more of an anomaly; he was both loved and respected, although the practical aspects of operations were way out of his ken; but he was an Indiana boy and possessed the homeyness expected of a Hoosier. One incident will serve as an example of the local resentment against New York domination.

In October 1933, fifty-seven-year-old Charles W. Tippy, probably Consumers Power's most popular general manager of all time, suffered fatal injuries in an automobile collision. Sitting on the right side of the front seat, he took the full blow when the other car hit midships. The accident happened on a

Saturday, and Tippy died on Sunday. On Monday Dan E. Karn, an experienced operating utilities man then serving as Tippy's assistant, was promoted to take his place.

Karn had started his career as a steam-heating engineer at the Central Illinois Light Company in Peoria in 1915, soon thereafter joined Consumers Power in Grand Rapids, and later worked in Frank Newton's rate department at the general office in Jackson. Evidently he knew his way around the company. Tippy was buried on Wednesday, and on Thursday word came through that M. Wilson Arthur, a Commonwealth & Southern executive in New York, would be reassigned to Jackson as assistant manager under Karn. The general reaction was expressed by one Jackson veteran who shall remain nameless: "What's the matter with those guys in the East? Don't they think Karn knows how to run the company?"[13]

When Willkie moved into the presidency of Commonwealth & Southern in January 1933, he immediately went to work behind the scenes to take the management of the business out of the hands of the investment bankers and return it to those who knew most about it, the operating men. Just how he managed it no one knows today, but by June 20, 1934, he had obtained the resignations of four super-holding-company C&S directors: Landon K. Thorne and A. L. Loomis, of Bonbright & Company; C. E. Groesbeck, chief executive of Electric Bond & Share; and Ray P. Stevens, of Stevens & Wood, one of the protagonists in the Allied Power merger and Cobb's bane of 1928. In their place, Willkie's new board of directors included the operating heads of the major subsidiaries, including Dan E. Karn.[14]

The conflict between investment bankers and operating men within C&S (as indeed in other utility groups) was not so much a matter of philosophy as of practicality. True, Cobb didn't approve of Insull-type, paper-pyramid operations, and Willkie had no use for people who could think only of money. But both men (even Willkie, who had toyed with socialism in his youth) were fervent believers in private enterprise. They opposed its excesses, but they knew that no other socioeconomic system had done nearly as well by its people.

On the outside, however, in the country at large, it was a different matter. As Insull had said to his guard, the old system was on trial.

All life is based on polarity. In economics and politics, no less than in physics, each force creates its counterforce. Too great a concentration of power results in an imbalance that inevitably seeks to correct itself. From society's point of view, all-powerful business is no more desirable than an all-powerful government. Sooner or later there is a violent emotional reaction, and just as revolution ends in excesses, so does the process of economic compensation.

Very early in the development of utilities it had become clear that they were natural monopolies. For one thing, there just isn't enough room for the clutter that would result from the duplication of wires and mains. More important, utilities are a business of such high capital investment that the sharing of revenues to be derived from any given area cannot provide sufficient return to keep competition alive. Then, too, as utilities developed, they became essential to almost the entire population. Combine these aspects—the natural monopoly situation and the utter dependence on the services offered by the monopoly—and it is not surprising that utilities, by their very nature, have always been subject to attack. Now add to this basic situation the terrible frustration that must have overcome the people with the suspicion that all this monopoly power was concentrated in the hands of but a few invisible men—unreachable, untouchable, beyond the law—and you have a situation that's ripe for some powerful upheavals.

The drive for public ownership of the utilities had gathered momentum throughout the 1920s. Although the Socialist Party, as such, was unable to muster a substantial vote in the United States,[15] socialist concepts found increasingly wider acceptance among the voters and politicians of America's established parties. By 1927 the federal government was ready to get into the utility business with the construction of Boulder Dam, on the Colorado River at the border of Nevada and Arizona. That same year, Senator Thomas J. Walsh, a Republican from Montana, demanded an investigation of the utility industry, and Senator George Norris of Nebraska made his first bid to create a federal power project around the Muscle Shoals plant on the Tennessee River, foreshadowing the future Tennessee Valley Authority.[16] Newspapers, notably those of the Hearst chain, joined enthusiastically in the vitriolic campaign against utilities. Here was a ready-made answer to circulation problems: "Power Trust" became a common headline term, screaming out its accusations in 96-point type.[17]

Gifford Pinchot, the former progressive Republican Governor of Pennsylvania and a long-experienced headline hunter who knew how to make political capital out of controversies, published a pamphlet, "The Power Monopoly: Its Makeup and Its Menace," in which he charged that six groups controlled the thirty-five utilities that served most of the nation. Other rabble-rousers, vote seekers, and fellow journalists alike, gleefully quoted and requoted Pinchot's inside information without worrying about how much of it was true. Pinchot's six villains were Insull, the House of Morgan, General Electric, the Mellon interests, H. M. Byllesby, and H. L. Doherty. Pinchot further charged that a spiderweb of interlocking directorates concentrated the power over power even more. As it happened, General Electric had been completely out of the power business for five years when Pinchot published his diatribe in 1929, and the generalization about interlocking directorates was an inside joke to those who knew how much Insull and the House of Morgan hated each other—but then Morgan didn't kill off Insull until two years later, and when he did it, it was precisely because Insull wanted no truck with Morgan.[18]

Of course, there was a grain of truth in Pinchot's allegations, as there often is in the smear and the big lie. Morgan-Bonbright's United Corporation was certainly on the make, and interlocking directorships were an old Morgan technique. Indeed, power over the nation's utilities was being increasingly concentrated at that very moment—and for the next three or four years it became concentrated even more since all the hue and cry about the holding companies, being based mostly on guesswork, actually obscured rather than revealed their activities. While the politicians screamed themselves hoarse, the bond houses were having their heyday profiteering on utilities.

The operating companies, however, didn't do nearly as well as either the politicians or the brokers, especially as the Depression deepened in 1931. Senator Norris, in one of his more amusing speeches (amusing only in retrospect), accused the electric companies of overcharging their residential customers by some $750 million a year. The speech, of course, caused nationwide indignation, even though the "overcharge" exceeded by $100 million the *total* annual bill to the nation's domestic customers.

This was the climate as Cobb's reign at C&S drew to a close and Wendell Willkie took over in 1933. By that time, of course, it was too late to save the organization. The fact that Willkie got rid of the Tories on his board meant a lot to him and to his loyal co-workers in Jackson and at the other C&S subsidiaries, but it didn't impress the outside world one bit. Commonwealth & Southern would continue to exist until 1949—long after Willkie's time—but its fate was decreed in 1935, during Roosevelt's first term, and there was nothing Willkie could do about it, just as he couldn't do anything about TVA, except put up a good fight—which, it turned out, was his specialty.

16

Barefoot Boy from Wall Street[1]

It was late in February 1933, and Michigan's winter weather was living up to its miserable reputation. An icy, penetrating wind blew along West Michigan Avenue in Jackson, driving wet snow before it and powdering with white a small group of men who had just come out of the Consumers Power Company general office building.

Luckily the men did not have far to go, only to the Hayes Hotel next door, for one of them was without an overcoat and didn't even have his jacket buttoned. He was a tall man, and his jacket flopped around a midriff slowly filling out with middle age. He hurried along, loose-jointed as the scarecrow in *The Wizard of Oz* and dressed with almost equal informality. It was evident even at first glance that if there was one thing this fellow didn't care a hoot about, it was his appearance. The wind had whipped a heavy shock of brown hair across his forehead, and after he had rushed into the hotel, he shook himself like a big poodle to get rid of the clinging snow and brushed his unruly hair back with an automatic movement of his hamlike hand. The lobby of the Hayes Hotel, high-ceilinged and modestly ornate in Middle Western small-town elegance, was packed with Consumers Power executives and office staff, all waiting to meet the man with the ill-fitting clothes and touseled hair. All were dressed in their Sunday best, for he was their new boss.

The reception had much in common with a wedding party. Dan E. Karn, still assistant general manager, hovered over the assembly like the mother of the bride. He maneuvered the unlikely maiden—for Wendell L. Willkie was truly innocent only in his deepest core—over to where C. W. Tippy, the general manager, stood in a strategic corner of the lobby, smiling kindly like a proud father who is slightly bedazzled by the festivities that haven't yet been paid for. Then everybody filed by to be introduced and pump the hand that now steered Commonwealth & Southern's course. Introductions over, Willkie gave a short speech.

"Gentlemen," he said, "I am a Democrat. I'll take care of the politicians. I want you to know that our best defense of private enterprise, of our investor-owned company, is that we'll sell so much power and at such low cost that those politicians won't want any part of our job."[2]

The speech was in many ways typical of Wendell Willkie. It expressed his supreme confidence in himself, or at least the appearance of such confidence. It was short: Willkie believed in brevity, particularly when making important points. And it showed his courage: he came right out in the midst of the largely Republican assemblage and said he was a Democrat.

Seven years later, when his experiences with the New Deal had turned him into the country's most prominent ex-Democrat and he was running against Roosevelt in the 1940 election, he was not quite so brief anymore in his public pronouncements (he talked so much he lost his voice), nor was he seemingly so self-assured (he was at his best speaking off the cuff, and

WENDELL L. WILLKIE

"My God," said Peck's Bad Boy when he first came to New York as a young Commonwealth & Southern attorney, "there isn't a soul here I know." But by 1940, when they had finally made him comb his hair for this formal portrait, everybody in the country knew him. (Photo by Chidnoff, Consumers Power collection)

as a candidate many of his speeches were prepared). If nothing else, his cramped campaign larynx and his stumbling over script lines enhanced the Hoosier image with which press and party propaganda had endowed him — raw, tall, and shambling, strictly from Booth Tarkington on the Wabash, as nostalgically frontier American as a Norman Rockwell character on the cover of the old *Saturday Evening Post.*

Nothing could have been further from the truth.

Lewis Wendell Willkie (the Lewis wasn't transposed and abbreviated until later) was born in the small town of Elwood, Indiana, on February 18, 1892, the same year that W. A. Foote lost the Boland-line race against Hawks-Angus. When Willkie entered grade school, excavations for Trowbridge Dam on the Kalamazoo River had just begun, and high-voltage transmission was still some years off. He was not quite forty-one years old when he inherited the Commonwealth & Southern presidency from B. C. Cobb. During these four decades the power business had become one of the major forces in American economic and industrial life. Any man who could cope with all its ramifications, all the complexities and confusions of a business that had grown up too fast, was no simple farm boy, and Willkie hadn't even started out as one.

True, his father owned farms, but he wasn't a farmer. Herman Francis Willkie was a landowner and lawyer (and a sometime judge), and an idealist and intellectual at that, who leavened his lucrative practice whenever he could by taking on underdog cases. They called him "Hellfire" Willkie for his initials. Wendell's mother, born Henrietta Trisch, would have delighted today's lady liberationists. She was a practicing attorney too, and her husband's partner in the firm. She wore high French heels until her death in 1940 at age eighty-one; she hated to cook, had a housekeeper to run her ménage while she was busy in her law office and in court. She spoke French and Spanish, and found her relaxation in voracious reading and the now hippy arts of quilting, embroidery, and China painting. As Wendell told his newspaperman friend and biographer

Joseph Barnes, "My father had a library of some six or seven thousand books. Eight of us, my father, mother and six children, lived in a constant atmosphere of reading and discussion, so when you ask me questions of what was my favorite book, it is difficult to answer as we read and reread everything in those days."[3] Willkie never got over the reading habit. His luggage was always stuffed with books. When he flew to Colorado after his nomination by the Republican Convention in Philadelphia in 1940, he read the following books on the plane: Carson McCullers' *The Heart Is a Lonely Hunter*, Morris L. Ernst's *Too Big*, *The Dissenting Opinions of Mr. Justice Holmes*, Mason Wade's *Margaret Fuller: Whetstone of Genius*, and Carl Snyder's *Capitalism: The Creator*.[4]

Wendell's grandparents were all Germans—a fact that accrued to his disadvantage during the presidential campaign when Democratic propagandists tried to imply that on top of being an unregenerate capitalist, he might also turn out to be a Nazi sympathizer, or at least appeaser. What they didn't know, and surely would not have advertised had they known it, was that Wendell's ancestors had fled their homeland precisely because they opposed Prussian militarism; in fact one of his maternal grandfathers, Jacob von Hessen-Lois, a minor aristocrat and wealthy Hamburg merchant, barely got his family out into political exile alive in the turbulent year of 1848. In short, Wendell L. Willkie was the product of an extremely liberal family—but then, by the 1930s, definitions had begun to be mixed up, and "liberal" suddenly meant someone who believed in the regulation and regimentation inherent in strong government.

Nor was Indiana, by the time of Wendell's youth, the vision of rural tranquility as promulgated (even today) by press and publicists. The state was deep in the throes of industrial revolution. Wendell's own hometown, thanks to the discovery of natural gas in the area around Muncie in the 1880s, was the site of the country's first big tin-plate factory. The year of Wendell's birth had also seen the birth (in Omaha, yet deeper in apple-pie heartland) of the Populist Party, whose basic argument that "the toils of the millions are stolen to build up colossal fortunes" dogged Willkie all his life. Union trouble flared in peaceful little Elwood during Wendell's youth, and his father represented a union. Indeed, Indiana's mood was a lot less conservative than it is now.

Young Wendell wore a red sweater, preached socialism from soapboxes, and left the Methodist Church because he had an Episcopalian girl friend. With his three brothers, who were even bigger than he was, he fought what seemed to be the entire police department of Bloomington, Indiana, with bare fists during a student riot while they were attending the university. Wendell championed the poor, begged Clarence Darrow to defend arrested pickets, and worked part time in a steel mill. Meanwhile, he took all the scholastic prizes in college, amused himself playing Hamlet from memory wearing his mother's old petticoat for a cape, loved frying eggs and eating them (four to six at a time), and taught history in high school. As the *Bay City Times* described him in 1940, he was "a mixture of Peck's Bad Boy, a juvenile Norman Thomas, and a misplaced Oxford don."[5]

He worked for awhile as a chemist on a Puerto Rico sugar plantation; then he studied law. He enlisted in the Army; married Edith Wilk, an assistant in the Rushville (Indiana) Library; and went off to war (mostly to defend doughboys who couldn't resist going AWOL in Paris). He came out a captain; he had a son, Philip; and then by way of the legal department of Firestone Tire and Rubber Company he joined the Akron, Ohio, law firm of Mather and Nesbitt, whose clients included the Northern Ohio Traction and Light Company, which eventually became part of the Penn-Ohio Edison Company — the utility that married Commonwealth in the Allied Power merger.

When B. C. Cobb first met Willkie in 1926, he was so impressed that he wrote to an officer of that company, which at this point was called Northern Ohio Power and Light, "We should not let this young man get away from us. He is a comer and we should keep an eye on him."

How the fastidious, elegant Cobb could possibly have taken a liking to the sloppy, personally careless Willkie is a mystery. Cobb fussed over every little thing that was out of place and put it right. Willkie dropped everything he was through with, right then and there. No man of lesser intelligence could have accomplished anything within the mess he constantly created around himself. Even the way he read a newspaper was unique—not page by page from front to back, but sheet by sheet. He read first the front page of the paper and then the back page; then he peeled off the sheet, looked at its two inside pages, and when he was done he simply let it flutter to the floor. And so with the next sheet and the next, working his way toward the middle of the paper, until there was nothing left in his hands, and it was all scattered around his chair. The fact that some stories jumped to pages deep inside the paper didn't bother him; he kept them in mind and finished them when he got to their continuations. Willkie's inevitable trail of litter did not deter Cobb, however. He knew that he had discovered a rare personality in Willkie and had no intention of letting him slip out of his grasp. In August 1929 he persuaded Willkie to join Weadock's law firm in New York to handle the legal work of Commonwealth & Southern.

Cobb may have singled out Willkie as his successor almost from the beginning. Chances are he talked the matter over with old Weadock and that the two men agreed it would be best to let the young lawyer pile up a few years of experience in the field before drawing him into the inner circles of the corporate court. Good executives always keep their eyes open for successors. When Cobb resigned as president of C&S in January 1933 and Willkie took his place, Weadock immediately sought out a new legal associate in the person of Justin R. Whiting, who had handled many of the company's legal affairs in Michigan. Again there is hardly any doubt that Weadock, most likely with Cobb's agreement, considered Whiting as a potential top executive of C&S—and indeed he turned out to be Willkie's successor.

But this was a long way off when Willkie moved into the C&S presidency. Cobb, though no longer in good health, remained chairman of the board for a while longer. Already in the early summer of the previous year, Cobb had relinquished some of his duties; one of the hats he turned in at that time was that of president of Consumers Power. On June 28, 1932, that post went to Timothy A. Kenney, the production and transmission specialist who had been imported from New York State back in the Foote days to build the company's original dispatching organization.

As soon as Willkie, now moving in above Kenney, found his footing in the C&S organization, Cobb's chairmanship became almost a formality. He soon had to undergo a serious operation and then suffered a nervous breakdown. On July 24, 1933, he gave up all his remaining offices, and Willkie was immediately elected to replace him, making official what had been apparent for more than a year—that Willkie was firmly in control of the organization. Thus, at age forty-two, the former college rebel and intellectual nonconformist found himself acclaimed as the youngest chief executive of a major utility system. Almost overnight he had become one of the most important men in American industry.

The nation's assessment of Wendell Willkie as a grass-roots type—offered in glorification or denigration, depending on who was talking—wasn't all wrong, however. Willkie didn't just look like a farmer; he knew how to milk cows. And when he had first come to New York as attorney for The Commonwealth & Southern Corporation, this man who would challenge FDR for the nation's leadership in another decade—this clumsy, big-boned newcomer from the hinterlands—gazed with awe at the crowded Manhattan sidewalks so different from those in booming but tight little Akron, Ohio, and commented to a lawyer friend who had picked him up at the railroad station and was taking him to a hotel by taxi: "My God, there isn't a soul here I know!"[6]

By 1933, when Willkie assumed the C&S presidency, this had long been remedied. He was now a cosmopolite New Yorker, as at home on Fifth Avenue as he had been on Main Street. What made him cosmopolitan, of course, was that unlike so many other New Yorkers of Middle Western origin, he did not turn into a Manhattan provincial for whom the world stops at the Hudson River. The nearest operating company under his aegis lay nearly 500 miles from Gotham, and Willkie never lost touch. Much of his time was spent on the road traveling from one company to the next, visiting and revisiting every community served by his utilities. That's where his major interest lay—in the people who lived out there beyond the corporate offices and boardrooms. He realized that privately owned utilities had a chance against the drive for public ownership only if they could prove that they could give the best service at the lowest possible cost. This became his mission.

Willkie was not a technical man. On his first visit to the Battle Creek division of Consumers Power, he walked into Claude Mulligan's office and said, "All the others are in there with the manager [then Boyd S. Eppes, whom we remember from earlier days as one of the Kansas City men brought in by Foote and Hodenpyl to survey potential takeover candidates], and they're talking about electricity, and I don't understand the first thing that they're talking about. What I want to know is all about this town. How did it get started? What kind of people live here? What are the industries?" Often he deserted his executives altogether and prowled the local streets instead, dropping in on the newspaper editor, the town's librarian, a downtown store or two. That's how Willkie went about it everywhere, until he had a complete picture of his territories locked in his encyclopedic mind.

This was not easy. At the time of the formation of Commonwealth & Southern, its corporate structures had embraced 165 subsidiaries, and while it was possible to simplify the administrative framework by bringing most electric, gas, and kindred operations in each state under one company, this evidently did not reduce geographic dimensions.[7] Commercial aviation was still in its infancy, so Willkie did most of his traveling by automobile and train, whiling away the long hours in storytelling and much kidding. He also enjoyed playing hearts, at which he lost so consistently that after awhile he refused to carry money on his trips. He never drove automobiles himself; an early accident had cured him of that American preoccupation. One of Willkie's frequent travel companions was E. V. ("Ted") Sayles, boss of Consumers Power's general engineering department, whose sound advice Willkie sorely needed at budget time. "If I ask for something that is silly, be sure to tell me," Willkie always reminded Sayles. "Remember, I'm not an engineer."

Ted Sayles, now retired, remembers those days very well. "I'll tell you one thing about Mr. Willkie," he says. "He was very kindly. I was just a young fellow as far as he was concerned, and of course there were always those big shots around who wanted to be recognized by him and get close to him. He was always polite to them and everything, but by gosh he would do things for me, little things, that showed that he was really interested. Like, for example, down there at the Southern Indiana Gas and Electric Company they had a metal-type switchgear I'd designed for them before they had those things in the catalogs, and I was quite proud of the idea. I told Willkie about it one time just riding along on the train. He said, 'Ted, I'm glad you mentioned it; I would like to see it. Where is this thing you invented?' I told him it was at the Garvin substation, and he nodded and said 'That's dandy.' That was his favorite expression when he liked something, 'That's dandy.' Anyway, I thought he'd forgotten about it because he never said anything about it later. But down there in Evansville [Indiana] one afternoon, he looked at his watch—it was about three-thirty— and he told all the big shots, 'We got to hurry along now. I want to see Garvin substation.' And by gosh he did. Mr. Willkie took about an hour out of his busy afternoon just to look at this gadget I was so proud of. I know he didn't understand

AS LUCK WOULD HAVE IT, THE LIGHTS DIDN'T GO OUT

You can just hear some photog saying, "Hey, Mr. Willkie, how about putting your hand on that dial over there!" Consumers' chief executive admittedly didn't know the first thing about technical matters and must have been quite embarrassed when asked to pose for this picture. No wonder old Weadock (right) looked somewhat apprehensive. (Consumers Power photo)

it and care much about it, but he sure did his best trying to listen as I was explaining it to him, and he said, 'Ted, that's dandy—just dandy.'"[8]

But things were not always dandy. Willkie could be damn tough, and the higher up the ladder employees were, the tougher he was with them. Once, on a visit to Consumers Power's Alma division (now called Central division), the manager was not there, even though he had been advised of the forthcoming meeting. So Willkie sat with the staff and fired questions at them. One of them, Ray Painter, the local superintendent of electric distribution, was trying to answer for his absent boss and doing a lot of bluffing. It wasn't long before Willkie had him trapped.

291

"Young man," Willkie said, "I have to admire that you're protecting your superior, but you haven't got the facts and what you said is not true. I'll excuse you this time and again compliment you for your loyalty, but I would advise you never to do this again." And he turned around to Dan Karn and said, "I want that manager released from his job as of right now."[9]

That's how he wanted almost everything—right now. The world moved far too slowly for him. Like so many other men with restless minds, he had no patience for sports. Trundling around a golf course bored him to death. He much preferred to read or plow through business papers, all the while smoking furiously, up to five or six packs a day, forgetting more cigarettes in the ashtray than he finished, and lighting a new one after every couple of puffs.

He had no patience for nit-picking, hated to see time wasted on bookkeeping, and couldn't stand it when people in his organization were slow about making up their minds on details. Crusty old Cobb had seemed like a man who'd brook no contradiction, but it was possible with him to get away with back talk. Not so with Willkie, who was a lot tougher than he appeared. Once he had made up his mind on something, even if it was just a small, unimportant matter, he was a hard man to budge. One time, after a budget meeting in Evansville, Willkie and Sayles went to the railroad station to catch a train to Chicago. The train was late, and they stopped at a one-horse saloon across the street. Willkie had to have something to eat. He was a big, powerful fellow, and he ate that way too. So they sat at the bar, which didn't serve beer except off the record, and Willkie ordered: "I'll have two hamburger sandwiches and two cups of coffee." The bartender gave him one cup of coffee and told Willkie he'd fill it up again when it was empty. Willkie, hungry and tired, blustered, "Hell no, I said I want two cups of coffee, and I want them right here and right now."[10]

Most of all, Willkie disliked squabbles. There was the time when the engineering and operating departments of Consumers Power couldn't agree on the width of a right-of-way for a transmission line, and a lengthy agrument developed in Willkie's presence between Benjamin L. Huff, Harold Foote, and Frank G. Boyce (later a vice-president). Willkie listened for awhile. Finally he said, "Well, I've heard enough. I will come back here in April, and by that time you farmers should have that decided. I don't want any more of this horse manure."[11] He just couldn't understand that other men's minds didn't usually click along like his own. When he was confronted with a decision at a budget meeting, he listened to the proposal, asked questions, and listened some more. In the end, if he liked the idea, he said, "I approve the item" or maybe, if he were especially enthusiastic, "That's dandy. I approve the item," but he never engaged in argument and wished that other people wouldn't either.

Willkie's major ambition was to achieve the sale of 1,000 kilowatthours per customer. Before his time, the residential customer was basically a lighting customer, with the use of electricity limited to a few lines in the house, some extension cords, and maybe a couple of minor appliances. Willkie wanted to sell him electric washing, electric refrigeration, and electric cooking; in short, he wanted to make him into an electric power customer. Willkie couldn't have picked a worse time.

The stock market crash of 1929 was soon followed by the most severe depression this country has ever known. Michigan, because it was so highly industrialized, was particularly hard hit. By 1930, one out of every five of the state's nonagricultural workers was unemployed; the next year it was one out of three. In 1933, with automobile production off by 60 percent from 1929, only every other industrial worker had a job.[12] The cost of unemployment relief placed a tremendous strain on governmental units, and the problem soon snowballed, with most of Michigan's citizens unable to pay the taxes to support their local governments. Tax delinquencies throughout the state averaged about one-third, and in some cities as much as one-half.

While the situation was at first most critical in the industrial cities, the crisis soon spread through the rural districts. Farmers, dispossessed for back taxes and unpaid mortgages, threatened judges and sheriffs and sometimes assaulted them. Sometimes, the farmers employed less violent and more effective tactics. For instance, late in January of 1933, just about the time Willkie became C&S president, some 150 farmers near Howard City in Montcalm County picketed a sheriff's sale of farm machinery and furniture for unpaid taxes. The picketers warned other onlookers to refrain from bidding and then offered only a few cents for each item. A grand piano went for 4 cents, and a hay-loader for 11. Total proceeds of the sale came to $2.40, and the purchasers returned the items to the owner.[13]

President Herbert Hoover kept his fingers crossed that conditions would improve without federal intervention. He was afraid, perhaps not entirely without justification, that once Washington took a direct hand in manipulating the economy, local initiative might be destroyed, resulting in a superstate. Hoover did expand public works, however, and in January 1932 established the Reconstruction Finance Corporation. This body was first authorized to lend money to banks, commercial enterprises, railroads, and insurance companies and later was expanded to make loans to farmers' cooperatives, to cities for the construction of self-liquidating projects, and to states if they were otherwise unable to finance their relief costs.

Among the first banks to ask for an RFC loan was Detroit's Union Guardian Trust Company, part of the Guardian–Detroit Union group. In 1932, Union Guardian Trust borrowed $15 million from the RFC and in 1933 asked for $50 million more. Examiners were unable to find enough collateral to justify the second loan, but promised to provide part of the amount if large depositors would guarantee the remainder. General Motors and Chrysler, two of the bank's largest customers, agreed on the condition that Ford would do the same. Henry Ford refused, however, and even personal appeals by President Hoover couldn't budge him.

The crisis came to a head on Sunday, February 12, when government officials, directors of the automobile companies, and bankers from New York, Chicago, and Detroit gathered in Detroit in a last-ditch attempt to save the city's key banking institution. They had one day of grace: Monday was a legal holiday because Lincoln's birthday had fallen on that Sunday. But the extra day did not help. It became evident that Union Guardian could not open its doors on Tuesday. Nearly two hundred banks had already failed since December 1929. In Detroit, only six banks were left. Governor William A. Comstock, afraid that Union Guardian's inability to meet its obligations would cause a run on the few remaining institutions, declared a bank holiday until February 23. This was later extended. Meanwhile, other states followed Michigan's lead, and on March 5, the day after Roosevelt's inauguration, the President made the bank holiday national. This meant that millions of people couldn't pay their bills, even though they might have had the money in the bank. In turn, millions of others couldn't get paid. It was a wild situation.

Consumers Power was caught in the vise along with everybody else. For several weeks the company was forced to operate on a cash basis.[14] And not much cash was coming in—and wouldn't for a good many years. The company's credit and collections department was swamped by customers who had fallen behind on their bills and were trying to make some arrangement to keep the service going. Surprisingly, it seemed to be the radio that mattered most. Depression and poverty had become a fact of life. People could resign themselves to getting along without gas and without a telephone, but radio was the only contact they had with the outside world, their only entertainment and diversion, and they didn't want to let it go.[15]

Often there were bitter tears, but Consumers Power really had no choice. If the company had started to carry a few customers who couldn't pay their bills, word would soon have spread and such a large number of customers would have defaulted that the situation would have become untenable. Between 1929 and 1933, gross revenues dropped 22 percent, from $33,420,000 to $26,000,000. Net income after fixed charges and dividends on preferred stock were paid fared even worse. Over the same years, common stock earnings dropped 66 percent, from slightly over $8 million to less than $3 million, and most of this had to be held in reserves. Strict economies were enforced within the company, including a 10 percent pay cut for all employees and officers. It was typical of Charles W. Tippy, then still general manager and with only a few months left to live, that he took a voluntary cut of 20 percent, and did so without letting anyone on the staff know about it—a fact revealed only by a search of the minutes of directors' meetings. The bleak year of 1933 was the turning point. In 1934, revenues and earnings were slowly on the rise again.[16] By 1936, revenues were almost back to the 1929 level, although income still lagged far behind.[17] It would be nice, in the context of this history, to be able to credit Wendell Willkie with getting the company back on its feet. That, however, wouldn't be quite true. Roosevelt's pump priming through the Work Projects Administration (the famous WPA) and other deficit financing measures pulled the country out of the depths of depression, and while the economy sagged once more in 1938, it did not plummet quite so deeply into the abyss of misery and unemployment.

What would have happened had World War II not intervened is a matter of conjecture; some scholars have maintained that Roosevelt's actions only postponed the inevitable and that he would have been in Hoover's shoes by 1940 if it hadn't been for Adolf Hitler's megalomaniac dream of building a new German empire. The paradox of Roosevelt's time may well be that his anticapitalist depression tactics and social welfare programs, in buying time, combined with Hitler's aggression, which precipitated a war economy, served to save capitalism in the United States. Certainly another major depression of the early 1930s variety would have brought about great social upheavals, possibly even revolution, and it is doubtful that utilities, always the number one target, could have escaped public ownership under those conditions.

This is not to say that Willkie failed to contribute materially to the comeback of Consumers Power and his other companies under the C&S umbrella. Where B. C. Cobb had been a driver and organizer, Willkie was a crusader and salesman. His crusade was the survival of investor-owned public utilities; his salesmanship was directed toward giving them viability under this banner. His crusade was not totally successful; his salesmanship was, although it didn't really pay off, except in statistics, until after he had left industry for politics—indeed, not until well after his death in 1944.

During Willkie's reign as chairman of the board, Consumers Power's number of electric and gas customers increased steadily; as did, except for an intermediate dip in 1938, the amount of electric and gas sales.[18] Much of this gain could be credited to Willkie's highly personalized campaign for greater appliance sales. His visits to Consumers Power and the other C&S companies were mainly for the purpose of budget discussion and operating decisions. But between meetings he never failed to drop in on the nearest appliance showroom of whatever operating company he was visiting and to approach some unsuspecting salesman, who usually had no idea that this great big bumbling fellow was his commander in chief.

"I want to buy this," Willkie would say, "but I don't know anything about it. You've got to explain it to me." Lucky was the salesman who knew how to sell. Willkie bought every single item that was demonstrated properly, paid for it in cash, and if it was portable took it with him. He returned from every field trip with dozens of packages; nobody knows what he did with all those toasters, percolators, broilers, and irons. His New York apartment must have been a veritable warehouse if he kept them all, which, however, isn't likely because he was a generous man who enjoyed giving presents.

Willkie's shopping trips turned out to be excellent training devices. After awhile the older salesmen got to know him and took pride in their performance, and the younger ones—remember that this was in the days when people were not yet sanguine about their jobs—always kept in mind that Willkie might come into the store almost any time.

It had been a Consumers Power policy of long standing that the interest of the public was best served by the sale of high-quality appliances. Since the 1920s, a laboratory had been maintained to test the various offerings of the manufacturers. Over the years, these tests resulted in many suggestions that were then incorporated in the eventual design. Consumers Power advertised each new appliance at great expense, generating enough sales volume to help the manufacturer remain in business until general public acceptance became a fact. Among the appliances Consumers Power thus helped pioneer were the electric refrigerator, the electric range, the low-consumption gas water heater, the off-peak electric storage water heater, and the gas refrigerator, which Consumers Power placed on sale shortly following the invention's introduction to this country after early use in Sweden. Consumers Power sold appliances at manufacturers' list prices. Where such prices were not furnished, Consumers Power calculated markups of sufficient size to enable independent dealers to compete with the company's appliance department at a profit to themselves, for the cooperative dealer was recognized as an ally in promoting the use of utility services.

One morning in 1935, Howard Davis, the appliance sales supervisor, sat at his desk pondering the problem of getting more rural customers into the company showrooms. Here was a huge potential market for laborsaving devices, but how could this market be tapped? Suddenly it came to Davis: He remembered the truck Harry Bell had fitted out in Kalamazoo more than a decade earlier as a traveling repair shop and store to sell light bulbs, electric irons, and other small appliances. This was it! If the outlying customer found it hard to visit the showroom on Main Street, then, by gosh, Main Street must be brought to his door.

Davis, usually quiet and imperturbable, got so agitated that he jumped up from his chair and paced the office. Then he picked up the phone and called Del Ford, the head of the company's display department. "How about a real traveling showroom?" Davis suggested. "Something spectacular—right in your line." Ford enthusiastically agreed; the proposal passed through the next budget hearings with a "That's just dandy" from Willkie, and the first of several streamliners was ordered from the Aero-Car Sales Corporation. The vehicle, which was large enough to function as a compact showroom for all the important major appliances that take the drudgery out of housework, was finished in the sparkling-clean kitchen white popular at the time, and it created a stir wherever it went. Most important, it sold lots of ranges and refrigerators.

One reason why appliance sales were so important, especially in the early years of slow economic recovery, was that the company's generating equipment and its transmission and distribution systems, both gas and electric, had been built for the prosperity demands of 1929 and 1930, and Consumers Power thus found itself stuck with excess capacity. But this was only a part of the picture. The overriding consideration was to generate sufficient volume so that rates could be drastically reduced.

To this end, Willkie pushed for what he called the "objective rate," an innovation that made many of the operating men gasp. Say a householder was using X number of kilowatthours in an average month. Under the objective rate, he could add electric cooking and still not pay more for several months. After a time, the total bill he paid was raised, but the unit cost was lowered. From the standpoint of the company, the objective rate permitted putting into effect immediate rate reductions without decreasing sorely needed revenues; from the point of view of the consumer, it allowed the use of more electric energy without a corresponding increase in the bill.[19]

Total revenue per customer went up, just as expected. In the seven years from 1935 to 1942, despite a drastic drop in the price per kilowatthour, the average customer's monthly power purchase rose nearly 35 percent, from $28.52 to $38.41 — but while the customer's bill was higher by one-third, his use of electricity nearly doubled.

The older utility managers, at Consumers Power as elsewhere, hadn't believed it possible that Willkie's goal of 1,000 kilowatthours per customer per month could ever be achieved, but Willkie kept hammering away, and the Battle Creek division was the first at Consumers Power to go over the top in 1936. By 1937, the average for the whole Consumers Power territory was 1,004, and in 1939, the year before Willkie resigned to run for President, it reached 1,150, almost double what it had been in 1933. During this period, Consumers Power's kilowatthour sales per householder rose far more sharply than national consumption, while the average rate charged by Consumers Power fell far faster than the national norm. In 1939, the Consumers Power rate averaged 3.01 cents, as compared with the national average of 4.05 cents. In terms of percentages this meant that the company's sales exceeded the national utility average by 28 percent at a price that gave Consumers Power's customers a 26 percent break. With supersalesman Willkie's new low rate and the great increase in the use of appliances, the consumption of electric energy now truly became a measure of the Michigan family's high standard of living.

Of course, Willkie lowered rates all over the C&S system. Part of this strategy was prompted by his effort to save the Tennessee Electric Power Company — he wanted to undersell the government's Tennessee Valley Authority. As we shall see, he did not succeed in this attempt. And while his drive for lower rates firmly established electricity as a basic commodity in our civilization, it did so at a great cost to Consumers Power; the company almost got into serious financial trouble.

Willkie pushed the rates so low that despite the resultant increase in revenues, there was too little income in relation to expenditures. With the increasing use of electricity it was necessary to expand generating and transmitting facilities, and as a result the company found itself in a cash squeeze. Consumers Power did not wholly recover from this situation until after World War II, and then only because of Michigan's population increase, which resulted from defense production and the fabulous growth of the automotive and chemical industries that came with the postwar boom.

Meanwhile, however, much of the necessary expansion had to be halted in its tracks, especially during the recession which hit in 1938. Distribution lines had to be built to service the new customers, but it was possible to interrupt construction on two big new steam-electric plants that had been started in 1937. One was the John C. Weadock plant at the mouth of the Saginaw River, north of Bay City, Weadock's hometown; the other was the Bryce E. Morrow plant on the Kalamazoo River, near Comstock, which was named for the Edison pioneer associate[20] from New York State who had in earlier years assisted T. A. Kenney in organizing what became the production and transmission department of Consumers Power. Building was stopped on these projects in mid-1938 and did not resume until the following year.

Not that progress stopped, even during the worst of the Depression years. For one thing, as we already know, the company in 1930 commenced the changeover from 30 cycles to 60 cycles, taking advantage of the lower demand during the early slump that left part of the generating capacity idle. It was a laborious and complicated procedure—and even in the Depression far from cheap—since it was up to the company to rewire the motors of all its customers. Under the supervision of A. E. Kriegsmann, who was at that time assistant to the general manager, a special factory was set up in an old foundry building in Grand Rapids where the design engineering department rewound all the apparatus and often had to redesign it. The changeover was accomplished in steps, neighborhood by neighborhood. The customers' motors were replaced with previously rewired equipment; then the electricity, now 60-cycle, was turned on again, and the old motors were shipped to Grand Rapids, where they were reworked to replace someone else's motor in turn.

A number of other technical innovations were introduced during this period.[21] Not all of them were successful, however. Among the failures was what may well have been the first attempt to get away from unsightly overhead wires. This happened long before citizen groups did their breast-beating about visual pollution, when in fact most of today's ecology crusaders hadn't yet been born. It's probably too much to expect that today's anti-Establishmentarians would give credit to an Establishment company like Consumers Power for trying to come up with some of the answers many years ago, back in 1934 and 1935. In any case, an experimental underground line, which was installed for a distance of 3.25 miles in rural Clarendon Township, Calhoun County, soon began developing faults; in 1945, after its fifth break, it was abandoned.[22]

The fact that this experiment was tried in a rural area was no accident. Roosevelt's first Congress had given birth to the Rural Electrification Administration as a tool to bring electric energy to the nation's farms, and FDR made the project part of his 1936 platform. It was, like so many New Deal actions, essentially a political propaganda move. The story was that farmers had been crying for electricity all along and that the hardhearted utilities wouldn't give it to them because it was too expensive to put in the lines. Now the great and good government was going to rectify the situation and let social justice prevail.

There was just enough truth to this story to make smoke-smellers see fire. Putting in rural lines was inordinately expensive in terms of customer cost. Few farms were electrified. But the fault, if such it was, lay not wholly with the utilities. Of course they resisted making wholesale investments that were out of line with the return that could be expected. How should such a deficit be covered? By charging higher rates to city dwellers? By penalizing investors in utility securities? It was a dilemma, sure enough, but not nearly so much of a dilemma as it would have been if the farmers had really wanted electricity.

Farmers, by and large, are a conservative breed—or at least they were until recently, when farming became a technological industry. The steel plow is only a little more than 150 years old. The McCormick reaper cut its first swath of grain as late as 1834. Old men are still alive who remember working with sickle and cradle when they were boys. Few of these farmers wanted anything to do with that newfangled thing called electricity.

Willkie looked like a farmer, and he was a farmer in the sense that he owned farmlands down in Indiana. He understood farmers, and when he wanted to, he could make his mind work like that of a farmer. He knew how immensely important electricity could be to agriculture if it were only accepted. What's more, here was another area, now that the REA had become law, where private industry could show those bureaucrats that it could do a better job. "I would like to have us get out in front of this parade," Willkie told Dan Karn. A meeting was called in Jackson to decide how electricity could best be sold to farmers. Professor Herman J. Gallagher, later Consumers Power's farm supervisor, suggested refrigeration as the first important mechanization.

Willkie was enthusiastic. The barefoot boy was right in his element. Wall Street, now that he had bounced the bond-house lawyers, no longer was a problem. All he had to worry about was the government. You can't beat a farmer who has cottoned to book learning. Willkie would show them. "That's dandy, just dandy," he said to Karn and Gallagher. "I want to get right on it."

17

Meanwhile Back on the Farm

When a farmer is busy during haying season, he doesn't like to be bothered, especially by salesmen and college professors—not even if the salesman and the professor are one and the same guy. Walter Carven, sweating in his blue denim overalls that reached up almost to his armpits, was on the wagon with his hired man, taking up hay with a sling when that fellow came chugging down the dirt road in a black-box Model A.

"Mr. Carven," the visitor said after extricating himself from the vehicle, "I'm Herman Gallagher of the Michigan Agricultural College." Carven kept on working. "Pleased to meet you." he yelled down from the wagon, but he really wasn't. "I hope I'm not intruding," Gallagher said ("You sure are," thought Carven), "but I want to talk to you about getting electricity to your nice farm here."

Carven couldn't have been less impressed. He listened with only half an ear as Gallagher, himself a former dairy farmer, explained in plain language that this was an experiment, that the cost would be minimal and the benefits profuse. "You'll be able to load your wagon and fill your silo without breaking your back," Gallagher said. "We'll provide all the engineering help you'll need without charge. If we can get just a few farmers like you working with us along this stretch of road here, why, we'll have something going that'll make the country sit back and perk up its ears."

Carven still hadn't stopped working. "I'll sleep on it," he said.

This he did. As he told it later, "As I slept over it after Mr. Gallagher left me, I began to see the possibility of it. I became very enthusiastic about it and lost no time getting in touch with some of the farmers to let them know what was in the air."[1] Carven was then in his middle thirties, the age of business venture. He lived off the Dansville Road (now State Highway 36) between Mason and Dansville in the flat green country south of Lansing. It was a characteristic Michigan farming area, typical in the crops grown and with the farms neither too big nor too small. That's why it had been picked, that year of 1925, almost a decade before Willkie's meeting with Karn and Gallagher, to serve as Consumers Power's rural laboratory.

Already two years earlier, in 1923, Charles W. Tippy had declared in his annual address as president of the Great Lakes division of the National Electric Light Association that the industry stood ready to build extensions for rural service "wherever the business at reasonable rates will pay a reasonable return on a reasonable investment." It was evident that this could only be accomplished if and when electricity became the source of all power used on farms.[2] The problem was, of course, that farms were few and far apart, giving a low density of customers per length of line. In order to produce a reasonable return on the investment, you had to increase the rate, increase the quantity of electricity used, or decrease the construction cost of the line, or perhaps all three. The last possibility was the only one over which the company had complete control, and some progress was made toward lengthening spans for rural lines and otherwise lowering construction costs.[3] Raising the rates was out. Not only was it contrary to the upbringing of most utility men, but it also involved outside consent—that of the Public Service Commission, and of course of the potential customers who would be even less likely to buy if they felt that they were being charged too much. The answer lay evidently in increasing electric use, but this was easier said than done.

Consumers Power's first attempt along this line was planned in 1924 for a small rural community north of the village of Parma, just west of Jackson. That same year, a committee was formed on the "relation of electricity to agriculture," composed mostly of members of Michigan Agricultural College (now Michigan State University), the State Grange, Consumers Power Company, and the Michigan Public Service Commission. Herman J. Gallagher, of the agricultural engineering department of the college, was appointed project leader.

As usual, the first step was a survey. In this case the research revealed that less than 3 percent of the state's farmers were connected to high-line service and that only 30 percent of even those farmers adjacent to existing lines were hooked up. Other findings were no more encouraging. Farmers who did have electricity used it principally for lighting and averaged less than 200 kilowatthours per month. Use of electricity for farm production was quite generally ridiculed as impractical and was considered far too expensive.[4] Seeing these facts, black and white on a committee report, would have been enough, most assuredly, to discourage any hard-nosed utilities executive from investing much time and effort in such a losing proposition. Consumers Power had its hands full as it was: this was the time when the company was expanding into all the tiny crossroad villages and hamlets, buying up a lot of small power outfits, and building them up to give better service.

But Gallagher was not to be discouraged. He kept up the

pressure until Consumers Power agreed on a cooperative research project with the college. The company would build, at no expense to the farmers, a 7-mile rural extension immediately adjacent to thirty-three farms, the Mason-Dansville line.

Now that the years have passed, Consumers Power is not adverse to taking credit for this pioneering step. It's doubtful, however, that the experiment could have been taken too seriously at the time. It was just one of those marginal things one does mostly as a public gesture.

Nevertheless, Consumers Power was willing to make the investment, and the line was built. Indeed, the company was

HE BROUGHT ELECTRICITY TO MICHIGAN'S FARMERS

In 1938, Herman Gallagher posed at the unveiling of a plaque commemorating the pioneer Mason-Dansville electric line built eleven years earlier by Consumers Power to advance rural electrification. This service to farmers came largely as a result of Professor Gallagher's conviction that electric power would greatly improve rural life. (Consumers Power photo)

a lot more willing than the farmers. Of the thirty-three along the extension, only twelve agreed to take the service and to wire their farms for power. The remaining twenty-one were too skeptical even to wire for lighting. It may be hard to believe now that this was the situation less than fifty years ago, at the same time that Richard E. Byrd flew across the North Pole and Charles A. Lindbergh puddle-hopped nonstop from New York to Paris. The few adventurous farmers who did go for the proposition were all in Carven's age group, old enough to know what they were doing and yet young enough not to be bogged down in the past.

The historic Mason-Dansville line was energized on February

... AND WHERE IT ALL STARTED

The Mason-Dansville electric line, which still exists today, was 7 miles long and adjacent to thirty-three farms. At its beginning, only twelve of these farms took advantage of the opportunity. Not until October 1949 was the one-hundred-thousandth Michigan farm connected—a record never exceeded in any other state. (Consumers Power photo)

4, 1927, and the test farmers were equipped with a wide variety of power equipment and appliances consigned by manufacturers cooperating with the project, i.e., the machinery didn't cost the farmers any money to start with. All the motors were separately metered so that studies could be conducted on their use, and an experimental rural rate schedule was filed with the State Commission for 5 cents per kilowatthour for the first thirty hours, 3 cents per kilowatthour for additional use, plus a monthly $3 service charge. The participating farmers formed an association and awarded a single contract for all the wiring.

The mechanization thus accomplished was as experimental as the project itself. Almost everything was improvised, with most of the ideas coming from a young man named Robey—his first name has been forgotten—who was connected with the engineering department of the college. Some of the new devices operated smoothly; others created trouble. A make-shift hay-loader nearly burned down a barn when friction developed and sparks began to fly. Electric water heaters still were scarce, but one was built at Carven's place that would hold 10 gallons. This homemade appliance had a heating element on the bottom, and this was of course wired, but there wasn't any piping, and the water had to be carried in and out. Despite all the difficulties, the value of mechanization soon became apparent. Each test farm had a 5-horsepower motor, a little two-wheeled affair that could be moved around. With the aid of this peripatetic machine powering a small grain elevator, two men could fill a 40-foot high silo in about six days, which was a lot more convenient than the old system, under which a farmer had to help half a dozen of his neighbors to fill their silos before his own turn came.

On the basis of the Mason-Dansville experiment, the agricultural extension of the college decided on farm electrification as one of its major educational projects, and in the spring of 1928 a trailer truck was equipped to convey farm power machinery throughout rural Michigan for demonstrations. This truck, which was financed jointly by Consumers Power and Detroit Edison, caused a slow awakening among the farmers.[5] Thousands of them, sometimes in organized groups and sometimes on their own, visited the test farms, as did representatives from every state in the Union and a dozen foreign countries.

In 1929, Consumers Power came out officially for farm electrification. Under this policy, the company agreed to bring in service on a customer-deposit basis of $1,000 per mile. Following the construction of each extension, $100 was refunded for each of the first ten customers connected within five years.[6] Standard residential rates became available on a uniform basis to all rural customers—a very important factor, as we shall soon see. As the farmer's part of the bargain, he was required to install, a minimum service of three-wire 60-ampere capacity and to grant free right-of-way for the line. This policy, which had been originated by The Detroit Edison Company and was also used by them, soon gained national repute and became known as the "Michigan plan" or the "$1,000-a-mile plan."

But while the company seemed ready to get into the rural power business, the farmers still were not, even after all the Mason-Dansville publicity. Programs take awhile to get rolling, and in this case the program rolled right into the economic slump. Hard hit by the Depression, Michigan's farmers were less ready than ever to invest in the future.

Willkie well understood that the 1930s farmer couldn't afford to finance capital improvements. "If I was a farmer and was convinced that I wanted electricity," he told Dan Karn, "I'd surely go to my neighbor and start what they call a co-op, and I'd pull the leg of my congressman and say, 'come on boys, get me some electricity.'"

There was only one way to preempt the Rural Electrification Administration, and this was for Consumers Power to bring down the cost to farmers just as it was reducing the rates for its urban customers. In 1935, on Willkie's command, Consumers Power revised its rural policy to permit free extension

WOMEN'S LIB

Free of their menfolk, who naturally gravitated toward the electrical farm equipment display truck, the ladies congregated around the household appliances trailer of Michigan's rural electrification sales cavalcade. The trailer truck was financed jointly by Consumers Power and Detroit Edison. On the road in 1928, it preceded the government's REA by several years. (Consumers Power photo)

of service—without any construction deposit—on the basis of five farm customers per mile and a minimum monthly billing guarantee of $12.50 per mile.

It was a big gamble. The cost of rural line was then about $5,000 per mile. With a 100,000-farmer goal—and not all of the farms were only one mile from the road—this constituted a potentially huge investment. Not surprisingly, the company was now swamped with requests for rural extensions. It became necessary to establish a farm service department, and Gallagher was brought in as its supervisor in 1936.[7] The following year, Consumers Power won the Thomas W. Martin Rural Electrification Award for its "invaluable contribution" toward "stimulating the improvement of the economic and cultural advantages of farm life."

This public recognition could not have pleased the REA, which was ready to chomp into the Consumers Power pie whenever it could. With considerable acumen and political tail-wagging, a gentleman by the name of C. A. Winder had been manipulated by Washington into the position of chief engineer for the Michigan Public Utilities Commission. This was a key spot, not only for keeping track of what was going on at Consumers Power, but also, provided one felt so included, for delicately depositing sand in its gears. A new regulation was instituted whereby the company was required to supply the commission with certain information on each proposed line, such as length, voltage, prospective customers, and respective minimum monthly payments. Consumers Power then had to wait thirty days to see whether the line qualified — often enough time for REA groups to start construction of their government line in the area applied for by Consumers Power. Sometimes, when those thirty days were not enough, Winder

WHAT THE LADIES SAW

The inside of the trailer was equipped as an all-electric kitchen. Other appliances, including an electric washing machine and vacuum cleaner, were displayed outside. Farming would never be quite such a drudgery again. (Consumers Power photo by R. J. Gusenbar)

and the commissioners managed to hold up the applications even longer, giving the REA a still better chance to encroach on Consumers Power's potential territory. Many of these REA lines are still in existence today, although some of them were later taken over by Consumers Power at the request of their customers.[8]

In 1938, Consumers Power stepped up the fight by removing the five-farmers-to-the-mile requirement before putting in a rural extension. It now built them at its own expense, regardless of the number of customers. What's more, the rates all these farmers paid were the same as those charged to residential customers in the cities—and as we remember, they were coming down fast with Willkie's objective-rate campaign. In short, Consumers Power was giving the farmers exactly what the administration said only the government could give them.

What do you suppose happened as a consequence? Washington let out a howl of rage that Consumers Power was being unfair to the REA by undercutting its rates! But then, who can follow the mysterious rationales of bureaucrats?[9]

Eventually the government-sponsored REA associations had to raise their rates, and this put Consumers Power even further ahead. The company's rural electrification program boomed, even though at great expense to its treasury. Only as farmers became increasingly mechanized, thus requiring more electric energy, did the investment slowly come back to the company. In 1949, Consumers Power became the country's first and only company to achieve 100,000 farm customers. There was a big celebration, with door prizes (appliances, of course), music, and lots of refreshments, and everybody went home exhausted, as is the way after crowd events.

Today, Consumers Power no longer has 100,000 farm customers. Michigan no longer has 100,000 farms. That's the great irony of the rural electrification story: when the time comes in the development of an industrial society to electrify its farms, the end of old-fashioned farming is near. In a system of mechanized, energized agriculture, the 200-acre property ceases to prosper and goes out of business. Thus, in the very process of gaining farm customers, a utility is actually making sure of losing them eventually. Birth implies death. Like man himself, every one of his enterprises is self-limiting. *Sic transit gloria* Willkie.

18

Tonight at Midnight

Franklin Delano Roosevelt was reasonably adept at turning phrases. "We have nothing to fear but fear itself" caught the imagination, and still does. Some of his other pronouncements, such as "I hate war," depended for their impact less on originality than on his imposing presidential presentation. Certainly he was no Winston Churchill: the British warlord's oratory will never shrink in print. Nor, unlike Churchill, was Roosevelt a man of letters, except in the literal sense, and therein lay his linguistic legacy—the profligate use of initials in public life.

Not that anyone could digest today's bureaucratic menu without heavy draughts of alphabet soup. Beginning with the New Deal, governmental bodies became so numerous and their descriptions so complex that abbreviations and acronyms now offer the only escape from mile-long nomenclature. Besides, they suggest an air of brisk efficiency which may or may not be appropriate but which in any case tends to be reassuring.

Roosevelt's NRA (National Recovery Administration), PWA (Public Works Administration), WPA (Work Projects Administration), and REA (Rural Electrification Administration) were but a few of his alphabetic innovations. The one that concerns us in this part of our narrative is the TVA—the Tennessee Valley Authority, whose three initials almost broke the back of America's privately owned public utilities. Note that the A in TVA doesn't stand for Administration but for Authority, a word that wields considerably more clout.

One could, if one were whimsically inclined, blame it all on Kaiser Wilhelm II, the King of Prussia and Emperor of Germany, last ruler of the Second Reich. If Wilhelm hadn't gone to war in 1914 and (to be simplistic about it) sunk our *Lusitania*, the United States government probably would not have built

WOODROW WILSON DAM AT MUSCLE SHOALS

The federal government's first venture into the power business soon grew into the Tennessee Valley Authority. Commonwealth & Southern never recovered from this blow. (The Bettmann Archive, Inc.)

a power dam on the turbulent Tennessee River. This dam and appurtenant plant were to provide energy for making nitric acid, an essential component of conventional explosives, then much in demand. The site of the dam was Muscle Shoals, a 37-mile stretch of white water above Florence, Alabama.[1] Harnessing the angry river's force was but one of the project's objectives. Ever since the Civil War, the government had studied ways of damming the Tennessee to make it navigable and to halt its periodic, devastating floods. It is one of the ironies of history that the government bought the damsite from the Alabama Power Company, one of the building blocks of Commonwealth & Southern, the very organization destined to suffer the brunt of Roosevelt's subsequent attack on the utilities. Alabama Power, afraid at that time of being accused of war profiteering, collected only $1 for the $500,000 Muscle Shoals property. Insult interposed itself immediately between irony and injury. Alabama Power was fined $750 for running a photographic reproduction of the $1 check in a goodwill advertisement of the company's contribution to the war effort.

Alabama Power could well have saved itself this patriotic net loss of $500,749 without impeding the Allied victory. When Wilhelm threw in his crested towel and fled to the Netherlands, the government dam was not quite one-third finished. With gunpowder temporarily a drug on the market, construction was halted, and the dam just sat there, a monument to too much, too late. For some years, Congress resisted the temptation of pork-barreling the project to completion. It was during this ambiguous period that Muscle Shoals gained its first notoriety, and even then—long before Willkie—it became linked to Michigan in a sequence of events which contributed indirectly to what was to follow.

What happened was that Henry Ford proposed to buy the government boondoggle, now worth $236 million, at a slight discount, i.e., for $10 million, only half of which he proposed to put up in cash. Ford, who proclaimed that he desired the property "more than another billion dollars," was at that time intent on capturing the Presidency (not of Ford Motor Company, which he had already, but of these United States), and he saw in Muscle Shoals a magnificent campaign opportunity. He promised to make it the center of a huge power network that would "run" the United States without benefit of (or to) Wall Street, and after fifty years he would turn the whole thing over to the people. In addition, he would use the Muscle Shoals nitrate plant for the peaceful production of fertilizer and, in some fuzzy combination with the farm machinery he already produced in his factories, help the United States update its agriculture along the Soviet cooperative farm model. America always has had a weak spot for flagpole sitters and goldfish swallowers: Ford's fantasy sparked an unprecedented land boom in the Tennessee Valley, greatly benefiting real estate speculators. There was even to be a new city with a first name familiar to all Michiganders: Highland Park, Tennessee. This community was actually planned on paper and incorporated, with temporary offices in Detroit.

Ford's dream was endorsed by almost everyone, including most congressmen, in the lucrative business of proclaiming the virtues of motherhood and other worthy enterprises. But the Tennessee Valley scheme had one implacable enemy: Senator George W. Norris, the liberal Nebraska Republican who frequently lent his franking privilege to admittedly socialist causes. Norris would not budge from his position of public ownership for Muscle Shoals. Faced with this granitic handicap, Ford apparently made the decision that he'd rather own Muscle Shoals than move into the White House. In December 1923 he met with President Calvin Coolidge, who was immensely eager for a second term, and a few days after their private discussion Ford declared the country "perfectly safe with Coolidge," thereby fishing his own hat out of the ring. Tit for tat, in a message to Congress, Coolidge recommended the sale of Muscle Shoals to private interests, without, however, specifically naming Henry Ford. Not that he had to. Nobody else wanted it.

But Norris remained adamant despite the Presidential nudge.

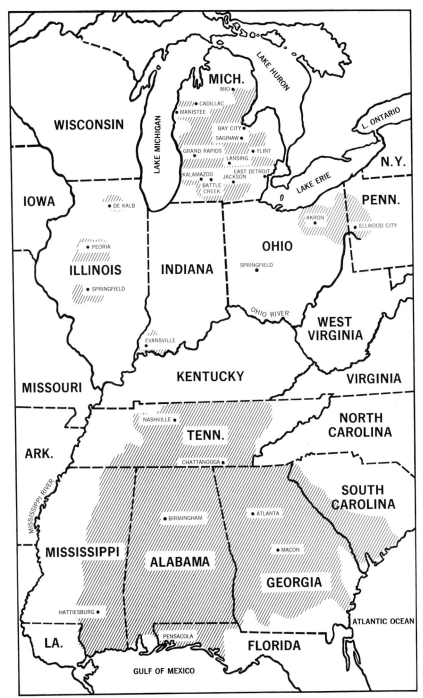

The far-flung domain of Commonwealth & Southern before the forced sale in 1939 of its Tennessee properties to the Tennessee Valley Authority.

After two different versions of a bill to sell Muscle Shoals to Ford had been passed by the Senate and the House, the single-minded senator jawboned the legislation to death in joint committee. Congress, meanwhile, appropriated funds for the completion of its hydroelectric project, now named Woodrow Wilson Dam. The dam's power plant finally started operating in 1925, and Alabama Power, still on friendly terms, bought all its output from the government.

This was not enough for Norris. His first bill to have Uncle Sam go directly into the power business, with government transmission and distribution lines, was killed by a Coolidge pocket veto in 1928. Norris tried again in 1931, and this time Hoover officially vetoed the plan. Hoover's opposition was based on two considerations. One was the cost of the project's modernization. By now the plant was six years old and based on blueprints devised fourteen years previously. Hoover's other objection was that such government competition would "break down the initiative and enterprise of the American people" and "negate the ideals upon which our civilization has been based." But Hoover's platitudes, however profound their rationale, could no longer stem the tide. Privately owned utilities were already in hot water to their waists and about to be immersed up to their necks.

The newspaper headline campaign against the "power trust" (see Chapter 15) was in high gear, fueled by the Federal Trade Commission hearings on public utilities that had been sparked by Senator Thomas J. Walsh, a Democrat from Montana. The FTC hearings lasted eight years, produced ninety-five volumes of testimony and reports, and cost the government some $2 million and the investigated companies probably even more than that. Most of the material arising from the hearings was irrelevant. Much of it was not at all unfavorable to the utilities, especially Consumers Power and other C&S subsidiaries.

But many of the FTC's findings were not exactly confidence-inspiring. You couldn't, for instance, blame the public for feeling resentment when they heard the government charge the National Electric Light Association with bribing school textbook authors to propagandize the arch-Tory point of view of the financiers who controlled most of the utility holding companies.

True, holding companies were not unique to the utilities. In 1932, about 70 percent of the country's 475 largest corporations in all areas of endeavor were holding companies. But as monopolies, the utilities were uniquely visible, and as every smart sharpshooter knows, you're bound to rack up a higher score when you can see your target.[2] Between 1919 and 1928, nearly four thousand individual public utility companies had disappeared by merger and absorption into holding-company structures. Before the collapse of the Insull system, thirteen holding companies controlled three-quarters of all privately owned utilities in the country. The three biggest superpyramids — The United Corporation, Insull, and Electric Bond & Share — alone controlled four out of five operating companies. Howard C. Hopson's New York-based Associated Gas and Electric Company system, although not one of the very biggest, provided an impressive example of the leverage thus achieved. By stacking holding companies in ten corporate layers, Hopson and others at the top, while owning only $300,000 worth of securities, had a firm grip on nearly $1 billion worth of assets.

This sort of pyramiding was ingeniously simple. Let's take a hypothetical case. If operating company A acquired property worth $1 million, it could issue bonds for half of that amount and voting stock for the other half. Thus holding company B could obtain control of operating company A by an investment of $1.25 million plus the price of a single additional share in order to have slightly more than 50 percent of the stock in company A. Through a similar operation, company B could, in turn, permit a super holding company C to control the entire million-dollar pyramid with an investment in a majority control of B common stock. Of course, several companies were always involved on the A, B, and other intermediate levels. By carrying this scheme through several layers of holding companies, it was possible to control many large operating properties with a relatively small investment.

In the case of Consumers Power and affiliated organizations in the C&S framework, there was a constant drive on the part of management, starting even before Willkie, to eliminate the intermediate holding companies as rapidly as practical considerations—mostly financing—would permit. Willkie himself desired nothing so much as corporate simplification.[3] But we must remember that his Commonwealth & Southern was but one of many utility holding companies, and revelations of such concentrated power as bared by the FTC hearings finally proved too much for a public pummeled by the stock market crash and sorely squeezed by the Depression. When Roosevelt declared himself for the Presidency, his platform called for strict federal regulation of utility holding companies.[4] Roosevelt also demanded federal supervision of utility rates where inter-

ROOSEVELT AND LINCOLN

On the campaign trail in 1932, FDR visited Muscle Shoals with other government power advocates, among them (left to right) Senator Kenneth McKellar, of Tennessee; Senator Clarence Dill, of Washington; Senator George Norris, of Nebraska; Roosevelt's daughter, then Mrs. Curtis Dall; and Governor B. M. Miller, of Alabama. The man behind the wheel is unidentified. The car is a Lincoln. (United Press International)

THE TVA BECOMES LAW
*On May 18, 1933, President
Roosevelt signed the Muscle
Shoals bill. The four men
standing immediately behind
him are (from the left) Sena-
tor McKellar; Representative
Miles C. Allgood, of Alabama;
Representative Lister Hill, of
Alabama; and, once again
Senator Norris, now finally
triumphant after his twelve-
year battle.* (United Press
International)

state connections were involved, and in general terms he
promised more electric power at cheaper rates—with the strong
implication of a federal program to provide it. Not surprisingly,
Senator Norris deserted the Republican Party to support FDR.
His reward was soon in coming.

On May 18, 1933, less than twelve weeks after Roosevelt's
inauguration, a new Tennessee Valley Authority bill, sponsored
by Norris in the Senate and by Representative John F. Rankin
in the House, became law. It charged the TVA with developing
the economic and agricultural life of the Tennessee Valley area
and with the production, distribution, and sale of electric power
in competition with private enterprise.[5]

Passage of the TVA legislation threw Commonwealth &
Southern into the main line of industry's defense against the

New Deal, and Wendell Willkie, as C&S boss, inevitably became the standard-bearer of privately owned public utilities.

It is doubtful that Willkie would have volunteered outright for this assignment had two of the C&S operating companies, Tennessee Electric Power and the aforementioned Alabama Power Company, not been the immediate targets of the administration's move. Not only had Willkie voted for Roosevelt, despite his platform, and even contributed $150 to his campaign, but he was also philosophically inclined to be on the side of the "people" rather than that of the holding-company barons. He was well aware, as Cobb had been before him, of holding-company abuses and, as will be recalled, was successfully fighting the bankers right within his own organization. He replaced the moneymen on his board of directors with operating men, broke with Bonbright & Company, and abolished, within C&S, the old holding-company strategem of assuring the loyalty of important local lawyers in operating territories by letting these attorneys have low-priced treasury stock and tossing enough legal business their way to keep them tame. Willkie was, in fact, so much in favor of a drastic housecleaning within the whole industry that he soon earned himself the sobriquet of the "Jesus Christ of the utilities business."

Even the arch-enemy of the power companies, Senator Burton K. Wheeler from Montana, who later introduced the legislation that doomed Commonwealth & Southern as a holding company, paid Willkie a left-handed compliment during an official hearing. He told Willkie that if all the utility companies had been as clean as C&S, the industry would not be facing its problems with the administration. Walter Lippmann, the eminent columnist, also cited Willkie as the leader of those men in the industry who "have been dismayed and angry at the kind of thing represented by the Insulls, and who fully recognize that the utilities are a public business. . . ."

But as much as Willkie was aware of the sins of the Tories in the power business, he wanted no help from Washington in setting the house in order. Such socialist ideas as he had espoused in his youth had gone up in smoke when he seriously studied Marxist concepts in college. Although Willkie never lost his drive for social justice, he had grown into a fervent believer in private enterprise and in the inalienable right of private property. His stance was especially firm since it was based on both philosophical and pragmatic foundations. Philosophically, Willkie could not agree with Roosevelt's contention that government has a right to compete with private enterprise; this would inevitably decrease, and perhaps wipe out, the value of investments by private citizens. Pragmatically, Willkie recognized that the waste and inefficiency inherent in most government operations could only result in higher cost to power customers, or if not directly to the customers then to the citizenry as a whole, since the government would be compelled to subsidize the resultant deficits by means of taxes.

Still, for the first eighteen months, it seemed as if Willkie could live with the TVA. It's safe to presume that this was only because, as Willkie often said, he was convinced that the New Deal would collapse after one term and that the TVA would go out of business. Alabama Power, as it had since 1925, kept buying the electric output of Muscle Shoals for distribution over it own lines. Shortly after passage of the TVA bill, Willkie worked out an agreement with David E. Lilienthal, one of the three initial TVA directors, whereby the Tennessee Valley area was divided into two spheres of influence.[6] Under this arrangement, Willkie agreed to sell to TVA a transmission line near the site of Norris Dam, on which construction had already begun, as well as various distribution properties in Alabama, Mississippi, Georgia, and Tennessee. Gross earnings of the properties sold to TVA amounted to approximately $1 million out of the $50 million total gross of the Southern companies in the C&S group.[7] Legal complications kept the sale from being consummated, except for the Norris Dam transmission line and the Mississippi properties, which were turned over to the government in June 1934. Most important among the provisions, however, was a territorial agreement which kept

C&S from selling power in counties where TVA had purchased distribution facilities and which conversely prevented TVA from selling to C&S customers outside those counties. This part of the compact remained in force until 1937.

Willkie and Lilienthal also agreed to work together on the sale of electric appliances. For his part of the bargain, Willkie offered help on arriving at designs of less expensive models. The government in turn agreed to finance appliance sales through its Electric Home and Farm Authority. Payments were added to the customers' monthly electric bills. Willkie didn't call himself the "world's greatest appliance salesman" for nothing. The scheme, which was strictly his idea, turned out to be the forerunner of installment-plan buying.[8] As soon as banks and private finance companies saw that the arrangement really worked, they got into the picture, and the country had taken another step forward in its consumer economy as we now know it.

On one vital point Willkie and Lilienthal could not come to agreement. Lilienthal proposed that TVA power sales should serve as a "yardstick" for the rates charged by privately owned utilities. Willkie objected to this unrealistic proposal from the outset—unrealistic, as we have already seen, because the government could always subsidize its rates, while private industry could not. Although this was a point of contention, the real collision did not come for some time.

Meanwhile, Willkie was busy pushing appliances and selling the objective rate. He even tried to sell it to Roosevelt. According to Willkie's biographer, Joseph Barnes, Willkie had dinner one night in October 1934 with Oswald Ryan, general counsel for the Federal Power Commission, and proposed to him that if Roosevelt should publicly declare himself for the objective rate (see Chapter 16) and promise that there would be no more TVAs in any region where utilities accepted this approach to lower electricity costs, Willkie would in return guarantee Roosevelt the backing of two-thirds of the industry. Ryan talked over the proposal with Frank R. McNinch, a member of the

Federal Power Commission, who conveyed it to the White House. Roosevelt reportedly said, "Well, maybe there is something to it," and asked McNinch to work it out.[9]

But it never came to that. Events were moving too fast for everybody. Not that Willkie's struggles to deal with the TVA problem took up all his time. Together with T. A. Kenney, who had taken over the presidency of Consumers Power at the time Willkie stepped into the presidency of Commonwealth & Southern, Willkie ran the Michigan show with as much energy as ever and with the same human touch that remained immune to the upheavals on the wider political and economic scene. At the other C&S properties, too, he was a favorite chairman of the board. At Georgia Power, for instance, he promoted the advertising manager because, as Willkie explained later, no man can do a good job if his wife is more important than he is—and that man's wife, Margaret Mitchell, had just published her immensely successful novel *Gone with the Wind*. Yet Willkie's good nature manifested itself less and less in his public speeches. He still remained on a personally friendly basis with Lilienthal, whom he considered, quite erroneously, "another farmer from Indiana." Indeed, he never attacked Lilienthal as an individual in all the bitter months that were soon to come.

At first there was still humor. On one occasion, Willkie produced a letter Roosevelt had written from Warm Springs on November 5, 1926, in which he had appealed to the Georgia Power Company, a subsidiary of Commonwealth & Southern, for help because the independent local system gave such poor service. Georgia Power had later taken over the system and improved service to Roosevelt's satisfaction. Pulling such a letter out of his pocket was fun for Willkie, and the irony behind it scored a dramatic point—any utility holding company that gave better service than a municipal system, even in Roosevelt's jaundiced view, evidently couldn't be all bad. But the fun soon stopped. As Norris Dam approached completion, which was scheduled for August 1936, the position on both sides hardened. Seven additional TVA dams were already under construction or on the drawing boards. Between the old Wilson Dam, the new Norris Dam, and the next dam, to be named after Senator Wheeler, TVA would have a capacity of 500,000 horsepower—1½ times as much as was then used in the Tennessee area altogether. Something obviously had to give.

The first skirmish in the battle had been fought back in September 1934, when holders of a small minority of the preferred stock of Alabama Power Company started litigation to invalidate the sale of fourteen of the company's municipal distribution properties to TVA. The suit, which eventually became famous as the Ashwander case, disrupted the working agreement that Willkie and Lilienthal had reached. Moreover, a lower-court decision gave reason to believe that this legal action might eventually result in the whole TVA's being declared unconstitutional. Much as Willkie insisted that C&S had not instigated the suit—that indeed he was an indirect defendant since he had been party to the sale that the Ashwander case challenged—Roosevelt regarded the suit as an assault by the utilities industry. On November 18, 1934, at Tupelo, Mississippi, the first town with a municipally owned power system fed by the TVA, Roosevelt announced that he would establish more TVAs all over the country. "What is being done here," he said, "is going to be copied in every state of the Union before we get through." With that speech, the cold war was heated up.

All through 1935, as the Ashwander case simmered its way through the courts, war talk on both sides grew more violent. On January 21, the White House announced the details of its Public Utilities Act, sponsored by Senator Wheeler and Representative Sam Rayburn, to regulate interstate transmission and sale of electric power. One of the bill's provisions, promptly dubbed its "death-sentence clause" by Willkie, spelled the doom of utility holding companies whose systems—like Willkie's Commonwealth & Southern's—were not contiguous and interconnected. As we shall see in the next chapter, the Wheeler-Rayburn Act, after years of legal and political fights, did finally force the dissolution of C&S and resulted in the emergence of Consumers Power Company as we know it today. But this was still some years off. For the time being the act merely added to the complexity of the struggle between the administration and private enterprise—between the new order and the old—and Willkie moved his desk from the C&S office on Pine Street in New York City to Washington, D.C., so as to be closer to the barricades.

The country was in the throes of immense social change. Corporate and entrepreneurial capitalism, normally thought to be to the right in the political spectrum, found itself pressed toward the center. Traditional socialism was still on the left, but a new collective, populist front, which combined socialist with nationalist and often racist concepts, such as those propounded by Detroit's rabble-rousing priest, Father Charles E. Coughlin, had suddenly formed on the right. Emotions ran high in all camps. Alliances formed and dissolved. Hatreds flourished. No one was immune. "Prolonged controversy," Willkie himself wrote at the time, ". . . is apt to engender such bitterness that fair and dispassionate consideration becomes extremely difficult."[10]

At the beginning of the controversy Willkie had been a moderate. He recognized the government's right to regulate public utilities, though he preferred state to federal regulation. Nor had he opposed TVA as a concept in earlier hearings before the House Military Affairs Committee, offering no objection to the government's construction of hydroelectric installations as long as they served primarily the flood control and navigation program. He had even, as we already know, voted for Roosevelt after the latter had proclaimed his TVA intentions. But now, driven increasingly into a corner, Willkie attacked all government business enterprise as inefficient, vulnerable to political manipulation, and unfair to private investors. "Such operations as TVA," he charged, were the works of men who "had become enamored with European economic and social concepts." He liberally quoted Norman Thomas, the perennial leader of America's Socialist Party, who had called the TVA "the only genuinely socialistic product of the New Deal." If Roosevelt could try his hand at oratory, then so could Willkie: "The Tennessee River waters four states and drains the nation," he declared.

Willkie spoke everywhere. He never overlooked an opportunity to carry his views to the public. "It makes no difference whether you be conservative, a liberal or a radical," he said, "you can subscribe completely [to the position of the utilities industry]. Neither Communism nor Socialism nor the social theories of 'share the wealth' nor 'distributing the wealth' are consistent with the 'destruction of wealth,'" which, he said, was precisely what the government was doing when it built power systems duplicating those already in existence and financed by the investments of private citizens. He pointed out that if one took into account all the factors, the rates of private utilities were lower than those of TVA. Willkie even cited figures to demonstrate that if his Tennessee Electric Power Company enjoyed subsidies like those which TVA had been granted, it could double its net income and still reduce rates to 35 percent below the rates charged by TVA.[11]

His contention was simply this: TVA managed to charge rates 50 to 60 percent below those of privately owned companies only because it didn't have to pay taxes, could obtain financing at lower interest rates than were available to private industry, faced fewer overhead expenses, and, to top it all off, was subsidized. "Whenever a householder in Tupelo, Mississippi, switches on a light, everybody in the United States helps pay for it," he said. "It is tax moneys that are being used to give Tupelo its well-publicized 'yardstick' rate."[12]

A classic comment by Thomas Edison, which Willkie liked to quote and expand on, stated the C&S leader's philosophy in no uncertain terms: "There is far more danger in public monopoly than there is in private monopoly, for when the government goes into business it can always shift its losses to the taxpayers. If it goes into the power business it can pretend to sell cheap power and then cover up its losses. The government never really goes into business, for it never makes ends meet, and that is the first requisite of business. It just mixes a little business with a lot of politics and no one ever gets a chance to find out what is actually going on."[13]

As may be imagined, Willkie's blunt tactics made him far from popular in Washington. Even some of his colleagues, fearful of reprisals from the administration, would have liked him to soften his approach. A little less dedication and a little more diplomacy, they felt, might help to nudge the New Deal from its extreme position. Roosevelt himself, like any politician, would have preferred compromise (more or less on his own terms, of course) to all-out battle. Indeed, he tried to achieve an agreement with the power industry and called in utility leaders for a series of behind-the-scenes White House conferences. But by then it was too late. "I am ready to sit down and work it out," Roosevelt complained privately to James A. Farley, New York's Democratic Party boss who served as his postmaster general and masterminded his second-term campaign. "But you can never pin them down . . . I had Wendell Willkie of Commonwealth & Southern in here for a talk, but I couldn't get anywhere with him. You can't get anywhere with any of them."[14]

Events have a way of escaping the control of their protagonists. Roosevelt saw his whole program threatened by the Damocles sword of unconstitutionality. The Supreme Court's February 1936 decision in the Ashwander case did not alleviate the New Deal's uneasy situation. The high court ruled against the stockholders, but avoided the basic constitutional issue. Worse yet, nineteen public utility companies affected by the TVA then filed suit under Willkie's leadership, seeking injunctions that would immobilize the entire TVA power program until the constitutional question was resolved. It was the most powerful weapon in Willkie's hands, and he had to use it. Once TVA started marketing its vast output of subsidized power to the public, the privately owned utilities in the area wouldn't have a chance. C&S was still operating at a profit, with earnings of 13 cents a share in 1936, but already the preferred stocks of its Southern companies were selling at up to 40 points below par.

With the completion of Norris Dam and the expiration of the Lilienthal-Willkie agreement, Tennessee itself became a battle ground. Cracker tempers ran high and hot. Construction men on both sides went out on the job with guns stuck in their belts. TVA crews pirated customers by building parallel lines and connecting them to private homes already served by

EVICTED BY THE TVA

The government had no compunction about moving families from their homes when land was required for a dam pond. Here a family is about to leave their condemned cabin in the Clinch River Valley to make room for the waters of Norris Dam. (United Press International)

the utility company. On more than one occasion, threats and abuses escalated into shoot-outs between the opposing crews. Even residents, whose sentiments were clearly on the side of TVA, became involved. They burned down private-company poles at night, and one Georgia housewife got out her husband's shotgun and warded off an Alabama Power crew until the TVA could get in.

One more attempt at compromise was made. The White House called for a truce to allow negotiations between Willkie and Lilienthal on a renewal of their earlier power pool. This truce also served to bridge the final months before the 1936 elections, a distinct convenience for the incumbent President, who expected a victory but could not be sure. When he finally walked off with a landslide, the roof caved in on the utilities.

Brain truster Thomas Corcoran declared that with FDR's victory at the polls, the utilities were now really "licked." Corcoran told Raymond Moley, then editor of *Today* and a former brain truster himself, that TVA would now try to take over Commonwealth & Southern "and all the rest of them too." He added that "twenty years from now the government will own and operate all the electric utilities in the country."

Roosevelt himself added fuel to this flame when, on June 3, 1937, he sent a message to Congress asking for six more TVAs all over the nation. One of these was to have jurisdiction of the whole Atlantic Coast area from Maine to Florida. Not surprisingly, the bill was introduced by Senator Norris and was immediately nicknamed the "seven TVAs bill," this number including the already existing project in Tennessee.[15]

It's interesting, and somewhat disquieting, to speculate what might have happened to the "seven TVAs bill" had the international situation not intervened. As it turned out, Congress shelved the bill a few months later, apparently at Roosevelt's own instigation, and he himself repudiated it on October 6, the day after his famous address that called for the containment of aggressor nations, by saying that all he'd really had in mind was "planning agencies."

While the administration thus did not launch further encroachments on the power industry, the TVA and the Public Utilities Act of 1935 were facts of life. Roosevelt himself called off the truce when Willkie refused to make a deal and to drop the suit by the operating companies under which TVA was enjoined from obtaining new customers until its constitutionality had been decided. TVA was already feeling the pinch: with the separation of the TVA and C&S systems upon completion of the Norris Dam, TVA had lost its biggest customer and almost two-thirds of its total revenue. On February 5, 1937, Roosevelt asked Congress to go along with him in reorganizing the Supreme Court so that it would support TVA and other New Deal programs.

Roosevelt did not get the Supreme Court legislation he asked for. It was defeated by just one vote in Senate committee; the bill probably would have passed had it reached the floor. But the Supreme Court, without being reorganized, suddenly began to reflect the mood of the times and handed down less conservative decisions. The court became even more "liberal" when Justice Willis Van Devanter's retirement gave Roosevelt the opportunity to replace this staunch anti-New Dealer with pro-New Deal Senator Hugo L. Black, the first of several such FDR appointments.

In January 1938, the Supreme Court stopped the injunctions of the power companies, and in March it upheld the provision of the Wheeler-Rayburn Act, which required utility companies to register with the Securities and Exchange Commission. Meanwhile, the U.S. District Court in Chattanooga, Tennessee, turned down Willkie's challenge to the TVA's constitutionality. This barrage of legal reverses marked the beginning of the end. As soon as the high court had barred Willkie's injunctions and backed government loans and grants to municipalities to build distribution systems to be fed by TVA, Secretary of the Interior Harold Ickes, as PWA administrator, announced allocations of more than $146 million for this purpose.

Willkie could do nothing but admit defeat. "No utility

company," he said, "can successfully compete with a municipal plant built with free money and upon which the municipality does not have to make a return. This is particularly true in areas such as the Tennessee Valley where a municipality can buy its wholesale supply of power at below cost from TVA. The decision is unfortunate . . . but the Supreme Court has spoken and it is the last word."

Up against the wall, there was only one thing left for him to do. As a "last resort in a desperate situation," he offered to sell the Tennessee Electric Power Company to the TVA.

It is not at all unlikely that Wendell Willkie had sensed, ever since Roosevelt's reelection, that this would be the outcome of the conflict. Probably his struggles had been less in the hope of victory than for the purpose of putting on enough pressure to get his stockholders a fair price for the doomed Tennessee company. Be that as it may, after having made his offer to sell, he continued to fight. On April 13, he appealed his suit on the TVA's constitutionality to the Supreme Court.

Willkie's first asking price for Tennessee Electric Power was $94 million. TVA countered with a $55-million offer, less discounts for depreciation, which were estimated at between $10 million and $15 million. Negotiations continued for a whole year, with both sides giving in a little at a time. Then, on January 30, 1939, the Supreme Court rejected Willkie's challenge of the TVA. Before the week was out, the show was over. Willkie agreed on a price of $78.6 million in cash and promised that there would be no more lawsuits against TVA.

Willkie had fought a brave battle and had accomplished the next to impossible in getting the government to pay this much. The fixed obligations of the Tennessee company amounted to about $72 million, and this was more than amply covered by the purchase price. Although the common shareholders lost quite a bit in the deal, Willkie's persistence had won the holders of bonds and preferred stock 100 cents on the dollar. Overnight, Willkie became the hero of the business community.

It took some doing to get Congress to appropriate funds for the purchase. Senator Norris held up the special bill until a provision was deleted that would have restricted TVA operations to the Tennessee River watershed. Not until August 15, 1939, less than three weeks before the outbreak of World War II, was the deal officially consummated.

On that day, flashbulbs popped and newsreel cameras whirred in the sixth-floor inner sanctum of the First National City Bank of New York as Lilienthal ceremoniously handed Willkie the government's down payment—a check for $44,-948,396.81.

"Thanks, Dave," Willkie said with a smile, for even in their bitterest days these two men had always gotten along pretty well. "This is a lot of money for a couple of Indiana farmers to be kicking around. For this I give you the deeds of The Tennessee Electric Power Company."[16]

"A COUPLE OF INDIANA FARMERS"
Wendell Willkie receives $44-million check from David E. Lilienthal (right), as down payment for Commonwealth & Southern's Tennessee property. The light-suited witness is E. E. Nelson. (United Press International)

That same evening, newspapers in many parts of the country carried an advertisement that accomplished something advertisements rarely do: it made the headlines and editorial pages and caused many citizens to wonder whether it was such a good idea after all for government to take over a private business.

Under the bannerline, "Tonight at Midnight . . . We Hand Over Our Tennessee Electric Properties and a $2,800,000 Tax Problem," the advertisement read:

> AT MIDNIGHT TONIGHT, The Commonwealth & Southern Corporation turns over to various public officials all its electric properties in the State of Tennessee.
>
> We have always believed, and still believe, that the interests of the public are better served by privately operated utilities than by publicly operated plants. Take our Tennessee properties for example:
>
> The State of Tennessee and most of the communities we have been serving have depended, in no small part, upon the taxes they have collected from us to pay the cost of their governmental activities, including school, water, fire, health and other services.
>
> Our Tennessee properties paid into local and state treasuries a total of $2,225,000 from electric revenues for 12 months ended June 30, 1939; with Federal taxes, the total for this period is about $2,800,000. That is more than 20 cents on every dollar received for electric service in Tennessee . . . it amounts to over $7,670 in taxes for every day of the year.[17]

The spectacular TVA war was over, but the laborious legal struggle for the survival of Consumers Power and the other Commonwealth & Southern companies had barely begun.

19

Metamorphosis

It was one of those days nobody ever forgets. Bay City bustled with excitement. Flags were flying and bands were playing as masses of people crowded the sidewalks around the Masonic Consistory, braving the hot summer sun of mid-July 1940. The occasion was the dedication of the John C. Weadock Plant on the shore of Lake Huron's Saginaw Bay, just north of the Saginaw River's mouth. Construction of this plant had been halted two years earlier as a result of the 1937–1938 recession, but now at last it was ready to go. Plant dedications are traditionally festive events. They are milestones of progress, not only for the utility company that built the plants, but even more so for the people, for the consumption of electric power is a measure of the nation's standard of living: power means prosperity.[1] No wonder that utilities pull all stops for such celebrations and turn them into carnivals, with food and drink, raffles and favors, music and orators, and appeals over the public-address system for lost children. As usual at Consumers Power dedications, the weather was as glorious as it should be on holidays. But it was not the blue sky, flecked with joyous white clouds, nor the party favors nor the significance of more steam-electric power that drew the crowds on this extra-special day. It was their chance to see the man who might well be their next President.

Only two weeks earlier, Wendell L. Willkie had been nominated at the Republican convention in Philadelphia, and his campaign was already under way. If it had been up to Bay City, Willkie would have been elected right then and there. Willkie buttons, worth a nickel at par, were going for $5. Some folks were even willing to offer $7 or $8.

Willkie and the other honored guests were picked up at the plant by the sleek Blue Boat of the Defoe Boat Works. The 150-foot motor yacht brought the dignitaries to the downtown harbor of Bay City, Weadock's old hometown, where Willkie was to speak at a festive dinner. Places had been set for 1,000 guests in the Consistory's huge hall, and all the lucky people with tickets were eager to hear Wendell (which is what they called him whether they knew him or not) deliver his first major political address. In this largely Republican assembly, the feeling was like that of a football team at half time when they're two touchdowns behind and Knute Rockne, that great coach, gets up and gives a rousing speech that sends them out there to win the ball game. Only this was politics, and the Republicans were behind by two elections, and they figured that with Wendell up there in the contest, they just possibly might make it this time.

Soon all the seats were filled except at the two-tiered head table. There were all those empty chairs up there, standing at attention, sixteen in a row, with the white linen and the silver and china sparkling in the light, but no Wendell. He was hanging on the telephone, talking with California, talking with New York, talking with politicos all over the map. Down in the banquet hall, the headwaiter nervously checked his watch for the tenth time. Finally, it was no longer possible to hold the food in the kitchen; the waiters fanned out with their fragrant trays, and the guests began eating. The main course was being served when at last the dignitaries marched in. The sound of a gavel hushed the clatter of knives and forks, the hall fell silent for a moment, and then a great roar of applause broke out.

Up on the podium, Wendell Willkie stood next to Weadock, the kingmaker, now approaching his eighty-first birthday but still with a lion's head and a mane to match, and Willkie smiled at the crowd when it came time for him to speak. Slowly he took off his rimless glasses and brushed a hand through his mussed-up hair. Here it comes, everybody thought, now "that man in the White House" is really going to catch hell. But Willkie, with his great poise and posture, let his eyes sweep across all those 1,000 faces staring at him from the main floor and the mezzanine balcony, and all he said was, "Ladies and gentlemen, I'm here only to do honor to John C. Weadock."

And that's exactly what he did. Not a word about politics, the government versus free enterprise, FDR, the brain trusters, or the New Deal. This wasn't the national arena but a Consumers Power family affair that honored the past and looked toward the future, and Willkie surely meant to keep it that way.[2]

One wonders whether Willkie would not have preferred to maintain the status quo all around and remain a utilities man. His ascendancy to the top rungs of America's political ladder had certainly been unexpected. The usual way up is on the slippery footholds of governorships and congressional elections, or at least by traverse from the upper reaches of the U.S. Army hierarchy. Willkie had never run for office before, although he had been approached to do so during his Akron days; and while he had served in the Army, and even in a war, he had never won a battle, only a few courts-martial. What had catapulted him to sudden political prominence, of course, was that in fighting the administration on behalf of

GREAT EXPECTATIONS

When Willkie came to Bay City in July 1940 after his nomination for the Presidency, the whole town turned out hoping to hear a blistering anti-Roosevelt speech. But Willkie was no man to mix politics with business, especially where his old friend, John Weadock (center, left), was involved. The occasion for Willkie's visit was the dedication of the Weadock Plant, and all he said at the banquet at the Bay City Consistory (above) was, "I am here only to do honor to John C. Weadock."

On the outdoor speakers platform, too, Willkie took a backseat to Dan Karn (left) and dreamily slouched against the balustrade.

Willkie did not start campaigning in earnest until after his total separation from Commonwealth & Southern affairs. His homespun Hoosier whistle-stopping (right) got him more votes than any other losing candidate had ever received before him, but when it was all over, FDR still sat in the White House. (Consumers Power collection)

his Commonwealth & Southern Corporation, he had found himself the spokesman not only for the utilities industry, but also for the whole American business community. True, in the last analysis Willkie had lost the fight, but no other man had opposed Roosevelt's policies so lucidly, and yet in a homespun style, as this Hoosier who ran the nation's third largest utilities organization.[3]

As early as May 22, 1939, columnist David Lawrence had discussed him as a Republican possibility, one from whom fair dealing in government's relation with business could be expected. Lawrence had pointed out that Willkie was precisely the kind of independent Democrat who would fit the pattern that nine out of ten Republicans really wanted but didn't dare ask for. In a thank-you letter to Lawrence, Willkie wrote that he was "utterly devoid" of political ambition, "but no man could be honest and at the same time indifferent to the suggestion from one such as you that he was qualified to lead the country in these times." His closing comment had wished Lawrence "all the luck in the world and, for myself, that no one takes you seriously."

A few months later, in November 1939, General Hugh S. Johnson, former head of the National Recovery Administration and now also a columnist, was answering questions about potential candidates after delivering a speech at the Bond Club in New York City. "How about Wendell Willkie?" someone in the audience called out. Johnson said he thought this was a fine suggestion. When newspaper reporters asked Willkie for a comment, he replied with the sense of humor so typical of him: "In view of the speed with which the federal government is taking over my business, I will probably have to be looking around for a new job. General Johnson's is the best offer I've had so far." And that's how Wendell Willkie found himself transmogrified from the business world's knight in shining armor into a dark horse.

Looking back, we can say with great assurance that Willkie obviously didn't stand a chance against FDR—and he didn't.

Yet it turned out that 22 million Americans voted for him, more than had ever before supported the losing Presidential candidate. Indeed, this dark horse's canter toward the White House looked deceptively easy at first. At Consumers Power, however, as well as at the other operating companies of Willkie's Commonwealth & Southern, the final months before his nomination and his almost immediate resignation from C&S on July 17 were an ambiguous time in which business found itself inextricably mixed with politics.

More than once, when Horace Brewer, then purchasing agent for Consumers Power, visited one of the suppliers, that company's sales manager would tell him, "Before we talk business, our president wants to see you." Brewer would enter the president's office, and that gentleman, if such he may be called under the circumstances, would say something like, "Well, Horace, old buddy, we like you Consumers Power people. You've bought this and that from us for a long time; you're good customers, and Horace, old chum, when you leave here you go right on back home and you tell Wendell that I'll be there in Philadelphia with $50,000." This sort of tail wagging and back scratching put Brewer and others in awkward positions, but the men solved the dilemma in the way they figured Willkie would have wanted them to, by paying no attention to such blandishments, by separating church from state, and by buying only when the bid itself was on the button.[4]

On May 31, 1940, practically on the eve of Willkie's nomination, he filed a thirty-six page brief with the Securities and Exchange Commission. His brief questioned once again the constitutionality of the order, given under the Wheeler-Rayburn Public Utilities Act, compelling Commonwealth & Southern to divest itself of ten of its subsidiaries. It was Willkie's last action in the holding-company battle; the final phases of defeat were in the hands of his successor.

That man was Justin R. Whiting, the attorney who had replaced Willkie as Weadock's associate in 1933 and who once again stepped into Willkie's shoes, now as leader of the organization. Weadock put him there, as he had Willkie, and before Willkie, Cobb. It was the last time that Weadock determined the royal succession at Commonwealth & Southern and Consumers Power. Neither he nor the holding company would survive the decade. But despite his advanced age, the kingmaker from Bay City was far from senile. He was still a genius at judging men.

Whiting's association with C&S dated back to the 1920s, when, as an independent attorney, he had handled much of the company's legal work in Michigan on a retainer basis. Among his labors had been the liquidations of the traction subsidiaries. At that time, Whiting had once suggested to B. C. Cobb that these operations be closed down as soon as possible, before they lost any more money.

"Justin," Cobb said, "I don't know why you of all people are making this recommendation. Once this traction business is finished, there won't be any work for your office. You are talking yourself right out of a job." Whiting replied very seriously, "Mr. Cobb, it's my responsibility to take care of the security holders and not to worry about whether my office will be retained." Cobb was immensely impressed by this answer. He decided then and there not only that he'd keep Whiting with the company after the liquidations but also that he'd move him closer to the center of power. That's how Whiting had come to join old Weadock in New York when Willkie took over C&S.[5]

Whiting's reply to Cobb on the traction matter sounds more than a little pompous to our modern ears. He might almost have been putting Cobb on. But this wasn't so. Whiting was that sort of man: quiet, precise, somewhat standoffish, responsible to the extreme. His mission as a corporation attorney, as he saw it, was to protect the stockholder—the man who risked his money to build America's future. This attitude, which was then still prevalent at least in smaller cities like Port Huron, where Whiting had been born and raised, had been instilled in him by his father, an old-time Democratic congressman of high purpose and apparently utter honesty.

WILLKIE'S SUCCESSOR

Justin R. Whiting was short in figure, but not of stature, as he unscrambled the complex affairs of Commonwealth & Southern and led Consumers Power through its first years of independence. (Fabian Bachrach)

Like his father, Whiting lived for his work. His wife, Patricia, once said that she never knew whether he had one suit or thirty. If indeed he possessed more than one, they were surely all of the same color, the same material, and the same cut, and they were all equally wrinkled. His shoes were always cracked, and his pants baggy. It is hard to imagine a less prepossessing chief executive. Moreover, Whiting was a very short man, a fussy gnome. His small frame, if not his attire, made him self-conscious; so much so, in fact, that he had a special long-legged chair moved into the boardroom so that he would look taller when the directors were in session. His letters were full of stilted, old-fashioned formalities, such as "I beg to state." Like Cobb, he was a stickler for details. Once he even gave someone hell for arriving fifteen minutes late at a cocktail party. Unlike Cobb, however, he was not an autocrat. Nor, evidently, was he a rousing, inspirational showman like Willkie.

All the Weadock protégés turned out to be exactly the right choices for their time. Cobb, the martinet, had been the logical man to pull the organization together. Willkie, the impetuous extrovert, had been the best man to expand the company's sales and to fight its pitched battles. Whiting, the methodical introvert, was ideally suited to see the company through its metamorphosis, to pick up all the pieces, and, in compliance with an overwhelming multitude of complex government regulations, to unscramble The Commonwealth & Southern Corporation.

While the Tennessee Valley Authority had merely threatened privately owned power companies in its own area of operation, the Wheeler-Rayburn bill, which emerged as the Public Utility Act of 1935, spelled the doom of C&S. The bill's "death-sentence clause"—so dubbed by Willkie at one of the congressional hearings—called for the dismemberment of all utility holding companies except those which controlled single, integrated systems of operating companies in single regions of the country.[6] C&S was evidently one of the bill's prime targets. Consumers Power, biggest and strongest of the C&S companies, sat by itself in Michigan. Equally isolated were C&S's Southern Indiana Gas and Electric Company and Central Illinois Light Company (whose operations, in fact, were not even contiguous within Illinois). The Ohio Edison and Pennsylvania Power Companies formed one relatively small clump that straddled the Ohio-Pennsylvania border. Then there was a big gap, and only in the South did the other six C&S properties constitute a single block—the Mississippi, Alabama, Georgia, South Carolina, and Gulf Power Companies, the last of these in Florida, hugging the north rim of the Gulf of Mexico, and of course the Tennessee Electric Power Company, which was eventually sold to TVA.

Paradoxically, it's possible that if Commonwealth & Southern had been even more of a giant and had owned *all* the operating utilities from Michigan to Florida, it might have survived as an integrated holding company, at least in the form specified in the original Wheeler-Rayburn bill. But that's idle speculation. No doubt, the bill would have taken a different shape in that case and forced the dismantling of C&S anyway.

Roosevelt wanted to kill off all holding companies. Indeed, he later claimed personal credit for the death-sentence clause. There is some indication, however, that the bill's authors, legislative aides Thomas Corcoran and Benjamin Cohen, had inserted this section as a bargaining counter. Be that as it may, the temper of the times was such that the holding companies didn't have a chance. The deck was stacked against them. The fact the Willkie ran a clean shop didn't help him one bit.

He emphasized in its defense:

> The Commonwealth & Southern Corporation has an exceedingly simple corporate structure; it has no intermediate holding company in either gas or electric business; it holds the common stock of its eleven operating companies directly. It makes no profit, direct or indirect, on management, supervision, financing, engineering or construction, and its entire income from the operating companies is derived from interest and dividends on securities which it owns in such companies. The Corporation has never borrowed any money from its operating companies, nor does it deal for profit in the securities of such companies.
>
> No officer of the Corporation received any bonus or compensation other than his salary and nominal directors' fees. No officer of the Corporation receives any profit from any company, or as a partner in any firm through which securities are marketed or from which this Corporation or its subsidiaries buy any service, merchandise, or any other material used by this Corporation or any other subsidiaries. Every officer and director of the Corporation is, by training and experience, particularly familiar with the operation and administration of utilities.[7]

These were all facts. An investigator for the Federal Trade Commission once even complimented Willkie on the fine way C&S was being managed. But when Willkie suggested that the commendation might be included in the investigator's report, the young man replied, "Oh, Mr. Willkie, I would be severely criticized if I put anything in my report favorable to a holding company."[8] As Senator Homer T. Bone from Washington, not altogether unkindly, pointed out to

Willkie during a Senate committee session on the Wheeler-Rayburn bill, "I am just wondering what the effect on the public mind is going to be right now when millions of people are demanding not this bill, but something infinitely more drastic with respect not only to your business but all other forms of business. You gentlemen will have to pay the price along with the rest of us. . . . We are dealing with forces over which we have no control."[9]

These forces swept over the utilities like a tidal wave: the market collapse, the Depression, and the dust bowl; the people's reaction to the abuses by arch-Tories in the utilities business and other big industries; the propaganda activities of admittedly socialist groups and their less forthright front organizations; the fervor of the young New Dealers; the political opportunism of Roosevelt. Even the folksy anti-Wall Street humor of Will Rogers contributed to the flood.

Yet the Wheeler-Rayburn bill was so controversial that Congress fought over it for seven months. The death-sentence clause itself passed the Senate by only a one-vote margin, and was then mildly softened for a compromise with the House. With the signature of the President on August 26, 1935, the Public Utility Act became law.

The act authorized the Federal Power Commission to regulate rates, facilities, and securities of all companies engaged in the interstate transmission of electric power, and it required the Securities and Exchange Commission to dissolve all utility holding companies except those limited to single, integrated systems. All holding companies were to register with the SEC by January 1, 1937. However, only the American Water Works Company complied. Instead, Commonwealth & Southern and other companies brought suit against the government to test the act's constitutionality.[10] One of these, by Electric Bond & Share, was picked for the test action, and the other actions were tabled pending its outcome.[11] On March 28, 1938, the Supreme Court sustained the act's registration provision, but said nothing about the legality of the death-sentence clause. In this decision, the high court declared that the use of the mails might be denied to a holding company which failed to register. That same day, C&S filed with the SEC.[12]

Then years of arguments and counterarguments began. Nobody could agree on the exact meaning of the law. Interpretations differed not only, as might be expected, between government and industry but also within government and within industry. Through 1940, the SEC viewed compliance with the integration provisions as involving an exchange of properties between different holding-company systems so as to make each more compact.[13] It was not yet understood by the utilities, nor at this point prescribed by the Commission, that any holding company would be limited to only one such system.[14] C&S took the stand that Consumers Power and its other companies constituted an efficient operating unit and thus complied with the requirements of the act. But this was not the way the SEC saw it. On March 19, 1941, the Commission filed an astonishing 317-page report whose findings were even more shocking than Willkie, in his day, would have expected. Nor had Whiting, at the helm now, ever anticipated anything like this.

C&S was given three choices. One was that Consumers Power could be retained, but all other properties disposed of. Another was that C&S might retain Alabama Power Company, and possibly also Mississippi and Gulf Power, but no others. The third choice was to retain Georgia Power and perhaps South Carolina Power. Moreover, the SEC made it clear that whichever course was elected, any of the resulting companies might still be too large and subject to further divestment.

It wasn't just the fate of the stockholders that was at stake here; they would of course be the losers in any such drastic dismemberment. An even more vital consideration was that the country could ill afford to do anything that would decrease the efficiency of the power industry. The year was 1941. The Japanese had not yet attacked Pearl Harbor, and America was not yet in the war, but the Lend-Lease agreement with Britain had been enacted barely a week before the release of the SEC report, and it was already clear that the United States would become the arsenal of the democracies. Perhaps it was because of this that the dissolution of Commonwealth & Southern was not pressed so hard by the government during the war years as it otherwise might have been. Certainly Whiting's presentations to the SEC, substantiating the holding company's efficiency, not only in customer service but also as a national power resource, must have given the Commission at least some pause.[15] Whiting proved beyond argument that Commonwealth & Southern's rates were lower than those of any other major privately owned utility group. He also pointed out that the C&S territory embraced several important industrial areas, especially Michigan, whose production was essential to the war effort, and that the C&S companies served a host of military installations, from Camp Custer at Battle Creek to the Naval Defense Area at Pensacola, Florida. It was only the foresight of the holding company's management, now under government attack, that had made it possible to meet the power demands of these establishments: since 1937, Commonwealth & Southern had put into operation at least one, and often several, new power-generating units every single year, increasing the group's capacity by some 300,000 kilowatts during that period.

While Whiting thus fought the C&S legal battle, a task for which he was equipped most admirably by temperament as well as by training and experience, the operations of Consumers Power were largely in the equally competent hands of Dan Karn and his assistant general manager, Wilson Arthur.

At the time it was a joke around Consumers Power that in order to make it with the company, you had to be either a redhead or a Purdue graduate. Karn was a redhead, and like his predecessor, Tippy, had gone to Purdue. The similarity didn't stop there. Tippy had been extremely popular, and so now was Karn. A big man, over 6 feet tall, he had a quiet sense of humor and a manner that inspired confidence. No one could have been better qualified to represent a company at public events. Karn didn't just earn his living as a front man, however. He was a highly experienced operating man who, except for an initial short stint with the Central Illinois Light affiliate in Peoria, had been with Consumers Power all his working life. He had started in Grand Rapids with the steam-heating department in 1916, had later joined Frank Newton's rate department in Jackson, and then had worked his way up through many other assignments to the general managership and a vice-presidency. But he was such a nice guy that he needed a disciplinarian at his side, and such a man was Arthur, who ran the kind of tight ship that Karn himself never could have managed.

When Delbert Ford, then in charge of Consumers Power's display department, first met Arthur, the latter gave him the following instructions: "One, I don't know anything about your business. You run it. That's what you were hired for. Two, live within your budget and save us some money if you can. Three, I don't like apple-polishers coming to me tattling on other guys, so don't you ever do that. And if you ever get into trouble yourself come directly to me and let me know."[16] Ford adored Arthur. Many other Consumers Power people didn't. They considered Arthur an autocrat, when actually he was just a mite bashful and thus reticent, and furthermore lacked the patience for visiting and passing the time of day without anything being accomplished. Arthur's competence, however, more than made up for any lack of popularity. His experience, in addition to a four-year C&S management stint in New York, encompassed just about everything from personnel matters and labor relations to rural electrification and sales of every description: power, lighting, gas, and appliance merchandising. He seemed to know every aspect of the utilities business. Whenever there was a problem, one could turn to him for an immediate answer.[17]

Karn and Arthur made an excellent team. They had to, for

theirs was no easy assignment. Because of the company's location in Michigan, the Allied center of production of combat vehicles and much other essential material, the wartime stresses on Consumers Power were enormous. Power-distribution graphs no longer showed pronounced peaks and valleys, depending on the hour of the day. Defense industries worked around the clock, and while brownouts conserved some power, there was hardly enough to go around. It was only by postponing maintenance and running units at greater than their rated outputs that requirements could be met; many times voltages were backed off to spread out the available supply. Any failure, whether in generation, transmission, or distribution, meant shutting down an assembly line whose products our fighting men were desperately waiting for. In the face of mounting shortages in manpower and supplies, it was a never-ending struggle to keep the operation going.

Foreshadowing today's power grid, additional interconnections were established between Detroit Edison and Consumers Power to help out in emergencies.[18] Women replaced men as substation operators.[19] Meters were read only every second month. With civilian production halted, the sales department closed out its remaining appliance stocks and concentrated on keeping existing appliances in working order. From 1943 on, for the duration, Consumers Power showrooms sold only bulbs, fuses, and occasionally extension cords. Construction came to a near standstill. Although utility service was essential to the war effort, only the most vital expansion projects received the necessary priorities. Basic materials were almost impossible to obtain.

Nor did the end of the hostilities in 1945, with V-E Day in May and V-J Day in August, immediately alleviate these problems. On the contrary, demobilization brought with it unprecedented demands for power, as the returning veterans founded new families and homes, and industry tried to catch up with the pent-up demands of the war years. Until 1949, material was still allocated on the basis of priorities.

Power lines could not be extended more than 50 feet without permission from Washington. Such authorizations were not easy to get. First one had to prove that manpower was available to handle the job.

There was the time, for instance, when Consumers Power wanted to add to the Weadock Plant, an expansion project that had been stopped by the war. Horace Brewer succeeded in getting the bricklayers' union agent drunk, which wasn't too difficult, and then persuaded him to write a letter saying that enough bricklayers were on hand for the project. Next, Brewer repeated the procedure with the agent of the steam fitters' union. Brewer then took these letters to Washington and finally obtained a permit.[20] But even with the necessary priorities granted, the project was still postponed for several months while Consumers Power purchasing agents scoured the country for materials as far afield as the Pacific Northwest.[21]

By that time, on the corporate level, the eventual fate of Commonwealth & Southern was resolved. Whiting's struggles with the Securities and Exchange Commission had been to no avail.[22] As soon as the wartime pressures were off, the government made it clear that C&S would not be permitted to survive. Divestment of certain properties was not enough. Nothing short of complete dissolution could satisfy the SEC's requirements for compliance with the Public Utilities Act.

On March 25, 1946, Whiting filed the sixth of eight different plans for changes in corporate structure that were designed to meet the government's demands while fulfilling the company's obligations to its stockholders. One of the complicating factors was that the common stocks of the operating companies were held by C&S. For example, there had never been any common stock of Consumers Power on the market, and there was thus no way to determine a fair market price for these securities. Plan No. 6, the first to face up to the inevitability of complete dissolution, provided for the liquidation of C&S and the creation of a new holding company, to be called The Southern Company, which would receive all the common stocks of the Southern operating companies. As far as Consumers Power and the other Northern companies were concerned, Whiting suggested two alternatives: distribution to the preferred stockholders of C&S or sale on the open market. To determine the market's acceptance of the securities, 200,000 shares of The Ohio Edison Company were sold in June 1946, and 500,000 shares of Consumers Power in November of that year. By the end of 1946, application had been made to the New York Stock Exchange for the listing of 4,123,432 shares of Consumers Power no-par common at $33.54 a share.[23]

But the struggle continued for another two years. Plan No. 6 faced government opposition in regard to the size of The Southern Company, even though it would serve a single, integrated territory. Whiting's Plan No. 7, modified to meet these SEC objections, then ran afoul of the stockholders. Plan No. 8, filed on July 7, 1948, effected a compromise that seemed to satisfy all the interested parties except a small minority of shareowners. To overcome their objections, it became necessary to obtain a court order, and not until July 15, 1949, was the way cleared for the orderly dismantling of The Commonwealth & Southern Corporation.

The final dissolution plan made South Carolina Power a separate organization, apart from The Southern Company. Each share of C&S preferred was to be exchanged for 2.8 shares of Consumers Power common, 55/100 of a share of Central Illinois Light common, plus $1 in cash. All remaining assets were to go to C&S's common shareholders.[24]

And so, after fourteen years on death row, Commonwealth & Southern was executed on October 1, 1949.[25] By then, even the condemned almost welcomed the release. The highly efficient organism that had been created by men like W. A. Foote, Anton Hodenpyl, Henry Walbridge, George Hardy, and B. C. Cobb no longer existed—but its cells lived on. At the same moment that C&S passed from the scene, Consumers Power became an independent entity, with a life all its own.

The situation was not necessarily to its liking. Serious

struggles lay ahead that could have been eased with the support of a parent body. But at least Consumers Power inherited the parent's brain. Justin R. Whiting remained Consumers Power president and moved to Jackson.[26] Two years later, on November 29, 1951, when Whiting became chairman of the company's reconstituted board of directors, Karn was made president. Continuity was preserved. Life could go on.

No event ever stands alone in history. It is born of its time, sibling to countless other events, all shaping one another even as youngsters do when they grow up together. The Tennessee Valley Authority and the Public Utility Act of 1935 had been but two of the many children of the Depression era. Another of its offspring was militant unionism.

The American Federation of Labor (AFL) dated back to 1881, when Samuel Gompers had founded its parent body, the Federation of Organized Trades and Labor Unions. Despite several violent episodes, however, the AFL was basically tradition-oriented. In 1935 a group of unions that were impatient with Gompers's cautious policy formed the Committee for Industrial Organization. Thrown out of the AFL two years later, this became the Congress of Industrial Organizations (CIO). Under the leadership of John L. Lewis, head of the United Mine Workers, the CIO set out to organize industries that had until then resisted unionization.[27] Among these were the steel, automobile, and textile industries—and the public utilities.

Consumers Power was hit by sit-down strikes in 1937 and 1938 as the AFL and the CIO battled each other for dominance among the company's operating, maintenance, and construction employees. The internecine union struggle was finally decided in a September 1940 runoff election in which the AFL's International Brotherhood of Electrical Workers came out the winner.[28]

To claim that prior to this time labor relations at Consumers Power had always been ideal, one would have to be a liar or a fool. Human relationships just don't work that way, especially where differences of interest are involved, as with employer and employee. But at Consumers Power the relationship between management and labor had been unusually good, far above average. Hodenpyl had earned his nickname "Father Anton" for good reason.[29] There had been a real sense of belonging in all ranks. To a large extent, unionism brought this to an end.[30]

The picture was the same throughout the country. Labor's revolt of the 1930s had liberated it from paternalism, from personal dependence on the employer. This newfound independence was illusory, however. Revolution is an exchange of bosses; you trade in one and get another. America's old boss had been the entrepreneur. Its new boss was the organization. With the Depression and World War II, the nation had completed its own metamorphosis into a mass society.

Who is to say which life-style—the individualist or the collective—makes men happier? Be that as it may, the vast changes in the country's social and economic philosophy brought with them some important material benefits. More security was one. Even at Consumers Power, which, like many other companies, had usually followed the practice of paying monthly sums to retired employees, this stipend had been considered on an individual basis and was nothing anyone could count on. Now, starting in 1944, there was a guaranteed pension plan, with cash reserves accumulated during the period of employment to cover payments after retirement. More leisure was another: workweeks grew shorter, and vacations longer. Paychecks grew too. Willkie, at $75,000 a year, probably had not been overpaid, considering his responsibilities as head of Commonwealth & Southern. But the average utility employee, making then $34 a week, surely was underpaid, not perhaps in relation to the Depression economy's ability to pay him, but in terms of his needs. Now mass production plus mass consumption spelled mass affluence.

For the men involved in future building, the satisfaction of the wants created by this new affluence (and in turn feeding it) became the main concern. Growth was the byword of the fabulous Fifties, and so also at Consumers Power Company, as Michigan's leadership as a great industrial center became even more pronounced in the postwar years.

Population growth and general prosperity kept pace with industrial expansion. The state's census, 5.3 million in 1940, rose to 6.4 by 1950 and rocketed to nearly 8 million by 1960. Most of this growth took place in Consumers Power territory. While some of its major cities—among them Jackson, Battle Creek, and Muskegon—lost inhabitants, the booming suburban areas far more than made up the difference.

Oakland County, north of the Eight Mile Road boundary, which had been so providently preempted by James Brown from Michigan Consolidated Gas, doubled its population between 1945 and 1960. Oak Park, one of its communities, increased its population sevenfold and became a city in its own right. Midland, Lansing, and Flint boomed. Grand Rapids and Kalamazoo annexed fringe districts. Several communities where Consumers Power had acquired gas territory in June 1934 were central to areas where some of the biggest growth took place: Plymouth and Wayne, just west of Detroit, and Mt. Clemens, in the burgeoning Macomb County stretch along Lake St. Clair.[31]

Consumers Power itself participated in stimulating the state's growth. It was a particular concern of the company's industrial development department to stimulate economic progress in areas that had not yet benefited from industrialization.[32] Consumers Power thus brought Corning Glass to Albion, General Electric to Edmore, Hooker Chemical to Montague, and U.S. Plywood to Gaylord. Similar industry locations were arranged in other communities.

Meanwhile, less than a year after the breakup of Commonwealth, Consumers Power had extended its electric operations to the Straits of Mackinac. With the purchase on September 8, 1950, of the Michigan Public Service Company, it acquired the property serving the areas of Traverse City and Cheboy-gan,[33] and thus now covered most of the Lower Peninsula, all the way from its northern tip down to the Ohio and Indiana boundaries, from Lake Michigan to Lake Huron and Lake Erie.[34]

But territorial expansion was the least of it. By 1955 Consumers Power found itself serving nearly 788,000 electric customers, an increase of more than 50 percent since the end of the war, and nearly 427,000 gas customers, up from 253,-880. Even more impressive was the increase in the number of gas space-heating purchasers, up from 25,640 to 198,005 in the same period. The number of customers, however, told only part of the story. Each customer demanded far more service than he ever had before. Kilowatthour sales nearly doubled, and gas sales quadrupled between 1945 and 1955. This rapid expansion presented big problems. Generating capacities had to be increased to meet the demand. Existing plants, such as the B. C. Cobb Plant near Muskegon, built in 1947, were enlarged, but this was not enough. Three new steam generating facilities—the James H. Campbell Plant near Grand Rapids (biggest in the system to date), the Justin R. Whiting Plant at the head of Lake Erie, and the Dan E. Karn Plant on Saginaw Bay—went into construction. Meanwhile, costs kept going up, for inflation is the inseparable companion of rising affluence.

While the resulting rate problems were familiar to the Consumers Power staff, it now had to cope with many of the challenges that had formerly been handled at the holding-company level. Prominent among these was the raising of new capital.[35] This is always a major concern of the utilities industry since expansion cannot be financed out of earnings: customers pay only for the service of equipment already in existence.

But the most overwhelming question of all, as Consumers Power looked ahead to its future in an affluent society, was how to find new sources of power. By 1970, Michigan's population would reach nearly nine million. That same year the total United States population would top 205 million. Already in the 1950s it became apparent that with current resources, there would be barely enough electricity and gas to go around to meet the booming demand.

Thus, not only had society changed, and Consumers Power with it, but the whole postwar world—with its population explosion, affluence, and rising costs; its huge cold-war budgets; and its depleting resources—brought entirely new challenges to the utilities industry. The world was a new ball park, it was a new ball game, and nobody had yet written the rules.

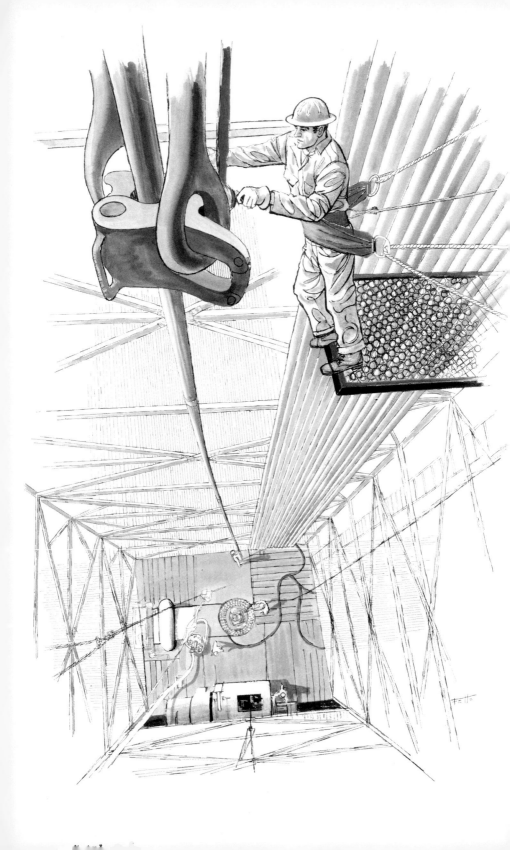

20

Earth Fire

Not one lonely tree shades the banks of the Sabine River as it flows south through marsh-grass flatlands that have no horizons, squeezed between the bayous of Louisiana and the rice fields and derrick-studded wastes of south Texas. At Sabine Pass, the river empties sluggishly into the Gulf of Mexico. It is here, at this ghost port of abandoned rusty barges, derelict car hulks, and clapboard shacks whose paint peeled off long ago, that oil and gas exploration men change helicopters for their flights to offshore drilling rigs. Under their choppers' beating blades, the water changes from a muddy beige to green to white-capped blue. Soon the sight of land is lost in sunny haze, the Gulf a trackless sea. But it only seems to be without dimension. On geologists' charts, the bottom beneath the waves is plotted into blocks of 5,000 acres each, as orderly in their invisible design as corn fields on the prairies. One day in March 1971, the gigantic rig *Ocean Driller* rode in 370 feet of water above Block 639. This chunk of suboceanic real estate lies some 130 miles south by southwest of Cameron, Louisiana, and is the farthest out that offshore drilling has ever been attempted. Captain Rudy Plaisance was in command.

To understand what happened that day under the blazing subtropical sun, one must first know that a deepwater semi-submersible drilling rig is just about the biggest single piece of self-contained equipment designed by man. *Ocean Driller* is basically a platform, roughly triangular in shape, with two sides of 348 feet each and one of 375 feet. This platform, a maze of shuffled decks and catwalks, looks as though it had been built by a playful giant hung up on Erector sets. It sits 92 feet above the water, riding on vertical bottle-shaped pontoons whose bulges extend 70 feet below the surface. The derrick, which is the whole reason for a driller's existence, rises another 142 feet from the main deck of the platform, so that the whole rig from derrick top to pontoon bottom measures 304 feet, about the height of a modern thirty-four-story skyscraper. Water ballast, pumped in and out of the pontoons, keeps the 1,140-ton monster on an even keel so stable that it takes a storm to make you realize you are afloat. Once the rig has been towed to the drilling site, nine 20,000-pound anchors, three at each corner, hold it in place. Each anchor line goes out nearly 2,000 feet, so that the spread between anchors is about three-quarters of a mile. Keep these figures in mind, for now suddenly this man-built mammoth turns into nature's toy.

The ocean floor bursts. A vast bubble of methane gas, as big as *Ocean Driller* itself, boils to the surface, right next to the rig. Waves rise in a fountain twice as high as the derrick. The churning ʼsea fizzes like carbonated water as far out as the anchors. *Ocean Driller* tilts. The side away from the bubble almost dips into the sea, and then the big rig begins to slide sideways through the waves, pushed by the immense pressure of rising gas. Captain Plaisance grabs the nearest stanchion. He is short and roundly built, a sturdy man. In his twenty-five years offshore, he has never seen anything like this. But he knows his business, and he can move fast.

"Cut her loose!" he yells. "Cut those anchors!" And he gives the order to abandon ship. By now, he and his men are gasping for air. Methane is not poisonous, but it has displaced the oxygen they need to breathe. Choking, their eyes running, nearly blinded, they clatter down the catwalks, racing for boats tied to the pontoons. The fifty-four men harbor a desperate fear: one little spark, and their world may end in a blinding flash.

Luck was with the drillers that day. Their world did not ignite. Everybody got off safely.[1] The $12-million rig did not sink. It drifted a mile, and then the gas eruption slowed. Nobody was even hurt—nobody, that is, except Consumers Power and its partners in this venture to find a new source of the most efficient and desirable of all known fuels: highly combustible, nontoxic, nonpolluting natural gas.

The rental of *Ocean Driller* from the Ocean Drilling and Exploration Company (ODECO) runs more than $13,000 a day, including operating costs. Drilling an offshore test well takes twenty to thirty days; thus the blowout cost Consumers Power Company's exploration subsidiary and its partners somewhere in the neighborhood of $250,000. This sounds like a lot of money and it is, but even a lot of money is peanuts in the high-stakes adventure of natural-gas exploration.

Just the right to drill Block 639 cost $15.5 million. At that, there was no guarantee the drillers would ever hit anything but rock. For an offshore well to be worthwhile, it must be capable of a controlled output of at least 1 million cubic feet of gas a day, with a reservoir sufficient to last for about twenty years, and, oilmen hope, even longer. If the well turns out to be a "Big Mother," as oilmen call a real bonanza, it might put out as much as 20 million cubic feet of gas a day. But that's one of those keep-your-fingers-crossed, once-in-a-lifetime propositions. The chances against it are 99 in 100. Yet, that's what it takes.

Consumers Power needs new sources of gas that can provide trillions of cubic feet for its customers over the next decades. Otherwise, the company's very existence as a gas utility is at

OCEAN DRILLER

Safely back aboard after the March 1971 blowout, Captain Rudy Plaisance relaxes on home-away-from-home porch swing (above), and oil geologists disembark from a helicopter (below) to go back to work. To get an idea of the rig's size, visualize a thirty-four-story highrise superimposed on the picture at the right. The building would top out at the tip of the derrick. (Aerial photo courtesy of Panhandle Eastern; others by the author)

stake, along with Michigan's future as a prosperous industrial state.

Take the "Mother" bubble that almost capsized *Ocean Driller* at the peak of the eruption. It was at least 300 feet across, and it rose some 50 feet above the waves, with water clinging to it by surface tension, before it blew into the sky. The crater on the ocean floor was 600 feet wide and 180 feet deep. Luckily, after five days it bridged itself, and the gas flow stopped. Geologists estimated that at least 200 million cubic feet must have blown out each of those days, for a total somewhere in excess of 1 billion cubic feet. This may seem an astronomical figure, but actually it was a relatively modest loss. Consumers Power needs almost that much every day to

GAS FROM THE GULF

Piping natural gas from offshore wells is hard work all the way. Here, the barge L. B. Meaders lays 30-inch pipe into the Gulf of Mexico for Trunkline's offshore system, a major supplier of Consumers Power. (Panhandle Eastern photo)

serve more than 860,000 residential and industrial gas customers.

An accident like the blowout at Block 639 can happen any time. It is but one of the many risks of drilling. What happened was simply this: when *Ocean Driller* sank its test probe 3,950 feet into the ocean bed, it tapped a sizable reservoir of natural gas. Not that natural gas—methane from life forms that decayed millions of years ago, with an admixture of other, usually inert gases like nitrogen—sits down there in a big cavern. Rather, the gas exists in highly porous sandstone called "gas sand," whose minute cavities are filled with gas in much the same way that a sponge is filled with water.

There is one big difference, however. Gas molecules are in a constant state of violent motion, tending to drive farther and farther apart from one another. This inherent pressure of gas is increased by underground "waterheads" that continually push against the gas sand. The deeper down a gas reservoir is, the greater these hydrostatic pressures.[2] The only reason the gas stays down there at all is that the sandstone formation is capped by harder, less porous rock, which acts like the cork in a champagne bottle. It's this cap that the drill must punch through to tap a reservoir; then the gas is vented up the drill pipe.[3] What happened at Block 639 was that the gas pressure, as any pressure always does, took the path of least resistance. Near the newly drilled hole in the rock cap of the reservoir was a slanting crack, and up came the gas.

Natural gas sometimes seeps on its own from the bowels of the earth. That's how it began its history as man's servant, when the ingenious ancient Chinese used reeds and bamboo for piping it. This art—even knowledge of natural gas itself—was lost over the ages, not to be rediscovered until about a century ago.

One of the first things that was a bit worrisome to Michigan's earliest settlers in the areas of Monroe and Wayne counties was that gas bubbled up from their ponds, usually in the spring. Because natural gas and petroleum often come together, these people sometimes found a nasty, oily scum on the ponds, and cattle refused to drink the water, which had a peculiar smell and taste. Later, when Oakland County was settled, residents in the Royal Oak area encountered an even more perplexing problem. Their drinking wells often yielded gas-filled water. It was potable, if not exactly pleasant. Nevertheless, it provided a great trick for dull parties: if you put that water in a small-neck bottle and struck a match over it, there was a pop as the free gas ignited. Later, of course, when people began to understand the phenomenon, some home-owners in Oakland County drilled their own little natural-gas wells in their backyards and used the gas for cooking.

In the first years of the century, some shallow oil wells were started in the Port Huron area by the G. B. Stock Xylite Grease & Oil Company, which turned the petroleum into greases of various kinds, among them axle grease, thus fore-shadowing the multiple uses of petroleum products in transportation. The first boomlet came in 1912. Saginaw, by then down-and-out as a lumber and mill town, was sitting on an earthfold (called "anticline") that showed some promise of containing hydrocarbons. A group of bankers, lumbermen, and wellmen went into business together, and they did bring in one well near Bristol Street Bridge, where they struck both gas and oil.

The next oil boom, also in Saginaw, came along in about 1925. It lasted a few years, but nobody made any money. Everybody started drilling holes in their city lots, making four holes in one block when there should have been perhaps one hole in several blocks. All that the well owners succeeded in doing was to put so many holes in a relatively small barrel that it quickly ran dry without yielding much of a return to any one individual for his effort and investment.

In the Muskegon area it was a different story. Where the Saginaw wells had yielded in the range of 10 to 30 barrels a day, the first Muskegon hole produced 330 barrels of oil daily, plus a lot of natural gas. But again the reservoir was quickly exhausted as everyone crowded in to make a fast fortune. The gas company in Muskegon, for instance, converted from manufactured gas to the cheaper and more efficient natural gas, only to find itself without supplies a few months later.

At last the big strike happened. It came near Mt. Pleasant, and thereby hangs a sad little tale. A wildcatter whose name, like those of most unlucky men, has been forgotten, obtained some leases in the Broomfield area and started drilling. He hit several dry holes and was just beginning to run into what looked like a promising sandstone structure when other business called him back to Kansas. He left his partner in charge of the Michigan operation. This was a big mistake. The partner ran up big debts, and when the luckless promoter returned, he faced so many creditors that all he could do was sell his leases. Six weeks later, on these very leases, the big Broomfield gas field was brought in.

Consumers Power Company was not in the drilling business then. While the transmission and distribution of natural gas are public utility services, the producing end is more in the nature of a mining proposition, and nobody in the company seriously considered venturing into that strange domain. But in 1931, Consumers Power began buying natural gas for distribution, and for that purpose it laid a 40-mile pipeline between the Broomfield wellheads in Isabella County and the town of Midland. Soon after Midland customers began using natural gas, other communities requested similar service. Consumers Power then decided to make a thorough test of this new commodity, not just as gas to be sold to customers but also as a fuel to make steam for electric generation. The company also wanted to find out whether the pressure in the Michigan gas fields would hold up under such continued demand.

A 6-inch pipeline for manufactured gas between Midland, Bay City, and Saginaw was reinforced and brought to the

Saginaw River steam-generating plant, and one of the plant's boilers was equipped with gas burners. For several months, the new "invisible coal" sent 120,000 pounds of steam into the rolling turbines every hour. The test was judged a success, and soon the announcement was made that sufficient gas lay underground in Michigan to supply customers in Bay City and Saginaw. By July 1933, Bay City distribution mains were fed with natural gas. By Labor Day of the same year, Saginaw customers also were hooked up.[4] The age of methane had arrived.

Like anything else, it brought with it a host of problems. Some were merely mechanical, and could be solved without difficulty. For instance, natural gas possesses nearly double the heat value of manufactured gas. Thus, adjustments in customers' appliances had to be made as homes were changed over from one type of gas to the other. Other problems were not so easy to deal with. While manufactured gas was produced

NATURAL GAS CLEANED THE ENVIRONMENT

That's how the Mt. Clemens gas works looked in 1928. Since then, with the advent of natural gas, Consumers Power has torn down all its ugly gas holders and eliminated air-polluting coke-oven stacks. Unfortunately, such monstrosities are still a fairly common sight in some other sections of the country. (Consumers Power photo)

locally, natural gas had to be brought into a community from central sources of supply. In effect, the gas business found itself in a stage of development similar to that of the electric business when W. A. Foote decided to bring power from distant rivers. Like its electrical counterpart, gas service now required a transmission system.

Erecting towers and stringing wires is one thing. Laying pipe is quite another. You have to dig a ditch that goes on for miles and miles, crossing roads, hedgerows, fences, and rivers. Then you have to weld the pipe together in sections, put it in the ditch, cover it up, and repair all the damages you wrought en route. Any change in the weather can play hell with your timetable. The pipeline which brought gas to Lansing in 1936 was particularly beset by troubles. Gullies and drainage canals turned into solid ice. Equipment floundered in snowbanks. Construction crews, battling blizzards, hacked at the frozen ground. Then in February came a sudden thaw. Ice turned to mud. Caterpillar tractors handling the heavy pipe crashed through melting ice crusts and plunged into streams and marshes. From morning to night men wallowed in mud and water up to their hips. But all this could be coped with. It was just part of the job.

The real difficulties came because the gas end of the company was now no longer in control of its own production. True, Consumers Power had to buy coal from outside suppliers to make manufactured gas, and still does so to fire its steam plants. But, barring strikes and other emergencies, these supplies are relatively assured; in any case, coal can be stockpiled. With natural gas, the situation is entirely different. Its availability depends not only on the largess of nature but also on man's ability to find the hydrocarbon reservoirs. No one could tell for sure, especially in the very early days, just how much gas there was under the ground of Michigan. Yet the economics of the business made it necessary to pump gas at the maximum possible rate. With the higher heat value of natural gas, a smaller quantity does more work. Hence, it was only by extending gas service to many additional homes and industries and by putting gas to work in new ways that the utility could make up for the smaller unit use.

Above all, industrial companies in Michigan had to be convinced that the gas flame could do a better and cheaper job than existing heat-generating processes on the production line. Only industry could guarantee the year-round consumption of gas without which Consumers Power's investment in natural-gas development would never pay off. Thus, from the very start, the methane business was a precarious gamble on the future.

At the beginning, this problem was not yet so obvious. More and more gas fields were being discovered, and as they went into production, additional communities were served. It was the development in 1934 of the Montcalm field in Hinton and Belvidere Townships of Montcalm County, now usually referred to as the Six Lakes field, that eventually led to the construction of the weather-troubled 60-mile line to Lansing.[5] In 1936 natural-gas service was extended to the Alma district, from the Crystal–New Haven field.[6] As the system grew, gas transmission lines were interconnected, just as electric transmission lines are, enabling the company to distribute natural gas as if it only had one source, even though the gas came from different places. Development of the Riverside-Winterfield and Cranberry Lake gas fields in Clare, Osceola, and Missaukee Counties in 1940 added considerably to available resources.[7] These now were enough to provide for widespread use of natural gas in the areas served—the central part around Saginaw and Bay City—and to reduce the cost of gas service in these areas anywhere from 44 to 79 percent. But it was already apparent that there wasn't enough Michigan gas to meet the needs of most of the Consumers Power territory. Manufactured gas was still being supplied to the industrial regions of Flint and Pontiac, the suburbs of Detroit, and the areas around Jackson, Marshall, and Kalamazoo. What's more, with the uncertainty of Michigan reserves, standby plants to make manufactured gas had to be installed in the communities served by natural gas.[9]

If Consumers Power wanted to get into this new business in a big way, there was only one way to do it. Gas had to be imported from out of state. The biggest known reserves of methane lay in the deep gas sands of America's oil country — the tornado-whipped Panhandle region of Texas, Kansas, and Oklahoma. Hydrocarbon reservoirs in that area were then immense, almost inexhaustible it seemed. And, with the land so sparsely settled, the real market for its wealth lay 1,000 or more miles to the east.

Back in 1929, a group of men in Kansas City had decided to bring resource and market together by pumping gas through a pipeline that would cross half the country. No such project had ever before been attempted. The Panhandle Eastern Pipe Line Company was a big gamble, based on meager financing and on the hope, not yet a certainty, of finding customers. In 1931 the first 1,411 miles of main through Kansas, Missouri, and Illinois were completed, together with connections to wellheads at the production end and laterals to customers along its route. The pipeline terminus was at Dana, Indiana, on the Illinois state line. Five years later, in July 1936, the pipeline was extended to Detroit, and Detroit City Gas (now Michigan Consolidated) became Panhandle Eastern's first major customer in the industrial Middle West.

With war clouds already darkening on the horizon, the time of decision had come for Consumers Power Company. It could stay with natural gas on a limited basis, keeping its fingers crossed that Michigan supplies would last for a few more years. Or it could take the big step, stop the old and dirty process of making manufactured gas, and get into the natural-gas business all the way.

In retrospect, it seems surprising that there was any hemming and hawing at all; the choice to go whole hog was clearly indicated. But Dan Karn was an electric man at heart, who considered the gas business 10 percent income and 90 percent trouble. He faced the gas issue at a time when it was difficult for him to make decisions. He had fallen ill with amoebic dysentery at the Chicago World's Fair and had been a sick man ever since. He came to work sometimes two or three hours a day, and sometimes not at all. Prompted largely by Wilson Arthur, his right-hand man, Karn finally made the decision for natural gas. But even then, he got his feet only a little wetter. Instead of giving Consumers Power its own guaranteed high-volume source of methane with a pipeline, of which Consumers Power would be the major (if not the only) customer, he made a deal to tap a lateral line into the Michigan extension of the Panhandle Eastern system. Nor did he push for expanding the Consumers Power gas territory, which the company's new capacity to distribute natural gas would have made fairly easy.

All this, of course, is Monday-morning quarterbacking; yesterday's answers are always cheaper tomorrow. There is no way to tell whether the investment to go into new markets would have been worth the return in those days: a company doesn't expand just to shade a map in its colors. By the same token, Karn may well have been advised that Consumers Power did not yet need the major portion of a pipeline's output and that an investment of such magnitude so early in the game might backfire on the company.

In any case, the connection to Panhandle's main line did put Consumers Power into the natural gas business, albeit just in the nick of time, for the war clouds were now sweeping in with threatening speed. In 1941 Consumers Power contracted with Panhandle for the purchase of up to 25 million cubic feet per day and converted Flint, Owosso, Pontiac, Jackson, Marshall — and, most importantly, the Detroit suburban area — to natural gas. In the winter of 1942–1943 these areas also were tied into Michigan's indigenous supplies.

Hesitant as Karn may have been about this enterprise at the time, conversion to methane was one of the most important events that ever happened to Consumers Power. It came precisely at the right time to take advantage of Michigan's phenomenal growth. The company long had been one of the country's leading utilities; it was soon to be among the most successful. At the peak of its prosperity, in the middle 1960s, Consumers Power achieved an almost unique position of being able repeatedly to lower its rates to customers, raise the wages paid to its employees, and increase the dividends to its shareholders. Indeed, the advent of natural gas launched the company into its truly golden years.

At first Consumers Power received 70 percent of its natural gas from the Panhandle line and 30 percent from Michigan fields. By the end of 1945 it was evident that the state's existing reserves were being rapidly depleted and that no substantial additional fields were about to be discovered.[10]

Just then the end of the war brought a tremendous surge in all areas of gas use. Most prominent among these was space heating, as more and more homeowners converted their old furnaces to gas and as builders of new homes installed gas furnaces to start with. This meant a lot of business for the company, but in view of the dwindling local supplies produced a serious problem at the same time. Heating demands are primarily seasonal, and Panhandle Eastern could not deliver gas to Consumers Power in sufficient quantities to take care of the winter peaks. The only answer was to store excess gas delivered in warm weather, and to store it in enormous quantities.

You will recall, from earlier in this chapter if not from long-ago science classes, that gas has an inherent desire to expand. If there is gas—any gas—in a container, and you let some out of it, the container will still be filled with gas, though at a lower pressure. Michigan's gas fields were being depleted: the pressure in all these natural containers was being decreased as gas was taken out. Why not put gas back into the fields and bring them up to their former pressure? The gas could be pumped in through the wells in the summer, when the Panhandle deliveries exceeded demand, and then pumped out in the winter, when Michigan customers needed to heat their houses. This ingenious system of underground storage of natural gas had been practiced before, but never on so large a scale as Consumers Power was about to try.[11]

It purchased the interests of Taggart Bros. and other companies in the Winterfield and Cranberry Lake fields for the not inconsiderable sum of $4,678,636.[12] By May 1946, these properties were turned over to a newly created subsidiary, the Michigan Gas Storage Company, of which Consumers Power owned 75 percent, and Panhandle Eastern the rest.

It was during this period that A. H. Aymond, an ambitious young attorney fresh out of the Navy, decided that now was the time for him to seek a new career. Al Aymond had been with a Chicago law firm for five years prior to going in the service. What he wanted now was a challenging job with a big company that might give him a chance to work his way to the top. He went back to his alma mater, the University of Michigan, at Ann Arbor, to ask an old law professor, Paul Leidy, for advice. It so happened that Leidy was a friend of Justin Whiting and knew that Whiting was searching for a young man who might someday lead the company.

Not without cause, this was one of Whiting's major concerns. Consumers Power Company, about to emerge from the Commonwealth chrysalis, was rich in operating know-how but desperately thin in management. If Whiting had died right then, there would have been no one who could have guided the company through the labyrinth of legal, financial, public relations, and general management problems that any utility must face successfully in order to survive. A meeting between Aymond and Whiting was arranged. Whiting liked the young man and assigned him for a start to the New York legal staff of the Commonwealth & Southern service corporation. It was exactly the kind of opportunity Aymond had been looking for, and he plunged right in to help handle Consumers Power's natural-gas storage application with the Federal

Power Commission. He was involved also with gas rate hearings before the state Public Service Commission.

These were Aymond's first—and far from last—experiences with government bodies in control of utility operations. The insolence of officials and the law's delay, which long ago bugged Hamlet, had since been developed to perfection. Even though the FPC did not look with disfavor on the storage project, the better part of a year went by before all the necessary approvals were granted, not only by the FPC itself, but also by the Michigan commission and the SEC. Eventually the company did manage to obtain interim certification, so that the fields could be used for storage even before final approval was granted. This saved the situation, for otherwise Consumers Power could not have maintained its gas service during the bitter winter of 1946. At about the same time, the state body granted rate relief sufficient to encourage the company in its struggles to meet increasing demands. Al Aymond thus was launched on a career that eventually would carry him to the chairmanship of Consumers Power Company.[13]

Some 247 wells were now drilled in the storage fields and connected to gathering lines, for it was necessary to move large quantities rapidly in and out of the reservoirs. But the gas situation still was touch-and-go. The postwar shortage of materials also had affected Panhandle Eastern and had slowed pipeline expansion needed to accommodate the additional Consumers Power load.[14] Deliveries fell behind schedule, and after the heavy demands of the winter of 1947 depleted existing supplies, the situation became desperate—so desperate, in fact, that Consumers Power had to resort to the expensive expedient of pumping propane into its gas storage fields.

Starting in mid-July, a procession of 1,200 railroad tank cars, bringing in liquid propane from Texas, filled the company's new siding at Pennock, an old timber-camp station north of Temple. The schedule called for twelve cars a day for a 100-day period ending in October, followed by three cars a day throughout the winter. The liquid propane was vaporized in a specially built plant and was injected into the Winterfield storage area along with the Texas natural gas.[15] It was another first for Consumers Power, and it worked: the company managed to get through another winter without having to interrupt service to its quarter of a million customers.[16]

But even after this crisis was overcome, and Panhandle Eastern managed to increase its deliveries, there still was not enough natural gas available to allow Consumers Power to serve all the new residential, commercial, and industrial customers who wanted it. Throughout the 1950s space-heat-

SOMETHING NEW UNDER THE OLD SUN

Modern arc-welding equipment joined sections of steel pipe during construction of the Mt. Pleasant to Zilwaukee gas line in 1955. Welding crews still use an old-fashioned farm-implement umbrella to shield themselves from the hot summer sun. (Consumers Power photo)

ing customers were added only as additional supplies permitted. In 1956 the Northville Field was purchased to supplement the company's reserves, and in 1957 the Overisel Field was bought, the first in the western part of the state that could be converted to storage use.[17]

An event that occurred nearly 2,000 miles from Consumers Power's Jackson headquarters took the company one further step in this direction. In 1950, a Panhandle Eastern subsidiary, the Trunkline Gas Company, was formed in Houston, Texas, to tap the vast new natural gas discoveries in the Texas and Louisiana Gulf Coast areas. Trunkline's operating vice-president, King Sanders, had been born in Oklahoma when it was still Indian territory. A granitic giant of a man, with a knowing grin and an oil-field drawl, he had bulldozed his way up from roustabout to the top-executive ranks and eventually was destined to become chairman of Panhandle Eastern's board.[18] He was exactly the kind of man it took to push the new 1,300-mile pipeline through in just fifteen months, from the southern Texas town of McAllen, near the Mexican border, to Tuscola, Illinois. That's as far as it was profitable to build it, and that's where it stopped. At the time no one considered that if this pipeline could be extended into Michigan, Consumers Power's gas supply could be assured for many years.

But it was precisely this sort of direct connection to the wellheads of the Southwest that came to Aymond's mind when Whiting assigned him in the mid-1950s to explore new sources of natural gas. Aymond's months-long search took him to the biggest producers in Kansas, Oklahoma, and Texas, among them Clint Murchison, who proposed building a combined oil-and-gas conduit to Consumers Power's doorstep. The contract with the Murchison interests had advanced into the serious negotiation stage when King Sanders, by then president of Trunkline, went to Dan Karn in October 1957 with a very interesting proposition.

"We don't want to go into Michigan with our pipeline," Sanders told Dan Karn, "but I'll tell you what we can do."

He reached for a map, his big, rough hands dwarfing whole states. "We'll extend Trunkline to the Michigan border at White Pigeon. You meet us there with a transmission main of your own. That way we'll be able to give you about 130 million cubic feet a day. I guess you can get along on that for awhile."[19]

Trunkline's offer looked extremely promising. In effect, Consumers Power would have its own direct connection to the Gulf Coast wells. Construction costs were estimated at $81.5 million, including 204 miles of pipeline to be laid from Tuscola to the Michigan state line and the enlarging of Trunkline's capacity so that it could carry the Consumers Power load. This expense would have to be borne by Consumers Power; not in a lump sum, but by paying nearly half again as much for each unit of the Trunkline gas as it paid for the Panhandle Eastern Pipe Line deliveries.

Aymond, by now executive vice-president of Consumers Power, was concerned about the Michigan Public Service Commission's attitude toward the inevitable rate increase that would have to be passed on to the company's customers. There also were some questions about the Federal Power Commission's approval of this highly unusual venture. These difficulties were overcome with surprising speed, however, and on January 27, 1958, at Panhandle Eastern's office, then at 120 Broadway, New York City, Karn and Aymond signed a twenty-year contract with Sanders and William G. Maguire, then Panhandle-Trunkline's top boss, laying the basis for a partnership, which as we shall see, eventually went far beyond its original provisions.

The old Panhandle contract had called for delivery of 120 million cubic feet a day, plus 45 billion cubic feet extra during the warm months for storage, or about 90 billion cubic feet over a year's period. Almost overnight, the new Trunkline contract would increase natural gas delivery to Consumers Power to nearly 150 billion cubic feet a year. All the brakes were off now. With the new pipeline, Consumers Power could really go.

Aymond is a man with an easy smile, and he smiled that day when Sanders told him that the new line would be completed by December 1959. Unfortunately, just a few months later the steelworkers' union went on strike.

This strike, the longest in that industry on record, lasted through the summer of 1959 and way into the fall, right through the pipeline-building season. Winter came, and there was no way to meet the target date: steel pipe was impossible to obtain in sufficient quantities. In fact, construction didn't really get fully under way until after the proposed delivery date.

Under ideal conditions two miles of pipeline can be laid in a day.[20] That winter of 1959, construction crews sometimes couldn't make even 300 feet. Down South, where the main trunk had to be expanded with nearly 850 miles of auxiliary pipe loops, the men battled torrential rains. Louisiana, Arkansas, and Tennessee turned into quagmires so deep that crankcases and oil breathers got clogged with mud, and tractors lay abandoned along the construction site like shot-up tanks on a battlefield. Southern Texas turned into one solid sheet of water, and construction here had to be stopped altogether for several months. Up North the weather was so fiercely cold that workers often dropped their tools and quit.[21] Virgil Kincheloe, then chief inspector for Trunkline, will never forget the frozen peat bogs near the Michigan border. He'd have fifteen or twenty pipe welders one day, and then only three or four would show up the next. Kincheloe and his assistants were on the phones almost every day, calling union hiring halls all over the country, flying men in from wherever they could be found, and hoping that they'd stick it out on this miserable job.[22]

At last spring came, and the pipeline was completed. Trunkline and Consumers Power were connected at the pipelines' junction, under a hedgerow that marked the Indiana-Michigan state line. The inauguration ceremony took place on May 18, 1960, and was treated as an important public event, as indeed it deserved to be, complete with all the ballyhoo that conscientious press agentry provides for such occasions. Michigan's governor, G. Mennen ("Soapy") Williams, then very much in the national political picture and a Presidential hopeful, lent his photogenic presence, green polka-dot tie and all, to the festivities. He flew down to White Pigeon from Kalamazoo between off-year election speeches and posed with Aymond and Sanders turning the valves that controlled the flow of the new gas into his state.[23] An improbably big dial, with a pointer more than 2 feet long, showed the increasing volume of the

NOTHING SO RARE AS A DAY IN JUNE

The weather wasn't always this kind during the Trunkline construction from the Gulf Coast states to Michigan. Under ideal conditions, as pictured here, about 2 miles of pipeline can be laid in a day. But in the winter of 1959, torrential rains in the South and hard-frozen ground in the North delayed the project for many months. This photograph shows trenching operation for expansion of the Trunkline system with 36-inch pipe in 1967. (Photo by Jim Thomas, courtesy of Panhandle Eastern)

BIG DAY AT WHITE PIGEON

On May 18, 1960, Consumers Power Company was officially connected to the new Trunkline natural-gas transmission system, with the pipelines joining on the Michigan-Indiana border. This development, bringing vastly increased quantities of natural gas to the Wolverine state, was a vital factor in Michigan's economic development of the 1960s. Happy smiles were the order of the day. In this picture they belong (left to right) to then Governor G. Mennen Williams; King Sanders, of Trunkline; and A. H. Aymond, then executive vice-president and now chairman of the board of Consumers Power Company. (Panhandle Eastern photo)

flow as the smiling dignitaries worked the valve wheels. Truth of the matter was that gas already had been rushing through the new pipeline for several days. The dial was a dummy affair, discretely cranked by a pipeline employee for the benefit of news photographers and TV cameramen. Not that this sleight of hand mattered. Reality lies in essence rather than appearance, and the reality was that Michigan had now truly become a natural-gas state.

During the 1960s, as gas consumption in Consumers Power's territory increased beyond all expectations, the Trunkline–Consumers Power pipeline system continued to grow until

GAS STORAGE WELLHEAD

St. Clair storage field operator blows a well to test gas pressure.
(Consumers Power photo)

most sections had three pipes lying side by side, each succeeding installation of a larger diameter than the one before.[24]

By 1963, too, Consumers Power had taken over the producing properties and exploration leases of Panhandle Eastern in Michigan. The price was $20 million, offered by carefully calculated sealed bid. One purpose of this purchase was to enlarge Consumers' capacity for natural gas storage, but even then Aymond and others in the company were flirting with the prospect of obtaining some of their own hydrocarbon resources. The deal paid off almost immediately. No sooner had the sales contract been signed than several Panhandle gas wells started blowing in St. Clair County. Before they ran dry, Consumers Power had recouped most of its investment — and there were yet other properties in the package still to be explored and developed.

Thus this transaction was of great significance. With one stroke of a pen upon a check, Consumers Power was no longer a gas utility in the ordinary sense, merely transmitting and distributing energy. It was now in the production end of the

ST. CLAIR FIELD CONTROL ROOM

Flow of stored gas into pipelines is controlled from a central console.
(Consumers Power photo by Tony Kelly)

business, and thus was one step closer to actual gas and oil exploration. In fact, the exploration rights purchased from Panhandle Eastern included several Michigan properties that would someday yield Texas-size wells. Years were yet to pass before Consumers Power would actually engage in drilling, but even then this future development was already inevitable, and the company was launched on a new course that would determine its survival.

By 1971, Consumers Power served more than 860,000 natural gas customers, and Trunkline's deliveries had been increased to 226 billion cubic feet a year. Panhandle still delivered 92 billion, for a total of 318 billion—nearly twenty times as much as Consumers Power sold in 1946. The price difference between Panhandle and Trunkline gas had long been equalized. Trunkline gas was only 1 cent higher, a gap easily accommodated in the rate.[25]

But a vastly more serious problem than cost considerations now faced the gas people at Consumers Power. Trunkline's 1971 contract called for 775 million cubic feet a day; yet the system could deliver only 700 million. The pipeline capacity was there—but the gas was not available at the wellheads.

Beset by a crisis of confidence not only in its government but also in itself, rent by new hatreds, and plunging into the ever-widening abyss between its generations, the nation barely noticed that an energy shortage was about to be added to all its other woes. In many parts of the country, although not yet in Michigan, electric power generation could barely keep up with the demand, and many attempts to increase capacity were thwarted by interventions of environmentalist pressure groups. There has been less opposition in the area of gas operations. After all, even the most vehement of ecological crusaders will admit, albeit perhaps reluctantly, that methane does not pollute. However, objections have been raised against drilling for hydrocarbons; some environmentalists are alarmed by the possibility that occasionally a well might get away from the drillers and spew out oil. So far, at least, this has not seriously hampered the production of natural gas, but even so, demand has far outstripped supply. The huge gas reserves of the Southwest and Gulf Coast are being rapidly depleted, and the exploration for new reserves has failed to keep pace with the need.

Not that the world has burned up all the gas stored by provident nature over the eons. There are still immense quantities bottled up under the earth's crust, probably enough to keep modern society going for several decades. It isn't even much of a secret where these energy treasures are hidden. Geologists have a pretty good idea about the general areas that might be drilled with good results. The basin of the Gulf of Mexico is one. The northern shelf of our continent is another. Scandinavia's offshore is a third. And there are more. But these are vast regions, and the difficulty lies in sinking the drills in precisely those spots where they will hit reservoirs. Every test well is an expensive gamble. On dry land, the cost of a wildcat—one that's far enough from a producing well so that it won't tap the same pocket—ranges from $300,000 to $750,000 depending on depth. Only about one in twelve such wildcats is successful; by the time it comes in, the prorated cost averages at around $12 million, and that's before further investment to develop the field. Offshore wildcatting is yet more expensive. Drilling a test well into the continental shelf can cost as much as $1 million, and only about one in fifty results in a strike worth exploiting. That's just the drilling cost and does not include the price, usually in the millions, the government collects for the lease of a likely offshore block.[26]

Obviously, natural gas exploration is an enormous gamble, and if this gamble at best can yield only a relatively small return, a wise investor will put his money elsewhere. That's the major reason why, as the 1960s became the 1970s, methane suddenly was in short supply. Oil economists generally agree that the Federal Power Commission had set the rates natural gas producers could charge so low that the producers were unwilling to invest heavily in developing desperately needed new reserves.[27] While this attitude on the part of the big oil companies is understandable enough as a practical business consideration, energy utilities like Consumers Power cannot afford to take a similar position. With them, it's not a matter of choosing between investments, but of securing their lifeblood.

As incremental supplies of natural gas grew more and more uncertain, Consumers Power Company looked for ways to protect its customers and its competitive position in the energy business. In this, it was aided by earlier foresight.

Three years previously, in 1967, the company had formed a wholly owned subsidiary, Northern Michigan Exploration Company, to prospect for natural gas and other hydrocarbons in the northern part of Michigan's Lower Peninsula. Now, under the direction of John B. Simpson, senior vice-president for Consumers Power gas operations and general services, the exploration subsidiary began a wider search for gas.[28]

Meanwhile, in the summer of 1970, Consumers Power

assessed the mounting demand for natural gas and concluded that drastic action would be required. With a definite limit on future deliveries from its interstate suppliers, it was clear that sales would have to be restricted. This was authorized by the Michigan Public Service Commission in the autumn of 1970, and severe restrictions were imposed on all commercial and industrial customers. Residential space-heating customers could be added, but only as long as supplies held out.

Now, it became a race to develop new sources of supply. Northern Michigan's earlier explorations had been disappointing. Although there was abundant reason to believe that substantial oil and gas reserves existed in a wide belt across Michigan's Lower Peninsula, there were no actual discoveries.

John Simpson now turned elsewhere, to partnership explorations in southern Louisiana and in the Gulf of Mexico. But even there, the first efforts were disheartening. In partnership with Anadarko Production Company, the exploration subsidiary of Panhandle Eastern, Northern Michigan drilled four wildcats, one as deep as 18,500 feet. All were dry.[29] For Consumers Power's subsidiary, this meant a $1.6-million loss; there's no high-low split in this variety of poker. But one day in October 1970, while these Louisiana wells were being drilled, Simpson got an exciting telephone call from Houston, Texas. The gist of the call was this: On December 15, the Bureau of Land Management of the U.S. Department of the Interior would auction 172 oil and natural-gas leases in the Gulf of Mexico, off western Louisiana. Sun Oil Company had formed a group of independent producers to bid in at this auction. Two members of the group had dropped out at the last minute. Would Consumers Power and Panhandle be interested in picking up their shares?

This was the chance that Simpson, a fifty-three-year-old no-nonsense New Englander, had been waiting for. Offshore auctions don't happen very often. The December sale was to be the first since 1962 for that particular area of the continental shelf. Sun Oil's geoscience surveys, conducted over a period of three years in anticipation of the auction, looked extremely promising. Simpson took the proposition to his bosses, A. H. Aymond and James H. Campbell. They took it to the board of directors. Finally the answer was "yes."

Consumers Power and Panhandle cut in for 12.5 percent each, and after the auction they found themselves partners in nine offshore leases that cost the group slightly in excess of $64 million. The Consumers Power share was over $8 million. A few weeks later, *Ocean Driller* was on its way to Block 639 and its rendezvous with the methane bubble that almost sank it.[30]

By early 1971, Consumers Power had committed $40 million to its natural-gas exploration program. *Ocean Driller* was working the Gulf. On land, Northern Michigan Exploration Company had agreed with Quintana Production Company of Houston to pay the cost of developing wells in the South Gibson field of southern Louisiana, 50 miles west of New Orleans. These two wells had a proved reserve in the neighborhood of 250 billion cubic feet, about the equivalent of eight months of Consumers Power gas distribution. Also in partnership with Quintana, the company was wildcatting two wells in other parts of Louisiana.[31] And right in its own home state, the exploration subsidiary was searching for new reserves of Michigan natural gas, drilling its own wildcats in Kalkaska and Otsego Counties and exploring other potential gas sites in Grand Traverse County in partnership with Amoco, subsidiary of Standard Oil of Indiana.[32]

Then it happened—the almost unbelievable happened.

All statistical chances to the contrary, Northern Michigan Exploration Company hit gas in one well after another. Out of seven wildcats drilled onshore and offshore by the summer of 1971, six came in.

Even the Michigan wildcats struck it rich. Drilling down to 7,000 feet, far below the depths that had been explored here in earlier years, Northern Michigan found reserves in the billions of cubic feet. In one Kalkaska County well alone, an initial investment of $200,000 eventually may produce $15 million worth of gas.

As each day showed more promise that Consumers Power's gas discoveries would be able to supply most of the company's needs for some years, restrictions on new customers were relaxed. But it was clear that the gas business would never be the same again. No single source—not even the biggest off-shore "Mother"—could indefinitely fill the demands of Michigan's expanding economy. Diversification of supplies was essential. It was thus that Consumers Power added another first to its impressive list of pioneer accomplishments.

On July 8, 1971, under a lowering sky that threatened to wash out the festivities, John Simpson clambered into the cab of a backhoe parked in a forest clearing near Marysville, just south of Port Huron, and after a couple of abortive attempts at handling the earthmover's complicated gears, broke ground for America's first "reforming" plant—a $70 million refinery that will take a mixture of assorted liquid hydrocarbons and turn it into synthetic natural gas. The plant will purify the raw butanes, propanes, and other similar substances of the "feedstock"; take out the polluting sulfur (for sale as a by-product); and inject the stock into a reaction vessel where heat and pressure will gasify the liquids and release gaseous methane.[33]

Establishment of this new installation constituted a multiple coup. One lay in obtaining the license for the reforming process from the British Gas Council.[34] Another was to pin down the feedstock supplies, and here again the Consumers Power move was exemplary of the initiative required of those who would build for the future: the company committed itself to a fifteen-year contract for 50,000 barrels of hydrocarbon liquids a day, enough to produce 220 million cubic feet of gas, or about a quarter of the company's needs.

Fifty thousand barrels is an immense amount of liquid— about 140 railroad tank cars' worth a day if you use the biggest

INNOVATOR JOHN SIMPSON

At a Marysville press conference, Consumers' senior vice-president of gas operations explained the economics of turning liquid hydrocarbons into natural gas. Seated with him at the speakers table were D. Richardson (left), of Humphreys & Glasgow, the London engineering firm consulting on the plant's construction, and Harry R. Hart, of the British Gas Council, which has operated reforming plants on a smaller scale for several years. (Consumers Power photo by Don Cunningham)

cars available (each holding 15,000 gallons). How could Consumers Power be sure that the deliveries would stay on schedule to keep this essential plant going?

It so happens that one branch of Canada's Interprovincial-Lakehead pipeline, which carries oil nearly 2,000 miles from Edmonton, Alberta, to eastern Ontario, cuts through Michigan's Lower Peninsula and reenters Canada at Sarnia. If an arrangement could be made for Interprovincial to ship the liquid hydrocarbons, and if a plant could be built right alongside the pipeline, the supply problem could be licked. Complex negotiations were held, all at the same time, for each hinged on the others—with the British Gas Council, the oil companies at Edmonton, the Canadian pipeline people, the landowners, and civic officials at Marysville. In the end everything fell

395

into place, making the project possible. Edmonton would produce the hydrocarbons. The pipeline would ship them. The plant would refine them.

Yet this still left a challenging question unanswered. Since the feedstock batches couldn't be processed all at once as they arrived, they must be stored. Now, what would be the safest way to do this, with no possibility of pollution or accidental fire? Simpson's men came up with the answer to that question too. The delivered feedstock would be pumped into artificial caverns some 4,000 feet down in salt formations below the Marysville plant. Underground, there could be no spillage; what's more, without oxygen, there could never be a fire. All the plant's major possible environmental problems had been solved with one stroke.

Consumers Power's reforming plant will be completed by early 1973, manufacturing initially about 100 million cubic feet of methane a day. The plant will double that output when it achieves full production in the fall of 1974. The following year, the discoveries in the Gulf of Mexico should be developed to the point where they will begin to augment natural gas supplies from the Michigan ,and Louisiana wells and the reforming plant. Together with purchases from the traditional Panhandle and Trunkline sources, this should enable Consumers Power to meet anticipated gas demands for at least a decade. If Simpson's men keep on bringing in wildcats—and of course there is no guarantee of that—the pressure may indeed by off for many more years than that. True, there won't be enough gas ever for massive steam and electric power generation. In any case, why waste a dwindling natural resource when nuclear fuel can do the job?

Beyond drilling and reforming, Simpson's men are exploring other options to keep the gas mains filled. The day may come when Consumers Power will import natural gas from the North Slope of Alaska, or even from other continents, shipping liquefied methane across oceans in cryogenic tankers that keep it supercooled.[35] And if coal is mined in large-enough quantities, coal gasification may again become part of Consumers Power's imaginative production arsenal.[36]

Imagination and initiative—that's what it takes. Consumers Power's bold approach had overcome the gas crises of the 1950s and 1970s. The coming 1980s and 1990s could present even more difficult problems; but give future builders half a chance, and they'll find a way.

21

The Power Struggle

When James H. Campbell flew back to Michigan from California that autumn night in 1958, he brought back with him the future. In the light of subsequent events, that future wasn't all rosy, but no future ever is.

Jim Campbell had never been so fired up in all his life. That's saying a lot, for Campbell was a man who got fired up easily when he found a good reason for it, and then there was no stopping him because he had that rare quality of infecting others with his enthusiasms. That morning after his flight in from California, he didn't even bother to check in at his own office. He had taken an uncomfortable night flight from San Francisco rather than waste a whole day; the company driver picked him up at Detroit Metropolitan Airport and sped him on the Interstate to Jackson. Now Campbell dashed along the fifth-floor corridor of the Consumers Power General Office Building. Even when he walked normally, most men found it difficult to keep up with his long strides, let alone when he was in a hurry. All the secretaries felt just a little more giggly as Campbell rushed past them, for he was tall, Scottish-handsome, and a gentleman besides. He strode into the office of his executive assistant, Robert D. Allen, leaned against the door frame, grinned, and said, "Bob, how would you like to get into the nuclear business?"[1]

This was a portentous question. It foreshadowed one of the most important decisions—perhaps the most important decision—that Consumers Power was to make in all its history. Campbell had just attended a high-level meeting conducted by Ralph Cordiner of General Electric at Woodside, California, and what he had learned there had convinced him that the future of electric utilities lay in nuclear power generation.

James H. Campbell then was forty-seven years old and senior vice-president of Consumers Power Company. Within two years he would be the company's president and chief operating officer, succeeding Dan Karn.[2] Like A. H. Aymond, who followed Whiting as board chairman and chief executive officer, Campbell was of the new generation. Son of B. G. Campbell, Sr., the Pontiac division manager in the days when Consumers Power extended its gas territory down to Eight Mile Road, Jim Campbell had grown up with and into the company as much as any man could. He'd worked for Consumers Power during school vacations. Like Tippy and Karn before him, he had been educated at Purdue.[3] But he was not married to the idea that electricity could be generated only by falling water and burning coal. There hadn't been enough waterpower to keep all the necessary generators whirling for some time, and fewer and fewer men in the hills of West Virginia, Pennsylvania, and the other coal states were willing to spend their lives digging in dangerous subterranean darkness. Moreover, it was not at all unlikely that coal eventually might become too expensive a fuel to produce the base load of an electric generating system.[4]

Base load, as the term implies, is the basic quantity of

THE LATE
JAMES H. CAMPBELL

*Forceful and persuasive
as ever, this is how
the Consumers Power
president looked in
1971, sixteen years
after his company's
fateful decision to get
into the nuclear energy
business. Campbell died
less than six months
after this photograph
was taken.* (Consumers
Power photo by Rus
Arnold)

PHYSICIST ENRICO FERMI

He started the chain reaction.
(Photo courtesy of The Detroit
Edison Company)

◄

DAN KARN AT FERMI
PLANT DEDICATION ►

Karn was flanked on the
speakers platform by
Admiral Lewis Strauss
(left), then head of
the Atomic Energy
Commission, and Walker
Cisler, president and later
chairman of Detroit Edison.
(Consumers Power photo)

electricity a system has to generate around the clock. Intermediate load is the next increment added when more power is required. Peak load is that extra margin necessary only at certain times, like the late afternoon of a winter weekday, when lights blaze and machines turn everywhere, or a hot summer day, when all air conditioners are blasting away. The important thing about meeting peak load is to have generating capacity you can turn on and off in a hurry. Peak-load plants therefore must be cheap because they stand idle so much of the time; by the same token, higher fuel costs are acceptable. So it's at peak times that Consumers Power employs its old, low-cost hydro plants and adds the power of relatively small, expensively fueled gas-and-oil-fired internal-combustion units, the first of which was installed at Gaylord in 1966.

At the opposite end of the scale, of course, are the huge base-load plants. The capital investment here can be high because the plants get so much use, but the fuel cost must be as low as possible. That's where coal was, and still is, the basic energy source.[5] But Campbell knew even in the 1950s that the economies of coal were running out. The nuclear reac-

tors he wanted to build would be far more expensive per kilowatt of capacity than the biggest coal-fired steam plants. But nuclear fuel, while infinitely more expensive than coal if measured pound for pound, held real promise of being the least expensive and—with proper safeguards—the cleanest fuel of the future.

Already back in 1954, shortly after President Eisenhower signed the amended Atomic Energy Act, which provided for private use and development of nuclear power, Jim Campbell, with Karn's backing, had been the driving force behind Consumers Power's participation with Detroit Edison and some twenty-four other corporations in organizing the Power Reactor Development Company.[6] PRDC built an experimental nuclear installation, the still extant Enrico Fermi plant, in Monroe County near the head of Lake Erie.[7] This plant was not intended as a commercial power-production facility—though it did house a generator—but rather as a base for research and development of a "breeder" reactor. The Fermi plant concept was way ahead of its time. A breeder reactor produces (i.e., breeds) additional fissionable fuel even as it consumes fissionable material. Even today, breeder reactors are billions of dollars and many drawing-board years short of commercial realization. Yet Campbell probably was right even then: there is little doubt among men who know about such things that sooner or later breeders will replace the boiling-water and pressurized-water reactors of today.

But in 1958, boiling-water reactors were new, and as Campbell had just learned in California, they would work. Nuclear energy wasn't theory any longer. It was time for Consumers Power to build a plant and learn more about it.

Not everyone in the company agreed with Campbell. There was, in fact, considerable debate, and for a while it was uncertain whether Campbell would carry the day.[8] In the end he did, again with Karn's support, and in 1959 contracts were signed with Bechtel Corporation of San Francisco and with General Electric, as equipment supplier, for the $25-million construction of the company's Big Rock Point nuclear plant near Charlevoix. Big Rock, the fifth investor-owned nuclear reactor in the country, started producing electricity on December 8, 1962, and two years later achieved its maximum generating capacity of 75,000 kilowatts. This is small potatoes as atomic plants go today, but it taught Consumers Power how to work with a boiling-water reactor.[9]

The principle is simple enough. Several dozen "fuel bundles" of uranium oxide are submerged in a water-filled vessel, the "reactor." Subatomic particles radiating from these bundles produce a controlled chain reaction, and as the uranium atoms split, they release energy in the form of heat. This heat brings the water circulating through the reactor vessel to a boil, and the resulting steam drives the turbine generator. The important point to remember is that all this takes place in a closed system: the alternately steaming and condensing reactor water never leaves its sealed and heavily shielded premises, and no significant amount of radiation can get out. What is discharged from the plant, however, is the water needed to condense the steam. This water circulates through a separate system and is never in contact with the reactor. You will recall from the first part of the book that environmentalists object to the alleged "thermal pollution" from this condenser water, which is returned to nature at least as clean as it was but admittedly somewhat warmer than when it came into the plant.

The warmed-up condenser water, flowing back into Lake Michigan, never presented a problem at Big Rock Point. In the 1960s, America was still a relatively happy land, and its people were not yet looking for causes on which to vent their frustrations. But such was no longer the case when the Palisades nuclear plant—far bigger than Big Rock—was built in

BIG ROCK POINT NUCLEAR PLANT

Fishermen come here by the droves and try to cast their lines as close to the plant's outflow channel as possible. It seems that most fish species like it here. (Consumers Power photo)

the late 1960s on Lake Michigan, 35 miles west of Kalamazoo. By that time, the world had spun out of control. Nothing seemed to go right anymore. Our country was divided against itself: hawk versus dove, white versus black, old versus young, labor versus capital, citizen versus government, permissiveness versus law and order, consumer versus producer. None of the issues held simple boob-tube solutions, if indeed they held solutions at all. In this confounding, frightening, wiretapping, computerized new world, there was just one thing almost everyone could agree on, namely, that mankind had been raising hell with its natural home and that something had better be done about it before it was too late.

This was a good and necessary cause indeed, and long over-due at that. But having at last come to recognize their heedless abuse of the environment, the American people now were trying frantically to make up for their transgressions and in the process were lashing out in all—and often wrong—directions. No other public issue in history had offered such a wonderful opportunity for passing the buck. You could de-nounce the makers of phosphate detergents while voting down the bond issue for a new sewage plant; you could drive your pre-1969 smogger past an oil refinery and curse the installa-tion's stench; you could campaign against insecticides, energetic from a bellyful of food that was there only because insects hadn't gotten at the vittles first; you could collect your paycheck from a company whose productivity depended on electric power, return to your air-conditioned home, and, over a dinner cooked on an electric range, condemn those dirty polluting utilities. Moreover, you could be an authority without knowing what you were talking about. If anything, knowledge was destructive, for it took the fun out of ecology by removing it from the realm of purgative passion and showing it for what it really is—modern man's most perplexing scientific-economic problem: how to keep the world livable without turning off life.

By the time Consumers Power Company sought to obtain

PALISADES UNDER CONSTRUCTION

This nuclear plant took more than three years to build and then stood idle for two more years, until finally, in early 1972, it was allowed to start producing power. (Photos on this and the two succeeding pages by Consumers Power. View of dome by Tony Kelly)

Dome of the Palisades nuclear plant reactor containment building topped out at 193 feet above the dunes. Steel-reinforced, prestressed, and post-tensioned concrete is 3.5 feet all around and is lined with steel plate.

Reactor pressure vessel being lowered past steam generator into its own reinforced-concrete housing. The pressure vessel has an inside height of 40 feet. The second steam generator is out of the picture to the right.

an operating license for its first major nuclear installation, the 700,000-kilowatt Palisades plant, it had become evident that society was no longer able to assess rationally its needs and determine appropriate priorities. The Palisades installation,[10] built on an isolated, dune-sheltered 487-acre site, 5 miles south of South Haven, was completed and ready to go when, just two weeks before the Atomic Energy Commission hearing on the operating license, a hastily activated environmentalist group registered its objection. The organization, which called itself the Michigan Steelhead and Salmon Fishermen's Association, intervened on the grounds that the warm condenser water returned to Lake Michigan from the Palisades plant could hurt the ecology of the lake — not that it *would*, but that it conceivably *could*. Several other environmental groups, including the Sierra Club, soon joined the fray.

The water to be discharged would be a maximum of 28° F warmer than it had been at its intake 25 feet below the lake surface. Now, they don't call Lake Michigan a Great Lake for nothing. It covers 22,400 square miles and has an average depth of 270 feet. This works out to 1,261,000,000,000,000 (1,261 trillion) gallons of water, much of it in a state of flux, flowing in from tributaries, flowing out into Lake Huron, receiving rain and snow, giving up moisture in evaporation. Palisades would discharge 390,000 gallons in a minute — a drop in a bucket. Scientists have pointed out repeatedly that on a sunny summer day, the surface water warms up without any help from anybody.

Consumers Power offered to conduct the plant's operation under strict and impartial scientific observation and to modify it promptly if any detrimental effect became apparent.[11] The environmentalists' answer was that ecological damage might not become apparent until 100 years from now. Maybe so. But while interminable arguments were going on at Atomic Energy Commission hearings in the Kalamazoo Public Library, fishermen, as they had for years, zeroed in on the waters around

GENERAL COUNSEL
GRAVES

His ordeal began with
Palisades and continues with
Midland, and there's more on
the way. (Consumers Power
photo by Rus Arnold)

Big Rock Point nuclear plant. It's a favorite rendezvous for fish, which evidently like the warm current flowing in, and the only provable ecological effect so far is a bigger fish kill by means of hook and gaff and net.[12]

The day-to-day burden of the environmental hearings sat on the shoulders of Harold P. Graves, the general counsel of Consumers Power, a taciturn lawyer of powerful build and serious mien who disdains legal theatrics and likes to stick to cold realities.[13] Not the company's most Pollyannaish executive to start with, Graves became increasingly frustrated as he saw the hearings rapidly deteriorate into what the law calls "adversary proceedings" instead of remaining, as they should have been, a rational, objective examination of facts. As the calendar flipped by, pressure mounted to get the case settled. Palisades standing idle was costing Consumers about $1 million a month in interest on capital investment and maintenance expenses. Moreover, the company had to make up for its generating shortage by buying electricity from Detroit Edison and other power-pooled utilities.

Week after week, Graves and his staff worked without

letup—often up to sixteen hours a day, Sundays included—
trying to arrive at a settlement formula that would get the
plant on line. Even when, after some nine months, Consumers
was willing to make what it considered unwarranted con-
cessions just to stop the continuous, debilitating financial
drain, Graves found that he couldn't get the various interveners to agree on language. Finally, on March 3, he went to
Aymond and asked to be given a deadline: if no agreement with
the company's adversaries could be reached by midnight of
March 12, Consumers Power would simply make the disputed
environmental modifications on its own, and the company's
announcement wouldn't even mention the interveners. Graves's
shrewd move threatened to deprive the environmentalists
of public recognition—and that, not surprisingly, did the
trick.

In the resulting peace pact, Consumers Power consented
to put up two horizontal "cooling towers," each some 650
feet long, in which the condenser water would be cooled by
forced air draft before being returned to the lake. The cooling
towers would take three years to build and were expected to
cost approximately $20 million. Their operation would take
3 to 4 percent of Palisades' power output, reducing the plant's
efficiency and raising its operating costs by $4 million to $5
million a year. The agreement with the interveners also called
for the installation of an additional containment system for
liquid radioactive wastes which will cost in the neighborhood
of $7 million. In return, while these additions were under
construction, Consumers Power could operate the nuclear
plant without further hindrance from the interveners.

But the Palisades troubles were far from over. Shortly
after the agreement with the interveners was reached, the
Atomic Energy Commission decided on the basis of an experiment, questioned by many engineers as to its validity, that
safety standards for emergency cooling systems of radioactive
cores in nuclear plants may have to be reevaluated. Consumers

Power's nuclear people are convinced that Palisades as planned will meet any new requirements imposed by the AEC in this regard, but even so the evaluation involved will add many months to the waiting period for a full operating license.

Jim Campbell was not destined to witness the operation of his big nuclear project. He died on January 24, 1972, of a heart attack. He was confident to the end that nuclear power eventually would find acceptance, despite the fact that in the last months of his life the obstacles seemed insurmountable.

In July 1971, Consumers Power's program for nuclear expansion—as indeed the plans of all utility companies—had suffered a further blow when a U.S. Court of Appeals in Washington ruled against the Atomic Energy Commission in the Calvert Cliffs test case brought by the Environmental Protection Fund.[14] The court decided in effect that the AEC had not properly complied with the Environmental Protection Act of 1970 in exempting some sixty nuclear plants currently planned or under construction from the provisions of that act. The court said that the AEC's concern had been with radiological aspects at the exclusion of other environmental considerations and that it had not been sufficiently responsive to objections in these areas, relying instead on the findings of other regulatory bodies. The net result of the court decision was that all nuclear plants—no matter in what stage of planning, construction or operation—were now wide open to challenges by anyone who felt so inclined, and quite regardless of scientific credentials. Electric utilities could look forward to years of litigation—while the country's energy shortage grew more critical by the day.

Thus, regardless of all opposition, Consumers Power will have to try and fight it through. Michigan's energy requirements rise some 7 or 8 percent a year. With Palisades finally in production, the company's generating capacity now stands at about 4.3 million kilowatts. Midland Nuclear Plant will add another 1.3 million, hopefully no later than 1977.[15] By 1982, to support the state's growing population, whose

MIDLANDERS FOR NUCLEAR POWER

More than 10,000 concerned Midlanders of all ages—nearly half that city's population—turned out for a rally on October 12, 1971, in support of the planned Consumers Power nuclear plant. The rally made it clear that the less than 100 intervenors, who had succeeded in halting the plant's construction, were in a distinct minority.

Still, the issue dragged on in the hearing rooms, while Midlanders continued to breathe fumes from soot-belching chimneys which the nuclear plant was intended to obviate. Worse yet, Midlanders were worried that their city's economy might seriously suffer if the plant were not built and Dow Chemical thus deprived of essential power and process steam.

Prominent among speakers at the Chamber of Commerce-sponsored rally were Art Linkletter (above), TV and radio personality; and U.S. Senator Robert P. Griffin from Michigan (below). (Midland Daily News photos)

HARD-NOSED AT THE CONFERENCE TABLE

Harry Wall, vice-chairman of Consumers' board of directors, started as an electric substation operator during the Depression and is not the kind of man to go overboard on new notions. At first negative on nuclear power, he too is now convinced that it is the only practical answer to our country's energy problem. But Wall acts the bulldog only during office hours. He melts on the way home to his young daughter, offspring of a late marriage. (Consumers Power photo by Rus Arnold)

livelihood depends on turning raw materials into manufactured products by means of applied energy, Consumers Power must be able to generate nearly 9 million kilowatts. A third major nuclear plant will then be essential.

This plant, if it is ever allowed to exist, will be the grand-daddy of light water reactor plants, with two units capable of producing a total of 2,300 megawatts, more than the combined capacity of Palisades and Midland. The plant is to be built on a 1,200-acre site near the village of Quanicassee, on the southernmost point of Lake Huron's Saginaw Bay, at a cost which by then could approach $1 billion, the way the inflation is going. Environmental studies at Quanicassee were launched in 1970, with surveys of aquatic organisms, fish, and bay ice formations. Announcement of the project came in the summer of 1971. By that time an environmental survey team from Michigan State University, working with Consumers Power, was conducting research on soil, vegetation, and animal life. Whether or not the team's findings will be trusted by environmentalists remains to be seen.

There is no one at Consumers Power who does not wish there were another, easier way to close the energy gap. But there isn't—not when it comes to base load. When Jim Campbell first spearheaded Consumers Power's entry into the nuclear business, Harry Wall, then vice-president in charge of electric operations and now vice-chairman of the company's board of directors, had been one of the men with serious reservations about the practical economics of nuclear power generation. Wall, born in 1909, is a contemporary of Campbell and by now one of the grand old men of electricity.[16] But where Campbell had been born into the utility business, Wall had always wanted to get into it from the outside, even as a kid. After working with line crews between terms at Carnegie Tech, Wall got his first real job as a substation operator for the Cleveland Illuminating Company at the depth of the Depression. Like anyone who has come up in business the hard way, Wall tends to be conservative and hard-nosed. Immediate realities count far more with him than the distant future. A company is no better than its balance sheet. Yet even Wall, who may be less of a visionary than Campbell was but who is no less a brilliant man, today admits, however reluctantly, that nuclear power is the main hope for electric service in the future.

"Yes sir," he says, in his friendly, old-fashioned way. "There is nothing else in the picture. The coal supply is becoming critical. Even coal that's full of sulfur is hard to get. Oil and gas are limited. There isn't enough of either available to carry a system like ours. The fuel cell is not developed to the point where it could be a central-station source [as opposed to individual use, as in a space capsule], and solar energy isn't developed at all to my knowledge. I can't see any other fuel at the moment except nuclear that can take care of large supplies."

Even if Quanicassee manages to jump all the hurdles, however, only some 45 percent of Consumers Power's total generating capacity will be nuclear by 1980. To help provide the additional power that will be needed to fuel the state's economy, Consumers Power has taken two giant pioneering steps.

It will be recalled from the previous chapter than one branch of Canada's Interprovincial-Lakehead pipeline crosses lower Michigan. At one point it passes within 10 miles of the Weadock and Karn plants near Bay City. Here, in the form of low-sulfur oil, was a potentially new source of minimum-pollution energy right at the company's doorstep. Like John Simpson's reforming plant arrangement with the same pipeline for liquid hydrocarbons, which followed some months later, the decision faced by the electric people was one of major proportions. A long-term commitment in the hundreds of millions of dollars would be required to assure the flow of sufficiently large fuel supplies over a sufficiently long period of time.

In March 1971, both the oil world and the utility industry were agog when Consumers Power signed a contract for nearly 25,000 barrels of low-sulfur oil a day from Canada. No other United States electric company had ever before so decisively grabbed the bull by its horns and sewed up part of the output of one of the world's major oil-producing areas for nearly a generation. With the stroke of a pen, the agreement relieved Consumers Power of some of its fretting about the decreasing availablility and ever-increasing cost of coal and enabled it to produce cleaner power in the bargain. As you read this book, six of Weadock's eight boilers are being converted from coal to oil, two 660,000-kilowatt oil-fired units are being installed at the Karn plant, and the Canadian oil deliveries from far-off Alberta are under way. By 1975, the oil will help fire a new 400,000-kilowatt generating plant in Zilwaukee. This will replace the old Saginaw River coal-fired steam plant, which was removed from service in early 1972.

Consumers Power's other major step in the electric area also had a counterpart in the gas business—the idea of storing natural gas from the Southwest and the Gulf Coast in Michigan's depleted gas fields. Unfortunately, you can't do that with electricity. Nor can you stuff the vast amounts involved into batteries. But there is a way to stockpile it for when it's needed most. Excess generating capacity can be used at off-peak hours, such as late at night and on weekends, to pump water into an elevated reservoir. During peak hours, when everybody turns on the switches, you let the water flow downhill again, through turbines that turn the falling water's energy into electricity. This ingeniously simple system is called "pumped storage." Switzerland, Germany, and Japan have several such installations, all relatively small, and there's a fair-sized one in the Ozarks.[17]

By now it must have become apparent that Consumers Power has lately been doing things in a really big way. So also here. In 1969 it joined with Detroit Edison to build the world's biggest pumped-storage hydroelectric plant, a project capable of adding more than 1.8 million kilowatts to the Michigan pool during hours of peak demand. Consumers Power and Detroit Edison are sharing all costs; both companies will put their excess base-load output into it, and both companies will withdraw from it.

For more than two years an army of 120 earthmovers with supporting heavy equipment scooped out the 27-billion gallon 1.3-square-mile reservoir from the undulating tableland above Lake Michigan, 4 miles south of Ludington, and built up a dike around it that's 170 feet tall at its highest point. As this book goes to press, construction is still in progress, for there is more involved than digging a hole and piling up dirt around it. To avoid leakage, clay must be compacted to a depth of 5 to 8 feet at the bottom of the reservoir. The inner slope of the dike embankment is being lined with asphalt, and the outer surface seeded to prevent erosion and to give the reservoir a pleasing appearance—for there will be parklands around it for camping and picnicking. Six slanting side-by-side steel pipes, each 1,400 feet long and up to 28.5 feet in diameter, will take water from Lake Michigan up to the reservoir and back down when extra power is needed. Six reversible pump turbines, one to each pipe, will suck in the water from Lake Michigan and push it up into the reservoir; when the water flows back down, these same turbines will drive the generators. Big as the reservoir is, its intake won't make a dent in Lake Michigan. The rise and fall of the great lake will not be measurable. That's how huge it is.

Visitors from all over the world have come to gawk at the spectacular Ludington project, almost unequaled as an earthmoving job since the Panama and Suez Canals were built, although these were of course infinitely bigger. Among the visitors has been a Russian power expert who told a Consumers Power employee assigned to host him that Russia had enough nuclear plants so that it didn't need pumped storage. "But," the Russian said, completely serious, "now that you have one, we will show that we can build a bigger one." Russia hasn't started yet, as far as anyone knows, but Consumers Power already has plans for another pumped-storage plant with several times Ludington's capacity for construction in the eighties if the concept continues to have economic attraction. Meanwhile, the Ludington operation is expected to start in mid-1973, and falling water, the oldest, purest, and most aesthetic way of making electricity, will once more do its job for Michigan.[18]

Regardless of the ultimate outcome of the nuclear power struggle, it is evident that for at least the next two or three decades, and probably longer, Michigan's electric energy will have to be derived from a complicated mix of sources—from coal, oil, gas, uranium, and water. Yet the components and percentages of this mix must be predicted, and while the predictions are being made, the company must keep all options open.

Harry Wall has made the point that an optimum planned program for adding economical sources of generation to take care of load growth can be prepared but that unforeseen obstacles such as have occurred at Palisades and Midland can badly disrupt the program's progress. Alternative programs must be on hand to permit a quick change in the type of generating-capacity addition to be adopted in order to be able to carry the load when it comes. Once any plan is authorized, the engineering and construction of the addition must be urgently and some-

AN ARMY OF EARTHMOVERS

In its first stages of construction, the Ludington pumped-storage reservoir looked like a war-movie setting. By 1973, a man-made lake, 1.3 square miles in area, will sparkle here above Lake Michigan, surrounded by public parks with campsites and picnic areas. (Consumers Power photo)

times frantically pursued in order for the capacity to be available when needed.

This task falls on Russell C. Youngdahl, part of whose assignment is the execution of all generating-plant projects. Then the company's youngest senior vice-president, Russ was handed this task in April 1970, a few days after his forty-sixth birthday.[19] Midland and Quanicassee are Youngdahl's babies, and if they are aborted by public edict, it will be the biggest disappointment of his life. But he faces up to that possibility, and in his new capacity—since June of 1972—as boss of all electric operations, it is now his major concern to create alternatives. Even if these alternatives cannot replace all the power lost, they will at least keep the company and its customers in business until society comes back to its senses and agrees on a workable set of priorities. Such alternatives could include using another combined-cycle oil-fired plant like the one at Zilwaukee, for example. Even if the alternatives prove to be immensely expensive to operate, that's okay with Youngdahl. If this is what the country wants, it will have to pay for it.

Just as Jim Campbell was the young generation in the early nuclear days of the 1950s, so Youngdahl today typifies the young thinking in the company. He is tall, slender, and boyish, and he loves baseball almost as much as the electric energy business. Not quite, though. He was, like so many other utilities people, born into that life: his father had been an electric man in southern Illinois, and ever since Russ Youngdahl's youth, utilities work has meant more than just paychecks to him—it has been a mission. "It's my job to provide power," he says. "I know that nuclear generation at this point makes the most sense, economically and ecologically, but we are here to serve the public, and if the public doesn't want nuclear power we'll have to try to go another route. Just tell us the rules in advance. Tell us what's acceptable and give us time to work on it."

Youngdahl knows that time is running out. Generating plants can't be built overnight. Technological development is not subject to the whims of man. No one can rewrite the laws of nature. "We're going through some real tough times," he says, "and maybe we'll make it, and maybe we won't. But when you're three runs behind in the last of the ninth with the bases loaded, I don't want to be warming the bench. I want to be up there batting."

Tomorrow

In the real-life serial that is the story of Consumers Power Company, the settings haven't altered much over the years; only the script and the actors have changed. As in the long-ago days of Anton Hodenpyl, New York City still remains a key locale. Here, Walter Boris occupies front-stage center, against an updated backdrop of glittering glass towers that camouflage the decline of Fun City on the Hudson. Youthful, although he recently celebrated his fiftieth birthday, tight-muscled like the skier that he is, gray-templed, handsome, and Establishment-urbane, he looks computer-picked for the part of "Our Man on Wall Street." But Boris is no central-casting cutout. His role as Consumers' vice-president of finance, for which Al Aymond and other senior executives had prepared him with much deliberation,[1] makes Boris a principal protagonist in the drama now being played: the company's battle for survival. Without the money Boris brings back from Wall Street, there'd be no next act.

Despite sophisticated plotting, however, the play doesn't always follow its scenario. *Dei ex machina* keep popping up offstage, ready to gremlinize the action. Take what happened when Consumers Power went to the market with a big bond issue in the summer of 1971. Boris had carefully selected Monday, August 9, as a day when conditions for financing would be relatively favorable. He had projected that during this week—and he hoped on this date—the comparatively small supply of bonds being offered to the market would result in a lower interest rate. Such timing is extremely important. Every fraction means a fortune when you borrow $60 million.

As usual on his frequent New York trips, Boris spent the night at the Essex House on stubbornly elegant Central Park South. After breakfast he cabbed downtown for final negotiations with Morgan Stanley & Co., the investment house interested in moving this particular bond issue.[2] The deadline was four o'clock. By that appointed hour, Morgan Stanley and Consumers Power would have to arrive at a mutually agreeable price—low enough so that the interest would not be too costly for the company, and yet high enough to attract bond buyers. In its understated, matter-of-fact business way, this was the climax of tense preparations. Up to the last possible moment, the Morgan Stanley representatives remained in constant touch with their partners and market traders, picking up every signal of the market until they finally committed themselves.

When they did, it appeared as though Boris had been right on target in recommending Monday as the day for the transaction. Indeed, bond interest rates had come down from the previous Friday, and where Boris had fully expected to pay 8¼ percent interest, he managed at the very last to get the quote shaved to 8⅛.[3] It was a real triumph—for six days. Then one of those offstage gremlins, in the person of Richard M. Nixon, tossed a firecracker that almost made Boris jump through the ceiling. Perhaps it was a good thing that, as a young pilot, Walt Boris used to walk on Nazi flak. Flying a riddled B-17, whose fuselage resembles a sieve, tends to teach a man to keep his cool. Boris surely needed his cool that Sunday night following the bond sale, as he listened to the President on TV.

For on Sunday night, August 15, Richard Nixon, after consistently (and convincingly) disavowing such action, announced his wage and price freeze. Not that Boris and most other Consumers Power top executives disagreed with Nixon's unexpected step. Like the rest of the country, their company had been sorely squeezed by rampant inflation. They felt that, if anything, the freeze had come too late. But as a result of Nixon's announcement, bond interest rates took a dive. They plunged to 7½ percent, a development that even the most astute assessment of market behavior could not have foreseen in the light of the President's previous stance.[4] Had Boris, against his own and everybody else's good judgment, set the date for the bond issue just one week later, Consumers might have saved $11.25 million in interest costs—$375,000 a year over the thirty-year life of these bonds.[5]

VICE-PRESIDENT WALTER R. BORIS

"When I go to Wall Street," he says, "I'm the beggar. That's what the people on the Public Service Commission don't understand." (Consumers Power photo)

Expensive as that blow out of the White House blue turned out to be, it was almost a trifle in Consumers' huge financing program. Young W. A. Foote thought in terms of hundreds of dollars. Anton Hodenpyl could still reckon in the tens of thousands. Cobb and Willkie—probably at their own stunned and delighted surprise—slowly learned to think in millions. But since World War II, the leaders of Consumers Power have been faced by investment decisions involving the kind of multimillion-dollar figures that used to strain even the federal puse. By 1971, interest payments alone on outstanding bonds topped $50 million in Consumers' annual budget.

Hardy Dam, biggest of the company's hydroelectric works, had cost $5.29 million in 1931. The B. C. Cobb Plant, completed in 1957, already required an investment of $67 million. The J. H. Campbell Plant, the company's newest coal-fired steam plant, swallowed nearly $90 million in construction money by the time its last power unit was installed in 1967. The Palisades Nuclear Plant, including its environmental safeguards and the added costs of delay, will run about $180 million. The Ludington pumped-storage project will cost Consumers about $190 million;[6] the twin-reactor plant at Midland, $550 million; and Quanicassee, if it comes to pass, nearly $1 billion. Partly because of inflation, but more importantly because of the economies of scale dictated to keep rates as low as possible, Consumers can't afford to even think of electric base-load projects anymore that cost less than $100 million. The gas side of the business also requires continual capital infusions. The Marysville Reforming Plant, dictated by the wellhead shortage of natural gas, will probably end up as a $70-million investment.

Consumers' 1972 budget calls for about $380 million worth

THE LAST AND BIGGEST OF THE DAMS

Hardy Dam, finished in 1931 at a cost of a little over $5 million, is still operating, but in Michigan natural waterpower is a thing of the past. (Photo by Abrams Aerial Survey Corp.)

of construction; and over the five-year period ending December 31, 1976, the company must contemplate an investment of nearly $2 billion. That's what is required to keep up with Michigan's workaday needs.

In 1950, with a population of just over 6 million, Michigan consumed 18.2 billion kilowatthours of electricity. In 1970, with the state's population at 8.6 million, electric energy consumption stood at 59 billion kilowatthours. By 1980, unless all forecasts are wildly out of whack, Michigan will have 9.9 million people using 112 billion killowatthours. The projection for 2000 is yet more awesome. Michigan's 15 million residents probably will need more than 300 billion kilowatthours that year.

Even at that, these figures do not fully factor in the additional power that may well be required to clean up Michigan's

THE BIGGEST AND PROBABLY LAST COAL-FIRED STEAM PLANT

The J. H. Campbell plant required an investment of $90 million. Completed in 1967, it could well be the last of its kind on the Consumers Power system. (Consumers Power photo)

environment. Up-to-date, nonpolluting sewage and solid-waste disposal facilities alone can increase the average community's energy consumption by 10 to 15 percent.[7]

Any reader who, at this stage of the book, thinks those projections were dreamed up by Consumers Power Company to enrich its stockholders either has been skipping pages or belongs to that now so fashionable faction that discounts anything industry says, even when it's documented.[8] To repeat: the earnings of utilities have long been limited by state regulation—so severely limited, in fact, that utility stocks have dropped drastically in recent years simply because investors know that they can make more money elsewhere.

Nor is Consumers' expansion program based on corporate pride. When, not very long ago, the chance arose to merge a smaller utility into Consumers Power, Aymond told his board of directors, "Before we go for this, let's really ask ourselves what we're in business for—is it just to get bigger?" The answer was a predictable "no," and since the acquisition would have done nothing for Consumers except to increase its size, the merger went out the window. As Walt Boris puts it,"We're in business to be reasonably big, commensurate with the efficiency and economy it gives us, and that's all." So much for aggrandizement as a motive for expansion.

This leaves one popular argument against increased energy production, namely, that our society, egged on by utility propaganda, consumes much more power than it needs. This is patent nonsense. Women don't buy self-cleaning ovens because utilities tell them to, but because they're sick and tired of kitchen slavery. In any event, incontrovertible statistics prove that about two-thirds of the energy Consumers Power sells (and most other investor-owned utilities operate in the same ball park) goes to industry and business. That energy keeps paychecks coming and gets taxes paid. Only about one-third is used by residential customers, and of this only 1 percent—i.e., about one-third of 1 percent of total energy production—powers such affluent-society gadgets as vacuum cleaners, radios, clocks, blankets, electric lawn mowers, toothbrushes, can openers, carving knives, razors, and hair dryers. Dispensing with these luxuries wouldn't make a microscopic dent in our modern society's energy requirements; it would only deprive the people who make these gadgets of their jobs.

Air conditioning, at least in a generally comfortable state like Michigan, is another matter. But Consumers Power stopped trying to sell that service some years ago, long before environmentalists began raising objections, when the company saw that air conditioning creates uneconomical peaking problems. Indeed, the challenge of B. G. Campbell, Jr.'s job in his recent position as Consumers' vice-president in charge of marketing[9] lay not in selling *more* power, but in adding load selectively where additional use will take up the slack during low-consumption hours. This is extremely important, for when an expensive plant is not used around the clock, the cost per kilowatt-hour to the customer inevitably must go up to pay for the idle overhead.[10]

Still, there remains the question of why Michigan's electric energy needs are expected to show such a phenomenal increase over the next decades. Why not, as Stuart Udall, John F. Kennedy's Secretary of the Interior, has suggested, inhibit the uses of electricity by charging progressively higher unit rates, the more power a customer uses? This sounds reasonable enough until you start to think about it. True, turning the rate structure upside down would discourage the use of electric toothbrushes and swizzle sticks. But remember: that isn't the real problem. The big users of electricity are not families, but commerce and industry, and it's commerce and industry that over the next ten years will have to provide employment for 650,000 additional people in Michigan who are already born and racing toward the day when they'll have to make a living.[11] Ironically, the same social philosophers who want to crimp the uses of power also insist on full employment and a better life for all. How this is to be accomplished simultaneously, they have not explained.

But let's be more conservative than they are and stipulate

that somehow or another Michigan will have to provide jobs for a work force increasing at the modest rate of 1 percent a year. This doesn't mean we can get by on increasing our industrial power consumption by only 1 percent a year. Since World War II, our nation's productivity has grown at an annual average rate of 3 percent — not a bad showing, but recent events have demonstrated that it isn't enough. Other countries, notably Japan and Germany, have far outstripped us in productivity. As a result, they undersell us, preempt us in the world market, and take jobs away from American workers. As has been pointed out in an earlier chapter, and as every economist understands, a leisure-oriented, highly unionized technological society like ours can only increase its productivity by letting machines do more work — and that means increasing the applications and quantitative use of manufactured energy. Since the sole alternative to increased productivity is a national decision to accept high unemployment, Consumers Power and Detroit Edison can only go on the assumption that Michigan's economic output in 1980 will be some 50 percent higher than it is today and — still only figuring a minimal and probably far from sufficient annual growth rate of 4 percent — that the state's productivity will have more than doubled again by the year 2000. Thus, Michigan's energy utilities must build up their capacity correspondingly — plus 17 percent for reserve to protect against unexpected failures of equipment and another 9 percent to replace older, inefficient generating units.[12] Anything short of that would be irresponsible, not so much toward utility stockholders, who might do quite well on more limited operations, but to the public Michigan's utilities serve.

Even in a less confused society than ours, raising the money for such vast expansion would be far from easy, but it could be accomplished with fewer headaches and fewer moments of suppressed despair. Logic would seem to dictate that when a society requires a service, it will pay for that service, and that investors who provide money to make this service possible will earn a reasonable dividend. Moreover, such investment in an obvious necessity would seem to entail minimal risk. But you can discount logic; it's not a factor any longer. If it were, Aymond and Boris and other Consumers Power executives wouldn't toss and turn many a night, wondering where it's all going to end.

The problem is that no public utility can earn enough to finance its growth. Most of the money must come from the outside, from bond issues and sales of common and preferred stock. Once a utility looks for such outside financing, it is in competition with other utilities and with nonregulated companies for the same relatively fixed dollars—the savings of individuals, institutions, insurance companies, pension funds. It's a fact of life that these savings will go where, all risks considered, they may be expected to win the largest possible return. When investors are doubtful about a good return, the interest rates a company must pay on its bonds go up, and the price of its stock goes down. This marketplace reality has apparently escaped the attention of the Michigan Public Service Commission, which, in recent years, has consistently refused to grant Consumers the rates it needs to show earnings that will continue to attract investors.

In saying this, I am giving the commission the benefit of doubt; for if its members understood the marketplace, the only explanation of their attitude would be that they are playing politics of the easiest sort: giving the public what it wants regardless of the consequences. Quite naturally, rate increases are unpopular. The average homeowner couldn't care less about the financial health of the utility he depends on. He wants to turn on the switch when he feels like it, and he doesn't want his bill to be higher than it was last month. The relationship between the flip of his switch and the utility's financial ability to keep the switch working is not within his understanding. Quite rightly, he leaves such esoteric matters to the public officials he elects, and through them to the commissioners whom they appoint. It thus becomes the responsibility of the regulatory agency to protect the citizen in two ways: to keep the rates he pays as low as possible but, at the same time, to guard the financial health of the utility so that it can keep functioning and supply him with the energy that he needs. In day-to-day political life, these two functions are difficult to reconcile: the exercise of public responsibility is a high-wire act over the abyss of public disapproval.

Not surprisingly, regulatory bodies almost always give the utilities less than they ask for. Still, the general growth of utilities until about a decade ago wasn't greatly hampered by unfair rate treatment. Even today, utilities in some jurisdictions fare better than those in others.[13] Consumers Power, however, is not among the most fortunate.

Let's look at the company's experience over the last fourteen years. In January 1958, it asked for $15.3 million in additional electric revenues. Eighteen months later, it got a little less than $6.8 million. In June 1960, it asked for $13.5 million in additional gas revenues. Nearly a year later, it got about $8 million. Slashed and delayed as these rate hikes were, they did not handicap Consumers too much at the time. It was under these rates that the company blossomed into its golden years of the early 1960s, during which it did so well that it *voluntarily* (although admittedly nudged by the Public Service Commission) reduced its electric rates by $7,300,000 and its gas rates by $4,487,000. But while a company can cut its rates from one day to the next, it takes, as you'll have noted, a year or more to get them increased.

For the first time in eight years, this became necessary in April 1968. Consumers Power then applied for gas rate relief in the amount of $28 million. The company eventually got $21,308,000. The order became effective in October, nearly two years later.[14] By that time, Consumers could see more thunderheads piling up on the horizon and already was preparing its next electric rate increase application. This was filed just a few months later, on August 13, 1970, requesting an increase of $28.5 million.[15] When it became apparent that no decision could be expected in the reasonable future, the company, hard pressed by rising costs, asked for interim relief in the amount of $7 million, the sum actually recommended by the commission's professional staff after its analysis of Consumers' financial situation.[16] The request, as may be recalled from the introductory chapter, was denied. Not until December 14, 1971—sixteen months after the original application—did the commission finally issue a rate order, and then it granted the company only $10.5 million, or slightly more than one-third of what Consumers had asked for. Meanwhile, a gas rate case Consumers had filed in April 1971 for $26,082,664 was still pending, although a few days after the electric rate boost, the PSC did grant Consumers an interim gas rate increase of $6.5 million to help make up for recent hikes in the wholesale price of natural gas.

In our inflationary times, these long delays in granting rate increases make the new rate structures obsolete even as they go into effect. This lag problem is compounded by the fact that rate relief is granted not on the basis of reasonable future expectations but on the basis of past experience—the company's financial situation during a twelve-month period all of which has already passed by the time the evidence is completed. Thus, the electric rates Consumers may charge in 1972 are partly based on costs that prevailed in 1970, an absurdity that should be evident to anyone who's been buying groceries during these years. Moreover, nonrecurring profits—such as a gain on Consumers Power bonds bought back by the company for its sinking fund when their price dropped as a result of rising interest rates—are allowed to inflate the earnings of the year on which the new rates are based.[17]

As an inevitable result of this rate squeeze, Consumers' return on common equity has been dropping steadily ever since 1967. The erosion was slow at first, from 12.5 percent on underlying book value to 11.6 percent by June 1970. But then, in the next twelve months, it plunged to 10.6 percent and from there to 10.2 percent in December 1971. That kind of negative growth performance doesn't look good to anyone buying stocks. The effect on the price of Consumers Power common was predictable. It fell from a high, equivalent to $54 a share in 1965, to about $30 at the end of 1971. Of course, the general deterioration of the market during this period entered into the picture too, but utility issues do not usually reflect large fluctuations; they are, for the most part, reasonably stable, slowly growing, safe investments.[18]

Nor did the bond market overlook the Consumers Power Company's predicament. Standard & Poor's reduced Consumers' rating from AAA to AA, and Moody's, the other major rating agency, followed Standard & Poor's in June 1972. The effect of a lower bond rating is higher interest rates — and, eventually, higher costs to the company's customers.

In effect, Consumers Power finds itself caught in a vicious cycle whose spin only a healthy rate hike can stop. Faced by declining earnings, the company should reduce its $2 dividend but can't afford to, since it must go back into the market year after year with additional common equity to finance a significant part of its expansion.[19] At the same time, of course, retained earnings are shrinking, making outside financing of new projects that much more important. And, to top it off, there is a limit to how much capital the company can borrow by means of bonds. Under the company's indenture, funds available for the payment of interest must be at least two times the actual interest payments. At the end of 1971, the coverage ratio stood at 2.46. If the electric rate increase — however small — had not come through in the nick of time, the $250 million of new securities planned for 1972 would have run the well dry. Consumers would then have been unable to issue more bonds until the coverage was built up again.

The electric rate increase authorized for 1972 stemmed the decline in the rate of return earned but did not reverse the trend. The return earned remains far from adequate to put Consumers on a sound financial footing for its required expansion. As this is written in early 1972, the company is preparing to file a new rate application, once again seeking an increase that would bring Consumers' return up to a point where it will attract capital. Using comparable utilities as a standard, it appears at present that a return of about 13.5 percent on common equity would be required.

The man who is stuck with the difficult job of dealing with the Public Service Commission is a surprisingly jolly fellow named John W. Kluberg, who came to Consumers from the public accounting firm of Arthur Andersen & Co.[20] Kluberg, vice-president and controller of Consumers Power as well as of its Michigan Gas Storage subsidiary, resembles a white-haired, pixielike professor of nineteenth-century literature— until you notice his eyes, which gleam like sharp new computer buttons, and then you know if he taught anything, it would have to be higher mathematics. Indeed, more than any other Consumers Power executive, Kluberg carries every minute

CONTROLLER KLUBERG

The man who knows all the figures. If he's smiling, it's not because they are amusing.
(Fabian Bachrach)

financial statistic on the tip of his tongue and is ever ready to deliver it, correlated with all pertinent data, like a computer print-out. This comes in mighty handy when Kluberg, backed up by Boris and Graves, argues with the Public Service Commission and its staff.

Not that these are violent arguments. The commissioners and their staffers are personally always pleasant. Rather, it must be a little like punching pillows. Kluberg makes his telling points, only to see them sink into a tepid sea of essential miscomprehension. Even assuming goodwill on the part of the PSC, the tenure of its appointed officials is never really long enough for them to gain deep insight into the problems of the many businesses they regulate. The PSC's work load is tremendous; there isn't just Consumers Power, but also Detroit Edison, Michigan Consolidated Gas, and Michigan Bell Telephone, plus nearly a dozen small electric and gas utilities, several independent telephone companies, and all the railroads and trucking companies doing business in Michigan. Every one of these companies has problems, similar in their own way to those of Consumers Power. While the PSC's staff has more professional experience, part of its function is that of the civil service naysayer, akin to that of the IRS man who audits your income tax return. In such a climate, it is almost inevitable that PSC staff recommendations usually will not be too favorable, and the easiest thing for the commission to do is to go along. To overrule the staff's recommendations, as has happened on occasion, leaves the commissioners in an unpopular position that they wouldn't have the precise knowledge to defend.

Kluberg, however, is an optimist. "There's some indication that there might yet be light in Lansing," he says, referring to a PSC order that gave the General Telephone Company almost all it asked for, including a 12.75 percent rate of return on common equity. Indeed, there had better be light in Lansing, or there won't be much light in Michigan.

Artificially low rates, coupled with such political boondoggles as a bill introduced in the 1971 Michigan Legislature asking for a 50 percent rebate on utility bills of low-income people over sixty-two, without providing for compensatory increases elsewhere,[21] are of course only part of the overall problem. Obtaining environmentally acceptable fuels to produce the energy needed in the future is another serious, seemingly insurmountable challenge.

On one hand, Consumers Power and other utilities are confronted with more and more delay in obtaining licenses to build and operate nuclear power plants; on the other, it's blatantly apparent that future energy supplies will depend absolutely on nuclear power. All cost considerations aside, there simply is neither enough low-sulfur coal and oil nor enough pollution-free natural gas around to do the big job that lies ahead with fossil fuels. Consumers Power Company has a long, proud record of environmental responsibility and was among the first utilities to start installing electrostatic precipitators in its generating station stacks back in the 1950s. Yet it stands condemned by the easy slogan that "all power pollutes," along with those energy utilities that keep fouling the atmosphere with black clouds of fly ash and the stinging stench of sulfur. Consumers' construction plans through 1975 call for about $100 million of pollution-control equipment that until two years ago not even the most ardent environmentalists thought of asking for. Still, this huge expenditure for ecological safeguards will scarcely impress those who'd like to see the United States return to the simple life of 150 years ago, when, incidentally, the average workweek was seventy-two hours (you've got to work a lot harder and longer when you make your living strictly by hand) and the life expectancy of the average male was thirty-eight years.

Ray Bradbury, perhaps the greatest and certainly the most poetic of our science fiction writers, once penned a tale set in the year 2026, entitled "There Will Come Soft Rains."[22] The story's central character is a fully automated house programmed by computer tapes. A voice-clock calls out wakeup time, announces the date, and tells what bills are payable this day. The food center ejects a breakfast of toast, eggs, and bacon, with coffee for the parents and milk for the kids. The garage door lifts, the garden sprinklers turn on, rooms vacuum themselves, the kitchen produces lunch as it had breakfast, three-dimensional movies are projected on the nursery walls, the bathtub fills itself with water, martinis materialize at cocktail hour, and dinner is served even as the beds warm up automatically for the cool night. The kicker is that there are no people—their shadows have been etched into the patio wall in yesterday's nuclear holocaust.

Remember, this is science fantasy: somehow, somewhere, power was still generated to run this house. If Bradbury were writing the story today, he might consider turning it around. The way things are going, it would seem more likely that by the year 2026, there will be people but no energy. New York City and its adjoining areas have already faced forms of energy rationing, and teetered on the brink of prolonged blackouts. Continued interventions by environmentalist groups against the expansion of Consolidated Edison's generating facilities bring the ultimate crisis for that city ever closer.

But even on their bitterest days, Consumers' executives refuse to give up hope. They can't believe that in the long run public opinion will tolerate a blacked-out Michigan or, for that matter, a blacked-out United States, especially since it's not at all unlikely. New York's situation will eventually sound a most dramatic warning. Nor can they really believe, although they are frequently worried about it, that the Michigan energy picture will be allowed to deteriorate to such a degree that power may have to be rationed. And here we arrive at the ultimate irony: if a generating shortage forced Consumers Power to restrict its sales, it would first have to ask the PSC for permission to do so![23]

Optimism and irony notwithstanding, that day may yet come. In fact, unless realistic measures are taken throughout the nation, it may be here as early as 1973 or 1974. This prospect, tragic for the general economy in its implication, harbors an additional specific threat for investor-owned utilities like Consumers Power. For if and when utilities fail to meet the country's energy demands, the blame inevitably will fall on the companies, not on those who prevented their orderly expansion. Certainly the government will not confess to having retarded the utilities' growth through unrealistic regulation, nor will the public accept industry's compliance with ecological demands as an excuse when the lights go out, the wheels slow down, and the paychecks peter out. Then the utilities will find themselves the villains once again, as they did in the 1930s, and this next time the voice for government ownership may well carry the day.

About 23 percent of the country's electric energy is now supplied by government-owned installations, such as the Tennessee Valley Authority and Bonneville Power Authority (federal), the New York Power Authority (state), and any number of municipal operations. Service by government utilities has not been necessarily bad, though on the average it has been no better and generally a little worse than that by investor-owned companies. But government ownership has a number of serious drawbacks.

Most important, perhaps, is the fact that while public service commissions have not always exercised their function with the greatest acumen, they have performed a necessary service: without them, utilities would be uncontrolled monopolies, with all the excesses monopolies are prone to. Government power, however, is also monopoly power. Worse yet, it is not subject to any regulation whatsoever. This means that government-owned utilities may be as inefficient as they like, and the unprotected customer and taxpayer must foot the bill for their inefficiency.

It is true that government power often sells for less than "private" power. But that's deceiving. Big chunks of utility revenues go for interest on capital investment and for taxes. Government power is cheaper only because it can be financed at lower interest rates and because it pays no taxes. Taking these advantages into consideration, it is actually more expensive, with the difference made up out of tax revenues. As Senator Norris, the arch-foe of the utilities, himself admitted in the 1930s, "the TVA would be out of business in three months" if it had to pay the same taxes imposed on investor-owned utilities. Thus, government ownership would not only be a drain on tax revenues, but at the same time would reduce these revenues because of its tax exemption. The inevitable result of a government take-over of utilities would be increased rates and/or increased taxes.

What's more, if the federal government were to finance a wholesale take-over of investor-owned utilities, the cost of expropriation would come so high—somewhere in the neighborhood of $150 billion—that to sustain the interest on the required bond issues and to carry the utilities' existing indentures, the government would be forced to reduce the value of the payback dollars. In short, more fuel would be added to inflation. As for outright confiscation—and there may even be voices that will demand that—not only would this be contrary to all American tradition, but it would also be like robbing yourself. While only about four million individual investors own utility issues, their immediate families constitute almost 10 percent of the population. Even more significant is the actual spread of utility ownership through pension funds, investment companies, and insurance companies: almost everyone in the United States has an indirect financial interest in investor-owned utilities.[24]

So let's assume that our country will come to its senses and entrust future building to those who have proved they know how to go about it. This still leaves investor-owned utilities—and indeed all growth industry—facing a tremendous problem: the ever more pinching shortage of available capital for conventional financing. There's a real question in moneymen's minds about how much longer bond buyers will be willing to buy bonds, and preferred stock buyers to buy preferred stock.

Walt Boris is among the people who keep pondering such matters, and he has already come up with a few possible answers. Leasing instead of building is one of them. This practice is not new to the company, but has been confined until now to relatively small equipment, where leasing is a convenience rather than a financial consideration.[25] Certain types of office equipment, for instance, fall into this category. But Boris is now considering leasing some of the really big stuff, such as generating plants. "Maybe we can stretch our money," he says, "by looking for an entirely new kind of investor—a bank maybe—that's not interested in buying our bonds but might be willing, for the depreciation leverage, to arrange for the financing of a major facility and to build it for lease to us. That way we'd have to rely less heavily on conventional financing, and at the same time we'd expect to encounter little opposition from the Public Service Commission in getting the lease fee in our rates as a cost of service since no return on capital investment to the stockholder is involved."

Boris has another, similar idea regarding expensive pollution safeguards. "There's a state law," he says, "that allows municipalities to issue revenue bonds for pollution-control equipment. When they passed that law, they probably weren't thinking of what I'm thinking about—which is that local townships or counties or some state agency could finance such projects much more cheaply than we can, while giving the investor a tax break that we can't give him. We'd lease the pollution-control equipment for the period it takes to pay off the bonds plus interest, and everybody'd be ahead: the community, the investor, and the company."

Whether or not these particular plans are realized is not so important. What matters is that it's this sort of innovative thinking which enables Consumers Power to keep building for the future. The company's vigorous—and highly successful—efforts to help itself and its customers by exploring and developing new sources of natural gas are a dramatic example of the attitude with which the leaders of Consumers Power are imbued.

Indeed, the company's new leadership draws on technological and administrative experience that goes far beyond the traditional concept of utility operations. In July 1972, Astronaut James A. McDivitt, who had been on Consumers' board of directors since January of the previous year, resigned from his NASA and Air Force posts and joined the company as a senior vice-president. He assumed a number of Aymond's responsibilities in the corporate area, for which—as head of the multibillion-dollar Apollo Program—McDivitt appears eminently qualified.[26] In turn, the reduction of Aymond's burdens gives him, as chairman of the board and president more time to concentrate on the critical decisions of entrepreneurship that are vital to the company's survival.

In a very real sense, the company has come full circle. Once again, just as in its earliest years, when every forward step was an adventure into the unknown, Consumers Power must

FUTURE BUILDER YOUNGDAHL

At the penstocks of Ludington, Senior Vice-President Russell Youngdahl ponders his assignment of bringing in Consumers' huge new electric projects in time to meet Michigan's power needs. (Consumers Power photo by Don Cunningham)

EX-ASTRONAUT McDIVITT

EX-ASTRONAUT McDIVITT

James A. McDivitt, 43, former boss of Apollo Program and orbital command module pilot, is another of the new generation of executives Aymond has moved into leadership positions at Consumers Power. (Photo courtesy NASA)

stake its existence on immense courage, imagination, and initiative.

But a utility cannot write the rules. Society must point the way. The time may well be here when as a nation, even as a world, we must balance our resources. If we do not have the fuel or the technology to sustain today's living standards without doing irreparable damage to the earth that feeds us, then we must reassess our values and arrive at a new definition of what constitutes a "better life." But such a new definition cannot be based on guesswork and nihilistic slogans. It must have its roots in a rational assessment of human needs. As Russ Youngdahl, the young senior vice-president of Consumers Power, has said, "Tell us what's acceptable and we'll go to work on it." If society can pull itself together in time to work out a set of viable goals, then the history of Consumers Power Company has only just begun.

Notes and Comments

Today

1. Alphonse H. Aymond, a native of St. Louis, Missouri, was graduated from Northwestern University in 1936 and earned his juris doctorate at the University of Michigan in 1939. After five years with a law firm in Chicago, he served as a Navy officer before joining the New York legal staff of Commonwealth & Southern in 1946. He was transferred to Consumers Power in 1947 and became the company's general attorney in 1951 and general counsel in 1955. He was named vice-president in 1956 and elected to the board of directors the following year. In 1958 he was appointed executive vice-president, and on Whiting's retirement in May of 1960 he became chairman of the board of directors and the company's chief executive officer. (See Chapter 20 for Aymond's early history with Commonwealth & Southern and Consumers Power.)

2. In terms of day-to-day work load and worry, this strike, with its sporadic outbursts of violence, was especially hard on Ralph C. Bretting, Consumers' vice-president in charge of personnel, who supervised all union matters until his resignation in May 1972. Bretting was then succeeded by B. G. Campbell, Jr., previously vice-president in charge of marketing (see Tomorrow, Note 9).

3. In August 1970, Consumers Power had filed for a $28.5-million electric rate increase. This did not come through. Instead, the Public Service Commission's staff recommended a maximum of $7 million. Consumers Power promptly asked for intermediate rate relief in that amount. The commission refused this request, inform-

ing the company that it would reach a final decision in the case in a few months. Since, however, the original application dated back to 1970, the facts which the commission would consider in late 1971 would be long superseded by more recent cost figures. Moreover, it would then take twelve months before the effects of the increase would be fully realized by the company.

Consumers Power previously had been granted an electric rate increase in 1969 in the amount of $16 million. Even with that increase, Consumers Power's average rate per kilowatthour was less in 1970–1971 than it had been since the mid-sixties. This may seem impossible, but it is the result of a combination of factors, most prominent among which is increased use. The more electricity a customer uses, the more he takes advantage of the lower incremental steps of the rate. The crucial fact for the company is that it costs X dollars to generate, distribute, and sell 1,000 kilowatthours, and the number of dollars received by the company for these 1,000 kilowatthours keeps going down.

4. This is predicated on the fair return on common stock being pegged at 14 percent, which with Consumers Power's capitalization at that time would have worked out to about $3.70. The Michigan Public Service Commission's idea of a fair return is 12 percent, which would come out to $3.20, some 13 percent more than Consumers Power was actually earning. The fact that per-share earnings as seen on a utility's financial summary may be increasing from year to year can be misleading, since the earnings, while up in dollars and cents, may well be down in relative terms of the return on the capital invested.

5. Distribution of electric energy between the two companies is handled by computers at the jointly built Michigan Electric Power Pool Control Center, outside Ann Arbor. Pooling power like this not only helps to forestall blackouts in case one of the companies has a major equipment failure but allows greater economies of operation. As generating units grow bigger, a failure becomes more serious; hence a system's reserve capacity must increase with the size of its generating units. Beyond a certain point, this becomes economically inefficient and therefore puts a limit on the size of the generating units that may be built within a single system. When, however, two or more extensive systems are tied together, the randomness of failure probability decreases, and each company can get by with less reserve, thus enabling it to install larger machines that come in at a cheaper cost per kilowatt.

6. Other companies in the MIIO group include Indiana & Michigan Electric, Commonwealth Edison of Chicago, Toledo Edison, Ohio Edison, Northern Indiana Public Service, and American Electric Power. The MIIO group is in turn tied into a power grid, the East Central Area Reliability Coordination Group (ECAR), which includes all the twenty-six electric companies in Michigan, Ohio, Indiana, West Virginia, Kentucky, and Pennsylvania. The ECAR companies are in turn connected with the CANUSE grid, which extends to the East coast and includes much of eastern Canada. Major members of the CANUSE grid (in addition to Consumers Power, Detroit Edison, and Ontario Hydro) include Niagara Mohawk, New York State Electric & Gas, Power Authority of the State of New York, Consolidated Edison Company of New York, Long Island Lighting, most of the New England companies, The Aluminum Company of America, and Quebec Hydro. The present interconnections are mainly for emergencies. The future will no doubt bring about power pooling on a wider scale. In fact, even now the whole Eastern United States is connected to the West, but the ties are rather weak.

7. The Hydroelectric Power Commission of Ontario (HEPCO), more commonly known as Ontario Hydro, has been tied in with Detroit Edison since 1953. Ontario Hydro's capacity in 1970 stood at about 10,000 megawatts; i.e., it was about the same size as the Michigan pool.
8. Responsibilities for planning these bulk power resources and making the power pools work lie with W. Jack Mosley, who joined Consumers Power in 1962 as director of power pooling, two years later became executive manager of electric operations, and in 1969 was elected a vice-president. Mosley was born in Hickory, Oklahoma, in 1912, and he earned his electrical engineering degree at the University of Washington, Seattle. Prior to joining Consumers Power, he was general engineering consultant for Ebasco Services, Inc., in Portland, Oregon, and was closely involved with power-pooling operations in the Pacific Northwest.

As of July 1, 1972, Roland A. Lamley, former executive manager of bulk power operations, has served as vice-president of bulk power operations. It is his job to boss Consumers' production of electric power and to supervise its electric transmission system.
9. Here, as an example of Consumers Power's financing, are the programs for 1969, 1970, and 1971.

	Shares	Principal amount
1969		
First Mortgage Bonds:		
7⅝% series due 1999		$50,000,000
8¼% series due 1999		$55,000,000
1970		
Common Stock:		
Offering Price $26.50 per share	1,264,938	$33,520,857
First Mortgage Bonds:		
8¾% series due 1976		$60,000,000
8⅝% series due 2000		$50,000,000
1971		
Preferred Stock:		
Offering Price $100 per share	700,000	$70,000,000
First Mortgage Bonds:		
8⅛% series due 2001		$60,000,000
7½% series due 2001		$60,000,000

10. As a dramatic illustration of a modern nation's dependence on its power supply, see Albert Speer's comments in his fascinating book entitled *Inside the Third Reich* (Verlag Ullstein GmbH, © 1969; New York: Macmillan, 1970). Speer, Nazi Germany's wartime production chief, reports that the May 1943 raid by nineteen British aircraft on the Ruhr dams and their hydroelectric power installations almost accomplished what previous attacks on factories and cities by many thousands of British planes had failed to do: immobilize the gigantic industrial complex of the Ruhr Valley. The only reason why this raid was not a total success was that it destroyed but one of the three dams and left the others virtually intact. Surprisingly, the British never repeated the attempt.

There may be one rational explanation—the same that could well apply to the Viet Cong's selective rocket attacks on targets around and even behind power stations. Perhaps military planners realize that generating facilities should not be destroyed, lest the occupation forces be unable to sustain life in the enemy's territory after victory. Who knows, but that this might also be the reason why the United States bombers and artillery in 1945 spared Manila's famed San Miguel beer brewery, although it was being used by the Japanese as an observation post.

11. The planted areas are maintained, thinned, and generally managed by the company's forestry department. Products from these timbered areas include a portion of the company's annual requirements of distribution poles, as well as fence posts, cabin logs, flooring, and pulp for paper mills.

Yesterday

Chapter 1

1. Opening verse of the "Emigrant's Song," which compares the rugged life on New England's rocky soil with the promise of a better future in rich and fertile Michigan.
2. The theory was that the loose texture of flannel absorbed the body's waste products, which otherwise would stay on the skin. See Catherine E. Beecher, *A Treatise on Domestic Economy for the Use of Young Ladies at Home and at School* (New York: Harper, 1847), pp. 112–114.
3. F. Clever Bald, *Michigan in Four Centuries* (New York: Harper & Row, 1961), pp. 8–9.
4. *Ibid.*, p. 155.
5. For fascinating detail on the Chippewa reservation, see Edmond G. Love, *The Situation in Flushing* (New York: Harper & Row, 1965), pp. 5–9. This book is worth reading altogether: it is a great bit of Americana.
6. This newspaper was first published in 1837.
7. The leaders of this group were Jeremiah P. Woodbury, Stephen S. Cobb, Allen Potter, James A. Walker, and William B. Clarke. Woodbury served as the first president until 1884, when Potter took over for a one-year term, after which Woodbury again assumed active management. See "A Brief History of the Manufacture and Distribution of Gas in Kalamazoo," Kalamozoo division files of Consumers Power Company.
8. W. W. France Company of Utica, New York, built the plant and necessary utilization equipment. The designer was A. J. Lathrop.
9. B. G. Campbell, "History: Jackson Gas Plant," Consumers Power Company files.

Chapter 2

1. Eliot Jones and Truman C. Bigham, *Principles of Public Utilities* (New York: Macmillan, 1931).
2. Winsor was probably an Austrian or German by birth, and was originally named F. A. Winzer. See *ibid.*
3. Thomas King, *Consolidated of Baltimore: 1816–1950.*
4. Jones and Bigham, *op. cit.*
5. Among them were New York City (whose Gas Light Company was franchised in 1823), Boston (1822), Detroit (1848), and Chicago (1850).

6. Stephen S. Cobb was not related to B. C. Cobb, the later president of Consumers Power Company.
7. The pertinent facts and figures here are taken from the Kalamazoo Gas Light Co. minutes. The quotations used in the text are evidently reconstructed, as are most of the other conversations in this volume, but they are nonetheless accurate in terms of the essentials involved.
8. The four "able and capable" businessmen were William M. McConnell, Levy Bacon, Jr., Horace C. Thurber, and Michael Crofoot. They apparently inherited a gas company franchise that had been granted earlier that year by the village corporation of Pontiac to "Enos T. Chappell and such other persons as may associate with him." It seems that Chappell was unable to form his company and more or less willingly allowed the other men to take over.
9. The East Saginaw Gas Light Co. was started on June 17, 1863, on a capital of $5,000. Local stockholders and directors were John F. Driggs, James L. Ketcham, and Julius K. Rose. The Saginaw Gas Light Co. (serving the community of the west side of the river, which was then a separate city) was established on May 21, 1868. In addition to D. L. C. Eaton, Thomas Merrill, M. S. Lockwood, and George L. Burrows, of Saginaw, its list of stockholders and directors included Alex and Edwin Swift, of Cincinnati, Ohio. Alex Swift was destined to play a prominent role in the electric business as well, in both Saginaw and Bay City. The Bay City Gas Light Company was organized with $40,000 of capital on February 15, 1868. It had thirty-two stockholders, nearly all residents of Bay City or Ann Arbor. The largest single stockholder was James Clements of Ann Arbor, father of W. L. Clements, who was later a regent and benefactor of the University of Michigan. The Bay City Company was reorganized in 1882 with a capital of $60,000. Clements still remained the largest stockholder. The exact date in 1870 of the incorporation of the City of Flint Gas Light Company is not known, nor are the names of its original incorporators. Local citizens prominent for many years in the destinies of the company included J. W. and C. M. Bergole, J. B. and W. A. Atwood, James Van Fleet, G. L. Denham, F. W. Judd, William Hamilton, Ira Wilder, Dr. J. C. Willson, A. D. McColl, R. J. Whaley, and W. C. Orrell.
10. Jones and Bigham, *op. cit.*

Chapter 3

1. Campau also founded Saginaw and platted it in 1822. See F. Clever Bald, *Michigan in Four Centuries* (New York: Harper & Row, 1961).
2. Albert Baxter, *History of the City of Grand Rapids, Michigan* (New York: Munsell & Company, 1891).
3. This multiple operation was possible because Brush's new arc light had an ingenious but simple mechanism which automatically short-circuited the lamp when it failed and thus maintained the path of the current to the other lamps.
   Brush, an 1869 graduate of the University of Michigan, was but one of several innovators of those days who concerned themselves with arc lights. In 1875, Charles J. Van Depoele, a native Belgian who manufactured church furniture in Detroit, built a dynamo and arc lamp for use by the Holy Trinity Roman Catholic Church during its Christmas celebration of that year. But Brush's light was the first to gain wide public notice.
   In 1877 the Franklin Institute of Philadelphia invited builders of dynamos to send

in their makes for comparative trial, and the Brush model was the one chosen for experimental use at the institute. Brush secured financial backing from his friend George W. Stockley, vice-president of the Cleveland Telegraph Supply Company, and soon merchandised his lighting equipment through that company.

Among the dozens of inventors, scientists, and engineers attracted to arc lighting by Brush's success was Elihu Thomson, a chemistry teacher at Philadelphia's Central High School, who teamed up with a professor, E. J. Houston, to develop their own arc-lighting system. The Thomson-Houston system went into production by the American Electric Company of New Britain, Connecticut, in 1880. Eventually the Thomson-Houston Electric Company was organized, led at the business end by C. A. Coffin, a top salesman and organizer who was destined to head General Electric Company in later years. By 1885 Thomson-Houston had begun making complete incandescent systems, including dynamos, and had developed a new filament-treating method that probably made their lamp superior to the Edison lamps of the time. In 1888, Thomson-Houston started manufacturing electric railway systems.

Another early electrical firm was the Weston Dynamo Electric Machine Company, founded in New York City by Edward Weston, an Englishman who had come to this country seven years before at the age of twenty. Weston's company was purchased in 1882 by the United States Electrical Lighting Company, incorporated by Hiram Maxim and William Sawyer. Maxim had invented his own type of incandescent lamp, but his fame in industrial history came as the builder of the Maxim machine gun, widely used in World War I, an accomplishment which earned him a British knighthood.

For details on the above and other general historical background of the electrical industry, see Eliot Jones and Truman C. Bigham, *Principles of Public Utilities* (New York: Macmillan, 1931), and Harold C. Passer, *The Electrical Manufacturers: 1875–1900* (Cambridge, Mass.: Harvard, 1953).

4. In 1935 Fred Powers, by then an elderly man himself, described his grandfather's ill-fated incandescent lamp (which had been conceived previous to Edison's lamp of 1879) to L. L. Benedict, later a vice-president of Consumers Power Company. Fred Powers told Benedict that the apparent problem was that the glassblowers had been unable to achieve a vacuum. As a result, the filaments burned out almost immediately, rarely lasting longer than three minutes.

5. In addition to William T. Powers and his eldest son, William H. Powers, the incorporators included A. B. Watson, James Blair, Henry Spring, John L. Shaw, Thomas M. Peck, and Sluman S. Bailey.

6. These were the E. S. Pierce Clothing Store, the Spring & Company's Dry Goods Store, A. Preusser's Jewelry Store, the Mills & Lacey Drug Store, and the Star Clothing House.

7. Baxter, *op. cit.*, p. 215.

8. Passer, *op. cit.*, and Charles M. Coleman, *P.G. & E. of California* (New York: McGraw-Hill, 1952).

9. Swift held 10,800 of the 12,000 shares of the Swift Electric Light Company stock. Other shareholders were Benton Hanchet and Norval Cameron, both of Saginaw; Benjamin F. Orton, of East Saginaw; and Charles F. Orton, of Bay City. The articles of association provided franchises for operations in Saginaw, East Saginaw, St. Charles, Buena Vista, Carrollton, Zilwaukee, and Swan Creek, in the County of Saginaw; in Bay City, West Bay City, Banks, Salzburg, Standish,

Deep River, and Sterling in Bay County; in the city of Flint, in the County of Genesee; and in the villages of Tawas City, East Tawas, Au Sable, and Oscoda, in Iosco County. There is no record that such an ambitious territory was actually ever covered. Swift Electric did, however, serve both the Saginaw and Bay City areas.

10. According to Passer, *op. cit.*, pp. 147–148, "In the fall of 1881, approximately one year after Edison first made a successful lamp, Maxim announced that he had invented a practical incandescent lamp. One of Edison's laboratory assistants who worked at Menlo Park during the incandescent lamp period has stated that Maxim drew on Edison's work for both ideas and techniques. Subsequently, Maxim hired one of Edison's skilled workmen, a glass blower, to supply the details on exactly how the Edison lamps were made. . . ."

11. The *Saginaw Daily Courier* was published in East Saginaw.

12. These gaslights were Bray burners, putting out 16 candles each.

13. Willett was secretary and general manager. George R. Hoyt was president, and C. W. H. Conover was treasurer. The first plant was established in the planing mill owned by Beardsley Gillis & Co. and remained there until 1884, when it was moved to a small building on the site of the recent division office building of Consumers Power Company on Saginaw Street. The present office is on Court Street.

The first operation consisted of a d-c series arc plant with one thirty-five-lamp arc-light generator. After the plant was completed in 1884, the service was d-c series arcs, a-c single phase, 133 cycles, 1,100 volts. The plant installation consisted of three 100-horsepower tubular boilers, two 6-by-6 simple Atlas engines, two 60-kilowatt alternators, either two thirty-light arc generators or one thirty-five-light arc generator, and one fifty-light arc generator.

14. N. L. Devendorf, "Electrical Pioneering in the Kalamazoo and Upper Grand River Valleys," the *Au Sable News* (internal organ of the Consumers Power Company), March–April 1935.

15. The Kalamazoo plant was in the area bounded by Burdick, Kalamazoo, Water, and Edwards Streets. The equipment consisted of three 100-kilowatt d-c generators, three low-pressure boilers, and one Corliss engine. See Devendorf, *op. cit.*, and the *Kalamazoo Gazette*, Jan. 24, 1937.

16. In 1886, two years after the Grand Rapids Electric Light and Power Company had absorbed the Michigan Iron Works Electric Light and Power Company, the new Edison Light Company of Grand Rapids became a competitor. Then in 1893, the Peninsula Light, Power and Heat Co. entered the race, and a municipal plant to serve street lighting and later water pumping joined the field in 1900.

17. According to Dean Mortimer E. Cooley, of the University of Michigan, the Swift Electric Company of Saginaw was organized in 1881, with an actual investment in cash of $200.00 Cooley wrote:

This company operated from 1881 to 1900, a period of 19 years, during which time it never paid a single dividend. At the end of this period it was sold to the Bartlett Illuminating Company for $100,000.

Another striking instance is presented by the Edison Electric Company of Jackson, organized in 1885 with an investment of $97,700 in cash. This company operated until 1893, never paid a dividend and sold its plant to the Jackson Light & Power Company . . . for $20,000. The Edison Electric Light & Motor Power Company of Pontiac had a similar experience. It was organized in 1888, with an investment of $20,000 of local capital. This company operated for ten years without paying a dividend, and was finally sold at a receiver's sale to Lucetta R. Medbury in 1898 for about $7,000. The Peoples Electric Light Company of Flint, organized in 1882 with an investment of $75,000, had a similar experience. It paid only a few negligible dividends during this period and finally sold out at a very considerable loss in 1903.

See M. E. Cooley, "Appraisal: Steam and Hydro-electric Power Plants, Transmission Lines, Gas Plants, 1913–1915," no. 5 (now in possession of Jensen, Bowen & Farrell, Ann Arbor, Michigan).

18. There was a "rapid succession of types of machinery necessitating the scrapping of equipment long before the end of its useful life, as based upon expectations at the time of purchase. It has not been possible to determine from the accounts the amount of machinery abandoned prematurely, but in many cases the profits from operation would have been adequate to yield a handsome return on the investment had it not been for the constant necessity of replacing obsolete machinery with new and more expensive types. The Swift Electric Company made earnings from operations as large as $30,000 in a single year. This constituted 15% upon the original investment of $200,000, but the constantly recurring necessity of making replacements in order to keep the plant in efficient operating condition always prevented the company from paying a dividend during the nineteen years of its corporate existence." Cooley, *op. cit.*

19. So termed by Martin Glaeser in his *Public Utilities in American Capitalism* (New York: Macmillan, 1957).

Chapter 4

1. The original Foote ancestor in America was Nathaniel Foote, who was born near Colchester, England, in 1630. He landed at Massachusetts and settled near Hartford, Connecticut. The family eventually moved to western New York State, and then Milton Foote, father of Augustus, migrated to the Michigan Territory. After a brief stay in Adrian, Milton married Louise Briscoe, settled near North Adams in the 1820s, and in 1849 returned to Adrian with his family. Augustus, who had been born in 1823, married Sarah Susan Barks, of Vermont. They had six children: William A. Foote and James B. Foote, the two brothers who figure so prominently in the early history of Consumers Power; a daughter, Netta, born in 1855; Catherine (Mrs. Will Darling), born in 1869; Della (Mrs. John Lawrence Schoolcraft), born in 1876; and a child, sex and name unknown, which probably died in infancy. Daughter Della's marriage to Schoolcraft, great-nephew of historian Henry Schoolcraft, was her second; her first husband's name was Holmes. The Schoolcraft marriage produced two sons, James and John Schoolcraft (both since deceased), and a daughter, Della Schoolcraft Beebee (Mrs. Fred Beebee), born in 1895, who at the time of this writing lived in Sherman Oaks, California. For descendants of W. A. Foote and J. B. Foote, see Notes and Comments, Chapter 11.

2. Fargo Engineering Company, "Valuations of Physical Properties of the Citizens Light & Power Company" (copy in possession of Consumers Power Company).

3. James Harold Foote, the son of J. B. Foote, credits an uncle by marriage—a brother-in-law of the Foote brothers—with persuading W. A. to get into the electric business. This brother-in-law, who had married Foote's sister, Della, after her first husband died, was a great-nephew of Henry Schoolcraft, the famed historian. His

name was John Lawrence Schoolcraft, and by profession he was an attorney, although by inclination he was an electrical engineer. According to his daughter, also Della by name, John L. Schoolcraft invented a circuit breaker which is now in the Smithsonian Institution. This circuit breaker worked quite well even when wet, and it's the story on the J. B. side of the family that whenever the Foote brothers got into trouble in the early days and the weather was too wet for their equipment to function, Schoolcraft came promptly to the rescue. Schoolcraft died in 1902, at quite a young age. James Harold Foote says that in recognition of Schoolcraft's services, W. A. and J. B Foote gave their sister a lifetime job, and her children some monetary compensation.

4. Captain Fee sold his part interest in the *Adrian Times and Expositor* to buy Foote's electric plant.
5. Foote's demonstration was not the first electric arc-lighting exhibit in Jackson, however. A few years earlier, the Forepaugh Circus, then making its stand on Murphy Hill, had illuminated its tents and adjacent grounds by means of Brush-system arc lights.
6. Hugh L. Smith was vice-president of the Jackson Electric Light Works, and John W. Allen, presumably W. A. Foote's former Adrian associate, was a director. The company used Thomson-Houston equipment, and according to the 1888 *Jackson City Directory* it was even known for a time (apparently before its incorporation) as the Jackson T. & H. Electric Light Company.
7. The North Monroe Street hydro plant in Battle Creek, built in 1888, was the third commercial plant of its kind in Michigan (following those of Grand Rapids and Allegan), and it was the first built by the Footes. A waterwheel 6 feet 2 inches in diameter was connected to two arc machines. Soon a 500-volt d-c Edison generator was installed to carry the commercial power load that was beginning to develop. By 1890, a single-phase 1,100-volt 100-horsepower alternator was added, and commercial incandescent lighting was begun. The plant remained in use until 1953. See N. L. Devendorf, "Electrical Pioneering in the Kalamazoo and Upper Grand River Valleys," the *Au Sable News*, March–April 1935.
8. The original operation was a six-light arc unit on the 30-horsepower waterwheel of the Albion Milling Company, owned by William D. Knickerbocker. This furnished power until the contract for streetlighting was obtained. The sample lighting system was set up on Main Street. It consisted of six Thomson-Houston single-carbon (one set of carbons) arc lights. After the demonstration's success, a roller-skating rink was made over into a power plant. This plant at first housed two arc machines, the original six-light arc plus one thirty-light arc, together with a 1,200-volt single-phase alternator. A 200-horsepower Lansing engine furnished power. All but the electrical equipment came from the Jarvis Iron and Engine Works, Lansing.
9. Interview with Grover Hemstreet, who retired from Consumers Power in 1952 at the age of sixty-five. Hemstreet, a native of Saratoga, New York, joined the Hudson River Electric Power Company at Albany when he was nineteen and first began working with Consumers Power in 1910, when he and others from Eastern power plants were assigned to help local Michigan men with the formation of the dispatching department of Foote's Au Sable Electric Company at its Trail Street plant in Jackson.
10. Michigan's population stood at 749,113 in 1860; 1,184,059 in 1870; and 1,636,-331 in 1880.
11. Interview with Grover Hemstreet.

12. The Ceresco Mill and Hydraulic Company, Ltd., was organized in 1895 by George Preston, of Grass Lake, who was chairman; Harry R. Hall, of Jackson, who was secretary; and Charles H. Frisbie, also of Jackson, who was treasurer. Almost immediately, Preston and Hall resigned as directors of the company, and the real entrepreneurs, W. A. Foote and Augustus N. Foote, were "chosen" to fill their places. W. A. then emerged as chairman, and Augustus as secretary. Frisbie was the only one who stayed on, and he was later associated with W. A. Foote in other enterprises.

13. The Kalamazoo Electric Company was organized in 1885 and started operations in 1886. The officers of this company were Frederick Bush, president; Charles L. Cobb, vice-president; Harry C. Potter, secretary; and Jacob K. Wagner, treasurer. Its offices were in the same building that Potter occupied as general passenger and freight agent of the Chicago, Kalamazoo and Saginaw Railway. The plant, bounded by Burdick, Kalamazoo, Water, and Edwards Streets, housed three return tubular shell boilers and a Lane and Bodley simple Corliss engine to drive three 100-kilowatt Edison bipolar generators. Later two more Lane and Bodley engines were added. One of these engines drove four 500-volt bipolar d-c generators, furnishing power to the street railways. The other two supplied power to a 150-kilowatt three-phase 2,300-volt generator (later moved to Albion), a single-phase 1,100-volt generator, and two small 500-volt bipolars for d-c shop power. See Devendorf, *op. cit.*

14. This term, confined to the Middle West, was probably a corruption of Taintor, a man's name, though no one knows who he might have been. A more proper technical term is "radial" gate, which refers to a gate which is shaped like a segment of a horizontal cylinder shell and which can be turned up and down to open and close.

15. The hydraulic unit consisted of four pairs of 42½-inch Leffel horizontal open-pit turbines connected in tandem so that their eight wheels drove a single horizontal shaft, yielding a total of 2,000 horsepower. With sufficient depth of water over the turbines to make a formation of air vortices unlikely, a horizontal unit was more desirable than the more common vertical geared drive of the period.

The generator was 60 cycles, three-phase, 2,500 volts, 1,500 kilowatts, directly connected to the horizontal shaft of the turbine unit, which passed through the end wall of the wheel pit, made watertight by a packing gland. The floor of the generator room was at the same level as that of the wheel pit. Two Lombard oil-pressure governors, one for each four turbines, controlled the load and frequency.

16. Up to that time, governor design had been based largely on mill and factory requirements; such governors, while demanding steady speed, carried a very steady load without any sudden variations. In the early hydroelectric plant, there was the same requirement of steady speed for close-frequency regulation of factory load and steady voltage for lights. But this was also the time of peak electric streetcar and interurban loads, which were extremely variable and noticeable on a small generating unit. The inherently poor regulation of the Trowbridge iron transmission line, plus the then little-understood complications of power factor and line losses, added to the problem, and regulators had to be redesigned to cope with it.

According to N. L. Devendorf, the leads from the generator were carried to the floor above and thence to a transformer house at the other end of the dam, where a delta-connected transformer bank stepped the voltage up to 22,000. This passed out of the building through the oil circuit breaker designed and built by J. B. Foote and George Stecker (see Note 17 below).

It is said that the basic principles of the Stecker regulator, which was built in the Kalamazoo plant of the Shakespeare Fishing Reel Company, were incorporated later by the General Electric Company in the design of the Tirrill voltage regulator.

17. The blade of the wagon-box switch was clamped on a porcelain bushing. This was mounted on a vertical wood shaft driven by bevel gears from other shafts, so that the three units controlling the three-phase circuit opened or closed when the operator moved the lever through a quarter turn. Clips for double break were mounted on the tops of line insulators from which the wide outer bell had been removed. These were set in two diagonally opposite corners of the container. When open, the blade was at right angles to its closed position, pointing to the other two corners of the case. The case (or box), as well as the insulator pins and operating shafts, were of hardwood. The bevel gears, of which there were two pairs for each unit, were of cast iron. Owing to the difficulty of making the wooden case oiltight, the unit was set in a galvanized iron tank, which was supported on line insulators on wood pins cemented into the concrete floor.

Remarkable as this early development of an oil circuit breaker was, its true significance can scarcely be appreciated unless one is familiar with other early types of pioneer switching equipment for high voltages. The usual practice in 1901 was to let the high-voltage lines alone as far as possible, arranging switches, fuses, cutouts, and the like on the low-voltage side of the transformers. When high-tension switches had to be used, experimental evidence pointed to the desirability of using oil as the breaking medium. Not only was the danger of arcing greatly reduced, but there was far less chance of producing unpleasant resonance effects on the line than there was with an air-break switch. *Electric Power Transmission* stated in 1901:

> In some recent experiments at 40,000 volts, it was possible to draw an arc nearly 30 feet in total length from a quick break long-armed air switch and breaking a circuit in this manner gives surging electromotive forces two or three times the normal voltage of the system. With an oil break switch having its contacts in separate oil receptacles, currents at 44,000 volts representing more than 1,000 kilowatts, could be opened instantly and certainly without a flash or any surging rise of potential.

While the author of *Electric Power Transmission* does not say so, these experiments, as nearly as can be determined, were carried out at the Trowbridge hydraulic plant by Charles P. Steinmetz, L. W. Robinson (no relation to the Lyman Robinson of Consumers Power), J. D. Hilliard, and others of the General Electric Company in cooperation with Foote and his organization. This also probably marked the first of several visits of these men from General Electric to Michigan to see the experimentation that was going on there.

In *High Voltage Oil Circuit Breakers* (New York: McGraw-Hill, 1930), R. Wilkins and E. Crellin report that in 1901, oil circuit breakers were introduced on the 60,000-volt line between the Colgate plant on the Yuba River and Oakland, California. The first of these switches was built in the halves of wood oil barrels and broke the arc first in water. Above the water was a mixture of oil and water, with oil on the top in which to make the final break. This plan was used because some engineers of the period had the idea that breaking the circuit in oil would open it too suddenly and start serious surges on the line. The water would offer resistance, the oil would offer a higher resistance, and the arc would finally break in oil after a considerable attenuation. The breaker was successful at the start, but after being opened several times in quick succession, it "blew up" and set the surrounding structure on fire, so that this particular type was discarded. The idea was there, however, and it was not long before a more satisfactory model was brought out.

18. Today, no one can be quite certain who exactly was present at Trowbridge during these events of 1899, nor precisely how Kalamazoo managed to communicate with Trowbridge. At the time, telephonic connection must have been extremely tenuous, if even possible. *Encyclopedia Americana* as well as William L. Langer's *Encyclopedia of World History* both date the development of induction coils (loading coils) by Michael I. Pupin, an American inventor of Serbian extraction, as 1899. These coils were of great help in long distance telephone communication, but they came too late to benefit the Foote group in rural Michigan.

Perhaps telegraph was used, but such a message undoubtedly would have been received in Allegan and carried from there to Trowbridge. Since a horsedrawn wagon—let alone a walker—would have been too slow, the supposition becomes inescapable that a horseman brought the good word to the dam.

Chapter 5

1. At one time there were as many as thirty-eight three-unit sets of wagon-box switches in use on the Kalamazoo Valley properties alone, plus more in other areas.

2. The windmill transmission towers were manufactured by the Aermotor Company of Chicago for many years and remained in use for several decades.

3. The directors of the new concern were W. A. Foote, J. B. Foote, George Mechem, Charles Frisbie, Frederick A. Bush, V. Weston, and S. S. Hulbert.

4. To start with, the conductors were of No. 4 iron. It will be recalled that Foote could not get his backers to finance anything more expensive in so risky a venture. Foote, however, did get them to agree to provide the means for purchasing better conductors should the experiment be a success. Thus, the Trowbridge line poles provided a short crossarm at the top and a longer arm below, with the three iron wires in a triangular arrangement on one side of the pole. This permitted the later installation of more adequate conductors on the other side of the pole without service interruption.

The original insulators for the iron wire were of glass, with a single groove for side tying, but no grooves across the top. They were 7½ inches in diameter and 2 inches deep. The aluminum line was supported on "Provo-type" insulators, so called because they were designed for the original 40,000-volt line of the Telluride Power Company at Provo, Utah, built in 1899 or 1900. These insulators were 7 inches in diameter and 6 inches high, with two inner bells, 4½ and 2½ inches in diameter and 1½ and ¾ inches deep, respectively. In Michigan's wetter climate, they were satisfactory on 22,000 but not on 40,000 volts.

A bank of delta-connected transformers, with the high voltage controlled by a wagon-box oil switch, stepped the 22,000-volt transmission down to 2,500 volts for local distribution in parallel with the existing steam-driven alternator. Lightning protection was provided by use of General Electric unit-type cylinder gap and resistance arresters. Each unit was designed for 2,500 volts, and ten units were connected in series for 22,000 volts. One inherent fault of these arresters was that their designers had assumed that lightning would turn several square corners in its passage to ground. It didn't always happen that way, and often the strikes discharged across the open end of the units, limiting and sometimes terminating their usefulness. This was partially offset by horn gaps installed over the open ends to make the shortcut to ground less destructive.

Power to Kalamazoo's street railway was supplied through rotary converters, the first machines of that type to operate on 60 cycles and produce 600 volts direct current. The rotary converter was at that time a comparatively new development, the first ones having been installed at the receiving end of the 25-cycle Niagara-Buffalo transmission line in 1896. Six-hundred-volt converters had come into use on 25, 30, and 40 cycles and on some of the odd frequencies in between. Sixty-cycle converters had been introduced in 250-volt d-c service, Edison or factory, but use of 600 volts on the higher frequency with the sudden load changes of railway power introduced an element of instability that presented quite a problem.

This was largely overcome and though the 60-cycle 600-volt converters may have seemed a bit more "temperamental" at times than the lower-frequency 600-volt ones or the lower-voltage 60-cycle machines, they gave excellent service in street and interurban railway service for more than a quarter of a century.

5. This coincided with the building of the electric interurban railway between Kalamazoo and Battle Creek by the Kalamazoo Valley Traction Company, an allied concern. For the proper handling of the power requirements of the railway, it was necessary to establish a substation halfway between the two cities. Augusta was the point chosen for its location.

Wood pins supported the insulators on wood crossarms with strap-iron braces. No guys were used on this line, but wood pole push braces were installed at sharp corners. Where the angle was slight, the poles were set to lean toward the outside of the curve.

When the transmission line reached Battle Creek in 1900, it was carried across the millpond and through the streets to the North Monroe Street hydraulic plant. While there is no record of the exact equipment installed, it is reasonable to assume that the usual sequence was followed: open-tile entrance air-break disconnects, wagon-box oil circuit breaker, cylinder gap and resistance lightning arresters, and a delta-connected transformer bank with 2,300-volt secondaries connected to the bus through an oil circuit breaker in parallel with the water-driven alternator.

In the partially completed South Monroe Street steam plant, two rotary converters were operated as d-c generators, belt-driven from Westinghouse engines. We do not know just when the original steam plant that supplied the streetlighting service was discontinued, but during 1900, a 500-kilowatt vertical steam turbine generating unit was placed in service at South Monroe Street, and the streetlighting and transmission equipment was moved.

It was on March 5, 1903, that the Trowbridge–Battle Creek line was raised to 40,000 volts. This was after the line had been extended from Kalamazoo to Battle Creek. After several hours' operation at 40,000 volts, some of the Provotype insulators failed. The line was cut back to 22,000 volts and was operated at that voltage until March 25, when the change of insulators from the Provo type to a larger, porcelain insulator was completed, and the voltage was again raised to 40,000, this time permanently.

6. E. Hardy Luther interview with George Erwin, 1954; transcript in Consumers Power Company files.

7. The corporate developments leading to the Grand Rapids–Muskegon Water Power Electric Company (and ultimately to the Grand Rapids–Muskegon Power Com-

pany) proceeded as follows: first, a Muskegon Realty Company was organized on August 13, 1903, with an issue of 5,000 shares, of which 3,400 were controlled by David D. Erwin, George Erwin's older brother, a Muskegon attorney. Other stockholders were C. W. Sessions, H. J. Hoyt, George D. Vanderwerp, and Joseph E. Montgomery, all from Muskegon. All the Erwin flowage rights, easements, and other land interests along the Muskegon River in Newaygo and Mecosta Counties were conveyed to this company. Soon thereafter, while still investigating additional property and flowage rights, the company bought an interest in the Big Rapids Gas Company. At about this time William M. Eaton, then superintendent of the Grand Rapids Gas Company, temporarily became their consultant. (This was presumably the same W. M. Eaton who later served as the first president of General Motors.) The Big Rapids Gas property, however, was soon sold, and the Muskegon people then concentrated strictly on the electric business.

In 1904, the Grand Rapids–Muskegon Water Power Electric Company was organized as a construction firm, whose executive committee was soon joined by W. A. Foote. At the same time, Foote served as a vice-president. Other officers were Thomas Hume, president; John G. Emery, Jr., treasurer; and Thomas Munroe, vice-president. Emery, Erwin, and Bradley M. DeLamater were on the executive committee with W. A. Foote.

On June 14, 1905, at a special meeting of stockholders of the Muskegon Realty Company, a resolution was adopted providing, among other things, that W. A. Foote would be permitted to subscribe to the remaining 2,500 shares and that the realty company would then sell to the Grand Rapids–Muskegon Water Power Electric Company all its accumulated real estate and landrights on the Muskegon River.

The following year, 1906, the Grand Rapids–Muskegon Water Power Electric Company ran into financial difficulties. The dam was not yet completed, and there was no money to go on. Nor could additional funds be borrowed since all the property, present and future, was pledged under a Michigan Trust Company mortgage. So it was suggested that a new company, the Grand Rapids–Muskegon Power Company, be created to pick up the pieces. There would be a new bond issue and a new mortgage, this time with the First Trust and Savings Bank of Chicago as trustee. N. W. Harris and Company of Chicago would purchase the new bonds, and the old bonds would be retired. The new company was certified on April 2, 1906, and everything was rosy again. N. W. Harris and Company of Chicago (later the Harris Trust and Savings Bank), which bailed Foote out in the Grand Rapids–Muskegon venture, became the financial backer of many of Foote's ventures.

8. Each penstock had a Leffel quadruplex central-discharge horizontal turbine unit of four 45-foot waterwheels of 750 horsepower each, giving a total of 6,000 horsepower on an effective head of 35 feet. The speed was 225 rpm.

Each turbine unit was direct-connected to a three-phase 30-cycle 6,600-volt Westinghouse generator of 2,250 kilowatts capacity, giving a plant capacity of 4,500 kilowatts, the largest yet undertaken by the Foote interests. Exciters were direct-connected to each generator. The generating equipment was housed in a gabled brick and steel building, 48 by 40 feet, set at the base of the penstock structure.

Current from the generators was led through oil circuit breakers to bus bars back of the switchboard on the downstream side of the generator room. At one end of the board was a feeder panel with an oil circuit breaker controlling the distribution to Big Rapids, which was supplied at generator voltage. In the center was a panel for each generator with the usual indicating instruments and controls, and at the east end was a fourth panel with a Tirrill voltage regulator, synchroscope, and other instruments.

The Big Rapids circuit was carried on a pole line to a substation located in the back of the present office building in Big Rapids. Here, after passing through an induction voltage regulator, energy was distributed at 7,200 volts, an early example of the use of higher-distribution primary voltages, in which the Foote people were leaders. The standard distribution voltage at the time was 2,300. The higher primary voltage brought about a much lower line loss.

Three 1,000-kilowatt transformers were installed in a separate brick building with a homemade "dropout" or vertical-brake oil circuit breaker on the line side. These transformers stepped up the generator voltage to 72,000, then considered the upper limit because of the mechanical limitations of the pin-type insulator, the only kind available.

The Westinghouse transformers were oil-insulated and water-cooled. They operated during the life of the original plant, but were discontinued when the plant was destroyed by fire in 1922, since the new installation included an outdoor substation, for which these transformers were not adapted. Later, however, they were arranged for outdoor use, and after a season of lightning tests at Croton they were installed at Kent City and replaced with new ones in 1933.

Wood pins and crossarms with strap-iron braces supported the 14-inch Thomas pin-type insulators on cedar poles. The line conductors were No. 2 solid hard-drawn copper. A private telephone line was carried on brackets below the bottom crossarm.

9. At the Kent City substation, the high-voltage equipment consisted of three wagon-box oil circuit breakers with disconnects, mounted in a double cellular brick structure. These wagon-box switches were similar to the ones in the southern part of the state, but were set in the center of the room instead of along the walls.

For the fourth annual convention of the Michigan Electric Association, held in Battle Creek in August of 1907, a paper prepared by J. B. Foote covered the first year's operation of the 72,000-volt transmission line extending from Rogers Dam to Grand Rapids and Muskegon. The line was "located entirely upon a private right of way, four rods wide, cleared of all trees and underbrush, and a large portion fenced . . ." the paper read. "Almost the entire distance from Rogers Dam to Croton, the line runs through the pine stumpland, which only a few years ago helped to make Michigan famous, but is now a dreary waste of blackened stumps and brambles." In the questioning that followed, F. E. Greenman, who had presented the paper on J. B.'s behalf, was asked what he thought of this new type of insulator, which had been described in some technical papers, made up in length and suspended from the crossarm. His reply was, "That will be used on our 100,000-volt line that we are putting up now." The reference was to the Croton developments, which are described in this chapter.

City distribution at 7,200 volts in Grand Rapids and Muskegon began with the Rogers to Grand Rapids and Muskegon installations. Here, as well as at Big Rapids, this was considerably higher than had been commonly used, 2,300 volts being standard at the time and considered high voltage to carry through the city streets.

In two substations in the heart of the business district, 30-cycle energy was converted to direct current for the Edison system, one in Campau Street near the

Pantlind Hotel, and the other in the basement of the old office building at 47 Monroe Avenue, in each of which a six-phase 1,000-kilowatt 275-volt rotary converter was installed.

At the time the dams were built on the Muskegon River, the question arose as to what frequency should be used. Since much of the output of these plants was to be used in interurban operation, and since 60 cycles was not as adaptable to that use, it was determined that they should be installed as a 30-cycle system. Thus, the service in Grand Rapids at this time consisted of two types of service, this 30-cycle a-c system and the d-c service of the Grand Rapids Edison.

10. Among them were W. H. Filman, commercial manager; A. F. Walker, superintendent; and F. E. Greenman, assistant superintendent.

11. J. B. Foote described the insulator problem in an article in the *Au Sable News* in September 1921. He had been in Schenectady looking after some apparatus which was going through the General Electric Company factory when E. M. Hewlett called his attention to the new type of insulator which he, in collaboration with Harold W. Buck, was developing. After some testing, J. B. Foote became convinced that a great advance had been made in the art of line insulation and that this advance would permit the use of much higher voltages than had heretofore been possible. With the old pin-type insulator, a unit of about 14 inches was the largest economical size. This seemed to limit the possible transmission voltage to around 70,000. But Foote was convinced that by using the new five-unit suspension insulator, a voltage of 110,000 could be achieved, practically doubling the capacity of the transmission line.

J. B. Foote obtained the authorization of the board of directors to go ahead and build a tower line from Croton to Grand Rapids using the five-unit Hewlett insulator. The line was being built mostly during the year 1907, as it took about six months to get any insulators delivered after the order was given. This delay was due largely to the interference of an order by the Central Colorado Power Company for the same insulators. P. T. Hanscom, engineer for that company, had designed a line from Glenwood Springs into Denver, using an 88,000-volt maximum potential and four Hewlett-type insulators in each string, the conductors being spaced horizontally side by side on one crossarm.

The suspension and strain insulators for Foote's line were of slightly different design; both, however, were 10 inches in diameter. The Foote suspension unit was made with a flat top, a small projection at the upper edge, and a deep skirt below to shed water. The strain insulator was made with a V-shaped rim having a wide projection on both sides, thus giving additional creepage surface. No provision was made to prevent water standing in the upper connection hole, nor was it considered that ice in this hole would cause any damage.

12. Croton's original hydraulic equipment consisted of two octuple-turbine units, each with four pairs of 45-inch Leffel wheels in open pits, mounted tandem on a horizontal shaft for direct connection to horizontal generators installed at the level of the wheel-pit floor.

The two generators were Westinghouse, 4,500 kilowatts, three-phase, 30 cycles, 6,600 volts with direct-connected exciters. This arrangement of turbines continued for quite a period of time, the first changes having been made in 1915, when one pair of turbines was removed from each unit and two 1,500-kilowatt Allis-Chalmers vertical units were installed in their place.

The pioneering feature of this plant was the installation of transformers to raise the voltage to the unprecedented value of 110,000 for the transmission to Grand Rapids. These transformers were of 3,000 kilowatts each, 6,600 to 100,000 volts, delta-connected. The generator voltage was raised from 6,600 to 7,200, which gave approximately 110,000 volts on the high taps of the transformers. When the plant was started, the line was not ready, nor was the Grand Rapids substation equipment completed. So for a time, service was supplied at 72,000 volts through the Rogers line.

J. B. Foote's new insulators gave no trouble for about a year and a half, but about then failures became frequent, and upon testing all the units on the line it was found that the problem was not in their design but in their manufacture, most of them being cracked in the head. By that time the feasibility of using 110,000 volts had been demonstrated, and the line voltage was reduced temporarily to 72,000 volts for parallel operation with the Rogers pole line.

The towers that were used on the Croton–Grand Rapids line were modeled after the three-legged towers for pin-type insulators first used in 1906 on the Webber-Lansing line. In April of 1906, H. R. Wager, of Ionia, had conveyed to Commonwealth Power Company rights and contracts for a 28-foot dam across the Grand River in Lyons Township, Ionia County. Work was started at once, and the new plant, known as Webber Dam, named for a banker in Portland who handled some of the land purchases, went on the line on March 12, 1907. The dam followed the usual Michigan construction, earth embankment with concrete core wall. Three transformers of 1,000 kilowatts each connected the generator to the transmission line through wagon-box oil circuit breakers and blade disconnects. The 40,000-volt transmission line marked the first use of steel towers by any predecessor of Consumers Power Company.

The conductor employed on the 110,000-volt Croton–Grand Rapids line consisted of six strands of No. 10 medium hard-drawn copper, cabled about a hemp center. This gave the copper wire a cross-sectional area something less than that of No. 2 wire with an overall diameter slightly less than that of No. 1 stranded wire. This wire was stranded of No. 10 rather than of the size of strand necessary for making No. 2 for the reason that manufacturers were not equipped to draw medium-hard copper of the size necessary for the latter, but did have the dies suitable for No. 10.

13. A glimpse at the financial situation of the Grand Rapids–Muskegon Power Company at about that time is extremely interesting in this respect. At the directors' meeting of the company held in Portland, Maine, on September 12, 1906, W. A. Foote reported that the trial balance of the company's assets as of May 31 of that year amounted to $2,978,308, including stocks of controlled corporations. Against this there was capital stock in the amount of $2,100,000; bonds, $800,000; accrued interest on bonds, $10,000; and accounts payable, $68,308. Already customers of the company were preponderantly traction lines. The gross earnings for August showed $3,141.65 from the Grand Haven and Muskegon Railway Company and $4,523.22 from the Holland and Chicago Railway, for a total of $7,664.87, more than 3½ times as much as gross earnings during the same period from industrial concerns whose payments ranged all the way from U.S. Gypsum's $1,264.87 down to the just-starting Pittsburgh Plate Glass Company's $3.08 tab. (The Pittsburgh Plate Glass payments were eventually expected to amount to at least $200 a month.)

More Grand Rapids–Muskegon Power Company bonds were authorized at a special meeting of directors on July 21, 1907. The president and secretary were authorized and directed to deposit pledged securities with the First Trust & Savings Bank, Chicago, securing an authorized issue of $7,500,000 worth of first mortgage twenty-five-year 5 percent gold bonds. The stocks listed as pledged were 6,025 shares of common stock, of which a block of 6,014 shares was owned by W. A. Foote, J. G. Emery, Jr., and B. M. DeLamater. In addition, there were 1,075 preferred shares issued in the joint names of W. A. Foote, J. G. Emery, Jr., and B. M. DeLamater.

A special meeting of the directors was held on August 19, 1907, at which time it was decided to submit a proposal to the city of Grand Rapids in connection with pumping water from Lake Michigan. At the same meeting, the executive committee set new rates applying to arc and carbon filament incandescent lighting: the first thirty hours of monthly use of connected load—8 cents per kilowatt; the second thirty hours of monthly use of connected load—6 cents per kilowatt; and all over sixty hours of monthly use of connected load—4 cents per kilowatt. There was a minimum charge of 50 cents per month to each individual light customer. Carbon filament lamp renewals were to be furnished free to lighting customers. The power rate varied considerably depending upon the connected load, but the rate ran all the way from 3 cents down to 1 cent, the 1-cent charge applying in the case of 300 hours' monthly use of maximum demand where the customer was using 150 horsepower or more.

At the adjourned annual meeting of the board of directors on September 25, 1908, a communication from the Muskegon Realty Company was read, pointing out the fact that the company, at its own cost, had secured rights-of-way for pole and tower lines that had been conveyed to the Grand Rapids–Muskegon Company and that the Muskegon Realty Company had purchased and still held title to certain lands on which transmission lines of the Grand Rapids–Muskegon Power Company were located. The company also paid the salary and office expenses of George L. Erwin, while he was securing some of these lands and rights-of-way. The Muskegon Realty Company proposed to convey to the power company all the rights-of-way now owned by them for the sum of $59,251.31. The proposal was accepted.

W. A. Foote filed an annual report of operations at the directors' meeting at Portland, Maine, in 1909. According to his report, the following types of business were being transacted: Grand Rapids, commercial light and commercial power; Muskegon, commercial power; Big Rapids, streetlighting, commercial lighting, and commercial power; Coopersville, streetlighting, commercial lighting, and commercial power; Grandville, streetlighting, commercial lighting, and commercial power; and Lowell, commercial lighting. The company also had been operating in Ada for five months. A big block of business, as usual, was with electric railroads.

Chapter 6

1. *Jackson Citizen Patriot,* Sept. 19, 1937.
2. *Ibid.*
3. Originally it was called the Jackson City Railway. Hiram H. Smith was the first president of the corporation, and Henry H. Smith, his son, was the first general superintendent.
4. *Jackson Daily Citizen,* Sept. 21, 1891.
5. The first city in Michigan to have electric streetcars was Port Huron. Its line, started

in 1886, was about 1.5 miles long. The following year, electric cars powered by storage batteries were tried in Detroit, but they were not successful. It is interesting to note that even today, despite extensive research by almost all automobile manufacturers, the problem of prolonged transportation through battery power has not yet been solved.

6. Later still, Boland, having made his fortune, relinquished his office in the Bank of Commerce Building, 31 Nassau Street, New York City, and returned to the family home near Grass Lake, east of Jackson, to build a magnificent residence called Grey Towers. This property is now occupied by the Romanian Orthodox Episcopate of America.

7. The term "cars," although possibly misleading, is entirely appropriate. In the early traction days there was only one car per "train." Additional carriages were hooked on only later.

8. E. Hardy Luther interview with W. G. Fargo, recorded in "Song of Service," on file in the library of Consumers Power Company, Jackson.

9. *Ibid.* According to the late William G. Fargo, the construction engineer, this was a very important moment in W. A. Foote's career. Foote had been practically commuting to the cities of the East—New York, Philadelphia, and Boston—trying to interest various sources in providing capital for his electric utility ventures, but this apparently was his first contact with E. W. Clark & Co.

Chapter 7

1. It may be recalled that the Michigan Iron Works Electric Light and Power Company, established as competition in the early days, had soon been taken over by Powers (see Chapter 3).

   In addition, in 1886, the Edison Light Company of Grand Rapids was organized. (The original name of the new concern was the Edison Light and Fuel Company.) It acquired property at the corner of Fulton and Calder Streets, the present site of the Fulton Street heating plant, and constructed an electric generating plant at that location. Some time later the name of the company was changed from the Edison Light and Fuel Company to the Edison Light Company.

   The Grand Rapids Edison Company was organized in April of 1902. At the first meeting of directors the purchase of the Edison Light Company (referred to as Edison Light and Power Company in the minutes) and William T. Powers' Grand Rapids Electric Light and Power Company was authorized, a transaction consummated by November.

   As usual, there was an almost insatiable demand for capital. At a spcial meeting of the board held on April 28, 1902, an increase in capitalization from $125,000 to $1 million (by August increased again to $1.2 million) was authorized. Officers were Daniel McCoy, president; W. D. Breed, vice-president; Thomas F. Bechtel, secretary; and Rufus T. Goodell, treasurer. By June, Goodell resigned as director, and Daniel McCool took his place—the same Daniel McCool who was one of the Newaygo Portland Cement people Erwin had run into in connection with the flowage lands on the Muskegon River. Bechtel became treasurer, and McCool became vice-president. It was at this same June 23, 1902, meeting that the first steps were taken that resulted, by the end of August, in the purchase by the Grand Rapids Edison Company, from F. G. Bigelow and his associates, of the Lowell Water and Light Company, West Michigan Electric Company, and the Peninsula

Light, Power and Heat Co. The agreement called for $100,000 and interest at 5 percent from the date of the contract Bigelow and his associates had made with the Michigan Trust Company.

The generating equipment used by the Grand Rapids Edison Company was for 110- and 220-volt d-c service in 1902. The Grand Rapids Edison Company board on January 24, 1903, decided that the company should proceed at once with construction of a power dam on the Flat River on property bought from the West Michigan Electric Company, with the energy to be transmitted to Grand Rapids and adjoining territory. It was also apparent that the company would need, especially during the winter of 1903–1904, additional storage batteries and facilities, at least equal to its present storage capacity. So it was decided to construct an additional storage battery in the company's plant at Station 1 in the city of Grand Rapids. Furthermore, the decision was made to construct new conduits on both the west and the east sides of the Grand River and to install new waterwheels for the more efficient use of its waterpower at Station 2. In addition, there were to be some new pole lines. All this was expected to cost in excess of $250,000. The thought was that $50,000 of this would come from earnings and that $200,000 would come from bonds.

In connection with the resolution concerning this action, steam-heating mains were also mentioned, so apparently the company was in the steam-heating business in Grand Rapids at this time.

At the directors' meeting of the Grand Rapids Edison Company held in Chicago on September 4, 1903, Daniel McCoy resigned as president; McCool took his place, and McGeorge Bundy (grandfather of McGeorge Bundy, president of the Ford Foundation) was chosen as vice-president to replace McCool. Harvey J. Hollister, having become a stockholder, was chosen a director.

When, in 1902, the Grand Rapids Edison people purchased three properties from F. G. Bigelow, apparently a Milwaukee man, and his associates, it marked their first connection. The association was rather short-lived, for the minutes of an executive committee meeting held on April 29, 1905, spoke of a verbal report made by McCool on a visit he and Bundy had made to Milwaukee to determine the extent to which Grand Rapids Edison was involved in an F. G. Bigelow "defalcation." As a result, F. G. Bigelow and Gordon Bigelow were requested to resign from the board of directors. In their places, Clay F. Hollister and A. F. Walker became directors.

By the time a special meeting of stockholders was held in Jersey City on March 30, 1907, W. A. Foote, J. G. Emery, Jr., and B. M. DeLamater were represented by proxy indicating ownership of 4,850 shares—by far the dominant influence. There were resignations from the board and transfers of stock, and J. B. Foote, W. A. Foote, J. G. Emery, Jr., and William Munroe became the new directors of the company.

2. In Muskegon there was a company which generated electricity by means of a steam plant and which also operated the street railway and distributed gas. In the early 1900s, this Muskegon Traction and Light Company was part of the American Light and Traction Company, an Emerson McMillin interest, along with the gas properties of Grand Rapids and Detroit. Interurban lines were also being constructed in the Grand Rapids and Muskegon areas at this time. It was in 1901 that Frederick W. Walker, who was field engineer for Westinghouse-Church-Kerr, out of Detroit, had started work toward the construction of the Grand Rapids, Grand

Haven and Muskegon Railway. Furthermore, in 1904, the Grand Rapids, Holland and Chicago Railway had been established. See E. E. Nelson, "Predecessor Companies," in Consumers Power Company files.

3. Henrietta M. Larson, "E. W. Clark & Co., 1837–1857: The Beginnings of an American Private Bank," *Journal of Economic and Business History*, vol. 4, no. 3, May 1932.

4. The neighbor was Frederick T. Hepburn. Quotations from an interview in Consumers Power Company files.

5. As told by Woodcock to Claude Hamilton, a later president of the Michigan Trust Company.

6. Albert Baxter, *History of the City of Grand Rapids, Michigan* (New York: Munsell & Company, 1891).

7. Michigan Trust's original officers were Lewis H. Withey, president; Willard Barnhart, vice-president; Darwin D. Cody, second vice-president; and Anton G. Hodenpyl, secretary.

8. These men were John Canfield and E. Golden Filer, of Manistee; Charles H. Hackley and Charles T. Hills, of Muskegon; W. W. Cummer, of Cadillac; Dwight Cutler and William Savidge, of Grand Haven; and Thomas Gilbert, Willard Barnhart, Julius Houseman, James M. Barnett, Harvey J. Hollister, Daniel H. Waters, Thomas Hefferan, Noyes L. Avery, A. D. Rathbone, Henry Idema, T. Stewart White, and Darwin D. Cody, of Grand Rapids. See Claude Hamilton, "Cool Head and Warm Heart: Two Qualities Which Make Mr. Hodenpyl Great," *Michigan Tradesman*, Nov. 10, 1926.

9. *Ibid.*

10. This rather ambiguous description of Walbridge as a "floater" originated with Charles B. Hays, of Kalamazoo, one of Walbridge's cousins.

11. The Grand Rapids Gas Light Company was incorporated in 1857 with Francis B. Gilbert, president; Hiliary Martin, secretary and treasurer; and Noyes L. Avery, George Kendall, and Charles C. Rood, directors. The superintendent was Thomas Smith, who was also connected with the Kalamazoo Gas Light Company. In 1859, Thomas D. Gilbert became secretary and treasurer and held the post for many years.

12. Walbridge operated the Grand Rapids Gas Light Company through a committee consisting of W. H. Barthold, superintendent; A. D. Mackie, in charge of sales; John Helen, in charge of distribution; and H. B. Wales, secretary-treasurer and office manager. Glen Chamberlain was the chief clerk.

This committee operation lists names of several individuals who later became associated with Consumers Power Company, its predecessors, or its affiliates. W. H. Barthold, later on, was a partner in the firm of Hodenpyl, Hardy & Company of New York. He was an officer of Commonwealth & Southern, as well as an officer of Consumers Power Company and various of the other affiliated companies.

For a time A. D. Mackie was in the Detroit office of Hodenpyl-Walbridge & Company and later became manager of a Springfield, Illinois, affiliate. While John Helen was never with Consumers Power Company or its affiliates, his brother, Bill Helen, was for many years gas distribution superintendent at Kalamazoo. Charles Barthold, brother of W. H., was in charge of gas production in Kalamazoo for many years. H. B. Wales was, at one time, manager in Pontiac. Glen Chamberlain remained with the gas company in Grand Rapids and later rose to prominence in that firm. There are still others, however, who although they were at one time connected with the gas business in Grand Rapids or Detroit subsequently came with the Consumers Power group.

At a later time, in 1903, William Eaton was manager of the gas company in Grand Rapids. In 1906, B. O. Tippy, brother of C. W. Tippy, who had been superintendent of manufacturing in Detroit, went to Grand Rapids as manager of the gas company there. C. W. Tippy himself was later chemist and assistant superintendent at Detroit City Gas.

J. A. Brown first started with the gas company in Grand Rapids. B. C. Cobb, at one time, was with the same company and still later was general superintendent of Detroit City Gas. Yes, and Anton Hodenpyl was a director of the Grand Rapids Gas Light Company in 1895. Furthermore, Anton Hodenpyl became a director of American Light and Traction Company, which was a company organized of Emerson McMillin properties, and it may also be mentioned that, subsequently, Emerson McMillin was a director of Commonwealth Power Railway & Light Company, one of the early holding companies of Consumers Power Company.

13. Charles B. Hays.

14. Grand Rapids Gas Light Company in 1895, Jackson Gas Company in 1897, Kalamazoo Gas Company in 1899, and the Grand Rapids Railway Company in 1900.

15. The office was at No. 7 Wall, at the corner of New and Wall Streets. Across from it, on the north side between Broadway and Nassau, at what was probably No. 10 (and is now the Bankers Trust Company at No. 14), was the office of King, Hodenpyl & Co., a stockbrokerage and investment firm, which Hodenpyl had joined as a partner in 1901, the same year Walbridge returned to Grand Rapids. This firm continued in existence until September 1, 1905, when Hodenpyl left it and its name reverted to John C. King & Co. In 1940, after some further partnership changes, it became part of Goodbody & Co.

16. As may be recalled, gas had first come to Pontiac in 1860 with the organization of the Pontiac Gas Light Company. In 1874, on a foreclosure sale, the property came to Lucetta R. Medbury, the widow of Samuel Medbury. In 1869, Samuel Medbury and a group of other Detroit men had organized the Street Railway Company of Grand Rapids for the purpose of taking over the existing street railway system. This marked the entry of the Medburys in the utility field in what later became Consumers Power territory. The affairs of the Grand Rapids concern were thrown into some disorder about 1875, when Samuel Medbury, by far the major stockholder as well as president, died. It developed, however, that the widow, Lucetta, would take over. She apparently became a very capable businesswoman. Though Samuel Medbury was in Pontiac occasionally prior to his death, it was she who started operating the Pontiac Gas Light Company in 1874.

The first electric company in Pontiac was Edison Electric Light and Motor Power Company, organized in 1887. This company was taken over by Mrs. Medbury in 1898, under the name of Medbury Electric Light Company. The following year it was merged with Pontiac Gas Light Company, under the name of Pontiac Gas and Electric Company.

Mrs. Medbury had brought in a William H. Morgans, probably from Detroit, as superintendent of her Pontiac properties. When Pontiac Gas and Electric Company was organized, the first stockholders were listed as William H. Morgans, 1,995 shares; F. G. Jacobs, one share; Chauncey Brace, one share; G. L. Seagrave, two shares; and F. E. Morgans, one share. So Mrs. Medbury was out, and William

Morgans, sometimes called Frank, and his daughter, Florance Morgans, called Flossie, were in control. Flossie Morgans, a buxom woman, became manager. Thus, for the second time, a woman conducted the affairs of the utilities in Pontiac.

Meanwhile, in 1891, the incandescent streetlamps furnished in Pontiac by the Edison Company were found unsatisfactory, and steps were taken to install arc lamps for streetlighting. Bids were asked by the city, and the contract was awarded to a Detroit firm, the Commercial Electric Company. This concern was a sales and construction organization and did not want to function as a public utility, so after an unsuccessful campaign to sell the city—a bond-issue election turned down the municipal ownership idea by a vote of 303 to 225—the Pontiac Standard Electric Company was formed to operate the plant. This company continued to furnish streetlighting until 1905, when it was sold to W. A. Foote and Nathan S. Potter, of Jackson, who, in 1906, transferred it to W. M. Eaton, by that time associated with Hodenpyl-Walbridge.

17. After the take-over, the company's officers were Walbridge, president; William H. Morgans, vice-president; Florance Morgans, secretary and treasurer; and Claude Hamilton, assistant secretary and treasurer. Michigan Trust Company was appointed fiscal agent and registrar. This was before the formation of Hodenpyl-Walbridge & Company, and the hand of the Michigan Trust group is seen in the offices held by Hamilton, a Michigan Trust executive who later became the trust company's president. (See Note 5 above.)

18. Commonwealth Power included Foote's old Ceresco Mill and Hydraulic Company, Ltd., the Jackson Light and Power Company, the Albion Electric Light Company, the Kalamazoo Electric Company, the Battle Creek Electric Company, the Plainwell Power Company, and the Otsega Power Company. (As the Foote interests grew in size, the accounting function became bigger and more complex. Early in their history W. A. Foote's father, Augustus N. Foote, had supervised most of the office affairs, but with the consolidation of properties into the Commonwealth Power Company, Foote made inquiries at General Electric Company about finding someone with experience to help him. It was in this way that Robert Davey came into the organization.)

Chapter 8

1. F. Clever Bald, *Michigan in Four Centuries* (New York: Harper & Row, 1961).
2. The Loud family first came to the Au Sable in 1865. The firm was then called Loud, Priest and Sheppard. Like other outfits, they first built a small mill to saw the lumber needed to build a bigger one. In 1866, the firm was reorganized under the name of Loud, Priest and Gay, which in turn was followed by Loud, Gay and Company, with sawmills in Au Sable and Oscoda. In 1876, a mammoth salt block was built as an ancillary operation. The reason for this joint operation, common to lumber mills in those days, was that the slab wood and other scrap from the mills could be used profitably that way as fuel for the evaporation of water from brine. Michigan at that time was making about half the salt in the nation. In the case of the Loud operation, the brine was pumped up from East Tawas through large wooden pipes. After various reorganizations, the firm name became H. M. Loud and Sons' Lumber Company in 1887 and H. M. Loud Sons' Company in 1898.
3. Edward F. Loud, "How the Power Development Came to the Oscoda Area," *Consumers Power News*, May–June 1941.

4. Lee Day and Jimmy Donahue, "The Mighty Au Sable," *Bay City Times,* July 22, 1951.
5. Loud, *op. cit.*
6. In those days visiting ballplayers donned their uniforms in their hotel rooms and rode to the ball park in a horse-drawn omnibus. Before going to the game, they used to "strut around the hotel lobby in full diamond regalia, spiked shoes and all. Some of the spike marks [were] still visible in the flooring of the lobby" when the old Cadillac Hotel was torn down in 1920, yielding to the Book Cadillac. For this and more on the old hotel, see *Detroit Sunday Night,* June 16, 1923, p. 8.
7. Loud, *op. cit.*
8. The Loud-Weadock encounter was not the only peculiar juxtaposition of time and persons in this history. Representing the Hodenpyl-Walbridge interests—and indirectly the Clark interests—in the negotiations with W. A. Foote was William M. Eaton, later president of General Motors, who had become manager of the gas company in Jackson shortly after Foote had started electric operations in that city in 1886. They were competitors of long-standing, but they were also friends. At one point, Eaton had even installed a complimentary gas range in the home of his electric competitor.

  William Eaton was born in Cambridge, Ohio, in 1856, the same year the first gas predecessor of Consumers Power Company started operations in Kalamazoo. He moved to Jackson with his parents in the early 1870s, went through the tenth grade, and joined his father in a pottery business which collapsed in 1881. After that, he held a number of short-lived jobs, until finally Alonzo Bennett, head of the Bennett Clay Machinery Company, asked him to run the Jackson Gas Light Company, in which the Bennett family held considerable interest. Eaton told Bennett quite truthfully that he knew nothing about the gas business, but Bennett said, "All right, I know you won't close the doors, so get up there and run it." Thus, in 1887, Eaton started to learn the gas business the hard way, working night and day. What's more, he came into the business at a very critical time. The Jackson Gas Light Company had been incorporated in 1857 for a period of thirty years, with a three-year grace period, and this term was now coming to an end. At the same time, the Jackson National Gas Light & Fuel Company, with home offices in Chicago, Illinois, had started competitive operations, and this competition was less than gentle. According to James Eaton, Will's son, "the way of the new company was to take our meters right out of cellars, disconnect them and throw them out the back door . . . and then hook into the service with their mains." In 1898, the National Gas Light & Fuel Company took over the Bennett operation, and in later years Eaton worked for the McMillin people in both Grand Rapids and Jackson before joining the Hodenpyl-Walbridge operation.

Chapter 9

1. Prior to Durant's involvement, James H. Whiting was the largest single stockholder of Buick. Next came David D. Buick and his son, Thomas. The third largest was Charles L. Begole, who was connected with the gas business in Flint.
2. The original incorporation of General Motors on September 15, 1908, was as a holding company, not an operating company, as was the case later when it became the General Motors Corporation. It is hard to imagine in retrospect that the initial capitalization was for only $2,400 (which, of course, soon increased) and

that apparently nobody except those directly involved in the venture noticed the new company. There wasn't even a mention in the *New York Times* the following day, September 16, 1908. More important news on that date was that Charles Evans Hughes had been nominated for governor of New York on the Republican ticket and that the White Star Company announced the construction of two new ocean liners, one of them the *Titanic*.

When Durant organized the original General Motors Company, he wanted to stay somewhat in the background or at least be freed of the normal operation as president. The certificate of incorporation was signed by George E. Daniels, Benjamin Marcuse, and Arthur W. Britton and was filed in the office of the Clerk of Hudson County, New Jersey. Daniels was the first president, and Marcuse the first secretary and treasurer. For good reading on the history of the automobile industry, see Arthur Pound, *The Turning Wheel* (New York: Doubleday, Doran, 1934).

3. Durant offered $8 million for the Ford property. Ford, in poor health at the time, agreed to sell for cash, but Durant couldn't raise that much, and Ford stayed independent.

4. For Eaton's earlier history, see Chapter 8, Note 8. His connection with Hodenpyl came via Walbridge. By 1897, Emerson McMillin had gained control of the gas company in Jackson, which eventually became the Jackson Gas Company. Harry Walbridge was the company's first vice-president. (Nathan S. Potter, W. A. Foote's early backer, was second vice-president.) Eaton stayed with the new organization as manager, and he and Walbridge came to know each other well. In 1903, Eaton went to Grand Rapids Gas Light, another McMillin property, as director, general manager, and second vice-president. The following year he joined Hodenpyl-Walbridge, assuming the office of vice-president and general manager of the Rochester Railway and Light Company in Rochester, New York, a property of the then newly organized Hodenpyl-Walbridge concern. In 1907, he transferred to Hodenpyl-Walbridge & Company itself, where he later became a member of the operating committee for the gas and electric properties of Commonwealth Power Railway & Light Company, an office he held until his retirement in 1914. Part of his job was to sell gas and electricity to automobile companies. His presidency of General Motors in the two-year period from October 20, 1908, to November 23, 1910, did not seem to conflict, however, with his Hodenpyl-Walbridge function; it was an unpaid position, and Eaton assumed it largely as a personal favor to Durant, who still preferred to remain in the background.

5. From an interview by E. Hardy Luther with his cousin, D. W. Hardy, son of George E. Hardy, of Hodenpyl, Hardy and Company, which later took the place of Hodenpyl-Walbridge. Interview in Consumers Power Company files.

Of course, if Hodenpyl had become involved in General Motors, life for both General Motors and Consumers Power would have become even more complicated in later years, when the federal government went on the warpath against trusts, monopolies, and holding companies.

6. Allan Nevins, *Ford: The Times, the Man, the Company* (New York: Scribner, 1954).

7. Other makes advertised in Detroit newspapers at that time included Abbott-Detroit, American, The Detroit Electric, Anhut, Brush Runabout, Catercar, Chalmers, Demotcar, Detroit-Dearborn, E.M.F. (which had just been bought by J. P. Morgan), Empire, Great Western, Herreshoff, Hudson, Hupmobile, Jackson,

Kisselkar, Krit, Maxwell, Metz, Mitchell, Oakland, Overland-Elmore, Parry, Patterson, Pierce-Arrow, Rapid, Regal, Sterns, Stevens-Duryea, Warren-Detroit, Paige-Detroit, Welch, and Whiting.

8. Woodrow Wilson, then still president of Princeton University, told the American Bar Association at its annual meeting in Chattanooga, Tennessee, in 1910 that he felt the corporate concept should be changed. "Corporations do not do wrong. Individuals do wrong, the individuals who direct and use them for selfish and illegitimate purposes, to the injury of society and the serious curtailment of private rights." He further said, "I regard the corporation as indispensable to modern business enterprise. I am not jealous of its size or might, if you will not abandon at the right points, the fatuous, antiquated, and quite unnecessary fiction which treats it as a legal person. . . ." He pled earnestly "for the individualization of responsibility within the corporation. . . ." See William Z. Ripley, *Main Street and Wall Street* (Boston: Little, Brown, 1927).

9. Thomas W. Lamont, "Henry P. Davison," *Colliers,* May 6, 1933.

10. The pertinent part of the decision reads as follows:

> If the King or subject have a publick wharf, unto which all persons that come to that port must come and unlade or lade their goods as for the purpose, because they are the wharfs only licensed by the Queen . . . or because there is no other wharf in that port . . . in that case there cannot be taken arbitrary and excessive duties for cranage, wharfage, pesage, &c. neither can they be inhanced to an immoderate rate, but the duties must be reasonable and moderate. . . . For now the wharf and crane and other conveniences are affected with a publick interest, and they cease to be *juris privati* only.

For more information on this subject, see William E. Mosher and Finla G. Crawford, *Public Utility Regulation* (New York: Harper, 1933).

11. In 1873, when the Legislature of Michigan created the office of the Commissioner of Railroads, with limited police control over railroad operations but with no power as yet to fix rates, the principal contact that gas and electric men had with any form of regulation was still the local franchise of the particular municipality involved. By 1905, utilities were beginning to outgrow the local boundaries of their municipalities, and the state Legislature passed an act allowing electric companies to use streets and roads outside municipalities. Under this statewide franchise, many companies then in existence invested in extensions of their lines. The law was, in effect, repealed by the Michigan Constitution of 1909, but the State Supreme Court held that the constitution could not take away the rights of companies which already had gone ahead and invested their money in accordance with the law. Thus the act works practically as a perpetual franchise for those companies which took advantage of it, and Consumers Power still operates in several cities on that basis.

In 1907, the legislators created the three-man Michigan Railroad Commission, whose members were appointed by the governor, by and with the advice and consent of the Senate for a term of six years. This commission now had rate-making powers, as did a similar three-man commission which took its place in 1909 and eventually developed into the Michigan Public Service Commission.

Credit for the first development of such commission-type control is shared jointly by Wisconsin and New York, both of which had passed the necessary legislation in 1907. The contest over the relationship between the state and corporations had culminated two years earlier under Wisconsin Governor Robert

W. LaFollette, and the task of the Wisconsin Legislature was not so much to decide a policy of control as to arrive at some method for carrying it out. Those drafting the New York Public Service Commission Act profited from the work of the Wisconsin Legislature. See Mosher and Crawford, *op. cit.*

12. In the gas field, there were the Jackson Gas Company, The Bay City Gas Company, the Saginaw Gas Company, the Flint Gas Company, the Pontiac Light Company, and the Kalamazoo Gas Company.

The Jackson, Flint, and Kalamazoo companies were already in existence. In 1910, the electric and gas functions of Pontiac Light Company were separated, with the Pontiac Light Company remaining a straight gas property, and the electric properties being conveyed to the Pontiac Power Company. In Bay City, the electric properties had already been conveyed to the Traction & Power Company in 1903. In Saginaw, gas operations now were handled by the Saginaw City Gas Company. All these companies were part of the Michigan Light Company.

In the field of electricty, there was—and we mention it first, not because of its overall importance, but because of its confusing name—the Consumers Power Company (Michigan), which had no relation to Consumers Power Company (Maine) other than it was, of course, one of the underlying companies. No one knows how this name duplication came about. It certainly had no corporate significance. Consumers Power (Michigan) took over the properties of The Owosso and Corunna Electric Company, the Charlotte General Electric Company, and the Shiawassee Light and Power Company, which also served as an electric operating company in other nearby communities.

Other electric companies that emerged were the Au Sable Electric Company, which owned the distribution lines from the Au Sable dams; Foote's Commonwealth Power Company of 1904 (again not to be confused with the Commonwealth Power Railway and Light Company of Maine, the overall holding company); the Grand Rapids–Muskegon Power Company, which grew out of the Grand Rapids–Muskegon Water Power Electric Company in 1906 and finally became the electric utility of the Grand Rapids and Muskegon areas; the Central Power Company, which held certain distribution facilities; the Flint Electric Company of 1908; the Saginaw Power Company, which in 1910 took over the Bartlett Illuminating Company, which had operated in this city; the Pontiac Power Company, which in 1910 assumed the electric properties of the Pontiac Light Company and of the Pontiac Standard Lighting Company; the Bay City Power Company, which in the same year absorbed the electric properties of the Bay City Traction and Electric Company; and the Economy Power Company, which held title to certain generating plants and which here deserves a separate paragraph.

The Economy Power Company ultimately became the holding company for the Cooke, Five Channels, and Loud Dam developments, and also for the new Battle Creek steam plant, later known as the Elm Street plant; the Grand Rapids steam plant, later known as the Wealthy Street plant; and the Rapid Street plant in Pontiac, which had already been built by a predecessor company of General Motors. Economy Power also incorporated the former Allegan Light and Power Company.

Eastern Michigan Power Company was set up as a construction concern under the same Consumers Power of Maine umbrella, and there were also several underlying landowning companies, such as the Prudential Land Company and the Iosco Land Company, the latter having been purchased from the Loud brothers by the Foote and Hodenpyl interests.

Chapter 10

1. The upper Au Sable has also been revitalized, thanks to George W. Mason, who gave 14 miles on both banks to the state; William B. Mershon and others, who initiated individual and corporate reforestation programs; and the federal and state governments, whose efforts were given impetus by the work of such famous conservationists as Gifford Pinchot, of Pennsylvania, and John Muir, of California. For more on the Au Sable's ecology, see Hazen L. Miller, *The River That Came Back,* published as a public service by Consumers Power Company.

2. In his "How the Power Development Came to the Oscoda Area," *Consumers Power News,* May–June 1941, Edward F. Loud presents a beautiful summary of his feelings:

> It is the customary procedure for a lumberman to come to a town, erect a mill and for a period of years lay waste the forest, convert the logs into lumber which he ships away. In most cases it must follow that when his final tree is felled, he too must gather up his gains and move away, and in the great majority of instances, in lieu of the wealth he has thus acquired, he can leave behind nothing of benefit or compensation to the community in which he has lived and labored.
>
> I speak now for all of us when I say that, as a Company, we were and are profoundly grateful for the rare good fortune which gave to us the priceless opportunity to leave behind a legacy that has brought renewed life to our community and should enable it to live and prosper throughout the coming years.

3. The story goes that on his inspection of the river some years earlier, Cooke had called attention to that particular location as a possible site. The location had not previously been considered, and subsequent surveys bore out Cooke's amateur but nonetheless valid conclusion. It is more likely, however, that W. A. Foote decided to name the dam after Cooke in gratitude for his presentation on behalf of the Au Sable venture to Hodenpyl-Walbridge.

4. The line was later operated at 132,000 to 150,000 volts at various times. It is now termed a 138,000-volt line, which is the nominal standard for the industry.

5. For more detail on the technical factors, see J. B. Foote, "The History of the Evolution of the High-voltage Power Transmission Lines of the Consumers Power Company," the *Au Sable News,* September 1921.

6. This statewide operational concept was new for many of the company people. Indeed, when a meeting was held in Detroit at which a uniform classification of accounts was to be set up, the general feeling stubbornly clung to the traditional method of handling accounts as if they were based on decentralized operations. Accounting, sales promotion, and distribution, as well as production and transmission accounts, were all to be separated into local areas. Robert Davey, who was later to be secretary of Consumers Power Company, but who was still a young man at that time, realized that this fractionated concept did not mesh with the thoughts W. A. Foote had expressed to him. Somewhat timidly he suggested that production and transmission expenses should be set up on the basis of a centralized operation for the whole state. None of the older men paid much attention to him. When the session closed for the day, Davey took the interurban to Jackson, where he consulted with Foote and confirmed his view. Back in Detroit for the next day's session, he spoke with more conviction and succeeded in winning Ernest J. Bechtel over to his way of thinking. (Bechtel, a railroad engineering specialist, was responsi-

ble to the company's executive committee.) Davey and Bechtel then finally persuaded the others.

7. The Owosso substation housed 140,000- to 40,000-volt transformers. At Kalamazoo a frequency changer was required because the Grand Rapids system worked on 30 cycles. The Kalamazoo–Grand Rapids line was originally energized at 70,000 volts from Grand Rapids.

8. T. A. Kenney was born at Mechanicville, New York, on January 5, 1882. After leaving school, he was employed by the Hudson River Power Transmission Company, one of the original properties of what became the New York Power and Light Corporation. At the time, this company was building a dam and power plant on the Hudson River 2 miles below Mechanicville, in which were installed the first 12,000-volt generators built by the General Electric Company. Kenney worked at various jobs about the dam and powerhouse, finally entering the construction office, where he learned shorthand, typing, and office methods. When the plant went into operation, he became office assistant to the superintendent. In 1902, when the Mechanicville plant was taken over by the Hudson River Electric Power Company in connection with its larger development of Spier Falls, farther up the Hudson, he became assistant to Bryce E. Morrow, who was the operating manager of the company. Morrow later joined Kenney in Michigan and eventually succeeded him as manager of production and transmission, the company's centralized generation and transmission organization, when Kenney was transferred to New York to become assistant to the president of Consumers Power.

9. Since the early dispatching in Michigan was based primarily on the lessons learned by the Hudson River Electric Power Company, let us review the experience of the New York concern. Central dispatching here started at about the turn of the century. At first, the dispatching was part of the duty of the operator of a central station, or where there was more than one generating station, it was usually the switchboard operator in the principal or controlling plant. As transmission extended, however, it was found that if the station operator were to work with any degree of efficiency, he must be free to concentrate on his own station, especially in time of storm or other trouble. This led to the establishment of a new branch of operating engineering and created a new position variously called "chief operator," "load dispatcher," or "system operator."

The main office of the Hudson River companies was established at Glens Falls, New York. These several companies had been organized for the development of the waterpower of the upper Hudson with electric transmission to Schenectady, Albany, Troy, Glens Falls, Saratoga Springs, and a number of smaller communities. In the summer of 1903, while making plans for the starting of the Spier Falls plant, the president of the Hudson River Power Transmission Company, who was a prominent lawyer, told Bryce E. Morrow, the operating manager, that he wanted a couple of good men in the office—one to be on duty days, and the other nights—to take care of the operating details of the system. Of course, in those days, there were no eight-hour shifts or relief days. These men were to take care of the operating details of the system. They were to be familiar with the system layout so that they could handle the high-voltage switching safely, and they had to be familiar with all load requirements, operating methods, and conditions. He also wanted a detailed record of every order that was issued and of every telephone conversation with customers; in addition, he wanted every report kept in duplicate and both copies of this log record to be in ink and signed by the man on duty. This record had to be in such form that it could be taken into court and presented as evidence at any time, on the day of occurrence or twenty-five years later. He apparently anticipated considerable litigation as the system developed, and he insisted on a legally accurate and complete record of operations.

N. L. Devendorf, who later came to Michigan and to whom the author of this book is greatly indebted for his early work on the history of Consumers Power Company and its predecessors, became the night switchboard operator for the Hudson River Power Transmission Company in 1902. He has written that in the early days of their pioneer dispatching system "there was grief good and plenty!" In addition to the usual difficulties of starting a new and, in this case, a very incomplete plant and getting it adjusted to carry regular and important service, such as a good part of the load of the General Electric works in Schenectady, there was considerable trouble that showed up on the transmission line, which was designed for 30,000-volt operation. While 15,000 volts had been utilized with fair success, when the voltage was raised to 30,000, the "Redlands" type of insulators began to fail in all directions, and the line had to be cut back to 15,000 volts, pending a change in insulators. As Devendorf tells it:

As the insulator job approached completion, there was some apprehension as to what might take place when we again went up to 30,000 volts. One day, however, we read in the *Electrical World and Engineer* [this was the name, from 1899 to 1905, of the magazine which preceded *Electrical World*] that a man by the name of J. B. Foote, in Michigan, was already using 40,000 volts and was planning a 70,000-volt system in another part of the state. We had also read of a 60,000-volt system in operation in California.

"Oh well," I remarked that night to Malone [an associate], "if those fellows in Michigan can handle 40,000 or 70,000 volts, we ought to be able to get away with 30,000 with these new insulators." "Sure," he replied, "we'll get along all right. I'll bet we'll have 100,000 or more before we reach the limit. They're talking it at Niagara."

When the voltage was raised, nothing happened until the lightning season began with a grand celebration in June. As Devendorf said, "It was a wholesale test of equipment and old Jupiter Pluvius cleaned up on us." Imperfect insulators were found and broken down, with resulting burned poles and interruptions to service. In addition, bushings, current transformers, and lightning arresters were thoroughly weeded out. As Devendorf said, "In the old-style arresters, made up of banks of fourteen or fifteen 2,300-volt units, a streak of 'greased lightning' was expected to turn something like sixty square corners in its passage through resistances and over spark gaps to ground—something it was generally in too much of a hurry to do!"

This account of the lightning troubles in New York State is interesting since electrical men tend to feel that lightning is more severe in their territory than elsewhere. Later on, some of the same Eastern men were operating in Michigan and experiencing considerable lightning difficulties. It caused Art Goulet to remark, "But I don't think they figured on Michigan lightning, and of course when they got that, their insulation broke down." But apparently they had considerable lightning in New York State too. At least Devendorf wrote, "We were a tired pair by the time the lightning eased off after another grand cleanup late in August."

10. In 1920, the Jackson dispatching office was moved from the Trail Street steam

plant to the so-called Hayes Street building, which used to stand back of the general office building. Parnall Road was started in 1956, and the dispatching office eventually moved out to this suburban complex.

11. T. A. Kenney's dispatching organization superseded the old station-to-station method of handling switching with load, frequency, and voltage control of the Kalamazoo River dams from the Battle Creek steam plant, and of Webber from the Trail Street steam plant at Jackson. The Muskegon River dams were operated under the direction of the substation operators at the Wealthy Street substation in Grand Rapids. The Kalamazoo tie-in through the frequency changer and the later developments on the Manistee River made it necessary to extend the dispatching system to Grand Rapids. These assistant dispatchers were called "chief operators" and reported to the Jackson dispatchers. Their duties for the western section were similar to those of the Jackson dispatchers for the Southern and Eastern divisions. The substation operators at Zilwaukee handled much of the Eastern division dispatching under the direction of the Jackson dispatchers until the building of the Saginaw River steam plant and the connection of the hydraulic plants of the Wolverine Power Company, with extensive additions to the transmission system, made it necessary to relieve them of substation operation.

The system diagram is an important tool of the dispatcher's trade. It would hardly be possible to operate a modern interconnected system without such a diagram. From the beginning, all the connections of the system have been shown on such a board. The first one, which occupied most of the west wall of the Trail Street office, was built under Kenney's personal supervision—it was a large white panel made of plank. All the generating plants, transmission lines, and substation connections were shown in heavy black lines, each switch location being designated by a suitable symbol indicating the type of switch. In the center of each of these symbols was a hole reinforced with a brass tube, in which was inserted a plug to indicate the closed switch. The plug was removed when the switch was opened. Later, in 1920, a new type of system diagram was worked out. This was rather similar to the previous one, except that it was smaller; it originated the method of having the switches indicated by holes through a thin panel with lights at the rear. A black rubber plug inserted in a hole indicated a closed switch. When the switch was opened, the dispatcher pushed the rubber plug through the panel, and the light shining through the hole indicated an open switch. Through the years there have been many improvements in the system diagram. At one time it was laid out on a metal panel covering the entire side of the room occupied by the dispatchers, with lines indicated on the metal panel and various symbols magnetized and attached to the panel to indicate different methods of operation. Since the move of power control to Parnall Road, the single diagram of the entire system has given way to slides bearing segment diagrams. A push-button projector throws on the screen any selection from a possible group of fifty such diagrams.

12. Kenney brought in J. Grover Hemstreet, of the dispatching department of the Hudson River Electric Power Company at Albany, and Harry J. Burton, of the General Electric Company's power plants at Schenectady and Schaghticoke, to work with local men in the formation of the dispatching department of the Au Sable Electric Company. Men worked regular twelve-hour shifts with weekly relief. H. J. Burton was relief dispatcher two days a week, the balance of his time being devoted to the study of the system and the formulation of transmission-line rules

and operating instructions. This was followed up with accident prevention and instruction work among the station operators and other employees of the Au Sable Electric Company. It was not long before these duties occupied Burton's entire attention and marked the beginning of a personnel and instruction department.

13. Despite their personality conflicts, Walbridge had a great respect for Hodenpyl, as is evidenced by the fact that his son was named after him. The son's name was Anton Emerson Walbridge, the Anton being after Hodenpyl, of course, and the Emerson after Emerson McMillin, Walbridge's former associate in the gas business.

One of Walbridge's annoying characteristics was that he habitually took the opposite point of view on a question. This trait is good in terms of drawing out all sides in a discussion, but if carried to an extreme, it becomes frustrating. George Hardy once told of an incident that illustrates rather amusingly this particular Walbridge characteristic. All the members of the Hodenpyl-Walbridge firm except Walbridge were in agreement on a certain point. When it came time to make the official decision, George Hardy, who went along with all the others in favor of the particular action—whatever it was—very seriously presented all the arguments against it. The other men at the meeting were rather shocked; on the face of it this seemed to represent a complete reversal of Hardy's views. Before long Walbridge, until then opposed to the action, entered the discussion very heatedly in favor of the proposition he had originally opposed. Ultimately George Hardy "allowed" himself to be won over to Walbridge's point of view, and the final decision was unanimous for the action that Hardy and the rest had really favored from the beginning.

14. B. C. Cobb's parents were Sanford H. and Mary E. (née Capen) Cobb. He was born August 13, 1870.

15. The Grand Rapids and Indiana Railroad no longer exists. Its remaining tracks are now part of the Penn Central System.

16. For Tippy's complete biography, see Chapter 12.

17. Barthold had started with the Grand Rapids Gas Light Company in 1896 and became its superintendent in 1898. In 1901, he was also placed in charge of the Hodenpyl-Walbridge gas companies in Kalamazoo, Bay City and Saginaw. In 1904, he joined the general staff of Hodenpyl-Walbridge and stayed with that organization and its successors until his retirement. His first major appearance as a power within the organization came in October 1910 when Hodenpyl's Michigan Light Company arranged to take over bonds of the Flint Gas Company previously owned by Claude Hamilton for resale. Before the end of that year, Hamilton and the other Michigan Trust people, Lewis H. Withey and George Hefferan, retired from the scene, and Walbridge, Barthold, and H. S. Brown, of Hodenpyl-Walbridge, took over.

18. Laraway held positions in Kalamazoo, Saginaw, Pontiac, and Jackson, as well as in Rochester, New York, and Williamsport, Pennsylvania. In 1919 he left Consumers Power as manager of the Jackson district, and after that he was a banker until his retirement from active life.

19. Others included George E. Luther, Ernest J. Bechtel, and James A. Brown.

George Luther was a specialist in land and title work, formerly with the Michigan Trust Company, whose expertise became an important factor in the acquisition of flowage lands. Luther joined Hodenpyl in 1909. His wife was the sister of George Hardy, whose family name is still borne by their son, E. Hardy Luther, a longtime executive of Consumers Power Company. George Luther had charge of land titles for the Michigan properties until his death in 1929.

E. J. Bechtel, who had been with the Toledo Edison Company, was an expert in rail operations, but he soon learned to double in other utility matters after joining the Hodenpyl-Walbridge organization. After the consolidation he served on the operating committee of Consumers Power Company, but made his headquarters at the Hodenpyl-Walbridge offices in New York and Detroit. Bechtel, a native of Toledo, Ohio, had no connection with the Bechtel Corporation of San Francisco, the worldwide construction firm which later acted as architect-engineer at the Big Rock Point and Palisades nuclear plants of Consumers Power.

J. A. Brown, like so many others, had started with the Grand Rapids Gas Light Company. In 1910, he was assigned to the newly established Detroit office of Hodenpyl-Walbridge to assist Barthold, who was in charge of gas operations.

In addition to Barthold, Bechtel, and Brown, the Detroit office consisted, to start with, of George Dobbin and Carl C. Wilcox and an industrial gas engineer whose last name was Harling. Dobbin had originally been employed by Laraway as a bookkeeper for the Rochester (New York) property. Wilcox, along with Barthold and Brown, later was one of the original incorporators of Hodenpyl's Michigan Light Company of New Jersey, as was Frank A. Newton, who also served in the Detroit office at one time, having been brought in from the Wisconsin Railroad Commission after thorough training in the newer concepts of general utility regulation and rate making. Rate regulation by the Michigan Railroad Commission was just coming into play, and the fact that each company of the Consumers Power group had its own rate schedule meant that considerable groundwork was necessary in order for there to be a gradual attainment of uniformity. There was also the consideration that the rates had to be set low enough to stimulate business without depriving the organization of sorely needed income.

Barthold and Bechtel moved to New York in 1911, when Hodenpyl-Hardy was formed. Fred Caldwell, who had been in the newspaper business in Kalamazoo, joined the Detroit office as publicity man at about that time. Caldwell later became director of public relations for Consumers Power Company. Arthur Mackie, formerly with the Grand Rapids Gas Light Company, eventually joined the Detroit office to head up sales activities, and still later C. I. Weaver came as Mackie's assistant. Charles W. Tippy also served briefly in the Detroit office between assignments in New York State and Texas. H. E. Broughton ultimately replaced Harling in charge of industrial gas activities. By 1914 the end of the Detroit office was in sight, and the staff was moved to Jackson.

20. In order to obtain uniformity of operations, it was the usual practice to place two Hodenpyl New York men as assistant secretary-treasurer and general auditor with the subsidiary companies. Before the Hodenpyl-Walbridge split, these two men were H. S. Brown and F. E. Haag. With the formation of Hodenpyl-Hardy, Brown and Haag resigned, and S. E. Wolff and H. G. Kessler occupied the posts of assistant secretary-treasurer and general auditor, respectively.

S. E. Wolff came originally from Jackson, was connected with the Jackson Gas Company, and later served with the Hodenpyl-Walbridge people in various locations in Michigan as well as in Rochester, New York.

Harry G. Kessler was born in Mount Vernon, New York. After his schooling, he started in the utilities business with the Westchester Lighting Company, but entered the Michigan scene in the service of The Saginaw Gas Company in Saginaw and became secretary of the properties in Saginaw as well as in Bay City. Apparently, it was in 1911, when Hodenpyl, Hardy & Company was organized, that Kessler returned to New York. Subsequently, he became controller and the chief accounting officer of all the subsidiary properties during the period of Hodenpyl, Hardy & Company, and on through the formation of The Commonwealth & Southern Corporation, remaining until his death on April 7, 1934.

For a general picture of the organizational structure that emerged, *Circular Letter No. 1980,* issued by B. C. Cobb from New York on January 2, 1913, is the best available source (Consumers Power Company files).

21. A letter from William A. Boland to W. A. Foote dated November 3, 1897, refers to Foote's proposition—apparently made to Boland as the potential financier of the venture—to "consolidate the electric and gas companies in the cities of Kalamazoo, Battle Creek, Albion and Jackson together with the proposed water power under one control and management. . . ." Boland evidently didn't come up with the money.

Chapter 11

1. J. B. Foote's public recognition in later years included an honorary degree from the University of Michigan.

2. E. V. ("Ted") Sayles, later in charge of Consumers Power's general engineering department, used to read J. B. Foote's mail for him in the mornings. Sayles, seventy-five years old and retired at the time of this writing, tells the story of how one day he was working with J. B. on the engineering budget for the coming year. Some of the items were fairly formidable, such as $700,000 for a transmission line. When everything was down on paper, Sayles offered to add it up. Hilda Pickett, J. B.'s secretary, told him, "Oh, don't bother, I'll do it," and so she did. The budget came to $7 million. J. B. signed it, although he could not read it, and the budget was proposed in this form and okayed. Later it turned out that Hilda had made a mistake and that the total should have been $8 million. J. B.'s department had to get along on $1 million less than it needed, but somehow they seemed to have managed all right.

3. J. B. Foote was survived by two sons, James Harold, born in 1891, and Kenneth, born in 1901, and by two daughters, Elinor (Mrs. Carl Soderbeck), born in 1893, and Margaret, born in 1898. Kenneth married Thelma Stecker, daughter of George Stecker, his father's longtime friend and associate. At the time of this writing, James Harold Foote, retired from the engineering subsidiaries of Commonwealth & Southern, lived just outside Brethren, Manistee County, on a 150-acre property, part of the flowage lands of a small hydroelectric project on Big Bear Creek which was envisioned in 1909 but which never came to fruition. He is married and the father of a son, James H. Foote, Jr. All J. B. Foote's other children were deceased at the time of this writing.

4. The Saginaw–Bay City Railway & Light Company, incorporated in 1903, controlled the stock of Bay City Consolidated Railway, The Bay City Gas Company, Saginaw City Gas Company, Saginaw Valley Traction Company, Bartlett Illuminating Company, Bay City Traction and Electric Company, and the Interurban Railway of Saginaw. The officers were Anton G. Hodenpyl, president, New York; C. M. Clark, vice-president, Philadelphia; George E. Hardy, treasurer, New York; G. L. Estabrook, secretary, Philadelphia; and B. C. Cobb, general manager, Saginaw.

5. The Grand Rapids Railway Company was organized in 1900 as successor to the Consolidated Street Railway Company.

6. Edna, born in 1883, had two sons, William and Edward. W. A. Foote's other mar-

ried daughter, Ethel (Mrs. William Walcott Tefft), born in 1881, had a son, Richard, who died in infancy; her second child, also a son, Robert Foote Tefft, was not born until 1915, the year of W. A. Foote's death. In addition to the two daughters, W. A. Foote and his wife Ida (née Westerman) had been the parents of two children, a boy, Raymond, born in 1880, who died at the age of seven months, and a daughter, Elsie, born in 1885, who lived only four years.

7. The Michigan United Railways Company, organized in 1906, took over the Jackson–Battle Creek Traction Company, which had been developed by the Foote interests; the Lansing and Southern Traction Company, built by the Mills people in the Lansing–St. Johns area; and the Michigan Traction Company and Michigan Traction Extension Company, both of these under the control of the Railway Company General and comprising street railways in Kalamazoo and Battle Creek, as well as their connecting interurbans and a spur to Gull Lake. Michigan United also absorbed the Lansing and Jackson Railway Company, which at that time connected the rail properties of Jackson to those of Lansing with an interurban line. In 1908, there was added the Jackson Consolidated Traction Company, which consisted of the Jackson and Suburban Traction Company, and the Wolf Lake Railway and Resort Company, Ltd., as well as a grouping of street railway operations in Jackson. Interestingly enough, before its take-over by Mills, Jackson Consolidated was a grouping of former competitors: J. D. Hawks, S. F. Angus, and W. A. Boland were all members of its board of directors—the bitter race between Foote-Boland and Hawks-Angus had apparently been forgotten, at least by Boland.

Early in 1911 Michigan United—before its take-over by the Foote interests—leased the lines of the Kalamazoo Lakeshore and Chicago Railroad, a steam line connecting Kalamazoo and South Haven, with the idea of electrifying it. This plan, however, was never carried out.

8. Officers of Michigan United Traction Company and Michigan Railway Company were George Hardy, Anton Hodenpyl, Jacob Hekma, B. C. Cobb, S. E. Wolff, E. W. Clark, C. A. Pearson, Jr., and Frank Silliman, Jr., plus a Jackson contingent consisting of John F. Collins, Robert Morrison, Jr., and John W. Glendening. Collins, who had been in Saginaw, was transferred to Jackson to manage the newly acquired traction system. Glendening, also formerly of Saginaw, assisted Collins. The original name of Michigan Railway Company was Michigan and Chicago Railway Company. The designation was changed in 1913.

9. It was felt that by utilizing 2,400 volts, a saving could be effected since it would not be necessary to have intermediate substations. The power sources were to be the Wealthy Street plant in Grand Rapids, the Elm Street plant in Battle Creek, and the Kalamazoo steam plant. It was found, however, that the third-rail operation at the higher voltage was not satisfactory in a Michigan climate. Snow and sleet in the especially severe winter of 1917–1918 caused the voltage to be cut back to 1,200, still double that of most interurbans. The only other 1,200-volt operations in Michigan were the Saginaw-Flint and the Holland-Saugatuck lines, which were part of the Grand Rapids, Holland and Chicago Railway.

10. From an E. Hardy Luther interview with Grant Cochran (in Consumers Power Company files) and expanded with prosaic license.

11. *Ibid.*

12. The Detroit, Toledo and Milwaukee Railroad belonged to the Michigan Central Railroad and the Lake Shore & Michigan Central Railway Company.

13. In his first Manistee River venture, Holmes was working with two men by the

names of C. J. Wheeler and C. J. Updyke. Holmes bought out Updyke, and Golden Filer, of Manistee, bought out Wheeler. Holmes and Filer hired an engineer who recommended three small dams rather than a big one. For financing, Holmes turned to the Dewitt-Trembell Company of Chicago and granted it a ninety-day option on the deal in 1906. Spreckels was the principal client of Dewitt-Trembell.

14. Manistee County Electric Company was organized in 1908, but the articles of association were not signed until January 22, 1909.

15. Stronach's first unit went into service October 1, 1912, supplying 30-cycle power to Manistee. This service was then expanded into Cadillac in 1915. The dam's power was supplemented by a 400-kilowatt unit at Manistee and one of similar capacity in the Cadillac steam plant (see Note 16 below).

16. Although the Manistee and Cadillac properties were not predecessor companies of Consumers Power in a true sense, it is appropriate here to review their early history.

In the 1880s Louis Sands was a prominent businessman in Manistee. He operated the Sands Salt and Lumber Company, had a timber operation, and built a logging railroad. Some of his lumbering was done in the vicinity where Tippy Dam now stands. Sands was instrumental in starting the gas and electric as well as the traction business in Manistee. It didn't cost him anything to steam his electric plant; he simply used leftover timber from the mill and driftwood. For gas manufacture, he used coal rather than resin. In 1882, a franchise was granted by the city of Manistee to the Manistee Light, Gas & Coke Company, of which Sands was one-half owner, to light the streets of the city. Two years later Sands became sole owner of the gas plant. In 1897, the Manistee Fuel and Gas Company was organized, of which he again was the principal owner. Then in 1889, Sands established an incandescent electric plant in his gasworks building. It consisted of a 500-light dynamo. Sands Electric Lighting Company, as it was named, then installed an arc-light plant in a new building at the rear of the gasworks, and on Christmas night of 1890, River Street was illuminated for the first time by brilliant arc lights which Sands had placed in position without cost to the city. A contract for electric streetlighting followed in 1891, and yet another new plant was built.

Actually, Sand's electric operation was not the first in Manistee. John Bowie, the predecessor of the Manistee Iron Works, had installed a private Edison incandescent system in his machine shop in 1882. It was the second in Michigan. The first such system had been installed a few months earlier by O. N. Taylor in his sawmill at Ludington. (See James W. Bishop, "Electric Lighting in Michigan," *Michigan History Magazine,* Autumn 1939.)

The operation in Cadillac had an even more colorful beginning. In 1879, what is now the city of Cadillac was a tiny lumber camp known as Clam Lake. Electricity was almost unheard of, but there was need for a waterworks. H. M. Green, father of the later Michigan Governor, Fred W. Green, thus built a small pumping station. It was a rough wooden structure on the north shore of Lake Cadillac. There were two small steam pumps and about ½ mile of 4- and 6-inch wood mains. One man operated the plant. He was on duty twenty-four hours a day, seven days a week. He had an alarm clock to awaken him when it was time to fire the boilers during the night.

Fire protection was the most important function of the waterworks. In those early days, Cadillac was one big tinderbox. The sole industry of the town was lumber; there was dry pine everywhere, and the marshes along the lake were filled with sawdust. The buildings themselves were flimsy lumber-camp structures. Quick action was essential in case of fire lest it destroy the whole town. When a blaze broke out, someone would run to the waterworks and pull a whistle cord to call out the populace. The plant operator would get up, make as much steam as he could, and start pumping. The little pumping station served its purpose well until 1884, when it burned to the ground itself. One of the first things to go was the cord of the fire whistle, so no alarm was given.

The rebuilt waterworks had to move in 1887 when the Ann Arbor Railroad came through, and it was also at this time that the Grand Rapids branch of Tomson-Houston sold Green an electric arc-lighting system. The employee Tomson-Houston sent to Cadillac to install the equipment was George D. Westover, who then remained as operator, later becoming manager of the property when it became part of Consumers Power. He continued as manager until his death in 1920.

17. Today the W. A. Foote Memorial Hospital stands as a monument to the father of Consumers Power, the land having been given by his widow. There is also a monument in the form of a bronze figure in the Woodlawn Cemetery at Jackson. This figure, entitled, *Memory,* is the work of sculptor Lorado Taft.

Chapter 12

1. F. Clever Bald, *Michigan in Four Centuries* (New York: Harper & Row, 1961).
2. After the death of W. A. Foote, B. C. Cobb was elected to the Consumers Power presidency at a special meeting of the board of directors on June 8, 1915. At the same meeting, J. B. Foote was chosen a director of the company to fill his brother's seat.
3. The plans to make Consumers Power an operating company dated back to 1910, at which time they were thwarted by regulations enforced by the Michigan Railroad Commission. In 1913, federal enactment of the first income tax gave a renewed push to the company's attempts to change its status: the simpler the organization, the fewer its tax liabilities would be. At the time, George Hardy pointed out that the par value of the capitalization of the subsidiary companies practically coincided with that of the Consumers Power Company of Maine, suggesting that this fact might help sway the state to authorize Consumers Power to do business in Michigan. "When this order is obtained," Hardy said, "all properties of all subsidiary companies will be conveyed to the Consumers Power Company (Maine), which will then buy the direct owning and operating company, with exactly the same standing as if it had been originally organized under the laws of Michigan. . . ." Nearly a year later, on November 12, 1914, petitions were presented to the Michigan Railroad Commission for an order approving the issuance of stocks and bonds and to the Secretary of State for permission to do business in this state. On July 22, 1915, B. C. Cobb could report to a special meeting of the board of directors that the petitions had been granted. At the same meeting, C. W. Tippy was appointed general manager.

By September 1915, the officers of the company emerged as follows: B. C. Cobb, president; E. W. Clark, vice-president; George E. Hardy, vice-president; Jacob Hekma, secretary; C. A. Pearson, Jr., assistant secretary; S. E. Wolff, assistant secretary; Robert Davey, assistant secretary; F. C. Potvin, assistant secretary; Jacob Hekma, treasurer; C. A. Pearson, Jr., assistant treasurer; S. E. Wolff, assistant treasurer; C. E. Rowe, assistant treasurer; and Alice B. Simoneau, assistant treasurer. J. B. Foote and F. T. Masterson were appointed engineers, and C. W. Tippy continued as general manager.

4. The Michigan Light Company (New Jersey), organized in 1904 as a holding company, initially acquired all the common stock, except director's qualifying shares, of Jackson Gas Company, Kalamazoo Gas Company, and Pontiac Light Company. Hodenpyl-Walbridge at that time turned over to Michigan Light the stock of these operating gas properties against the issuance of securities which were in turn sold to the public. Hodenpyl-Walbridge retained common stock control. Subsequently, Michigan Light acquired the capital stock of the gas companies in Flint, Manistee, Saginaw, and Bay City, the last two from the Saginaw–Bay City Railway & Light Company.

When Michigan Light Company, the Michigan operating corporation, was organized, the initial capitalization was $3,000,000 in common stock and $2,144,000 in preferred. The original incorporators were William H. Barthold, James A. Brown, Frank A. Newton, and Carl Wilcox. As was common practice in setting up such corporations, the original officers soon resigned, and the helm was turned over to the real power: B. C. Cobb became president; Barthold and J. A. Cleveland, vice-presidents; F. C. Potvin, secretary; Alice B. Simoneau, treasurer; and S. E. Wolff, assistant secretary and assistant treasurer. At this time all the preferred stock was held by the Michigan Light Company, which also owned all but thirteen of the 30,000 outstanding common shares. Each of the directors of the company held one of the remaining shares. Later, Robert Davey was elected assistant treasurer, with G. H. Bourne assistant secretary and assistant treasurer. Still later, C. W. Tippy was appointed general manager, and H. G. Kessler was named general auditor.

The parent holding company, Commonwealth Power, Railway & Light, was paid $1,500 per annum for the services of gas operating experts and $2,100 per annum for the services of sales experts. Commonwealth Power was also paid 6 percent of all construction expenditures as compensation for engineering and general supervision of construction work.

W. A. Foote was named vice-president of Michigan Light Company (Michigan) at a special meeting of the directors on June 9, 1914, less than a year before his death. At this time, The Bay City Gas Company, Saginaw City Gas Company, and Pontiac Light Company already had common offices with the electric properties of those particular cities. Similarly, the gas operations of Flint and Jackson were combined with the electric operations. There was some delay in working out details with the Kalamazoo Gas Company, and this property did not actually become part of Michigan Light Company until the end of 1916, although the general operations of Kalamazoo Gas had been taken over prior to that time.

5. The D-type retorts in use at that time required an average of 319 pounds of the best grade of coal or coke for each ton of coal that was carbonized in the process. The average yield was 4.98 cubic feet of gas for each pound of carbonized coal.

6. In relation to their size, the old water-gas plants had very small connections and a low input of air and steam. Consequently, their capacity was small, and they were wasteful in their use of raw materials. On the average, the manufacture of 1,000 cubic feet required 3.92 gallons of the best grade of oil and 43 pounds of the best grade of fuel.

7. James A. Brown served as director of Consumers Power from April 1935 through September 1949.

8. The new oven units were built by the Improved Equipment Company of New York. According to the late James A. Brown (in an interview with E. Hardy Luther, in Consumers Power Company files), the steel-plant coke ovens were modified "by adding producers for making gas for underfiring, changing the design somewhat to decrease sizes, and adding self-sealing doors on all openings into the oven." The Jackson installation proved to be the forerunner of other such plants, each with some minor improvements.

9. At the end of 1914, the company's exact capitalization stood at $22,995,477.99, according to the application for operating-company status filed with the Michigan Railroad Commission. For the purposes of this application, a financial history and analysis of the properties had been prepared by Dean Mortimer E. Cooley, of the University of Michigan. (By coincidence, the charming young woman taking dictation on this part of the book is Mrs. Ruth Houston, wife of the great-grandson of Dean Cooley, which only goes to show that Michigan can still be a small world.)

10. The additions were planned for the Wealthy Street plant in Grand Rapids, the Elm Street plant in Battle Creek, the Trail Street plant in Jackson, and the St. Johns plant in Flint.

11. Alcona Dam originally was named Bamfield Dam.

12. Financing was so hard to come by that, at one point, the funds for building electric lines and gas mains had to be borrowed from the customer to whom these lines were to supply service. The customer was General Motors, which was carrying on a development in Flint and needed utilities for this installation. Getting a new industrial customer was, of course, a most welcome occasion for Consumers Power and Michigan Light. But to get the funds needed for construction, Consumers Power had to pledge some of its 6 percent preferred stock to General Motors as security.

The interest rates Consumers had to pay climbed as high as 7 percent on other occasions. This was a remarkable rate for that time in history, although it pales in comparison with the interest required on bond issues in recent years. When an issue of 7 percent debentures was sold to National City Company (later the First National City Bank of New York), George Hardy commented: "They're making us pay through the nose for that money." We may surmise that had he lived to see 1970, his language would have been a mite stronger.

13. The 1921 recession, while not nearly so severe as the Great Depression of the thirties, was sufficiently serious to result in a great number of business dislocations. William C. Durant, for example, lost control of General Motors at that time, being forced out of the organization he had founded.

14. Ed Washburn, onetime Owosso superintendent, told this to George Clark, now retired, who became head of electric distribution in 1931 after serving with Michigan Light and Consumers Power since 1919.

15. Interview with Leroy L. Benedict, summer 1970.

16. Much of the credit for restoring service goes to the fast work of the Aermotor Company of Chicago in bringing tower steel to the storm area. An Aermotor engineer was dispatched to Michigan to help in determining what parts were required. In turn, Walter H. Sammis, then in the Consumers Power engineering department, was sent to Chicago to follow the shipments through. He reported that the entire transmission tower department of Aermotor had been put on Consumers Power work in the emergency.

17. The *Au Sable News*, April 1922.

18. In countries such as Switzerland that are blessed with mountain scenery and roaring glacier streams, most of the power even today is derived from hydro installations. Industrialized as Switzerland is, and with resultant heavy load requirements, its hydropower is so cheap that the country's amazingly extensive railroad system is totally electrified, with extremely frequent runs and comparatively low-cost ticket rates.

19. The *Au Sable News,* December 1920.

20. Raymond C. Miller, *Kilowatts at Work* (Detroit: Wayne State University Press, 1958).

21. The urgency for selling utility service required rates that were as low as possible. Cost factors had to be studied to make the rates attractive to customers of varying characteristics and still protect the company. Although there were early attempts at storing electricity, as in Grand Rapids, these were never satisfactory. Thus a characteristic of the electric business in particular, and of the gas business to a lesser degree, is—and always has been—that service has to be produced as needed on demand. Regardless of how many watts or kilowatts the individual customer has connected to the lines, it must be possible for him to turn on everything at once. This creates a metering problem, and as a result metering was developed along two lines. One was the perfection of meters to record energy as it was used. Originally called "watthour meters," these began appearing in the 1890s and became the recorders of kilowatthours. The other route of meter development covered those for the normal measurement of demand—in terms of kilowatts rather than kilowatthours—the customer was making on the system. For more information on this subject see Harold C. Passer, *The Electrical Manufacturers: 1875–1900* (Cambridge, Mass.: Harvard, 1953).

22. The *Au Sable News,* May–June 1919.

23. The *Au Sable News,* March–April 1918.

24. In the fall of 1921, B. C. Cobb, then president of Consumers Power in a statement released by Dow-Jones & Company, said that most public utilities had been unable for several years to earn an adequate rate of return on their investments. Cobb said that, comparatively speaking, Commonwealth's electric light and power business had managed to make a good showing under the adverse conditions created by World War I, but that its gas and traction properties, which contributed about half of the company's gross, were extremely hard hit. Cobb foresaw the day when street railway operations might stop: "The question of continuing to advance funds to non-earning traction properties is quite a problem for companies holding their securities, particularly in cases where [rate] relief is not forthcoming. It may be that some properties will have to be left to work out for themselves, without further financial help from holding companies. In the case of the Commonwealth company, the dropping of non-earning traction properties would help its earnings."

25. F. A. Newton, "A Standard Rate Schedule for Consumers Power Company," the *Au Sable News,* August 1923.

26. In the fall of 1904, Tippy had joined Hodenpyl-Walbridge to become superintendent of gas manufacture at the Rochester (New York) Railway & Light Company, where he worked under the management of W. M. Eaton. Two years later he was made general manager of the Williamsport (Pennsylvania) Gas Company, replacing Burton Laraway, who had originally looked after the property subsequent to its purchase by the Hodenpyl-Walbridge interests. In 1909, Tippy became man-

ager of the Dallas (Texas) Gas Company. He moved to Detroit in 1910 and to Jackson in 1914.

27. This device actually had been introduced by Jay Cooke at the time of the Civil War, although, of course, he worked on a much smaller scale.

28. P.G. & E.'s original offering was 125,000 shares of 6 percent preferred capital stock, according to Charles M. Coleman, *P.G. & E. of California* (New York: McGraw-Hill, 1952). The program was carefully devised, providing full information about the company and its properties and stressing the mutual interest of the company and its customers. Shares were offered on the installment plan. Eliot Jones and Truman C. Bigham, in their *Principles of Public Utilities* (New York: Macmillan, 1931), report that this action was widely imitated especially after 1919 "when capital was very difficult to obtain and public relations work took on an added importance, because of the need of the utilities for higher rates to compensate for higher costs. . . ." Jones and Bigham point out that Central Maine Power Company already had sold preferred stock to customers in 1905 and that Central Hudson Gas and Electric Corporation and Interstate Public Service Company had taken similar actions in 1912. P.G. & E., however, was the first large company to employ the device, and its action in 1914 is generally considered the birth of so-called customer ownership.

29. Hoover obtained this information from John Britten, P.G. & E. manager in Oakland, who apparently had launched the customer-ownership project at his company.

30. The selection for customer ownership of preferred stock of the underlying property may not have been entirely idealistic. It was probably tempered by sound, practical judgment, based in part on bitter experience. Early in 1916 employees of Commonwealth Power, Railway & Light Company had been given an opportunity to become shareholders. The plan provided for the issuance to each subscribing employee of a limited amount of common stock, payment for which was to be made at the rate of $1 a month, to be deducted from the employee's salary. The stock in this case was that of the holding-company common, which traded in the open market and subsequently went down in value. This naturally caused considerable dissatisfaction among the employees. Hodenpyl-Hardy no doubt remembered this venture when they decided on the selection of Consumers Power preferred stock for customer ownership.

31. B. C. Cobb strenuously objected to Insull's dubious practice. According to Fred Hoover, Cobb even carried the fight to the National Electric Light Association convention floor. But Insull persisted, and Cobb and others of a like mind could never get him to discontinue selling holding-company common shares. Not that Insull was doing anything illegal; it was just very risky for investors. Some years later, on a visit to Europe, Cobb ran across Samuel Insull, who was then a refugee from the Justice Department. Insull, then seventy-three years old, reportedly admitted his mistake to Cobb (see Chapter 15).

32. Employees received $2 for each sale on the time-payment plan of one through four shares; $3 for each similar sale for cash; $4 for each sale to one customer on the time-payment plan for five shares of stock, plus 50 cents for each additional share; and $5 for each cash sale to one customer of five shares of stock, plus 50 cents for each additional share.

33. At that time, the authorized preferred stock was $20,000,000, of which $12,775,800 had been issued and was outstanding. For the remaining $7,224,200

of authorized and unissued preferred shares, the officers of the company were authorized to petition the Michigan Public Utilities Commission to issue and sell 7 percent stock. (At the same meeting Hoover was unanimously elected vice-president.) By September 16, 1920, a total of 1,349 shares of this stock had been sold to 324 customers. Of these transactions, 975 were for cash, and the remainder on time. By December 20, a total of 4,933 shares had been sold to customers (3,802 of these for cash), 527 to Consumers Power employees (80 for cash), and 575 to time-payment subscribers of the Employee Subscription Plan of Commonwealth Power, Railway & Light. In addition, 142 shares had been sold for cash and 121 on time to existing stockholders of Consumers Power, making up the total of 6,378 shares.

34. Between 1922 and 1924 the number of stockholders increased from approximately three thousand to more than eighty-five hundred. In 1922 the 7 percent preferred was in good demand at par, and, with continuing improvement in market conditions, it was the opinion of the directors that preferred stock bearing less than 7 percent dividend could be sold at par. It was at a meeting on September 21, 1922, that lower dividend rates for the additional $10-million issue were decided on. The sale of the 7 percent cumulative was thus discontinued in October 1922, and a new issue put out at 6.6 percent. During that year, 1,471 shares of earlier 6 percent cumulative preferred were reacquired by direct purchase or exchanged at $94 for 6.6 percent preferred stock. During the same period, the balance of Michigan Light Company's preferred stock in the hands of the public was acquired prior to the merging of that company with Consumers Power.

The tally of the stock outstanding for the years 1922 and 1923 was as follows:

	December 31		
	1922	1923	Increase (or decrease)
6% Cumulative Preferred	$12,739,000	$12,694,200	$ (44,800)
6.6% Cumulative Preferred	527,100	5,466,800	4,939,700
7% Cumulative Preferred	3,654,100	3,335,600	(318,500)
Common	16,175,900	16,404,300	228,400
	$33,096,100	$37,900,900	$4,804,800

A note in the audit explained decreases in 6 and 7 percent preferred stock as representing shares reacquired in exchange for 6.6 percent preferred at 94 and 105, respectively, and cancellations of some partially paid subscriptions as well as purchases in the open market. Aside from the relatively small proportion of 6.6 percent issued in exchange for stock of the other two issues, the increase in the amount of 6.6 percent preferred represented sales to the general public at par, practically all of which was to customers of the company. In March 1923 common stock of $228,400 par value was sold to the Commonwealth Power Corporation at par.

By the end of 1924 there had been an increase of $6,837,200 in the amount of 6.6 percent preferred stock outstanding or subscribed for, representing the net result from total sales during the year of $7,465,800 par value, less what was taken back from stockholders and some reacquired in exchange for 6 percent. Any 6.6 percent preferred stock reacquired was immediately reissued in paid-up subscriptions or new cash sales. Another block, this time 14,000 shares, or $1.4-million par value of common stock, was sold to Commonwealth Power Corporation at par on August 22, 1924. The authorized common stock was changed from 200,000 shares of $100 par value to 1.4 million shares of no-par value.

The sale of 6.6 percent preferred stock was discontinued in 1925, and in its stead 6 percent preferred was offered to the public. The financing of capital requirements for the year was by capital stock sales. Preferred stock, outstanding and subscribed for, increased 155,565 shares, while 40,000 shares of no-par common were sold at $30 per share to the Commonwealth Power Corporation.

At a special directors' meeting on March 3, 1925, it was stated that the $9.5 million of the company's preferred stock, bearing dividends not exceeding 6.6 percent per annum, authorized by the Michigan Public Utilities Commission in January of that year, would probably all be sold by April, as $5 million of it had already been sold to Bonbright & Co., Inc., and sales under the customer-ownership plan were progressing at a rapid rate.

At the same meeting, it was disclosed that the officers were arranging to discontinue the sale of 6.6 percent preferred stock under the customer-ownership plan and to sell instead, commencing April 1, 1925, the company's 6 percent stock at $95, with the idea that the price would be advanced to par later in the year. Under the orders of the Michigan Public Utilities Commission, the company was required to obtain par for its preferred stock. It was announced that Commonwealth Power Corporation, in order to facilitate the sale of 6 percent preferred stock at $95, had agreed to make payments to Consumers Power of the difference between the price at which the stock was sold and par. The chairman submitted a draft of an offer proposed to be sent to all stockholders of the company with a subscription blank attached affording opportunity to purchase the company's 6 percent preferred stock with dividends payable monthly or quarterly at the election of the stockholders at $95 and dividends accrued to date of payment.

Business now was on the upgrade, capital was getting easier to raise, and in the mid-1920s the outlook was bright. In 1927, the company sold 16,336 shares of its 6 percent preferred stock at $103 a share. The premium, amounting to nearly $50,000, was credited to the cost of selling preferred stock. That same year, 125,000 shares of no-par common were sold at $40 per share to Commonwealth Power Corporation.

Net sales from January 1 to April 30, 1928, of the 6 percent preferred under the customer-ownership plan covered 12,356 shares. By August 31, the total had grown to 18,074 shares. At this point the sale of the 6 percent preferred was discontinued. Starting on September 17, $5 preferred was sold at $95. On February 1, 1929, the selling price of this issue was raised to $98. Net sales of 50,000 shares at that price were contemplated for 1930. At the end of August 1930, nearly 27,000 had been marketed.

Customer-ownership selling continued into 1933. By that time, of course, the big stock market crash had come, followed by the Great Depression, and customer buyers increasingly cancelled their subscriptions. In 1933, for example, 1,535 subscriptions of 2,299 shares of the preferred were cancelled and during the first three months of 1934 another 1,950 subscriptions for 2,933 shares were dropped. For Consumers Power and other utilities, this particular method of raising money had outlived its usefulness, and it has not been tried since.

35. Among others who were involved with customer ownership in the course of time were M. C. Dowling, H. H. Koelbel, S. B. Morton, and J. R. Thomson. Early in the program, D. M. Mackie was brought back to Michigan from Springfield, Ohio, where he had been associated with C. I. Weaver after the Alcona Dam construction job was postponed and the Eastern Michigan Power Company had been discontinued (see Note 38 below). Mackie handled publicity and developed an advertising department, later being assisted by L. A. Fleming. In 1926 Karn took complete charge of the customer-ownership program and became a vice-president. When Karn was assigned to Kalamazoo as district manager on January 1, 1927, Koelbel, formerly in appliance sales work, replaced him in customer ownership.

36. The appliance aspect of the business grew so much that for a time, separate appliance companies were established, the United Appliance Company (1920 to 1927) for the Commonwealth Power, Railway & Light properties, and the Electric Shop Company for the northern Ohio properties. These were first under the guidance of C. W. Johnson and later under that of L. R. Parker. Originally, the appliance companies had direct supervision of all merchandise activities, though eventually they served primarily as purchasing units. (There was a time when appliances were sold under the Unesco label. This, of course, had nothing to do with the later UNESCO. Rather, it was the acronym for United Appliance and Electric Shop Companies.) In 1922 the Federal Profit Sharing Company was organized, which issued its customers coupons with appliance purchases. These coupons could be redeemed in payment for premiums, somewhat on the order of the United Cigar Store coupons then prevalent, and they were precursors of the trading stamps that are now in vogue.

37. Here is a step-by-step account of how this was done: At the annual meeting of Michigan Light, April 24, 1919, there were approximately 450 stockholders; in other words, the stock was relatively widely held. At that time, 28,526 shares of preferred stock and 31,759 shares of common stock were outstanding. The largest concentration of stockholding was that of Commonwealth Power, Railway & Light Company, with 31,746 shares of common stock. This constituted all but the director's qualifying shares. The preferred stock, however, was scattered.

In response to a petition of the Consumers Power Company, the Michigan Public Utilities Commission, on January 12, 1920, issued an order authorizing Consumers Power Company to issue Consumers Power Company common capital stock in exchange or payment for a like amount of Michigan Light Company common stock and Consumers Power Company preferred capital stock in exchange or payment for a like amount of Michigan Light Company preferred capital stock. In addition, there was authorization to Consumers Power Company to acquire Michigan Light Company bonds, and this was subsequently done.

By the time of the annual stockholders' meeting of April 15, 1920, the number of preferred stockholders had been reduced to between 50 and 100, and 24,078 shares of preferred stock and 31,759 shares of common stock were now owned by Consumers Power Company and pledged under its indenture to The National City Bank of New York as trustee under Consumers Power Company general and refunding mortgage dated January 1, 1920. By April of the next year, 26,634 of the preferred shares of Michigan Light, as well as the 31,746 shares of common formerly held by Commonwealth Power, Railway & Light Company, were pledged to The National City Bank. A little more than a year later (June 24, 1922), there were only thirteen shares of preferred stock outstanding with the public and not pledged to National City.

The situation in June of 1922 was that Consumers Power Company was the owner of all the common stock, 31,759 shares issued and outstanding, and of 27,545 out of a total of 27,558 shares of the preferred stock issued, outstanding, and pledged under its mortgage. In addition, certain of the Michigan Light Company first and refunding mortgage 5 percent twenty-year gold bonds, issued under an indenture dated March 1, 1916, with the Union Trust Company as trustee, had been pledged under the Consumers Power Company mortgage. The National City Bank of New York, as trustee, consented that the Michigan Light stock deposited and pledged with it be voted in favor of the sale of all the company's property and franchises to Consumers Power Company on the condition that prior to the culmination of the sale, the property and franchises should have been validly conveyed under, and made subject to, the lien of the general and refunding mortgage dated January 1, 1920, executed by Consumers Power Company, subject only to the prior lien of the first and refunding mortgage dated March 1, 1916, executed by Michigan Light Company to the Union Trust Company as trustee.

In effect, this meant that the company was pledging property rather than securities and that the Michigan Light Company was going out of existence, with its property being taken over by Consumers Power Company.

38. As a further part in the simplification of corporate structure, it was decided to eliminate the Eastern Michigan Power Company, which had been the construction unit. C. I. Weaver, Eastern's Michigan manager, was then transferred into the managership of the Springfield (Ohio) Light, Heat & Power Company, another of the Hodenpyl-Hardy-Clark Commonwealth properties.

Chapter 13

1. The scouting of likely properties took about three months, after which the four men originally thought of returning to Kansas. However, they were offered other jobs around the company. R. E. Richardson, who had been general manager of the Kansas City (Missouri) Electric Light Company before taking on the scouting assignment for Consumers Power, became general manager of the distributing company serving Charlotte, Owosso, Corunna, and other communities in the area. (This is now the Owosso district of the Flint division.) Eppes became district manager and later division manager in Battle Creek. Thomson briefly served as local manager and later as district manager in the same division. Lang became local manager in Kalamazoo and then went back to Kansas for awhile before returning once more to Consumers Power several years later.

2. Here, in brief, is the early history of Reed City's electric operations. Electricity was first produced in that community by James H. Andrews at an unknown loca-

tion. On June 24, 1892, Andrews bought a 10-acre site on the millrace, including a dwelling house, a mill building with machinery, a small dam, and appurtenant water and flowage rights. He moved in his generating equipment, added some more, and began operations on the millrace in about September 1892. George Westover purchased the site in 1908. He sold his interest to the Osceola Light and Power Company in 1921, and this company, in turn, almost immediately conveyed the property to the village of Reed City.

3. The purchase agreement for the Reed City property seemed to have been fairly typical for such take-overs. It was a long-term contract to be paid off as follows: $40,000 on the date of settlement, $2,000 per year for fifteen years at 6 percent interest, and $3,000 per year for ten years, also at 6 percent.

4. The earnings increases of the 1920s were not without reversals, however. There was a 14.86 percent rise in net earnings before depreciation in 1923 over 1922. The increase in 1924 over 1923 was 12.2 percent. In 1924, kilowatthour sales to large power customers declined, but this was practically offset by increases in other power sales. Business conditions in certain localities were not as favorable during 1924 as they had been in 1923, and there was again a considerable drop in energy consumption by some of the large manufacturing establishments. Again, too, this decrease was largely compensated for by more sales to smaller customers, principally to additional customers connected during the year. As a result, there was a higher average revenue per unit of energy sold because a larger proportion of the total sales were billed at the higher rates applicable to the smaller customers. The increase in net earnings continued its relative decline in 1925, but was 9.52 percent greater than in 1924. In 1927 there was a 9.56 percent increase in the net, and that year the gross earnings were $2,476,971.87 higher than for 1926, or a 10.26 percent increase. An increase of 19.71 percent in net earnings before provision for retirement reserve was recorded for the year of 1928 as compared with 1927, and 1929 showed an 11.47 percent increase over 1928.

The exact figures for 1929 were $33,420,538.87, gross earnings; $17,200,462.42, gross income after operating expenses and taxes; $14,347,139.62, net income after fixed charges; and a balance of $8,249,213.07 after provision for retirement reserve and dividends on preferred stock. (See Consumers Power Company stockholder reports for the respective years.)

5. Other minor acquisitions of the 1920s included the properties in Goodrich, Atlas, Greenville, Belding, Spencer (municipal), Athens, Shepherd, Ovid, Dimondale, Farwell (municipal), Beaverton, St. Charles (municipal), and Wyoming.

6. Each time a property was acquired, a general pattern of events ensued. The system being added usually required strengthening to improve service. Its load was built up through intensive selling, and rates to the customers were reduced. Often, too, the wages paid to former employees of the acquired properties were increased. These actions did not necessarily follow immediately upon purchase. Often it took awhile to get the property in shape.

Not all the new properties came directly into Consumers Power. Some came through other corporate organizations, such as the holding company, as exemplified by the acquisitions of Thornapple Gas and Electric and Southern Michigan Light and Power, which are discussed here in detail.

The Thornapple Gas and Electric Company had operations centered on Hastings, in Barry County. The property was acquired by the Commonwealth Power,

Railway & Light Company, and in November 1922 Consumers Power entered into a contract with that company, leasing the property. By December of 1922, Consumers Power Company had purchased 4,600 shares of Thornapple from Commonwealth Power, Railway & Light, and also $1 million worth of bonds. In this particular case, for reasons connected with the financing, it was decided to keep the Thornapple corporate structure intact. The property was pledged under a first mortgage of Thornapple, and the bonds issued under this mortgage were in turn pledged as collateral for Consumers Power Company general and refunding bonds. While Thornapple Gas and Electric was almost immediately integrated into the operations of Consumers Power, it remained structurally a subsidiary until its dissolution in 1928.

During the existence of Thornapple Gas and Electric Company, the property acquired in the vicinity of Alma and Mt. Pleasant, as well as the property for the generating station at Zilwaukee, was carried by Thornapple. Once again it was desirable that these properties not come immediately under the Consumers Power mortgage, so they were put in Thornapple instead of Consumers Power.

The Southern Michigan Light and Power Company was another of the major acquisitions of Consumers Power Company. It illustrates an entirely different type of situation. Organized in the fall of 1915, The Southern Michigan Light and Power Company immediately took over the properties of Hudson Electric Light Company and Morenci-Fayette Light and Power Company. Southern Michigan was led by George F. Avis and his two sons, Floyd D. and Clyde J. Avis.

Consumers Power Company people became interested in this property in about 1926. In fact, July 1 of that year, at a special meeting of the board of Southern Michigan, there was a change in the directors and officers of the company, with the new directors emerging as George F. Avis, C. W. Tippy, Robert Davey, C. J. Holmes, and W. W. Tefft. Officers were president, C. W. Tippy; vice-president, George F. Avis; secretary, Robert Davey; and treasurer, C. E. Rowe.

That same day the president of The Southern Michigan Light and Power Company received a communication from G. H. Bourne, secretary of Commonwealth Power. It seems that Commonwealth Power Corporation, at this point, owned 840 shares of The Southern Michigan Light and Power Company preferred stock and 6,857 shares of common, as well as all the property and assets of the Southern Michigan Supply Company (a co-partnership). It had also contracted to acquire all the property and assets of the Avis Light and Power Company (another co-partnership), as well as those of Community Power Company (a corporation). These holdings, except for the preferred stock, would be surrendered to The Southern Michigan Light and Power Company in exchange for a stipulated number of no-par common shares. The transaction involved amending the articles of association, increasing the authorized capital stock, and issuing additional common stock, all with the consent of the Michigan Public Utilities Commission.

Steps were taken that same month to effectuate these transactions, the new company becoming Southern Michigan Light and Power Company, and in August 1926, at a special meeting of the directors, the list of officers and directors was enlarged and changed. Except for members of the Avis family, all the officers and directors were old-time Consumers Power men. George F. Avis was made vice-president, director, and district manager at Hudson; Clyde Avis became superintendent of new business, appliances, and house wiring; and Floyd D. Avis was made assistant general manager.

Again the corporate structure was continued rather than being merged into Consumers Power Company at the outset. In this particular case, however, the reason was that time was needed for rebuilding the system and increasing load to a point that would warrant a change in the standard Consumers Power Company rates.

During the ensuing years, Southern Michigan Light and Power Company was enlarged considerably over its original size, and many of the acquisitions of property throughout the state actually came into Southern Michigan Light and Power rather than into Consumers Power for the same reason that Southern Michigan Light and Power was continued in existence. Not until September 1, 1931, were the properties of The Southern Michigan Light and Power Company completely integrated into the Consumers Power Company, and the standard rates applied.

7. Not included in the acquisitions was the Adrian gas plant, an oversight which Consumers Power now realizes was a mistake.

8. There was no precedent for the construction of a dam as high as 41 feet on such a difficult foundation. Alcona sat on sand underlaid with 10 or 12 feet of quicksand, below which the coarse sand again appeared. The cost of pumping out the quicksand, it was felt, was prohibitive, so it was decided to confine it. The powerhouse and spillway were designed as a unit. Rather than being beside the powerhouse, the spillway was under the building. The first use by Consumers Power of this so-called conduit spillway, which recently had been patented by W. W. Tefft (United States Patent No. 1,281,706, issued October 15, 1918), was at Mio Dam. This design was just right for Alcona because the powerhouse and spillway, nearly a cube, could be carried on a monolithic slab, heavily reinforced.

The slab was supported on round wooden piles driven 2.5 feet apart at their centers each way to a depth of 70 feet below the slab, the top of each piling extending 6 inches up into the concrete slab (total number of linear feet, of piling is 101,000). These piles were driven, partly through clay, in the winter, with temperatures at times as low as 20 degrees below zero. Jets were used, connected with rubber hose and with occasional small steam injections, to assist the driving up to the last 10 feet. Interlocking steel sheet piles enclosed the periphery of the concrete slab. These piles were driven 55 feet below the bottom of the concrete to form a watertight box, which was enclosed at the top and on all sides but which was open at the bottom. This box, representing the plan of the powerhouse spillway unit, was 115 by 170 feet lengthwise of the stream. In addition, the sheetpiling cutoff was carried both ways from the powerhouse across the river valley underneath the concrete core wall connected to it by a watertight joint which allowed for any settlement that might occur.

The conduit spillway, which was also used on later dams, had the advantage of being operated from the turbine room, thus eliminating the necessity for the operator to leave this active machinery, as is the case with most other types of spillways. For more details, see the *Au Sable News*, March 1924.

9. There were actually a few households in Royal Oak that cooked with natural gas obtained from their own ground. They had little private wells to which their ranges were connected.

10. James A. Brown's tenure as vice-president spanned the years from 1944 to 1948.
11. Substantially similar accounts of this Consumers Power–Detroit City gas deal were given to the author during interviews in the summer of 1970 with E. Hardy Luther (official historian of Consumers Power), Lyman Robinson, and Horace Brewer. Robinson had retired from Consumers Power as assistant controller in 1963 after forty years of service with the company. Horace Brewer's career with Consumers Power and affiliated companies spanned the years between 1926 and 1967, mostly in purchasing and industrial development. None of the three men were directly involved in the imputed event and had heard about it from different reliable sources. Chances are that the account is substantially accurate, though, perhaps luckily, it couldn't possibly be proved. In any case, the situation by now is so stabilized, and the territorial claims of the companies is so taken for granted, that not even the most eager beaver among trustbusters could possibly be interested in launching an investigation—it would be akin to trying William Randolph Hearst *in absentia eterna* on charges of conspiring to start the Spanish-American War of 1898.
12. From the point of view of the utilities, this instantaneous heater, with its high load but poor load factor, was not very desirable either.
13. W. H. Barthold was named president of the Handley-Brown Heater Company; Brown, vice-president; and Handley, general manager. The factory was located on Park Avenue in Jackson.
14. The *Au Sable News*, July 1927.
15. In the very early days—that is, around the turn of the century—free lamp renewals were not at all uncommon, but Consumers Power soon stopped this practice, as did most other companies. Detroit Edison, however, still allows its customers to turn in their burnt-out bulbs for new ones free of charge, and since March 1, 1932, when Consumers Power's rates in Pontiac were made identical with those of Detroit Edison, Consumers Power's customers in this area have also had free lamp renewals. Basically, it is against Consumers Power's philosophy to make people think that these lamps are free. The cost of the renewals is part of the cost of doing business, which in turn is inevitably reflected in the rates customers pay.
16. The *Au Sable News*, July 1927.
17. The quartet was composed of C. C. Day, J. A. Peterson, L. A. Fleming, and Burt Burnett. *Ibid.*, October 1926.
18. *Ibid.*, March 1927.
19. Forms of sales activities were as old as the early predecessor companies. From early gas sales for streetlighting, it was but a step to general lighting and piping premises for gas. Electric sales also generally started with streetlighting and then moved into the commercial field.

      George Stecker, J. B. Foote's assistant, might be termed the first lighting engineer of any of the predecessor companies; he was often involved with attempts to stimulate the use of arc lighting (see below). Then, at the time the Detroit office of Hodenpyl-Walbridge was in existence, Arthur D. Mackie was in charge of new business, and he shortly acquired an assistant, Chauncey I. Weaver, who worked with coal mines and other prospective power users. An industrial gas engineer by the name of Harling (his first name is not on record) was also connected with this Detroit office about 1910, and he was shortly replaced by Harry E. Broughton in the same capacity. Toward the end of World War I, William

King and others were calling on customers in connection with power and lighting problems, and in April 1919, Dan E. Karn, later Consumers Power president, had one of his first jobs with the company in Grand Rapids as combination heating superintendent and power engineer.

Walter H. Sammis, later a vice-president of Consumers Power and still later president of The Ohio Edison Company, is generally credited with first organizing a system-wide power sales effort. In 1922, when he was made power sales engineer, he employed a staff in various districts throughout the state. Among them was C. H. Purdy, who was assigned to the Grand Rapids district in 1923. Purdy later moved to the general office as head of power engineering, and still later was in charge of both power and lighting sales. Lighting engineering was inaugurated on a statewide basis also in the 1920s, with Joseph F. Mayo in charge.

The industrial gas part of new-business direction was retained in the New York organization, starting originally in the Detroit office and later moving to Jackson, and it was combined with the industrial gas activities of the smaller territories of affiliated companies in Indiana and Illinois. Harry Haroldson, who eventually was in charge of this work on behalf of the New York office, wasn't transferred to the Consumers Power payroll until 1948, shortly before the dissolution of Commonwealth & Southern.

We have referred to the late George Stecker as the first lighting engineer of the predecessor companies. It might be appropriate here to have a look at what he had to deal with when, after spending a few years in Albion, he was moved to Jackson "to take up studies in connection with advanced lighting conditions." That was about 1893 or 1894—at least the Jackson Light and Power Company had been organized just recently.

The first lights that Stecker dealt with were d-c arc lights, some two- and some single-carbon arcs, which he described in an interview with E. Hardy Luther, official historian of Consumers Power Company, as follows: "They made a very good light but made a considerable amount of noise and were objectionable in several ways, and the competition they had from the Welsbach gaslight was quite keen." He told Luther that General Electric was then working on an arc enclosed in a glass bulb which would be somewhat quieter and which had greater illuminating power and was not hampered by the difficulties encountered with the other lights as the result of the carbon burning.

Charles Steinmetz, of General Electric, was one of those interested in improving the arc light, and as the nineteenth century neared its end, all his experiments centered upon a type of electrode composed of magnetite, an oxide of iron, mixed with a proportion of titanium. While the resulting light was far more brilliant than that produced by the carbon electrodes, it was very difficult to determine the exact quantities of magnetite and titanium that would work best together. A report of the common council proceedings in Jackson for January 4, 1904, told of a committee visit to Newton, Massachusetts, and Schenectady, New York, to examine experimental streetlighting installations. Among the lamps the committee saw were Steinmetz's magnetite lamps, which for commercial purposes were called "luminous arc lamps." The council report said that the Jackson Electric Light Co. had placed an order in October 1903 for 300 of these lamps, getting in far ahead of other electric companies. And when the magnetite lights first went into use under Stecker's supervision, the interest of electric light men from all over the country was focused on Jackson. See John Winthrop Hammond, *Men and Volts* (New York: Lippincott, 1941).

Electrical World and Engineer (vol. 45, no. 22, June 3, 1905) described the luminous arc lamps as follows:

The luminous arc lamp derived its superiority from the fact that it is a true arc of luminous vapor and does not depend on incandescent carbon points for its source of light. Apart from the high luminous efficiency of the iron vapor, a great gain in effective illuminating area is derived from the excellent shape of the light distribution curve, due to the long arc, which is six to eight times the length of the open and two to three times that of the enclosed arc. Thus, instead of a brilliantly illuminated area in the immediate vicinity of the lamp, rapidly changing to comparative obscurity, the area under and around the magnetite lamp is not excessively lighted, and points farther away receive ample and uniform illumination. Consequently, the substitution of these lamps for those previously installed at the same time improved the street illumination and greatly reduced the energy consumption. The claim of very long burning electrode, which has frequently been made for this lamp has been fully substantiated, as the stubs taken from the lamps are very even in length and have uniformly given close to 180 hours' light. The color of the light, being a brilliant white, shows in marked contrast to the violet color of the lamps burning in the immediate neighborhood, and seems to give the nearest approach to daylight of any artificial illuminant so far discovered.

But arc lighting for commercial establishments was still far from satisfactory. According to Stecker, "There were a great many things that an arc didn't do, and one of them was that we still had too much noise, and we had heat. On summer evenings it was almost impossible to stand it in a store where three or four arc lights were burning; yet it was the custom in those days to stay open until nine or ten o'clock." Despite all technical and promotional efforts, the Welsbach burner stayed ahead in the competition. Only with the advent of the tungsten light did the situation brighten for electric salesmen.

20. In the period 1921 to 1932, kilowatt sales rose from 294,408,610 to 979,542,316. Gas sales in cubic feet increased from 2,289,078 to 6,786,105. (Consumers Power Company *Report to the Stockholders* for the year ended December 31, 1929.)

21. One of the major technological developments of the early 1920s lay in the area of tripping circuit breakers in a hydro-electric generating station while the generators were carrying full load. Such a condition resulted in the overloading of the hydraulic turbine, with the consequence that until the governor could bring the unit back to normal speed and a reduction in excitation could be effected, all apparatus connected to the generator was subject to high voltages. To meet this condition, some of the first overvoltage protective schemes to be used in hydroelectric stations were developed. In 1920 an effective means of controlling overvoltage was devised: In case of overvoltage, an overvoltage relay inserted a relatively high resistance in the main exciter field circuit, thus reducing the machine excitation and voltage. Backup overvoltage protection was also provided by a second voltage relay, which tripped the field switch and the main generator oil circuit breaker if the overvoltage exceeded a predetermined value. This type of overvoltage protection has since been used by other power supply companies. (See The Commonwealth & Southern Corporation, "Outline of Engineering Services and Facilities," 1940, in Consumers Power Company files.)

Probably the most important development in excitation systems for generating plants was the use of pilot exciters. As early as 1920 the engineering organization recognized the advantages of having a separate source of excitation for the main exciter of a synchronous machine. In fact, in 1921 a storage battery and motor-generator combination was used as a supply for the main exciter field of a 10,000-kilowatt frequency changer of Consumers Power Company. Pilot exciters were installed on two large hydrogenerators of the Consumers Power Company system at Hodenpyl Dam and also on the first unit installed at the Saginaw River steam plant in 1923.

That year, too, saw the development of high-voltage oil circuit breakers whose general design is followed to this day. (The Commonwealth & Southern Corporation, "Outline of Engineering Services and Facilities," 1940, in Consumers Power Company files.)

22. The new gas plant for Saginaw and Bay City, for instance, no longer consisted of hand-operated benches, but utilized nineteen Koppers cross-regenerated combination ovens of the Becker type. Each oven had an average width of 13½ inches with a ¾-inch taper, a height of 9 feet 11 inches, and a length of 20 feet 7½ inches. The space between ovens was 3 feet 6¼ inches, center to center, and the capacity was 5.4 tons of coal. The ovens were equipped with vertical flues in the sidewalls, and reversing took place from one side to the other over the top of the ovens. The ovens were heated by producer gas or coal gas and were so arranged that any part of the battery could be used on either gas at the same time. The producer gas, as it came to the ovens, had been cleaned and cooled and was distributed through steel lines and controlled with cast-iron cocks, enabling accurate adjustments of heats at all times. The producer gas was preheated in the regenerators before combustion; the oven gas was not. The regenerators were so divided and arranged that at no time was the incoming flue gas counterflowing to the outgoing flue gas in the adjacent regenerator chamber. There was, therefore, no danger of wasting the gas through possible leakage. (See the *Au Sable News,* October 1923.)

W. W. Klyce, who was superintendent of gas production at Pontiac, described a new back-run gas-making method in 1923: "Back Run Gas, so-called, is made in an ordinary water gas set so modified that steam is introduced into the off-take at the superheater, passing back through the superheater and carburetor in a superheated condition to the generator, where combining with carbon, it forms blue gas, the blue gas being then conducted to the wash box and thence to the relief holder. . . . [While several sets on the West Coast using soft coal with this process have reported excellent results, the] first back run installation east of the Rockies was made at the Gas Plant of the Consumers Power Company, Pontiac, Michigan, purely as a manufacturing experiment. . . ." It developed, during the tests of this back run, when using coke, that there was a decided saving of generating fuel per 1,000 cubic feet and an increased capacity per run. (The *Au Sable News,* November 1923.)

O. G. Yeager, superintendent of gas distribution in the Jackson division, described the 1924 Jackson plant installation of fifteen Baker-type coke ovens of 4.4 tons capacity each: "In efficiency, these ovens were an improvement on any coal carbonizing equipment used anywhere previously. The yield of gas was higher, the quality of coke was equal to any produced and the operation and maintenance costs were reduced to a minimum not previously considered possible." (See *Consumers Power News,* March 1939.)

That changes in production methods were beneficial is noted in the Arthur Andersen audit of 1924, which stated: "Closing of old gas plants in Bay City and Saginaw in May, 1924, and supply requirements for these districts from the new

Saginaw River Plant [resulted] in a marked reduction in labor, fuel, and other expenses [as well as] a marked increase in the quantity of gas produced per ton of generated fuel used."

Improvements continued. In April 1925, J. A. Brown reported in the *Au Sable News* that the Kalamazoo gas-oven plant had been enlarged and equipped with a new gas producer to heat this extension which was so designed that the producer gas would be carried to the existing ovens when they were renewed. The same year, additional coal-gas ovens and a new 2,000,000-cubic-foot gas storage holder were installed at the Pontiac gas plant, and a 10-foot Stere Engineering Company water-gas set was brought in to supplement the existing 7-foot UGI contracting company's water-gas maker. The new gas holder was designed by J. A. Brown. (The *Au Sable News*, November 1925.)

23. W. W. Tefft married Ethel Foote, daughter of W. A. Foote, in 1910. By that time, though barely out of the University of Michigan, he was already an old hand in the electric business. On graduation from high school, he had worked for the Commonwealth Power Company as a rodman on electric railway location and hydroelectric topography and as a groundman on electric railway trolley construction. Later he was dredging inspector on the Lime Kiln Crossing of the Detroit River and transit man and chief of party on waterpower surveys that preceded the hydroelectric developments on the Muskegon River, meanwhile continuing his studies. After a stint as assistant to Gardner S. Williams, head of the University of Michigan's department of civil engineering, he joined the Fargo Engineering Company and eventually Consumers Power Company. He became vice-president of Consumers Power in 1922 and served on the board of Commonwealth Power Railway and Light. Tefft resigned in 1929 to go into private engineering practice. He died in 1932, within the week following the death of Mrs. W. A. Foote.

24. The change to 60 cycles cost about $6 million and was essentially completed by 1936. (Ironically, the last changeover, which did not occur until 1959, took place at Croton.) The Depression years were of course a good time to do the major part of the work, since it was not only cheaper then but also easier, with much of the generating power shut down as a result of lower demand.

When alternating current came into use in the early days of the electric business, there were no standards of alternation. Consequently, a wide variety of frequencies developed. Since many early frequencies were based on alternations per minute, they resulted in fractional cycles per second. This is shown in the following tabulation:

Alternations per minute	*Cycles per second*
2,000	$16\frac{2}{3}$
3,000	25
3,300	$27\frac{1}{2}$
3,500	$29\frac{1}{6}$
3,600	30
4,000	$33\frac{1}{3}$
4,800	40
6,000	50
7,200	60
8,000	$66\frac{2}{3}$
10,000	$83\frac{1}{3}$
15,000	125
16,000	133

Michigan had its share of these frequencies. The early 125 and 133 cycles of Jackson were soon changed to 60 cycles. The territory in Grand Rapids had several frequencies. The Edison d-c system gave way to 60-cycle alternating current; the hydro plant on the Flat River, however, generated at 25 cycles. Interurban lines between Grand Rapids and Muskegon, as well as between Grand Rapids and Holland, operated at 3,500 alternations per minute, or approximately 29⅙ cycles per second. When Rogers Dam was built in 1905, it was decided to use 27½ cycles so that a 25-cycle load could be taken on by speeding up the motors by 10 percent, and yet the railway load could be readily taken on by slowing down the rotary converters by 6 percent. When Croton was added two years later, it was decided to increase the frequency to 30 cycles, which could be readily converted to the 60 cycles existing in Grand Rapids and Muskegon and would cause less lamp flicker than either 27½ cycles or 25 cycles.

After several years, the 60-cycle service in Grand Rapids and Muskegon was changed to 30 cycles. When Stronach Dam was built in 1914, and 44,000-volt lines were run to Cadillac and Manistee, it was necessary to change those cities to 30 cycles since Stronach and later Junction (Tippy) were to tie into the western 30-cycle system.

Direct current resulted in fewer transmission losses, and the fewer the cycles of alternating current, the lower the losses. So 30 cycles had some advantage in that respect over 60 cycles. But the 30-cycle fluctuation became objectionable with incandescent lighting. Also, in the course of time, there was more standardization on 60 cycles throughout the country. Thus 30 cycles became a nonconforming standard for equipment, and at times customers had difficulty in providing equipment for 30 cycles.

So, every now and then, the idea of changing the 30-cycle system to a 60-cycle system was presented. Finally, the 1928 budget included an item for such a changeover.

In a press release, C. W. Tippy pointed out that the existing 30-cycle equipment meant superior operating economies for the company and that the changeover would not increase capacity, but actually reduce it. Tippy pegged the cost of the changeover at $60 per 100,000 customers.

When the project commenced in 1929, a great deal of preliminary work was necessary: surveying customers' requirements, providing 60-cycle feeds, etc. One thing that brought the changeover to a head at this particular time was the contemplated construction of Oxbow (later called Hardy) Dam, which was to be the world's largest earth dam. The question arose as to whether it should be a 30-cycle or a 60-cycle operation and whether the transmission line from it should connect into Grand Rapids or should go cross-country to Lansing so as to become part of the then existing 60-cycle system.

25. The McEachron experiments at Croton lasted until 1932 and resulted in a number of other findings which are still being applied today. For instance, the idea of using a static wire over the transmission line was revived. In the very early days of the Trowbridge Dam line, a barbed wire had been installed over the conductor wire, on the assumption that the points of the barbed wire would attract the lightning. This wire, however, deteriorated so rapidly that it caused more trouble than it seemed to prevent. It was soon taken down, leaving behind a bad reputation that lasted for many years. The Croton tests rehabilitated the original idea by revealing that a ground wire, properly installed and separated from

the line conductors, as well as properly grounded at the towers, was indeed very effective in protecting the transmission line.

Another discovery was that lightning flashover on insulators could be reduced sharply by spacing the insulators farther apart. Before this finding, the disks on suspension insulators had been spaced rather closely to prevent cascading of the discharge from one insulator over the next. Now it turned out that a longer string assisted materially in lightning protection. The use of wood insulation on steel towers was also found to be effective.

26. To build and operate the electric transmission between Consumers Power and Detroit Edison, a new firm, The Electrical Interconnections Inc., was formed. This new company was owned equally by Consumers Power and Detroit Edison, and its board of directors consisted of three men from each company. Alex Dow, of Detroit Edison, became president, and B. C. Cobb, of Consumers Power, became senior vice-president. The jointly built line ran between Cement City and the town lines of Saline and Bridgewater. At either end, Consumers Power and Detroit Edison built their own links, each approximately 18 miles long.

27. The *Au Sable News,* October 1926.

28. *Ibid.* January 1929.

Chapter 14

1. The telephone conversation as reported in the text, while not fictitious, is an extrapolation based on the characters of the two men involved. Fact is that Cobb sprang the news on Martin without any preliminaries. The conversation was brief, and as usual Cobb was all business. (Author's interview with Lyman W. Robinson, summer 1970, in Consumers Power Company files.)

2. Hodenpyl-Walbridge (later Hodenpyl-Hardy), together with Commonwealth Power Railway & Light, also furnished the underlying operating properties with experts in such areas as purchasing, sales, and rates, thus fulfilling the service-company functions.

3. The *Au Sable News,* September 1921.

4. Justin R. Whiting, later head of Consumers Power, played a very important role in the liquidation of the railway properties.

5. A full account of the Tennessee electric power development can be found in the Princeton University thesis by Philip H. Willkie, son of Wendell Willkie, president of Commonwealth during the TVA period, entitled "The Story of Commonwealth & Southern." The thesis is in the university library in Princeton, New Jersey.

Here is a brief summary of the Tennessee background: at about the turn of the century, E. W. Clark & Company had acquired the electric distribution system of the city of Chattanooga, and in 1906 it acquired some damsites on the Ocoee River. The Nashville Railway & Light Company was there, bought from H. M. Byllesby & Company of Chicago in 1912. In 1913, in connection with the construction of a dam on the Ocoee River, the Clark people made an arrangement to supply the Alcoa Tennessee plant of the Aluminum Company of America with power for its electric furnaces. In return, the aluminum company was willing to finance construction of the dam. Clark thus controlled two Tennessee properties, the Chattanooga Railway & Light Company (electric distribution and traction) and the Tennessee Power Company (hydroelectric generation).

Meanwhile, other interests had been concerned with harnessing the power of the Tennessee River. The pioneer here was Joseph C. Guild, Sr., who late in the 1890s succeeded in getting permission from Congress to build a hydroelectric dam at Hales Bar. But financing was hard to come by, and it was not until 1905 that Guild and his associates managed to interest Anthony M. Brady in backing the project. Because of difficulties with the dam's foundation, Hales Bar was not completed until 1913, at which time Brady's Chattanooga and Tennessee River Power Company leased the dam's output to the Clark property.

At this time, the Clark people brought Hodenpyl, Hardy & Company into the Tennessee Power Company as their financial associates. The debt to the aluminum company troubled the management, particularly during World War I and the postwar periods. The Clarks were determined to effect a consolidation between their property and that of the Brady people, and the Brady group were glad to join in the consolidation because they were afraid their lease for the output of their dam would expire, leaving them a dam but no market. As a consequence, The Tennessee Electric Power Company was formed by the consolidation of the Chattanooga Railway & Light Company, the Chattanooga and Tennessee River Power Company, and the Tennessee Power Company.

6. In tabular form, the Commonwealth Power holdings in 1927 were as follows:

> Commonwealth Power Corporation
>> Central Illinois Light Company
>>> Pekin Light, Heat & Power Company (property leased to Central Illinois Light Company, April 19, 1913)
>> Commonwealth Power Corporation of Michigan (nonoperating)
>> Consumers Power Company
>>> Iosco Land Company
>>> Thornapple Gas and Electric Company (property leased to Consumers Power Company, November 1, 1922)
>> Illinois Electric Power Company
>> Illinois Power Company
>> The Ohio Edison Company
>> Southern Indiana Gas & Electric Company
>> Springfield & Eastern Railroad Company (nonoperating)
>> The Tennessee Electric Power Company
>>> Lookout Inclined Railway Company
>>> Lookout Mountain Railway Company
>>> Nashville Railway & Light Company
>>> Toccoa Power Company
>> United Appliance Company (nonoperating)
>> Utilities Coal Corporation

7. Interview with Claude Mulligan, now retired, summer 1970, in Consumers Power Company files.

8. Interview with George Clark, spring 1970, in Consumers Power Company files.

9. This secretary, who was at that time assigned to John A. Cleveland, manager of the Saginaw division from 1916 to 1924, later married Leroy L. Benedict after many years of keeping company. Needless to say, their long courtship occasioned much intramural kidding until their wedding in 1942. L. L. Benedict eventually became a vice-president and served from 1950 until his retirement in 1952. (Interview with Mr. and Mrs. L. L. Benedict, summer 1970, in Consumers Power Company files.)

10. Interview with Claude Mulligan, summer 1970, in Consumers Power Company files.
11. Consumers Power Company, "Minute Book," January 8, 1925.
12. Specifically, the contract with Bonbright & Company dated December 6, 1928, provided for the creation of these thirty-year bonds under the Consumers Power Company's deed of trust to the National City Bank of New York as trustee (this deed dating back to January 1, 1920) to bear interest at $4\frac{1}{2}$ percent per annum and to be sold to Bonbright at $93\frac{1}{2}$ percent plus interest, $11,415,100 being the principal amount of the new issue.
13. The Northern Ohio Power & Light Company was the successor to Northern Ohio Traction & Light Company. Its holding company was the Northern Ohio Electric Corporation.
14. The officers were the same for both the Allied Power & Light corporations. Once again the Delaware company was the holding company, and the New York company was the operating company—in this instance a service company. The address of Allied Power & Light was 20 Pine Street, New York City.
15. Federal Trade Commission, *Utility Corporations,* Senate Document 92, part 77, 70th Cong., 1st Sess., 1927.
16. *Ibid.,* part 78.
17. Commonwealth & Southern Corporation (New York) was organized primarily to render a general supervisory, financing, and purchasing service to the operating subsidiary companies of The Commonwealth & Southern Corporation (Delaware), the holding company. These services had formerly been rendered by Allied Power & Light Corporation (New York). On April 1, 1930, Stevens & Wood, Inc., changed its name to Allied Engineers, Inc. *(Ibid.)*

    The chronology of events was this: In May, June, and July of 1929, shares of common stock and option warrants of The Commonwealth & Southern Corporation were sold for cash. These shares and option warrants were subscribed and paid for at a price of $20 for one share and one option warrant, which amounted in the aggregate to $45 million. The interests purchasing these securities for cash were Allied Power & Light Corporation; The American Superpower Corporation; The Electric Bond & Share Company; Bonbright & Company, Inc.; Tucker, Anthony & Company; The United Corporation; and The United Gas Improvement Company. Under a plan and deposit agreement dated May 24, 1929, provisions were made for the exchange of common stock and option warrants of The Commonwealth & Southern Corporation for common stock of Commonwealth Power Corporation and for common stock and option warrants of Southeastern Power & Light Company and of Penn-Ohio Edison Company.

    As of December 31, 1929, approximately 97 percent of the total outstanding stock of each of these three companies had been acquired. Over 98 percent of these shares so acquired were entered on the books of The Commonwealth & Southern Corporation at values authorized by a meeting of the board held June 11, 1929, which were substantially the same as the then current market value of the securities. A plan of merger and consolidation dated January 7, 1930, provided for the acquisition by The Commonwealth & Southern Corporation of all the assets and the assumption by it of all the liabilities of its three subsidiary holding companies—Commonwealth Power Corporation, The Ohio Edison Company, and Southeastern Power & Light Company—and also the acquisition of all the assets and the assumption of all the liabilities of the Allied Power & Light Corporation.

The latter and the Penn-Ohio Edison Company were consolidated with The Commonwealth & Southern Corporation as of February 11, 1930. The Commonwealth Power Corporation and the Southeastern Power & Light Company came into The Commonwealth & Southern Corporation as of February 14. *(Ibid.)*

At a meeting of the directors of The Commonwealth & Southern Corporation on June 11, 1929, there was a description of an offer of exchange contemplated by the plan and deposit agreement of May 24, 1929:

> The chairman stated that he had been informed by the committee under a certain plan and deposit agreement, dated May 24, 1929, between George H. Howard, Alfred L. Loomis, and Landon K. Thorne, as parties of the first part, and J. P. Morgan & Company, as depositary of the terms of said plan and deposit agreement, a copy of which is presented. Said plan and deposit agreement provided for the deposit thereunder of common stock of Commonwealth Power Corporation and common stock and option warrants of the Southeastern Power & Light Company and of Penn-Ohio Edison Company, and authorized the committee, upon said plan and deposit agreement being declared operative, to make an offer for the exchange of common stock and option warrants deposited with it for common stock and option warrants of this corporation. . . . *(Ibid.)*

18. The following tabulation shows the distribution of officers of the companies of Commonwealth & Southern as of February 18, 1930:

[D-Director; ChB-Chairman of the Board; P-President; VP-Vice President]

Directors of The Commonwealth & Southern Corporation February 18, 1930	Commonwealth Power Corp.	Southeast Power & Light Co.	Penn-Ohio Edison Co.	Allied Power & Light Corp. (Delaware)
B. C. Cobb	D-P	D	D-P	D-ChB-P
F. P. Cummings	—	VP	—	—
C. E. Groesbeck	—	D	—	—
Jacob Hekma	D-VP	—	D-VP	D-VP
George H. Howard	—	D	—	—
T. A. Kenney	D-VP	—	D-VP	VP
Alfred L. Loomis	—	—	D	D
T. W. Martin	D	D-P	—	—
S. Z. Mitchell	—	D	—	—
R. P. Stevens	—	—	D	D
Landon K. Thorne	—	—	—	D
E. A. Yates	—	D-VP	—	—

19. Cobb's daughter, Alice (Mrs. Charles G. Quinlan), told this to Claude Mulligan that morning when he called to find out whether his old boss and friend was still alive. (Interview with Claude Mulligan, summer 1970, in Consumers Power Company files.) Cobb died on September 30, 1957, at the age of eighty-seven. In addition to Alice, two other daughters survived: Mary (Mrs. Carl F. Muller) and Alby (Mrs. L. E. Brownson, Jr.). His wife had died in 1939.

Chapter 15

1. Forrest McDonald, *Insull* (Chicago: University of Chicago Press, 1962). The Insull comment is quoted verbatim on pp. 1 and 2 of this excellent book, possibly the most fascinating ever written on the American utilities industry; the Insull quote, in turn, was derived from a document entitled "Mr. Samuel Insull," a typescript record of Insull's conversations with Burton Y. Berry, third secretary of the American Embassy at Istanbul, who served as Insull's guard on the trip.
2. *Ibid.*
3. *Ibid.*, p. 294
4. *Ibid.*, pp. 319–333
5. Early in the 1930s there were strong advocates of reform of the public utilities. These ideas of reform were not confined to those outside the utilities industry. In a talk before the National Electric Light Association convention at Atlantic City in 1932, Cobb made this statement: "Ours is a great industry. Surely it cannot be destroyed by those mischievously inclined. To keep it together, however, so that it may render service and so that it may be inviting to our customers and others for the investment of their money, we must conduct it so that it may be clean in thought and purpose and so that whatever we do in its operation may be kept above reproach." At this convention the utility leaders demanded that the industry divest itself of all semblance of propaganda activities, that it assume an attitude of frankness and ready cooperation in its dealings with the public and with regulatory bodies, and that complete and frequent financial reports be made by all companies.

   As a consequence, the Edison Electric Institute was organized in 1933, replacing the National Electric Light Association, which had long been the official body of the industry.

   Consumers Power Company became a charter member of the Edison Electric Institute, and B. C. Cobb was one of its original twenty-two trustees. President of the association was George B. Cortelyou; vice-president, William J. Hagenah; executive secretary, Bernard F. Weadock; and treasurer, Edward Reynolds, Jr.

   That this new association was determined to bind itself by a rigid code of ethics was shown in its constitution, which gave the membership committee authority, under the board of trustees, to consider and investigate the business practices of any member company and to expel, suspend, or take other disciplinary action against any member who was guilty of violation of proper or ethical business practices, or who failed to furnish required information. By virtue of becoming members, companies were deemed to have recognized the right of the institute to impose such disciplinary action.

   The institute's objectives were:
   1. Advancement in the techniques of producing, transmitting, and distributing electricity and the promotion of scientific research in these areas
   2. Making available to the public factual information, data, and statistics relative to the electric industry
   3. Furnishing aid to its operating-company members to generate and sell electric energy at the lowest possible price commensurate with safe and adequate service and with due regard to the interests of consumers, investors, and employees

   This housecleaning and self-regulation of the industry came too late, however.

The industry had been under attack for years by propagandists, others of socialist persuasion, who advocated everything from municipal to national ownership of the utilities. With the Depression, and with the heavy losses suffered by people who had invested in some of the utility companies, such as Insull's, the attackers made headway, and there was very little the Edison Electric Institute could do about it.

6. The other two were Henry L. Doherty's Cities Service group and the late H. M. Byllesby's Standard Gas and Electric.

7. In 1930, Consumers Power held 21,508 shares; Georgia Power, 14,663 shares. (Federal Trade Commission, *Utility Corporations*, Senate Document 92, part 77, 70th Cong., 1st Sess.

8. The only specific charge ever brought against C&S in later hearings before the House Interstate and Foreign Commerce Committee and the Senate Committee on Interstate Commerce was the allegation that it had carried some $500 million in watered capital values on its books from 1930 to 1932, thereby increasing the book value of its securities. This charge, however, was never proved, and the very accusation recognized the fact that the company voluntarily wrote off this watered capital, if indeed that's what it was.

9. *Ibid.*, parts 23 and 24.

10. American Superpower also dabbled in traction. It will be recalled that when Commonwealth Power was organized, the rail properties of the old Commonwealth Power Railway & Light were taken over by the Electric Railways Securities Company. In 1925, this company organized the Utilities Shares Corporation, which then acquired certain assets from Electric Railways Securities in exchange for Utilities Shares stock. This was evidently an attempt to salvage properties that still had an earnings potential. In 1927, The American Superpower Corporation made an offer to the stockholders of Utilities Shares for an exchange of stock. Another offer was made in 1928, and on June 4, 1929, the stockholders of both companies adopted an agreement of merger and consolidation whereby The American Superpower Corporation continued in existence and Utilities Shares Corporation ceased to exist as a separate entity.

11. According to the Federal Trade Commission, *op. cit.*, part 52, the statement released by J. P. Morgan & Co. read as follows:

The United Corporation has been organized under Delaware laws by J. P. Morgan and Co. and Drexel and Company and Bonbright and Company, Inc., and has made arrangements to acquire certain minority interests in the United Gas Improvement Company, Public Service Corporation of New Jersey, and Mohawk Hudson Power Corporation, held by the organizers and American Superpower; the directors being Thomas S. Gates of Morgan and Co. and Drexel and Company, George Whitney of Morgan and Co., and Landon K. Thorne and Alfred L. Loomis of Bonbright and Company

In November of 1930, The United Corporation reported to the Federal Trade Commission on the purpose of the company:

1. To acquire and hold securities of the Electric Power and Light and Gas Company and other public utility companies and companies owning the stock or securities of the public utility companies.

2. To acquire and hold the securities of companies engaged in the business of managing or operating or supervising the management or operation of public utility companies and of the companies doing a general construction, engineering or contracting business with Public Utility Company and other companies.

The *New York Times*, on January 11, 1929, stated that at the start The United Corporation became interested in companies with securities valued at more than $2 billion and that financial circles were anticipating many important readjustments of holdings in eastern states, this belief being based on the existing relations of the Bonbright interests to the Electric Bond & Share group and of the Morgan interests to the Mellon Utilities, including the Koppers Company as well as the United Gas Improvement Corporation.

The Federal Trade Commission *loc. cit.* reported:

The United Corporation is the largest of the type of corporation superimposed upon electric and gas operating and holding companies during the recent boom which broke in 1929. This type is the so-called "investment" company which does not acquire the majority of the stock of holding or operating companies and which does not openly take control of the companies in which they invest. They appear to have been formed primarily as vehicles for the working out of mergers and regroupings.

Previous large utility corporations included numerous groups of operating companies in widely separated areas which generally were not physically interconnected. These companies were controlled either through the actual ownership of a majority of voting stock as in the case of the North American Company, or through the control of voting proxies, as in the case of Electric Bond & Share Company and Middle West Utilities Company. The familiar argument for this type of aggregation was the advantage of diversification of economic conditions arising from a wide variety of localities including different industrial, commercial and agricultural characteristics. This diversification was held strongly, to insure a greater steadiness in the use of power and, therefore, greater stability of earnings.

Conditions in the stock markets beginning in the last quarter of 1929, brought mergers in the electric and gas utility fields to a practical standstill.

(George Roberts, partner in the Bonbright law firm of Winthrop, Stimson, Putnam & Roberts, was quoted by the Federal Trade Commission as saying that American Superpower, a company controlled by Bonbright and Co., was the largest stockholder of The United Corporation and that J. P. Morgan & Co. was the second largest. In referring to American Superpower as being controlled by Bonbright & Co., Mr. Roberts said that as long as the stockholders included friends of Bonbright & Co. and those who had confidence in Bonbright & Co., the latter would control general policies. Federal Trade Commission, *loc. cit.*)

12. The United Corporation held directly more than 20 percent of the total stock of three large public utility holding companies: The United Gas Improvement Company, of which it held 25.1 percent, and the Niagara Hudson Power Corporation and Columbia Gas & Electric Corporation, in each of which it held 21.7 percent. It also held stock in two other companies in which it and The American Superpower Corporation, The Electric Bond & Share Company, and the United Gas Improvement Company held a combined total of more than 25 percent. These two were the Public Service Corporation of New Jersey and The Commonwealth & Southern Corporation. (Federal Trade Commission, *loc. cit.*)

According to the Federal Trade Commission (*op. cit.*, part 78):

It has been stated by an official of The Commonwealth & Southern Corporation that those who are mostly responsible for the organization of that company were B. C. Cobb and T. W. Martin. At that time B. C. Cobb was a director of each of the four companies which as hereinafter explained were consolidated in 1930 and president of three of them. T. W. Martin was at that time president of the Southeastern Power & Light Company and one of the directors of Commonwealth Power Corporation. It appears, however, that others who were closely identified with The United Corporation, The American Superpower Corporation, Electric Bond & Share Company, The United Gas Improvement Company, Bonbright & Company, Inc., were active in the organization of The Commonwealth & Southern Corporation.

13. It seems, however, that in this particular case the adverse reaction to New York management was unjustified. Tippy himself had been trying for some time to arrange for Arthur's transfer to Consumers Power, but had been unable to get him. Arthur, a native of North Carolina and a graduate of Clemson Agricultural College with a degree in electrical engineering, worked for Westinghouse for seven years before joining the Commonwealth group of companies. His first job with Commonwealth was as commercial manager with the Northern Ohio Traction & Light Company in Akron. After five years, he advanced to manager of electric sales and distribution. In 1929, he was assigned to the C&S staff in New York. At Consumers Power, he served as vice-president from April 1934 until his death on January 3, 1952, and as a director from 1949 until 1952.

14. In addition to Karn, of Consumers Power, Willkie's new directors were Preston A. Arkwright, president of Georgia Power Company; A. C. Blinn, general manager of The Ohio Edison Company; Jo Conn Guild, Jr., president of The Tennessee Electric Power Company; and R. S. Wallace, president of the Central Illinois Light Co.

15. For many years Eugene V. Debs was the Presidential candidate of the Socialist Party. His biggest triumph at the polls came in 1920, when he managed to get a little over 900,000 votes. By the 1930s, Norman Thomas had become the quadrennial Socialist candidate. In 1932, despite the Depression, he was able to muster just short of 900,000 votes. By the end of World War II, so many socialist concepts had been incorporated into the platforms and practices of the Democratic and even the Republican parties that the Socialist Party as an entity ceased to be even a minor political force.

16. Congress passed Norris's first Muscle Shoals bill in 1928, but President Coolidge vetoed it. The Tennessee Valley Authority was enacted in 1934 (see Chapter 18).

17. These were the general conditions. Now the question arises: What did business and professional people, and particularly public utilities, do about this situation?

Beginning in 1919, a series of state committees on public utility information was organized throughout the country. The number reached twenty-eight by 1925, and they covered thirty-six states. The names of these groups varied from state to state. Some of the typical names were Committee on Public Utility Information, Public Utility Information Bureau, and Public Service Information Committee. These information bureaus assembled, initiated, and circulated publicity desired by the business-managed utilities. They were financed by contributions from the holding companies, as well as the utility operating companies in the particular territories. Normally, each bureau functioned under the direction of a full-time director, who was especially selected for his qualifications in the conduct of publicity work. These committees functioned under the supervision and with the direct personal assistance of leading utility executives.

In Michigan, the first director of this type of work was Henry H. Tinkham, a newspaperman of long experience, who was subsequently employed by Consumers Power Company as director of public relations. The underlying objective of this work was to create more favorable public opinion with respect to utility companies and their activity. Attempts were made to disseminate information so that the public would become more aware of the nature of the public utility business and its accomplishments.

Under the auspices of the Michigan Bureau of Public Utility Information, the utilities throughout the state had an annual open-house week in the communities served by them. The general public, service clubs, school classes, and other groups and individuals were invited during this week to make tours of the company properties and plants.

In the public utility business, good public relations are perhaps more vital than in other businesses. Such companies are commonly monopolies, and customers and public alike often have been critical of their prices and service almost as a matter of principle. In addition, utilities have been targets for political attacks. It is scarcely surprising that utilities took advantage of every opportunity to present themselves in a favorable light. Activities of the information bureaus, however, did not meet with universal acceptance, and undoubtedly there were areas in which the utility operators carried things to extremes. For instance, the utilities were accused of trying to influence the content of school textbooks.

Revelation of so-called public utility propaganda efforts came as a by-product of an investigation into the "power trust" forced by certain so-called liberal senators. That earlier investigation by the Federal Trade Commission was directed chiefly at alleged monopolistic control of electric utilities by General Electric Company. Even though the resultant report was that in 1924 ". . . neither the General Electric Company nor any other single power interest, or group of allied power interests, substantially monopolized or controlled the generation, transmission and sale of electricity in the United States."

On February 28, 1927, Senator Walsh of Montana introduced a resolution for Senate investigations following a speech on capitalization of utilities. The investigation was to be directed at the growth of the light and power industry, the volume and character of security issues, and the operation of holding companies. Irsten Robert Barnes, in *The Economics of Public Utility Regulation* (New York: Crofts, 1942), says: "Almost as an afterthought, the resolution called for an investigation of the extent to which the industry was attempting to influence opinion against municipal or public ownership." There was considerable opposition to the resolution, but it was reported and recommended for adoption. Before its adoption, the resolution was amended so as to have the investigation conducted by the Federal Trade Commission.

The resulting investigation proved to be a long one. Bernard F. Weadock, John Weadock's nephew and business associate, left the firm of Weadock & Weadock of New York and moved to Washington. On January 6, 1930, after eighteen months of investigation by the Commission, the utilities were granted an opportunity to present their side of the picture. Bernard Weadock, as special counsel for the utilities, began his presentation by clearing up certain misconceptions regarding relations between the utilities and the schools. He showed that the material introduced into the schools, which had been said to be an attempt to propagandize schoolchildren, consisted of eight-page leaflets describing in a factual and scientific way the methods by which electricity is generated and distributed. He called attention to the fact that the only instance of controversial matter adduced lay in a few paragraphs in one leaflet, issued in but one of the states, which declared that private operation is better than public operation of utilities. He also pointed out that these leaflets had been made available to the schools at the request of teachers who knew their contents. In reviewing publicity activities of the utilities, Weadock declared that a great part of them were undertaken to offset the hostile campaign of the government-ownership advocates. He said:

> It is my plan to call your Honor's attention to the activities of certain groups already named in the record and to their effort toward public ownership and democratic control, centering upon the basic industries of the country, but particularly directing their attention, as a step in that larger program, upon the electric utilities of the country; and that these organizations are the League for Industrial Democracy, the National Popular Government League, the People's Legislative Service, and the Public Ownership League of America.

The presiding commissioner declared that the Federal Trade Commission was required to investigate only what the utilities had done and not what anyone else might have done. Mr. Weadock tried to point out that without a full and complete knowledge of the extent of these activities, including their publicity and their manner of injecting the different legislative bodies into this picture, it was incomplete. He concluded with the statement, "I say that every industry in the United States is under fire in this situation." The presiding commissioner, however, for technical reasons connected with the authorizing Senate resolution, refused to accept the exhibits which Weadock offered to him as proof of his assertions. All that the commissioner would accept was a list of the exhibits which he permitted in the record as "an undisputed list of those who had advocated government ownership."

Soon, open-house weeks were a thing of the past, and the work of the information bureaus also declined. Now, about the only time the public is invited to visit facilities of Consumers Power plants is at the time of the opening of a new plant or operation. However, there have been many occasions over the years when school groups, at their own request, have been permitted to tour company facilities.

18. This was not Pinchot's only error. As Forrest McDonald (*op. cit.*) points out, the hearings of the Federal Trade Commission at the same time were producing evidence that General Electric had been out of the power business since its sale of Electric Bond & Share in 1924, that the Mellon interests had sold their holdings to Cyrus Eaton in 1926, and that the House of Morgan had not begun its raids on utility holding companies until just a few months before the Pinchot pamphlet was published. As for Byllbesby, he had been dead since 1924. (Lest this totally discredit Pinchot, it must be emphasized that he performed a number of valuable services in other areas; he was, for instance, one of the country's earliest and most outstanding conservationists. His attack on privately owned utilities may have been motivated partly by the fact that he wanted the federal government to build dams not only for power but also for the dual function of irrigation.)

Chapter 16

1. That's what Harold L. Ickes, Roosevelt's Secretary of the Interior and the most militant among FDR's anti-utility brain trusters, once called Wendell Willkie in a wisecrack. The description was so astute that it is difficult to imagine it coming

from the mouth of a politician. Sure enough, Ickes had borrowed it from a news-paper columnist, Jay Franklin; so here it is, third hand, and back in the realm of journalism.

2. Delbert Ford, a showman at heart, has a phenomenal memory for what people say, and since Ford is a colorful speaker, the quotes he quotes tend to be just as colorful as his impressions. It was precisely because of Ford's talent to select the relevant and to phrase it pertinently that he turned out to be one of the best inter-view sources on recent Consumers Power history. Del, who looks like a com-pressed version of the actor William Holden—shorter and rounder, but with the same ski-jump nose and smile-crinkled ironic eyes—joined the Battle Creek United Appliance department in 1925 at the age of twenty after one abortive week at Albion College. His first job was sweeping off the sidewalk and hosing down the street first thing every morning. George Westerman was then in general charge of Consumers Power display, and Del eventually worked for him as assistant. When Westerman was promoted to director of display for Commonwealth & Southern, Ford became general supervisor of Consumers Power's display department, which in 1930 consisted of one man—himself—and has since grown to a staff of thirty-two. The department is in charge of seventy-five appliance showrooms and assists also in office design and all functions that involve stage management, such as plant dedications, open houses, shareholder meetings, parades, and floats. Ford retired in the summer of 1970, but remains Consumers Power consultant for special events.

3. Joseph Barnes, *Willkie* (New York: Simon and Schuster, 1952: © Joseph Barnes, 1952) a most delightful book, is the source not only of this quote but also of much other background material in this chapter, particularly about Willkie's early life.

4. *Ibid.*

5. *Bay City Times*, June 1940.

6. Barnes, *op. cit.*

7. It was decided that these state companies should have only three classes of secu-rities: bonds secured by mortgages, preferred stock with shares of equal rank in case of liquidation, and common stock of one class. It was also proposed at that time to eliminate all intermediate or subpublic utility holding companies and as many of the nonfunctioning companies as possible. In order that each operating company would be in a position, as far as could be foreseen, to finance itself com-pletely with sufficient working capital, C&S was to increase its investment in the common stocks of the operating companies and, where such existed, surrender as much second preferred and unfunded debt as possible. Rail operations, which often showed losses, were to be separated into distinct companies, thus removing their burden from the gas and electric operations and rates.

8. Interview with E. V. Sayles, summer 1970, in Consumers Power Company files.

9. Interview with Delbert Ford, summer 1970, in Consumers Power Company files.

10. Interview with E. V. Sayles, summer 1970, in Consumers Power Company files.

11. This quote has been cleaned up somewhat for the sake of propriety. For its orig-inal version, assuming you can't guess it, see author's interview with George Clark, summer 1970, in Consumers Power Company files.

12. F. Clever Bald, *Michigan in Four Centuries* (New York: Harper & Row, 1961).

13. *Ibid.*

14. Almost immediately after the bank holiday was declared, Congress passed an emer-gency act that gave the Controller of the Currency power to examine all national

banks and to open those appearing to be sound; conservators were appointed for those banks in less trouble, and they were permitted to release a percentage of their deposits.

In many cases, large depositors waived their rights to immediate payment of a portion of the amount which they would be entitled to receive. As a result, many banks soon were able to pay off the smaller depositors. The Controller of the Currency declared that this self-denial by the large depositors represented "one of the most outstanding public-spirited actions coming before this office during the several years of the emergency." Consumers Power Company cooperated with banks in this situation and later assigned some of its claims in the establishment of new banks.

At the beginning of the bank holiday, Consumers Power made do with safe-deposit boxes and in some cases arranged for the use of money chests in various bank vaults. Soon there was a rumor that the conservators would be required to freeze such moneys, and so a plan was worked out whereby all the money from the different areas in the state would be transferred to Jackson under state police protection. This was done, and the cash so accumulated amounted to about $500,-000. It was put in several safes in the general office, special insurance was taken out, and there were officers who stayed with it in the building all night. This currency was then transferred to the Detroit Bank as a step in its getting to the Federal Reserve Bank so that credit could be given in New York.

Some banks opened with certain percentages of deposits available, and receivers were appointed for those which did not open. During this period, Consumers Power had no real checking accounts for some time. Employees were paid by check, but the checks were cashed at company offices from cash that had been taken in.

The first payday of this sort occurred on February 16, the third day of the bank holiday declared by the Governor. It was necessary on this occasion to liquidate government securities and to have actual currency shipped from New York to meet the payrolls. Liquidation of the bank accounts went on for a period of years. Consumers Power ultimately realized 80.65 percent of the deposits.

15. Interview with Louis McDowell, now executive assistant to Anson Hedgecock. vice-president for divisions and customer service. McDowell served in the credit and collections department at that time. He had joined the company in 1928.

16. The financing situation also improved, though not quite so soon. Customer ownership, as a program, had ended in 1933 after taking a turn for the worse in 1931. (Herman H. Koelbel, vice-president in charge of the program, resigned his post at this point and was made head of the new cooperative merchandising program.) When in 1936 market conditions improved and it became apparent that the preferred stock outstanding carried a higher dividend rate than conditions warranted, steps were taken at a stockholders' meeting on January 18, 1937, to retire all the outstanding shares of 6 percent, 6.6 percent, and 7 percent preferred stock. On March 20, 1937, all the dividends on those issues were to end, rights of the holders of the stock were to cease and terminate, and the holders were to be entitled to receive only their redemption price of $105. The company deposited the aggregate redemption price with The National City Bank of New York, irrevocably in trust for the several holders of the preferred stock, payable on or after March 20, 1937, to the respective holders of the shares upon surrender of the certificates.

In January of 1937, an application was made to the New York Stock Exchange for listing the new Consumers Power Company $4.50 preferred stock. This was in line with previous policy, for in October 1935 the directors decided to apply for a listing of the first lien and unifying mortgage bonds on the New York Stock Exchange.

The minutes for the 1930s are full of items bearing upon new financing, indicating applications made both to the Michigan Public Service Commission and to the Securities and Exchange Commission. At times the two regulating bodies were not in complete accord, and the company had to make adjustments in the various programs of financing in order to satisfy both regulations.

17. The following is a summary for the years 1927 to 1936 as shown in the Consumers Power Company Report to the Stockholders for the year ended December 31, 1936:

Year	Gross revenue	Operating expenses provision for retirement reserve and taxes	Interest on funded debt and other income deductions	Dividends on preferred stock	Balance
1927	$26,612,448.96	$15,259,064.58	$2,552,943.63	$3,349,334.52	$5,451,106.23
1928	30,464,127.41	17,033,896.85	2,826,026.08	3,551,863.18	7,052,341.30
1929	33,420,538.87	18,520,076.45	2,853,322.80	3,752,926.55	8,294,213.07
1930	32,512,048.80	17,394,155.11	3,161,390.44	3,882,535.62	8,073,967.63
1931	30,860,143.00	15,785,320.90	3,928,671.98	4,121,862.31	7,024,287.81
1932	27,931,248.88	14,491,977.88	4,498,059.96	4,165,000.95	4,776,210.09
1933	26,000,000.19	14,371,658.41	4,660,527.41	4,168,437.04	2,799,377.33
1934	28,685,138.05	16,678,876.31	4,793,497.32	4,189,839.21	3,022,925.21
1935	30,477,295.12	17,493,271.58	4,990,614.12	4,207,954.64	3,785,454.78
1936	33,051,899.73	19,732,825.78	4,283,422.35	4,208,001.40	4,827,650.20

The general earnings picture at C&S was even grimmer. Earnings had plummeted from 40 cents a share in 1929 to 12 cents a share in 1932. By 1933, C&S showed a loss of 1 cent per share. In 1934 this loss grew to 5 cents per share. Earnings turned around in 1935 and then climbed back to 13 cents a share in 1936.

18. These were the figures from 1933 to 1940:

Year	Number of electric customers	Electric sales in kilowatthours	Number of gas customers	Gas sales in cubic feet
1933	309,799	732,018,395	138,316	5,207,294,600
1934	329,681	865,132,787	162,478	6,141,604,800
1935	344,115	1,014,116,860	171,472	6,660,291,100
1936	364,406	1,236,879,072	182,237	7,669,174,100
1937	392,857	1,434,445,087	192,761	8,904,645,800
1938	425,424	1,250,931,440	195,108	8,391,376,400
1939	446,039	1,442,258,814	201,302	9,244,337,700
1940	467,163	1,751,991,019	209,781	10,699,588,700

19. This rate plan was devised in 1932 and made effective by Alabama Power Company and Georgia Power Company. It was also proposed for adoption by The Tennessee Electric Power Company. The plan attracted nationwide attention, and by 1936 it had been approved by the utility commissions of thirty-three states. It set up two separate, distinct residential rates that were effective coincidently. One of the rates was designed as the immediate rate, and the other as the objective rate. The objective rate was naturally lower than the immediate rate. Base sales were established for each customer by applying the fundamental rate to the customer's consumption for each month of the year preceding the adoption of the plan. Whenever a customer increased his use so that his bill, figured under the objective rate, was equal to, or greater than, his base bill for the month, the objective rate was automatically applied. The plan was utilized by Consumers Power in 1936 and applied not only to the electric business but also to portions of the gas territories.

20. Edison Pioneers were those who worked with Thomas Edison prior to 1886, while Edison Pioneer Associates were in the Edison organization between 1886 and 1900.

21. In 1935 the general engineering department developed a new fabricated steel type of bus structure — "bus" being short for bus bar (or omnibus bar), which in electric parlance refers to a carrier of current. This new type, which had many advantages, differed distinctly from other metal-enclosed structures in that it was so designed that it could be assembled from structural materials available in the ordinary steel-fabricating shops and could be easily erected in the field. In that respect it was entirely different from the so-called metal-clad structure produced by equipment manufacturers, which was fabricated at the factory and shipped complete as a unit with equipment installed. Furthermore, the new bus structure permitted use of any manufacturer's equipment. The structure consisted of a steel framework enclosed by a finished type of furniture steel with doors that provided accessibility to equipment. The designs were partially standardized, and several standard widths and heights were used. The doors on one side of the structure served in place of a separate switchboard panel, and upon them were mounted such items as control switches and relays. Thus the necessity for a separate switchboard and costly control cable and conduit was eliminated. Use of the innovation spread rapidly, principally because of its ease of installation and its low cost, which was approximately one-half the cost of previous, conventional types.

Another technical problem tackled during this period was that of melting sleet from transmission lines. It had been recognized for several years that sleet melting was desirable, but it was not until the mid-1930s that spare capacity in generators, transformers, and transmission lines was available for this purpose on the Consumers Power Company system. During 1932 and 1933, a plan was formulated and tests made on the Consumers Power Company transmission system which indicated that sleet melting from the transmission lines could be carried on successfully. Strangely enough, after the necessary preparations were made, there were no ice storms of any consequence, with the exception of a few deposits during the latter months of 1935. These were not serious sleet conditions, but they did present opportunities to test out the effectiveness of the sleet-melting scheme.

As a rule, heavy deposits of ice occur with rain or mist when temperatures are but a few degrees below freezing. This condition may continue for several hours, even up to half a day or longer in extreme cases. It is during this period of formation that sleet can be melted to the best advantage because it is usually followed by dropping temperatures with increasing winds, both of which reduce the effectiveness of melting operations. It is necessary that the ice be removed from the line during its formation in order to prevent trouble on the line. That's because lines, while designed to withstand heavy ice loading, cannot practically also be designed to withstand the high winds which almost invariably follow an ice storm.

The Consumers Power Company system was organized to melt sleet on all the 140,000-volt main transmission lines in the Eastern division, as well as on the 22,000-volt lines supplying the Bay City and Saginaw substations. In the Western division, the company was prepared to melt sleet on the 140,000-volt lines out of Grand Rapids to Kalamazoo, Croton, Hardy, and Muskegon. It was also possible during light-load periods to extend the melting on the 140,000-volt lines from the Eastern division to points as far south as Charlotte and Jackson in the Southern division. Thus, under favorable conditions, it was possible to protect a good portion of the main system from severe ice storms.

The actual process of melting sleet was not especially complicated. For the most part, a 20,000-kilowatt turbogenerator was used to supply the current, as at the Saginaw River steam plant in the Eastern division and at the Wealthy Street steam plant in the Western division. In order to melt sleet, a line was first taken out of service and short-circuited at the far end from the generator station. This, of course, requires at least two lines feeding the substation; otherwise, service would be interrupted. The 20,000-kilowatt generator was then connected to feed directly into the line. The voltage on the generator was raised, which caused the current to flow through the short-circuited line. The current used on most lines would run from 400 to 500 amperes, which caused enough heating effect to raise the temperature of the wire. This resulted in melting the ice coating. The length of time required depended on a number of factors, for example, the amount of current, the size of the wire, the outside temperature of the air, and the wind velocity. As a general rule, fairly good results were obtained in about one-half hour, although more time was required if temperatures were considerably below freezing, accompanied by a high wind.

22. The Clarendon Township underground line operated at 2,400 volts, single phase, with one side grounded. The cable, a development of the Anaconda Wire & Cable Company, was plowed into the ground by means of a cable plow designed especially for that purpose. The cable consisted essentially of an inner No. 6 solid-copper conductor, insulated with 0.10-inch impregnated paper and with an overlapping of oiled and moisture-impervious sealing tape and a corrugated, impervious cylindrical copper sheath used as a grounded return conductor. Over the copper sheath was a nonmetallic protective cover of the Duraseal type; except at road crossings, it was installed on private rights-of-way at a depth of 18 to 22 inches. At road crossings the cable was installed in a 1¼-inch iron pipe under the traveled way and set at a depth so that it would not be distrubed by any normal future grading of the highway. Elsewhere in the highway limits the cable was protected by a 1½ by 6-inch plank laid directly over it. The cable was first reeled out and laid on the ground in the approximate location of the installation. Then the cable was threaded through the plow so that as the plow was pulled along, it also guided the cable into the trench. The cost was $2,357.23 per mile, exclusive of the right-of-way. Originally, there were twenty customers, resulting in a per-customer cost of $383.05. About a year after the installation, a fault developed.

In trying to locate this fault, a second fault developed. In July 1936, a third fault appeared. A fourth appeared in December 1940, and a fifth in July 1945. Ultimately, it was decided to abandon the use of underground lines for rural extensions.

Chapter 17

1. Interview with Mr. and Mrs. Walter Carven by E. Hardy Luther, sometime in the late 1950s.
2. The *Au Sable News,* October 1923.
3. George A. Clark, who retired in 1958 as general supervisor of electric distribution, was deeply involved in Consumers Power's rural electrification program. He devised a system by which it was possible to eliminate one lightning arrester and one fuse cutout on each transformer. This was done by replacing the old delta system (in which none of the conductors were grounded) with a four-wire grounded system. As he explains it, "Then you could hook up a transformer between one of the three hot wires and the neutral grounded conductor, and in that way you could eliminate one fuse cutout and one lightning arrester every transformer, which meant maybe $35 to $40 per transformer, and you get four of those to the mile. There's a couple of hundred bucks right there." At the same time, higher-strength conductors replacing the original copper conductors made it possible to stretch the line between towers up to 350 to 400 feet instead of 125 or 150 feet, without the line's sagging.

    Clark, unlike others, was always sold on bringing electricity to farmers. He made a bet with Dan Karn one day that the company was going to build over 3,600 miles of rural line. Karn bet him a new hat. "Well," says Clark, "we built 3,800 miles and I got a new hat from Oppenheim's." (Interview with George A. Clark, spring 1970, in Consumers Power Company files.)
4. H. J. Gallagher, "100,000th Farm," an unpublished manuscript.
5. From 1929 to 1935 the truck was used at 255 demonstrations, attended by 22,179 people. In addition to the public demonstrations, 206 electric schools were conducted, with a total attendance count of 8,812. Other activities included forty-one radio broadcasts, nine fair exhibitions, and participation in twenty-six county agricultural agents' conferences.
6. The refund was equivalent to a free extension on the basis of an average of ten customers per mile, or to an average cost to the customer of $100 each on the basis of five customers per mile.
7. The main jobs of the farm service were, and still are, largely to educate farmers about the economics and other advantages of electric service and to develop an aggressive dealer organization for the sale of equipment. To conduct the work out through the Consumers Power territory, rural service engineers were placed in the various divisions. These men, mostly agricultural engineering graduates, work with farmers, county agricultural agents, county home demonstration agents, high school agricultural teachers, and 4-H clubs in educational programs determined cooperatively by Michigan State University and the company.

    The educational program includes various types of group meetings, demonstration farms, and field projects with high school students and 4-H clubs. An essential part of the educational program involves using dealer equipment in the course of the demonstrations and discussions and making the dealer an active part of the program. Advertising, publicity articles, personal contacts, and group meetings with dealers further augment the company's relations with the dealer. In addition, many of the

farm visits that the rural service engineers make to assist the farmer with his individual problems result in dealer sales.

The farm service activities are a definite benefit to the farmer. In fact, they constitute virtually the same kind of farm electrification program conducted by land-
grant colleges, with the big difference that land-grant colleges generally lack
sufficient personnel to render as complete a service as is rendered by Consumers
Power Company.

8. Interview with George A. Clark, spring 1970, in Consumers Power Company files.
9. In March 1939 the *Grand Rapids Press* commented:

If a saving sense of humor existed among the economic planners in Washington,
they might avoid some of their inconsistencies. The current blast from the rural
electrification administration against a Michigan power firm is a ludicrous case in
point.

The REA, it seems, is exceedingly wroth because the private utility in this state
is offering to serve farmers at rates which are lower than those which the REA
Cooperatives can offer. Ignoring the fact that private farm rates have been the same
as city rates for 10 years — long before the REA came into existence — the administration attempts to create the impression that the power firm has to be condemned for
giving the people power at low cost.

The inconsistency of the situation is to be found in the frequent utterances from
Washington demanding lower rates by consumers on the part of the private utilities.
Government competition, it has been widely heralded, would provide a yardstick
which would measure the private rates, and force them down to a point at which
the customer might enjoy the benefits of service to a larger extent.

Now that a Michigan utility is discovered to be offering low rates, a howl goes up
in Washington to the effect that they are not fair to the government sponsored lines.
The REA Associations, furthermore, are facing the prospect of raising their rates
in order to make ends meet. . . .

Chapter 18

1. According to Henry Gamett, *American Names* (Washington: Public Affairs Press,
   1947), the name Muscle Shoals derives from the fact that many marine bivalve
   mollusks are found in that area of the Tennessee River, just south of the Tennessee
   border. On the face of it, "Muscle" appears to be a misspelling of "mussel." Ety-
   mologists know, however, that the form "mussel" is derived from the Latin *muscul-
   us*, meaning "muscle," and anyone who has ever tried to chew an overcooked
   mussel can appreciate the reason for this derivation.

2. One of the biggest reasons why the young utility industry resorted to holding
   companies was that its securities were hard to sell: new and somewhat speculative
   enterprises always face financial and promotional problems. Centralized corporate
   management of scattered properties provided an answer to both.

   In this connection it is interesting to note that the congressional and Federal
   Trade Commission investigations of the utility business in the 1920s and 1930s
   were a direct outgrowth of earlier investigations of other types of businesses,
   arising primarily from antitrust investigations. Indeed, the first investigation of
   the utilities business was based on this antitrust premise and came from the use
   of the holding company as a means of furthering the use of manufactured equipment as exemplified by the interest in utilities held by equipment companies.

In the early years of the electric business, after inventions by Edison and others had made the central station possible, the great electric equipment companies such as Westinghouse and the General Electric predecessors, notably Thomson-Houston Electric Company, had difficulty in securing the desired market for their station and distribution equipment. Financial interests were doubtful of the success of this new and untried experiment, and operating utilities lacked the confidence of the investing public necessary to secure their credit and enable them to place their stock and bond issues. So the equipment companies decided to take a hand themselves and give financial support to potential and struggling clients or, if necessary, even to create such clients.

The Westinghouse Company took public utility stocks, bonds, and notes in payment for equipment in order to lend support to utilities. Thus, it became a "parent company" for various public utility enterprises.

A different policy was followed by General Electric and its predecessors—perhaps an even more successful policy—which was to form separate holding companies for public utilities and even promote the formation of new utilities. These holding companies were then controlled by the equipment company through ownership of all or a majority of their common stocks.

During the period shortly before and shortly after World War I, the preoccupation with physical growth that had marked the industry's earlier years gave way to regulatory problems. As recognition of the need for public regulation of such a naturally monopolistic service became widespread, state regulatory commissions, which had been set up by legislative action mostly in the decade from 1907–1917, began to raise questions concerning the propriety of controlling holding companies. The Supreme Court in 1923 ruled that a state commission, unless there appeared to be bad faith or the exercise of improper discretion, had no power to alter or examine the reasonableness of the terms of a contract made by a subsidiary company for services performed by its own parent holding company.

This view was virtually reversed in later decisions, as the battle raged between those who felt there was a gap in the jurisdiction of state bodies that could be remedied only by extension of federal controls and those who felt state commissions had ample powers of protection through strict regulation and control of accounting for operating expenses.

The main argument against public control over utility holding companies is based on the premise that the only excuse for regulation of utilities lies in the public interest in adequate service at reasonable rates. The argument goes that the control of the holding company has little or no bearing upon the regulation of the service and rates of the operating company. To be sure, other people, the investing public, for example, have other interests in the utilities that may, on occasion, require some degree of public protection. But these other interests are not unlike those in steel, automobile, or airplane manufacturing companies and in many other types of business. It is only the actual consumer who requires the special protection against unrestrained action by a public utility. The utility holding company, by its nature, is not an operating company and does not supply the consuming public with service or charge the public any rates for service.

It seems a bit incongruous that the monopolistic phase of these investigations should have been the starting point, for against the somewhat familiar antimonopoly background, there remained almost unquestioned a regulatory principle that public utilities are natural monopolies. The economics of the business are such that the public is best served by a limited monopoly, and the fundamental underlying principle of public utility regulation is the exercising of monopoly power under adequate and effective government regulation. Thus the situation differed from that surrounding the earlier campaigns against steel, oil, and tobacco trusts. "But," as *Public Utility Reports* commented, "it is doubtful if the public at large understood the difference."

Further, when emotional overtones and suggestions of public ownership are extracted, it might well be that the residue of the political struggle against the power industry was essentially a fear of size—causing an attack on bigness as such.

The problem then became one of retaining monopoly, an accepted reason for public regulation, but one of keeping it in relatively small local units, in spite of claims of the many advantages of large-scale centralization.

For detailed analyses of this subject, see *Federal Utility Regulations, Annotated* (Public Utility Reports, Inc., 1942), as well as James C. Bonbright and Gardiner C. Means, *The Holding Company* (New York: McGraw-Hill, 1932).

3. In 1929, under Cobb, there were still 165 C&S companies. By 1935, under Willkie, the number had shrunk to eleven operating units that owned some twenty-five companies. For the most part these subsidiaries were continued in order to hold real estate or franchises or to meet mortgage requirements. Two other companies owned by The Commonwealth & Southern Corporation (Delaware) were, in effect, asset-realization companies for twenty subsidiaries owning transportation, ice, water, and other properties and securities, thus making a combined total of sixty companies, including The Commonwealth & Southern Corporation, both Delaware and New York.

Corporate simplification went on apace in the fall of 1935 and early in 1936, as shown by two items in the minutes of the directors' meeting held on January 14, 1936. The Iosco Land Company, which had been established by the Loud interests and later became a landowning company for Consumers Power, ended its corporate existence on November 6, 1935, with the conveyance of its holdings to Consumers Power Company. Also, Electrical Interconnections, Incorporated, which had been organized in connection with the interchange of energy between Consumers Power Company and The Detroit Edison Company through Cement City, ceased to exist on November 20, 1935. Its entire capital assets were sold to the two operating companies; Consumers Power Company thereby acquired 11.46 miles of transmission line, and The Detroit Edison Company acquired 12.87 miles of line.

For more details, see The Commonwealth & Southern Corporation, "Outline of History and Development," Feb. 26, 1935, in Consumers Power Company files.

4. Roosevelt's first-term platform also called for regulation of the security and commodity exchanges. The resultant Securities Act of 1933, better known as the Truth in Securities Act, called for the disclosure of material facts regarding all securities publicly offered and sold in interstate commerce. It was followed in 1934 by the Securities Exchange Act, which was further designed to eliminate abuses in the securities markets and to make available to the public current and sufficient information concerning the management and financial condition of corporations whose securities are traded in the securities markets, so as to enable the investor to act intelligently in making or retaining his investments and in exercising his rights as a security holder.

5. More specifically, the purpose of the Tennessee Valley Authority was to stimulate

the development of agriculture and industry in the Tennessee Valley, to improve navigation of the Tennessee River, and to control the floodwaters of both the Tennessee and the Mississippi Rivers. The incidental power generated at the TVA's multipurpose dams was authorized for distribution and sale to private corporations, states, counties, municipalities, corporations, partnerships, and individuals, with preference given to states, counties, municipalities, and cooperative organizations. See *United States Code*, 1946 ed. (Washington: GPO, 1947), vol. 2.

As it turned out, the Tennessee Valley Authority has become impressively successful in its own right—that is, apart from considerations of the principle of private versus public ownership. The scheme has become a model for similar projects in many parts of the world. TVA, which now has thirty-one dams in its system, is unique among federal agencies. Its headquarters are not in Washington but right in its own territory, and it functions as an independent corporation, almost as if it were privately owned. In addition to deriving income from the sale of power and fertilizers, it has issued its own bonds to finance expansions. Interestingly enough, private enterprise has become involved in the scheme. Some of the dams are owned by the Aluminum Company of America and are only operated by the TVA.

Hydroelectric power is no longer the TVA's main product. By far the largest share of the power it now sells—some 70 percent—is steam-generated. Total capacity of the system is in the area of 12 million kilowatts. A navigation channel, 630 miles long and with a minimum depth of 9 feet, extends from the river's mouth to Knoxville and has resulted in a tremendous increase in river traffic. The region, once an Appalachia, is now prosperous.

Only in recent years has the TVA known political peace. During the Eisenhower administration, the Atomic Energy Commission, which until then had bought all power for its Oak Ridge installation from the TVA, made a deal to obtain additional power with a privately owned utility group controlled by Edgar H. Dixon and Eugene A. Yates. This became a bone of contention between advocates of public and private power, and after much congressional battling, the Dixon-Yates contract was eventually voided. In 1960, the TVA attained maturity when it gained the right to float its own bond issues rather than seek congressional appropriations. In turn, its area of operation was sharply delineated; it cannot now expand beyond these borders.

6. The other two original directors were Dr. Arthur E. Morgan and Dr. Harcourt A. Morgan (no relation).

7. At the end of 1932, the total assets of Commonwealth & Southern and its subsidiaries amounted to $1,136,542,942.

8. Lilienthal credited Willkie with this innovation. See Joseph Barnes, *Willkie* (New York: Simon and Schuster, 1952), p. 65.

9. *Ibid.*

10. *Ibid.*

11. "Wendell L. Willkie," *Fortune*, May 1937.

12. Willkie's technical position on this issue was summarized in an address he gave over Station WEAF and the Red Network of the National Broadcasting Company (as opposed to the Blue Network, with obviously no political or moral connotations implied in these designations). The address was reprinted under the title "The Utilities and the Tennessee Valley Authority" in the *Au Sable News*, April 1936. Willkie said:

Why am I talking to you and what is it I am seeking? Merely this—that Congress define the limits of the operations of the TVA instead of letting it go its way unhampered and uncontrolled. I proposed at the last session of Congress and I again propose—

First—That the TVA in its utility operations be required to pay taxes at the same rate and on the same basis of property valuation as the private utilities;

Second—That it be required to keep a uniform system of accounts such as is required of the utility companies;

Third—That it be required to charge rates for the electric energy which it sells so as to produce a fair rate of return on the value of the property which it uses in that business;

Fourth—That before it duplicates the transmission or distribution lines of companies already in the business that it be required to condemn the property thus sought to be duplicated and pay the companies owning such properties the value of the same as determined by a just tribunal;

Fifth—That it be required to charge uniform rates to all customers of the same class and file such rates in the same manner as utilities are required to do, either with the public utility commissions of the states or the Federal Power Commission at Washington.

In the same address, Willkie said that the question naturally arose as to why the United States was developing electricity and entering the field of private business. He asked whether there was not already an adequate supply of electricity available in the territory and whether the power companies were not supplying service to the people at uniform and reasonable rates. He said, "I know if I answer these questions you will think me self-interested and prejudiced. Therefore, I shall call as my witness a man whom no one would accuse of being a friend of the power companies."

He then cited comments made by Franklin D. Roosevelt on June 1, 1931, at French Lick, Indiana, before a conference of governors. Roosevelt had said, "In northern Alabama they have all the power in the world at a very cheap cost," and he had referred to the Alabama rule that ". . . just because a man happened to have been born and brought up on a farm in southern Alabama was no reason for penalizing him greatly over his cousin or neighbor who happened to have been brought up in the northern part of the state. . . ." Willkie explained that as a result of the rules of the Alabama commission, "rates were made uniform throughout the state for farmers and city dwellers." He further explained that the organization of which he was president was "interested in the power companies in Alabama, Georgia and Tennessee, and the methods of operation and the rates in all three of those states are uniform and power is cheap. Therefore, we can apply the President's statement to the operation in all three states."

Willkie further said that the reason the TVA desired to go into the electric business was that they believed, or pretended to believe, that they could sell electric energy more cheaply than private power companies could or even would. He said that in pursuance of that policy at Tupelo, Mississippi, the government put into effect rates 50 to 60 percent of those of the private power companies, thereby greatly increasing the use of electric energy by the ordinary domestic consumer. He did not dispute the increase: "If they gave the power to the domestic consumer, he would still use more." It was at this point that he raised—and answered—the question as to who was paying the Tupelo bill.

13. "Wendell L. Willkie," *Fortune,* May 1937.
14. Barnes, *op. cit.*
15. Roosevelt's "seven TVA's bill" called for the "legislation for national planning and development of natural resources" through an Atlantic seaboard authority spanning the East from Maine to Florida; a Great Lakes–Ohio Valley authority; a Missouri River authority; an Arkansas Valley authority; a Columbia Valley authority for the Pacific Northwest; and a Southwestern authority centered on the Colorado River basin.

    The story went—and it may well have been a vicious rumor—that the reason Roosevelt attacked the utilities with a passion that often seemed highly personal was that in 1928, before running for Governor of New York, he had asked Howard C. Hopson, of Associated Gas and Electric, for a top-executive job and that Hopson had not only rejected Roosevelt's offer of association but also ridiculed it. On the other side of the coin, Roosevelt, in private, sometimes claimed that the underlying motivation of his antibusiness legislation was to save capitalism from itself. "One of my principal tasks," he wrote to Newton D. Baker shortly before the Tupelo speech, "is to prevent bankers and businessmen from committing suicide!" Another interpretation of Roosevelt's economic-political stance, which changed considerably over the years, is that economic theory was far less important to him than political fact: he pursued those policies which promised to produce the most votes, and he was probably hopeful that things would balance off in the long run and work out for the best. Roosevelt was at once the most familiar and most enigmatic of Presidents. Despite all his fireside chats, incessant press conferences, and apparent camaraderies with intimates, he was his own best-kept secret, and despite all the literature on him he still is. Like most political leaders, he was probably neither so much a villain as his enemies made him out to be nor quite the saint that his supporters claimed he was.
16. Willkie's official comment, quoted here in part from the *Consumers Power News,* September 1939, was this:

    > With the purchase of these properties, the government acquires, at about 80 percent of its real value, one of the best electrical services in the world. I sincerely hope that our former customers in the State of Tennessee will continue to enjoy the benefits which The Tennessee Electric Power Company originally made possible. Whether or not the quality of service is maintained, these customers will, of course, enjoy the lower rates made possible by government subsidy—but they and all the people in the United States, will pay the higher taxes which tax-exempt and heavily subsidized government operations inevitably require.
    > We sell these properties with regret. We have been forced to do so because we could not stay in business against this subsidized government competition. . . .
    > From now on, this business is in the hands of governmental agencies. The participation of private management and private investment is at an end. Another business is removed from the tax rolls. While this sale does not represent the true value of this investment, at least, we have received enough to make full payment to the owners of the bonds and preferred stock. The common stockholders, principally The Commonwealth & Southern Corporation, are taking all of the loss.

17. *Ibid.* (The *Consumers Power News* is the successor of the company's *Au Sable News* and is still its house organ today.)

Chapter 19

1. Another steam plant, this one on the Kalamazoo River near Comstock had been "put on the line" just two months earlier, in May 1940, with two 35,000-kilowatt turbogenerators instead of only one, as originally planned. This installation was named after the late Bryce E. Morrow, who had replaced T. A. Kenney as head of the Consumers Power transmission department when the latter was reassigned to become B. C. Cobb's assistant in the New York office. Morrow came to Michigan from the Hudson River Electric Power Company in New York State, where he had at one time been Kenney's boss.

2. Interview with Delbert Ford, summer 1970.

3. Typical of Willkie's style was a speech he gave on February 28, 1938, before the Economic Club of Detroit, shortly after the Supreme Court had stopped the injunctions against TVA. The speech is quoted here in part from Joseph Barnes, *Willkie* (New York: Simon and Schuster, 1952 © Joseph Barnes, 1952):

> If it is my baby that's hurt now, it may be your baby later. With all the earnestness of which I am capable, I want to state that those who wish to prevent government invasion of their business had better begin to preach the doctrine now. At the same time, I might as well warn you what will happen to you if you do. From personal experience I know very well what happens to those individuals who defend their causes against government attack. You may, for example, have your income tax examined several times with a magnifying glass. You may be called an economic royalist. You may be chastised in official speeches. You may be called down to Washington to be questioned as to your personal affairs. You may have your name dragged into political investigation by a legislative committee of this or that state. You may suffer and your families may suffer by having your reputation smeared with the mud of false insinuations. All of that may happen to you and I can assure you that it is not pleasant.
>
> But isn't the risk worth it when you consider what is at stake? Isn't a personal discomfort and annoyance a far less important thing than the preservation of a free enterprise which has been responsible for the extraordinarily high level of the American civilization?

4. Interview with Horace Brewer, spring 1970.

5. Interview with Delbert Ford, summer 1970.

6. The final form of the "death-sentence clause"—Section 11 of the Public Utility Holding Company Act of 1935—read as follows:

> (a) It shall be the duty of the [Securities and Exchange] Commission to examine the corporate structure of every registered holding company and subsidiary company thereof, the relationships among the companies in the holding-company system of every such company and the character of the interests thereof and the properties owned or controlled thereby to determine the extent to which the corporate structure of such holding-company system and the companies therein may be simplified, unnecessary complexities therein eliminated, voting power fairly and equitably distributed among the holders of securities thereof, and the properties and business thereof confined to those necessary or appropriate to the operations of an integrated public-utility system.
>
> (b) It shall be the duty of the Commission, as soon as practicable after January 1938:
>
> (1) To require by order, after notice and opportunity for hearing, that each registered holding company, and each subsidiary company thereof, shall take

such action as the Commission shall find necessary to limit the operations of the holding-company system of which such company is a part to a single integrated public-utility system, and to such other businesses as are reasonably incidental, or economically necessary or appropriate to the operations of such integrated public utility systems: *Provided, however,* That the Commission shall permit a registered holding company to continue to control one or more additional integrated public-utility systems, if, after notice and opportunity for hearing, it finds that—

(A) Each of such additional systems cannot be operated as an independent system without the loss of substantial economies which can be secured by the retention of control by such holding company of such system;

(B) All of such additional systems are located in one State, or in adjoining States, or in a contiguous foreign country; and

(C) The continued combination of such systems under the control of such holding company is not so large (considering the state of the art and the area or region affected) as to impair the advantages of localized management, efficient operation, or the effectiveness of regulation. The Commission may permit as reasonably incidental, or economically necessary or appropriate to the operations of one or more integrated public-utility systems the retention of an interest in any business (other than the business of a public-utility company as such) which the Commission shall find necessary or appropriate in the public interest or for the protection of investors or consumers and not detrimental to the proper functioning of such system or systems.

(2) To require by order, after notice and opportunity for hearing, that each registered holding company, and each subsidiary company thereof, shall take such steps as the Commission shall find necessary to ensure that the corporate structure or continued existence of any company in the holding-company system does not unduly or unnecessarily complicate the structure, or unfairly or inequitably distribute voting power among security holders, of such holding-company system. In carrying out the provisions of this paragraph the Commission shall require each registered holding company (and any company in the same holding-company system with such holding company) to take such action as the Commission shall find necessary in order that such holding company shall cease to be a holding company with respect to each of its subsidiary companies which itself has a subsidiary company which is a holding company. Except for the purpose of fairly and equitably distributing voting power among the security holders of such company, nothing in this paragraph shall authorize the Commission to require any change in the corporate structure or existence of any company which is not a holding company, or of any company whose principal business is that of a public-utility company.

7. The Commonwealth & Southern Corporation, *Report to Stockholders,* Dec. 31, 1935.

8. Barnes, *op. cit.*

9. *Ibid.*

10. Besides Willkie, the directors of Commonwealth & Southern (Delaware) at that time included:

William H. Barthold, who in 1896 entered the employ of the Grand Rapids Gas Light Company and who in 1901 was placed in charge of various gas companies in Michigan—forerunners of the gas operations of Consumers Power Company.

Clarence M. Clark, of Philadelphia, member of the E. W. Clark & Co. firm and long associated with Consumers Power Company and its predecessors.

S. Sloan Colt, president of the Bankers Trust Company in New York.

William H. Hassinger, director of the Alabama Power Company and the First National Bank of Birmingham, Alabama.

Jacob Hekma, who came from the Michigan Trust Company of Grand Rapids to the Hodenpyl-Walbridge organization in 1905 and was from that time connected with predecessors of Commonwealth & Southern, thus being closely associated with Consumers Power Company and its predecessors.

Timothy A. Kenney, who entered the utilities business in 1897, in 1912 came to Michigan and was connected with Consumers Power Company and its predecessors, and in 1916 moved to New York, where he was connected with predecessors of Commonwealth & Southern.

Eugene A. Yates, who started with the Pennsylvania Railroad in 1902, in 1912 went with the Alabama Power Company, and was a consulting engineer from 1914 to 1920, but who then returned to the Alabama Power Company, later becoming general manager of the Southeastern Power and Light Company, one of the firms that merged into the holding company.

The service company, Commonwealth & Southern (New York), as described elsewhere, was owned by the operating companies which it served, and on the board of directors of the service company were the operating heads of the underlying properties. In this capacity, Dan E. Karn, vice-president and general manager of Consumers Power Company, was a director. In addition to these directors, there were also Barthold, Hekma, Kenney, Willkie, and Yates, who also were directors of the holding company. Further, there were James A. Brown, who entered the employ of the Grand Rapids Gas Light Company in 1905 and who from 1910 on was actively engaged in the supervision of public utility companies, now a part of the Commonwealth & Southern system, and Benjamin L. Huff, who came from the General Electric Company to Consumers Power Company in 1911, subsequently serving it as well as associated companies and the Commonwealth & Southern system.

11. Charles Tippy, "The Commonwealth & Southern Corporation (1929–1949)," thesis, University of Michigan, Ann Arbor, 1956. The author of this study is the grandson of C. W. Tippy.

12. *Ibid.*

13. According to Barnes, *op. cit.,* Willkie, starting in the summer of 1938, was negotiating for the purchase of Michigan and Ohio utility properties of Cities Service Company, a corporation that was primarily in the oil business and therefore now needed to divest itself of its utility holdings.

14. The Commission served upon C&S and each of the subsidiary companies an order, dated March 6, 1940, requiring them to file their joint or several answers which "may include a statement of the claim of the respondents or any of them as to (a) the action, if any, which is necessary and should be required to be taken . . . to limit the operations . . . to a single integrated public utility system . . . (b) the extent to which [the corporation] *should be permitted to continue to control one or more additional integrated public utility systems* as may meet their requirements of clauses (A), (B), (C) of Section 11 (b) (I) of the act." [Author's italics.]

15. Lest it be felt that the opposition to the holding-company dissolution stemmed entirely from holding companies, it may be noted that Merwin H. Waterman, of the faculty of the School of Business Administration at the University of Michigan, made an extensive study under the auspices of Michigan Business Studies, which was published in 1941. Among his observations, later published in the *Con-*

sumers Power News (May–June 1938), was that control and operation of public utilities by holding companies did not appear to impose a detrimental influence on either the operating utility's customers or its investors. He felt that the attitude of the law embodied in Section 11 (b) (1) of the Public Utility Holding Company Act was "unrealistic and unreasonable." He found that holding-company subsidiaries were as effectively regulated as their independent contemporaries. He further said: ". . . any pseudo reasoning to the effect that big utilities, or even big utility holding companies, are necessarily uneconomic, inefficient, and detrimental to the public interest is squelched by the consistent array of facts relating to the utility industry."

Dr. Waterman also had some thought-provoking recommendations, although he apparently put no stock in their being accepted because of the many "legal and politico-economic barriers" that existed. He was correct in this feeling. Such views did not prevail, although his economic studies were proffered as evidence before the Securities and Exchange Commission, August 18, 1941.

16. Interview with Delbert Ford, summer 1970.
17. M. Wilson Arthur, a North Carolinian by birth, graduated from Clemson Agricultural College with a specialty in electrical engineering. He first joined Westinghouse and remained there for seven years before coming into the C&S group as commercial manager of the Northern Ohio Traction and Light in Akron. After five years he was advanced to manager of electric sales and distribution, serving in that capacity for another five years. In 1929, Arthur transferred to the C&S staff in New York, and in October 1933, immediately after Tippy's death, he was assigned to Consumers Power as assistant to Karn. He became a vice-president the following year and remained in this position until his death of a heart attack on January 3, 1952. In his last years Arthur spearheaded the vast postwar marketing operation in industrial gas, lighting, and appliances.
18. The new interconnection points were in the areas of Genesee and Oakland Counties and in Shiawassee and Monroe Counties.
19. Actually this was no revolutionary innovation. Some women had been employed as Consumers Power station operators as far back as 1912, and World War I had also seen a temporary increase in their ranks.
20. Interview with Horace Brewer, spring 1970.
21. By 1947, the maximum demand on the Consumers Power system was 20 percent greater than the demand during the war peak, in the early days of 1945. This necessitated not only increased generation but also expansion of transmission and distribution facilities. One of the principal items in this network is the distribution substation where energy is stepped down from high-voltage lines to lower-voltage lines to lower voltage suitable for transmission along city streets and through rural areas.

The need for additional substations had been anticipated. During the "construction holiday" of the war years, a number of studies had been conducted, and plans made. Immediately after cessation of hostilities, fifty new substations were authorized for 1945 and 1946, and an equal number were planned for 1947 and 1948. It was by far the biggest substation program in the company's history.

It was helpful that some engineers, who had not forgotten playing with Mechano or Erector sets during their boyhood, created the Erecticon design for substations after a full year of concentrated study. The supporting structure was made up of standard prefabricated welded sections of uniform cross section (12 by 30 inches) which were bolted together to give the desired length. Lengths of individual sections were standardized at 4-foot intervals with 12-, 16-, and 20-foot lengths most commonly used, although 8- and 4-foot lengths were available. All other items of miscellaneous structural parts were standardized so that each standard part might serve a variety of structural purposes. The flat surfaces of all structural members had holes at regular 3-inch intervals to permit the bolting of cross members at any desired location or the attachment of equipment at any location. This made it possible to assemble standard units in a wide variety of combination of heights and widths to accommodate the particular requirements of any substation.

22. The effort to maintain the integrity of Commonwealth & Southern to the greatest extent possible under the Public Utilities Act of 1935 was not Whiting's only Washington battle. Another grave concern was the wartime excess-profits tax. As Whiting saw it, this levy—which in 1942 constituted the largest single item in the C&S tax picture—was misapplied when it came to public utilities since the purpose of the tax was to dilute the abnormal profits arising from war contracts. From 1936 to 1942, the year the excess-profits tax went into effect, Commonwealth & Southern taxes (federal, state, and local) increased eight times faster than the rate of the company's growth.

At Consumers Power during this period, the tax total rose from about $2.5 million a year to $16 million, a sum greater than the company's entire annual payroll. In 1942, taxes amounted to about $37 for every home supplied with electricity and thus practically consumed the entire year's electric revenue. While Consumers Power earnings still covered bond interest and preferred stock dividends, the company's cash safety margin was reduced by more than half, to about $1.3 million for the seven months ending July 31, 1942. (See Karn's statement in *Consumers Power News*, September 1942.) If a real emergency had arisen, there evidently would not have been enough money around to pay the bills. Another sleet storm like the one in February 1922 would have been disastrous. Luckily, nothing like that happened.

The excess-profits tax created a peculiar situation with respect to customer charges in both 1944 and 1945.

By a divided court, in the case of *City of Detroit v. Michigan Public Service Commission*, the Supreme Court of Michigan held that the commission had the right to exclude in whole or in part "excess profits" of the character defined in the Revenue Act as operating expenses which would place unnecessary burdens upon the consumer. As a consequence, the Michigan commission ordered reductions in the revenues of Consumers Power Company in avoidance of amounts which otherwise would be paid to the federal government in the form of the so-called excess-profits tax. Similar orders were issued in proceedings against other utilities in the state. These reductions were ordered without any investigation on the part of the commission as to whether or not the companies were earning a reasonable return on the value of their properties. The nature of the reduction was a 75 percent credit on the December 1944 bills.

Similar reasoning was employed in December of 1945, when a 20 percent reduction was ordered. The principal reason for the smaller credit in December 1945 than in 1944 was the reduction in 1945 taxable income resulting from expenses relating to redemption of bonds in that year.

23. Notice of public invitation for proposals for the purchase of shares of common stock of the Consumers Power Company, without par value, was published on

November 7, 1946, in the *New York Times, New York Herald Tribune, Wall Street Journal, Detroit Free Press,* and *Chicago Journal of Commerce.* The resultant proposal which specified the highest price for the stock was submitted by Morgan Stanley & Co. This firm acted as the representative of several purchasers named in the proposal. The price per share was named as $33.5399. When this was announced at the Consumers Power Company directors' meeting held on November 13, 1946, waiver by The Commonwealth & Southern Corporation of its preemptive right as a stockholder to purchase or subscribe for shares of this stock was also submitted.

24. The initial per-share distribution on the common stock consisted of 35/100ths of a share of The Southern Company common stock. This was to be followed by distributions, in kind or in cash, of common stock of Ohio Edison and of other assets remaining after liabilities and expenses had been met. There was also a provision that with SEC approval, remaining assets could be contributed to The Southern Company. (See The Commonwealth & Southern Corporation, *Report to Stockholders*, Dec. 31, 1948.)

25. The Commonwealth & Southern Corporation (Delaware) deposited its holdings of Consumers Power Company common stock with the First National Bank of New York as trustee, for distribution to the holders of C&S preferred stock, in accordance with the plan approved by the Securities and Exchange Commission and the Federal District Court of Wilmington, Delaware. The 16,000 former holders of C&S preferred stock became, under the plan, holders of common stock of Consumers Power Company, as well as of Central Illinois Light Company.

The mutual service company, The Commonwealth & Southern Corporation (New York), which had been owned by Consumers Power and other C&S operating subsidiaries, became an independent service company known as Commonwealth Services, Inc. Its stock now was owned by its officers and employees, of whom there were about three hundred in Jackson, Michigan, and about one hundred in New York City. Commonwealth Services was to provide services, including consultation and design engineering in public utility, industrial, and municipal fields; assistance in rates and rate audits, taxes, insurance, purchasing, public and stockholder relations, merchandising and display, and finance and accounting; consultation on general operating and construction problems; and representation before regulatory bodies. Such services had previously been available only to the companies of the C&S system, but now would be offered throughout the country and in other parts of the world.

26. Ever since the early days of Consumers Power Company, the controller function had been performed by the New York office, notably in the persons of Harry Kessler and his successor, Granville Bourne. It was for this reason that the move of H. B. Hardwick from the office of controller in New York to that of controller of Consumers Power Company was especially important. Hardwick was a native of Alabama and had begun his career in the utility industry in 1918, when he joined the Alabama Power Company. He entered larger fields of utility operation in 1925 with the Southeastern Power & Light Company system and went into The Commonwealth & Southern Corporation when that corporation was organized. He became controller of Consumers Power Company in 1947 before the C&S dissolution, and in 1949 he was elected to membership on the Consumers Power Company board of directors.

On June 1, 1949, the top-executive echelon at Consumers Power, in addition to Whiting, consisted of Karn, vice-president and general manager; Arthur, vice-president and assistant general manager; Frank G. Boyce, vice-president in charge of electric power and transmission; Hardwick, controller; Archie J. Mayotte, secretary; and Clyde E. Rowe, treasurer.

By April 1950 the composition was as follows: Whiting, president; Karn, first vice-president; Arthur, vice-president; James H. Campbell, vice-president; L. L. Benedict, vice-president in charge of electric power and transmission; Hardwick, controller; Mayotte, secretary; and Lewis J. Hamilton, treasurer.

The most important addition to these ranks in 1950 was that of Campbell, who ten years later became the company's president and chief operating officer (see Chapter 21).

27. It's the interrelation of events that makes history so fascinating. John L. Lewis supported Franklin D. Roosevelt for President in 1932 (as Willkie did in his own way); then he split with him and threw his weight behind Willkie in 1940, staking his CIO presidency on the latter's victory. When Willkie was defeated, Lewis resigned; Philip Murray emerged as the CIO's new leader, and in 1942 Lewis and his United Mine Workers withdrew from the CIO. In short, the UMW as a separate, independent union can be traced to Willkie's defeat.

28. In the spring of 1937, a series of slowdown and sit-down strikes, at first confined to automobile plants, began in the eastern section of Michigan, principally in Flint, Saginaw, and Bay City. The trouble eventually spread to Pontiac, Muskegon, Battle Creek, and Kalamazoo. Riots occurred, and it was necessary to call out the National Guard to help to restore order in some localities. At the peak of this unrest, in April 1937, Consumers Power received a demand from the United Automobile Workers of America (CIO) that it enter into collective bargaining with that organization for the company's employees in Saginaw. While these negotiations were in progress, the CIO called three strikes, which resulted in the seizure of some of the company's property and the shutting off of light and power service in Saginaw, Bay City, and Flint. On June 8, 1937, Consumers Power entered into an exclusive contract with the CIO, covering all operating employees.

Soon, however, an independent union was formed by a group of employees. In addition, the International Brotherhood of Electrical Workers (AFL) also became active in organizing Consumers Power. Both unions petitioned the National Labor Relations Board to determine the majority status of the competing labor organizations. Concurrently, the CIO union filed a complaint against the company charging that it dominated the independent union.

The independent union was ordered disestablished. Meanwhile, the contract with the CIO union had expired, and the company refused to renew it until the question of majority representation was settled. This refusal resulted in another sit-down strike on April 1, 1938. As a result of this strike, the CIO agreement was extended to September 4, 1938, and thereupon expired.

A representation election was finally held by the National Labor Relations Board on January 10, 1939. It was inconclusive, and there followed an active battle between the CIO and the AFL unions for supremacy among the company's operating, maintenance, and construction employees. This controversy involved resort to the courts and other legal procedures. A second inconclusive election and another strike by the CIO union in September of 1939 followed.

Ultimately, in September 1940 a runoff election between the two unions was held, resulting in the certification of the AFL union as the sole agency for collective bargaining among Consumers Power employees. Recognition of this union as the exclusive bargaining agent followed, culminating in an agreement with the International Brotherhood of Electrical Workers.

The present union representation for operating, maintenance, and construction employees is the Utility Workers Union of America (AFL-CIO). Aside from occasional flare-ups, usually at the time of contract negotiations, management-union relations were generally quite amicable until 1960, when Consumers Power went through its first long postwar strike, a stoppage of 42 days. In 1969, however, the situation changed for the worse. That year, the union went out for 83 days, and in 1971 it staged another major strike that lasted 112 days and included numerous acts of sabotage and physical assaults on supervisory employees.

It is interesting to note in this connection that sometimes the most militant of union men eventually realize that management-union relations are a two-way street on which collisions don't have to happen when traffic is properly supervised. Garland Sanders, the original boss after 1940 of the Consumers Power local of the International Brotherhood of Electrical Workers, turned out to be one of the best union leaders in industry. It was under his tutelage that labor peace reigned for so many years. Yet in the unionization struggles of the late 1930s he had once thrown a steel chain over a transmission line near Saginaw, causing a power failure over a wide part of the system.

29. Hodenpyl died in 1933, which seems almost symbolic. He was a member of a generation that had run its course, yielding to new men with new attitudes.

30. Throughout the Consumers Power territory, back through the years, there had been employees who got into various little scrapes, were short of finances, or had other problems. Managers and department heads at times had helped these employees over their difficulties, and it came as a real shock to see some of those very same employees in the front rank of a picket line at the time of the first strike. Some executives never got over this. But the 1930s were abnormal times — unemployment was rife, agitators were at large, various isms came into being, everyone was groping for cures, and goon squads were employed to coerce. America was at war with itself — a war from which it never really recovered.

31. In the same acquisition, Consumers Power obtained electric territories of Wayland north of Kalamazoo and in the Frankfort area and additional gas territories around Northville, Marshall, Owosso, St. Johns, Sault Ste. Marie, and Alpena. The latter two properties were subsequently released. Transfer of these properties to Consumers Power occurred in the following manner.

Shortly prior to the organization of The Commonwealth & Southern Corporation, the Southeastern Power & Light Company, one of the firms consolidated into C&S, owned some collateral trust notes and stock of Central Public Utilities and its predecessor Central Public Service Corporation. These were assigned in consideration of delivery of Michigan Federated Utilities and Lower Peninsula Power Company to Consumers Power Company, and of other properties to the South Carolina Power and Gulf Power companies.

32. Horace Brewer took over the company's industrial development department in 1950 and remained its head until his retirement in 1967. The first industrial development program in the company's territory had been conducted in 1913 in the days of the Detroit office of the Hodenpyl group. Fred M. Caldwell was then in charge. He later moved to the office in Jackson, and after his death was succeeded by Eugene Holcomb. Fred W. Hoover, the executive who had handled the

company's customer-ownership program, was also in charge of industrial development for the entire Commonwealth group at one time.

33. While this latest acquisition included about 30,000 customers, it also brought considerable headaches. Aside from the Old Mission Point area out of Traverse City, practically the entire newly acquired territory was competitive with municipal plants, REAs, or cooperatives.

Consumers Power Company again went through the customary process of rebuilding the facilities, increasing sales per customer, and reducing rates. In this particular case, arrangements were made to bring the electric rates in the area into line with Consumers Power's standard rates in a series of four reductions beginning in September of 1950 and ending in September of 1953. The total effect of the four annual reductions in the area was to reduce the average electric bill for all classes about 24 percent.

An interesting aspect of this acquisition was that the company came into possession of the Slackwater Navigation Company and its system of locks. The chief role of the locks is to carry navigation around the Cheboygan hydro plant, which was built originally to secure power from the strong rapids that existed at this point and made boating impossible. The locks had been constructed after a special enabling act of the state Legislature in 1867. The first principal use of the locks was to bring lumber down the Cheboygan River to Lake Huron. While it's been many years since they performed this function, they now admit the vacationer to one of the most delightful water routes in the world—the inland water route of the southern peninsula of Michigan. More than four hundred boats a season lock through from Lake Huron to Cheboygan to take this trip.

34. Before the acquisition of Michigan Public Service Company, Consumers Power Company had fifteen operating commercial divisions: Cadillac, Manistee, Muskegon, Grand Rapids, Kalamazoo, Battle Creek, Jackson, Hastings, Lansing, Alma, Pontiac, Flint, Owosso, Saginaw, and Bay City. All fifteen division managers reported directly to Karn, and the acquisition of the new area would make a total of sixteen. This was evidently too much for proper "span of control," as it is called in business-organization parlance. It was therefore decided to cut down on the number of divisions, combining some of the previous smaller ones and making them districts under larger divisions. For a few years the number stood at twelve, but eventually became fifteen again, this time with a vice-president in charge of division operations, under Karn. The first was Claude A. Mulligan, who was succeeded by Anson Hedgecock in 1964.

35. The first two Consumers Power common stock offers were made even before the C&S dissolution was completed. The initial sale, in 1946, as will be recalled, involved 500,000 shares at $36 a share. Then in November 1948 another 400,000 shares of common stock were sold at $33 a share. Additional issues were brought out in later years, and several of these were offered to employees on a payroll deduction plan.

For example, the *Consumers Power News* of February 1950 announced that every full-time regular employee could buy up to 100 shares of the company's common stock for cash or on payroll deduction with a down payment of 10 percent or more. Arrangements were made with banks in division headquarters cities so that employees could purchase shares on an installment loan basis, the company paying the interest and service charges on the notes. While the 454,457 shares authorized by the Michigan Public Service Commission had to first be offered to existing stockholders because of preemptive rights, any shares not subscribed for by the stockholders were available for purchase by employees.

Nearly one-fifth of the employees of Consumers Power Company and its subsidiary, Michigan Gas Storage Company, took advantage of the stock-purchase opportunity. Stock subscriptions were signed by 1,304 employees, or about 19 percent of full-time regular employees. The subscriptions covered 21,287 shares. At the price of $34.25 per share, the total amount subscribed was $729,080, of which nearly half was paid in cash. In 1951, a similar type of offer was made to the employees. After this offer, nearly one-fourth of the employees emerged as shareowners of Consumers Power Company, and of those who purchased at the time of the February 1950 plan, 706 again purchased stock in October 1951. In January 1954, some 679,000 shares were offered to stockholders and employees. With this sale, more than 38 percent of the employees became stockholders.

The laws of Maine required that official annual stockholder meetings be held in that state, and this was done. But since most Consumers Power shareholders resided in Michigan, it was decided also to hold regional stockholder meetings in the company territory. The first of these meetings, in April 1949, were staged in Flint, Saginaw, Grand Rapids, and Jackson. Stockholders turned out in large numbers, some having come many miles to attend. Whiting and Karn addressed the stockholders, and at the conclusion of their talks they invited questions. Secretary Archie J. Mayotte also reported on the annual meeting held in Portland, Maine. Each regional stockholder meeting closed with light refreshments. The meetings were so successful that the program was expanded in succeeding years.

Chapter 20

1. Offshore drillers work at the edge of eternity, seven days on, seven days off, twelve hours a day. Aboard, they live in relatively luxurious barrack style. Food is plentiful (steak for lunch almost every day), and the pay is good, as it had better be. *Ocean Driller,* one of three rigs capable of conducting deepwater exploration, is now equipped with two bright red Brucker survival capsules, made by the Whittaker Corp. of La Mesa, California. Each capsule, looking somewhat like a fat flying saucer, holds twenty-eight men, is equipped with motor and radio, and is stocked with enough food, oxygen, and water to last five days. It is waterproof and airtight and can stand 1200° F heat. Not inappropriately, the *Ocean Driller* crew has christened its capsules Apollos I and II.

2. Petroleum, although it is a liquid, is under similar pressure, since it is lighter than the water that presses against its reservoir—hence the gushers of the oil business.

3. To avoid a real blowout through the pipe, it is necessary to compensate for the pressure of the sediment that has been removed in drilling. This compensatory pressure is maintained by means of mud suspended in water which presses down into the pipe casing. Normally the drill, which rotates at about 140 to 170 rpm, depending on depth, is under 2,500 to 3,000 pounds of pressure per square inch. Maintaining the proper mud mixture for precisely the pressure required is one of the major operations aboard a driller.

4. In connection with the construction of the natural-gas transmission main from the Broomfield gas field through Midland to the Saginaw area, an incident occurred that illustrates the problems of business operation within the framework of government regulation and the response of such regulation, sometimes, to politics.

In September 1934, criminal proceedings were initiated against Dan Karn, who was then vice-president and general manager; Clyde J. Holmes, vice-president and general counsel; and A. L. Watkins, the same man, now old and sick, who served W. A. Foote in his negotiations with Loud for the Au Sable flowage lands. Criminal suit involved an alleged violation of Act 9 of the Public Acts of 1929. It was claimed that the gas main was constructed without first obtaining permission from, and filing maps with, the Public Utilities Commission.

Let us first place the incident in relation to its time. Less than two years had passed since Roosevelt's first election, which had also swept in William A. Comstock as Michigan's first Democratic governor since 1917. As we have already seen in the preceding chapters, this was hardly the heyday of investor-owned utilities. Now let us see what happened.

In 1931 Consumers Power had contracted with Isabella Oil Development Company to purchase gas from the Broomfield field and had constructed an 8-inch line from that field to Midland. Two years later, the company entered into contracts for the sale of natural gas to the citizens of Bay City and Saginaw. For some time, this gas was delivered through the new line to Midland and through an old 6-inch line to Bay City and Zilwaukee, which had been constructed originally for serving manufactured gas to Midland. When natural gas came in, the flow of the line was simply reversed. In the fall of 1933, to increase the pressure of the natural gas in Saginaw, a 10-inch line was constructed from Midland to Saginaw. This line was tied into the Consumers Power main at Midland.

Consumers Power continued to buy gas from the Isabella Oil Development Company, which later changed its name to the Michigan Cities Natural Gas Company. Consumers Power purchased gas from just this one company, and its sale of gas was confined to its own customers.

It transported no gas, except for its own use. The company's main did not extend beyond the meter house at the wells, at which point Michigan Cities Natural Gas Company made delivery.

While Act 9 of the Public Acts of 1929 did call for the approval by the state commission of natural-gas-main construction, one section specifically excluded lines constructed by individual business for their own use. In any case, the commission had been apprised at all times of the natural-gas project.

After the change in state administration, a new chairman took office in February 1934 with the express responsibility of reorganizing the commission. The criminal proceedings were initiated in September 1934, a matter of weeks before the prospective fall election. In the *Saginaw Daily News* of September 4, Governor Comstock was quoted as saying: "It may be perfectly true the commission knew all about the illegal action of the Consumers Power Company, at least the commission had, made no attempt to enforce the Natural Gas Act. I found it necessary to institute removal proceedings and reorganize the commission."

Next day's *Jackson Citizen Patriot* introduced an interesting element in the case:

Although neither Karn nor Holmes would discuss this angle of the situation, political discussion in Lansing linked the prosecution of power company officials with the Metzger case in Greenville. It will be recalled that the son of Samuel Metzger, state agricultural commissioner and political power in the Comstock administration, was arrested following an assault upon Joseph E. Stanton, local manager for the Consumers Power Company in Greenville. Stanton, a man of more than 60 years, was badly beaten. He instituted court action against young

Metzger. The story is that various efforts were made to coerce the power company into "calling off" Stanton and forcing him to abandon the action against Metzger. However, neither threats nor persuasion prevailed, the power company contending that Stanton's charge against Metzger was his personal business and not the affair of his employer, and that, at any rate, the company didn't propose that anybody, even a politician's son, should beat up its employees with impunity. Following a hectic court trial, Metzger was found guilty of assault and sentenced to jail. But Governor Comstock pardoned young Metzger. The state-wide protest, which followed this pardon, is said to have incensed the governor and his close friend, Attorney General O'Brien, with the result that the state administration has been sharpening its ax for the power company. . . .

In the fall election of 1934, the state administration changed. Ultimately the criminal case was quashed by an order of the circuit judge on October 21, 1935. There was, however, an additional civil case, the type of procedure that would have been the more normal one to follow. This civil case clarified the question of PSC permits.

5. Shortly after the changeover had been started in Lansing, the Grand Rapids Gas Light Company applied for a permit to construct a line from the Six Lakes field to the city of Grand Rapids and to serve 100 percent natural gas to its customers there. To obtain gas for this operation, Grand Rapids Gas Light entered a contract with producers and leaseholders in the Six Lakes field.

   Soon, Consumers Power also became interested in this gas-producing area: the company needed additional supplies to meet the requirements of the cities to which it was furnishing service. And so, in March 1936, it purchased the Petroleum Transportation Company, which operated in the Six Lakes field, and changed its name to Hinton-Belvidere Natural Gas Gathering Company. This meant that there were now two utilities drawing gas from the same field, which in the long run was really inadequate to supply either.

   In May 1936, Consumers Power and Grand Rapids Gas Light, in order to avoid duplicate investment in the gathering system, made a contract by the terms of which each provided an equal amount of money for constructing gathering lines in the Six Lakes field. The contract provided that Consumers Power would operate the field and divide the cost of operation on the basis of the wells connected. A similar agreement was later negotiated to cover the construction of a compressor station.

6. This addition was made possible by Consumers Power's purchase in 1936 of a 4-inch line between the Crystal–New Haven field and Alma from the Refiners Fuel Supply Company.

7. A 12-inch 600-pound natural-gas line, 58 miles long, was constructed to connect this area with Consumers Power markets.

8. The daily open flow for all the Michigan fields used by the Public Service Commission on March 31, 1941, for proration was 5,323,907 thousand cubic feet. This may be compared with the remaining reserves as of December 31, 1940, of 67,766,-109 thousand cubic feet. Reserves were only about thirteen times the daily open flow.

   Anyone in the natural-gas business today would find this very small ratio of reserves to daily open flow utterly astounding, but this type of improvident operation was general in the Michigan fields in those days. Producers, always anxious to maximize current revenues, were pushing for additional outputs that existing reserves simply did not warrant.

Consumers Power Company was very much concerned about the reserves in sight for its already connected markets. Had the company hooked up additional markets with requirements of, say, 3 billion cubic feet per year, the margin of reserves over requirements would have been severely curtailed. The failure to meet its requirements would make it necessary that some or all of the communities return to manufactured gas at a greatly increased cost of service. Not only would the company's investment be rendered useless, but also the customers' investment would prove to be greater in amount than the company's investment. Careful consideration had to be given constantly to this condition, and resolute handling was required to avoid the making of serious errors in judgment.

Consumers Power Company constantly sought, aided, and encouraged producers to develop and extend new reserves for the present and for additional markets. This was done by keeping competent men in the field and by making loans to producers for drilling and constructing other facilities of production. These loans usually took the form of advanced payments for gas when and if produced. (For more detail on this period, see a 1941 analysis by Jensen, Bowen & Farrell, engineers of Ann Arbor, Michigan, entitled "History and Development of the Gas Operations of Consumers Power Company," in Consumers Power Company files.)

9. Already with the beginning of natural-gas service in Saginaw and Bay City, consideration was given to a standby plant in case of failure of the natural-gas supply. The gas manufactured in such a standby plant would have to work well in natural-gas appliances without adjustment.

   In January 1934, a series of tests was started on a 7-foot 6-inch hand-operated water gas machine in the Saginaw River gas plant. After months of trial, a process of making a substitute gas was developed to such an extent that the larger 10-foot automatically operated water-gas machine was equipped to produce this gas. The machine was heated by a coke fire in the generator, and during the down run, oil was injected into the top of the generator, this oil being cracked as it passed down through the coke fire, thus forming large quantities of hydrogen. This gas was mixed with the oil gas that was formed in the carburetor by the admission of considerable quantities of oil. After many tests, it was found that the best operating cycle consisted of blasting the set until the carburetor and superheater reached the proper temperature, in the neighborhood of 1500 to 1600 ° F, and then admitting oil into the top of the generator. This oil was cracked by the fire as it was forced down through the firebed into the wash box. The gas made on this part of the cycle was of a very low specific gravity and of comparatively low Btu. On the other so-called volume part of the cycle, large quantities of oil were sprayed into the carburetor, thereby being cracked and passed up through the superheater into the wash box. The final purge of the water-gas machine was made by making a steam run, up through the fire, forcing the oil gas out of the carburetor and superheater into the wash box. It was found that a satisfactory oil gas could be made, using approximately 10 gallons of oil and approximately 18 to 20 pounds of fuel per 1,000 feet of gas. The gas formed had a specific gravity of approximately 0.64 and a calorific value of 975 Btu per cubic foot. A gas with such characteristics was found to satisfactorily replace natural gas when tried on sample appliances. In order to determine whether this gas was satisfactory for general use, tests were made in Zilwaukee, Michigan. Oil gas made by this process was distributed for a period of approximately one week, and very few complaints were received. In fact, most of the people did not know that they were being served with oil gas instead of natural gas. When Lansing was changed over to natural gas in 1936, a large water-gas machine in the Lansing plant was immediately equipped to make a substitute gas by this process.

10. Jensen, Bowen and Farrell, *op. cit.*

11. The earliest successful operation for underground storage of natural gas on this continent was in Welland County, Ontario, Canada, in 1915. In 1916 the Zoar field near Buffalo, New York, began operations. Some important storage fields were devloped in the late 1920s and 1930s, but the big expansion has taken place since 1937. Today, Consumers Power's underground storage has a capability of 93.5 billion cubic feet, making Michigan the leading gas storage state of the nation.

12. The Taggart purchase totaled approximately $2,695,000. Acquisitions also included rights of the Sun Oil Company ($260,000) and Michigan Consolidated Gas Company ($223,636), as well as several other rights among them, some owned by the state of Michigan (for a total of $1,500,000).

13. The position of the chairman of the board of Consumers Power was unfilled from the time of Whiting's retirement on May 1, 1956, until May 1, 1960, the date of Karn's retirement from the company's presidency. During this period Karn was the chief executive officer, presiding at meetings of directors and stockholders and in general taking charge of the company's business and operations. Wilson Arthur had died of a heart attack in January 1952, and Karn was now backed up by James H. Campbell, the senior vice-president who was to succeed Karn as president, and Robert P. Briggs, a University of Michigan business administration professor who had joined Consumers Power as a director and financial vice-president in 1951 and who, after Arthur's death, was named executive vice-president, a position he held until he retired in 1969.

During the late 1950s, even though Karn was the chief executive, Whiting continued to maintain his grip on the company's reins as chairman of the executive committee. It was he who supported the election of A. H. Aymond as chairman and chief executive officer and of Campbell as president upon Karn's retirement in 1960.

Justin R. Whiting died on February 28, 1965, at the age of seventy-eight while on a Mediterranean cruise. He was still a director of the company and chairman of its executive committee. After his death the mandatory retirement age for directors was set at seventy-two. It is sixty-five for officers and employees.

14. Panhandle Eastern established its own underground storage facility in a gas field it had pumped for sixteen years near Howell, Michigan. This helped to alleviate the shortage, but did not overcome it.

15. The propane was received in a 30,000-gallon receiving tank. The liquid propane was then pumped 4½ miles to another 30,000-gallon tank at the Muskegon River compressor station in the Winterfield storage area. When the liquid propane left this second receiving tank, it was pumped through heat exchangers to raise its temperature to the vaporization point. It was then transferred to a tower and mixed with heated natural gas and air. In its gaseous form, the propane contained 2,526 heat units per cubic foot, but the combination of natural gas, propane, and air that left the mixing tower had the standard natural-gas Btu content—1,000 per cubic foot. It was this mixture that was then introduced into the regular stream of natural gas flowing into the storage field from the Hugoton field in Texas, Oklahoma, and Kansas and carried under pressure into the underground formation of the field.

In addition to the use of propane, the new arrangement with Panhandle brought in 8 to 10 million cubic feet of gas per day rather than the earlier 4 million. Furthermore, Michigan Consolidated Gas agreed to supplement Consumers Power's supplies by selling the company some 100 million cubic feet of natural gas over the next few months. This was to be paid for by Consumers Power's giving Consolidated enough propane to enable them to manufacture an equivalent amount of gas in Detroit.

A Michigan Public Service Commission ruling enabled the company to pass along the $1.6 million extra expense of the propane operation to its larger customers as a surcharge during the eight months beginning with August and ending with March. Customers using no more than 2,500 cubic feet of gas per month were not affected, since the first 2,500 cubic feet of each customer's monthly usage was exempt. This meant that the surcharge was confined largely to industrial, commercial, and home-heating customers, where it amounted to about 14½ cents per 1,000 cubic feet on gas used in excess of 2,500 cubic feet a month.

In order to speed gas on its way to and from the fields, it was necessary to install some temporary compressor capacity at Flint. The Flint compressor station was built in record time by the Storage Company. The gas that had already traveled some 1,200 miles when it reached Flint was pushed on its way to the Chippewa station near Midland, en route to the storage fields 100 miles distant at the intersection of the boundaries of Clare, Missaukee, and Osceola Counties.

During this period, large-size steel pipe was scarce. In the winter of early 1949, a pipeline 120 miles long was being constructed to help carry Texas gas to the central Michigan storage fields of the area. The line was to have been built of 24-inch piple, but a switch to 20-inch pipe was made in order to obtain immediate delivery. This particular line started at Freedom Junction near Chelsea, where the Storage Company receives Texas gas, and was projected to a point near Mt. Pleasant to connect with the Storage Company's existing pipeline system. It was designed to carry pressure of 700 pounds per square inch.

For more information on the unusual propane operation and early gas storage problems, see *Consumers Power News*, May, July, and August 1948, and January 1949.

16. Up to this time, all the gas area of Consumers Power had been served with natural gas with the exception of Manistee. Manistee was an isolated area, not connected with the transmission systems involved in the Panhandle gas supply and Michigan storage. Steps were taken, however, to serve Michigan natural gas in Manistee in the spring of 1949. The natural-gas supply was very short-lived; however, after enjoying natural-gas service for only three months, it was necessary that Manistee switch in June to propane-air gas. (See *Consumers Power News*, July 1949.) The Manistee gas operation was subsequently sold.

17. In order to facilitate the transmission of larger quantities of gas, pipeline construction went on. For instance, a new natural-gas pipeline, 40 miles long, connecting the Oakland, Macomb, and Wayne County areas with the main gas transmission lines of the Michigan Gas Storage Company at a point near Laingsburg, northeast of Lansing, was completed in the late fall of 1952, under the direction of D. E. Herringshaw, then vice-president of gas operations. This new 24-inch pipeline more than doubled the ability of Michigan Gas Storage to deliver natural gas to Consumers Power customers in the heavy growth areas of Pontiac, Mt. Clemens, Royal Oak, Berkley, Birmingham, East Detroit, Ferndale, Hazel Park, Livonia, Plymouth, Roseville, St. Clair Shores, Wayne, and other communities. The line

also reinforced service to Flint by relieving other pipeline facilities that had been serving both the Pontiac and Flint regions. In the summer of 1955, to bring increased volumes of gas from the company's underground storage fields in central Michigan to Flint and Saginaw Valley cities, work started on the new 16-inch gas main, 36 miles long, from Mt. Pleasant to Zilwaukee.

18. At the time of this writing, Richard L. O'Shields was president and chief executive officer of Panhandle Eastern Pipe Line Company.

19. There were several reasons behind Trunkline's decision to stop at the Michigan border. For one thing, it wanted to avoid exposure to yet another regulatory body, in this case the Michigan Public Service Commission (not because of the MPSC per se, but because it would just add complications). There also would be the local problems of conducting business in a new state; ad valorem taxes, right-of-way negotiations, etc. In any case, it made sense for Consumers Power to own and operate the facility within Michigan. If the Michigan portion were owned by Trunkline, the Federal Power Commission would become involved every time Consumers Power wanted to tap into the system at a new delivery point.

20. Pipeline construction works like an assembly line in reverse. Machinery and men move instead of the product. At the head of the parade marches the "fence gang," which removes fences. Then comes the "right-of-way gang," which grades, bulldozes, and cuts out the sides of hills. Then the ditching machine rolls up: it's a rotary digger whose conveyor belt deposits the dirt from the ditch to one side, cutting a trough 6 feet deep and 4 feet wide. This machine is followed by the "stringing gang," which links the 40-foot joints of pipe, and the "bending crew," which bends the pipe where necessary. Next comes the welding crew to weld the pipe sections, and then the "clean-and-prime" machine and the paint machine, which coats the pipe with a spiral layer of tar (in marshes the pipe is coated with concrete). During all this work, the pipe lies alongside the ditch. As this procedure is progressivley finished, the pipe is lowered into the ditch by tractors with wide booms. The pipe generally is buried at a depth at pipe top of between 36 and 42 inches. Once the ditch is filled, a "clean-up gang" forms the tail end of the procession, putting fences back up and making similar repairs.

When the pipeline is in operation, compression stations along its route push the gas along at a pressure that usually ranges from 800 to 1,200 pounds per square inch.

Planes regularly fly along pipeline routes to check for leaks. A big leak will actually blow out dirt because of the pressure, and that's easy to see. Small leaks can be spotted from the air because of the dead vegetation over it: the methane displaces oxygen, and the plants die. On plowed fields, leaks can be detected after rain: the gassed area is drier than the rest because the gas absorbs moisture. In a dry, plowed field, a leak is hard to find, and sometimes crews have to walk the line. Pure methane is almost odorless, tasteless, and invisible, although a trained nose can smell it. (The odor of natural gas sold to customers is added artificially as a warning device.)

21. Originally the project had been undertaken in three "spreads," as pipeline men call construction areas. One spread worked south from the Michigan border, another north from the Illinois-Indiana border, and the third north from Tuscola. These spreads were subcontracted to construction firms on a bid basis. Engineers Limited, a California construction company, bid in low on the two northern spreads of the Michigan extension. Its bid underestimated the additional costs resulting from the

adverse weather conditions; it could not carry out its job at the quoted price and went out of business. The whole extension was then handled by the Contract Material Company of Evanston, Illinois, which was working north from Tuscola.

22. Interviews with Virgil Kincheloe, manager of construction; J. B. Sellers, manager of compressor station design; and Thomas McPherson, senior engineer, all of Trunkline, spring 1971.

23. Another valve turner was S. A. Petrino, general manager of Michigan Gas Utilities, which also received Trunkline supplies, although of course in a much smaller measure.

24. The original extension between Tuscola, Illinois, and the Michigan border was 26 inches in diameter. This has since been looped with 36-inch pipe. The original 26-inch main line was first looped with 30-inch pipe to take care of the Consumers Power extension, and has now been looped with additional 36-inch pipe practically all the way.

25. In early 1971, Panhandle delivery took place at the rate of 92 billion cubic feet a year at an average price of 34.3 cents per 1,000 cubic feet. Trunkline's annual 226 billion feet averaged out at 31.55 cents per 1,000 cubic feet. Consumers Power absorbed nearly one-third of the Panhandle-Trunkline's annual trillion-foot capacity, making it the biggest by far of the pipeline system's 137 customers in twelve states.

26. Offshore oil and natural-gas leases are good for five years. An additional charge of $3 per acre per year—$15,000 for a 5,000-acre block—is made during the drilling period. If and when production starts, the rental stops, but then the government collects a 16.6 percent royalty off the top.

27. The Supreme Court in the 1954 Phillips decision had extended the FPC jurisdiction to producer prices. The economic implementation of the Natural Gas Act flowed historically from the concept of regulating the *transportation* of gas by pipelines. Transportation was viewed in the context of providing a service such as electric and telephone under the general concept of utility regulation as developed within the states.

The marketing of gas, as viewed by the industry, involved both transportation and selling a commodity. Regulation of producer prices by the FPC since 1954 has failed to recognize the commodity aspect of gas. While at the retail level, utility service might be an acceptable premise for state regulation, it does not square with the economic circumstances prevailing in the search for gas, the product itself. The producer is providing no "service"; he is merely seeking a commodity which pipelines transport.

The major fallacy in FPC producer regulation is the imposition of economic regulation on a "service" basis. This approach results in "cost-of-service" machinations in order to fix a "just and reasonable" price at the wellhead.

But when cost determinations are sought, certain compromises with the reality of risk have to be made. This has resulted in the difficulty the FPC has experienced in finding a producer rate which would adequately compensate the explorer but which would be no higher than that necessary to get the exploration accomplished. At no point in the methodology or criteria utilized by the FPC has any commodity value for gas been recognized. Hence, the regulated price has been at levels which produce conflicting results—surging demand because of artificially low prices and the dwindling of the investment needed to meet that demand.

In essence what the nation is now experiencing is not so much a supply shortage but a demand excess. Those who zealously guard the "public interest" against necessary upward price adjustment may someday also be presiding over a prolonged gap in supply versus demand. At that point the danger of extreme remedies may appear, and we shall be debating the wrong subject at the wrong time.

28. John B. Simpson, a native of Milton, Massachusetts, is a 1940 graduate of the Massachusetts Institute of Technology with a B.S. degree in petroleum engineering. After two years with Stanoline Oil and Gas Co. at Stafford, Kansas, he spent 3½ years in the Civil Engineering Corps of the Navy. He joined Consumers Power as a junior engineer in the gas department in 1946, transferred to the Michigan Gas Storage subsidiary as an engineer in 1947, became assistant general superintendent of the Storage Company in 1951, and returned to Consumers Power as general supervisor of gas operations in 1952. He was elected vice-president in charge of gas operations in 1958 and has been senior vice-president since 1968. At the same time he serves as vice-president of the Storage Company and director of both the exploration and storage subsidiaries.

With Consumers Power's executive reorganization in 1972 (see Tomorrow, Note 26), Simpson also assumed direct responsibility for general services, including its data processing, which takes place at the company's huge computer center at the Parnall complex in Jackson.

29. Two of these unsuccessful test wells were in the Hackberry zone of Calcasieu Parish, one was in Plaquemaines Parish, and the fourth was in Terrebonne Parish.

30. When Northern Michigan Exploration and Anadarko joined the exploration group, its other members were Sun Oil Company, the operator, which held a 35 percent interest; Clark Oil Producing Company; and Acquitaine Oil Corp., a French company. It was then called SCAAN, an acronym made up of the initials of its members. After the auction, Diamond Shamrock Corp. joined the group, and it was then called SCAAND. It is expected that another 100 blocks in the same southwest Louisiana offshore area will become available at an auction in late 1972 and that the Sun Oil Company group will again bid for leases. According to plans as this is written, Consumers Power's Northern Michigan Exploration Company is to have a 15 percent share in this new venture, and Anadarko 25 percent. Diamond Shamrock and Acquitaine are not expected to participate, and the exploration group's name presumably will be SCAN.

The 1971 auction, held at the Sheraton-Charles Hotel in New Orleans, attracted hundreds of bidders, including the world's biggest oil companies. Bids exposed totaled nearly $3 billion and resulted in $850 million worth of sales. The exploration managers of the SCAAN group—including Richard J. Burgess, of Consumers Power, and Raymond E. Fairchild, of Anadarko—had ranked seventy-two tracts on the basis of Sunoco's surveys and prepared bids on forty-seven of these blocks, with a total exposure of $201.7 million. Since such auctions are held on the basis of secret bids handed in before the sale starts, the group had entrusted the calculation of its bids to computers, hoping to arrive at figures which would not be too high for the potential of the respective desired leases but which would be high enough to beat the sums competitors were likely to offer. In the first twenty tracts auctioned, SCAAN's bids proved to be too low. Humble Oil Co. outbid the group for its top-ranked tract. The group also lost out on its second most desired drilling site. Burgess and Fairchild had just lost all hope (Fairchild blurted something like, "My God, something went wrong with our computers. We've blown the whole deal!") when suddenly the bids started falling their way. The group walked off with ranked tracts numbered 3, 4, 7, 9, 15, 18, 24, 25, and 28. Its most expensive purchase was 3, which cost $15.5 million. That was Block 639.

31. These two Louisiana wildcats were located in North Freshwater Bayou, 30 miles southwest of New Iberia, and in Cherokee Prospect, 15 miles south of Morgan City. Consumers Power's share of exploration costs was estimated at $2.5 million.

32. Northern Michigan was fifty-fifty partners with Amoco in a wildcat southeast of Traverse City. It also held a 25 percent share in an oil property at Pigeon River field with Amoco and Shell.

33. Since the Marysville announcement, several other United States utilities have followed Consumers Power's footsteps. At the time of this writing, plans to build reforming plants are under way at Boston Gas Co., Public Service Electric and Gas Co. of New Jersey, Brooklyn Union Gas Co., Algonquin Gas Transmission Co., Texas Gas Transmission Corp., Columbia Gas System, Inc., and Northern Illinois Gas Co.

34. The British Gas Council has some forty such plants in operation. The plants in Britain, however, produce natural gas of a heat value of only 850 Btu, which is then thinned down to 500 to 600 Btu to be compatible with manufactured coal gas. At the Marysville plant the methane will be stepped up to 1,000 Btu, the heat value of methane in its natural form. The engineering of the Marysville plant has been contracted to Lummus Co. of Bloomfield, New Jersey, a subsidiary of Combustion Engineering. The feedstock will be furnished by Amoco and Dome.

35. Plants to liquefy natural gas by cooling it are being built and planned in increasing numbers in foreign oil-producing countries, including Algeria and Venezuela. Only a few small cryogenic tankers operate at this writing, plying between Africa and Europe. Eventually cryogenic supertankers will be built, but these huge ships of 200,000 tons and over will not be able to go up the St. Lawrence Seaway for direct delivery to Consumers Power. When that time comes, the liquefied natural gas, after being gasified again on leaving the tanker, may have to be fed into a pipeline to reach Michigan from the port of delivery.

36. Consumers Power is supporting coal-gasification research through the National Institute of Gas Technology, Chicago.

Chapter 21

1. Interview with Robert D. Allen, winter 1970, shortly after his resignation from Consumers Power Company, where he had worked his way up to the position of senior vice-president in charge of general services, personnel, plant construction, and engineering. He is now vice-president of Bechtel Corporation, the huge international construction firm based in San Francisco. Allen, who was born in 1921 and is a native of Bessemer, Michigan, is an electrical engineering graduate of the Michigan College of Mining and Technology at Houghton.

2. Karn retired on May 1, 1960. He spent his remaining years in Jackson and died on June 20, 1969, at the age of 79.

3. In 1945, Jim Campbell was a lieutenant colonel of artillery with the U.S. Army in Italy. When the atomic bomb exploded over Hiroshima, his unit was relaxing at the resort village of Gardone Riviera on lovely Lake Garda, and all he could think of was that now he didn't have to go and fight another war in the Pacific. He had no idea that practically his whole future career would be devoted to the peaceful application of the nuclear forces that science had just unleashed. It is ironic that

over the years there has been more public opposition to the constructive uses of the atom that to its ever-more sophisticated development as a war tool.

Campbell was born in Jackson in 1910 and spent his youth in Springfield, Illinois, and in Pontiac. He joined Consumers Power as a power and lighting engineer in Lansing in 1933, immediately after earning his bachelor of science degree in mechanical engineering. Six years later, he was awarded a Sloan Fellowship for advanced studies at the Massachusetts Institute of Technology. Later he worked briefly as power engineer for Ohio Edison before going into the service. In 1946, he was assigned to Grand Rapids as assistant to the division manager, was promoted to division manager the following year, and became assistant to the president (then Justin R. Whiting) in 1949. Campbell was named vice-president in 1950 and was elected to the board of directors in 1952. He became senior vice-president in 1956 and president in 1960.

Despite a serious illness, which necessitated open-heart surgery in 1969, Campbell refused to give in to his frequently severe pains and continued full force in the chief operating post of the company until his death in 1972.

4. Not only the rising price of coal but also the cost of shipping it places a great burden on Consumers Power. Michigan, being quite distant from major coal sources, has always had the shipping-expense problem. In fact, the aluminum industry considered the state as a potential site for plants after World War II and then abandoned the idea precisely because the cost of fuel would be too high.

5. As of the fall of 1971, the generating lineup of Consumers Power stood as follows:

Fourteen hydroelectric plants: Alcona, Allegan, Cascade, Cooke, Croton, Five Channels, Foote, Hardy, Hodenpyl, Loud, Mio, Rogers, Tippy, and Webber.

Ten steam plants: Campbell (two generating units), Karn (two), Weadock (eight), Whiting (three), Morrow (four), Cobb (five), Saginaw River (three), Elm Street (two), Wealthy Street (one), and Kalamazoo (one).

Twenty-three oil- and/or gas-fired internal-combustion units: Allegan (three), Campbell (one), Gaylord (five), Morrow (two), Straits (one), Thetford (nine), Weadock (one), and Whiting (one).

Two nuclear generating plants: Big Rock and Palisades.

6. The Power Reactor Development Company was an outgrowth of Atomic Power Development Associates, a research and development group of forty-five corporations, including thirty-three electric utilities. APDA's organizer had been Walker Cisler, chairman of Detroit Edison, one of the industry's first crusaders for atomic energy. (See Raymond C. Miller, *Kilowatts at Work* (Detroit: Wayne State University Press, 1957, pp. 407ff). Consumers Power was one of the original members of APDA. Consumers Power's contributions to PRDC and APDA have totaled approximately $9 million.

7. Named after Dr. Enrico Fermi (1901–1954), the Italian-American physicist who first demonstrated how the atom's power could be harnessed for practical use. It was he who in 1942 built the original atomic "pile" at the University of Chicago and achieved the first nuclear chain reaction.

8. The basic objection to the construction of a pilot nuclear plant stemmed from the fact that there was no way that it could stand on its own feet financially. A plan was eventually evolved to allow the project to finance itself to the extent that the facility produces power for the system, basing this capital amortization on what the plant's cost would have been had it been coal-fired. The surplus was written off over a period of years as a research and development expense. It was

considered to be an important step in the progression toward commercial boiling-water nuclear reactors.

9. Looking back at it nine years later, Campbell told me, "Big Rock was something of a gamble in a way. There was no guaranteed prize at the end, no way to know for sure that you were going to come out all right. You might have found yourself with a plant that was either so plagued with trouble that you couldn't run it—and that's happened to some reactor plants, and they never will run—or so costly that you couldn't afford to run it. Well, that's not the case at Big Rock. It has some relatively attractive economic advantages going for it now, so that it has been decidedly worth our while to run it."

Big Rock Point's fuel core consists of eighty-four bundles, each containing eighty-one zirconium alloy tubes filled with pellets of uranium oxide (UO_2 with the uranium slightly enriched in its U-235 isotope). The steel reactor vessel is about 30 feet high and 8 feet in diameter and is designed for a steam pressure of 1,715 pounds per square inch and a steam temperature of $650°$ F. The turbine generator produces electricity at 13,800 volts, which is stepped up to 138,000 volts before being fed into the Consumers Power transmission system.

But, at the beginning, electric generation was not the plant's prime purpose. The point was to learn how to handle a boiling-water reactor and to prove out an important link in the chain of development. The lessons learned put Consumers Power way in the forefront of the electric power utilities. There were indeed plenty of problems to learn from. As Bob Allen puts it, "Big Rock has a tremendous facility for demonstrating things in a negative way." Nobody, for example, could foresee the difficulty of the mass flow of fluid through the reactor. The flow of water caused a serious vibration in the neutron-absorbing safety shield within the reactor, and it took a whole year to lick this vibration problem.

The use charge on the uranium owned by the federal government was waived by the government as its research and development contribution during the early months of the plant's operation. In return, Big Rock conducted experiments on the use of fuels. Since those early days, however, Big Rock has ceased to be a pilot plant and is now a full-fledged production facility.

Needless to say, the interior of a nuclear plant is not a sightseeing attraction, but visitors are welcomed at Big Rock's information center, where guides give illustrative lectures on how a nuclear reactor generates electricity.

The new Palisades nuclear plant also has an information center, with appropriate lectures and exhibits.

10. That was the cost of the plant itself. Its core of fuel bundles came to about $25 million, which seems a lot, but isn't: the 90 metric tons of enriched uranium dioxide provide the power equivalent of 6.7 million tons of coal. The plant can operate for a full year between refuelings, at which point one-third of the bundles are replaced.

Economic studies on nuclear versus conventional power plants show that the fixed charges on a nuclear unit are larger than those on a conventional unit. These charges include the carrying charges on the capital investment, interest during construction, insurance, maintenance, and operating and personnel costs. These larger fixed charges are more than offset by the lower nuclear fuel costs so that the net result is that the overall generation costs attributable to the plant are less for a nuclear unit.

Most of the nuclear fuel used by Consumers Power at Big Rock so far has been fabricated by General Electric. Combustion Engineering supplied the first Palisades fuel load. There are now several other manufacturers in the field, including Westinghouse, Babcock and Wilcox, Gulf-United Nuclear, Nuclear Fuel Services Corp., and Jersey Nuclear. Reload fuels will be bought by Consumers Power on a competitive bid basis.

The contractor for the nuclear steam system at Palisades was Combustion Engineering. Bechtel Corporation handled the architectural and engineering services and plant construction.

11. In laboratory experiments, some scientists have observed detrimental effects on fish when water temperature is raised. However, this is hardly conclusive evidence since, in the laboratory, all the water has been heated and not just the surface, as is the case in nature. Interestingly enough, Dr. Merrill Eisenbud, professor and director of the Laboratory for Environmental Studies of New York University Medical Center and the former environmental protection administrator of the city of New York, says that there is ample evidence that the average temperature of Lake Michigan was 5 degrees higher at the turn of the century than it is today. Not that nuclear plant effluents would ever be sufficient to bring the lake's temperature back up to anywhere near that level.

12. Not included in the harvest are lake trout, which indeed dislike the warm water and shun it.

13. Harold P. Graves, vice-president and general counsel of Consumers Power Company, was born on February 11, 1917, at Groton, New York. He earned his B.A. at Calvin College, Grand Rapids, in 1938, and a juris doctor degree from the University of Michigan Law School in 1941. He was research assistant with the Honorable Edward M. Sharpe, chief justice of the Michigan Supreme Court, in 1941 and 1942, and assistant prosecuting attorney of Bay County, Michigan, in 1943, and again from 1946 through 1948, his career having been interrupted by wartime service as a special agent in the Counter Intelligence Corps of the Manhattan (atomic bomb) Project at Oak Ridge, Tennessee.

After a brief stint in private practice in Bay City, Graves joined Consumers Power as an attorney in 1953. He became the company's general attorney in 1955 and general counsel in 1958. He was elected vice-president and general counsel in April 1970. Graves is member of the Jackson County Bar Association, the State Bar of Michigan, and the American Bar Association.

14. The Calvert Cliffs project was a nuclear power plant being built on Chesapeake Bay by the Baltimore Gas and Electric Company.

15. The Midland intervention was led by the Saginaw Valley Nuclear Study Group, headed by an ardent lady by the name of Mary Sinclair. Mrs. Sinclair was joined by the Sierra Club (headquartered in California), Trout Unlimited (although trout is not only limited but altogether nonexistent in the sluggish Tittabawassee River), and the Environmental Law Student Society in forming a coalition to retain Myron Cherry, the same Chicago attorney who had spoken for the Palisades intervenors. In addition, two other separately financed organizations entered the Midland case: the Environmental Defense Fund and a group of private citizens of Mapleton, Michigan, just south of Midland near the proposed plant's location.

It seemed as if the Midland hearings might be conducted in a much more businesslike atmosphere than those at Kalamazoo. In the Palisades controversy, the three-man Atomic Safety Licensing Board panel was headed by Samuel Jensch, who, although he is a member of the AEC's permanent stable of hearing examiners, apparently had never encountered this type of drastic intervention before and seemed at a loss as to how to handle it. Almost any statement was accepted into the record, regardless of its scientific validity. Such was not the case at Midland, at least in the early stages, where Arthur W. Murphy was chairman of the hearing panel and kept a tight rein on admissible evidence.

This was just as well, for the Midland hearings were considerably more complex. Not only were the AEC's radiological safety standards challenged, but the thermal-pollution problem presented totally different aspects. At Midland, there is no Great Lake to absorb the plant's output of warm water. Instead, an artificial pond, covering 880 acres, would be used to cool the water, which would then be recirculated through the plant.

However, there would be a certain amount of discharge into the Tittabawassee River, and under certain climatic conditions, fog might rise from the pond. All these aspects, of course, had been studied by Consumers Power before the Midland plans were made, and the pond was specifically designed to minimize any environmental effects. Additional cooling facilities were added to eliminate any thermal effect on the river.

Much of the opposition to Midland and other nuclear installations has an emotional base. Some people are worried about radiation, knowing that since it can't be seen or felt, one never knows whether it's there. It's easy enough to blame these objections on the claims of John W. Gofman and Arthur R. Tamplin in their widely publicized book, *Poisoned Power* (Emmaus, Pa.: Rodale Press, 1971), that nuclear plant radiation would result in thousands of additional cancer deaths, an allegation based on unsupported theory. But there is more to the public's attitude than that. Basically, it may have been the initial use of atomic power as a weapon in war that spoiled its acceptability as an industrial energy source. If nuclear power had been used for peacetime projects to start with, there is little doubt—at least in this author's mind—that the situation today would be entirely different.

Even the most serious problems have their humorous aspects, however, and the public's fear of radiation is no exception. During the public hearings on the Dresden Unit 3, a nuclear power project of the Commonwealth Edison Company of Chicago, Dr. Tamplin (one of the authors of the book mentioned above) was asked whether he had any idea of the annual radiation dose one receives as a result of sleeping with one's wife. Even though Dr. Tamplin did not cite a specific amount, he acknowledged that it could approach the potential radiation dose from the Dresden plant. This provided food for some irreverent but soundly scientific thoughts by Grady B. Matheney, a Consumers Power Company radiology expert, who prepared the following extracurricular memorandum regarding Midland's potential dangers:

I have performed such an analysis and find that the annual dose to you from the potassium-40 in your wife's body is about 0.14 mrem. Potassium-40 is a naturally occurring radionuclide which enters the body by the ingestion of food.

Our calculations concerning the Midland plant reveal that a person standing at the low population zone for a year (1 mile from the plant) who obtains his annual supply of water and fish from the Tittabawassee River would receive an annual dose of no more than 2 mrem. This is an upper-limit dose because it is based on the unrealistic assumption that both plants will operate for one year with 1 percent failed fuel and that 12,000 curies of tritium will be released each year. It is now believed that the annual tritium release will not exceed 1,200 curies, because of the zircaloy cladding, and therefore it is expected that the dose at the low population will not exceed 10 percent of the predicted 2 mrem.

Thus it can be concluded that the risk from radiation while sleeping with your wife is about the same as the risk from our Midland plant.

I certainly do not intend to imply that you should sleep in twin beds, but caution should be exercised in sleeping with two women at the same time because your risk from *radiation* will then exceed the risk from the radiation release from our plant.

The Midland nuclear power plant is to have two generating units, each with its own reactor. Each reactor will be fueled with a 90-metric-ton core of enriched uranium dioxide. (When both generating units are operating at maximum capacity, uranium atoms will be splitting at the rate of 144 million trillion fissions a second.) The Midland plant will serve the dual purpose of providing process steam to the nearby manufacturing installations of Dow Chemical Company. The reactor system contractor is Babcock & Wilcox.

16. Harry R. Wall, a native of Shreveport, Louisiana, was graduated from the Carnegie Institute of Technology with a degree in electrical engineering. He held a variety of jobs with the Cleveland Electric Illuminating Company, The Tennessee Electric Power Company, The Commonwealth & Southern Corporation, and Commonwealth Associates before joining Consumers in Jackson in 1951 as assistant general supervisor in the production and transmission department. He was elected vice-president in 1954, senior vice-president of electric operations in 1958, and in July 1972 assumed the newly established office of vice-chairman of the board of directors as part of the executive reorganization following Jim Campbell's death.

Wall is a member of the National Society of Professional Engineers, and of CIGRE (International Conference on Large High-tension Electric Systems) and is a fellow in the Institute of Electrical and Electronic Engineers. He is currently serving on national committees of Edison Electric Institute, the Association of Edison Illuminating Companies, and the National Association of Manufacturers. He is president and director of the Michigan Electric Association. In 1963 and 1964, he served on the Transmission and Interconnection Advisory Committee for the National Power Survey of the Federal Power Commission. In 1966, he was a member of the United States Electric Utility Study Mission to Japan, the purpose of which was to interchange information with the Japanese regarding design, operation, and reliability of electric power systems.

17. The Ozark installation, known as the Taum Sauk pumped-storage plant, is owned by Union Electric of St. Louis, Missouri. It has a capacity of about 400,000 kilowatts. There are also smaller storage operations in New Jersey, Colorado, and Pennsylvania.

18. Ludington's power will be fed into the Michigan power pool and will be shared by Consumers Power and Detroit Edison. During the first few years, the plant's capacity is expected to exceed the peak-period requirements of the two companies, and this surplus will be sold.

Fargo Engineering, the firm Bill Fargo had formed in the Foote days, handled the original surveys on 1,200 acres of land that Consumers Power had purchased for the project in the early 1960s. The site was later augmented by another 600 acres. When the magnitude of the enterprise became apparent, the project was turned over to Ebasco Services, an engineering consulting firm that is one of the outgrowths of Electric Bond & Share, of the holding-company days.

Ludington's immense reversible pump turbines, each with a capacity of 312 megawatts, are being supplied by Hitachi of Japan, low bidder in a competition that involved Westinghouse, General Electric, and Allis-Chalmers, as well as Brown Boveri of Switzerland. It will take six ships coming up through the St. Lawrence Seaway after their ocean voyage from the Orient to deliver the turbines and their ancillary equipment.

The units will be set in a powerhouse, 26.5 feet below the level of Lake Michigan. When pumping, each unit will lift 11,000 cubic feet per second, or 5 million gallons per minute. When generating, the entire plant discharge will be about 75,000 cubic feet per second. This flow is equal to that of the Ohio River about Cincinnati.

The average maximum depth of the pond will be 95 feet at maximum intake, but at the dam the level will be 162 feet, putting the maximum pressure head at 362 feet above the level of Lake Michigan. The "drawdown"—letting the water out—will lower the pond's surface by 67 feet. Refilling the pond will require utilizing all six units for 9.9 hours. Of course, neither the filling nor the drawdown will occur all at once. The average pond level will decrease during the week, as each day more water is let out than is pumped in at night. On the weekends, the reservoir will be brought back to maximum capacity.

19. Russell C. Youngdahl, a 1945 University of Michigan graduate with a degree in electrical engineering, joined Consumers Power in 1946 as a distribution technician. He served in various engineering and supervisory capacities in the company's Central and Flint divisions, and in 1961 he moved to Jackson to become general supervisor of electric distribution. In 1963, after attending the Massachusetts Institute of Technology on a Sloan Fellowship, he was awarded the degree of master of science in industrial management. A promotion to executive manager of electric operations came the following year, and in 1966 Youngdahl was appointed executive manager of engineering and construction.

He was elected vice-president in August 1967 and was placed in charge of electric construction and the purchasing and stores operation, all of which remain his responsibilities as senior vice-president. On Harry Wall's elevation to vice-chairman, Youngdahl assumed the added responsibility for all electric operations (see Note 16 above, and Tomorrow, Note 26).

Tomorrow

1. Walter R. Boris, a native of Amsterdam, New York, was born on September 7, 1921. Boris was a World War II bomber pilot and joined Consumers Power at the age of 29, equipped with degrees in engineering and law from the University of Michigan. His first job with the company was that of title examiner; soon he was assigned to more important legal work. In 1953, he became Whiting's executive assistant, and three years later was elected assistant secretary. From here he advanced to the dual post of secretary of Consumers Power and its Michigan Gas Storage subsidiary. He was elected vice-president of finance in 1968, and also serves as vice-president and as a director of Michigan Gas Storage.

Boris was a member of the Jackson Board of Education from 1962 to 1964, and was its president in 1965. He has been a member of the Jackson Metropolitan Regional Planning Commission since 1956, serving as its chairman from 1965 to 1970.

He is a director of the Citizens Research Council of Michigan, a director of the S. H. Camp Company, and a trustee of the Samuel Higby Camp Foundation. He has been a member of the Michigan Council for the Arts since 1969, and trustee of the Michigan Foundation for the Arts since 1970, and he is vice-president of Michigan Artrain, Inc. He also belongs to The Economic Club of Detroit, the Michigan and New York State Bar Associations, and the American Finance Association.

2. Consumers Power Company does not generally negotiate with only one underwriting group, but considers the bids of several, usually three. The bidding takes place in the offices of Winthrop, Stimson, Putnam & Roberts, the legal firm that represents Consumers in Wall Street transactions. An open telephone line connects Boris with the boardroom at the Consumers Power building in Jackson, where the directors are in simultaneous session to consider the best offer and okay it on the spot if it is acceptable. In turn, private offices with telephones are provided for the bidders so that they can confer with their head offices.

Even in an age when government and industry seem to handle huge sums as if they were only play money, $60 million is an enormous amount of cash, and not at all easy to come by. Few underwriting firms can afford to take on that much alone, even though their ultimate function is to resell the bonds to investors. Underwriters thus pool their resources and form themselves into groups that may include as many as forty or fifty investment banking firms. There is usually a lead underwriter in each group who will take on about $5 million as his personal responsibility. The others go for considerably smaller shares; they'll agree to move anywhere from a few hundred thousand to 1 or 2 million dollars.

Singling out the most favorable bid requires a computer. While the coupon rate on a bond issue is expressed in eighths, the principal amount the bidders are willing to pay is expressed in decimals, often running to three or four digits. For instance, if Consumers has an 8 percent bond for which a bidder is willing to pay $100, it's easy enough to tell that the cost to Consumers will be precisely 8 percent. But take the case where a bidder wants $8\frac{1}{4}$ on the coupon but is willing to pay Consumers $101.342 per bond. Now the arithmetic becomes more difficult. To complicate matters further, there is a sinking fund on these bonds. After the fifth year they can be called at a price equal to the reoffering price plus the coupon divided by $\frac{1}{29}$ for every one of the years left to maturity. The range of possible combinations on all these factors become too unwieldy for immediate pen-and-paper calculation, and that's where an offshoot of old Commonwealth & Southern comes into the picture.

Commonwealth Services, the service company remnant of C&S, operates a computer bank in New York, which Consumers contracts for on occasions of this sort to spit out immediate answers not only on the lowest cost of the money but also on the relative redemption provisions and prices throughout the life of the bonds. With the computer results in hand, Boris phones the best bid to Aymond. The board or executive committee then votes whether or not to accept the bid and attends to the necessary paper work to make it official. Bidding time is usually set for 11 A.M. By noon at the latest, the bond issue is generally all wrapped up.

3. This was well below the recent bond-interest peaks of more than 9 percent, and it even beat the $8\frac{3}{4}$ and $8\frac{5}{8}$ series Consumers had issued the previous year. See *Today,* Notes and Comments, Note 9.

4. A few days later, a securities analyst called Boris from New York. "I want to find out something," the man said. "Did the President talk to the utilities before his wage

and price freeze speech?" Boris answered, "I can't tell you if he talked to the utilities, but I can tell you whom he didn't talk to. He didn't talk to Consumers Power."

The effect of a freeze was obvious to anyone in the money business—it had to drive down interest rates—and nobody in his right mind would have issued bonds that week if such an order had been even remotely expected.

5. Consumers' bond issue moved rather slowly the first day or two, and then it quickly picked up speed. Investors who were astute or lucky enough to buy the 8⅛s came out way ahead. After the President's announcement, the bonds jumped to 106½ on the open market and were out of sight. Boris has received many letters from Consumers Power stockholders, complaining that they usually buy the company's bonds several days after they are issued and never have any trouble getting them without paying a premium. This time, suddenly, there weren't any around. Several writers accused Consumers of having directed the bonds to a few favored people. All Boris could do was to answer the disgruntled stockholders that they had run into a peculiar situation this time—one that had hurt the company much more than it had hurt them.

6. Ludington's total cost will be about $376 million, with the investment and ownership shared by Consumers Power (51 percent) and Detroit Edison (49 percent). See Chapter 21.

7. Here are two examples involving electric energy needs for fighting pollution.

First, electric melting furnaces in foundries, replacing dirty cupolas, require about 20,000 kilowatts each; a fair-sized foundry needs several of these furnaces and can easily absorb 50,000 kilowatts. That foundry's annual need would be about 100 million kilowatthours.

Second, a crusher to press junked automobiles into scrap-steel packages uses a 2,000-horsepower motor, requiring about 1,200 kilowatts to run. That's relatively small potatoes, but its annual consumption comes to about 1 million kilowatthours.

You could keep citing the energy requirements for environmental control, ad infinitum.

8. Consumers Power makes it a special point to thoroughly document all its public statements, whether in executives' speeches, press releases, educational films and brochures, or advertisements. The meticulousness of the company's efforts to always tell the straight story is in no small measure due to Aymond's insistence on having only professional newsmen in top public relations jobs. His vice-president for public relations is Romney Wheeler, formerly London news director for NBC and president of NBC International, Ltd., and later senior public relations executive for The Radio Corporation of America. Wheeler's right-hand man and director of public information is Ty Cross, who went to Jackson as a PR man from the *Detroit Times* in 1950, but who never lost the no-nonsense attitude of a scholarly, deep-digging reporter who can smell a lie coming almost before a man starts to talk.

Wheeler, who was born on February 11, 1911, and is a native of Huntington, New York, joined Consumers Power in 1964 as assistant director of public relations; the following year, upon the retirement of Donald J. McGowan, he took over the latter's post as director of public relations. He was elected vice-president in April 1970.

As a public relations executive for Consumers Power Company, Wheeler has served in various capacities in national industry organizations. These include the public relations committee of the American Gas Association (chairman, 1969–

1970); the public relations committee of the Edison Electric Institute (chairman, educational materials subcommittee, 1969–1972); and the public affairs committee of the Atomic Industrial Forum. He is also chairman of the Film Exhibition Division for the Ninth World Energy Conference, to be held in Detroit in September 1974. His civic contributions have included service as a member of the board of managers of W. A. Foote Memorial Hospital, Jackson. He was chairman of the board from 1970 to 1972.

9. Like his brother Jim, the late president of Consumers Power, Birum G. Campbell, Jr., grew up into the company. It will be recalled that their father, B. G. Campbell, Sr., was Pontiac manager during that interesting and important period when Consumers established its gas franchise in Oakland County.

B. G. Campbell, Jr., was born in Pontiac on September 12, 1917, attended Pontiac High School, and joined the sales department of the southeast division in 1939 after attending the University of Michigan. Following World War II, during which he served nearly five years with the Army Signal Corps in Europe, he returned to the company in 1946 and worked for several years in personnel. In 1949, Campbell, Jr., became local manager in Royal Oak; in 1950 he became district manager there and, in 1951, assistant to the division manager in Kalamazoo. The next year he was promoted to head of the Kalamazoo division, and he held this position until his election to the marketing vice-presidency in 1957.

In the late spring of 1972, the marketing department ceased to operate as an entity, and B. G. Campbell, Jr., was elected vice-president of personnel. At the same time, Consumers Power went out of the appliance business. Campbell Jr.'s other marketing functions were distributed among W. Anson Hedgecock, vice-president for divisions, who absorbed the sales department; Harry R. Wall, now vice-chairman of the board of directors, who took over area development, i.e., the promotion of new industry in Michigan; and Romney Wheeler, vice-president for public relations, who was placed in charge of advertising and display.

10. The summer peaking problem created by air conditioning is by now almost impossible to rectify. The villain here is not so much home air conditioning, which is used a good deal at night and thus actually increases the economic operating efficiency of base-load plants, but the air conditioning of office buildings, commercial establishments, and factories. Practically all such structures built in the last dozen years, and many erected as long as a generation ago, were designed around electricity-powered climate control. Windows often can't be opened, and large interior areas have no windows at all. If continuous air-movement systems were to be eliminated, the United States would have to rebuild large sections of most of its cities—another utopian solution that loses its glamour when it's stripped to the buff.

11. Another big problem that those in favor of upside-down rates apparently haven't thought about is that large users of power would be tempted to install their own generating facilities. Big as these individual power plants might be, they would not be big enough to warrant the tremendous investment necessary for nuclear operation and would have to rely on fossil fuels, which are not only dirtier but also in increasingly short supply. In other words, the suggestion to increase bulk rates doesn't make sense, no matter which way you look at it.

12. In the summer of 1971, the peak demand made on the power-pool resources of Consumers Power and Detroit Edison reached 9.8 million kilowatts. This was the actual amount of generating capacity that had to be producing power at the

moment when industrial, commercial, and residential users all made maximum demands for energy. By the summer of 1980, the peak demand is expected to hit 19.4 million kilowatts, an increase of 9.6 million. But the actual amount of new generating capacity that must be added to the power pool by that time totals 12.3 million kilowatts, including 1.6 million reserve capacity and 1 million to permit retirement of antiquated plant.

13. Utilities in Ohio, Illinois, Indiana, Florida, and California operate in relatively favorable regulatory climates.

14. The Public Service Commission authorized this increase in September 1969, but did not approve the rate schedules to implement it until April 1970. In the meantime Consumers Power went to court for authority to put the new schedule into effect. This court approval was actually granted several months prior to the PSC's final order.

15. How laborious such rate cases turn out to be can be seen from the number of pages of testimony that get on the record. In round numbers, the 1960 gas rate case went to 2,600 typewritten pages of testimony, or about four times the length of this book. Records of the 1958 electric rate case covered 1,500 pages; the 1968 electric rate case, some 2,000 pages.

16. The Michigan Public Service Commission is composed of three members. They are, as this is written, Willis F. Ward, the commission's chairman, who has served since 1966, Lenton G. Sculthorp, who had been Director of the Department of Licensing and Regulation prior to joining the PSC in 1969, and William Ralls, a new appointee who in 1971 replaced William A. Boos, Jr. All these men are lawyers. None has a utilities background.

The commission's civil service staff, composed of 185 members, examines requests for rate increases (and other applications for utility service modifications) and on the basis of its findings makes recommendations for action. These recommendations are usually followed by the commissioners.

17. Consumers' 1970 earnings included a profit of about $2 million on the discount of reacquired securities. The company had two options for income tax purposes. It could treat the gain as taxable income and pay out about half of it in taxes, or it could look on the $2 million as a reduction in the company's tax-cost basis. The latter approach would spread the profit (and the taxes due on it) over a period of several years; i.e., the property would thus be depreciated at a lower rate over its remaining life. The PSC insisted on considering this gain current taxable income, with the result that the earnings for 1970, test year in the electric rate case, were inflated. However, the commission—prodded by John W. Kluberg, Consumers' controller (see text below and Note 21)—did recognize the problem and agreed that in this particular instance, Consumers Power would be permitted to average its profits on reacquired securities over the five-year period from 1965 to 1970. This mitigated the inequity to a degree.

Actually the PSC has been reasonably fair in accepting sound accounting principles. Take the alternatives of handling investment credit. The tempting way is to take the credit on the spot and to reduce current taxes, with the result that the year's earnings are increased by the amount of the credit. The other, sounder principle is to treat investment credit as a reduction in the cost of the acquired item. This method doesn't provide an immediate earnings windfall, but spreads the saving over the life of the property. Here, the Michigan PSC allows the latter accounting method, thus enabling the companies it regulates to guard themselves against the fate that overtook many companies elsewhere when the investment credit was cancelled in 1969. The earnings of these companies had been inflated year after year, which didn't hurt as long as the credit was in effect, but when the credit stopped, their earnings suddenly dropped dramatically.

It's interesting to note that while the investment tax credit on new equipment was set at 7 percent for nonregulated companies, utilities could claim only 3 percent. A similar provision, with a 4 percent tax credit for the utilities, is written into the 1971 bill which revives the credit.

18. Consumers Power's earnings per share on common stock dropped from $2.87 in 1966 to $2.71 in 1971. That's 16 cents per share less and doesn't seem so terrible, but Wall Streeters who understand such matters look at financial statements more carefully, for the bottom line—contrary to the popular saying—tells far from the whole story.

To wit: Consumers' underlying book value in 1967 stood at $22.83 per common share. By 1971, because of increasing plant investment, it had risen to $26.39 a share. Thus, per dollar invested, the company was earning considerably less.

This wasn't the only thing that caused anxiety. Factored into earnings is an item known as "interest charged to construction," a bookkeeping device that allows a company to add back on the plus side a certain amount of dollars relating to plant being built which is not yet producing. This is done by capitalizing the interest and other expenses of maintaining the nonoperative facility. While this income shows up on the books, it is not cash income earned from production. Carried ad absurdum, a company could be totally nonproductive and yet show a plus item in this category as long as capital plant stood around unused.

With the rapidly accelerating expansion of Consumers' productive facilities the construction-interest item has been growing by leaps and bounds in recent years. This is as it must be, but when you deduct these plus-side figures, the cash earnings look a lot worse than the bottom line would indicate. In fact, the company's cash earnings have dropped by nearly 25 percent since 1967. The chart below traces the relationship.

Year	Per-share earnings	Interest during construction	Earnings exclusive of interest
1967	$2.87	$.11	$2.76
1968	2.60	.22	2.38
1969	2.79	.37	2.42
1970	2.95	.60	2.35
1971	2.69	.91	1.78

You'll have noted that for 1971, the company's per-share earnings exclusive of interest charged to construction stood at $1.78—i.e., within 22 cents of the company's $2 common stock dividend. Now, if real earnings drop just a little more, part of the company's debt financing would have to be used to maintain this dividend, a not too healthy situation. To reduce the dividend would further erode investor confidence in the company.

19. The company's 1972 construction financing plans call for the sale of about $70 million worth of preferred stock, $120 million worth of bonds and approximately $60 million of common stock. In addition, the company probably will have to take out $30 million in short-term loans and generate around $100 million in retained earnings, tax accruals, and depreciation in order to meet its goals.

Bonds are the cheapest way to finance construction: with the interest tax-deductible, the actual cost comes to only about 50 cents on the dollar. But it is far from safe when too much reliance is placed on this vehicle. Interest must be paid out on certain dates, principal is due on other dates, and if any of these payments are not met, creditors can put a company into receivership, as has happened to a number of overbonded railroads, among them most notably Penn Central.

In any event, bondholders protect themselves by means of limitations contained in the indenture place on the issuance of additional debt.

The way Aymond and Boris see it, a utility company, for maximum safety and financial efficiency, should derive about 40 percent of its capitalization from risk investment, i.e., common stock, and not much more than 50 percent from bonds. The remaining 10 percent can be raised by means of preferred stock, a type of security which, even when it is not convertible, is popular with certain investors. At the end of 1971, Consumers Power was lighter on common equity (about 35 percent) and somewhat higher on bonds (about 57 percent) than the company likes to see. It became necessary to sell common stock in 1972 in spite of low earnings and a depressed market. The fundamental problem is that the PSC has not permitted rate increases sufficient to cover increasing costs with the resulting deterioration in interest and preferred stock dividend coverages.

20. After his graduation from the University of Illinois School of Commerce, John W. Kluberg was associated from 1937 through 1950 with Arthur Andersen & Co., first in their Chicago office and later in Detroit. Kluberg joined Consumers Power early in 1951 as controller, and was elected vice-president and controller in 1964. He is a certified public accountant in the states of Illinois and Michigan and a member of the American Institute of Certified Public Accountants and the Financial Executives Institute.

21. The bill was to apply to individuals and couples with total yearly incomes of no more than $6,000. The majority of retirees fall into this category. It is estimated that some 150,000 Michigan homeowners are now over the age of sixty-two and that another 100,000 are renters.

22. Copyright 1950 by Crowell-Collier and included in Ray Bradbury, *The Martian Chronicles* (New York: Doubleday, 1950), which has since been reprinted several times by Doubleday in hard cover and by Bantam Books in soft cover.

23. Such was the case in the summer of 1970, when a critical shortage of natural gas necessitated the imposition of restrictions on Consumers' commercial and industrial gas customers (see Chapter 20). These restrictions have since been modified.

24. As of April 23, 1971, Consumers' 24,033,838 common shares were in 94,654 hands, as follows:

	Holders	Shares
Men	15,378	2,284,124
Women	25,258	3,528,750
Joint accounts	43,803	4,183,407
Fiduciaries	7,234	995,200
Institutions	579	434,656
Stockbrokers	225	868,394
Nominees (many of these are banks and insurance companies)	1,138	9,549,154
Other	1,039	2,190,153

Slightly more than one-third of the common stock was voted from Michigan: 8,468,908 shares by 63,959 owners or their representatives. This was the distribution:

Area	Holders	Shares
Battle Creek division	2,363	261,833
Bay City division	3,178	314,525
Central division	2,301	215,199
Flint division	9,041	1,444,891
Grand Rapids division	11,646	1,296,789
Jackson division	4,176	499,565
Kalamazoo division	4,560	565,869
Lansing division	4,526	506,401
Muskegon division	4,149	449,134
Northwest division	2,222	226,057
Pontiac division	1,084	104,083
Saginaw division	3,765	348,167
Macomb division	984	98,003
South Oakland division	2,014	287,348
West Wayne division	620	57,917
Greater Detroit area	3,429	1,317,478
Other Michigan	3,901	475,649

NOTE: Division refers to the division territory of Consumers Power.

Not surprisingly, the largest number of Michigan shares is in the hands of relatively small investors in areas served by Consumers Power Company. This fact is in no small measure attributable to the easy familiarity of most of Consumers' customers with the company. Good public relations on the service level, where it counts (and the only thing that counts here is good service), has always been emphasized by the company, and its local and division managers have been selected with much care.

Currently in charge of divisions and customer service is W. Anson Hedgecock, a vice-president since 1965, who joined the company in Flint during the Depression. He worked his way up in the Flint division, and after a series of promotions there he became district manager at Cadillac. In 1955, he went to Pontiac as assistant division manager and later became district manager at Royal Oak. He was named manager of the company's customer services in 1959, and in 1961 he took the post of division manager at Saginaw. In 1964 he became general executive in charge of divisions, and the vice-presidency came to him the following year.

25. One notable exception was nuclear fuel, which until 1969 had to be leased from the Atomic Energy Commission.

26. James A. McDivitt, Jr., son of a retired Consumers Power engineer, was born in Chicago and grew up in Kalamazoo and Jackson. He joined the U.S. Air Force in 1951, flew 145 combat missions in F-80s and F-86s during the Korean conflict and was selected as an astronaut by the National Aeronautics and Space Administration (NASA) in 1962. Three years later, he served as command pilot on the 66-orbit, four-day mission of Gemini IV and in 1969 commanded Apollo 9 in an earth-orbital

mission. Later that year, he first became manager of lunar landing operations in the Apollo Spacecraft Program and then was named manager of the entire Apollo project. In early 1972, he got his star as an Air Force brigadier general.

At the same time that 43-year-old McDivitt was elected to his senior vice-presidency of Consumers Power in June 1972, a number of other upper-echelon changes took place in the company. In this executive reorganization, Harry R. Wall was named vice-chairman of the board of directors; B. G. Campbell, Jr.'s vice-presidential responsibilities were shifted from marketing to personnel; additional functions were assigned to senior vice-presidents John B. Simpson and Russell C. Youngdahl, and to vice-president W. Anson Hedgecock. (See Index for location of biographies.)

Three new vice-presidents also were elected: Roland A. Lamley, Eugene B. Hedges, and Stephen H. Howell.

Roland A. Lamley, vice president for bulk power operations, joined Consumers Power in Adrian in 1938 as assistant substation supervisor and in 1940 went to the electric dispatching department in Jackson. After a stint with the bulk power department in Grand Rapids, he returned to Jackson in 1950 to hold a variety of assignments, culminating in his appointments as manager of bulk power supply and later executive manager of bulk power operations, both in 1970. He is a graduate of the University of Toledo.

Eugene B. Hedges, 53, vice president for gas operations, started as a gas transmission engineer in the Saginaw division in 1949. He moved to the general gas department in Jackson in 1954; and since then he has served as manager of gas production and transmission, executive manager of gas operations, general superintendent of the Michigan Gas Storage Company, and as vice president of the Northern Michigan Exploration Company. On assuming his new post, Hedges continued his functions with the subsidiaries. He is a graduate of Purdue University and served in World War II as an Air Corps pilot.

Stephen H. Howell, 40, vice president, electric plant projects, came to Consumers in 1961 as a geologist with the gas storage subsidiary. He was promoted to executive assistant, then assistant manager of gas production and transmission, and finally manager of gas production and transmission before being named executive manager of electric and generating plant construction in 1971. Later that same year, he was promoted to executive manager of electric plant construction. He is a graduate of Princeton and was a Sloan Fellow at the Massachusetts Institute of Technology.

Appendix A

Officers and Directors
(From April 15, 1910)

*Date of Death

NAME   TERM (Inclusive)

First Vice-President

D. E. Karn   April 14, 1950–November 29, 1951

Senior Vice-President and Assistant to the Chairman of the Board

J. B. Simpson   July 2, 1969–September 2, 1969

Senior Vice-President

James H. Campbell	April 26, 1956–April 30, 1960
W. C. Schmidt	January 27, 1966–November 1, 1967
H. R. Wall	April 9, 1968–June 6, 1972
J. B. Simpson	April 9, 1968–July 1, 1969
R. D. Allen	April 9, 1968–May 8, 1970
J. B. Simpson	September 3, 1969–
R. C. Youngdahl	April 14, 1970–
James A. McDivitt	July 1, 1972–

Executive Vice-President

R. P. Briggs	January 24, 1952–April 30, 1968
A. H. Aymond	January 1, 1958–April 30, 1960

Financial Vice-President

R. P. Briggs   January 18, 1951–January 23, 1952

Vice-President and Controller

J. W. Kluberg   April 23, 1964–

Vice-President and General Counsel

A. H. Aymond	January 1, 1956–December 31, 1957
H. P. Graves	April 14, 1970–

Vice-President

E. W. Clark	April 15, 1910–September 12, 1929
H. D. Walbridge	April 15, 1910–April 28, 1911
Geo. E. Hardy	April 28, 1911–August 22, 1928
T. A. Kenney	July 7, 1920–June 28, 1932
F. W. Hoover	July 7, 1920–May 12, 1926
C. W. Tippy	June 21, 1921–September 15, 1933*
W. W. Tefft	June 26, 1922–December 19, 1928
W. H. Barthold	September 12, 1922–June 24, 1941
D. E. Karn	May 12, 1926–January 4, 1927
	September 18, 1933–April 14, 1950
R. P. Stevens	June 26, 1928–December 11, 1929

*Date of Death

NAME	TERM (Inclusive)
Jacob Hekma	August 22, 1928–February 17, 1949
C. J. Holmes	December 19, 1928–January 31, 1945
W. H. Sammis	May 3, 1932–June 27, 1944
M. W. Arthur	April 24, 1934–January 3, 1952*
F. G. Boyce	June 22, 1937–February 28, 1950
J. A. Brown	April 28, 1944–April 20, 1948
L. L. Benedict	March 1, 1950–November 1, 1952
James H. Campbell	April 14, 1950–April 25, 1956
H. S. Richmond	January 24, 1952–May 1, 1964
D. E. Herringshaw	January 24, 1952–January 15, 1958
C. E. Arvidson	November 1, 1952–October 20, 1954*
C. A. Mulligan	November 24, 1953–January 1, 1965
H. R. Wall	October 28, 1954–April 8, 1968
B. G. Campbell, Jr.	January 15, 1958–
J. B. Simpson	January 15, 1958–April 8, 1968
W. C. Schmidt	May 1, 1960–January 27, 1966
R. D. Allen	April 23, 1964–April 9, 1968
W. A. Hedgecock	April 22, 1965–
R. C. Bretting	April 22, 1965–July 1, 1972
F. C. Fisher	April 11, 1967–
R. C. Youngdahl	August 2, 1967–April 13, 1970
W. R. Boris	May 1, 1968–
W. J. Mosley	July 2, 1969–
E. R. Wheeler	April 14, 1970–
E. B. Hedges	July 1, 1972–
S. H. Howell	July 1, 1972–
R. A. Lamley	July 1, 1972–

Assistant Vice-President

David H. Gerhard	December 1, 1961–August 1, 1964

Secretary

George E. Hardy	April 15, 1910–September 3, 1913
Jacob Hekma	September 3, 1913–August 4, 1920
Robert Davey	August 4, 1920–May 5, 1937*
A. J. Mayotte	June 1, 1937–May 31, 1956
W. R. Boris	June 1, 1956–April 30, 1968
P. A. Perry	May 1, 1968–

Treasurer

George E. Hardy	April 15, 1910–April 28, 1911
Jacob Hekma	April 28, 1911–August 4, 1920

* Date of Death

C. E. Rowe	August 4, 1920–March 1, 1950
L. J. Hamilton	March 1, 1950–February 1, 1958
G. E. Olmsted	February 1, 1958–June 30, 1964
H. J. Palmer	July 1, 1964–

Controller

H. G. Kessler	September 12, 1922–April 7, 1934*
G. H. Bourne	April 24, 1934–July 22, 1947
H. B. Hardwick	July 22, 1947–December 28, 1950*
J. W. Kluberg	January 18, 1951–April 22, 1964

General Counsel

C. J. Holmes	August 1, 1915–February 1, 1945
W. D. Kline	February 1, 1945–June 30, 1948
W. R. Roberts	July 1, 1948–August 31, 1955
A. H. Aymond	September 1, 1955–January 1, 1958
H. P. Graves	January 1, 1958–April 13, 1970

General Manager

| C. W. Tippy | August 1, 1915–September 15, 1933* |
| D. E. Karn | September 18, 1933–April 14, 1950 |

Assistant General Manager

| D. E. Karn | April 1, 1931–September 18, 1933 |
| M. W. Arthur | November 1, 1933–April 14, 1950 |

Assistant to the President

| R. D. Allen | May 1, 1960–April 23, 1964 |
| R. E. Kettner | July 23, 1964–June 15, 1968 |

Former Directors

M. W. Arthur	September 28, 1949–January 3, 1952*
W. H. Barthold	July 14, 1924–June 24, 1941
Arthur L. Blakeslee	October 25, 1949–September 22, 1960
G. H. Bourne	February 23, 1938–October 25, 1949
Lindsay Bradford	October 26, 1943–July 22, 1954
J. A. Brown	April 9, 1935–September 28, 1949
James H. Campbell	January 24, 1952–January 24, 1972*
C. M. Clark	April 15, 1910–August 4, 1920
	September 16, 1920–June 29, 1937
E. W. Clark	April 15, 1910–August 6, 1929
C. Sewall Clark	October 26, 1937–March 22, 1938

*Date of death.

Percy H. Clark	April 12, 1938–October 25, 1949
B. C. Cobb	August 28, 1911–July 24, 1934
H. H. Crowell	April 12, 1919–June 11, 1919
W. M. Eaton	April 15, 1910–December 17, 1913
Robert M. Farr	July 19, 1949–September 23, 1954
J. B. Foote	June 8, 1915–May 3, 1924
W. A. Foote	April 15, 1910–April 14, 1915
H. B. Hardwick	September 28, 1949–December 28, 1950*
George E. Hardy	April 15, 1910–June 30, 1949
Jacob Hekma	December 26, 1919–February 17, 1949*
Anton G. Hodenpyl	April 15, 1910–June 19, 1929
Robert L. Hoguet, Jr.	July 22, 1954–June 23, 1955
	May 27, 1964–September 1, 1965
Clyde J. Holmes	December 19, 1928–February 1, 1945
Lee Wilson Hutchins	October 25, 1949–June 17, 1956*
D. E. Karn	September 18, 1933–April 11, 1967
T. A. Kenney	May 10, 1928–January 19, 1938*
H. G. Kessler	August 6, 1929–April 7, 1934*
W. D. Kline	February 19, 1945–September 28, 1949
Thomas W. Martin	June 19, 1929–June 28, 1932
James A. McDivitt	January 6, 1971–June 30, 1972
Don T. McKone	January 14, 1953–April 10, 1965*
Ralph C. Morley, Jr.	September 23, 1954–March 19, 1966*
E. E. Nelson	November 28, 1938–December 17, 1943
	March 1, 1949–October 25, 1949
Paul A. Perry	April 13, 1965–May 27, 1965
	April 12, 1966–April 12, 1966
Donald J. Porter	July 19, 1956–April 13, 1971
W. H. Sammis	June 28, 1932–June 27, 1944
Arthur H. Sarvis	December 17, 1943–April 11, 1967
Frank Silliman, Jr.	December 17, 1913–December 26, 1919
R. P. Stevens	May 10, 1928–December 11, 1929
W. W. Tefft	June 26, 1922–December 19, 1928
Edwin Thorne	October 25, 1949–January 28, 1965
C. W. Tippy	June 26, 1922–September 15, 1933*
D. B. Varner	April 11, 1967–January 7, 1970
H. D. Walbridge	April 15, 1910–April 28, 1911
J. C. Weadock	August 3, 1920–September 16, 1920
Wendell L. Willkie	December 11, 1929–July 17, 1940
Justin R. Whiting	April 12, 1934–November 28, 1938
	July 17, 1940–March 1, 1965*

*Date of death.

CURRENT DIRECTORS

A. H. Aymond	December 19, 1957–
R. P. Briggs	January 18, 1951–
E. Newton Cutler, Jr.	September 1, 1965–
L. D. Ferden	February 19, 1945–
Daniel M. Fitz-Gerald	April 11, 1967–
Richard M. Gillett	April 11, 1967–
John F. Gordon	June 24, 1965–
Frank Hamilton	June 23, 1955–
C. S. Harding Mott	July 22, 1965–
L. C. Roll	October 25, 1962–
Dr. E. Gifford Upjohn	May 27, 1965–
H. R. Wall	July 1, 1972–

Appendix B

Bibliography

The author has drawn heavily on the books listed
below for background on the utilities industry,
for the history of Michigan, and for information on
prominent figures whose lives influenced directly
and indirectly the course of events at Consumers
Power Company, its predecessors and associated
companies. Citations of other books used as source
material, as well as of numerous periodicals,
newspapers, theses, interview transcripts, and
government and industry documents may be
found in the main text where appropriate, and/or
under Notes and Comments.

Bald, F. Clever: *Michigan in Four Centuries* (New York: Harper & Row, 1961).
Barnes, Irsten Robert: *The Economics of Public Utility Regulation* (New York: Crofts, 1942).
Barnes, Joseph: *Willkie* (New York: Simon and Schuster, 1952).
Baxter, Albert: *History of the City of Grand Rapids, Michigan* (New York: Munsell & Company, 1891).

Bonbright, James C., and Gardiner C. Means: *The Holding Company* (New York: Mc-Graw-Hill, 1932).

Coleman, Charles M.: *P.G. & E. of California* (New York: McGraw-Hill, 1952).

Dunbar, Willis Frederick: *Michigan: A History of the Wolverine State* (Grand Rapids, Michigan: Eerdmans, 1965).

Furnas, J. C.: *The Americans: A Social History of the United States: 1587–1914* (New York: Putnam, 1969).

Glaeser, Martin: *Public Utilities in American Capitalism* (New York: Macmillan, 1957).

Jones, Eliot, and Truman C. Bigham: *Principles of Public Utilities* (New York: Macmillan, 1931).

Love, Edmond G.: *The Situation in Flushing* (New York: Harper & Row, 1965).

Luther, E. Hardy: "Song of Service: A Century of Consumers Power Company and Predecessors," in Consumers Power Company files.

McDonald, Forrest: *Insull* (Chicago: University of Chicago Press, 1962).

The Michigan Energy Service Committee: *Energy and the Michigan Economy* (Ann Arbor: University of Michigan Press, 1967).

Miller, Raymond C.: *Kilowatts at Work* (Detroit: Wayne State University Press, 1958).

Morison, Samuel Eliot: *The Oxford History of the American People* (New York: Oxford University Press, 1965).

Mosher, William E., and Finla G. Crawford: *Public Utility Regulation* (New York: Harper, 1933).

Nevins, Allan: *Ford: The Times, the Man, the Company* (New York: Scribner, 1954).

Passer, Harold C.: *The Electrical Manufacturers: 1875–1900* (Cambridge, Mass.: Harvard, 1953).

Pound, Arthur: *The Turning Wheel* (New York: Doubleday, Doran, 1934).

Ripley, William Z.: *Main Street and Wall Street* (Boston: Little, Brown, 1927).

Wilkins, R., and E. Crellin: *High Voltage Oil Circuit Breakers* (New York: McGraw-Hill, 1930).

Vennard, Edwin: *Government in the Power Business* (New York: McGraw-Hill, 1968).

Index